WITHDRAWN

Physics of the Earth's Upper Atmosphere

Active Auroral Forms Over Churchill, Manitoba

CONTRIBUTORS:

R. E. BARRINGTON
J. S. BELROSE
B. C. BLEVIS
T. R. HARTZ
L. HERZBERG
R. MONTALBETTI
I. PAGHIS — Defence Research Telecommunications Establishment, Defence Research Board, Ottawa, Canada

W. I. AXFORD — Department of Astronomy, Cornell University, Ithaca, N.Y

W. C. COLLINS — Division of Pure Physics, National Research Council, Ottawa, Ontario

J. A. FEJER — Southwest Center for Advanced Studies, Dallas, Texas

W. J. HEIKKILA — Southwest Center for Advanced Studies, Dallas, Texas

C. O. HINES — Department of the Geophysical Sciences, University of Chicago, Chicago, Illinois

G. C. REID — Central Radio Propagation Laboratory, National Bureau of Standards, Boulder, Colorado

Physics of the Earth's Upper Atmosphere

EDITORS:

Professor of Aeronomy
University of Chicago
Chicago, Illinois
C. O. Hines

Superintendent, Radio Physics Laboratory
Defence Research Telecommunications Establishment
Defence Research Board
Ottawa, Canada
I. Paghis

Consultant, Radio Physics Laboratory
Defence Research Telecommunications Establishment
Defence Research Board
Ottawa, Canada
T. R. Hartz

Professor of Atmospheric and Space Sciences
Southwest Center for Advanced Studies
Dallas, Texas
J. A. Fejer

Englewood Cliffs, N. J. **Prentice-Hall, Inc.**

PRENTICE-HALL INTERNATIONAL, INC., *London*
PRENTICE-HALL OF AUSTRALIA, PTY., LTD., *Sydney*
PRENTICE-HALL OF CANADA, LTD., *Toronto*
PRENTICE-HALL OF INDIA (PRIVATE) LTD., *New Delhi*
PRENTICE-HALL OF JAPAN, INC., *Tokyo*

Library of Congress Catalog No. 65–14942
Printed in the United States of America
67227C

Preface

This book is concerned with the earth's atmosphere above the regions that are usually associated with the discipline of meteorology. This upper atmosphere supports what is, perhaps, the broadest range of physical processes within any single discipline, and gives rise to complex interactions among them. Our fundamental goal has been to provide a broad view of the entire subject. To achieve this, a division of subject matter into chapters was determined editorially; the various chapters were then written by workers in different branches of the field, and the whole was integrated by the editors. The emphasis throughout has been toward portraying a meaningful picture rather than presenting a wealth of observational detail.

Recent years have witnessed an explosive development of upper atmospheric investigations. This has been accompanied by a surge in the number of scientists who devote themselves to studies within the discipline, and who find it necessary to acquaint themselves with the great range of processes and interactions that bear upon their own particular investigations. For some time, Mitras' classic, *The Upper Atmosphere*, provided much of the broad view, while more recently a number of new texts have appeared that have treated one or another of the phenomena—or indeed, a range of phenomena—in great depth. It was our experience, however, that newcomers to the field often found themselves immersed in a wealth of detail before the general picture became clear, and were in consequence inhibited from pursuit of the subject in its broader aspects. Too often they channeled their thoughts into their own particular path of investigation, with the hope that time would broaden their scope, and, as a result, they failed to acquire the most elementary concepts that would have expedited the broadening process. At the universities, where this situation might have been improved, the teaching of upper atmospheric physics has been inhibited to a large extent by a shortage of suitable texts.

It was in an effort to mitigate these problems that the present book was prepared. A firm background was available in a lecture series already given within the Defence Research Telecommunications Establishment, Ottawa, Canada, and that background was expanded by the presentation of an extension course at Carleton University, Ottawa. From these beginnings the format of the book took shape and the selection of appropriate authors emerged.

In a field as broad as upper atmospheric physics, it is difficult to limit one's scope in any but an arbitrary fashion. In the present instance, as in all, a limitation was implicit in the fields of broad interest or specialization of the available authors, but that limitation did not seem to provide a legitimate final guide when the objective of the book was kept in mind. Accordingly, we have attempted to provide at least minimal coverage of all processes that play an intimate part in the clarification of other processes, and have left more isolated phenomena (such as the formation of meteor trails) to others. In doing so we have been guided in part by the availability of good texts (as in the example cited) that make up for our deficiency. We would not claim adequate coverage of all subjects that are treated, either, for we have excluded much that is pertinent in order to provide the general view that is our fundamental goal. Once this view has been acquired, a wealth of reference material awaits the student who wishes to proceed further, and bibliographies are presented to direct his next steps.

Conflicting views as to the selection of material, presentation, emphasis, and objective invariably enter the preparation of a multiple-author book, and the present volume provided no exception. The maintenance of good relations between editors and authors, and the editors' view of their responsibility to the intended readers, are factors that were not always readily reconciled. With the good will of the authors the first of these has been achieved; it is our hope that the second has been put into effect with equal success.

THE EDITORS

Contents

1 INTRODUCTION 1

by C. O. Hines, I. Paghis, T. R. Hartz & J. A. Fejer

1.1. The Earth's Upper Atmosphere 1
1.2. Structure of the Book 2
1.3. Structure of the Atmosphere 6
1.4. The Geomagnetic Field 13
1.5. Ionospheric Research 20
1.6. Energy Propagation in a Dispersive Anisotropic Medium 24
1.7. The Sun 27
1.8. Related Phenomena 28
1.9. International Cooperation 28
Bibliography 29

2 SOLAR OPTICAL RADIATION AND ITS ROLE IN UPPER ATMOSPHERIC PROCESSES 31

by L. Herzberg

2.1. Introduction 31
2.2. The Solar Radiation Incident on the Earth's Atmosphere; the Emitting Layers of the Sun 32
2.3. Transmission through the Atmosphere 35
2.4. Absorption 37
2.5. Airglow 42

3 THE LOWER IONOSPHERIC REGIONS 46

by J. S. Belrose

3.1. Introduction 46
3.2. The Formation of Ionized Layers 46
3.3. The Ionospheric *D* Region 51
3.4. The Ionospheric *E* Region 59
3.5. Recombination in the *D* and *E* Regions 67
3.6. Collisional Frequencies in the *D* and *E* Regions 69

4 THE IONOSPHERIC *F* REGION 73

by J. S. Belrose

4.1. Introduction 73
4.2. Morphology of the *F* Layer 74
4.3. The Formation of Ionized Layers in the Quiet *F* Region 84
4.4. Parameters of the *F* Region 88
4.5. *F*-Region Irregularities 90

5 THE OUTER IONOSPHERIC REGIONS 96

by W. J. Heikkila & W. I. Axford

5.1. Introduction 96
5.2. Neutral Particles 98
5.3. Charged Particles of Thermal Energy 109
5.4. The Earth's Radiation Belts: Introduction 115
5.5. The Motion of Charged Particles in Magnetic Fields 115
5.6. The Radiation Belts 125
5.7. The Geomagnetic Effects of Trapped Particles 129

6 MOTIONS OF THE NEUTRAL ATMOSPHERE 134

by C. O. Hines

6.1. Introduction 134
6.2. Atmospheric Rotation 134
6.3. Prevailing Winds 135
6.4. Tidal Oscillations 138
6.5. Irregular Winds and Internal Gravity Waves 145
6.6. Turbulence 153

7 MOTIONS OF IONIZATION 157

by J. A. Fejer

7.1. Introduction 157
7.2. The Mean Velocity of Charged Particles in the Ionosphere; Conductivity and Diffusion 158
7.3. The Dynamo Theory 166
7.4. The Effect of Charged-particle Drifts on Electron Concentration 170
7.5. Vertical Drifts due to Horizontal Winds in the Neutral Gas 172

8 IONOSPHERIC NOISE AND GEOMAGNETIC MICROPULSATIONS 176

by R. E. Barrington & J. A. Fejer

8.1. Introduction 176
8.2. Ionospheric Noise 177
8.3. Geomagnetic Micropulsations 188
8.4. Observational Characteristics of Micropulsations 190
8.5. Theories of Micropulsations 194

9 SOLAR ACTIVITY AND SHORT-LIVED TERRESTRIAL EFFECTS (SID) 198

by W. C. Collins & L. Herzberg

9.1. Introduction 198
9.2. Sunspots; Spot Groups; the Sunspot Cycle 199
9.3. Solar Flares and Related Phenomena; the Solar Disk Observed in Monochromatic Light 202
9.4. Sudden Ionospheric Disturbances: Introduction 206
9.5. Type of Solar Radiation Producing SID's 207
9.6. Description of SID's 209
9.7. Ionization During SID's 211

10 PARTICLE EMISSIONS FROM THE DISTURBED SUN, AND THE SUN-EARTH ENVIRONMENT 216

by T. R. Hartz

10.1. Introduction 216
10.2. The Solar Corona and the Interplanetary Gas 218
10.3. Magnetic Fields in the Extended Solar Corona 222

10.4. Observations of the Solar Particles near the Sun 227
10.5. Observations of the Corpuscular Cloud in the Sun-Earth Space 236
10.6. Summary 240

11 SOLAR COSMIC RAYS AND THE IONOSPHERE 245

by G. C. Reid

11.1. Introduction 245
11.2. The Measurement of Ionospheric Absorption 246
11.3. Ionospheric Effects of Solar Cosmic Rays 248
11.4. The Nature of Solar Cosmic Rays 255
11.5. The Characteristic Features of Polar Cap Absorption 257
11.6. The Use of Ionospheric Sounding to Investigate PCA 265
11.7. Effects on Low-Frequency Radio Propagation 267
11.8. Conclusion 268

12 MAGNETIC AND IONOSPHERIC STORMS 271

by I. Paghis

12.1. Introduction 271
12.2. Upper Atmospheric Storms and Solar Activity 275
12.3. The Average Characteristics of Magnetic and Ionospheric Storms 282
12.4. Magnetic Storm Classification 284
12.5. Life History of a Storm 286
12.6. Worldwide Storm Characteristics 292

13 OPTICAL AURORA 299

by R. Montalbetti

13.1. Introduction 299
13.2. Geographical Distribution 301
13.3. Form and Brightness 302
13.4. Height 304
13.5. Orientation 305
13.6. Luminosity 307
13.7. Motion 307
13.8. Solar Influence 308
13.9. Associated Phenomena 309
13.10. Auroral Spectrum 309
13.11. Temperatures 312
13.12. Hydrogen Emissions 313
13.13. Auroral Particles 317

14 RADIO AURORA 319

by B. C. Blevis & C. Collins

14.1. Introduction 319
14.2. Reflection and Scattering in Radio Aurora 320
14.3. Auroral Absorption of Radio Waves 327
14.4. Radio Noise Emissions from the Aurora 330
14.5. Concluding Remarks 331

15 THEORY OF GEOMAGNETIC AND AURORAL STORMS 334

by C. O. Hines & G. C. Reid

15.1. Introduction 334
15.2. Geomagnetic Storms 335
15.3. Auroral Theory 351
15.4. Conclusion 360

16 EPILOGUE 363

by C. O. Hines, I. Paghis, T. R. Hartz & J. A. Fejer

APP. I WAVE PROPAGATION IN A HOMOGENEOUS IONIZED GAS 371

by R. E. Barrington

I.1. Introduction 371
I.2. The Hydrodynamic Approximation 372
I.3. The Dispersion Equation of Radio Waves 375
I.4. Graphical Representation of the Dispersion Equation 380
I.5. Reflection Conditions 384
I.6. QL and QT Approximations 385
I.7. Effects of Collisions on the Refractive Indices 386
I.8. Whistler Dispersion 390
I.9. The Dispersion Equation of Hydromagnetic Waves 392

APP. II WAVE PROPAGATION IN AN INHOMOGENEOUS MEDIUM 396

by J. A. Fejer

II.1. Introduction 396
II.2. Propagation in a Horizontally Stratified Medium 397
II.3. Ray Solutions 398

II.4. Limits of the Ray Approximation 403
II.5. Propagation in an Irregular Medium 407
II.6. The Phase-changing Screen 408
II.7. The Angular Power Spectrum and the Autocorrelation Function 412
II.8. Weak Scattering by Three-dimensional Irregularities 415
II.9. Multiple Scattering 418
II.10. Incoherent Scattering 418

INDEX 425

1

Introduction

1.1. THE EARTH'S UPPER ATMOSPHERE

The earth's upper atmosphere, for purposes of this book, extends upward in height from levels of 60 km or so. It grows ever more tenuous as greater elevations are attained and finally merges, either smoothly or abruptly, with the interplanetary gas beyond. It occupies a volume some thousand times the volume of the solid earth, but contains less than a thousandth of the mass of the atmosphere as a whole. Despite its relatively minute content, it supports some of the most fascinating and intricate of nature's phenomena.

The base level of 60 km is to some extent artificial, being determined in part by a transition from one class of observational techniques to another, and to that extent it may be considered anachronistic in these days of rocket-borne experiments. Indeed, one of the most significant developments in current atmospheric research is a growing emphasis on the treatment of the atmosphere as a continuous entity, subject to strong couplings between various levels from the ground on up, and indivisible into physically self-sufficient height ranges.

Nevertheless, the transition in observational techniques reflects a transition in the relative importance of various physical processes, and in this respect it is real enough. The physical transition is brought about by two major factors: the upward decrease of gas density, on the one hand, and the injection of energy from outside, principally from the sun, on the other. The decrease of gas density leads to a decrease of interparticle collisions, and hence to longer lifetimes for ionized, dissociated, and certain excited states of the atmospheric constituents, as well as a reduced selective absorption of the energy incident from outside. The incidence of energy from outside, both in photons and in particles, leads to certain energetic processes in the upper atmosphere that cannot occur at lower levels, because the necessary sources have been filtered out. In addition to these primary factors, certain secondary effects play important roles; for example, the high degree of ionization that is maintained leads to the introduction of electromagnetic forces which can dominate both the static and the dynamic properties of the atmosphere at great height. Hence much can be said of the atmosphere above 60 km without detailed reference to the much greater bulk below, and we adopt this level as a convenient, though sometimes ignored, base for our subsequent discussions.

The outer boundary of our upper atmosphere is less clearly specified, and indeed is the subject of much uncertainty. This is particularly true of the neutral constituent for which the boundary is not sharp and depends on arbitrary definition. The boundary between the ionized constituents and the interplanetary gas depends on electromagnetic interactions that can produce abrupt changes, and they will be discussed in due course. For the moment, to set some initial scale on our region of interest, it may be said that the boundary is frequently envisaged some 10 or so earth radii above the earth on the sunward side, and at some substantially greater distance in the anti-sun direction. This point will receive further elaboration shortly, and again in greater detail at a later stage.

1.2. STRUCTURE OF THE BOOK

The energy incident on the upper atmosphere from outside comes largely from the sun. The radiant energy is, of course, familiar to us by direct visual observation, although the actual incident spectrum is far broader than the eye alone can detect. In addition, ionized interplanetary gas moves outward from the sun and produces a continuous interaction and transfer of energy at the boundary of the atmosphere. When the sun is in a relatively quiescent state, a corresponding quiescent pattern of behavior is to be found in the upper atmosphere; the latter is then said to be 'normal' or 'undisturbed.' But the sun is also subject to severe and often violent disturbances of various types, during which the emission of radiation and matter is strongly enhanced. The upper atmosphere responds to these enhanced emissions in various ways, and when sufficiently altered from its normal state, it is said to be 'disturbed.' There is, of course, a continuous range of states between 'undisturbed' and 'disturbed,' but it is convenient to divide the discussion into two major parts based on this elementary distinction. Such a division is reflected in the over-all structure of this book.

1.2.1. The Undisturbed Upper Atmosphere. Granted the decrease of density with height previously remarked upon, the static features of the undisturbed upper atmosphere are determined almost exclusively by solar photon emissions. These are important over a broad spectral range and are excited at various levels in and above the sun's (photospheric) surface. They produce photochemical reactions in the earth's atmosphere and thereby affect its chemical composition. Their origins and subsequent reactions are discussed in Chapter 2, not only in relation to the 'upper atmosphere' as previously defined but also for somewhat lower levels (the 'ozonosphere') whose characteristics are pertinent to a part of the later discussion. Also described in Chapter 2 are the scattering and reemission of the solar radiation, which combine to produce an 'airglow.'

One of the major features of the upper atmosphere is its substantial degree of ionization, produced primarily by the solar radiation. This ionization is important, and sometimes dominant, in physical processes above the 100-km level, but it extends in diminishing quantity even below. It plays a crucial role in most long-distance radio communications, and it has been studied as much for this reason as for the scientific purposes of interest here. The whole region of significant ionization is termed the 'ionosphere.' The percentage ionization tends to increase with increasing height, although the absolute concentration of ions exhibits a layered structure associated with different photoionization and recombination processes. This structure permits a convenient division of the discussion in terms of height ranges, and three such ranges are adopted here. The lowest of these embraces the ionospheric *D* and *E* regions, which will be defined shortly, and extends up to a height of about 140 km; it is treated in Chapter 3. Chapter 4 is concerned with much of the ionospheric *F* region, from the 140-km level up to the level of maximum ionization density at 250–500 km. The regions above this *F*-layer maximum embrace not only the low-density residual gas of the ordinary ionosphere, but also include the energetic charged particles of the 'trapped radiation belts'; Chapter 5 treats both.

Motions in the undisturbed upper atmosphere are discussed in the next two chapters, first for the neutral gas (Chapter 6) and then for the ionized constituents (Chapter 7). The sun plays a dominant role in establishing these motions, but by less direct processes than those that arise in the preceding chapters. Much of the pertinent energy is introduced at lower atmospheric levels in the form of heat and reaches the upper atmosphere by dynamical coupling. Here the linkage of the various atmospheric regions is particularly noticeable, although the discussion is largely confined to its manifestation in the upper atmosphere proper. The motions of the neutral gas lead to motions of ionization, through interparticle collisions and subsequent electrodynamic forces, which extend some of the dynamical effects throughout the whole of the ionosphere to its very outer boundary.

At or near that boundary, interactions with the interplanetary gas appear to give rise to transient fluctuations in the movement of ionization, with a resultant production of electromagnetic oscillations at periods of 10^{-4}–10^{2} sec. Whether or not this is indeed their origin, such oscillations are in fact observed at ground level (as 'very low frequency ionospheric noise' and 'micropulsations') even when other manifestations of disturbance are missing. They are therefore discussed in Chapter 8, as a feature of the 'undisturbed' upper atmosphere. They grow in intensity and occurrence as certain disturbed conditions set in, however, and are geographically linked to those conditions; hence they provide a natural point of transition to a discussion of disturbances.

1.2.2. The Disturbed Upper Atmosphere. Disturbances in the upper atmosphere are intimately linked to disturbances on the sun, and often individual events can be associated unambiguously with particular solar features. Optical radiations provide a good indicator of the solar disturbances, but the direct atmospheric consequences of transient photon fluxes are relatively minor and certainly short-lived. The role they do play, both on the sun and in the atmosphere, is discussed in Chapter 9.

Particles ejected from the solar disturbances lead to much stronger and more serious modifications of the atmosphere, at least at high latitudes, and the remaining chapters of the book are devoted to them. The particles fall into two general categories: those that are highly energetic, but sufficiently low in concentration as to be noninteracting, and those of much lower energy and higher concentration whose collective interactions in 'plasma' processes are of prime importance. The ejection of both classes of particles is usually accompanied by radio emissions from the sun whose characteristics, if identified, can serve as advance warning of the oncoming disturbance. This early stage in the particles' history is discussed in Chapter 10, together with the factors that affect their flight from the sun to the earth's immediate environs.

The more energetic particles, often termed 'solar cosmic rays,' lead to quite a distinctive and fairly sharply defined pattern of disturbance, concentrated in the polar regions of the upper atmosphere. They and their effects are discussed in Chapter 11.

The less energetic, more numerous, particles lead to widespread consequences of diverse nature, which may be labeled conveniently as an upper atmospheric 'storm.' The ionospheric and associated magnetic disturbances are world-wide, and are discussed together in Chapter 12. Optical emissions from the upper atmosphere are greatly enhanced during storm events and altered in character, at least in a band of medium-to-high latitudes often referred to as the 'auroral zone.' These 'auroral emissions' are in fact present almost every night at the center of the zone and probably then reveal the continual outpouring of solar particles at a low level of activity, but they intensify to sometimes awesome levels during major storms. Their characteristics are described in Chapter 13, and those of the closely related 'auroral ionization' in Chapter 14. Theories of these storm processes are numerous, and still in a developing stage, but they provide many of the most challenging problems of current research; some of the more important are outlined in Chapter 15, which concludes the discussion of the disturbed upper atmosphere.

1.2.3. Summary of Structure. The structure previously outlined is not only convenient for purposes of presentation, but also useful as an outline of the scientific content of upper atmospheric studies. It is therefore repeated here in chart form, with further comments on the introductory and terminal chapters.

The present chapter will proceed shortly with introductory material of a general background nature, including, for example, a general discussion of the decrease of gas density with increasing height, systematic height variations of related parameters, a description of the earth's magnetic field, and resultant nomenclature. We then proceed to

THE UNDISTURBED UPPER ATMOSPHERE

- Photon Processes (photochemical, absorption, emission)—Chapter 2
- Ionospheric Structure
  - Lower regions—Chapter 3
  - *F* region—Chapter 4
  - Outer regions—Chapter 5
- Motions
  - Of neutral gas—Chapter 6
  - Of ionization—Chapter 7
- Fluctuations (ionospheric radio emissions, micropulsations)—Chapter 8

THE DISTURBED UPPER ATMOSPHERE

- Photon Processes (abnormal emission, ionospheric consequences)—Chapter 9
- Particle Processes
  - Ejection, and travel to earth's environs, of solar cosmic rays and storm plasma—Chapter 10
  - Solar cosmic rays and polar cap events—Chapter 11
  - Solar storm plasma effects
    - Ionospheric and magnetic storms—Chapter 12
    - Auroral emissions—Chapter 13
    - Auroral ionization—Chapter 14
    - Theory—Chapter 15

This completes the bulk of the book: there follow a short concluding chapter (Chapter 16) and two appendices on the propagation of radio waves in an ionized medium, first for homogeneous and then for varying properties. These appendices are included in part as amplification of points touched on in the main text, and in part because of the major role that radio techniques play in the measurement and interpretation of upper atmospheric processes.

1.3. STRUCTURE OF THE ATMOSPHERE

The gross structure of the atmosphere can be described in several different ways, and each leads to a classification of the height regions that is appropriate to the physical process under consideration. The main classifications, outlined here, neglect horizontal and temporal variations in these physical processes.

1.3.1. Thermal Structure of the Neutral Atmosphere. As we proceed upward from ground level, the temperature first falls throughout the 'troposphere' until a local minimum is reached at the 'tropopause,' usually

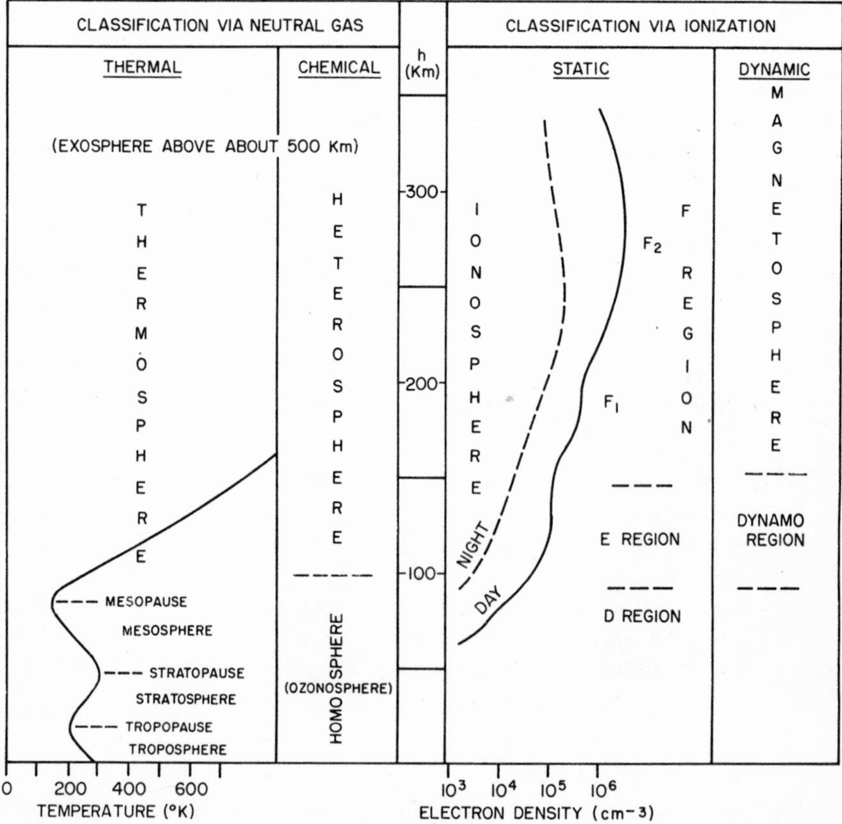

Fig. 1.1 Upper atmospheric nomenclature and the different ways of classifying the atmospheric structure.

at heights in the range 7–17 km. It rises again through the 'stratosphere' until the 'stratopause' is reached, at 45–55 km height, and then declines through the 'mesosphere' to a minimum at the 'mesopause' near 80–85 km. It rises again through the 'thermosphere,' rapidly at first, then more slowly, and finally reaches a relatively constant terminal value in the uppermost levels. These thermal domains and boundaries are indicated in Fig. 1.1, together with the other classifications of atmospheric structure. The stratosphere and mesosphere are sometimes combined under either name alone, or under the term 'middle atmosphere'; when termed the mesosphere alone, the temperature maximum near 50 km is called the 'mesopeak,' and the term 'stratosphere' is then applied to a height range immediately above the tropopause in which the temperature is nearly constant.

1.3.2. Classification of the Upper Atmosphere Based on Chemistry. The decrease of gas density with increasing height is governed, to great heights, by a hydrostatic equilibrium between the pressure gradient and the force of gravity:

$$0 = \rho g + dp/dh, \tag{1.1}$$

where ρ is the gas density, g the acceleration due to gravity, p the gas pressure, and h the height (above ground level, say). The pressure is related to the gas density by the gas law,

$$p = NkT = \rho kT/M, \tag{1.2}$$

where N is the number density of molecules, k is Boltzmann's constant ($= 1.38 \times 10^{-23}$ joule per degree absolute), T the absolute temperature, and M the mean molecular mass. The density may be eliminated from Eq. (1.1), by the introduction of (1.2), and the result integrated to yield

$$p = p_0 \exp - \int_0^h dh/H, \tag{1.3}$$

where

$$H = kT/Mg, \tag{1.4}$$

and p_0 is the pressure at ground level. If T/M were independent of height, then (1.2) and (1.3) would combine to yield

$$\rho = \rho_0 \exp - \int_0^h dh/H, \tag{1.5}$$

but in general

$$\rho = \rho_0(MT_0/M_0T) \exp - \int_0^h dh/H, \tag{1.6}$$

where zero subscripts again indicate ground-level values.

The parameter H occurs frequently in atmospheric studies, and is known as the (local) 'scale height' of the atmosphere. When constant, it represents the height interval over which the pressure or density decreases by a factor *e*, and also the total height to which the atmosphere would extend if compressed to the constant pressure p_0. It takes a value near 8.5 km at ground level, and somewhat lower values at greater heights (except for a recovery at the stratopause) up to about the 100-km level; a minimum value of about 5 km is found at the mesopause in summer, and a local minimum of 6.4 km is representative of the tropopause.

The foregoing analysis may be applied with constant M when the predominant atmospheric constituents are thoroughly mixed. They are so mixed, owing presumably to turbulence and convective overturning, up to heights of the order 100 km. This region is termed the 'homosphere' to indicate its homogeneous composition, predominantly of nitrogen and oxygen molecules, although it does contain trace constituents (such as water vapor, carbon dioxide, and ozone) that are not all homogeneously distributed. Above the homosphere, mixing no longer occurs or, at least, is no longer complete, and each constituent gas that achieves a static equilibrium is then supported only by its own partial pressure. Equations (1.1)–(1.6) could be rewritten for each constituent in turn, but because of the difference in molecular masses, each constituent would adopt a scale height of its own. At constant temperature each would decrease exponentially with increasing height, but the total gas pressure would decrease in a somewhat more complex fashion. The chemical composition of the region would change with increasing height, the heavier gases being left more rapidly behind and the lighter gases remaining. The situation is further complicated by the presence of chemical and photochemical reactions which remove and produce various molecules, and which then invalidate the basis on which Eq. (1.1) is assumed. In practice, nitrogen molecules give way to oxygen atoms and ultimately to hydrogen atoms, as the dominant neutral constituents; at certain epochs, helium is predominant between the oxygen and hydrogen levels. Because of the changing composition, this region is occasionally termed the 'heterosphere.'

At heights above 500–600 km, Eq. (1.1) is invalidated for a further reason: the gas density has diminished to such low values that the formalism of fluid dynamics is no longer applicable to the neutral particles. Instead, these particles—primarily oxygen atoms at the lower levels and hydrogen atoms above—follow ballistic trajectories under the influence of gravity alone, freed from the collisional interactions that lead to an isotropic pressure. This region is termed the 'exosphere,' and it marks a gradual transition of the terrestrial atmosphere to the interplanetary gas beyond, at least insofar as the neutral constituents are concerned.

1.3.3. Classification Based on the Static Ionization. The ionized constituents behave somewhat differently than do the neutral particles, and they provide a third means of categorizing the various height ranges.

Ground-based radio techniques provide a convenient method of studying ionization at heights of 90 km and above, and this level marks the base of the ionospheric *E* region. Ionization can also be detected below this level with suitable ground-based equipment, particularly during disturbances, and it has been found on occasion as low as 50 km even in normal conditions. The levels below 90 km constitute the ionospheric *D* region, to which no base has yet been assigned. A well-defined layer of ionization is formed during normal daytime conditions in the *E* region, and another two layers (or one double layer) above it in the *F* region. The demarkation between these two regions occurs at about 140 km. (Conventionally, a height of 160 km is often used for this demarkation. This choice was made many years ago on the basis of the limited data then available, and it is now known to carry little physical significance; more recent studies show that the ionization of the *F* layer extends below 140 km under suitable circumstances.) The ionization density normally reaches a peak in the *F* region at heights of 250–500 km, depending on location and conditions, and then gradually diminishes above. No conventional upper limit has been assigned to the *F* region.

The ionization well above the peak of the *F* layer is in large measure supported hydrostatically from below, the local production and loss processes being negligible. The collisional cross section of the ions is sufficiently great that, unlike the neutral particles, they tend not to follow ballistic trajectories and no 'ion exosphere' is believed to be formed. The earth's magnetic field is of importance here since it strongly inhibits intermixing of charged particles except by motion along the field lines. The pressure gradient of the ion gas must come into balance with the gravitational force only in the direction of the magnetic field, and the hydrostatic support then follows the field lines; height variations take on a different form from those given in Eqs. (1.3) and (1.6). This situation is further complicated by electrostatic forces in a manner to be discussed (Chapter 5), with the net result that protons, together with their attendant electrons, ultimately become the most numerous particles. A transition from atomic oxygen ions to helium ions takes place at heights of the order of 1000 km, and from helium to hydrogen ions at heights of the order of 3000 km. (These heights are for daytime conditions in the declining phase of solar activity; the corresponding nighttime values are about 600 km and 1000 km.) The region in which hydrogen ions (i. e., protons) predominate is often referred to as the 'protonosphere' or 'protosphere.'

1.3.4. Classification Based on Ionization Dynamics; Frozen-in Magnetic Fields. The importance of the earth's magnetic field is felt even at the lower ionospheric levels, when the dynamical state of the ionization is considered. Below and into the *E* region, ionization motions are controlled by the motion of the neutral gas through collisional interactions. Within the E region there is a transition, however, whereby the collisional processes give way to electrodynamic forces almost exclusively. Large-scale motions of the ionization tend then to be of a quasi-equilibrium nature, in which the electrostatic force and the Lorentz force just balance:

$$\mathbf{E} + \mathbf{V} \times \mathbf{B} = 0, \tag{1.7}$$

where $\mathbf{E}$ is the local electric field, $\mathbf{B}$ the local magnetic induction, and $\mathbf{V}$ the local mean velocity of the ionized constituents.* When combined with Faraday's law, $\partial\mathbf{B}/\partial t = -\text{curl}\,\mathbf{E}$, this leads to

$$\partial\mathbf{B}/\partial t = \text{curl}\,(\mathbf{V} \times \mathbf{B}). \tag{1.8}$$

This relation in turn gives rise to the hydromagnetic concept of 'frozen magnetic fields,' which plays a key role not only in the discussion of certain aspects of ionospheric dynamics but in the treatment of interplanetary and stellar plasmas as well. The concept is, simply, that whenever and wherever Eq. (1.8) is a valid approximation, lines of magnetic flux may be thought of as 'frozen' to the conducting medium; they may be carried about by the medium in the course of its motion, or they may control, or at least constrain, that motion, but in either event the field lines and the medium move together.

This description of events is to some extent arbitrary, for there is no unique means of identifying any particular line of force continuously in time. The statement just made, concerning the motion of the lines, in fact constitutes a specific prescription whereby one might choose to identify a particular set of lines continuously in time: the identification is made by means of the medium that lies along each line in turn. The fact that such a prescription is permissible is all that can be proved, and the proof clearly demands that two conclusions be reached. First, it is necessary that the portion of the medium that lies along a line of flux at one time should at all other times lie along a line of flux; second, a tube of flux whose bounding surface is identified by a set of such lines should always encompass the same number of flux lines (see Fig. 1.2). In establishing these conclusions, we shall start by showing that the flux through a closed contour that moves with the conducting medium does not change.

Consider some closed contour Λ drawn in the conducting medium, comprising elements $d\boldsymbol{\lambda}$, enclosing a surface Σ whose elements are $d\boldsymbol{\sigma}$. This contour encloses a certain magnetic flux Φ, given by

$$\Phi \equiv \int_{\Sigma} \mathbf{B} \cdot d\boldsymbol{\sigma}. \tag{1.9}$$

*Rationalized mksa units and formalism are used throughout the book in all relevant equations unless an explicit exception is made; in the body of the text, numerical values are given in the units most commonly employed for the parameter in question.

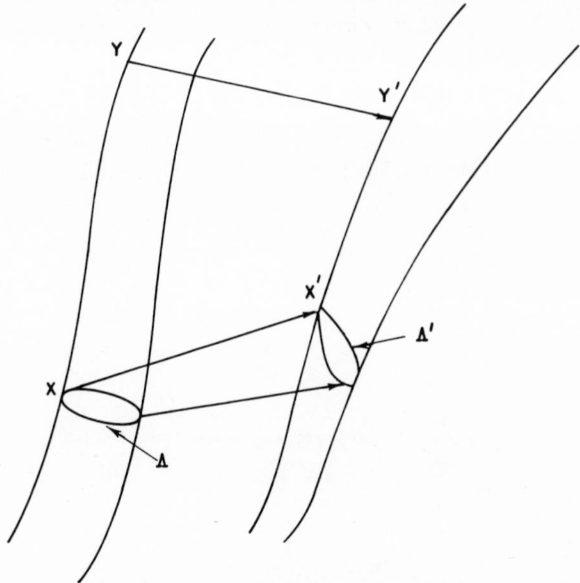

Fig. 1.2 A tube of conducting medium (defined at one instant by a cross-sectional contour Λ and by the magnetic flux lines, such as XY, that pass through Λ) moves in the course of time to a new position illustrated by Λ' and $X'Y'$. When the 'frozen-field' approximation applies, lines such as $X'Y'$ must still be magnetic flux lines, and the number of flux lines enclosed by Λ' must equal the number previously enclosed by Λ.

As the medium moves and deforms, so too does the contour Λ; we wish to establish the time rate of change of Φ. The change $\delta\Phi$ that occurs in a differential time δt may be separated into two parts: the first results from the change that occurs in **B** within the integral in (1.9), without allowing for any motion of Λ; the second accounts for the changed location and configuration of Λ, without allowing for temporal changes of **B**. Only these two changes are of first order in δt, and they are therefore adequate to establish the limit of $\delta\Phi/\delta t$, namely, $d\Phi/dt$. The first may be expressed as

$$\begin{aligned}\delta_1\Phi &\equiv \int_\Sigma \left(\frac{\partial \mathbf{B}}{\partial t}\,\delta t\right)\cdot d\boldsymbol{\sigma} \\ &= \delta t \int_\Sigma [\text{curl}\,(\mathbf{V}\times\mathbf{B})]\cdot d\boldsymbol{\sigma} \\ &= \delta t \oint_\Lambda (\mathbf{V}\times\mathbf{B})\cdot d\boldsymbol{\lambda},\end{aligned} \tag{1.10}$$

where (1.8) has been assumed and Stokes' theorem employed. The second is found by noting that each element $d\boldsymbol{\lambda}$ sweeps out a vector area $(\mathbf{V}\,\delta t)\times d\boldsymbol{\lambda}$ in time δt, and so transfers $(\delta t)\mathbf{B}\cdot(\mathbf{V}\times d\boldsymbol{\lambda})$ lines of flux from one side of Λ to the other—from without Λ to within, as may be confirmed by a check on vector directions—and the total transfer is then

$$\delta_2\Phi \equiv \delta t \oint_\Lambda \mathbf{B} \cdot (\mathbf{V} \times d\boldsymbol{\lambda}) \equiv \delta t \oint_\Lambda (\mathbf{B} \times \mathbf{V}) \cdot d\boldsymbol{\lambda} = -\delta_1\Phi. \quad (1.11)$$

Thus the total change in flux, $\delta\Phi = \delta_1\Phi + \delta_2\Phi$, vanishes to the first order of δt. This conclusion is valid irrespective of the time at which the analysis is performed, and so

$$d\Phi/dt = 0. \quad (1.12)$$

This establishes the preliminary step.

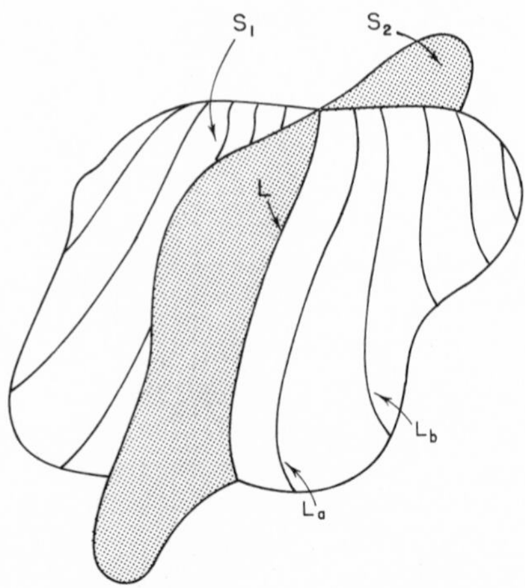

Fig. 1.3 S_1 is a segment of a surface comprising a set of flux-line segments (such as L, L_a, L_b); S_2 is a similar surface segment although, for clarity, its family of flux-line segments is not indicated. S_1 and S_2 intersect along some line segment L, which must be a flux-line segment. As S_1 and S_2 move with the (highly conducting) medium, they continue to comprise sets of flux-line segments, and L continues to be such a segment.

Consider now some material surface drawn so that $\mathbf{B} \cdot d\boldsymbol{\sigma} = 0$ everywhere on it, and containing, therefore, a set of flux-line segments (as in Fig. 1.3). If some closed contour Λ is drawn on this surface, the corresponding integral in (1.9) will vanish and, in accordance with (1.12), will remain zero despite the motion of the surface and of Λ with the medium. This is true for arbitrary Λ within the surface; hence $\mathbf{B} \cdot d\boldsymbol{\sigma}$ continues to vanish everywhere in the surface despite the latter's motion, and the surface itself continues to consist only of flux-line segments. Consider now a second such surface, intersecting the first along some line segment L; L must be a part of a flux line, and it must remain a part of a flux line despite the motion. Thus portions of the medium that are at one time connected by a flux line remain connected by a flux line, despite their motion; the first requirement of the 'frozen field' concept is established.

This done, it is clear that a tube of flux (defined by the material on its boundary at any given time) remains a tube of flux. If some cross-sectional surface Σ is drawn across it, then $\int_\Sigma \mathbf{B} \cdot d\boldsymbol{\sigma}$ yields the number of flux lines it contains, and by (1.12) this number remains constant despite the motion; the second requirement of the 'frozen field' concept is proved.

Although this formal development is somewhat tedious, the conclusion reached is a tremendous conceptual aid in many 'hydromagnetic' problems, and its application to a variety of situations is found in the following pages. In particular, its application to the upper atmosphere is straightforward for, in the E region and above, the energy density of the atmosphere is less than that of the earth's magnetic field, and in these circumstances, motions of the atmosphere or of its ionized components cannot seriously distort the magnetic field lines. Any 'frozen' motions of ionization at one point on a field line must then be accompanied by corresponding motions of the remaining 'frozen' ionization on the field line such that the configuration of the field lines remains relatively constant. These conditions prevail from heights of 130–150 km out to the boundary of the ionized atmosphere, and this whole region is known as the 'magnetosphere.'

The validity of Eq. (1.7) extends down to the height of 130–150 km when applied to the mean velocity of ions alone, but to a much lower height, 70–80 km, when applied to the mean velocity of electrons alone. Below these respective heights, the motion of ions and electrons is dominated by collisional interactions with the neutral gas. In the intermediate height range of 80–130 km, the ions move almost entirely with the neutral gas but the mean velocity of the electrons still closely satisfies Eq. (1.7); the mean velocity of electrons therefore generally is not the same in this region as the mean velocity of the ions, and there is a flow of electric current. The generation of ionospheric currents in this height region by atmospheric tidal oscillations is discussed in Chapter 7. These currents, caused by the motion of the conducting atmosphere across the geomagnetic field, are comparable to the currents generated in the moving conductors of a dynamo. They are therefore usually called 'dynamo currents' and the region in which they flow (about 80–150 km) is often labeled the 'dynamo-region.' The same region carries strong currents at times of magnetic storms, although in that case the driving mechanism is usually taken to be an electric field rather than a dynamo action, as discussed in Chapter 15.

1.4. THE GEOMAGNETIC FIELD

The magnetic field of the earth plays a major role in many upper atmospheric processes, as has already been indicated, and a short discussion of its main features is in order at this stage. The earth's magnetic field consists of a dominating component, whose sources lie within the earth and which varies only on a time scale of years or centuries, and a superimposed variation with time scales of days, hours, minutes, or seconds. The first of these components, the 'main field,' is the center of interest here. The second component, the 'variation field,' is attributed to sources in the upper atmosphere and to resultant induced currents in the earth; it therefore constitutes a topic of study later in the book (principally in Chapters 7, 8, 12, and 15) and is discussed here only to introduce a conventional nomenclature.

1.4.1. The Main Field; Coordinate Systems. The main field has been measured at ground level for many decades now, and even for centuries at some locations. Mathematical analysis reveals it to have its origins entirely, or almost entirely, within the earth, in current systems that are presumed to flow mainly inside the liquid core. Above the earth's surface, it approximates to the field of a magnetic dipole located at the earth's center,

$$\mathbf{H} = -\text{grad}\,(\mathbf{M} \cdot \mathbf{r}/4\pi r^3), \tag{1.13}$$

where $\mathbf{M}$ is the dipole moment ($M \simeq 8.1 \times 10^{22}$ amp-meter^2) and $\mathbf{r}$ a radius vector from the dipole to the point in question. The approximation is best if $\mathbf{M}$ is taken to be directed toward a point on the earth's surface at latitude 78.5°S, longitude 111°E. This point is known as the 'geomagnetic south pole,' and the antipodal point at 78.5°N, 69°W is the 'geomagnetic north pole'; the line joining them is the 'geomagnetic axis.'

A system of 'geomagnetic coordinates' can be established by use of these polar points, with latitude and longitude defined by an obvious analogy. The zero meridian is taken to be that which contains the south geographic pole, and geomagnetic longitude is taken to increase from 0° to 360° as a point moves eastward from this meridian. Diurnal variations of certain phenomena are often described in terms of 'geomagnetic time,' which is defined as the difference in geomagnetic longitude (measured as an hour angle) between the site in question and the anti-sun direction. Since the sun does not move uniformly in geomagnetic longitude, geomagnetic time proceeds throughout the day at a variable rate which is itself modulated throughout the year. A 'geomagnetic equator' is defined in an obvious manner. Despite this uniformity in the application of the term 'geomagnetic', it should be noted that the 'geomagnetic field' is normally taken to mean the main field, or the total field, and not the '(centered) dipole field' on which the geomagnetic coordinates are based.

The dipole approximation can be improved if the dipole itself is taken to be displaced from the earth's center, with the optimum offset some 342 km in the direction of 6.5°N, 161.8°E geographic. This provides an 'eccentric dipole field' that is useful for some purposes but not generally employed.

Certain major deviations from the dipole approximations exist, on spatial scales ranging up to thousands of kilometers. In some regions the deviations form in distinctive semi-isolated patterns, as viewed on contour charts of some representative deviation parameter, and these are termed 'anomalies.' They are attributed to relatively localized current systems deep within the earth in some cases, and to abnormal magnetic properties of rock and ore formations in the others, depending on the spatial scale and temporal variation (if any), or on observed crustal features. Because of anomalies, the actual geomagnetic field becomes normal to the earth's surface at points (or regions), termed the 'dip poles,' well removed from the geomagnetic poles. The location of the dip poles can change fairly rapidly as the anomalies undergo small changes. They are currently located in the regions indicated on the accompanying map (Fig. 1.4), and with the limitations imposed by the scale of the map, these locations should be valid for at least a decade.

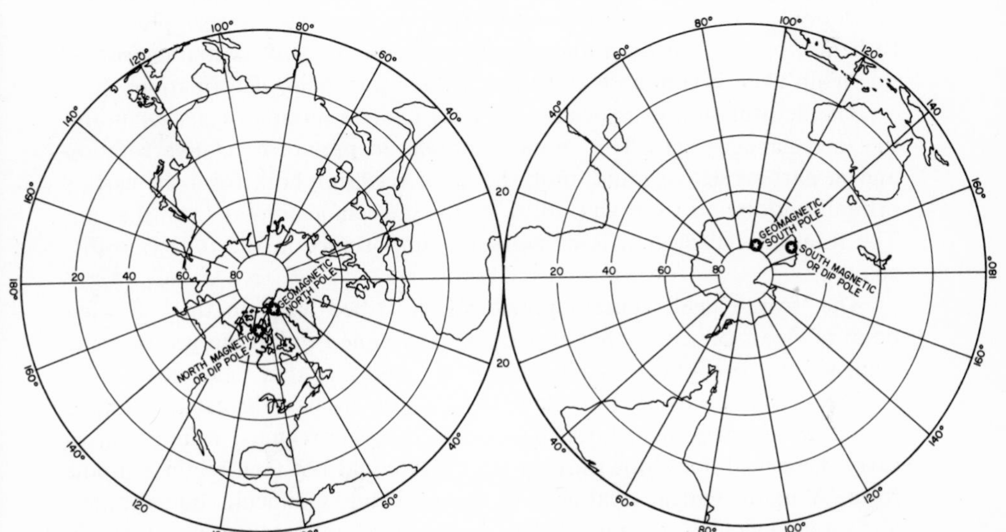

Fig. 1.4 Locations of the geomagnetic and magnetic or dip poles.

For certain studies of the upper atmosphere (cf. Chapter 4), it has been found convenient to organize observations in terms of 'magnetic latitude.' This term, which is not to be confused with 'geomagnetic latitude,' is applied in practice only at or near the earth's surface (specifically, *not* far out in the magnetosphere). It is often denoted λ, and is related to the dip angle I (the angle between the magnetic field vector and a horizontal plane) through

$$\tan I = 2 \tan \lambda. \tag{1.14}$$

It is therefore simply a scaled measure of the dip angle, with the significance that it represents the latitude at which the observed dip would have been found, had the geomagnetic field been a true dipole field aligned along the earth's axis. It is employed in the discussion of phenomena that depend more strongly on the dip angle than on the geomagnetic latitude or some other such parameter, and it is simply a convenient way of retaining some concept of the relevant latitudes in those discussions. A 'magnetic equator' is defined in keeping with this terminology, at $\lambda = 0$.

At great distances from the earth, toward the outer boundary of the magnetosphere, it is now known that the geomagnetic field lines depart from the dipole form that would be suggested by ground-level observations. The departure is in the form of a diurnal variation as seen from a point on the rotating earth, but is a constant deformation as seen by an inertial observer outside. (The outside observer would expect to see a small diurnal variation because the dipole axis and the rotation axis do not coincide; this has only a small influence on the major deformation, however, and will be ignored in the present discussion.) Since it constitutes not simply a perturbation of the field but rather a complete alteration of its characteristics, the 'main field' is commonly taken to include this major deformation.

The deformation is associated with the relative motion of the earth and the interplanetary gas. This motion consists in part of a relative rotation and in part a relative translation, the latter resulting both from the earth's orbital motion and from an outflow of the interplanetary gas from the sun. The translational motion is of particular importance in the following discussion.

The 'frozen field' concept previously described leads to the following point of view: ionization that at one time is confined within the geomagnetic field will be so confined at all other times, and any that lies outside that field will remain outside. Interplanetary gas moving past the earth, if linked to the geomagnetic field lines that rise from polar regions, would tend to carry these field lines 'downstream' and they could not then retain a dipole form. A mathematical treatment of the problem is difficult, but intuition and model calculations suggest that the geomagnetic field would ultimately be confined within a 'geomagnetic cavity' carved out of the interplanetary plasma. Two field-line configurations may be distinguished within this cavity—a low-latitude torus of dipole-like field lines, girding the earth, and a high-latitude configuration containing the field lines that rise from polar regions, stretching out into a 'geomagnetic tail' on the downstream side of the earth, as depicted in Fig. 1.5. This picture is by no means universally accepted—some authors take the polar field lines to extend indefinitely into interplanetary space (see Fig. 15.8)—but it will be adopted in most parts of the later discussion when the distant configuration of field lines becomes relevant.

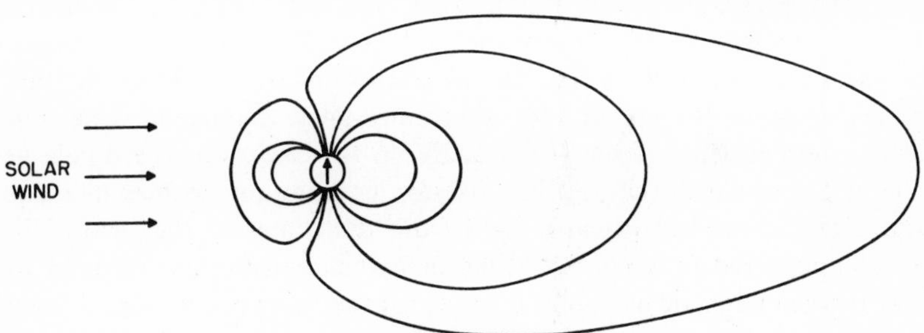

Fig. 1.5 A section of the magnetosphere, showing the low-latitude field lines as having a roughly dipole shape and the high-latitude lines swept round over the poles to form a geomagnetic tail.

Within the low-latitude torus of field lines, we have the familiar situation that a point on the earth's surface in the northern hemisphere is linked by a magnetic line to a point in the southern hemisphere. Such points are said to be 'magnetically conjugate,' and there is reason to expect that those upper atmospheric processes that depend on incoming charged particles might exhibit similar behavior at the two conjugate points. This situation also applies to polar stations if Fig. 1.5 correctly depicts the form of the field lines that rise at high latitudes, but there it is more suspect because of the uncertainty previously mentioned.

The field within the geomagnetic cavity has not yet been mapped in any detail with satellite-borne instruments. The values in use have been obtained by computations that involve a spherical harmonic expansion of the surface field. In an increasing number of instances such field values have led to a closer correlation with observed phenomena in the upper atmosphere than is possible with a dipole field. This applies particularly to the energetic charged particles that have been detected and measured by means of satellites in the outer regions. Experience has shown that a broad scatter of data points arises if the relevant measurements are organized in a coordinate system based on a dipole field model, but that the scatter can be markedly reduced if more accurate extrapolations of the surface field are employed.

In the case of the energetic particles, moreover, it has been found convenient to adopt the 'McIlwain coordinates,' (B, L), which are defined in terms of the geomagnetic field itself. For a general point A, the first of these is simply the magnitude of the local magnetic induction, say B_A, whereas the value of L depends both on B_A and on another parameter I_A, the 'integral (or longitudinal) invariant,' defined by

$$I_A \equiv \int_A^{A'} (1 - B/B_A)^{1/2}\, ds, \tag{1.15}$$

where ds is an element of path length along the magnetic field line through A, and the integration extends along that line from A to a complementary point A' at which $B = B_A$ once again (with $B < B_A$ in between). The defining function $L = L(B, I)$ is specified by McIlwain* in such a manner that L remains constant (to within 1%) along any given geomagnetic field line, and that it represents closely—or exactly, in the case of a true dipole field—the height to which the field line rises on crossing the geomagnetic equatorial plane (measured in earth radii from the center of the earth). Field lines characterized by a specific value of L then constitute a toroidal shell about the geomagnetic axis, and L is termed the 'shell parameter.' The shell would have circular symmetry about the geomagnetic axis if a true dipole field obtained, but in fact the departures from symmetry are significant.

The McIlwain coordinates may be transformed into pseudo-polar coordinates (R, λ) by use of the relations that would apply in a true dipole field:

$$B = \mu_0 M R^{-3}(4 - 3R/L)^{1/2} \tag{1.16}$$

$$R = L \cos^2 \lambda, \tag{1.17}$$

where μ_0 is the free-space permeability and M is the dipole moment as before; λ is sometimes called the 'invariant latitude,' and should not be confused with the magnetic latitude previously denoted by the same symbol. Although useful for some conceptual purposes, these pseudo-polar coordinates must be employed with caution since their relation to true polar coordinates in real space is indirect and irregularly longitude-dependent.

The great value of the McIlwain coordinates is intimately related to the departures of the true field from a dipole form, for they are designed to minimize the consequences of those departures when they are applied to the study of energetic trapped particles. These particles, whose motion is described in some detail in Chapter 5, spiral rapidly back and forth along the field lines from one hemisphere to another, and drift relatively slowly in longitude from one field line to another. For a given particle, these motions are closely confined to a given L-shell, and the field-aligned component of motion is reversed when a given value of B is reached on that shell, regardless of the detailed departures of the geomagnetic field from a dipole form. The McIlwain coordinates are also being tested in the organization of other types of data that are related to energetic particles, and preliminary results indicate that they may be of considerable value in those broader areas as well.

In addition to the foregoing coordinate systems, it is convenient to refer to certain latitude zones when considering geomagnetically controlled processes. The following classification of these zones is used frequently throughout the book:

*C. E. McIlwain, "Coordinates for mapping the distribution of magnetically trapped particles," *J. Geophys. Res.*, **66** (1961), 3681.

1. '*Auroral zone*' properly designates the zone in which the aurora occurs. As we shall see in Chapter 13, the observational statistics indicate that auroral emissions are found most frequently in two nearly circular rings at geomagnetic latitudes, north and south, of about 67°. At higher and lower latitudes the frequency diminishes, but not abruptly, so the full auroral zone in each hemisphere consists of a (nonuniform) belt of some substantial width. For the purposes of this book, we may think of the auroral zone as having the latitude limits where the auroral frequency is half that at the zone maximum, although the term often has been applied loosely to the maximum of the belt only.
2. '*Polar caps*' are roughly the regions bounded by the auroral zone maxima and containing the geomagnetic poles.
3. '*High latitude*' usually is less restrictive than 'polar cap,' and approximates those regions having geomagnetic latitudes greater than about 50°.
4. '*Low latitude*' usually refers to geomagnetic latitudes ranging up to about 30°, north and south of the equator. Within this zone an 'equatorial zone' is sometimes recognized. It extends to about 5° magnetic latitude, north and south, and embraces the region in which certain strictly equatorial phenomena (associated with nearly horizontal field lines) are observed.
5. '*Middle latitudes*,' accordingly, apply to the remaining geomagnetic latitude belts with approximate limits of 30° and 50°, north and south.

1.4.2. The Variation Field; Magnetic Indices. Varying currents flow in the upper atmosphere, with time scales that range from days to seconds, depending on the nature of the current sources. These external currents induce further currents inside the earth, and together they produce magnetic variations above the ground that are known as the magnetic 'variation field.' The precise nature and location of the variation currents is of considerable interest and will be discussed later in this book. It is sufficient to note here that currents flowing at or above E-region heights are the primary sources of the variation fields. Because of the ionospheric location of the source currents, it is not surprising that the magnetic variation field, like the upper atmosphere generally, is greatly affected by solar disturbances.

Magnetic variations at frequencies below about 1 cycle/minute have been recorded continuously on a world-wide basis for many decades. Higher-frequency recordings have also been made, particularly in recent years, for the study of micropulsations and magnetic impulses (Chapters 8 and 12). Experimental techniques at the higher frequencies are still changing rapidly and there has been little standardization of the data. The lower-frequency records, 'magnetograms,' are, however, taken by standard magnetometers and are essentially similar throughout the world. Three perpendicular field components are measured as functions of time: normally one of them lies in the mean direction of the horizontal component, H, of the main field; the other two are in the vertical and horizontal directions of the orthogonal plane. The unit employed for the variation field is usually the gamma, γ, equal to 10^{-5} gauss. To assist in the analysis of magnetic data and in the comparison of magnetic data with other geophysical measurements, international indices based on the standard magnetometer records have been established.

Since 1884, magnetic observatories have assigned a character figure, C, to their daily records. The three values $C = 0, 1, 2$, correspond to daily variations that are quiet, moderately disturbed, or highly disturbed. C values from about 50 observatories are then averaged to one decimal place, and this mean value is called the 'International Magnetic Character Figure,' C_i, for that day. The C_i index is admittedly crude, and when a 3-hr K index (described below) was introduced in 1940, a new planetary International Magnetic Character Figure, C_p, was derived from the K values. The C_p values, like C_i, range from 0.0 to 2.0 and this permits the use of C_i in the earlier years and C_p in the later years of long-term studies.

Since 1940, magnetic observatories have measured the *total* range of variation of the most active component of the magnetic field within a 3-hr interval. A quasi-logarithmic scale, increasing in integral steps from $K = 0$ to $K = 9$, is employed at each station, and the K values then include local effects. To obtain a planetary index, about a dozen stations, located in and near the northern auroral zone, prepare a 'standardized' index, K_s, from their local K values. The K_s values are largely free of local time variations and are averaged to form the planetary K_p. The K_p index also has a range from 0 to 9, but it is computed to the nearest third of a unit. The K_p values $0, \frac{1}{3}, \frac{2}{3}, 1, \frac{4}{3}, \ldots$, are usually written in the notation $0, 0^+, 1^-, 1, 1^+, \ldots$. The nonlinearity of K_p makes it inconvenient for some forms of analysis. The a_p index is a linear index derived from K_p, and it gives the range of total 3-hr variation in units of approximately 2γ. Daily indices can be obtained by summing the eight values of K_p, or by averaging the eight values of a_p; the latter average is called the A_p index.*

1.5. IONOSPHERIC RESEARCH

The history of research on the ionized regions of the upper atmosphere is long and very difficult to trace accurately. The term 'ionosphere' is due to Watson Watt, but the name of Balfour Stewart is usually associated with the earliest concrete suggestion (1882) of the existence of such a region.

*These indices are published annually by the International Union of Geodesy and Geophysics (IUGG); the earlier bulletins are labeled IATME (International Association of Terrestrial Magnetism and Electricity), but since 1955 the bulletins have been labeled IAGA (International Association of Geomagnetism and Aeronomy).

Many people have contributed to its study since that time, and the ionosphere has entered into the everyday life of most persons because of its role in long-distance communications and broadcasting. The operational requirements of these applications have so greatly accelerated upper atmospheric studies that it is not always possible to differentiate clearly between fundamental and applied research. The present volume deals primarily with the physics of the upper atmosphere and includes communications only incidentally.

Probably the most important single achievement in ionospheric research was the development of the ionosonde. This evolved from the experimental equipment of Breit and Tuve, who were the first to do pulse sounding of the ionosphere, although the continuous-wave method of Appleton also contributed much to the development. The present-day ionosonde, of which a variety of models exist and now operate in very many countries on a routine basis, consists of a pulse transmitter and receiver having an operating frequency that is swept, or stepped, over the range from about 1–20 Mc/s. The time delay between the transmitted and received pulse varies with frequency and represents propagation time to and from, including retardation within, various levels in the ionosphere. The resulting record of 'equivalent height' of reflection (h') versus frequency (f) is known as an 'ionogram,' or $h'(f)$ curve. From such a curve it is possible to compute the electron density (N) as a function of height (h), and so provide an 'electron density profile' or '$N(h)$ curve.' This last step, however, is not a simple procedure, and a great deal of the early research on the ionosphere involved the equivalent height (often called the 'virtual height') of reflection. An additional complication is introduced by the geomagnetic field which, in the ionized upper atmosphere, splits the radio waves into two differently polarized components which propagate more or less idependently and produce two echo traces on the ionogram instead of one. Despite these difficulties, for many years the ionosonde has been the main tool for research on the ionosphere.

Recently, the sweep-frequency sounding technique has been extended to satellite operation in the Canadian 'top-side sounder' satellite, Alouette I, which probes the ionosphere from above to determine its shape and structure above the level of maximum ionization. This work is at an early stage and no very detailed picture of the top side is yet available. The preliminary work would indicate that the physical processes and many of the features associated with the F-layer ionization peak extend to much greater heights. Differences in experimental techniques and inadequate understanding of this topic have led to a somewhat artificial division of the subject matter between Chapters 4 and 5.

Sample ionograms for the bottom and top sides of the ionosphere, taken at approximately the same time and geographic location, are shown in Fig. 1.6. The measured parameter is delay time, which in the one case is indicated by virtual height above the earth and in the other by virtual depth below the satellite, the latter itself being some 1000 km above the surface at the time. In Fig. 1.7 is shown the corresponding $N(h)$ profile computed for the entire height range. To facilitate comparison of these two figures, the abscissa of the latter shows the radio frequency at which reflection would occur (f) as well as electron density (N); these two quantities are related by

$$N = 4\pi^2 \epsilon_0 m f^2/e^2, \tag{1.18}$$

where e and m are the electronic charge and mass and ϵ_0 is the free-space permittivity (see Appendix I).

Throughout the book the reader will find frequent reference to ionosonde

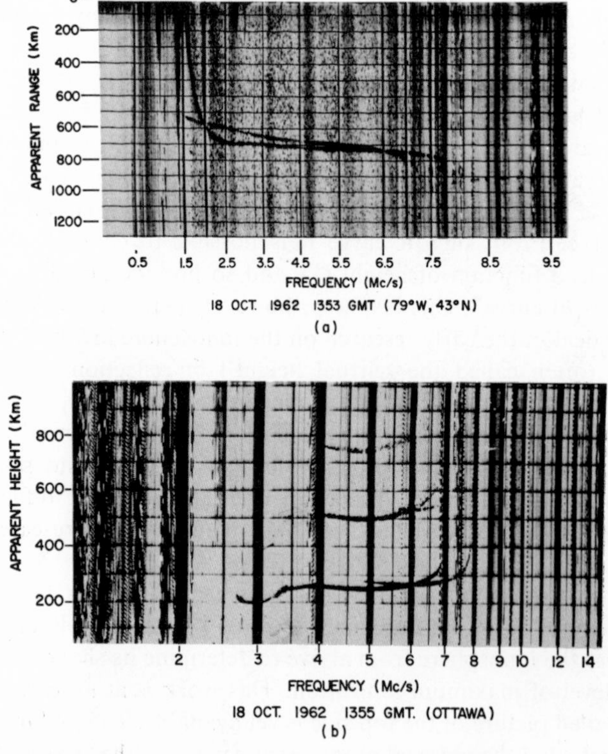

Fig. 1.6 Ionograms obtained with a satellite-borne top-side sounder, (a), and with a ground-based ionosonde, (b), at approximately the same time and geographic location. (From G. L. Nelms, Ionospheric results from the topside sounder satellite Alouette, Space Research IV. Amsterdam; North-Holland Publishing Company, 1964, Figs. 12, 13.) The bottom-side echo traces shown at about heights of 500 and 750 km are due to multiple reflections between the ionosphere and the ground.

data, since our understanding of the ionosphere rests in large measure on these data. Numerous other instruments, however, have been employed to explore our upper atmosphere, such as the auroral or backscatter radar, the riometer, the all-sky camera, the whistler receiver, and rocket and satellite probes. Succeeding chapters give little or no space to the techniques of measurement; rather the results of observations by any suitable technique are presented.

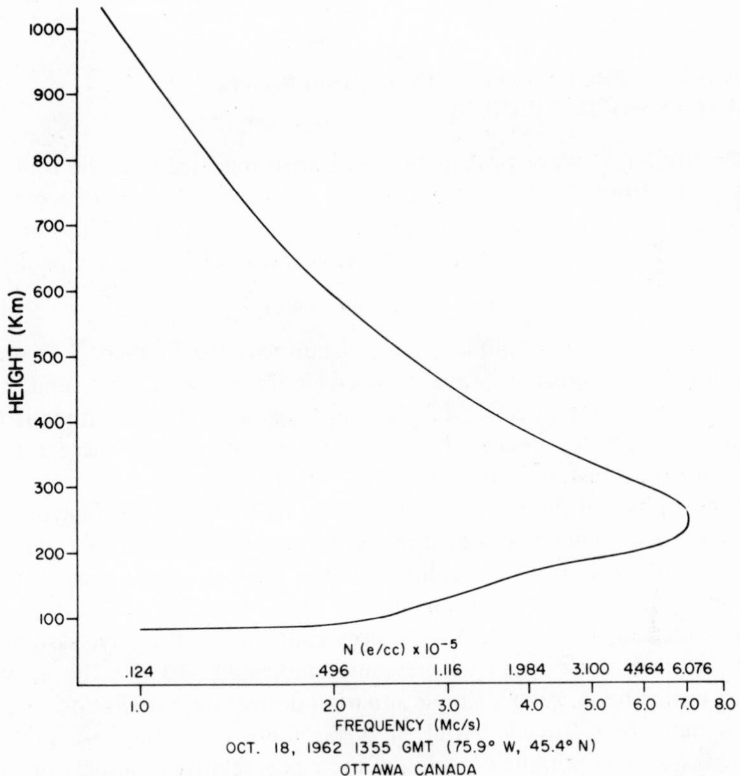

Fig. 1.7 The height profile of electron density computed from the two ionograms of Fig. 1.6. For ease of comparison with the preceding figure, the abscissa gives the reflection frequency as well as electron density. (From Nelms, *ibid.*, Fig. 14.)

In connection with radio studies, the reader will note the use of a standard nomenclature throughout the book to designate the various frequency bands of the radio spectrum. For convenient reference the main bands are identified in Table 1.1.

Table 1.1

Frequency Range	Band Designation	Abbreviation
300–3000 c/s	extremely-low frequencies	ELF
3.0–30 kc/s	very-low frequencies	VLF
30–300 kc/s	low frequencies	LF
300–3000 kc/s	medium frequencies	MF
3.0–30 Mc/s	high frequencies	HF
30–300 Mc/s	very-high frequencies	VHF
300–3000 Mc/s	ultra-high frequencies	UHF
3000–30,000 Mc/s	super-high frequencies	SHF

1.6. ENERGY PROPAGATION IN A DISPERSIVE ANISOTROPIC MEDIUM

The subject of wave propagation will arise repeatedly in the following pages, both from the hydrodynamic and electromagnetic points of view. In many wave systems commonly met in physics, the variation (φ) of some quantity can be expressed in terms of plane waves with the functional form

$$\varphi = A \cos (\omega t - kz), \tag{1.19}$$

where A is a constant amplitude, ω a constant 'circular frequency' or simply 'frequency,' k a constant 'wave number,' t the variable time, and z the space variable in the direction of phase propagation. The amplitude is then constant on surfaces defined by $\omega t - kz =$ constant, and these surfaces move with the constant 'phase speed' ω/k in the z direction.

In most physical situations the ratio of the frequency to the wave number, ω/k, is not a constant but is determined by some 'dispersion relation,' say, $\omega = \omega(k)$, which is itself determined by the physics of the process under consideration. There are certain special cases, however, where this ratio may be independent of k; then the energy contained in the wave system can move with the same speed as previously indicated, ω/k. In the areas of interest in this book, such a simple situation derives only in limiting circumstances that are relatively trivial. It is far more often the case that ω/k depends on k and upon the direction of the z axis, relative to gravity or to the geomagnetic field; then new considerations must be taken into account. These constitute a field of investigation in their own right, but the most important aspects for present purposes are outlined below. (See Chapter 6 for a more detailed consideration of the dispersion relation and some of its consequences in connection with the propagation of atmospheric gravity waves; for similar information concerning radio waves in the ionosphere see the appendices.)

If attention be confined still to propagation in a single direction, some insight may be gained by the (mathematical) construction of a 'wave group,' made up by the superpositioning of a number of waves of the form (1.19), but with A as a function of k:

$$\varphi = \sum_k A(k) \cos(\omega t - kz), \tag{1.20}$$

or more conveniently, by an integration over a continuous finite range of k's:

$$\varphi = \int [A(k) \cos(\omega t - kz)]\, dk. \tag{1.21}$$

A particularly simple case arises if $A(k)$ is taken to be unity over some range $k_0 - K < k < k_0 + K$ and to be zero outside that range, k_0 being some 'central' value of wave number. If K is sufficiently small, it may be supposed that

$$\omega = \omega_0 + \omega_0' \Delta k \tag{1.22}$$

for departures $\Delta k \equiv k - k_0$ that are less than K, where ω_0 and ω_0' are the values of ω and $d\omega/dk$ at $k = k_0$. The cosine factor in (1.21) may then be expanded as

$$\begin{aligned} \cos(\omega t - kz) &= \cos[\omega_0 t - k_0 z + (\omega_0' t - z)\Delta k] \\ &= \cos[\omega_0 t - k_0 z] \cos[(\omega_0' t - z)\Delta k] \\ &\quad - \sin[\omega_0 t - k_0 z] \sin[(\omega_0' t - z)\Delta k]; \end{aligned} \tag{1.23}$$

the variable of integration may be changed from k to Δk; and the integration itself may be completed to yield

$$\varphi = 2(\omega_0' t - z)^{-1} \sin[(\omega_0' t - z)K] \cos(\omega_0 t - k_0 z). \tag{1.24}$$

The wave then has a fine-scale structure provided by the $\cos(\omega_0 t - k_0 z)$ factor, contained within a more slowly varying group envelope given by $2(\omega_0' t - z)^{-1} \sin[(\omega_0' t - z)K]$. The maximum amplitude of the envelope occurs at

$$\omega_0' t = z, \tag{1.25}$$

and this plane, like the envelope as a whole, moves with the 'group speed' ω_0'. The energy of the wave system resides primarily in the vicinity of the maximum—it falls off roughly as $(\omega_0' t - z)^{-2}$ at points well removed from the maximum—and so must similarly move with the group speed. In the simple case $\omega/k =$ constant, it is readily seen that $\omega_0' = \omega_0/k_0$, so the group speed equals the phase speed.

The foregoing development may be generalized by the addition of waves propagating in more than one direction. For this purpose, it is convenient to express the individual components in the form,

$$\varphi(\mathbf{k}) = A(\mathbf{k}) \cos(\omega t - \mathbf{k} \cdot \mathbf{r}) = A(\mathbf{k}) \cos(\omega t - k_x x - k_y y - k_z z), \tag{1.26}$$

and to perform the integration over a range of variables dk_x, dk_y, dk_z. The analysis proceeds as before, except that now it is assumed that

$$\omega = \omega_0 + (\partial\omega/\partial k_x)_0 \Delta k_x + (\partial\omega/\partial k_y)_0 \Delta k_y + (\partial\omega/\partial k_z)_0 \Delta k_z. \tag{1.27}$$

The integral then yields a maximum at a point rather than a plane, and this point, like the envelope as a whole, moves so that

$$0 = x - t(\partial\omega/\partial k_x)_0 = y - t(\partial\omega/\partial k_y)_0 = z - t(\partial\omega/\partial k_z)_0. \quad (1.28)$$

The 'packet velocity' is then given by the vector components

$$(\partial\omega/dk_x)_0,\ (\partial\omega/\partial k_y)_0,\ (\partial\omega/\partial k_z)_0, \quad (1.29)$$

and the energy moves with this velocity. In the simple case when ω depends only on the magnitude and not on the direction of **k**, it is readily shown that the vector (1.29) lies in the direction of **k**, and that the magnitude of the packet velocity is equal to the group speed.

The form of (1.29) implies a particularly simple and useful result, for it shows that the packet velocity is just the gradient of $\omega(\mathbf{k})$ in a **k** space. It then follows that, if k_x, k_y, and k_z are measured along the x, y, and z axes of physical space, and surfaces of constant ω are depicted in that space, then the normals to such surfaces yield the direction of the packet velocity, often called the 'ray direction.' The construction may be effected equally well if the coordinates are normalized to n_x, n_y, and n_z, given by $k_x c/\omega$, $k_y c/\omega$, and $k_z c/\omega$, respectively, c being some characteristic speed (for example, that of sound or of light); for the shape of an $\omega(\mathbf{n})$ surface is identical to that of the corresponding $\omega(\mathbf{k})$ surface; $|\mathbf{n}|$ may be interpreted as the refractive index

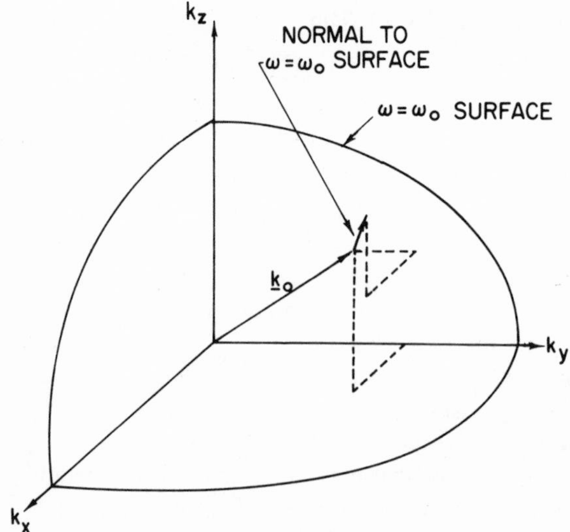

Fig. 1.8 Geometrical construction to determine direction of energy propagation (ray direction). A packet of plane waves is considered, propagating with phase normals centered on the $\mathbf{k}_0$ direction and with wave numbers (k) centered on k_0; they then have frequencies centered on ω_0. The surface $\omega(\mathbf{k}) = \omega_0$ is constructed, and the (inward or outward) normal to that surface at the point defined by $\mathbf{k}_0$ yields the ray direction.

for propagation in the $\mathbf{n}/|\mathbf{n}|$ direction. The graphical construction is illustrated in Fig. 1.8 for one type of $\omega(\mathbf{k})$ or $\omega(\mathbf{n})$ relation. Its application to the problems of this book is simplified through the occurrence of an axis of symmetry (governed by gravity in hydrodynamic oscillations and by the geomagnetic field in electromagnetic waves) such that the $\omega(\mathbf{k})$ or $\omega(\mathbf{n})$ surfaces may be generated by rotation. Attention may then be confined to a single plane containing the axis of symmetry, for the corresponding normals will lie in that same plane, and the complete picture may be regained by rotation of the two-dimensional cut. These planar constructions are illustrated for particular cases in Figs. 6.10 and 8.3. Note that these constructions yield only the axis of the energy flow, but not the sense (that is, direction along the axis); whether the outward or the inward normal is appropriate for the sense of energy flow can be determined only by establishing explicitly the sign of one of the components in Eq. (1.29).

1.7. THE SUN

The sun, of course, is the prime energy source for the processes in both the lower and upper atmosphere.

A number of atmospheric parameters show a cyclic variation with a period of about eleven years; this variation is a direct consequence of a varying solar emission and accordingly it is appropriate to think of an 11-yr solar activity cycle. It has been found that the number of sunspots appearing on the solar disk, averaged in some suitable fashion, can be used reliably as an index of solar activity so that 'sunspot cycle' and 'solar activity cycle' are used synonymously throughout the book. (Upper atmospheric phenomena do not show that the true sunspot cycle has a 22-yr rather than an 11-yr period, as discussed in Chapter 9.) Variations in ionospheric parameters are also found with a period of about 27 days, corresponding to the synodic rotation period of the sun—or, more accurately, to the synodic rotation periods of those latitude belts of the sun thought to be most closely associated with terrestrial phenomena. (See Sec. 9.2.)

The sunspot number is a quantity that has been used extensively in the study of solar-terrestrial relations. It was introduced by Wolf in 1849 and is still sometimes referred to as the 'Wolf number.' If there are seen on the sun s individual spots which are gathered into g groups, the corresponding sunspot number is

$$R = k(10g + s). \tag{1.30}$$

Here the factor k has a value between 0.5 and 1.0; it depends on the viewing conditions or image quality, the experience of the observer, and the nature of the instrument used. Consequently, a certain degree of arbitrariness enters into the data and the probable error of a single determination of R has been estimated at about 15 %. Efforts have been made at several observatories, and notably at Zurich where records are available back to 1749, to keep the sunspot number scale homogeneous (see Fig. 9.2). Alternative indices of solar activity have also been used, such as spot areas or the intensity of 10.7-cm radio noise, and these correlate well with sunspot numbers, but the former measurement is time-consuming and requires special photographs, while the latter data are available only from 1946.

Chapter 9 will note that sunspots are not the only manifestation of solar activity. The most violent effects in the upper atmosphere are probably associated with major flares, although not every major flare produces observable effects. Flare classifications are generally made according to an 'importance' scale, ranging from 1 minus to 3 plus, that is based primarily on the area covered on the solar disk but also takes into consideration such factors as flare brightness, suddenness of commencement, and spectral line width (see Sec. 9.3). In geophysical applications, major flares are usually considered to be those of importance at least 2 plus.

1.8. RELATED PHENOMENA

This book does not treat in any detail several items of fundamental interest in upper atmospheric research; these include cosmic rays, meteors, and lower atmospheric meteorology, all of which do play a role in the upper atmospheric processes. We shall see in Chapter 3 that cosmic rays are thought to be responsible for the ionization in the lowest part of the D region, sometimes called the 'C layer'; the role of 'solar cosmic rays' is discussed in Chapter 11. Meteors have been shown to contribute to the mean ionization in the lower part of the E region, and transitory ionized meteor trails in this height range are well known. Nevertheless, both these effects are thought to be of minor import to the large-scale processes of the upper atmosphere, and the reader is directed elsewhere for more information on meteors and cosmic rays. Also any discussion of meteorology is outside the scope of this book: it will be seen in Chapter 6 that the dynamics of the upper and lower atmospheres have certain linkages, but this topic has not yet been investigated in any detail.

1.9. INTERNATIONAL COOPERATION

In general, upper atmospheric phenomena must be studied on a global basis if they are to understood, and a world-wide array of research sites has been established for the purpose. A substantial number of the activities pursued at these stations is now well coordinated on an international basis, and examples can be seen in the global networks of magnetometer stations, ionosonde stations, and observatories maintaining a solar flare patrol. To a large extent international cooperation in upper atmospheric physics is carried on by direct contact between individuals, but it is furthered by certain formal organizations. Chief among these, for our purposes here, are the Union Géodésique et Géophysique Internationale (UGGI), Union Radio Scientifique Internationale (URSI), International Astronomical Union (IAU), and Committee on Space Research (COSPAR), all of which are now operating under the auspices of the International Council of Scientific Unions (ICSU). International cooperation was brought to new heights with the organization of an International Geophysical Year (IGY, 1 July 1957 to 31 December 1958), during which an extensive and coordinated observational program was carried out. This was followed by a year of International Geophysical Cooperation (IGC, 1 January–31 December 1959) for which coordinated observations continued on an only slightly reduced scale. These programs led to results of immense importance and provided masses of data of which the greater part has yet to be fully analyzed. Most of these data have been deposited in several world data centers and are available to the scientific community for study.

At the time of publication another extensive observational program, also coordinated on an international basis, is under way. Known as the International Years of the Quiet Sun (IQSY, 1 January, 1964–31 December 1965), it has been chosen to coincide with the minimum of the sunspot cycle so as to complement IGY. There can be little doubt that the IQSY program will add much to our knowledge of the earth's upper atmosphere, and will open new channels of investigation to challenge us in the years to come.

C. O. HINES
I. PAGHIS
T. R. HARTZ
J. A. FEJER

BIBLIOGRAPHY

1. Alfvén, H., and C. G. Fälthammar, Cosmical Electrodynamics, Fundamental Principles. 2nd ed. London: Oxford University Press, 1963.
2. Bates, D. R. (ed.), The Earth and its Atmosphere. New York: Basic Books, 1957.
3. Budden, K. G., Radio Waves in the Ionosphere. London: Cambridge University Press, 1961.
4. Chamberlain, J. W., Physics of the Aurora and Airglow. New York: Academic Press, 1961.
5. Chapman, S., and J. Bartels, Geomagnetism. Oxford: Clarendon Press, 1940.
6. CIRA 1961, COSPAR International Reference Atmosphere, 1961. Amsterdam: North Holland Publishing Company, 1961.

7. DeWitt, C., J. Hieblot, and A. Lebeau, (eds.), Geophysics: The Earth's Environment. New York: Gordon and Breach, Inc. 1963.

8. Dungey, J. W., Cosmic Electrodynamics, London: Cambridge University Press, 1958.

9. Ellison, M. A., The Sun and its Influence. London: Routledge and Kegan Paul, Ltd., 1955.

10. Evans, J. W. (ed.), The Solar Corona. New York: Academic Press, 1963.

11. Ginzburg, V. L., Propagation of Electromagnetic Waves in Plasma. New York: Gordon and Breach Science Pubs., Inc., 1961.

12. Harang, L., The Aurorae. New York: John Wiley & Sons, Inc., 1951.

13. Kuiper, G. P. (ed.), The Earth as a Planet. Chicago: University of Chicago Press, 1954.

14. ———, The Sun. Chicago: University of Chicago Press, 1953.

15. Massey, H. S. W., and R. L. F. Boyd, The Upper Atmosphere. London: Hutchison & Co., Ltd., 1958.

16. Mitra, S. K., The Upper Atmosphere, 2nd ed. Calcutta: Asiatic Society, 1952.

17. Odishaw, H. (ed.), Research in Geophysics, Vol. 1; Sun, Upper Atmosphere and Space. Cambridge: The M. I. T. Press, 1964.

18. Ratcliffe, J. A., The Magneto-Ionic Theory. London: Cambridge University Press, 1959.

19. ———, (ed.), Physics of the Upper Atmosphere New York: Academic Press, 1960.

20. Rawer, K., The Ionosphere. New York: Frederick Ungar Publishing Co., 1957.

21. Smith, H. J., and E. V. P. Smith, Solar Flares. New York: MacMillan Co., 1963.

22. Störmer, C., The Polar Aurora. Oxford: Clarendon Press, 1955.

2

L. Herzberg

Solar Optical Radiation and its Role in Upper Atmospheric Processes

2.1. INTRODUCTION

Electromagnetic radiation interacts with the earth's atmosphere, as with matter generally, by several different physical processes: it may interact with the free electrons in the atmosphere, with individual atoms and molecules, or with atomic nuclei. Since the relative importance of these different effects varies greatly with wavelength λ, one can divide the electromagnetic spectrum roughly into three regions, according to the dominant interaction process: (1) The radio-frequency region ($\lambda > 0.1$ cm) where interaction takes place mainly with free electrons of the atmosphere. (2) The so-called optical region comprising infrared, visible and ultraviolet light, as well as soft X-rays (0.1 cm $> \lambda > 10^{-9}$ cm). This is the part of the spectrum where the photon energies, $E = ch/\lambda$, (c = velocity of light, h = Planck's constant) are of the order of atomic and molecular energies, and where, as a consequence, the interaction between radiation and atmospheric atoms and molecules is most important. (3) The high-energy radiation of hard X-rays and of γ-rays ($\lambda < 10^{-9}$ cm). This radiation, like optical radiation, interacts with atoms and molecules, whereas its most energetic component (hard γ-rays) may also interact with atomic nuclei.

The present chapter is concerned with optical radiation in its relation to atmospheric processes generally and specifically with those interactions that are of interest in the height range of 30–120 km. Processes occurring at higher levels are treated in succeeding chapters (see in particular Chapter 4), as are the effects of high-energy corpuscular radiation (Chapter 11).

Hereafter, optical radiation comprising the spectral region from millimeter waves to X-rays will as a rule be referred to simply as 'light.' Although this term, as commonly understood, refers to a much narrower part of the spectrum, its more general use is justified in the present context, since in interaction with the atmosphere, radiation in the whole optical region behaves in much the same fashion. Variations with wavelength, although very pronounced and important, are essentially quantitative and do not correspond to fundamental differences in the physical processes involved.

Because light interacts with atoms and molecules, the optical properties and the chemical constitution of the atmosphere are closely interrelated. In the first place, attenuation of light by absorption at different wavelengths depends sensitively on the number and type of the atoms and molecules in the light path, so much so that the absorption spectrum of transmitted light is an important—in some cases the only—source of information on certain atmospheric constituents. Further, the absorbed radiation influences in varying degrees the chemical balance in the atmosphere, either by photodissociation of molecules or, more indirectly, by the initiation of photochemical reactions. Finally, some absorbed energy is re-emitted as optical radiation of the 'airglow' spectrum, whose characteristics are governed by conditions in the emitting regions.

These various interactions provide the main topic of the present chapter. Before they are discussed in detail, however, some background information on the incident solar radiation and its origin will be given.

We shall follow, as a rule, the established practice of using different units of length in the different wavelength regions of the optical spectrum: centimeters or millimeters at the longest wavelengths, microns ($1\ \mu = 10^{-4}$ cm) in the intermediate region, and Angstroms ($1\ \text{Å} = 10^{-8}$ cm) at short wavelengths.

2.2. THE SOLAR RADIATION INCIDENT ON THE EARTH'S ATMOSPHERE; THE EMITTING LAYERS OF THE SUN

The light emitted by the sun originates in three different and fairly well-defined layers: the photosphere, the chromosphere, and the corona. The outline of the photosphere is seen as the solar disk with its characteristic sharp limb. The chromosphere and corona are visible from ground level only when the light of the disk has been removed, either through an eclipse by the moon or through an artificial eclipse produced by an instrument (coronagraph) designed for this purpose. Under these conditions, the chromosphere appears as a narrow ring around the solar disk, with a very complicated irregular outline. The corona extends outward from the surface of the chromosphere to a considerable distance, partially in a rayed pattern.

The sun consists of hydrogen with a small admixture of the other elements. The bulk of the solar mass is contained below the photosphere. The temperature of the solar gas decreases from several million degrees at the center to a few thousand degrees at the boundary between photosphere and chromosphere, and then rises again very sharply. The increased temperature of the higher solar layers makes them practically transparent to radiation coming from below. For this reason, light from the photosphere penetrates into space, enabling us to 'see' the spectrum of the disk.

The energy lost by radiation from the surface of the sun is compensated for by energy released in the nuclear reactions that take place in the hot and dense central core. The upward transport of this energy poses a difficult theoretical problem. Up to the height of the chromosphere, that is, through the region of decreasing temperature, convection together with radiative transfer can account for the energy flux. Other means are necessary to explain the upkeep of the high coronal temperature, and energy transport by hydrodynamic and hydromagnetic waves has been considered in this connection.

The spectrum of photospheric radiation consists of a continuum with superimposed absorption lines, the Fraunhofer lines. The continuum extends from the microwave region ($\lambda \simeq 1$ cm) into the ultraviolet. Its intensity distribution corresponds approximately to that of a 6000°K black body in the visible region and to that of a 4200°K black body at the shorter wavelengths. The Fraunhofer lines are partly atomic absorption lines, especially Fe lines, arising from the ground state of the atom or from relatively low excited levels ($\lesssim 25$ ev), and partly absorption lines of molecules formed in the highest, coolest layer of the photosphere, for instance CN or CO. (Absorption lines produced in the solar spectrum by the earth's atmosphere are also called Fraunhofer lines. They are in general easily distinguished from lines originating in the sun, for example, by their variation with solar zenith angle.)

The chromosphere, the layer immediately above the photosphere, has a very complicated structure. This is obvious from its appearance, for instance as seen in a coronagraph picture, where, in addition to the irregular surface already mentioned, streams of luminous matter may be seen extending upward to a considerable height. These prominences, jets, etc., belong to the transient solar phenomena which are described more fully in Chapter 9. The chromosphere is a relatively thin layer of approximately 10,000 km thickness, (compared to the solar diameter of about 10^6 km), in which the transition from the photospheric temperature of about 5000°K to the temperature of the lower corona takes place. The most recent results indicate an increase to 400,000°K at the top of the chromosphere with a fairly smooth transition into the lower corona [3]. This is in contrast to earlier models in which the temperature at the top of the chromosphere was assumed to be only 30,000°K, with a sharp temperature increase at the lower boundary of the corona.

The solar corona extends above the chromosphere far out into space, perhaps beyond the orbit of the earth. The coronal temperature continues to rise from the top of the chromosphere outward and reaches its maximum value of about 2×10^6 °K at an altitude of approximately 50,000 km above the photosphere. There follows a gradual decrease in temperature to perhaps 50,000°K at the distance of the earth.

At wavelengths below 1500 Å where the photospheric intensity falls off sharply, chromospheric and coronal radiation dominate the solar spectrum. This radiation has been recorded spectrographically through the ultraviolet down to $\lambda = 80$ Å, and photometrically, in narrow wavelength bands, over the interval from 100 Å to 2 Å in the *X*-ray region. The solar emission at these shorter wavelengths is of great geophysical interest because it is the main source of energy for atmospheric ionization.

Of the very many emission features identified on the spectrograms, only the most important will be mentioned here: a group of strong emission lines between 1500 and 1000 Å, among them the Lyman alpha line of neutral hydrogen ($\lambda = 1215$ Å); the Lyman continuum of hydrogen, extending from $\lambda = 910$ Å to shorter wavelengths; and the resonance lines of neutral and ionized helium, at $\lambda = 584$ Å and $\lambda = 304$ Å, respectively. The Lyman α line carries the greatest energy flux of any individual line, of the order of 6 ergs cm^{-2} sec^{-1} at the earth's distance; the He^+ line ranks second [9, 10] with a flux estimated to be of the order of 0.5 erg cm^{-2} sec^{-1}. The high photon energy of the latter, 40 ev, renders it particularly significant to the physics of the ionosphere.

Observations over many years have shown that the total energy flux in the photospheric continuum fluctuates only very slightly about a constant mean value, the 'solar constant.' Similarly, local intensity variations on the quiet disk are only minor. In contrast, observations of the solar *X*-ray continuum below 100 Å, which extend now over almost a full solar cycle, have shown an approximately sevenfold increase of energy flux in the period between minimum and maximum solar activity. Measurements in separate wavelength bands have shown that the variation in energy flux increases with decreasing wavelength. In fact, the measurable intensity was found to extend at most to 10 Å during solar minimum, whereas it reached into the neighborhood of 6 Å during solar maximum. In addition, evidence for great intensity differences between different regions of the disk has been obtained both by direct *X*-ray photography of the sun and by eclipse observations. More particularly, it has been established that the intensity of *X*-ray emission is very high over the so-called active regions on the sun.

The coronal *X*-ray emission and certain coronal lines in the visible and near ultraviolet regions have revealed a further remarkable fact: even for a quiet sun, that is, even in the absence of flares and similar manifestations of local and temporary increase in emission, the coronal radiation is neither constant in time nor evenly distributed across the disk [5]. The behavior of the coronal emission differs therefore in important respects from the photospheric radiation and, as far as the evidence goes, from chromospheric radiation.

The coronal emission lines in the near ultraviolet and visible region of the spectrum, although they do not affect ionospheric conditions directly, are of interest in the present context for what one might call their diagnostic value. These lines are emitted by highly ionized atoms, such as Fe XIV ($\lambda = 5303$ Å, green), CaXV ($\lambda = 5694$ Å, yellow), or Fe X ($\lambda = 6375$ Å, red).* Since the distribution over the various states of ionization for each chemical element is very sensitive to temperature, intensity changes in the coronal lines are useful indicators of geophysically important variations in the state of the corona. This is discussed in more detail in Chapter 9.

2.3. TRANSMISSION THROUGH THE ATMOSPHERE

Radiation in the optical wavelength region undergoes considerable absorption and scattering when passing through the atmosphere. In the height region considered here, dust particles and droplets are of little importance and the attenuation is essentially a function of the number of absorbing and scattering molecules in the light path. For an extraterrestrial source like the sun and for a given distribution of the atmospheric constituents with altitude, this number depends on height above ground level and on zenith angle. Except for large zenith angles, where the curvature of the earth must be taken into account, the number of molecules per unit cross section in the light path is given by

$$N = N_0 \sec \chi , \tag{2.1}$$

where N_0 is the number of molecules per unit cross section above a given height and χ the zenith angle. For large values of χ ($> 75°$), the number of molecules in the light path is significantly smaller than that given by the

*Roman numerals following the chemical symbol indicate the degree of ionization, for example, Fe I stands for the neutral iron atom, Fe II, Fe III, Fe IV, etc., stand for the ions carrying 1, 2, 3, etc., positive charges (Fe^{+}, Fe^{++}, Fe^{+++}, etc.)

secant law [8] and becomes, for $\chi = 90°$ (horizontal incidence),

$$N \approx 36 N_0. \tag{2.2}$$

At sunrise and sunset, therefore, the attenuation at ground level corresponds to that due to 36 'air masses,' where one 'air mass' is the atmospheric mass per unit cross section through the zenith.

When the sun is below the horizon ($\chi > 90°$), illumination by direct sunlight occurs only above the height h_0 where the solid-earth shadow intersects the line to the zenith. If refraction is neglected, this height is given by

$$h_0 = r[\sec(\chi - 90°) - 1], \tag{2.3}$$

where r is the radius of the earth (6370 km), as can be seen in Fig. 2.1. The attenuation of radiation reaching this level exceeds that due to the 36 air masses previously mentioned, by a factor that reaches two in the limiting case of $\chi = 180°$.

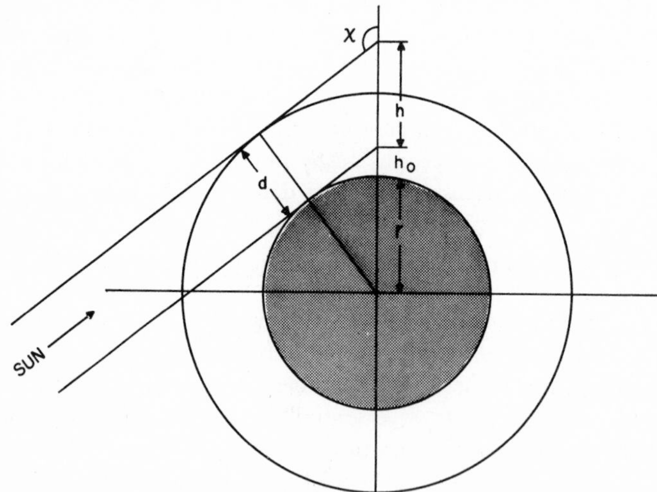

Fig. 2.1 Geometry of solar illumination at zenith angles, $\chi > 90°$.

In addition to the height h_0 of the solid-earth shadow, it is often of interest to know the altitude at which the atmosphere in the zenith is illuminated by light whose path avoids the lowest, most attenuating layers of the atmosphere. For a light ray that grazes an atmospheric level at height d, this altitude is given by

$$h' = h_0 + d \sec(\chi - 90°) \tag{2.4}$$

(Fig. 2.1). The quantity h' is termed the 'shadow height' corresponding to the level d.

The total attenuation of a light ray traversing the atmosphere is given by the exponential law

$$I = I_0 \exp - [\beta N/L + \sum_i \alpha_i N_i/L]. \tag{2.5}$$

Here I_0 and I are the intensities of incident and transmitted light; L is the number of molecules per unit volume at normal temperature and pressure (2.69×10^{19} cm^{-3}); N and N_i are, respectively, the total number of molecules and the number of molecules of different species in the light path, per unit cross section; β is the mean scattering coefficient which varies only slightly with changes in atmospheric constitution; and α_i is the absorption coefficient of the ith molecular species, per unit path length through the gas at normal temperature and pressure. (Instead of the absorption coefficient α, frequently the absorption cross section $\sigma = \alpha/L$ is used.)

The scattering coefficient β, according to Rayleigh's theory, is given by

$$\beta = \frac{32\pi^3(n-1)^2}{3L\lambda^4}, \tag{2.6}$$

where n is the index of refraction. The dependence of β on the fourth power of the wavelength causes a considerable variation in the importance of scattering in the different parts of the spectrum. There is, for instance, an approximately fourfold increase in β in the wavelength interval from the red ($\lambda \simeq 6500$ Å) to the blue ($\lambda \simeq 4500$ Å), with a corresponding difference in scattering intensity. This effect is quite obvious in the preponderance of blue in sunlight scattered from the sky and its deficit in the light of the setting sun. But even in the red, for large solar zenith angles, attenuation by scattering is by no means negligible. It reaches 80% at ground level at sunset and it can become as much as 96% for the radiation which strikes the atmosphere at high altitude when the sun is below the horizon. This fact is important in the discussion of ionospheric twilight effects.

Atmospheric absorption of optical radiation, unlike scattering, is not a simple function of wavelength and cannot be discussed in general terms. It is treated in detail in Secs. 2.4 and 2.5.

First, however, a few remarks should be made on atmospheric refraction. Its effect is relatively small in most circumstances but can become important when the light source is near the horizon. Since the index of refraction increases from $n = 1.0000$ above the atmosphere to $n \simeq 1.0003$ at ground level, light rays traverse the atmosphere along slightly curved paths. The main consequence of this for present purposes is a decrease in the apparent zenith angle of the sun amounting to 0.5° at the horizon. This effect has to be taken into account in computing the times of (apparent) sunrise and sunset.

2.4. ABSORPTION

Optical absorption is essentially confined to two wavelength regions which are separated from one another and from the region of radio wave absorption by spectral regions of relatively high transparency: the long-wavelength, mainly infrared, region of absorption between $\lambda \simeq 1$ cm and $\lambda \simeq 0.7\,\mu$, and the ultraviolet and soft X-ray region at $\lambda \leq 3500$ Å. Owing to the difference in quantum energy of the radiation, the character of absorption and its effect on the atmosphere differ considerably in the two regions. In the long-wavelength region, absorption takes place in bands of discrete spectral lines which are seen against the background of the solar spectrum; in the short-wavelength region, the absorption is continuous and leads to a complete cutoff at ground level of the solar radiation for wavelengths $\lambda < 2900$ Å. (The wavelength region $\lambda > 2900$ Å is frequently referred to as the 'accessible' region of the solar spectrum.)

2.4.1. Absorption in the Visible, Infrared, and Microwave Region: the Minor Atmospheric Constituents. The long-wavelength part of the atmospheric absorption spectrum consists of a large number of discrete molecular bands, corresponding to transitions in various molecules from very low energy states, mainly the ground state, to a stable state of higher energy (excited state). The excited state may differ from the ground state in rotational energy, in vibrational and rotational energy, or in electronic as well as in vibrational and rotational energy. Pure rotation bands occur in the centimeter and millimeter region of the spectrum, which is known as the 'microwave region.' Rotation-vibration bands, because of the higher energy of vibrational excitation, lie in the near infrared. Electronic bands are not restricted to any specific part of the optical spectrum, though they usually involve fairly high energy. In the case of the various atmospheric molecules, the intense ('allowed') electronic absorption features are confined to the ultraviolet. This accounts for the existence of the 'optical window' in the visible part of the spectrum.

The atmospheric absorption spectrum in the long-wavelength region has been studied in great detail and its origin is now very well understood. The two main constituents of the atmosphere, diatomic oxygen, O_2, and nitrogen, N_2, contribute very little to the total absorption in this region. These two molecules, owing to their symmetry, do not produce rotation or rotation-vibration bands, for the former occur only if the molecule has a permanent dipole moment, the latter only if the dipole moment changes during the vibration. As a consequence, N_2 does not absorb at all in the accessible region, and O_2 only in certain intrinsically weak bands which correspond to electronic transitions of low probability ('forbidden' transitions), more specifically in two bands in the millimeter region and in the important 'atmospheric' bands in the red and near infrared. Because of the great abundance of O_2 in the atmosphere, however, the red atmospheric bands (the strongest at 7600 Å) stand out very sharply against the background of the solar continuum. (Incidentally, it was in these bands that the oxygen isotopes O^{17} and O^{18} were discovered.)

Most of the atmospheric absorption in the accessible region is due to minor atmospheric constituents, namely, carbon monoxide (CO), carbon dioxide (CO_2), nitrous oxide (N_2O), methane (CH_4), ozone (O_3), and water (H_2O). Except in the case of O_3 (see below), H_2O, and possibly N_2O, spectroscopic measurements indicate that the rare molecules have the same distribution with height as the bulk of the atmosphere.

2.4.2. Absorption of Ultraviolet Radiation; Photodissociation and Photoionization. For observation from ground level, atmospheric absorption in the ultraviolet region of the spectrum sets in at $\lambda \simeq 3500$ Å with a series of diffuse bands which are known to be due to ozone. These bands soon merge into a strong continuum, and beyond $\lambda \simeq 2900$ Å the atmosphere is completely opaque. The physical processes underlying the ultraviolet absorption were originally identified on the basis of laboratory data combined with knowledge gained from observations in the accessible wavelength region. Rocket experiments at high altitudes now make it possible to refine the picture and fill in details.

In the ultraviolet absorption region the photon energy becomes high enough to make possible photodissociation and photoionization of the various atmospheric constituents. The combined effect of different absorption processes varies with wavelength, as does the altitude at which the incident radiation is reduced to a given fraction of its original intensity.

Conventionally, atmospheric absorption at a given wavelength is characterized by the 'penetration depth,' defined as the altitude at which, for vertical incidence, the intensity of transmitted light has been reduced by a factor e (see Eq. 2.5). For the main atmospheric constituents, whose abundances increase exponentially with depth, this altitude also corresponds to the level of maximum rate of absorption. Figure 2.2 shows, as a function of wavelength, the 'penetration depth' defined in this way. As seen in the diagram, the atmospheric absorption continuum sets in at $\lambda \simeq 3000$ Å and extends from there to shorter wavelengths. Between 3000 Å and 2000 Å, the absorption is relatively weak and is due almost solely to dissociation of ozone, O_3. In this part of the spectrum radiation penetrates to 50 km at the O_3 absorption maximum ($\lambda = 2500$ Å), and even farther at longer and shorter wavelengths. From 2400 Å to shorter wavelengths, diatomic oxygen, O_2, contributes to the total intensity of absorption; however, O_2 absorption between 2400 Å and 2000 Å, though continuous and producing dissociation, is very weak and does not prevent the radiation from penetrating deeply into the atmosphere. From 2000 Å on, the penetration decreases sharply, because of absorption in a series of strong O_2 bands with accompanying dissociation continuum. This O_2 continuum reaches maximum

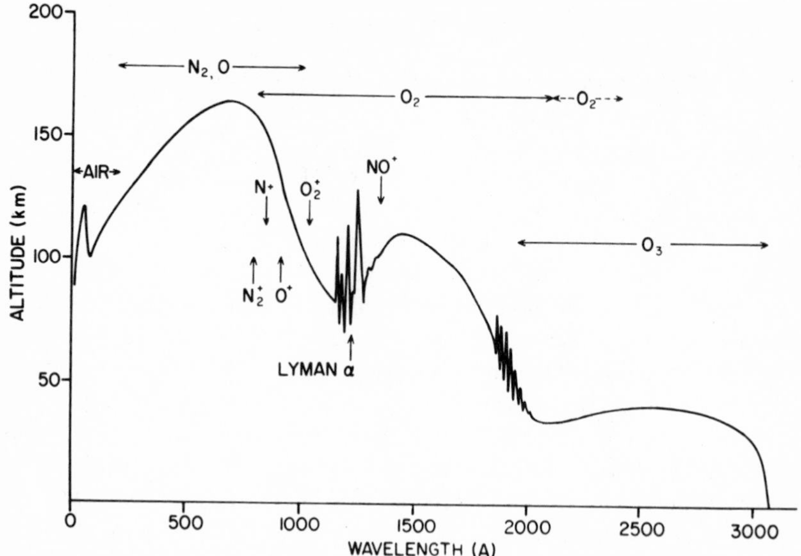

Fig. 2.2 Altitude at which the intensity of solar radiation drops to $1/e$ of its value outside the earth's atmosphere, for vertical incidence. (Based on Nawrocki, Watanabe, and Smith [7].)

intensity at $\lambda \simeq 1500$ Å. From here to $\lambda \simeq 1000$ Å, the penetration depth becomes very variable, owing to the superposition of strong discrete O_2 absorption bands on the diminishing O_2 continuum.

Although generally rather opaque, the 1500–1000 Å region contains a number of narrow 'windows' in which radiation may penetrate to an altitude of, perhaps, 70 km. One of these windows coincides in wavelength with the Lyman α solar emission line ($\lambda = 1215.7$ Å). This is of importance for the ionospheric D and E layers (cf. Chapter 3) since Lyman α has a sufficiently high photon energy to ionize certain rare atmospheric constituents, especially nitric oxide (NO).

Absorption at wavelengths shorter than 1000 Å can, in the main, be accounted for by photoionization of the dominant atmospheric constituents: of O_2 at $\lambda \leq 1026$ Å, of O at $\lambda \leq 910$ Å, of N at $\lambda \leq 852$ Å, and of N_2 at $\lambda \leq 796$ Å.

As far as is known, N_2 has no important dissociation continuum in the ultraviolet. Photodissociation, however, does occur by discrete absorption ('predissociation') in the wavelength region $\lambda < 1270$ Å, which includes the wavelength of Lyman α. Since Lyman α penetrates rather deeply into the atmosphere, as pointed out earlier, its absorption provides a source of free N atoms at moderate altitude (~ 85 km). This is important because the only other efficient source of N atoms in the atmosphere, dissociative recombination of N_2^+,

$$N_2^+ + e \rightarrow N + N,$$

is primarily a high-altitude process.

2.4.3. The Ozone Layer. Ozone in the atmosphere is produced predominantly by the addition of an oxygen atom to a diatomic oxygen molecule in a triple collision:

$$O + O_2 + M \rightarrow O_3 + M.$$

The O_2 molecule has two different dissociation continua in the ultraviolet, one between 2400 Å and 2000 Å (Herzberg continuum), the other between 1700 Å and 1500 Å (Schumann-Runge continuum). As shown in Fig. 2.2, the depth of penetration is very different in the two wavelength regions. As a result there are two widely separated regions of maximum atomic oxygen production: one at $\sim$ 100 km; the other at $\sim$ 35 km. Of these two levels, the lower one is much more favorable for the formation of ozone since the higher atmospheric density greatly increases the probability of triple collisions. The atmospheric ozone abundance, therefore, will be mainly concentrated in a layer centered at approximately 35 km altitude.

Above about 65 km, the effect of the ozone layer becomes negligible, and light of the sun and other extraterrestrial sources is observed to about 2000 Å, that is, to wavelengths well below the ground-level cutoff. The variation of the ozone abundance with height can be measured by observation of the solar spectrum at different altitudes. Figure 2.3 gives the results of three rocket flights which have taken place at different times. In each case a layer of ozone has been found, although there were some differences

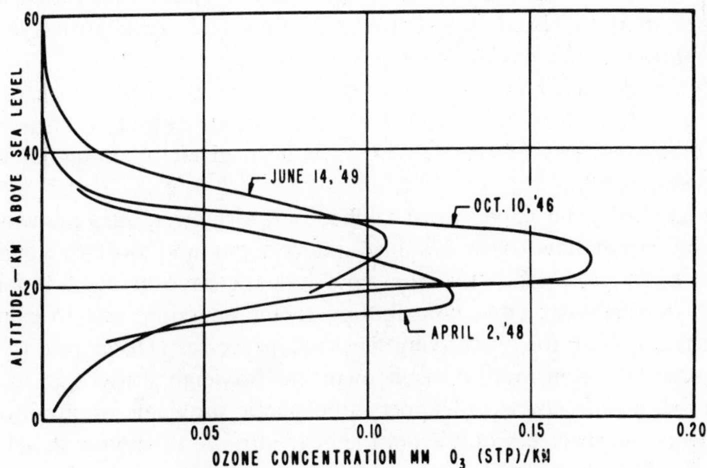

Fig. 2.3 Vertical distribution of O_3 from three rocket flights. (Johnson, Purcell, Tousey, and Watanabe [4].)

both in total abundance and in the altitude at which the layer was centered. The variability of the ozone layer is not surprising since the abundance of ozone at different altitudes depends, apart from the photochemical conditions, on a number of factors, among them the complicated and varying effects of turbulence and diffusion.

In a similar way, the abundances at different altitudes of the other atmospheric constituents depend on both photochemical and dynamic effects. For this reason no exact predictions can be made, on the basis of laboratory data only, as to the chemical constitution of the higher layers of the atmosphere. For instance, photochemical considerations cannot give precise values for the degree of dissociation of O_2 into O atoms at high altitudes. Different estimates put the height of the 'oxygen transition region' (50% dissociation of O_2) at various altitudes between 90 and 110 km.

2.5. AIRGLOW

The various phenomena involving the emission of optical radiation by the atmosphere, as opposed to absorption, are classified according to their general appearance and association with other phenomena either as aurora or as airglow. Aurora is the subject of a separate chapter (Chapter 13); the much less extensive observations on airglow and their interpretation are discussed here.

We designate as airglow the weak, generally widespread, and steady glow from the sky which is always present, though in varying degree. At high latitudes, airglow forms a background for the more intense, highly variable, and localized phenomenon called 'aurora.' It should be recognized, however, that the borderline between airglow and weak aurora is vague and is drawn differently by different authors.

We can discuss here only the most important and best-established data on airglow and their most widely accepted interpretations. Very complete and critical reviews of the subject have been given by Bates [1] and by Chamberlain [2].

In spite of great experimental difficulties, airglow spectra showing considerable detail have been obtained under night and twilight conditions. These 'night glow' and 'twilight glow' spectra have made it possible to recognize different factors contributing to the emission, and to gain some understanding of the underlying physical processes. Observations of the 'day glow' are even more difficult owing to Rayleigh scattering.

In the general context of upper atmospheric problems we are interested in the airglow spectrum only from the near infrared to shorter wavelengths, since the long-wavelength emission of the atmosphere ($\lambda > 5\mu$) is mostly thermal radiation originating in the lowest layers.

The airglow spectrum, though feeble throughout, is very rich and contains a number of important and very interesting features which have been definitely identified: the red and green lines of neutral atomic oxygen, at 5577 Å and 6300–6364 Å, respectively; the sodium D lines at 5893 Å; bands belonging to different systems of the O_2 molecule, which lie in the red and infrared and in the ultraviolet; the N_2^+ band at 3914 Å; and a relatively intense group of rotation-vibration bands of OH, extending from the infrared into the visible region. At times, the hydrogen Hα line at 6563 Å and the helium line at 10,863 Å are observed. There is probably also a continuum or group of unresolved bands in the 4000 Å region.

Various methods have been employed to determine, from the ground, the altitude at which the night glow is emitted. One, the van Rhijn method, is based on the variation of intensity with zenith angle. Other methods are based on emission temperature as determined from line width or from the intensity distribution in molecular bands. The results obtained by these methods are, as a whole, neither very clear-cut nor consistent. This is due both to experimental difficulties and to the uncertainty of related factors, such as absorption in the lower layers or the efficiency of exchange of kinetic energy.

Certain of the results, however, are quite reliable. The most important example is the emission height of the rotation-vibration bands of OH, determined from the intensity distribution among lines arising from different rotational levels in the excited state. Since the transition probability for this type of band is small, the molecule spends a considerable time in the excited state. Therefore, unless the pressure is very low, that is, unless the bands are emitted at very great heights, the number of collisions undergone by the molecule in its excited state is sufficient to produce a rotational energy distribution corresponding to the ambient temperature. Intensity measurements in a number of OH bands have given rotational temperatures of 150–250°K, corresponding to altitudes of 65–110 km.

More direct altitude determinations have been made recently with rocket-borne photometers. These experiments have shown that the infrared OH bands originate between 56 and 100 km, in good agreement with the spectroscopic results. Various other emission features, especially the green oxygen line at 5577 Å, were found to originate in the regions from 80–110 km. Significantly, emission of the red oxygen lines was found to occur much higher (above the maximum height reached in the experiment, 163 km). These lines arise from an excited state with exceptionally long radiative lifetime, which at the lower altitudes is depopulated by the more frequent collisions.

High-altitude experiments have led to the discovery of airglow radiation in the ultraviolet region, particularly the Lyman α line of hydrogen at 1215 Å and an emission at approximately 2700 Å believed to be due to the O_2 molecule. This ultraviolet radiation, which originates in the 100-km altitude region, does not reach ground level since it is absorbed by the lower atmosphere.

The various processes underlying airglow emission are gradually becoming clear. Cosmic rays are believed to play only a minor role, though there is some evidence [4] that the N_2^+ emission at 3914 Å may be due to ionization by cosmic rays. Sunlight scattered into the dark side of the earth by the gas high above the earth's surface is now thought to produce, by further resonance scattering, the hydrogen Lyman α night glow. Except for these mechanisms, most of the energy emitted by nightglow appears to derive from solar radiation which has been absorbed by the atmosphere during the day and which becomes gradually available through subsequent chemical reactions as chemiluminescence.

For example, absorption of solar ultraviolet radiation produces free oxygen atoms by photodissociation of O_2 molecules, as already mentioned, and under suitable circumstances ozone will be formed by association of O and O_2 in three-body collisions. Oxygen in the form of O and O_3, produced by solar radiation in daytime, forms therefore a reservoir of energy which, by various chemical reactions, can be transformed into airglow radiation during the night.

The simplest of these reactions is the association of two normal O atoms in two-body or three-body collisions with subsequent emission of radiation. The various band systems of oxygen observed in the airglow correspond to transitions from the different excited states of the O_2 molecule which can be formed of O atoms in their ground states.

The process underlying the emission of the rotation-vibration bands of OH is more complicated. The dominant mechanism consists of two successive reactions and involves both O atoms and O_3 molecules:

$$\mathrm{OH} + \mathrm{O} \rightarrow \mathrm{H} + \mathrm{O}_2$$

$$\mathrm{H} + \mathrm{O}_3 \rightarrow \mathrm{O}_2 + \mathrm{OH}^*.$$

(The asterisk indicates that the OH molecule formed in the second reaction is in an excited state.) The maximum possible excitation energy is equal to the energy of reaction, and is slightly less than the energy of the tenth vibrational level of the OH molecule in its electronic ground state. Significantly, the OH bands observed in the airglow correspond to the transitions only between the first nine vibrational levels.

Mechanisms proposed to explain the excitation of other airglow features are more complicated than the O_2 and OH processes described and are not discussed in the present survey. Similarly, we shall not discuss the twilight glow in detail. The spectrum of the twilight glow can be understood as a superposition of the night glow spectrum and atmospheric fluorescence caused by incident sunlight. The main twilight effect consists in the enhancement of certain airglow features, the most important of which is the N_2^+

band at 3914 Å. In addition, the twilight glow contains a few features which are not seen in the night glow, among them certain O_2 bands, and the He line at 10,863 Å.

REFERENCES

1. Bates, D. R., The airglow, in Physics of the Upper Atmosphere. ed. J. A. Ratcliffe. New York: Academic Press, 1960, p. 219.
2. Chamberlain, J. W., Physics of the Aurora and Airglow, New York: Academic Press, 1961.
3. Friedman, H., Ultraviolet and x-rays from the sun, Ann. Rev. Astron. Astrophys. Vol. I. Palo Alto, Calif.: Annual Reviews, Inc., 1963, p. 59.
4. Johnson, F. S., J. D. Purcell, R. Tousey, and K. Watanabe, Direct measurements of the vertical distribution of atmospheric ozone to 70 kilometers altitude, *J. Geophys. Res.*, **57** (1952), 157.
5. Kreplin, R. W., Solar X-rays, *Ann. Geophys.*, **17** (1961), 151.
6. Meinel, A. B., Origin of the continuum in the night sky spectrum, *Astrophys. J.*, **118** (1953), 200.
7. Nawrocki, P. J., K. Watanabe, and L. G. Smith, The Upper Atmosphere. Geophysics Corp. of America, GCA Technical Report 61-13-A, 1961.
8. Pressley, E. C., Air mass between an observer and outer space, *Phys. Rev.*, **89** (1953), 654.
9. Purcell, J. D., D. M. Packer, and R. Tousey, The ultraviolet spectrum of the sun, in Space Research, Proc. of the First Space Science Symposium, ed. H. Kallman-Bijl. Amsterdam: North Holland Publishing Company, 1960, p. 581.
10. Violet, T., and W. A. Rense, Solar emission lines in the extreme ultraviolet, *Astrophys. J.*, **130** (1959), 954.

3

J. S. Belrose

The Lower Ionospheric Regions

3.1. INTRODUCTION

The lower ionospheric regions are in some respects the most interesting of the whole upper atmosphere, for they support a wider range of physical phenomena than do any of the other regions. They are not well understood in detail, however, in part because of the complexity of their processes and in part because of observational limitations. The latter are such as to render direct studies of the neutral gas more difficult than those of the ionized constituents, and indeed observations of the ionization are often employed to infer characteristics of the background medium. This emphasis on the properties of ionization is reflected in the content of the present chapter, which treats in turn the ionospheric *D* region (Sec. 3.3) and *E* region (Sec. 3.4), following an introductory discussion of the formation of ionization layers (Sec. 3.2). Properties of the neutral gas necessarily enter the treatment, however, and the balance will be further redressed in Chapter 6 when the dynamical behavior of the atmosphere is considered.

3.2. THE FORMATION OF IONIZED LAYERS

Much of the study of the ionospheric regions concerns the detection and interpretation of the manner in which the free-electron concentration (N) varies with height (h)—the so-called $N(h)$ profile. This profile generally exhibits an increase of N to a peak value in the F region, followed by a decrease above. In addition, particularly during the day or during disturbed conditions, the $N(h)$ profile exhibits local peaks and ledges in the lower ionospheric regions. The more permanent or recurrent of these are attributed to overlapping 'layers' of ionization; the more variable are attributed to dynamical and disturbance processes. The latter receive fuller discussion later in the book, but a general appreciation of the formation of layers is essential at this point.

That layers are likely to form is clear from elementary considerations. The ionizing energy, be it carried by photons or particles, will be incident from above the atmosphere. It will encounter an increasing concentration of ionizable atmospheric particles as it penetrates and so will produce ionization at an increasing rate. It will suffer absorption in the process, however, and this will ultimately offset the increase of atmospheric concentration. A peak rate of production of ionization will be attained, and at lower heights the rate will decline until the flux of ionizing energy becomes negligible (see Fig. 3.1). The actual concentration of ionization will depend on the loss processes as well, but at least one peak is to be expected.

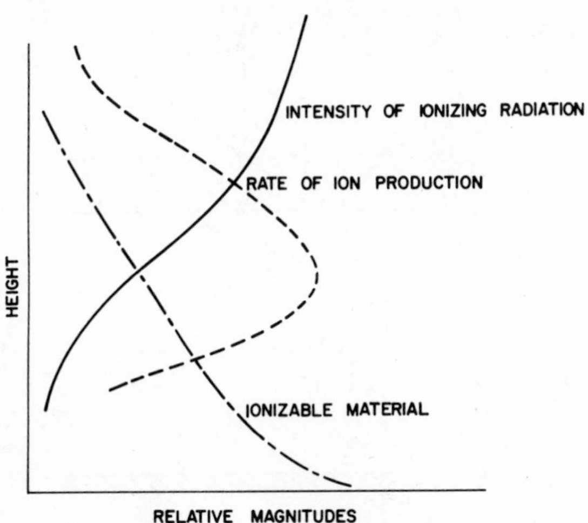

Fig. 3.1 Production of ionization in the atmosphere (schematic diagram).

To illustrate the operation of these factors, the production of a layer in relatively simple circumstances is discussed in this section, along lines explored first by Chapman [15]. Some of the complications that arise in practice are also touched upon, but for the most part they are left to their appropriate place in more specific discussions of the D, E, and F layers.

3.2.1. The Production of Electrons. A flat atmosphere will be assumed, in which the number density (n) of the ionizable molecules or atoms decreases with increasing height according to a simple exponential law:

$$n = n_g \exp(-h/H), \tag{3.1}$$

as in Eq. (1.5) with constant scale-height H assumed and with n_g = the number density at ground level (or at some other appropriate reference level from which h is measured). Radiation will be assumed incident from above, directed at an angle χ from the vertical; its intensity (S) will be measured in quanta per unit time per unit cross section (normal to the path), with an initial flux of S_∞ at $h = \infty$. A 'cross section for ionization' (A) may be defined, such that quanta are absorbed at the rate of nSA (per unit path length, per unit cross section normal to the path, per unit time) and electrons are freed at an equal rate, q (per unit volume, per unit time):

$$\cos\chi\, dS/dh = nSA = q. \tag{3.2}$$

(The differential of height, dh, corresponds to a differential of path length equal to $\sec\chi\, dh$, as illustrated in Fig. 3.2.)

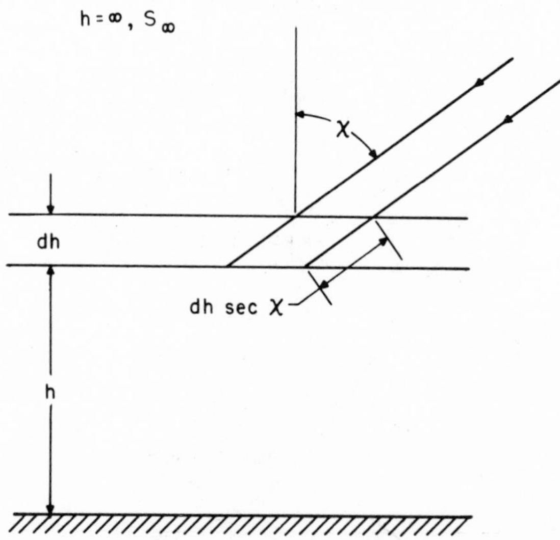

Fig. 3.2 Geometry of atmospheric ionization.

The first equation in (3.2) may be integrated to yield

$$S = S_\infty \exp(-n_t A \sec\chi), \tag{3.3}$$

where n_t is the total number of ionizable particles in a vertical column of unit cross section above the height at which S is measured:

$$n_t = Hn_g \exp(-h/H),$$

when (3.1) is adopted. The second equation in (3.2) now combines with (3.1) and (3.3) to show that q reaches a maximum value, given by

$$q_m = S_\infty \cos \chi / H \exp (1), \tag{3.4}$$

at a height

$$h_m = H \log_e (n_g A H \sec \chi) \tag{3.5}$$

where the ionizable constituents have a number density

$$n_m = \cos \chi / AH, \tag{3.6}$$

whereas in general

$$q = q_m \exp \left[1 + \frac{h_m - h}{H} - \exp \left(\frac{h_m - h}{H} \right) \right]. \tag{3.7}$$

Further, if q_0 and h_0 are the values taken by q_m and h_m when $\chi = 0$, then (3.5) and (3.7) may be rewritten as

$$h_m = h_0 + H \log_e (\sec \chi) \tag{3.8}$$

$$q = q_0 \exp \left[1 + \frac{h_0 - h}{H} - \sec \chi \exp \left(\frac{h_0 - h}{H} \right) \right]. \tag{3.9}$$

The normalized rate of electron production, q/q_0, is shown as a function of the normalized height, $y = (h - h_0)/H$, for various χ's in Fig. 3.3.

It is of interest to note from (3.4) that q_m is independent of the ionization cross section, A, as is the 'shape' of the layer given by (3.7), whereas the height h_m does depend on A but is independent of the initial intensity, S_∞.

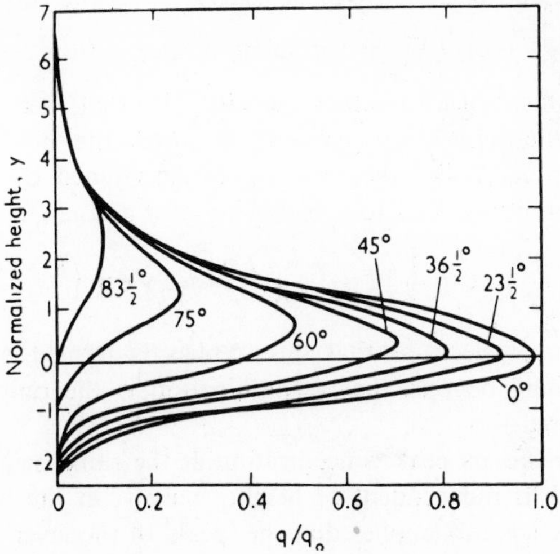

Fig. 3.3 The normalized rate of production of electrons, q/q_0, plotted against normalized height $(h - h_0)/H$, for different values of solar zenith angle χ [34].

3.2.2. The Loss of Electrons. Free electrons may be removed by recombination with positive ions or by attachment to neutral molecules, but in either case the removal rate is proportional to the electron concentration itself, N. In the case of recombination, the rate will also be proportional to the concentration of positive ions, and if no negative ions are present, this concentration will equal N (if the positive ions are singly charged). Thus the removal rate for recombination will in fact be proportional to N^2. The attachment process, on the other hand, will be dependent on the concentration (n) of neutral particles, which is essentially independent of N (for $n \gg N$). Depending on the process, then, the loss rate could have the functional form αN^2 or βN, and when written in this form, α is termed the 'recombination coefficient' and β the 'attachment coefficient' (see also Sec. 4.3.2).

In general, it is possible for both recombination and attachment to occur, and the loss rate can then be represented by $\alpha N^2 + \beta N$. In these circumstances, however, α and β become 'effective' coefficients whose relation to the basic processes may be quite complicated. For example, when negative ions are formed by an attachment process, the positive-ion concentration may remain proportional but no longer equal to N, and the factor of proportionality will depend both on the attachment rate β and on the recombination or charge-exchange rate of positive with negative ions. This and other complications will be discussed as appropriate in the later text.

3.2.3. Formation of an α-Chapman Layer. The equation of continuity for the electron concentration (N) in general takes the form

$$\partial N/\partial t + \operatorname{div}(N\mathbf{v}) = (\text{production rate}) - (\text{loss rate}) \tag{3.10}$$

where $\mathbf{v}$ is the local mean electron velocity. We shall here be concerned with a static situation ($\partial N/\partial t = \mathbf{v} = 0$) in which the production rate is given as in Sec. 3.2.1 and the loss rate is determined by recombination alone. These conditions lead to a balancing of q and αN^2, whence

$$N = \left(\frac{q_0}{\alpha}\right)^{1/2} \exp \frac{1}{2}\left[1 + \frac{h_0 - h}{H} - \sec\chi \exp\left(\frac{h_0 - h}{H}\right)\right]. \tag{3.11}$$

The distribution of electrons that this implies is termed an α-Chapman layer. (The α here denotes that recombination is the only electron loss process considered.)

Such a layer has its peak concentration at the same height as the peak production if α is independent of height, namely, at the height h_m given by (3.8). In practice, this implies that the 'peak' of the layer will descend in height from sunrise to noon and then rise again. In complementary fashion, the electron concentration at the peak will increase during the morning and decrease during the afternoon, being governed by the relation

$$N_m = (q_0/\alpha)^{1/2} \cos^{1/2} \chi. \tag{3.12}$$

The maximum attainable by N_m would be

$$N_0 = (q_0/\alpha)^{1/2}, \tag{3.13}$$

and this would be found at the subsolar point.

A radio wave of frequency f, vertically incident on a horizontally stratified layer, is reflected when it encounters a 'critical' electron concentration N_c which is proportional to f^2 (for the 'ordinary' component, see Appendix I). The 'penetration frequency' of a layer, f_0, is that frequency which will just escape reflection in the layer. It is evident that f_0 will be proportional to $N_m^{1/2}$, so

$$f_0 \propto \cos^{1/4} \chi. \tag{3.14}$$

Relations (3.8) and (3.14) are the ones most commonly employed in practice to test for the occurrence of a 'Chapman-like' layer.

3.2.4. Complications in the Formation of Layers. Many complicating features, beyond those touched upon in the discussion of removal processes, can affect the formation of ionospheric layers. Horizontal stratifications are spherical, rather than planar, and departures from horizontal stratification do occur. The temperature varies with height and so leads to a varying scale height in the exponential decrease of gas density. A number of ionizable constituents are present, and not all of them are subject to purely hydrostatic support. A number of ionizing radiations are present, with varying ionization cross sections. The number of free electrons produced need not equal the number of quanta absorbed; it could be greater, as a result of secondary emissions, or less because of competing absorption processes.

These various factors can, to some extent, be taken into account theoretically [16, 34], but in many cases they must be introduced empirically to account for multiple layers and abnormal characteristics. They will be mentioned again in later sections as they become pertinent.

3.3. THE IONOSPHERIC *D* REGION

It may be recalled from Chapter 1 that the *D* region includes the level of the mesopause, at 80–85 km height, where the temperature reaches a minimum variously estimated in the range 130°–250°K. Below this level, down to the stratopause at least, the atmosphere is subject to convective overturning and to the generation of turbulence. These processes apparently lead to a mixing of the atmospheric constituents, with the result that the relative concentrations of most chemical species are virtually independent of height. This conclusion has been confirmed by rocket-borne experiments which reveal, in particular, that N_2 and O_2 remain the dominant constituents and retain the approximate 4:1 ratio they exhibit at ground level.

The atmosphere above the mesopause is more stable, because of the increase of temperature with height, but nevertheless turbulence exists up into the base of the *E* region. This tends to maintain the uniformity of chemical composition throughout the *D* region, although it is debatable whether some separation of constituents might not occur even before the *E* region is reached. There is as yet no evidence for such separation.

In addition to N_2 and O_2, various trace constituents occur and must be taken into account for specific purposes. For example, CO_2 and O_3 are believed to play a major part (along with O_2) in maintaining the radiative energy balance, and so in controlling the temperature distribution [30]. If noctilucent clouds are due to water vapor, there may be sufficient H_2O to further affect the radiative balance. The ionization balance may be similarly influenced by trace constituents, and NO is particularly suspect in this regard. The uncertainty of its role will become clearer, however, as the discussion of ionization proceeds (both here and in Chapter 11).

The earliest studies of the ionosphere revealed directly the existence of the *E* and *F* layers, at heights above 90 km, but they also gave indirect evidence of underlying ionization in the *D* region. The first indications were provided by Appleton and Ratcliffe [4], who showed that this region must be responsible for a large part of the attenuation suffered by MF radio waves reflected from the daytime *E* layer. Subsequent studies have confirmed this deduction and added greater detail concerning the height variation of the electron distribution and collisional frequencies. The following pages outline the picture of the undisturbed *D* region that has emerged from these studies.

3.3.1. Electron Distribution in the *D* Region. The percentage ionization in the *D* region is exceedingly low and the properties of the neutral atmosphere have a significant influence on this ionization. Accordingly, it has been found rather difficult to carry out experimental studies of the electron distribution in this region. A number of techniques have been used in such investigations and the results indicate a variability that can be attributed both to observational limitations and to changes in atmospheric and ionizing conditions. Some of this variability in the experimentally determined $N(h)$ data is illustrated in Fig. 3.4. Curve 1 was obtained with the partial reflection technique which depends on the scattering of radio waves from irregularities in the electron number density distribution [10, 20, 23]; this is considered to be one of the best techniques currently available for the study of *D*-region ionization. Curve 3 was obtained by a rocket-borne Langmuir probe; curves 4, 5, and 8 by a radio propagation experiment that employed transmissions between a rocket and the ground facilities; and curve 6 by an ionospheric cross-modulation experiment. Curve 7 was derived from standard ionosonde data and does not extend below the *E*

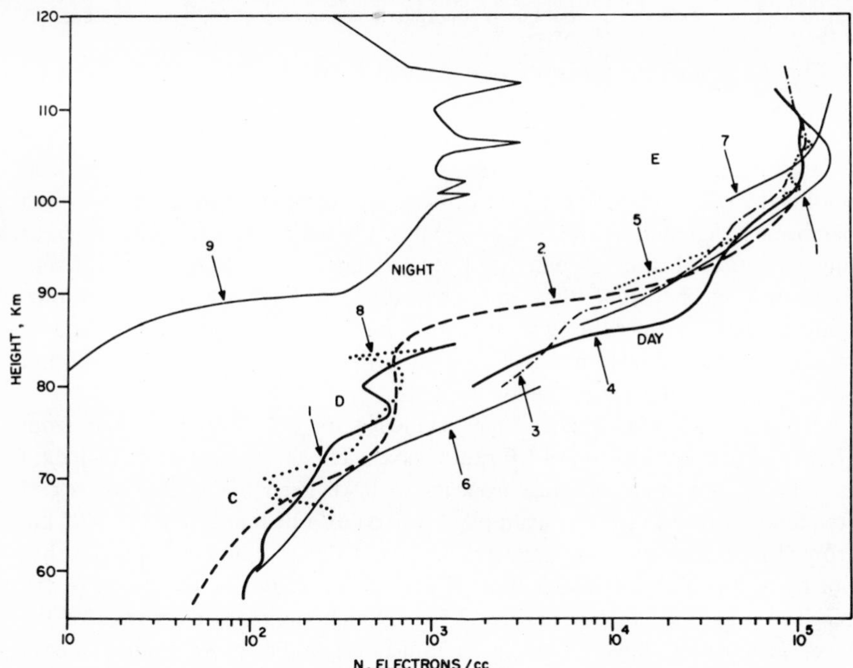

Fig. 3.4 Electron density versus height for the lower ionosphere. The various curves are as follows:

1. Partial reflection experiment, after Belrose and Burke [10], 1030 L.S.T., May, 1961, Ottawa, Canada.
2. Theoretical, after Aikin *et al.* [2], middle latitude, midday.
3. Rocket-borne Langmuir probe, after Yonezawa [46], 1532 L.S.T., 22 September 1960, Michikawa, Japan.
4. Rocket-borne radio propagation experiment, after Adey and Heikkila [1], 1237 L.S.T., 17 September 1959, Churchill, Canada.
5. Rocket-borne radio propagation experiment [21], 1730 L.S.T., 26 June 1954, U.S.S.R. middle latitude.
6. Pulse cross-modulation experiments, after Barrington *et al.* [5], 1000–1400 L.S.T., March–April, 1960, Kjeller, Norway.
7. Ionosonde experiment, after Robinson [35], midday, 27 March 1957, Cambridge, England.
8. Rocket-borne Faraday rotation experiment, after Aikin *et al.* [2], 1430 L.S.T., 8 March 1963, Wallops Island, U.S.
9. Rocket-borne Langmuir probe, after Smith [39], 0435 L.S.T., 27 October 1961, Wallops Island, U.S.

region, a limitation of this technique. Curve 9 represents a nighttime distribution obtained with a rocket-borne Langmuir probe; curve 2 is a theoretical distribution calculated for a quiet sun at a low zenith angle. It is not possible to say whether the illustrated differences result from changes of location, of time, or of solar conditions, or simply from observational errors.

Some general features of the *D* region can be seen in several of the curves in Fig. 3.4; these are probably best defined by the partial reflection experiment (curve 1) which shows them as three ledges of ionization. Clearly discernible from the electron number density curve are (1) the base of the *E* layer at about 80–85 km; (2) the *D* layer which reaches a quasi peak in the height range 75–80 km; (3) a distinct region below about 75 km which has been designated as the '*C* layer.' Since the ledges exhibit quite different diurnal patterns and, as will be discussed later, are ascribed to different ionization mechanisms, they are, according to our previous definitions, quite properly termed 'layers.' It should be noted that both the *C* and *D* layers are formed within the *D* region proper, as defined by convention (that is, the ionized region below 90 km).

To date, the best, albeit meager, evidence for a *C* layer has come from studies of the propagation of LF radio waves. The interpretation of such data is difficult, but some progress appears to have been made [28]. Waves of frequency near 80 kc/s, for example, received at a distance of 1900–2400 km from their transmitter, are reflected by the *C*-layer ionization by day but not by night. A characteristic diurnal variation is found in the phase of the received wave, as shown in Fig. 3.5(a), which indicates a growth of the layer just before dawn at the path mid-point, a far more gradual decay after sunset, and an almost constant height during the hours of sunlight.

This behavior differs markedly from that associated with Chapman-like

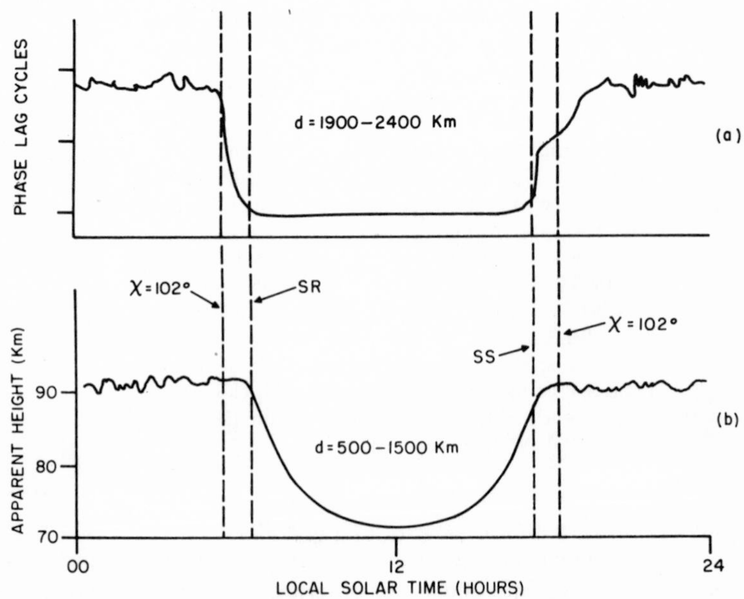

Fig. 3.5 Variation of phase height for low-frequency waves near 80 kc/s, propagated at middle latitudes to distances as shown.

layers. It could result, however, if some constant source of ionization were present and if the electron loss process differed sharply between the daylight and dark hours. Cosmic rays provide a suitable source of ionization, and at these heights, the removal process should indeed alter from day to night: the available electrons would disappear at night by attachment to form negative ions, but these ions are unstable in the presence of visible light and so could not remove electrons during the day. The principal negative ion is thought to be O_2^-. These mechanisms in combination provide a satisfactory basis of explanation for the *C*-layer characteristics.

The LF propagation studies also provide information on the *D* layer. For, over shorter path lengths (500–1500 km), the radio waves are more steeply incident on the ionosphere and are then able to penetrate through the underlying *C* layer. The apparent height of reflection in the *D* layer varies smoothly throughout the daytime hours, much in the fashion of an α-Chapman layer, as depicted in Fig. 3.5(b). At night the reflection height rises to the base of the *E* layer, which persists in a manner yet to be described (see Sec. 3.4.5).

The formation of the *D*-layer ionization appears to be a more complicated process than that operating in the *C* layer. Two different mechanisms are recognized during undisturbed conditions, each of which may be influenced by the existing atmospheric composition. As discussed in Sec. 2.4.2, solar Lyman α radiation can penetrate into this height region and is capable of ionizing nitric oxide molecules. Although NO occurs only as a trace constituent at these heights, its concentration, when taken with the known Lyman α flux, appears sufficient to explain the observed ionization during quiet solar conditions. Solar cyclic changes that are observed in the *D*-layer ionization, however, are not as readily explained by this process since the solar Lyman α does not appear to change substantially throughout the sunspot cycle. On the other hand, the solar *X*-ray flux is known to vary with the solar cycle—by some two orders of magnitude or more (see Chapter 9) —and *X*-radiation, acting on the major atmospheric constituents, N_2 and O_2, is an additional source of ionization for the *D* layer. This latter process becomes increasingly important as the maximum of the sunspot cycle is approached, when ionospheric observations suggest that the electron density gradients at the base of the *D* region become steeper and that the total electron content up to the base of the *E* region increases.

During times generally considered abnormal there are additional sources of ionization for the *D* region; these result in significant electron density increases over a substantial height range. Three main effects are recognized: the sudden ionospheric disturbance during which hard solar *X*-rays (< 8 Å) impinge on the sunlit atmosphere, as discussed in Chapter 9; the polar cap absorption events when energetic protons from the sun enter the polar atmosphere (see Chapter 11); and radio aurora and auroral absorption events that are attributed to an influx of energetic electrons into the auroral zones and possibly also to their accompanying bremsstrahlung X-radiation (Chapter 14). Although the solar-cyclic control previously discussed might be produced in part by disturbances of this nature, which occur more frequently at sunspot maximum, it is found even in the absence of any clear indications of these characteristic conditions.

3.3.2. Seasonal Changes in *D*-region Ionization. Only a few attempts have been made to measure seasonal changes in electron concentration in the D region. One set of measurements, obtained by a partial-reflection experiment at Ottawa, is shown in Fig. 3.6. Data taken on five magnetically quiet days each month were averaged, from November, 1961, to October, 1962. The winter curve is the average for November, December, and January; the summer curve is the average for June, July, and August; March and September are plotted separately. These data show a marked seasonal varia-

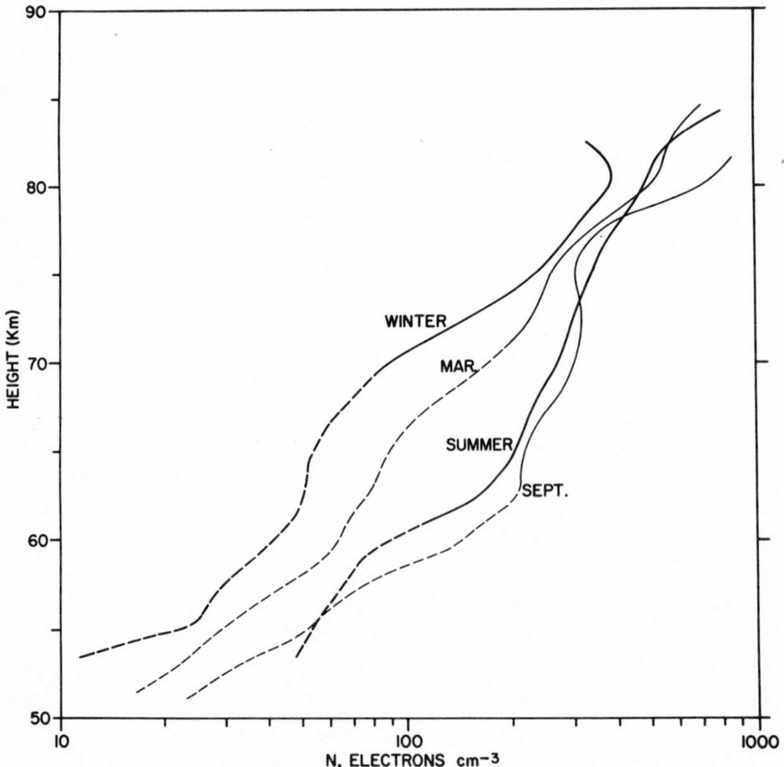

Fig. 3.6 Seasonal changes of electron densities in the D region. The dashed and solid portions of the curves correspond to different analysis of the data (See Ref. [10].), in the different height regions.

tion in *D*-region electron densities (particularly near a height of 65 km). Note that the September curve nearly resembles a summer month; this result is consistent with the 'November effect' discussed in Sec. 3.3.4.

3.3.3. The *D* Region at High Latitudes. It has already been suggested that the ionization low in the *D* region may be due almost entirely to normal cosmic rays. If so, then the electron concentrations there will depend on the geomagnetic latitude and can be expected to increase by about a factor of three in going from the equator to 60° [31]. So far only a few observations of electron densities in the *D* region have been made at high latitudes, but LF propagation studies have revealed that transmission over paths north of about 60° geomagnetic is quite different from that over paths at lower latitudes. Relative phase recordings of 80 kc/s transmissions from Ottawa, received at a distance of 740 km to the north, have revealed that the diurnal change is trapezoidal in shape, like Fig. 3.5(a), whereas propagation over similar distances in Europe showed a cosinusoidal pattern, like Fig. 3.5(b). Field strength records made at Churchill of 77 kc/s transmissions from Thule, indicate a very regular variation with practically no fading at night, whereas LF waves at lower latitudes reveal strong fading. These data suggest that the *C* layer becomes more important at high latitudes, and in fact, cosmic-ray ionization at very high latitudes ($> 70°$ geomagnetic) would be expected to be important even at night (at heights of say 80 km). However, some recent observations at Resolute Bay during the polar winter night using the partial reflection technique cannot be readily explained on the basis of galactic cosmic rays alone, but would require some additional fairly steady source of ionization above about 90 km, such as electrons with energies in the range 10–100 Kev.

3.3.4. *D*-region Meteorology. All observations which give evidence about electron number densities and physical properties of the *D* region indicate great regularity from day to day in summer; but in winter, in the northern hemisphere at least, there is considerable irregularity from day to day. In addition, seasonal changes in the propagation of LF and VLF waves are not symmetrical in their variation with the zenith angle of the sun. The winter irregularities and seasonal asymmetry are likely to be related to meteorological effects in the *D* region, rather than to changes in the ionization intensities from the sun.

On some days, marked increases in ionization densities are observed throughout the *D* region. This results in a marked increase in the absorption of high-frequency radio waves reflected at higher levels, to the point where a statistically significant 'winter anomaly' is recognized. This little-understood phenomenon has long been thought due to some sort of atmospheric meteorology [19], since it is not associated with magnetic activity, and on one occasion [45] the anomaly coincided with a dramatic increase in the temperature of the stratosphere. Although no satisfactory explanation yet exists, the absorption effects might be attributed to changes in the minor ionizable constituents in the lower *D* region.

A detailed study [43] of the winter anomaly in the northern hemisphere during the IGY reveals a maximum effect at a geographic latitude of about 55° in Europe. Since the anomaly is thought to be meteorological, it is likely to be related to geographic rather than magnetic latitude. In North America, the relevant latitudes lie in or near the auroral zone, and the anomaly is therefore likely to be masked by other phenomena. One case has been found, however, which does appear to be relevant: excess absorption was observed somewhat to the north of Ottawa on 21 and 22 February, 1961, during a period of solar quiet, and midday $N(h)$ profiles at Ottawa revealed excess *D*-region ionization as depicted in Fig. 3.7. February 20 and 23 (not shown) were normal.

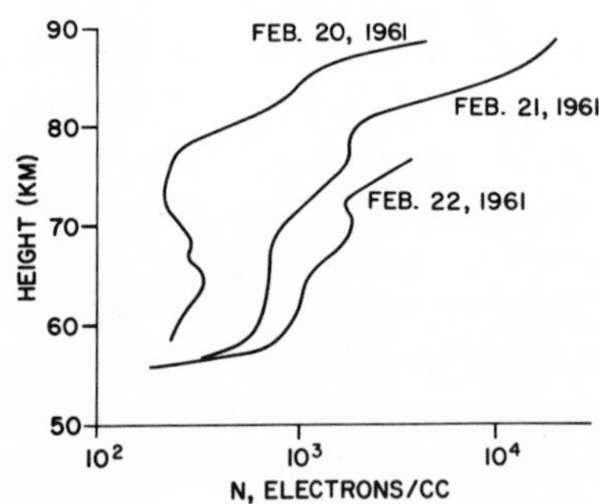

Fig. 3.7 Changes in the winter *D*-region electron number densities observed at Ottawa.

Rocket grenade measurements [40] have shown that the temperature profile in the mesosphere over Churchill is anomalous in winter, in that no strong temperature decline is found, and that stable temperature inversions occur in the 60–75 km height range. Partial reflection of radio waves scattered from *D*-region irregularities also suggests evidence for temperature inversions at the lower heights of 50–60 km for observations made at Ottawa.

One further variation, termed the 'November effect' in the literature of VLF and LF propagation, warrants comment: the received wave amplitudes are less in summer than in winter. The amplitude decrease begins gradually about February, and minimum values are reached in July and August. The amplitude increase in the autumn is more abrupt, beginning in September and reaching the highest amplitude in November. With the winter anomaly and other seasonal effects, this variation remains as yet unexplained.

3.4. THE IONOSPHERIC *E* REGION

The mixing processes of the lower levels appear to be quenched in the *E* region, at least at heights above 100 km or so, and a diffusive separation of the chemical constituents is then to be anticipated. The effects of this transition, and of changes in the transition height, are likely to show up most strongly in the *F* region and above, where minor constituents have greater importance, but no certain effects have as yet been established. A much more important chemical change is also believed to occur in the *E* region, resulting from the photodissociation of O_2 into O. It is thought to become appreciable at heights of 90–100 km, and to be virtually completed by the 150 km level. Direct determinations of the relative proportions are only beginning to be made with some degree of certainty [36].

A far greater body of information is available concerning the ionization of the region. Some of this has come from the rocket-borne experiments of recent years, but most stems from the conventional ionosondes mentioned in Chapter 1. These yield 'ionograms,' in which is displayed as a function of frequency (f), the 'virtual height (h')' at which a radio pulse is reflected, as determined from the delay between transmission and reception of the pulse at ground level. The interpretation of the resultant '$h'(f)$ curves' in terms of the height profiles of electron number density, $N(h)$, is by no means simple nor free from sources of error, but it can now be accomplished with a reasonable accuracy.

Normal daytime ionograms show the formation of an *E* layer, whose general behavior is similar to that of an α- Chapman layer. Detailed analysis reveals certain complications, however, when inferences are drawn about ionizable constituents, ionizing radiations, recombination processes, atmospheric scale height, geographic variations, and similar features. These complications have yet to be fully understood, but their various sources are becoming recognized and are touched upon in the subsequent discussion.

Superimposed on the normal *E* layer, and sometimes obscuring it in conventional ionograms, may be one or more ledges of additional ionization. Such ledges are almost invariably observed when high-power high-resolution ionosondes are employed, but they are often missed with more conventional apparatus. Their rather random appearance on the latter led to their designation as 'sporadic-*E* ionization,' or 'E_s', and several distinct categories are now identified empirically. Some of these appear on 'normal' days and are probably associated with dynamic processes as discussed in Chapter 7. Others are related to disturbance phenomena and are discussed in Chapters 13 and 14.

3.4.1. Electron Distribution in the *E* Region. Knowledge of the way in which the free electrons in the *E* region are distributed is of the greatest importance for the investigation of the physics of the ionosphere. Instrumentation carried in rockets has provided the most accurate measurements of electron densities, both by radio propagation and by probe techniques, but such measurements are severely limited in number and geographical distribution. Accurate $h'(f)$ soundings contain much of the information necessary for a determination of the electron distribution, since the equivalent height of reflection h' for radio waves incident vertically on the ionosphere is related to the electron density N by

$$h'(f) = \int_0^{h_r} \mu'(f, N)\, dh, \tag{3.15}$$

where h is the height above ground, h_r is the height of reflection, and the 'group refractive index' μ' is a complicated but known function of f, N, and the strength and direction of the geomagnetic field. Since the $h'(f)$ curve is measured, and the $N(h)$ relationship is to be calculated, an inversion of this integral equation is required [42]. This inversion is difficult because of the complicated mathematical formalism, and also because of the absence of data for frequencies below some minimum observed value, usually 1.5–2.0 Mc/s; some assumptions must be made concerning the low-lying ionization to make up for this shortcoming. A further limitation to the analysis is imposed by a requirement that the electron density profile must be assumed to increase monotonically with height.

The radio pulses actually propagate in two distinct modes, the 'ordinary' and 'extraordinary,' because of the effect of the geomagnetic field (as discussed in Appendices I and II). In principle, some of the difficulty just remarked upon could be avoided if the 'extraordinary' wave could be observed [41], but it is normally missing because of high daytime absorption. For this reason, and to gain improved height resolution, more sophisticated ionosondes have been developed and are now coming into use. A record made by one such ionosonde is shown in Fig. 3.8. Note that daytime reflections are observed down to about 700 kc/s and that both the ordinary (O) and extraordinary (X) traces are clearly observable. It is expected that new knowledge about the ionospheric E layer will be obtained when the use of these new equipments becomes more widespread.

The ionogram presented in Fig. 3.8 shows that the E-region reflections are complicated by cusps on both the O and X traces near the penetration frequency, and by the presence of partial reflections from a scattering region near 100 km. High-resolution ionosondes indicate in addition that the E-layer echo is seldom a 'clean' single return but is often made up of two or more overlapping signals of comparable amplitude, returned from almost the same height. Such overlapping signals are caused by small-scale variations in the otherwise horizontally-stratified ionosphere.

The 'partial reflection' experiment employed in D-region studies has also given results for the E layer. The information it provides is more limited

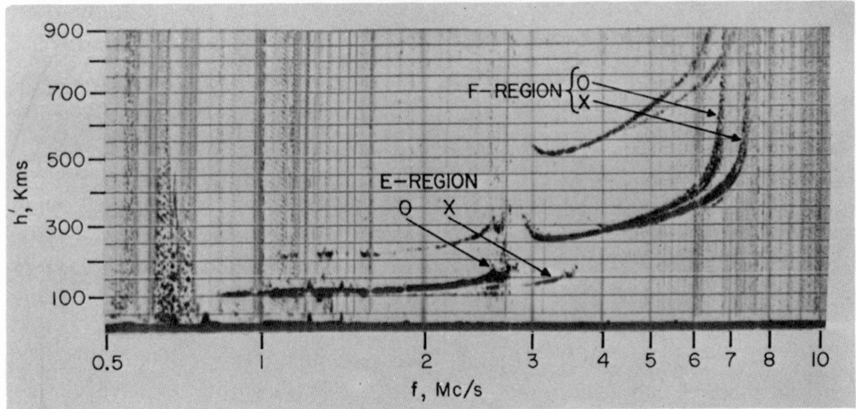

Fig. 3.8 Ionogram taken at Uppsala, Sweden, at about 1800 hours L.S.T., in June 1958, during an epoch of maximum solar activity. (The author is indebted to W. Stoffregen for this ionogram.)

here, however, and on some days the technique does not seem to work at all, owing to obscuration of the weak scatter echoes by echoes coming obliquely from preferred scatter heights (probably E_s reflections). On days when it has been possible to obtain clear-cut results, agreement has been found with the conclusions reached by other methods.

Some typical results of the most reliable measurements of electron distributions are illustrated in Fig. 3.4.

Robinson [35] has undertaken one of the most detailed studies of data obtained from ionograms. He attempted to take into account underlying ionization by assuming that the apparent reflection height for 16 kc/s waves is the real reflection height; hence that variations of it represent variations of the level where the electron number density is 300 cm^{-3}. He further assumed that the electron density increased exponentially from this height up to the height at which 1.2 Mc/s waves (the low-frequency limit of his ionosonde) were reflected. This permitted him to bridge the observational gap imposed by the low-frequency limitations of the ionosonde data, and so he was able to derive $N(h)$ curves for the E region whenever the ionograms were free from severe clutter. (One such curve is shown in Fig. 3.4, curve 7.) From a study of the $N(h)$ curves so obtained, he concluded the following:

1. To a first approximation, the diurnal behavior of the layer is in agreement with Chapman theory. The height of the maximum follows the elevation of the sun during the day, and values $h_0 = 108$ km and $H = 8$ km could be deduced from Eq. (3.8).
2. Deviations in the shape of the $N(h)$ distribution from that predicted by

simple Chapman theory could be explained if, with the recombination coefficient independent of height, the scale height was assumed to increase with altitude. The necessary gradient, dH/dh, was found to be 0.2, and the scale heights determined in this way agree closely with rocket measurements.

3. The magnitude of the recombination coefficient was estimated from the variation of the layer shape with time. (In a time-varying layer, finite recombination times cause the ionization density to lag behind the value that would be implied by the formulas previously given.) Recombination effects were found to be so small that drifts or other disturbances in the region could greatly modify the apparent α. The recombination lag could be measured only in spring and summer, and the mean value of the recombination coefficient in these seasons was found to be about 2×10^{-8} $\text{cm}^3\ \text{sec}^{-1}$. Studies of the decay of ionization during solar eclipses [33] have given values for α_{eff} which range from 0.5×10^{-8} to 2×10^{-8} cm^3 sec^{-1}.

3.4.2. Diurnal Variation of f_0E. The diurnal variation of the E-layer penetration frequency, f_0E, is closely controlled by the zenith angle of the sun. This regular variation of f_0E is shown for the ordinary mode in the world maps depicted in Fig. 3.9. It will be recalled from Eq. (3.14) that the f_0 of an α-Chapman layer should vary as $\cos^{1/4}\chi$. At low and medium latitudes, the monthly median values of f_0E are more accurately represented by the empirical expression $f_0E \propto \cos^{1/3}\chi$, and this expression also applies to individual days if the data are acquired and reduced with sufficient accuracy (see Fig. 3.10). The departure of the exponent here from the α-Chapman value can be accounted for easily by a height-variation of the scale height or of the recombination coefficient, but observations of the penetration frequency alone do not enable any distinction between these two cases. If H varies linearly with height, and if α remains constant, then the penetration frequency can be shown [35] to have the form

$$f_0E \simeq \left(\frac{q}{\alpha}\right)^{1/4} \cos^{(1+dH/dh)/4}\chi. \tag{3.16}$$

In the case illustrated in Fig. 3.10, the calculated value of dH/dh is 0.2 which agrees with the observed scale-height gradient. It then seems reasonable to attribute to the scale-height gradient the observed deviation of f_0E from a simple α-Chapman behavior. The same cannot be said for high-latitude deviations. In the auroral zone, the sensitivity of the E layer to solar control is very low (f_0E is approximately proportional to $\cos^{1/10}\chi$ [38]), and some other explanation must be found. At still higher latitudes f_0E is approximately proportional to $\cos^{1/4}\chi$, as expected for an α-Chapman layer.

The variation of the penetration frequency is nearly symmetric about

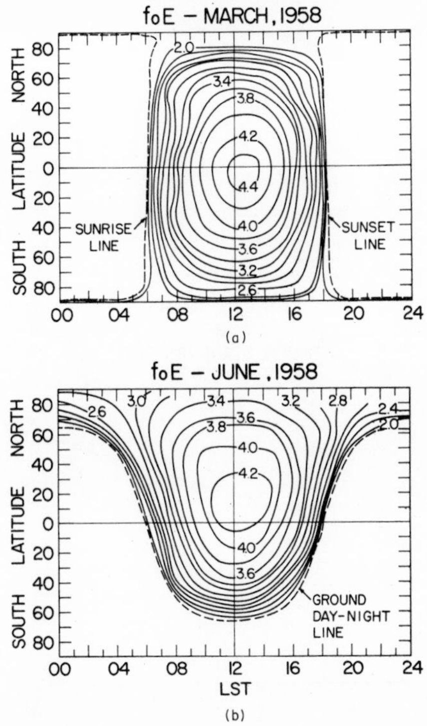

Fig. 3.9 Maps of f_0E (monthly median values) for (a) March and (b) June, 1958, during an epoch of maximum solar activity. (After Davies [18].)

noon. This implies a rapid recombination, such that the ionization follows the production function with little time lag. Appleton [3] has shown that the recombination coefficient can be estimated from the difference between the ionization at pairs of times in the morning and afternoon for which the same value of χ occurs. Robinson [35] has attempted to calculate α_{eff} in this way from accurate measurements of penetration frequency on individual days. On all winter and spring days studied, α_{eff} was reasonably constant for 3–4 hrs on either side of noon, being somewhat less than 1×10^{-8} cm^3 sec^{-1}. (See also the values of α_{eff} given in Sec. 3.4.1.) But data originating farther from noon led to sharply increased estimates of α_{eff}, and eventually the afternoon value of the penetration frequency fell below the morning value, in contrast to the implications of a recombination lag. This result led Robinson to suggest that there may be drift effects in the *E* region which are comparable to the effects of recombination. Vertical drift velocities of the order 5 m/s were suggested by him as being reasonable to explain the observational data, but their role has yet to be confirmed by other means.

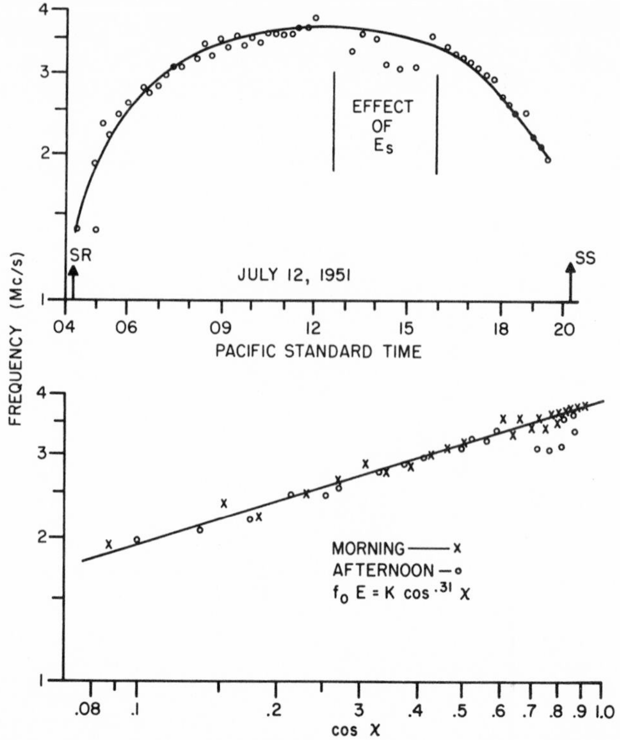

Fig. 3.10 Diurnal variation of f_0E measured at Vancouver, Canada [9]. Vertical arrows mark times of ground sunrise and sunset.

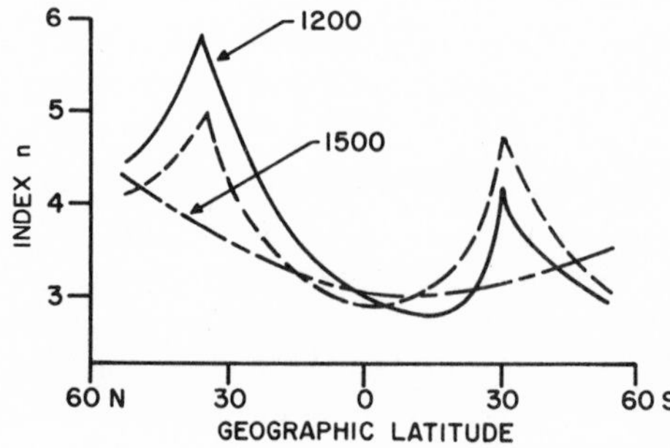

Fig. 3.11 Index n for stations centered on the 150°E meridian, derived from values of f_0E at times shown for 1952–54 (minimum epoch of solar cycle). The dashed curve is for noon values reduced to a common solar distance, correcting for the fact that the earth is closer to the sun in December than in June. (After Beynon and Brown [13].)

3.4.3. Seasonal Variation of f_0E. The index n in the relation $f_0E \propto \cos^{1/n} \chi$ has been derived for fixed hours by a number of workers, making use of the seasonal variation in χ. Beynon and Brown [13] find it to be strongly dependent on latitude at noon, with sharp peaks of n at latitudes $\pm 35°$, but the dependence decreases and the peaks disappear by mid-afternoon (Fig. 3.11). They suggest that this behavior might be attributed to an effect of the ionospheric current systems, which have foci located at the pertinent latitudes just before noon (as illustrated in Fig. 7.3, where they are discussed further). It is indeed the case that an upward drift will occur at latitudes below, and a downward drift at latitudes above, the daytime foci [29], and such drifts will alter f_0E. Seasonal variations in the location of the foci can be called upon to explain anomalous variations of n that have been found near latitudes $\pm 35°$ [13]. The full theory of these regular and anomalous variations has yet to be developed, however.

3.4.4. Variations of f_0E with Solar Activity. A direct relation exists between solar activity and the electron concentration of the *E* region. This is shown on occasion by a close correlation between day-to-day variations of the Zurich sunspot number, R, and the critical frequency of the *E* layer [12]. It is also revealed statistically, for the monthly mean noontime value of $(f_0E)^2$ is found to vary with the monthly mean of R. The variation in this case has the linear form

$$(f_0E)^2 = a(1 + bR), \tag{3.17}$$

where $(f_0E)^2$ and R are now the monthly mean values, a is a factor which varies from month to month, revealing seasonal effects, and b is a parameter which appears to have little seasonal dependence; b is found to be about 4×10^{-3}, whereas R may be as high as 100 or more, so the effect of solar activity is a pronounced one.

The most meaningful correlation may be greater even than this implies, for it should be found between f_0E and solar ultraviolet or X-ray emissions, and the latter are not fully correlated with R. Indeed it has been proposed that f_0E be employed as an index of the strength of the ionizing radiations, in the form

$$I_E \equiv (f_0E)^4/\cos \chi \tag{3.18}$$

which, from Eqs. (3.4) and (3.12), should be proportional to S_∞. Studies of this 'ionization character figure' have shown it to be closely correlated with the epoch of the solar cycle, but that there is not a one-to-one correspondence with the instantaneous values of any other solar index. Beynon and Brown [12] have shown that f_0E is dependent not only on R itself but also on the general level of background radiation which varies throughout the solar cycle. This is not surprising, in view of the loose correlation between R and the background radiation.

3.4.5. The *E* Layer at Night. There is little information available about the nocturnal *E* layer because its penetration frequency lies below the working range of most ionosondes. Some valuable data, however, have been obtained from a low-frequency (50–2000 kc/s) ionosonde at Boulder, Colorado [44], and these have been complemented by a few rocket-borne probe measurements.

An example of the Boulder ionograms is depicted in Fig. 3.12. It shows echoes from three distinct strata, with virtual heights of about 100, 150, and 250 km respectively. Each stratum is seen twice, by virtue of a splitting of the transmitted radio wave into its ordinary (*O*) and extraordinary (*X*) modes. The 100-km stratum normally appears patchy, and it must be fairly thin, since no substantial increase of apparent height is to be seen within it. The echo may result more from scattering than from reflection, in which case the interpretation of the penetration frequency is by no means direct. On the occasion illustrated, however, the observed penetration frequencies correspond to reflection at an electron concentration of about 3×10^3 electrons/cm^3, and this value is representative also of direct probe results (see Fig. 3.4). More often, the stratum at 100 km is seen at still higher frequencies and may extend into the normal ionosonde range where it would appear as sporadic-*E*.

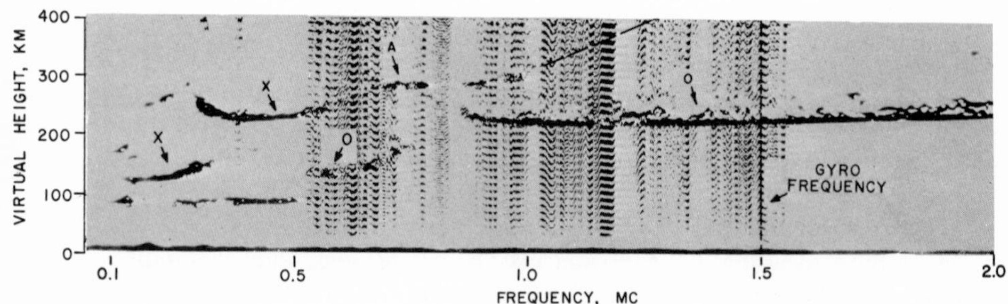

Fig. 3.12 Low-frequency ionogram made at Boulder, 2 December 1959, 2250 L.S.T. (The author is indebted to J. M. Watts for this ionogram.)

The stratum near 150 km seems to be the true nocturnal *E* layer, in that it shows continuity with the daytime layer and it exhibits a similar response to the influence of solar activity. Its penetration frequency for the *O* mode, f_0E, decreases by about 200 kc/s during the nighttime hours, to a predawn minimum of about 400 kc/s, although this latter value varies by about 250 kc/s over a sunspot cycle. The value 730 kc/s, found on the occasion illustrated here, corresponds to an electron concentration of about 6300 cm^{-3}. Direct observations of this nocturnal *E* layer are possible for only a small part of the time, because of blanketing by the underlying stratum. It will be noted, however, that the *X*-mode reflection from the *F* layer exhibits a cusp (marked *A*) at f_0E. The cusp is due to retardation of the *X* mode within the *E* layer (see Appendix I), and its location can be employed to determine f_0E even when blanketing of the *E* layer occurs [44]. On some occasions even the cusp is missing, and the *E*-layer peak is then believed to have merged with the tail of the overlying *F* layer.

3.4.6. Formation of the *E* Layer. The ionizing radiations responsible for the *E* layer must be of such a nature that they can penetrate the regions above without serious loss, and then be absorbed within the *E* region. Early attention was directed to the possibility that the pertinent radiation might be one specific to the ionization of O_2, for this molecule is virtually absent from levels above 150 km as already noted. More recent investigations have looked to *X*-rays as the more plausible source, with wavelengths in the range 10–100 Å being considered most seriously. These, together with ultraviolet radiation (Lyman α and Lyman continuum) appear to be adequate to account for the profile observed [6, 7, 24, 26].

The ionizing efficiency of *X*-rays is more or less independent of the species to be ionized, and a strong production rate of N_2^+ would then be expected. This contrasts with the fact that a substantial quantity of N_2^+ is not found spectroscopically or by rocket-borne measurements. The explanation appears to lie in an extremely high recombination rate of N_2^+, as compared with O_2^+, NO^+, or O^+, which effectively removes the N_2^+ ions as rapidly as they are produced; laboratory measurements do suggest that a recombination coefficient of 10^{-6} or 10^{-7} cm³ sec⁻¹ would apply to N_2^+, whereas the coefficient deduced for the bulk of the *E*-region ionization is lower by an order of magnitude or more (see below). On this picture, then, nitrogen molecules are responsible for about $\frac{4}{5}$ of the depletion of the ionizing radiation without at the same time providing any substantial contribution to the electron density [22]. This view is not held by all workers, and is discussed again briefly in Sec. 4.3.2.

3.5. RECOMBINATION IN THE *D* AND *E* REGIONS

If the effective recombination coefficient, α_{eff}, is to be deduced, it is necessary to know the time variation of electron concentration at each height, the rate of electron production at each height, and the magnitude of any vertical movements in the region. None of these is known with sufficient precision to provide results reliable to better than an order of magnitude, and for this reason it is not yet known whether apparent inconsistencies between various conclusions represent real physical variations or simply illustrate the current uncertainties.

Results to date have been obtained mainly from the nocturnal decay of ionization after sunset, from the corresponding decay during a solar eclipse, or from the diurnal asymmetry of some quantity, such as absorption, phase, polarization, or penetration frequency of probing radio waves. Values ranging from 10^{-6} cm^3 sec^{-1} at 70 km to 10^{-8} cm^3 sec^{-1} at 110 km have been deduced, and these suggest that the recombination process changes significantly from the *D* to the *E* region. They also imply that simple radiative recombination is not the controlling process in either region, for coefficients of the order 10^{-12} cm^3 sec^{-1} would have been expected in that case.

It now seems reasonably well established from laboratory observations that the loss process in the *E* region is one of dissociative recombination, with coefficient α_D say, as first suggested by Bates and Massey [8]. This reaction is of the form

$$(XY)^+ + e \rightarrow \underset{\text{unstable}}{(XY)^*} \rightarrow X^* + Y^* \tag{3.19}$$

in which a positive diatomic ion species (which in the *D* and *E* regions may be N_2, O_2, or NO) combines with an electron to form one or two excited atoms. The best values available at present for the rate of the dissociative reaction come from laboratory measurements [14] for $\alpha_D(N_2^+)$ and $\alpha_D(O_2^+)$, namely, 3×10^{-7} cm^3 sec^{-1} and 1.7×10^{-7} cm^3 sec^{-1}, respectively. Both coefficients are a factor of ten higher than the apparent rates for the *E* region, so neither is now thought to control there. Recent rocket data [25] have shown that a dominant ion in the *E* region is NO^+, so the recombination observations could be explained reasonably if $\alpha_D(NO^+)$ were about 2×10^{-8} cm^3 sec^{-1}. This value has yet to be confirmed by laboratory measurements, and at present it exceeds theoretical estimates by a factor of ten [31].

Below 90 km, the recombination coefficient is influenced by reactions involving the mutual neutralization of ions. Electrons become attached to neutral molecules to form negative ions, and the latter subsequently combine or charge-exchange with positive ions to form neutral products. If the latter process is markedly slower than the attachment process, it will determine the net rate of recombination in this sequence. The effective recombination coefficient then becomes

$$\alpha_{\text{eff}} = \alpha_D + \lambda\alpha_i, \tag{3.20}$$

where λ is the ratio of negative ions to electrons and α_i is the coefficient of ion-ion neutralization. Estimates of λ during the day range typically from 7.5 at 60 km to 10^{-3} at 90 km [31], whereas α_i might be as high as 10^{-7} [8], so this process may well be of importance low in the *D* region but is probably not relevant above 80 km. A variation is expected in λ from day to night, which will further complicate deductions about low-level recombination.

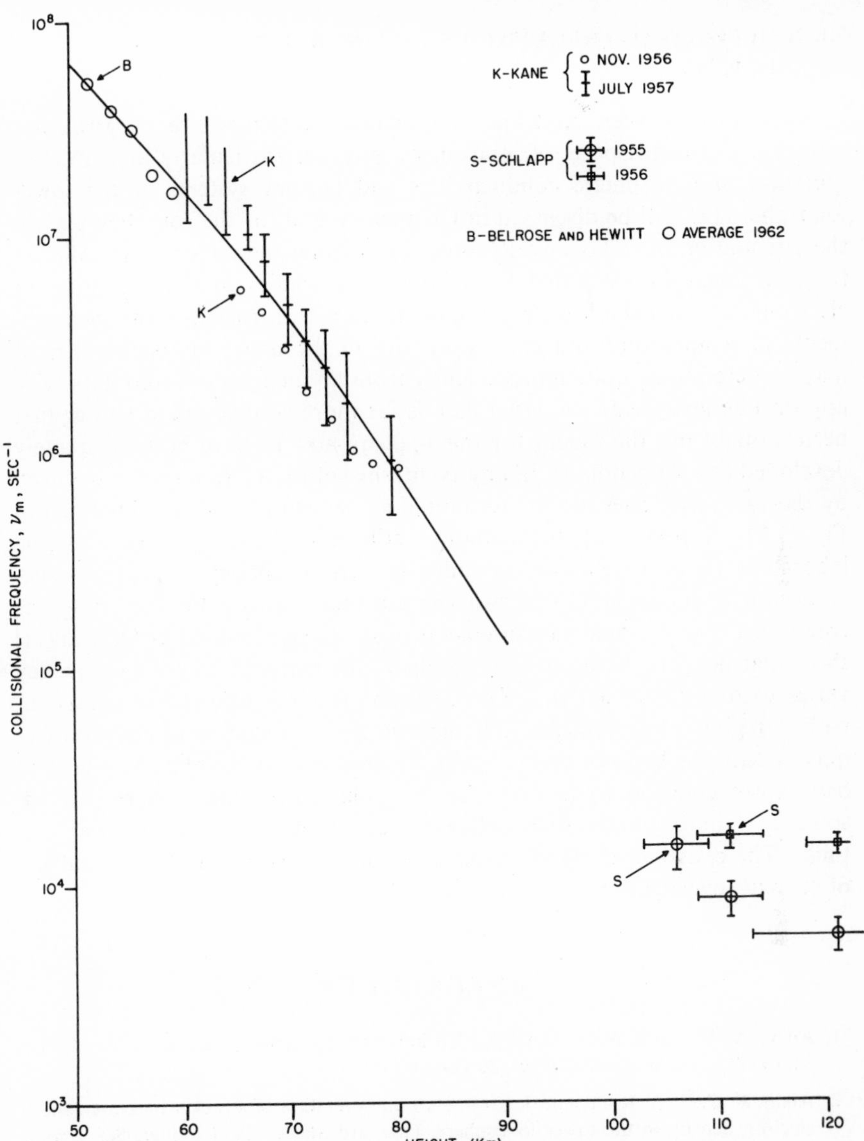

Fig. 3.13 Collision frequency ν_m of electrons plotted against height. The solid curve has been calculated using a formula based on work by Phelps and Pack [32] from laboratory measurements and by using the COSPAR international reference atmosphere [17]. The experimental points are taken from Belrose and Hewitt [11], Kane [27], and Schlapp [37].

3.6. COLLISIONAL FREQUENCIES IN THE *D* AND *E* REGIONS

Collisions between electrons and neutral molecules are of great importance to some aspects of ionospheric physics, particularly in the determination of ionospheric conductivities and current systems in the lower ionosphere (as will be discussed in Chapter 7), and for the role they play in the attenuation of radio waves propagating within the region. The collision frequency may be estimated from laboratory studies of the mobilities of electrons in atmospheric gases, in combination with rocket-borne measurements of temperature and particle density in the upper atmosphere; or it may be determined quite independently from an analysis of radio data. The appropriate analysis in the latter case is far more complex than had at first been thought but the theory for this appears now to have been adequately developed (see Appendix I). In any event, the collisional frequencies deduced by the two techniques are in substantial agreement [27, 32] as illustrated in Fig. 3.13. A period of consolidation still lies ahead, however, as the laboratory measurements are extended to various species of neutral molecules and as ionospheric observations are taken over a broader range of conditions. For example, measurements made during 1961–63 at Ottawa [11] show that near the base of the ionosphere, the deduced collision frequency varies with the solar activity. This *D*-region result appears to be consistent with *E*-region measurements [37] that suggest a variation of collision frequency with the sunspot cycle. Again, observations at Resolute Bay in 1964 have given collision frequencies for the polar winter mesosphere that are some 2–4 times greater than collision frequencies measured at lower latitudes. The causes of these variations are not understood, and are a subject of current investigation.

REFERENCES

1. Adey, A. W., and W. J. Heikkila, Rocket electron density measurements at Fort Churchill, Canada, *Can. J. Phys.*, **39** (1961), 219.
2. Aikin, A. C., J. A. Kane, and J. Troim, An interpretation of a rocket measurement of electron density in the lower ionosphere, Goddard Space Flight Center, Sci. Report X-615-63-159, (1963).
3. Appleton, E. V., Regularities and irregularities in the ionosphere I, *Proc. Roy. Soc. A*, **162** (1937), 451.
4. ———, and J. A. Ratcliffe, Some simultaneous observations on downcoming wireless waves, *Proc. Roy. Soc. A*, **128** (1930), 133.
5. Barrington, R. E., E. V. Thrain, and B. Bjelland, Diurnal and seasonal variations in D-region electron densities derived from observations of cross-modulation, *Can. J. Phys.*, **41** (1963), 271.

6. Bates, D. R., Mixed Commission in the Ionosphere—4th Meeting (Brussels, 1955), p. 82.

7. ———, and F. Hoyle, Origin of the E-layer, *Terr. Mag. Atmos. Electr.*, **53** (1948), 41.

8. ———, and H. S. W. Massey, The basic reactions in the upper atmosphere. II, The theory of ionized layers, *Proc. Roy. Soc. A*, **192** (1947), 1.

9. Belrose, J. S., The fine structure of the E region. M A Sc. Thesis, Univ. British Columbia 1951.

10. ———, and M. J. Burke, Study of the lower ionosphere using partial reflection. Part I. Experimental technique and methods of analysis, *J. Geophys. Res.*, **69** (1964), 2799.

11. ———, and L. W. Hewitt, Variation of collision frequency in the lowest ionosphere with solar activity, *Nature*, **202** (1964). 267.

12. Beynon, W. J. G., and G. M. Brown, Proc. Mixed Comm. on Ionosphere, Second Meeting (1951) p. 156; *Observatory*, **77** (1957), 94.

13. ———, and ———, Geomagnetic distortion of region-E, *J. Atmos. Terr. Phys.*, **14** (1959), 138.

14. Biondi, M. A., Low energy atomic collisions, in Advances in Electronics and Electron Physics, ed. L. Marton. New York: Academic Press, **18** (1963), 152.

15. Chapman, S., The absorption and dissociative or ionizing effect of monochromatic radiation in an atmosphere on a rotating earth, *Proc. Phys. Soc.*, **43** (1931), 26, 483.

16. ———, The atmospheric height distribution of band-absorbed solar radiation, *Proc. Phys. Soc.*, **51** (1939), 93.

17. CIRA 1961, COSPAR International Reference Atmosphere, 1961. Amsterdam: North Holland Publishing Company, 1961.

18. Davies, K., Ionospheric Radio Propagation, Monograph No. 80, U.S. Govt. Printing Office, Washington, D.C. (in press).

19. Dieminger, W., Short wave echoes from the lower ionosphere, in The Physics of the Ionosphere. London: The Phys. Soc. 1955, p. 53.

20. Fejer, J. A., and R. W. Vice, An investigation of the ionospheric D-region, *J. Atmos. Terr. Phys.*, **16** (1961), 291.

21. Friedman, H., Rocket observations of the ionosphere, *Proc. I.R.E.*, **47** (1959), 272.

22. ———, The sun's ionizing radiations, in Physics of the Upper Atmosphere, ed. J. A. Ratcliffe. New York: Academic Press, 1960, p. 191.

23. Gardner, F. F., and J. L. Pawsey, Study of the ionospheric D-region using partial reflections, *J. Atmos. Terr. Phys.*, **3** (1953), 321.

24. Houston, R. F., The effect of certain solar radiations in the lower ionosphere, *J. Atmos. Terr. Phys.*, **12** (1958), 225.

25. Holmes, J. C., C. Y. Johnson and J. M. Young, Ionospheric Chemistry, COSPAR, Proc. Fifth Intern. Space Science Symposium, Florence, Italy, May, 1964. Amsterdam: North-Holland Publishing Company, (in press).

26. Kallmann, H. K., Inst. Geophys., Univ. California at Los Angeles, Sci. Report No. 4, 1956.

27. Kane, J. A., Re-evaluation of ionospheric electron densities and collision frequencies derived from rocket measurements of refractive index and attenuation, *J. Atmos. Terr. Phys.*, **23** (1961), 338.

28. Krasnushkin, P. Y., and N. L. Kolesnikov, Investigation of the lower ionosphere by means of long radio waves and low frequency probes installed on a rocket. Detection of a new ionospheric layer, *Akad. Nauk Doklady* (USSR), **146** (1962), 596.

29. Martyn, D. F., Atmospheric tides in the ionosphere, *Proc. Roy. Soc. A*, **189** (1947) 241; *ibid.*, **190** (1955), 273.

30. Murgatroyd, R. J., and R. M. Goody, Sources and sinks of radiative energy from 30 to 90 km, *Quart. J. Roy. Meteorol. Soc.*, **84** (1958), 225.

31. Nicolet, M., and A. C. Aikin, The formation of the D-region of the ionosphere, *J. Geophys. Res.*, **65** (1960), 1469.

32. Phelps, A. V., and J. L. Pack, Electron collision frequencies in nitrogen and in the lower ionosphere, *Phys. Rev. Letters*, **3** (1959), 340.

33. Ratcliffe, J. A., A survey of solar eclipses and the ionosphere. Solar Eclipses and the Ionosphere, *J. Atmos. Terr. Phys.*, (special suppl.), **6**, (1956).

34. ———, and K. Weekes, The ionosphere, in Physics of the Upper Atmosphere, ed. J. A. Ratcliffe, New York: Academic Press, 1960, p. 381.

35. Robinson, B. J., Diurnal variation of the electron distribution in the ionospheric E-layer, *J. Atmos. Terr. Phys.*, **18** (1960), 215.

36. Schaefer, E. J., and M. H. Nichols, Neutral composition obtained from a rocket-borne mass spectrometer, COSPAR, Proc. Fourth Intern. Space Science Symposium, Poland, 1963. Amsterdam: North Holland Publishing Company, 1964, p. 205.

37. Schlapp, D. M., Some measurements of collision frequency in the E-region of the ionosphere, *J. Atmos. Terr. Phys.*, **16** (1959), 340.

38. Scott, J. C. W., The solar control of the E and F1 layers, at high latitudes, *J. Geophys. Res.*, **57** (1952), 369.

39. Smith, L. G., Rocket measurements of electron density and temperature in the nighttime ionosphere. Geophys. Corp. Amer., Tech. Report 62-1-N, 1962.

40. Stroud, W. G., W. Nordberg, W. R. Bandeen, F. L. Bartman and P. Titus, Rocket-grenade measurements of temperatures and winds over Churchill, Canada, *J. Geophys. Res.*, **65** (1960), 2302.

41. Thitheridge, J. E., The calculation of real and virtual heights in the ionosphere, *J. Atmos. Terr. Phys.*, **17** (1959), 96; The use of the extraordinary ray in the analysis of ionospheric records, *ibid.*, **17** (1959), 110.

42. Thomas, J. O., The distribution of electrons in the ionosphere, *Proc. I.R.E.*, **47** (1959), 162.

43. Thomas, L., The winter anomaly in ionospheric absorption, *J. Atmos. Terr. Phys.*, **23** (1961), 301.

44. Watts, J. M., The interpretation of nighttime low frequency ionograms, *J. Geophys. Res.*, **63** (1958), 717.

45. Wexler, H., A look at some suggested solar-weather relationships, in The Sun's Effect on the Earth's Atmosphere, Inst. Solar-Terrest. Res., Tech. Report No. 2, High Altitude Observatory, Univ. Colorado, October, 1956, p. 21.

46. Yonezawa, T., Probe measurements of electron and positive ion densities in the E and F regions by rockets, in Proc. NATO Advanced Studies Institute, Skiekampen, Norway, 1961, ed. B. Maehlum. New York: Pergamon Press, Inc., 1962, p. 80.

4

J. S. Belrose

The Ionospheric *F* Region

4.1. INTRODUCTION

The ionospheric *F* region begins at the top of the *E* region, at a height of about 140 km; there is no generally accepted upper height limit. The maximum ionospheric electron number density, the so-called *F*2 peak, occurs at heights varying from about 250 to 500 km. The bulk of the atmosphere consists of neutral gas even at these heights, but its composition is markedly different from that of the lower regions. As noted in Sec. 3.4, atmospheric mixing processes are of little significance above the *E* region. The composition of the *F* region is therefore determined by ionization production and loss processes, and by diffusive separation of the chemical constituents. In the lower *F* region, the principal constituents are atomic oxygen and molecular nitrogen, the latter predominating. With increasing altitude, the dominant constituent changes from nitrogen to atomic oxygen, to helium, and finally to atomic hydrogen (see Fig. 5.4). The scale height at the base of the *F* region is about 30 km, compared with a scale height of about 10 km for the *E* region.

It is sometimes convenient to consider that the *F* region is bounded by the height at which O^+ ceases to be the dominant ion. The authors of the present book have found it more convenient to discuss these upper levels in terms of two regions defined somewhat differently, the

F region up to the *F*2 peak (Chapter 4) and the outer ionosphere above the *F*2 peak (Chapter 5). This particular division reflects the fact already noted in Chapter 3; namely, direct studies of the neutral gas are more difficult than studies of the ionized constituents. Historically, most of our knowledge of the *F* region has been derived from observations of the ionization and, in particular, of the ionization up to the *F*2 peak.

Partly because it is responsible for most HF communications and partly because its thickness and minimal attenuation for probing radio waves make it most prominent in ionosonde recordings, the *F* layer has been the most studied of the ionized layers. Usually, but not invariably, the ionization of the *F* region exhibits two subdivisions, the *F*1 ledge below and the *F*2 layer above. The diurnal, seasonal, and geographic variations of the critical frequency of the *F*1 ledge, f_0F1, are quite like those of an α- Chapman layer (Sec. 3.2.3) whereas the variations of f_0F2 are 'anomalous'; that is, quite unlike and sometimes opposite to those that would be expected on simple theory. The variation of f_0F2 is much altered on days of magnetic disturbance, while that of the *F*1 ledge remains relatively unchanged. Perhaps the outstanding anomaly of the *F*2 layer is its symmetry with respect to the geomagnetic rather than to the geographic equator.

Solar ultraviolet radiation is the main ionizing agent in the *E* and lower *F* regions. The situation is less certain in the upper part of the *F* region, where some of the recent experimental data suggest the presence of an additional source of ionization at high latitudes. This additional source might, for instance, consist of an influx of energetic particles. Another complicating factor in the *F*2 region is that the lifetime of a free electron is of the order of hours, so that the ionization equilibrium can be strongly affected by the movements of electrons that result from electromagnetic forces, temperature changes, and diffusion (see Secs. 4.3 and 7.4).

This chapter outlines the global morphology of the *F*-region ionization during magnetically quiet times and discusses its structure in terms of the composition of the atmosphere. Physical conditions, such as temperature, effective electron loss rates, and collision frequencies, will be briefly reviewed. Finally, some *F*-region irregularities, not obviously associated with magnetic storms, will be considered. Most of the chapter concentrates on the *F* region below the *F*2 peak, but on occasion, the discussion is concerned with physical processes that are continuous across the *F*2 peak. This leads to a slight overlap between the subject matter of Chapters 4 and 5.

4.2. MORPHOLOGY OF THE *F* LAYER

4.2.1. The *F*1 Ledge. The *F*1 ledge, like the *E* layer, exhibits close solar control. It appears at dawn, reaches a daily maximum a few minutes after noon, and disappears at dusk. Only small perturbations from the behavior of an α-Chapman layer are found. This might at first seem surprising, since the $F1$ ledge is not at all well defined but instead merges with the $F2$ layer to such an extent that the two are often scarcely distinguishable (see Fig. 3.8). The $F1$ ledge is much more pronounced in its appearance on ionograms during the summer season, at the minimum of the sunspot cycle (Fig. 4.1), during ionospheric storms, and in fact at all times when low values of f_0F2 are observed during the day. At other times, and always at night, a single unbifurcated bank of ionization, designated the $F2$ layer, is present in the F region.

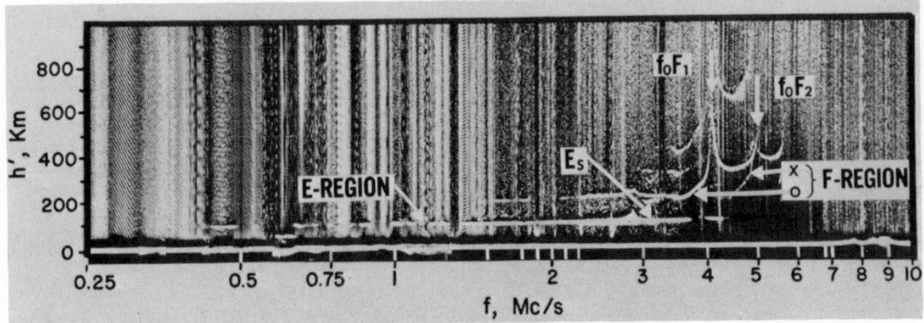

Fig. 4.1 Ionogram taken at Ottawa, Canada, at about 0930 L.S.T., 12 May 1964, during an epoch of minimum solar activity.

At noon near the equator, the peak of the $F1$ ledge is reached at about 160 km which is some 50 km or more lower than the virtual height indicated in the ionosonde records. The corresponding peak electron density is about 2.5×10^5 cm^{-3} at the equinoxes during sunspot minimum; this varies with the epoch of solar cycle according to the empirically defined relation [1]

$$N_m F1 = 2.5 \times 10^5 (1 + 6.2 \times 10^{-3} R), \tag{4.1}$$

where R is the sunspot number.

If f_0F1 corresponds to the peak of an α-Chapman layer, it should vary with the zenith angle of the sun diurnally and seasonally, according to

$$f_0 \propto \cos^{1/n} \chi,$$

where $n = 4$, (see Eq. (3.14)). It is found, however, that the diurnally determined index n is not a constant but has a seasonal variation. This effect appears to depend on latitude, but variations of this type have not yet been given detailed examination. Again, midday determinations of the index n show variations from station to station, and with the epoch of the sunspot cycle. It may be worth noting that n is generally greater than the theoretical value of 4 for the $F1$ ledge, whereas it is less than 4 for the E layer (see Secs. 3.4.2 and 3.4.3).

Local-time maps of f_0F1 for June, 1954, and June, 1958, are shown in Fig. 4.2 to illustrate the remarkable difference between conditions of sunspot

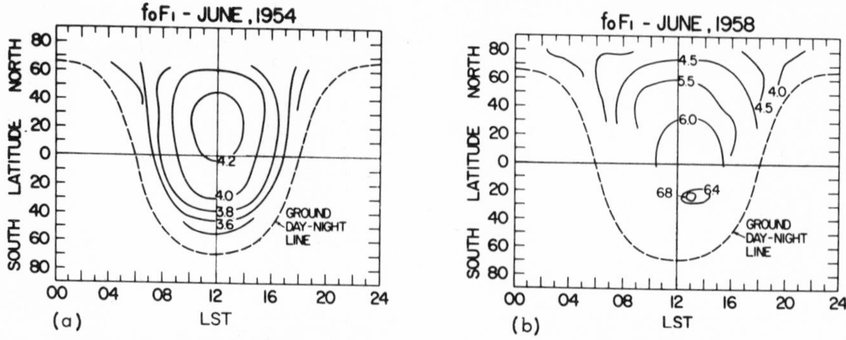

Fig. 4.2 Maps of f_0F1 (monthly median values) for (a) June, 1954 (epoch of minimum solar activity), (b) June, 1958 (epoch of maximum solar activity). (After Davies [10].)

minimum and maximum. At minimum, Fig. 4.2(a), the f_0F1 contours are roughly circular. They are approximately symmetric with respect to local noon, and the maximum electron density occurs in the summer hemisphere. This is the type of behavior to be anticipated from simple theory and is similar to the behavior of f_0E, Fig. 3.9. At sunspot maximum it is difficult to obtain f_0F1 measurements in the winter hemisphere. It is evident, however, that the partial contours plotted in Fig. 4.2(b) depart significantly from those in Fig. 4.2(a). In particular, the contours are more irregular; they are probably asymmetric with respect to local noon, and the maximum of f_0F1 occurs in the winter hemisphere. These results suggest that it is only during conditions of sunspot minimum that the behavior of f_0F1 is closely similar to that of an α-Chapman layer.

4.2.2. The *F*2 Peak. The morphology of the $F2$ layer is much more complex than that of the $F1$ ledge. Neither the critical frequency, f_0F2, nor the height at which it occurs can be explained on a simple physical model. The critical frequency can be measured much more readily than the height of the peak, and variations in f_0F2 provide some indication of what is happening within the $F2$ layer as a whole. Accordingly, the present section places emphasis on the f_0F2 variations.

Figure 4.3 shows world contours of f_0F2 for equinoctial and (June) solstitial months for two epochs of the solar cycle: 1947, a year of maximum sunspot activity, and 1943–44, which were years of minimum activity. The critical frequencies are plotted here on a grid of local time and geomagnetic latitude. Had geographic latitude been employed, the equinoctial contours would have been much more asymmetric about the equator, and additional diagrams would be needed to exhibit a longitudinal variation which then arises.

In spite of obvious differences in detail, certain large-scale features arising from solar control of the $F2$-layer ionization are common to the

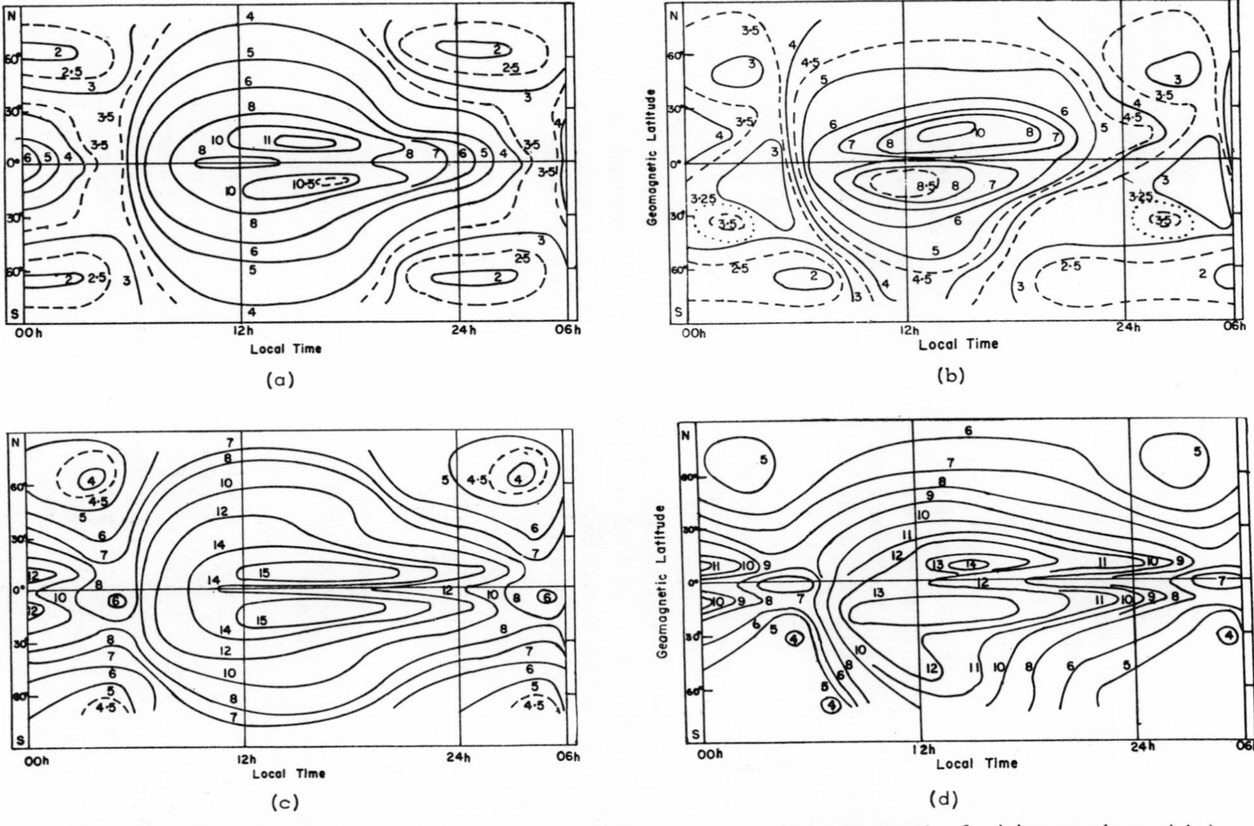

Fig. 4.3 Maps of f_0F2 (median values) for (a) equinox, (b) June solstice for 1943–44 (epoch of minimum solar activity), (c) equinox, (d) June solstice for 1947 (epoch of maximum solar activity). (After Martyn [25].)

four diagrams. The critical frequency increases after sunrise, the increase being most rapid at the lower latitudes. A maximum is reached in the early afternoon, and there is a relatively rapid decrease shortly after sunset. The critical frequencies are highest in the general vicinity of the equator.

Figure 4.3 also illustrates, in a compact way, the major anomalies in the variation of f_0F2. The near symmetry of the equinoctial curves about the geomagnetic equator is itself an anomaly, since according to simple theory, we should expect symmetry about the geographic equator. The variation of f_0F2 along a line of fixed time in the afternoon shows the *geomagnetic anomaly*, also called the 'equatorial anomaly': there is a trough in f_0F2 along the geomagnetic equator, and two peaks are formed about 10° or 15° on each side. The variation of f_0F2 along a line of fixed latitude shows the *diurnal* anomaly, which, for a particular station, depends on the season and epoch of the solar cycle. For stations near 10°–15° north and south of the geomagnetic equator, the maximum in f_0F2 is reached late in the afternoon in summer and in equinoctial months, but in winter the peak occurs near noon. The trough in f_0F2 near the equator produces there a so-called bite-out in the diurnal variation. At sunspot minimum, this occurs only during daylight hours, but at sunspot maximum it persists, in diminishing degree, until after midnight.

In moderate to high latitudes there is a gross *seasonal anomaly*, in that winter daytime values of f_0F2 are not smaller than corresponding summer values, and in fact, particularly at the maximum epoch of the solar cycle, the winter values are strikingly greater than the summer values. Detailed studies have revealed that there is also an annual component in the variation, sometimes called the *December anomaly*, such that f_0F2 tends to reach a maximum in December regardless of latitude [39]. In the northern hemisphere, the seasonal and December anomalies act in the same sense, so the recorded values of f_0F2 are greater then than at any other season of the year.

In Fig. 4.4 are shown some results of a detailed study of the winter anomaly. Here the electron number density at the $F2$ peak, N_mF2, is plotted against the magnetic dip angle for different epochs of the solar cycle. The broken lines are mirror images of the southern hemisphere curve about the magnetic equator. These data reveal that the winter anomaly is restricted in magnetic latitude (see Eq. (1.14) for the relationship between magnetic dip angle and magnetic latitude) and is most pronounced at times of high sunspot number. The additional peaks at dip angles of about 30° corresponding to magnetic latitudes of about 15°N and S, which are the predominant feature at the minimum epoch of the solar cycle, are the result of the geomagnetic anomaly and are best studied in equinoctial months. When values of N_mF2 are plotted against magnetic dip for other hours of the day or night, a similar maximum is found near 70° (corresponding to a magnetic latitude of about 55°) throughout the daylight hours. It appears at sunrise,

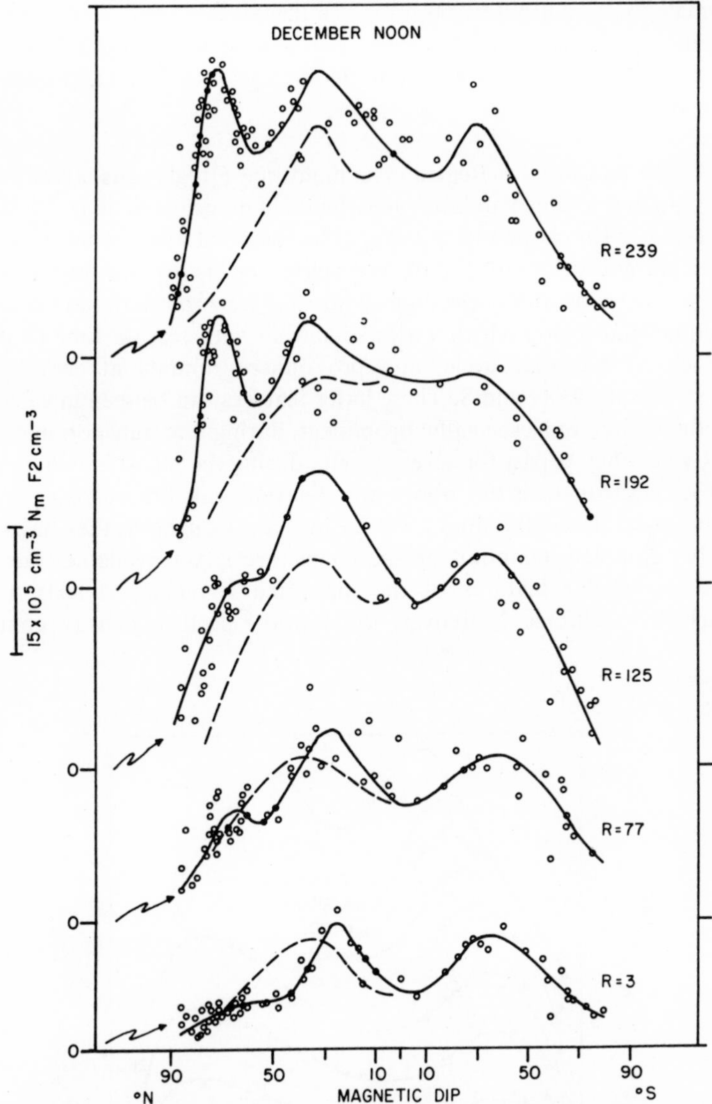

Fig. 4.4 The variation with magnetic dip of the median December local noon values of N_mF2 at different epochs of the solar cycle. (After Thomas [35].)

is most prominent near noon, and subsequently decreases until at midnight it disappears.

At the highest latitudes, the ionosphere may be in continuous sunlight or continuous darkness for long periods of time, depending on the season. A moderate diurnal variation may be due to small variations of the solar zenith angle, but a diurnal variation is still detectable at the south pole [21]. This confirms that, at high latitudes as well as low, factors other than solar illumination play an important role in determining the diurnal variations of the ionosphere.

4.2.3. The Nocturnal *F* Region. The nighttime *F* region, as already mentioned, contains a single unbifurcated bank of ionization; it is known as the *F*2 layer or simply as the '*F* layer.' The temporal and spatial variations of this nocturnal ionization for the respective epochs are illustrated in Fig. 4.3. For a fixed time during the night hours, f_0F2 exhibits a broad maximum in the equatorial region which varies somewhat with season, time of night, and epoch of the solar cycle, and pronounced minima at geomagnetic latitudes of about 63°N and S. These latter features can be seen in each part of the figure but are especially prominent during the sunspot minimum equinox when they persist for several hours during the night. Satellite observations of electron densities above the *F*-layer peak are currently giving more details on these minimum f_0F2 features, or 'troughs' as they have been called. No complete temporal or spatial picture is yet available, but they seem to be regular features of the nighttime *F* region, at least during undisturbed conditions. Moreover, the topside electron density contours

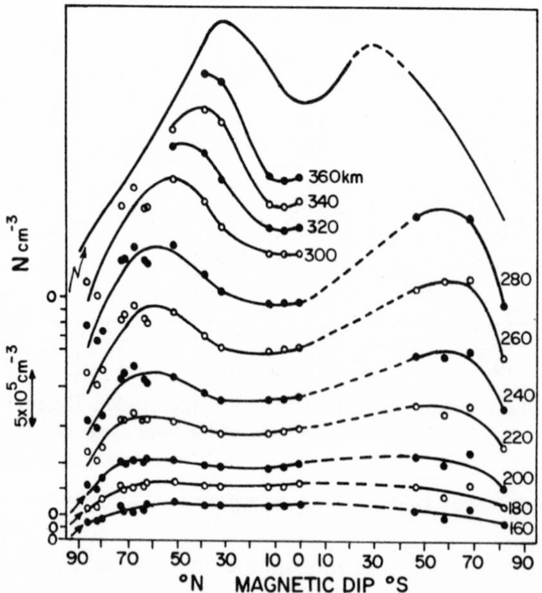

Fig. 4.5 Contours of electron number density at a series of fixed heights up to the *F*2 peak; median local noon values in September, 1957. (After Croom *et al.* [7].)

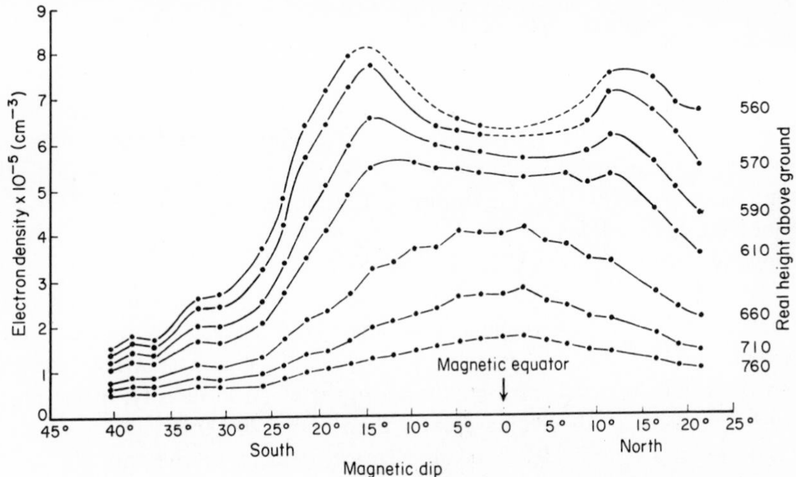

Fig. 4.6 Contours of electron number density at a series of fixed heights above the $F2$ peak; from satellite data recorded at Singapore between 1001 and 1012 L.S.T., 1 October 1962. (After King [20].)

(cf. Fig. 5.6) suggest that the trough is rather restricted in latitude, much more so than one might infer from the statistical bottom side data shown in Fig. 4.3.

In this connection it is interesting to note that the observations of cosmic radio noise at MF in Tasmania [12] during the past few years were probably related to this trough feature in the ionosphere. Such long-term measurements indicate consistently low penetration frequencies and strengthen the belief that the trough is a regular or permanent feature of the nighttime F layer.

4.2.4. The Distribution of Electrons in the *F* Region. Although the morphology of the F layer is most readily examined by means of the penetration frequencies, along lines previously indicated, improvements in the reduction of ionosonde data and the growing use of satellite observations have recently permitted more detailed studies to be made into the shape of the layer as a whole. Such studies are adding to our understanding of the various anomalies.

In Fig. 4.5, the electron number density at local noon is plotted against magnetic dip for a number of different heights up to the peak of the $F2$ layer. The geomagnetic anomaly is not evident at $F1$ heights, but first appears at about 200 km. Here maxima in electron density occur at dip angles of about 60° and as the height increases, these maxima shift gradually toward the magnetic equator. The sequence is continued above the $F2$ peak in Fig. 4.6, which is derived from a particular satellite pass over Singapore. The separation between the peaks continues to decrease as the height increases until, at about 700 km, a single maximum is formed on the magnetic equator. It thus appears that the equatorial anomaly takes the form of an arch with its top at about 700 km above the ground. Further plots of the type shown in Fig. 4.6 reveal that the top of the arch appears to be farthest from the ground, approximately 900 km, at about 20 hours local time [20]. The contours also show that the anomaly is then most pronounced. After 20 hours the arch begins to fall and, near midnight, the top is only 400 km above the ground and the anomaly has virtually disappeared.

In Fig. 4.7 data similar to those shown in Fig. 4.5 are plotted for December, 1957. The geomagnetic anomaly is much less pronounced, and is evident only for heights greater than about 300 km. The winter anomaly shows clearly, however, as a maximum in the electron density, in the northern hemisphere at all heights greater than about 200 km.

In Figs. 4.8 and 4.9, *F*-region electron density profiles are shown for quiet days in December, 1957, and June, 1958, at different magnetic latitudes, at local noon and midnight. In December at noon in the northern hemisphere the height, h_N, of a fixed value of electron density, N, is greatest near the equator and least near 72°; it increases again above that latitude.

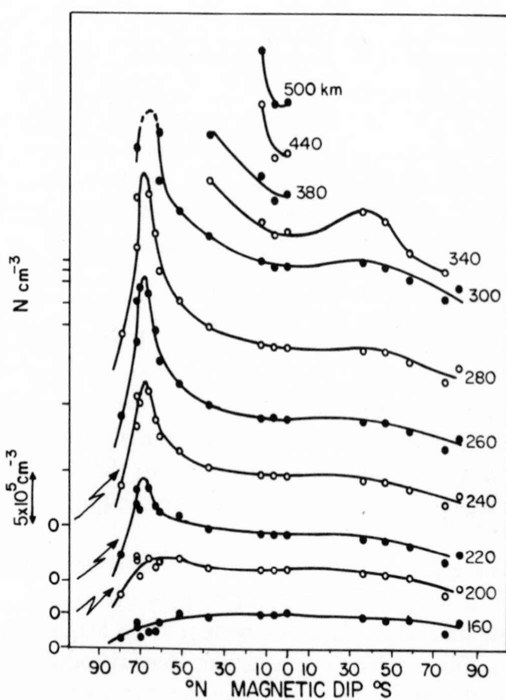

Fig. 4.7 Contours of electron number density at a series of fixed heights up to the *F*2 peak; mean local noon values in December, 1957. (After Croom *et al.* [8].)

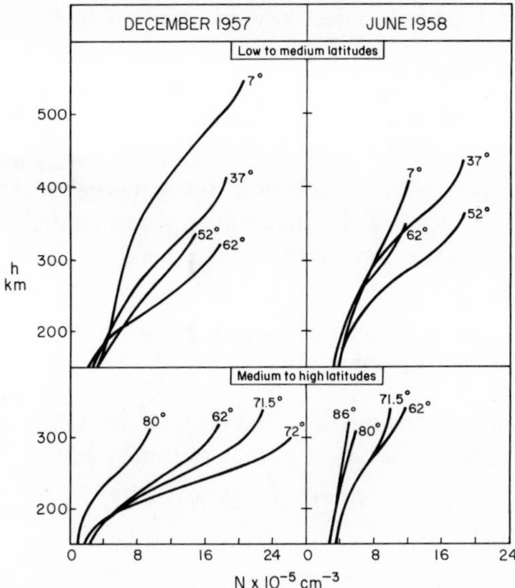

Fig. 4.8 *F*-region electron number density distributions, *N*(*h*) curves, at local noon in December, 1957, and June, 1958, for eight stations. The stations in order of decreasing magnetic dip are Thule (86°); Godhavn (82°); Pt. Barrow (80°); St. John's (72°); Washington (71.5°); Adoc (63°); Stanford (62°); Puerto Rico (52°); Maui (39°); Okinawa (37°); Conception (36°); Chimbote (7°); and La Paz (−5°). (After Croom *et al.* [9].)

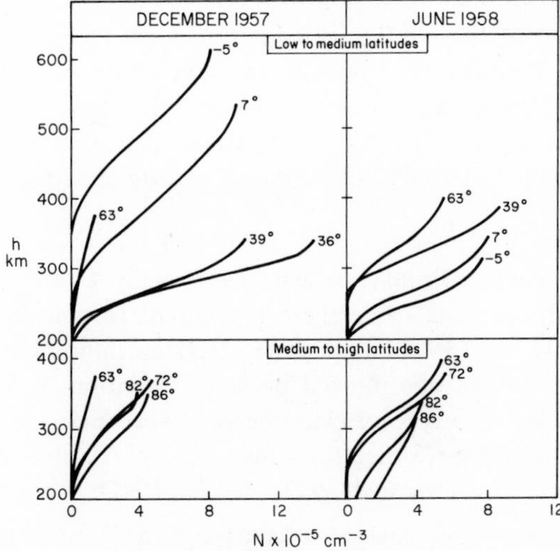

Fig. 4.9 *F*-region electron number density distributions, *N*(*h*) curves, at local midnight in December, 1957, and June, 1958, for eight stations listed in the caption of Fig. 4.8. (After Croom *et al.* [9].)

The same general latitude effect occurs at noon in June, except that the height variations are considerably reduced and the lowest heights occur at somewhat lower latitudes, near 52°. At midnight in December, h_N is greatest near the equator and near 63° and smallest near 36°. There is a marked difference between the December midnight curves for 7°N and 5°S, indicating rapid variations with latitude near the equator. At midnight in June, h_N is again greatest near 63° latitude but in sharp contrast to the December data, the equator is the site of the lowest heights.

4.3. THE FORMATION OF IONIZED LAYERS IN THE QUIET *F* REGION

4.3.1. The Continuity Equation. The electron density $N(h, t)$ at any height and time is given by the solution of the continuity equation,

$$\partial N/\partial t = q - L(N) - M, \tag{4.2}$$

in which the terms on the right-hand side stand for production, loss, and diverging movement of ionization, respectively. The movement term can be written as the divergence of a transport flux of ionization

$$M = \text{div}\,(N\boldsymbol{v}) = \text{div}\,[N(\boldsymbol{v}_{EM} + \boldsymbol{v}_T + \boldsymbol{v}_D)]. \tag{4.3}$$

Here three types of movement are recognized explicitly, namely, movement caused by electromagnetic forces, by temperature changes of the atmosphere, and by ambipolar or plasma diffusion. It is usually assumed* that horizontal movement makes little contribution to the term M, which is then just the vertical divergence $\partial(Nw)/\partial h$, where w is the vertical component of velocity of electrons and ions and h is a vertical coordinate.

The solution of the continuity equation is extremely complicated if all three types of ionization movement are taken into account, and to date only beginnings have been made to this complex task. The procedure followed has been to examine conditions when one or more of the terms of Eq. (4.3) are believed to be negligible, if indeed movements are included at all.

4.3.2. Free-electron Production and Loss Processes. In the *F* region below, say, 600 km, the neutral atmosphere is thought to consist primarily of O and N_2, with O_2 and N (and perhaps NO) as minor constituents. Each neutral constituent may be ionized by solar radiation or by collision with energetic particles. The type of electron loss process depends very much on the positive ions present. Electrons may be lost by dissociative recombination with molecular ions such as O_2^+, N_2^+, and NO^+, or they may combine

*This assumption does not hold at low latitudes, of course, where the field inclination is such that horizontal movements cannot be neglected; the significance of this in connection with the 'geomagnetic anomaly' is discussed in Sec. 4.3.5.

directly with atomic ions. The latter process is so slow as to be negligible compared to dissociative recombination, except possibly at heights well above the $F2$ peak, and even there electron losses occur at a negligible rate compared to losses at lower levels. The net result is that direct recombination with atomic ions is not considered to be a significant loss process. Instead, the atomic ions react with neutral molecules to form molecular ions, which then undergo dissociative recombination [2].

Since O and N_2 are the dominant constituents, the most important loss processes include the following:

Loss Reactions

$$O^+ + O_2 \rightarrow O_2^+ + O \tag{4.4a}$$

$$O_2^+ + e \rightarrow O^* + O^{**} \tag{4.4b}$$

$$O^+ + N_2 \rightarrow NO^+ + N \tag{4.5a}$$

$$NO^+ + e \rightarrow N^* + O^*. \tag{4.5b}$$

The rates of the general reactions (a) and (b) may be expressed in the form:

$$\frac{dn(O^+)}{dt} = -K_1 n(O^+) n(XY) \tag{4.6a}$$

$$\frac{dN}{dt} = -K_2 N n(XY^+) \tag{4.6b}$$

where K_1 and K_2 are constant rate coefficients, N is the electron number density, and $n(XY)$, $n(XY^+)$ are the densities of neutral diatomic molecules (O_2 or N_2) and positive diatomic ions (O_2^+ or NO^+), respectively. The parameters $K_1 n(XY)$ and K_2 play the role of the attachment and recombination coefficients, β and α respectively (Sec. 3.2.2), and when replaced by these symbols, they combine to yield a net loss rate [29] given by

$$L(N) = \frac{\beta \alpha N^2}{\beta + \alpha N} \tag{4.6c}$$

where α is a constant and β is height dependent.

If $\beta \gg \alpha N$, as is the case low down in the F region, then $L(N) \simeq \alpha N^2$, and the net loss rate is controlled by the dissociative recombination process, but if $\beta \ll \alpha N$, as is the case in the upper F region, $L(N) \simeq \beta N$ and the net rate is controlled by the attachment-like process.

The changeover from the quadratic rate of loss of electrons low down, to a linear loss rate high up, takes place at a transition level where

$$\alpha N = \beta\ . \tag{4.7}$$

The height at which this transition level occurs has an important influence on the shape of the electron density profile (as will be discussed further in Sec. 4.3.3).

The foregoing discussion has not considered what effect N_2^+ ions may have on the total loss rate. There is little doubt that an appreciable fraction of the solar ultraviolet radiation is consumed in producing N_2^+ ions. Available measurements indicate, however, that the main ionic constituents are O^+, NO^+ and O_2^+, and that N_2^+ ions are relatively scarce in the entire *F* region. This is usually taken to imply that the dissociative recombination of N_2^+

$$N_2^+ + e \rightarrow N^* + N^{**} \tag{4.8}$$

is so rapid that N_2 does not make a significant contribution to the observed ionization [31]. Norton *et al.* [27], however, postulate a reaction

$$N_2^+ + O \rightarrow NO^+ + N \tag{4.9}$$

which they think takes place instead of the direct dissociative recombination reaction, and which then prevents the rapid removal of the associated free electrons. In fact, on their hypothesis a substantial contribution to *F*-region ionization arises from the photoionization of N_2.

4.3.3. The *F*1 Ledge. The shape of the equilibrium electron number density profile depends on all three independent quantities, q, α, and β. If the transition level defined by Eq. (4.7) is assumed to occur near the peak of production, it is possible to explain the appearance, at times, of an *F*1 ledge which behaves rather like a Chapman layer [17]. This condition is most nearly attained when the solar zenith angle is small, the production peak being then at its lowest elevation. This explanation would account for the observed tendency of the *F*1 ledge to form during the midday hours. The analysis also shows that the increased production of ionization that occurs near sunspot maximum should reduce the likelihood of being able to observe an *F*1 ledge. Again, this is in agreement with observation, and it provides some insight into the departure of the index in Eq. (3.14) from the value of $\frac{1}{4}$ that would be appropriate for an α-Chapman layer.

It should be mentioned that some workers have suggested that bifurcation of the *F* layer might be due to temperature gradients such as are known to exist in the lower *F* region [5]; this situation might be expected to generate two peaks in the height distribution of the electron production function. It seems unlikely, however, that the detailed morphology of the *F*1 ledge can be accounted for in this way. Although the existence of temperature gradients may be important here, the splitting of the *F* layer would seem to be more dependent on the processes previously described.

4.3.4. The *F*2 Peak. In the *F*2 layer the loss coefficient β is thought to decrease so rapidly with height (because the concentration of diatomic molecules decreases rapidly with height) that the electron density increases with increasing height above the production peak. This explanation for a bifurcation into *F*1 and *F*2 was first suggested by Bradbury [4] and is often termed the 'Bradbury hypothesis.' It does not, of itself, set any limit on the upward increase of N, and so the existence of a maximum in the electron density must be explained on further grounds. There is as yet no general agreement on this subject, but the following points appear to be pertinent [31]:

1. Simple theory assumes that only a small proportion of the atmosphere is ionized. In analysis of the upper F region, this may become a poor approximation to use.
2. The continuing decrease of β with height does not lead to a corresponding continuous decrease of the electron loss rate, since at sufficiently great heights direct recombination of the electrons and ions must become the dominant loss process [29].
3. The ionization diffuses under gravity and assumes a hydrostatic distribution at great heights [37].
4. Even if it is assumed that the equilibrium electron density could increase indefinitely with height (until 100% ionization is achieved), the time constant $1/\beta$ would be sufficiently large to prevent equilibrium being reached during the day.

It is now believed that points (1) and (2) are not important below 300 km, a typical height at which the $F2$ peak is found in temperate latitudes. With regard to (3), if an equilibrium distribution is assumed, plasma diffusion can produce a peak in the electron density [32, 38]. The daytime $F2$ layer, however, does not attain equilibrium (see Sec. 4.4.2), and it follows that the behavior of the peak is influenced by transient effects. In summary, it appears that at heights well below the $F2$ peak, the electron density in the daytime approximates the equilibrium value it would have in the absence of diffusion; whereas above the peak, the electron density is largely controlled by diffusion. (It will be recalled that no diffusion is assumed in an α-Chapman layer; it is therefore not surprising that the morphology of the $F2$ layer differs substantially from that of an α-Chapman layer.)

4.3.5. The *F*-Region Anomalies. As already indicated, F-region variations that are inconsistent with the behavior expected of an α-Chapman layer are called ‘anomalous’ variations. This terminology arose early in the history of ionospheric research and has been perpetuated by sheer inertia even after a given anomaly has been satisfactorily explained.

The sense of the annual (nonseasonal) electron number density variation, previously referred to as the ‘December anomaly,’ can be explained: since the sun-earth distance is a minimum in December, the global ionization density might be expected to be greatest at this time. This is observed, but the magnitude of the effect (about 20%) is much larger than can be explained by this variation alone: the decrease in the sun-earth distance should not increase q by more than about 6%.

The geomagnetic anomaly (or equatorial anomaly) clearly shown in

Fig. 4.5 is consistent with the hypothesis that the ionization produced in the vicinity of the geomagnetic equator is raised to heights above the $F2$ peak and then transported to higher latitudes along magnetic field lines. This hypothesis is supported by the work of Duncan [11] who has shown that afternoon values of f_0F2 in the equatorial zone are negatively correlated with those on the same meridian in the subtropical belts. With a diurnal variation of the process taken into account, due probably to tidal effects (see Chapter 7), the diurnal anomaly can be considered as one aspect of the geomagnetic anomaly.

The seasonal anomaly has as yet no adequate explanation. Possible seasonal changes in photochemical processes have been suggested, and they undoubtedly play some part. For instance, the larger winter daytime electron densities might be associated with a variation in β if the latter were sufficiently temperature dependent. But since the anomaly is sharply dependent on magnetic latitude (being maximum near 70° dip in the winter hemisphere), this cannot be the sole reason. It has been suggested that the seasonal anomaly might be associated with transport processes, or with the exospheric trapped radiation. Both suggestions must at present be considered as conjecture.

There is a large seasonal change in the sunrise rate of increase in electron density ($\partial N/\partial t$) at heights near the $F2$ peak [33], the winter values being much greater than the summer values (by about the same factor as for N_mF2 from winter to summer). This appears to indicate a seasonal change in q, which might be due to a corresponding change of composition in the upper atmosphere. There is, however, no independent evidence for seasonal changes in composition.

4.4. PARAMETERS OF THE *F* REGION

4.4.1. Effective Electron Loss Rates. The most probable electron loss process at heights greater than 200 km has been discussed in Sec. 4.3.2. An atomic ion is first converted to a molecular ion, and the latter then undergoes dissociative recombination, conditions being such that the exchange process determines the net rate. Measurements made at night, when it may be assumed that $q = 0$, at places where it was believed that movements were not important, have suggested [30] that the effective attachment coefficient is given by

$$\beta = 10^{-4} \exp\left[\frac{300 - h}{50}\right], \tag{4.10}$$

where β is measured in (seconds)$^{-1}$ and h in kilometers above the ground.

The main difficulty with loss processes appears to be that loss coefficients suitable for explaining $N(t)$ curves by day and shortly after sunest are inapplicable in the later part of the night when electron densities decrease very slowly or even increase (see, for example, Fig. 4.3). The situation is undoubtedly complicated by movements. Changes in β could be caused by a temperature dependence of the rate coefficients involved or by a progressive change in the abundance of important constituents. The effective loss rate can certainly change from night to day because of the different height distributions of the main positive ions [18]. By day O_2^+ and NO^+ are found in comparable numbers, and the number density of both decreases with increase in altitude, whereas the number density of O^+ (the dominant ion in the $F2$ layer), increases with height. At night the distributions are quite different: NO^+ is the dominant ion in the lower F region, and O^+ ions are scarce below 200 km.

4.4.2. Temperature of the *F* Region. During the night, the electron temperature, T_e, and the neutral gas temperature, T_n, are generally thought to be equal at all altitudes. This equality is also believed to occur by day in the E region and below under quiet solar conditions, but probably not necessarily in the daytime F region [3]. It is of considerable importance to compare T_e and T_n as functions of altitude, since their interdependence is a sensitive index of the complex reactions that affect the rates of various photochemical processes. Unfortunately neither T_e nor T_n is known very accurately in the F region, and the positive-ion temperature, T_i, has not been studied at all.

Our knowledge of the behavior of the neutral gas temperature at F-region heights is based principally on atmospheric densities computed from satellite drag observations and assumed atmospheric composition. Values of T_n so derived are probably not very accurate, but the variations are certainly meaningful (see Sec. 5.2.2). The drag observations show that neutral gas temperature has its maximum in the afternoon and that the density variations are correlated with solar activity.

The electron temperature is even less accurately known. Langmuir probe data (acquired from rocket and satellite experiments) require careful interpretation because of the disturbance produced in the medium by the conducting vehicle body. In addition a Maxwellian velocity distribution is usually assumed in the analysis principally because no method has yet been developed to measure the actual distribution. Nevertheless, if T_e derived from Langmuir probe data is compared with T_n, then it is found that, at low latitudes and for quiet solar conditions, midday values of T_e and T_n are equal below 150 km and above 450 km. The thermal equilibrium that this suggests is not found in the lower $F2$ layer (near 200 km, where the electron production is believed to be a maximum), nor at sunrise.

Preliminary analysis of the Ariel satellite data [36] for altitudes above 450 km indicates that, except for a marked departure from equilibrium at sunrise, the diurnal maximum and minimum values of T_i at middle latitudes approximate the diurnal extremes of T_n. An observed latitude dependence of T_i, however, suggests that corpuscular radiation or hydromagnetic wave energy is an important heat source at high latitudes.

4.4.3. Collision Frequency. In the D and E regions, collisions of electrons with neutral particles predominate. This is not necessarily the case in the F region, where electron-ion collisions increase in importance, but there is little experimental evidence to tell us which type of collision predominates, nor in fact what the collision frequency is. The latter parameter is, however, required for any estimation of radio wave absorption or of the electric conductivity in the direction of the geomagnetic field. For most purposes, the important ion collisions are with neutral particles, and their frequency is required for calculations of the diffusion of all ionization (electrons and ions), the conductivity transverse to the magnetic field, and the absorption of hydromagnetic waves. Chapman [6] has given the following theoretical formulas for the various collision frequencies:

$$\nu_{ei} = [34 + 4.18 \log_{10} (T^3/N_e)]\, N_e T^{-3/2} \tag{4.11}$$

$$\nu_{en} = 5.4 \times 10^{-10} N_n T^{1/2} \tag{4.12}$$

$$\nu_{in} = 2.6 \times 10^{-9} (N_e + N_n)\, W^{-1/2}, \tag{4.13}$$

where W is the molecular weight of ions and neutral particles (assumed equal), subscripts e, i, n denote electrons, ions, and neutral particles respectively, and T is the temperature of all constituents (assumed equal). The concentrations N are measured in units of cm^{-3} and the collision frequencies in sec^{-1}.

It is interesting to note that ν_{ei} is proportional to $T^{-3/2}$ whereas ν_{en} is proportional to $T^{1/2}$. If electron collisions are mainly with ions, when the temperature increases during the day their collision frequency will decrease, whereas, if electron collisions are mainly with neutral particles, their collision frequency will increase. These changes have opposite effects on the absorption of radio waves.

Martyn [25] has estimated the values of ν_{ei} and ν_{en} to be 880 and 2300 sec^{-1} at the height of the $F1$ ledge, and 900 and 40 sec^{-1} for the height of the $F2$ peak (300 km), respectively. Ion-neutral collision frequencies were computed to be 96 and 1 sec^{-1} respectively at these same two levels. Thus in the $F1$ ledge, electron collisions would be mainly with neutral particles and in the $F2$ layer mainly with ions.

4.5. *F*-REGION IRREGULARITIES

4.5.1. Travelling Disturbances. Superimposed on the relatively slow and predictable diurnal variations of the F-layer ionization, there are found on occasion irregularities with quasi periodicities of 15 min to 1 hr. When observed at a single station these appear to move downward through the *F* region, though multiple-station observations show also a horizontal motion which can carry the disturbance over many hundreds of kilometers in the course of a few hours. Their horizontal directions of motion tend to be toward the equator or toward the east. They have been studied in several medium-latitude locations, most thoroughly in Australia [14, 15, 26].

The quasi-periodic variations they exhibit suggest an explanation in terms of wave motions, and various types of waves have been considered. Of these, the only acceptable combination of period and speed is provided by internal atmospheric gravity waves which are discussed in Chapter 6. These were first proposed in conjunction with a superimposed wind, to form standing 'cellular' waves in an atmosphere that was taken to contain winds moving with the speed observed [24], but later studies have favored an explanation based on purely progressive internal gravity waves, propagating through an atmosphere that is either stationary or only incidentally in motion [16]. In this latter view, the main source of energy lies below the *F* region and is ducted there, the *F*-region disturbance itself being a manifestation of energy that escapes upward from the duct. The apparent downward movement results from a peculiar relationship that exists between the directions of phase and energy propagation in the waves (see Chapter 6).

4.5.2. Spread *F*. In addition to the large-scale regular motions of ionization in the *F* region, other observations which suggest irregular or turbulent motions are obtained. The morphology of these irregularities has been extensively studied by many workers using routine ground-based ionosondes, and is currently under examination by ionosondes sounding from above.

The name 'spread F' has been adopted for this phenomenon because of the visual appearance of the ionograms, which show rather diffuse *F*-region traces. There are two main classes of spread *F*, frequency spreading and range spreading, which are obvious in the example of Fig. 4.10. Classic high and temporate latitude spread *F* is of the frequency-spreading type, and classic equatorial-type spread *F* is of the range-broadening type with little, if any, evidence for increasing virtual heights at higher frequencies. Both types may be found, however, at all latitudes.

At high latitudes, spread *F* is specifically associated with disturbed rather than with normal conditions; at low latitudes, the reverse is true. Moreover, the morphology of equatorial spread *F* is so different from that of spread *F* in the polar regions, that many doubt that the cause is the same.

Equatorial spread *F* is visible on ground-based ionosonde records only in the evening and at night. It is most prevalent before midnight, and occurs more frequently in sunspot minimum years than at sunspot maximum [34]. At sunspot maximum, a region about 20 degrees wide in latitude, centered

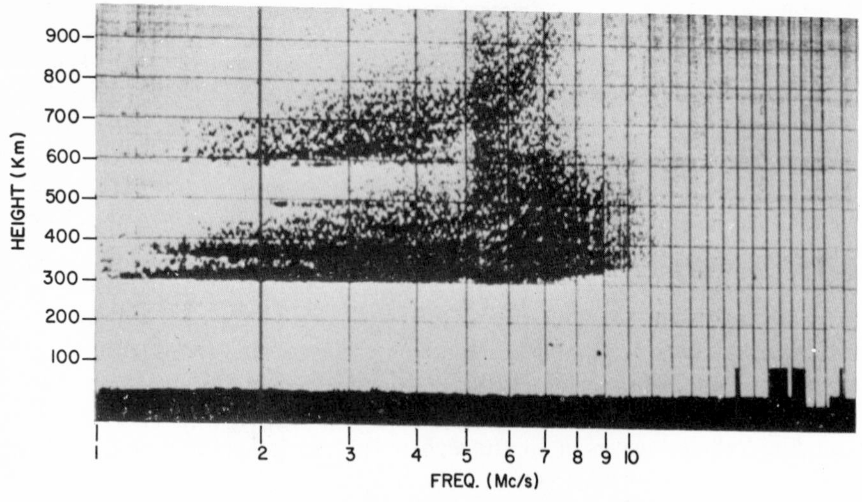

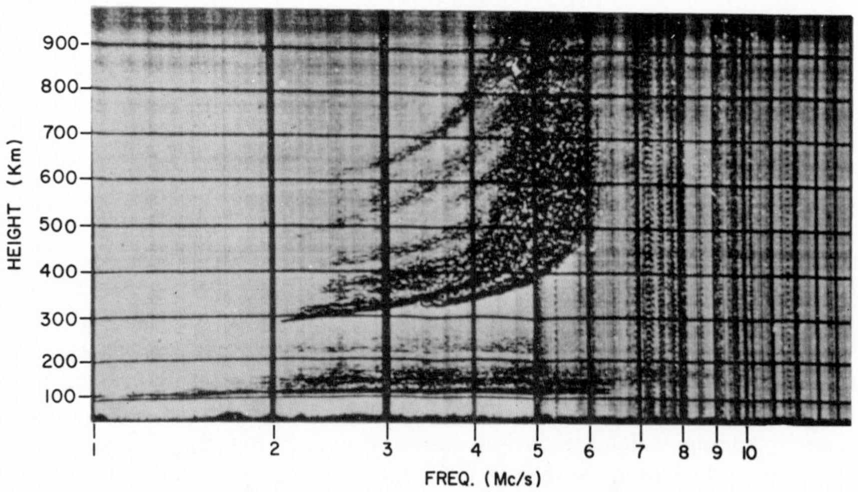

Fig. 4.10 Two types of spread *F*; the upper ionogram shows the type commonly observed in the equatorial region; the lower ionogram shows the type usually observed at middle to high latitudes. The echo traces shown at virtual heights of about 600 km are due to multiple reflections between the ionosphere and the ground. (Courtesy of J. W. Wright and R. W. Knecht.)

on the magnetic equator, has an incidence of spread *F* exceeding 90% for the early part of the night [23]. Throughout a 60° latitude belt centered on the geomagnetic equator there is a strong inverse correlation between spread

F and magnetic activity. There is evidence that the ionization irregularities that cause equatorial spread F, both on the bottom side [40] and on the top side [22] of the layer, are aligned along the geomagnetic field lines. These irregularities may form as a stage in the diurnal development of the geomagnetic anomaly.

High-latitude spread F appears on ground-based ionosonde records mainly, but not exclusively, at night, and is most frequent between midnight and sunrise, and in winter [34]. Satellite data [28] have shown that high-latitude spread F above the $F2$ peak occurs at all hours of the day, but that at night the irregularities causing spread F extend to lower heights than during the day. The sun's ionizing radiations appear to exert a stabilizing influence, reducing the probability that spread F will occur at low heights.

Satellite data show, in addition, that on magnetically quiet days high-latitude spread F begins at about 72° magnetic dip in both hemispheres, but it spreads into lower latitudes during magnetic storms. The range of heights within which spread F occurs is also a marked function of latitude. Near the low-latitude limit of spread F, the irregularities are confined to heights near (but definitely above) the $F2$ peak, but in a narrow latitude belt just inside the auroral zone maximum, the irregularities extend throughout the whole range of heights from the $F2$ peak to at least 1000 km (the satellite height in this case). At still higher latitudes, the upper height of the spread F irregularities again decreases to just above the $F2$ peak.

The specific physical processes causing the development of spread F are not understood. Among the proposed causes are atmospheric turbulence; convective diffusion; vertical transport due mainly to an irregular polarization field in the E region, which is communicated to the F region along the highly conducting lines of the geomagnetic field; hydromagnetic waves arriving from outer space; and charged-particle penetration.

REFERENCES

1. Allan, C. W., Variations of the sun's ultra-violet radiation as revealed by ionospheric and geomagnetic observations, *Terr. Mag. Atmos. Electr.*, **51** (1946), 1.

2. Bates, D. R., and H. S. W. Massey, The basic reactions in the upper atmosphere, Parts I and II, *Proc. Roy. Soc. A*, **187** (1946), 261; *ibid.*, **192** (1947), 1.

3. Bourdeau, R. E., Ionospheric research from space vehicles, *Space Sci. Rev.*, **1** (1962–63), 683.

4. Bradbury, N. E., Ionization, negative-ion formation, and recombination in the ionosphere, *Terr. Mag. Atmos. Electr.*, **43** (1938), 55.

5. Burkard, O., A new F layer model, *Geophys. Pure Appl.*, **37** (1957), 145.

6. Chapman, S., The electrical conductivity of the ionosphere; a review. *Nuova Cimento*, **4**, Ser. 10, Suppl. No. 4 (1956), 1385.

7. Croom, S. A., A. R. Robbins, and J. O. Thomas, Two anomalies in behavior of the F2 layer, *Nature*, **184** (1959), 2003.

8. ———, ———, and ———, Variation of electron density in the ionosphere with magnetic dip, *Nature*, **185** (1960), 902.

9. ———, A. R., Long, and J. O. Thomas, Private communication.

10. Davies, K., Ionospheric Radio Propagation, U. S. Govt. Printing Office, Washington, D. C. (in press).

11. Duncan, R. A., The equatorial F region of the ionosphere, *J. Atmos. Terr. Phys.*, **18** (1960), 89.

12. Ellis, C. R., The trapping of cosmic radio waves beneath the ionosphere, *J. Atmos. Terr. Phys.*, **13** (1958), 61.

13. Gliddon, J. E. C., and P. C. Kendall, The effect of diffusion and attachment-like recombination on the F2 region, *J. Geophys. Res.*, **65** (1960), 2279.

14. Heisler, L. H., Anomalies in ionosonde records due to travelling ionospheric disturbances, *Aust. J. Phys.*, **2** (1958), 79.

15. ———, Observation of movement of perturbations in the *F*-region, *J. Atmos. Terr. Phys.*, **25** (1963), 71.

16. Hines, C. O., Internal atmospheric gravity waves at ionospheric heights, *Can. J. Phys.*, **38** (1960), 1441.

17. Hirsh, A. J., The electron distribution in the *F* region of the ionosphere, *J. Atmos. Terr. Phys.*, **17** (1959), 86.

18. Holmes, J. C., C. Y. Johnson, and J. M. Young, Ionospheric Chemistry, COSPAR Proc. Fifth International Space Science Symposium, Florence, Italy, May 1964. Amsterdam: North-Holland Pub. Co., (in press).

19. Jacchia, L. G., The variable atmospheric density model from satellite acceleration, *J. Geophys. Res.*, **65** (1960), 2775.

20. King, J. W., Investigations of the upper ionosphere deduced from top-side sounder data, *Nature*, **197** (1963), 639.

21. Knecht, R. W., Observations of the ionosphere at the south geographic pole, *J. Geophys. Res.*, **64** (1959), 1243.

22. Lockwood, G. E. K., and L. E. Petrie, Low latitude field aligned ionization observed by Alouette top-side sounder, *Planet. Space Sci.*, **11** (1963), 327.

23. Lyon, A. J., N. J. Skinner, and R. W. H. Wright, The belt of equatorial spread-F, *J. Atmos. Terr. Phys.*, **19** (1960), 145.

24. Martyn, D. F., Cellular atmospheric waves in the ionosphere and troposphere, *Proc. Roy. Soc. A*, **201** (1950), 216.

25. ———, The normal F region of the ionosphere, *Proc. I.R.E.*, **47** (1959), 147.

26. Munro, G. H., Travelling ionospheric disturbances in the F region, *Aust. J. Phys.*, **11** (1958), 91.

27. Norton, R. B., T. E. Van Zandt and J. S. Denison, A model of the atmosphere and ionosphere in the E and F1 regions, *Proc. International Conference Ionosphere*. London: Inst. Physics and Phys. Soc., 1962, p. 26.

28. Petrie, L. E., Top-side spread echoes, *Can. J. Phys.*, **41** (1963), 194.

29. Ratcliffe, J. A., The formation of the ionospheric layers F1 and F2, *J. Atmos. Terr. Phys.*, **8** (1956), 260.

30. ———, F. R. Schmerling, C. S. G. K. Setty, and J. O. Thomas, The rates of production and loss of electrons in the F region of the ionosphere, *Phil. Trans. Roy. Soc. A*, **248** (1956), 621.

31. Rishbeth, H., Guide to the theory of the quiet F layer in the ionosphere and exosphere, in Electron Density Profiles, ed. B. Maehlum. New York: Pergamon Press, Inc., 1962, p. 284.

32. ———, and D. W. Barron, Equilibrium electron distribution in the ionospheric F2 layer, *J. Atmos. Terr. Phys.*, **18** (1960), 234.

33. ———, and C. S. G. K. Setty, The F layer at sunrise, *J. Atmos. Terr. Phys.*, **20** (1961), 263.

34. Shimazaki, T., A statistical study of world-wide occurrence probability of spread-F. Part I. Average state, *J. Radio Res. Lab.* (Japan), **6** (1959), 669.

35. Thomas, J. O., The electron density distribution in the F2 layer of the ionosphere in winter, *J. Geophys. Res.*, **68** (1963), 2707.

36. Willmore, A. P., R. L. F. Boyd, and P. J. Bowen, Some preliminary results of the plasma probe experiments on the satellite Ariel, Proc. International Conference Ionosphere. London: Inst. Physics Phys. Soc., 1962, p. 517.

37. Yonezawa, T., A new theory of the F2 layer, *J. Radio Res. Lab.* (Japan), **3** (1956), 1.

38. ———, On the influence of electron-ion diffusion exerted upon the formation of the F2 layer, *J. Radio Res. Lab.* (Japan), **5** (1958), 165.

39. ———, On the seasonal and non-seasonal annual variations and the semi-annual variation in the noon and midnight electron densities of the F2 layer in middle latitudes, II, *J. Radio Res. Lab.* (Japan), **6** (1959), 651.

40. Cohen, R., and K. L. Bowles, On the nature of equatorial spread F, *J. Geophy. Res.*, **66** (1961), 1081.

5

W. J. Heikkila
W. I. Axford

The Outer Ionospheric Regions

5.1. INTRODUCTION

We now continue upward in height to those atmospheric regions that lie above the electron number density maximum. Very little information indeed was available about these outer regions before the advent of rocket and satellite techniques. These regions of lower electron density are shielded by the underlying regions of higher electron density from observation by ground-based ionospheric soundings. Their natural emissions are of low intensity because of the very small ambient atomic and molecular densities, and such emissions as are observed (see Chapter 8) are only poorly understood.

Nevertheless, some speculations were possible even in the early years of upper atmospheric studies. The supposed rates of escape of terrestrial hydrogen and helium suggested fairly high temperatures at extreme altitudes. So too did the very presence of high sunlit aurora (see Sec. 13.4). The diffusive separation of atmospheric gases according to mass, with the lighter gases predominating at the greater heights, was known. The latitude dependence of auroral occurrence and the morphology of geomagnetic storms suggested a ring current circling the earth high above the equator. More recently, analysis of the propagation and dispersion of 'whistlers,' and observations of Faraday rotation of the plane of polarization of radio signals reflected from the moon, implied appreciable electron densities up to several thousand kilometers.

These ideas were often qualitative, sometimes erroneous, and at best incomplete. New information resulting from rocket and satellite experiments, mainly since the IGY, now permits a much fuller understanding. We shall summarize the present picture of the outer ionospheric regions in this chapter. The neutral and the charged components will be considered separately, and the charged components will be discussed according to their energies, whether low (thermal) or high (trapped).

Turning first to the neutral component, we recall that the atmosphere up to and into the *F* region can be treated as a rather simple gaseous fluid, subject to standard gas laws and fluid dynamics. The relevant theories are based upon the assumption of frequent collisions and small mean free paths. But the mean free path rapidly increases with height, being already approximately 1 km at a height of about 250 km. With continued increase it must soon become comparable to the local scale height, which is some tens of kilometers. We cannot then apply the simple gas laws without modification. Instead, we must consider the motion of the individual particles.

Proceeding in this vein, we can imagine that a neutral particle moving upward from some high enough level may proceed without encountering other particles. It therefore follows a ballistic trajectory in the gravitational field of the earth. Depending upon its energy, it may remain as part of the earth's atmosphere, falling back into denser regions, or it may escape from the earth's gravitational field and be lost. There is a critical level, defined later, above which collision-free trajectories are likely, and the region above this level is called the 'exosphere.' The exosphere is the region from which neutrals may escape directly. The magnitude of the escape flux depends upon the number of particles with velocities exceeding the earth's escape velocity. The atmospheric density variation within the exosphere is determined by the integrated effect of all particles whose trajectories intersect the region.

We have seen in previous chapters that a significant fraction of the upper atmospheric constituents is ionized. The distribution of ionization with height is greatly influenced by factors not important for the neutral particles, and so quite a different distribution results. Firstly, ions have a much greater collision cross section than neutrals, resulting from the long-range coulomb forces. Consequently, ion-ion collisions are frequent at heights well above the base of the exosphere, which is defined in terms of neutral-neutral collisions. Indeed, ion-ion collisions are never negligible for these purposes, and no 'ionic exosphere' exists; an isotropic pressure is maintained, and a form of hydrostatic law is applicable. Secondly, the strong requirement for electrical neutrality produces a buoyant effect of the very light electrons on the much heavier ions, with the result that, for equal electron and ion temperatures, the scale height for the ions is essentially twice that which would have applied to the parent neutral constituent. This fact, of great importance in the exosphere, leads to an ever-increasing percentage of ionization with height. Thirdly, the long-range forces between charged particles also lead to many-particle interactions and collective motions. These topics are studied by the techniques of plasma physics and are in general of great complexity. They may well be pertinent to the steady distribution of ionization at these heights, but their implications have yet to be fully examined. Finally, the earth's magnetic field has a dominating effect on the motions of charged particles at all but the highest energies. Charged particles of low or medium energy, both ions and electrons, have small gyro-radii in the geomagnetic field and, as a result, spiral tightly along the field lines between collisions. The field lines all lead back to earth, at least at moderate latitudes if not also in the polar regions, and there is normally no possibility of ion escape.

Besides the charged particles of thermal energies there are in the exosphere significant numbers of more energetic charged particles trapped in orbits in the geomagnetic field. Their presence was brought to prominence by the experimental data obtained by means of artificial satellites. These orbits are normally not accessible to particles originating from the lower atmosphere, or from the sun, or from outer space. They can be filled, however, by nuclear reactions, such as neutron decay in the exosphere, by deflecting collisions with other exospheric particles, by some other form of local acceleration, or by the entry of extraterrestrial particles when the magnetic field is perturbed. Particles are lost from these trapped orbits by similar processes, but especially by collisions and charge-exchange with thermal particles at the lower extremities of the orbit. The long lifetimes that are attributed to the more energetic trapped particles can lead to significant concentrations even with slow injection rates.

The complicated behavior of energetic trapped particles in the geomagnetic field is only imperfectly understood. Longitudinal drifts occur owing to the gradients in the field. Differential drifts of ions and electrons lead to electric currents and can supply the so-called ring current which will enter later discussion of disturbance phenomena. Severe modifications of the field, such as may occur when intense particle streams from the sun sweep past the earth, may cause dumping of the trapped particles into the atmosphere.

These various aspects of the exosphere will now be considered in more detail, with reference to undisturbed conditions.

5.2. NEUTRAL PARTICLES

The neutral particles make the major contribution to the total density for the first few thousand kilometers. This total density has now been studied extensively by observations of satellite drag. The related parameters —pressure, temperature, molecular weight, and scale height—can be inferred from the observed density distribution.

5.2.1. Satellite Drag Measurements of Density [1]. The density can be determined from the rate at which the orbit of an artificial earth satellite contracts (and the orbital period decreases), since this depends primarily on the drag due to the air density. If the satellite moves in an appreciably elliptic orbit, the air drag acting on it is a maximum at lowest levels, in the region of perigee. The resulting decrease in velocity near perigee leads to a reduction of the apogee height, so the orbit contracts and becomes more nearly circular. From the net decrease in orbital period, the value of the density near perigee can be obtained. A model (usually exponential) is assumed in the calculations, the choice not being at all critical. The more eccentric orbits permit the evaluation of an averaged density along an arc of the orbit some 20 degrees on either side of perigee, permitting studies of latitude and longitude dependence of the density as the perigee point moves. For orbits that are nearly circular, the derived density is an average over the whole orbit. Because of the very small magnitude of the drag force, no estimate of its instantaneous value can be obtained; instead, the average over several successive orbits is usually determined. The satellite drag measurements of density thus have somewhat coarse resolution in space and time.

When the perigee height exceeds 1000 km, other factors besides air drag may be of importance. These include an increase in the effective cross-sectional area of the satellite due to an electric potential on it in an atmosphere with a high percentage of ionized constituents; solar radiation pressure in the case of highly elliptic orbits, or orbits partly in the earth's shadow; odd harmonics in the earth's gravitational potential; and lunar or solar perturbations. Usually these can be evaluated and allowed for, so that the drag force can be determined quite accurately.

The air drag D on the satellite is proportional to the density ρ as shown by the usual aerodynamic formula [1],

$$D = \tfrac{1}{2}\rho V^2 S C_D .$$

Here V is the velocity of the satellite relative to the ambient air, S is the effective cross-sectional area, and C_D is the drag coefficient. In evaluating the relative velocity V, the rotation of the atmosphere with the earth must be taken into account. The effective cross-sectional area for an unstabilized satellite may be estimated by assuming that the satellite rotates about an axis of maximum moment of inertia. The direction of this axis in space may be unknown, but an average over all possible conditions usually entails a maximum possible error of less than 20% for long cylindrical satellites; for the many more nearly spherical satellites, the error is of course much smaller.

The drag coefficient for all satellites may be taken to be in the range 2.2–2.5. In deducing the drag force, it is necessary to know the mass of the satellite; in most cases, this is known accurately. With the leaky, deformable balloon type of satellite both the effective mass and area require careful consideration.

5.2.2. The Inference of Pressure, Temperature, and Composition. Once the density is determined as a function of height, the pressure can be inferred directly if the hydrostatic law, Eq. (1.1), is assumed to apply. At the lower exospheric levels, departures from this law are negligible insofar as the magnitude of the pressure is concerned. Caution, however, must be exercized in the interpretation of the 'pressure' so deduced, since it actually becomes a tensor quantity, only one of whose elements is revealed.

The temperature may be inferred from the vertical profile of density in a similar fashion, by the assumption of standard gas laws, but only if the mean molecular mass is known. This depends on the diffusive separation of the different gaseous constituents, which in turn depends on the temperature; the two must be deduced in conjunction with one another, and a certain degree of ambiguity then results. This is lessened by the following considerations:

The absorption of solar radiation, which leads to marked thermal structure at lower levels, is believed to be inappreciable in the exosphere. Similarly, the absorption of corpuscular energy, hydromagnetic waves, and internal gravity waves, which are thought to be pertinent to the heat budget of the E and lower F regions, is considered to be irrelevant at heights much above the F-layer peak. In contrast, as shown by Nicolet [2], the thermal conductivity increases rapidly with height, roughly inversely as the particle concentration. This high conductivity permits significant heat flow even with small temperature gradients and tends to maintain the whole of the exosphere at a single temperature whose magnitude is largely determined by the denser region below.

The preceding comments, of course, refer only to the temperature of the neutral gas. The temperatures of the ions and neutrals may be equal, but this has not been verified experimentally. Moreover, it need not be the case since there are negligible collisions between the ions and the neutral particles in the exosphere. The ion thermal conduction is determined by the magnetic field so that ion temperature gradients along the field are small, but gradients across field lines can be supported. A considerable smoothing of geographic variations will already have occurred at the base of the exosphere, however, so only large-scale variations (for example, day-night) can persist at greater heights. More specifically, height variations of temperature within the exosphere should be small, and isothermal conditions can reasonably be assumed in the determination of temperature and composition. This limits the ambiguity previously mentioned and indeed practically eliminates it when knowledge of the *F*-region composition is introduced.

The foregoing considerations also point up the usefulness of the temperature as a single parameter characteristic of the exosphere throughout its height, and so as an index of exospheric behavior. In this connection, it may be noted that the time required for heat conduction on a planetary scale in the exosphere is of the order of hours; any anomalous deviation should be carried throughout the region within a day.

5.2.3. Temporal Variations of Density and Temperature. Numerous satellite investigations of density and temperature have been carried out since the first Soviet launchings of 1957. They indicate a marked variability of exospheric conditions at a given point, consisting of at least four major components: One reveals a close correlation with solar activity; another constitutes a large diurnal variation; a third exhibits correlation with geomagnetic activity; the fourth comprises a semiannual change.

Irregular variations following solar activity were noticed first in 1958. A 28-day cyclical behavior suggested association with solar rotation, but even more convincing was the close correlation of the rate of change of period of all satellites with the flux of solar radiant energy, the latter being indicated by the intensity of microwave solar radiation. Major short-lived solar events, such as the solar flares of 10, 12, and 15 November 1960, resulted in immediate increases of exospheric density (within the resolution time of the observations, which of course equals one orbital period or more). In a similar manner, the exospheric density is correlated with longer-term solar activity and follows the course of the sunspot cycle.

Jacchia first established a simple relation between exospheric temperature and the flux of solar radiation at a wavelength of 10.7 cm, and this was confirmed by Harris and Priester [4]. It is illustrated in Fig. 5.1. There is certainly no suggestion that the 10.7-cm radiation is itself responsible for the exospheric temperature changes, even though empirically the relationship is very close. It follows, however, that the strength of the microwave radiation is a good measure of the solar flux producing the exospheric changes.

Owing to the combined effects of the precession of the satellite orbit about the earth, the rotation of the orbit in its own plane, and the movement of the earth around the sun, the perigee points for most satellites make day-night transitions every few months. After the irregular variations linked with solar activity are removed, there remain variations correlated with these transitions. These variations have clearly demonstrated a diurnal bulge in the contours of constant density, with a maximum density early in the

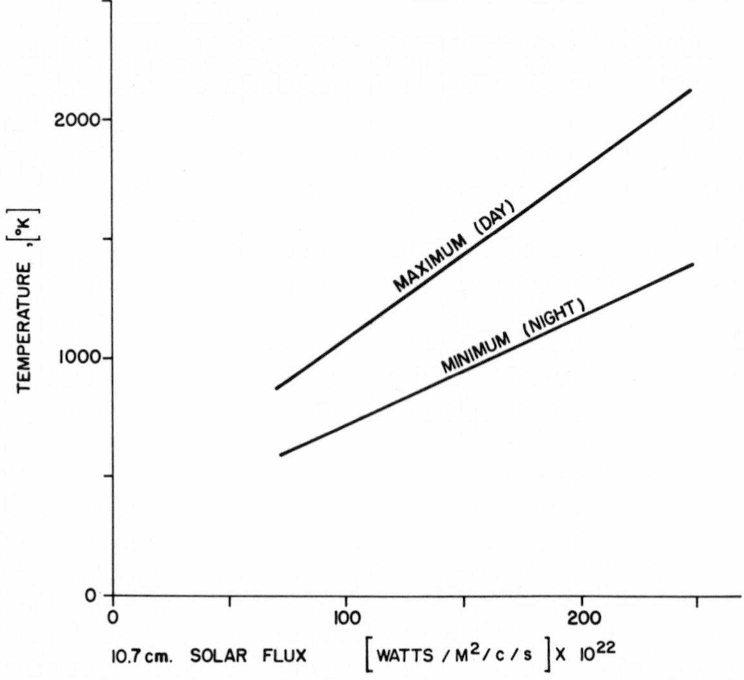

Fig. 5.1 The relation between exospheric temperature and the flux of solar radiation at 10.7 cm. (After Harris and Priester [4].)

afternoon and a minimum density between midnight and sunrise. The diurnal density variation increases with height: at 200 km it is only a few percent, whereas near 600 km it reaches a factor of ten, and near 1600 km it may reach a factor of one hundred. Maximum temperature occurs at mid-afternoon, and minimum temperature just before dawn; their ratio is approximately 3: 2.

From an analysis of the phase and amplitude of the diurnal variation of temperature Harris and Priester [4, 5] and Jacchia [6] concluded that the absorption of solar radiation (ultraviolet and X-rays, in the F region) cannot alone account for the observed features. A second heat source had to be postulated, with comparable strength and a maximum input at three hours before noon. Solar corpuscles were considered to be a possible agent, and of course they might account for the variability with solar activity that is represented by the correlation with 10.7-cm radiation.

An influence of geomagnetic activity on the upper air densities was noted by Jacchia [3]. He showed that the effect of magnetic storms can be approximated by the simple formula,

$$\Delta T = 1.2 a_p \ ^\circ\mathrm{K},$$

where a_p denotes the 3-hr geomagnetic planetary index and ΔT the deviation of temperature. This correlation also suggests a corpuscular heat source, or perhaps a hydromagnetic one.

Semiannual variations have been established [6, 7], with maximum temperature near the equinoxes. Here again an empirical link with geomagnetic and auroral activity is clear (see, for example, Chapter 13), and a corpuscular or hydromagnetic source seems plausible.

5.2.4. Observed Height Variations of Atmospheric Parameters. Height variations of the atmospheric properties may be determined by a combination of data from many satellites. An early, internationally recognized compilation of this type is provided by the 'COSPAR International Reference Atmosphere 1961' (CIRA, 1961), in which results are tabulated to a height of 800 km for conditions of medium solar activity [8]. Three sets of tables are in fact provided, representing average, average minimum, and average maximum conditions to be expected during a 24-hr period.

Since the CIRA, 1961, was drawn up, results have become available to greater heights by analysis of the drag on the balloon satellites 1960 Iota 1 and 1961 Delta 1. These satellites have a very small mass-to-area ratio, about 10^{-2} gm cm^{-2}, so even the minute atmospheric densities at 1500 km height are measurable by means of the drag exerted on them. They have the further advantage that their perigee height alters in a quasi-periodic manner under the influence of solar radiation pressure, and so they yield data over a range of heights repetitively. (The perigee of 1960 Iota 1, for example, fell from its initial height of 1500 km to 950 km, and then returned, in the first four months of flight.)

These recent data have been combined with earlier results by Harris and Priester [4] to yield an extensive set of tables of height variations at hourly intervals. The vertical profile of density and pressure is illustrated here in Fig. 5.2, under the representative conditions of noon, at low latitudes, and average solar activity (or more precisely, a flux of 10.7-cm solar radiation of 1.5×10^{-20} watt/m^2/cycle/second). In practice, this illustration is indicative of orders of magnitude only; values above 400 or 500 km exhibit variations by a factor of ten or more under different conditions of solar activity and time of day.

The height variations of temperature and mean molecular mass are illustrated in Fig. 5.3, for the same conditions as those adopted in Fig. 5.2. The degree of departure from the profiles shown, under changing conditions, is not so severe as in the case of density and pressure. The remarkably steep temperature gradient at heights of 100–300 km gives way to an isothermal region above for reasons already outlined. The high temperature ascribed to these levels is determined from the density profile on the assumption that atomic oxygen is the dominant constituent near the base of the exosphere. This assumption may be based on an extrapolation upwards

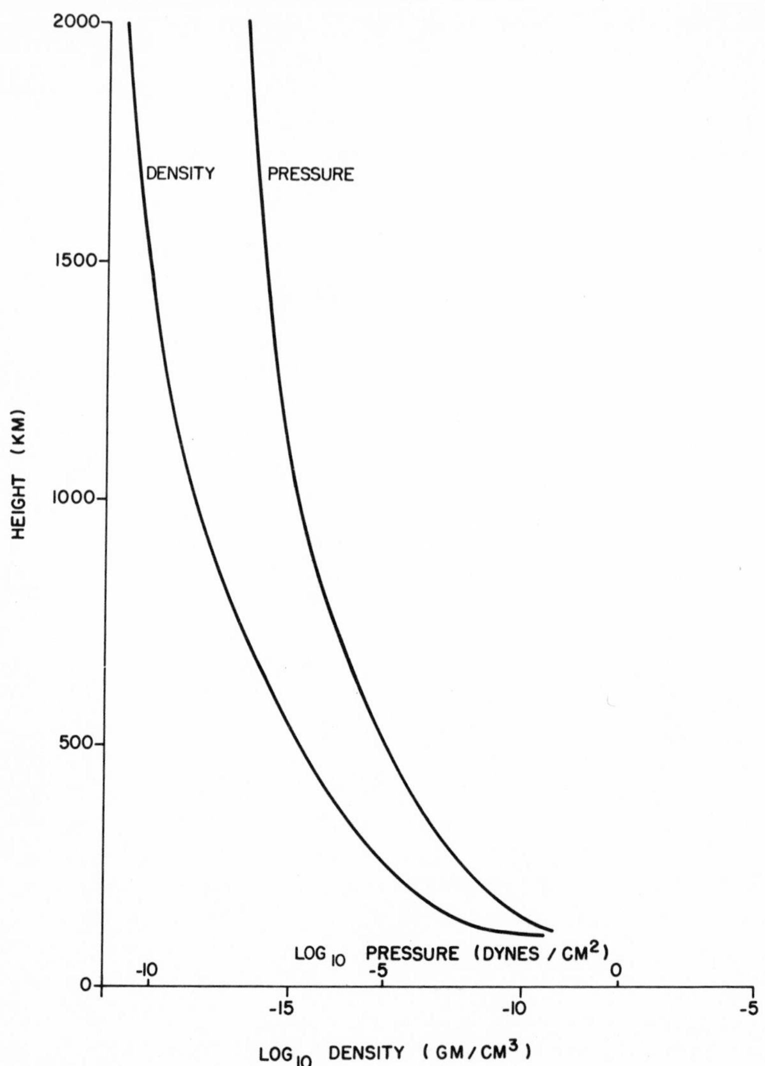

Fig. 5.2 Density and pressure variation with height under average midday conditions, at low latitudes.

from directly determined *E*-region data or on the internal consistency of its implications in the total temperature-composition analysis, and it is supported by other forms of evidence.

Once the temperature at the base of the exosphere is determined, the same value may be employed at higher levels to determine the mean molecular weights there. These in turn may be analyzed in terms of the individual gaseous species, each one of which must assume a vertical profile appropriate

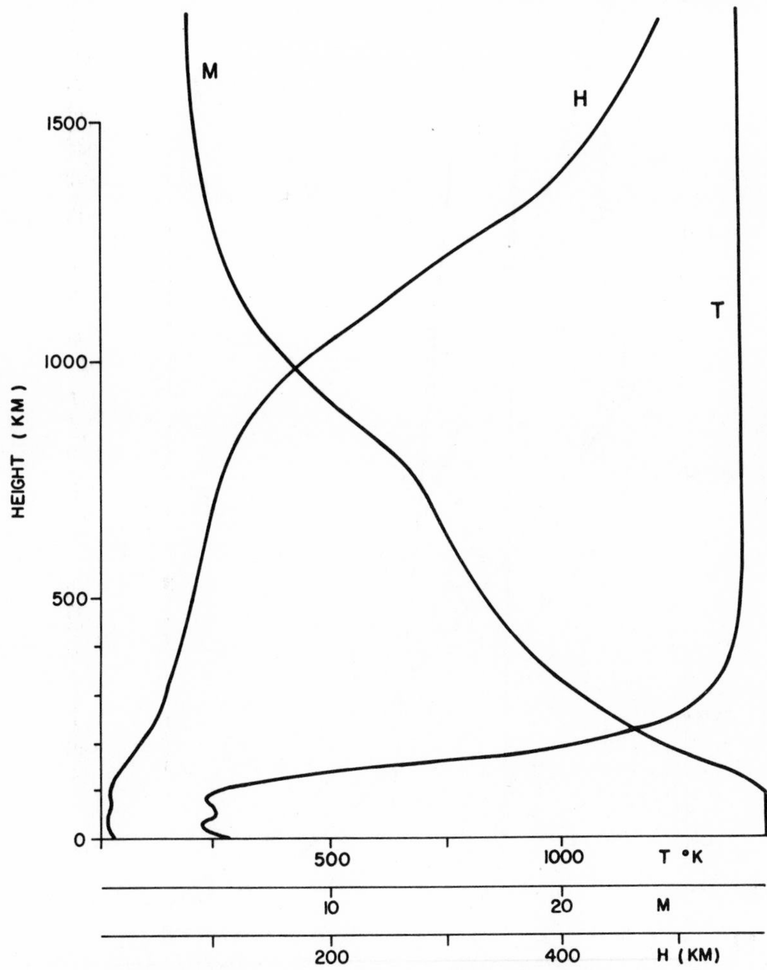

Fig. 5.3 Temperature (T), mean molecular weight (M), and scale height (H), under average midday conditions, at low latitudes.

to the common temperature and to its own molecular mass. It is at this point that the internal consistency of the method is exposed to confirmation, and that confirmation is indeed obtained.

The concentrations of the five main constituents, O_2, N_2, O, He, and H, are illustrated in Fig. 5.4 for the same representative conditions as before. The molecular constituents are seen to be of minor importance above the peak of the *F* layer. The concentration of atomic nitrogen is not known accurately but is undoubtedly well below the total particle concentration at all heights. Atomic oxygen is found to predominate up to about

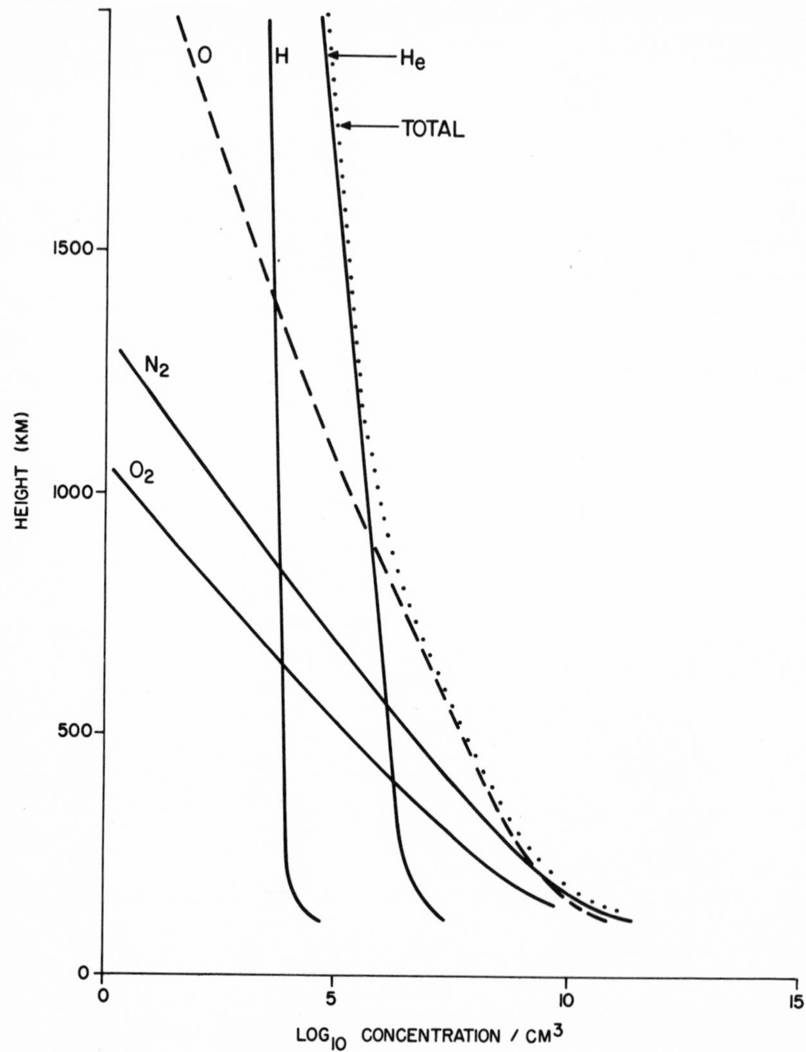

Fig. 5.4 The concentrations of the main exospheric constituents under average midday conditions, at low latitudes.

1000 km, where it is gradually replaced by helium. The transition from helium to neutral atomic hydrogen is shown here near 3000 km; but it is highly variable with temperature, and it is empirically uncertain because the hydrogen concentration has relatively little effect on the satellite drag measurements. (See also Sec. 5.2.5.)

At the greater heights that have now come under discussion, the present satellite data fail to provide adequate information for the observational determination of density and related parameters. Instead, theoretical extrapolation becomes of major import.

5.2.5. Theoretical Extrapolation of Density. Although continuum concepts are useful low in the exosphere, in principle they should be abandoned once the frequency of interparticle collisions becomes sufficiently low that thermodynamic equilibrium is no longer maintained. One criterion that is often employed for determining the transition height h_c, and so for marking the base of the exosphere, is provided by the following analysis:

A single species of particle is considered, of collisional radius a. A single member of that species is imagined to move vertically upwards from the height h_c, past its neighbors. It would collide with any other particles whose centers lie within a distance $2a$ of the line traced by its own center, and so within a vertical column of cross section $4\pi a^2$. If the particles were distributed in height according to the hydrostatic law for isothermal conditions, their concentration n would have the functional form

$$n(h) = n_c \exp (h_c - h)/H, \tag{5.1}$$

where $n_c = n(h_c)$ and H is the appropriate scale height, as discussed in Chapter 1. The number of collisions that would be experienced by the vertically moving particle is then given by

$$4\pi a^2 \int_{h_c}^{\infty} n(h)\, dh = 4\pi a^2 n_c H, \tag{5.2}$$

and h_c is taken to be the level for which this number equals unity. Thus the base of the exosphere is taken to lie at the height where

$$n = (4\pi a^2 H)^{-1}. \tag{5.3}$$

With $a = 1.5 \times 10^{-8}$ cm and $H = 100$ km as representative values, $n_c = 3.5 \times 10^7$ particles per cm^3. Reference to Fig. 5.4 shows that this value is to be found at heights of 500 or 600 km.

Each neutral particle in the exosphere will move along a trajectory determined by its initial motion and the earth's gravitational field, as already mentioned, simply because it is free from other forces and specifically from collisional interactions. Several distinct classes of trajectories may be distinguished.

1. *Elliptic ballistic trajectories* are followed by all particles coming up from the transitional level with velocities less than the escape velocity. For the temperatures involved in the earth's atmosphere, the great majority of all atoms and molecules in the exosphere belong to this class. Typical flight times are some minutes or tens of minutes, short enough that the particle is unlikely to be ionized before it falls back into the denser atmosphere again.

2. *Complete elliptic orbital paths* are followed by particles that have less than escape velocity but remain above the transitional level. A neutral particle originating in the atmosphere below must suffer a deflecting collision above the transitional level in order to enter such an orbit. These collisions are necessarily infrequent, but similar collisions to remove the particles from orbit are also infrequent. Thus, removal by collision with dust particles, or by ionizing under the influence of solar ultraviolet and X-rays, may determine the lifetime of the orbits. Although the concentration of this class of particles is difficult to evaluate precisely, it is thought unlikely that they contribute greatly to the exospheric density.
3. *Hyperbolic escaping trajectories* are followed by atmospheric particles with velocities greater than the escape velocity. Their number is derived from the high-speed 'tail' of the Maxwellian velocity distribution. Whether or not this escaping component is significant is determined by the temperature at the transitional level.
4. *Hyperbolic incoming trajectories* are present in the exosphere. This inward flux is an accretion of neutral particles from interplanetary space, and its magnitude has no a priori relation to the escaping flux; it may be smaller or larger. Since atoms in space are very likely to be ionized by solar radiation, it is probable that the interplanetary density of neutral particles is low and that the rate of accretion is small compared to the escape flux. The accretion of particles can therefore be neglected insofar as exospheric density is concerned.
5. *Hyperbolic external orbits* should be mentioned for completeness, but as their importance is also determined by the interplanetary neutral particle density they may be neglected until the exosphere itself is left behind.

In the light of these considerations, the distant exosphere may be expected to comprise almost only particles which had escape velocity or greater at the transitional level. These particles form the escape flux and stream outward with nearly radial velocity. The density must be asymptotic to an inverse square law in the absence of other gravitational fields or interplanetary matter. The velocity distribution of the escaping particles is not isotropic, and the usual concepts of temperature, pressure, thermodynamic equilibrium, and hydrostatic support are of course not meaningful.

The exospheric density problem has been treated quantitatively by several authors, notably Opik and Singer [9] and Herring and Kyle [10]. The results of such calculations for an atomic hydrogen exosphere at 1500°K are presented in Fig. 5.5, which shows that the concentration falls off more rapidly than it would under a purely hydrostatic law. The optical thickness of the atomic hydrogen corona above the E region was deduced [11] from rocket measurements of the intensity of scattering of solar Lyman α radiation; this in turn provided a normalization factor for the hydrogen number density profile.

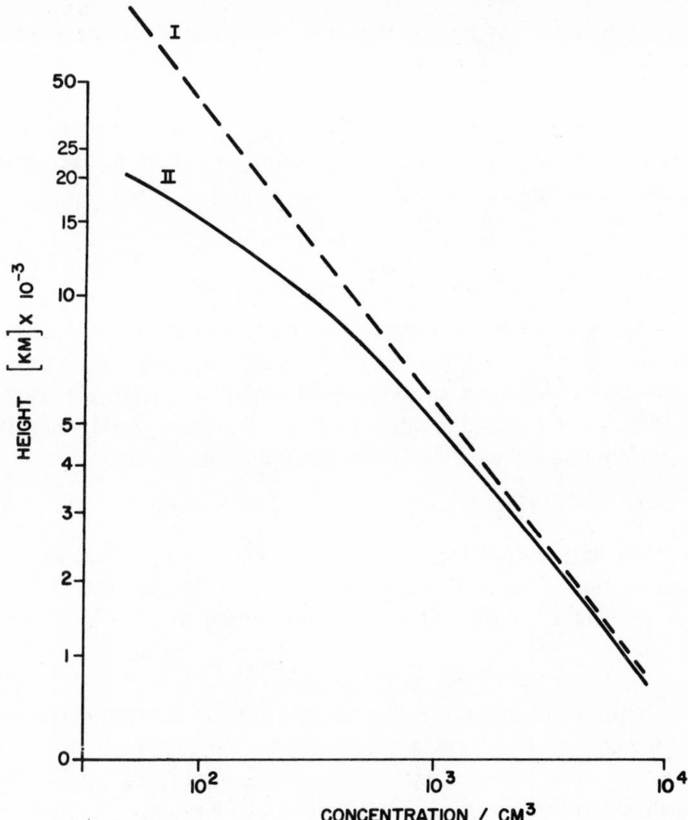

Fig. 5.5 The theoretical asymptotic behavior of the density of a neutral atomic hydrogen exosphere. Curve I represents the variation according to the hydrostatic law; curve II shows the departure from this law owing to the escape flux.

5.3. CHARGED PARTICLES OF THERMAL ENERGY

As we have seen in previous chapters, an appreciable fraction of the upper atmospheric constituents is ionized. The electron density reaches a maximum in the *F* region, and above that it decreases again. The rate of decrease, however, is slower than for the neutral component and the percentage ionization continues to increase. The long-range nature of the coulomb interaction is adequate to maintain frequent ion-ion collisions, and so a scalar pressure may be employed in the determination of the ion distribution. On the other hand, that distribution is complicated by the effects of an electric field and of the geomagnetic field, in a manner that has no counterpart in the case of the neutral gas.

5.3.1. The Equilibrium Ion Distribution. Well above the peak of the F layer, the ions and the electrons would each establish its own diffusive equilibrium distribution, were it not for the electric field that is produced when the two distributions differ. The equilibrium conditions may be established only if the hydrostatic equations are modified to take this field into account, as follows (for a single species of ion):

$$kT_i\, dn_i/dh = -n_i m_i g + n_i eE$$
$$kT_e\, dn_e/dh = -n_e m_e g - n_e eE. \tag{5.4}$$

Here the subscript i denotes values of the parameters for the ions, e for the electrons; E is the vertical electric field. As may be confirmed a posteriori, the relevant E is established by very small departures from electrical neutrality indeed, so the approximation $n_i = n_e$ is a very good one. If it is applied, the foregoing equations may be combined to yield

$$k(T_i + T_e)\, d \ln n_i/dh = -(m_i + m_e)g. \tag{5.5}$$

Since the electronic mass is negligible in comparison with that of any ion, and assuming that T_e and T_i are independent of height (Sec. 5.2.2.), the effective scale height for the ion distribution is seen to be

$$H_i = k(T_i + T_e)/m_i g. \tag{5.6}$$

If $T_i = T_e$, this is just twice the scale height for the parent neutral species.

The foregoing development applies only to the case of a single species of positive ion; that for a mixture is more complicated again [12]. For example, the distribution of a minor ion in the presence of another predominant ion is radically different. The complication occurs because the magnitude of the electric field is determined largely by the predominant ion. With only one type of ion present, the upward electrical force eE on the ions is one-half the downward gravitational force $-m_i g$. For a lighter minor constituent, the upward force will be the same, but the gravitational force will be less and may even be less than the upward force; the corresponding density would then increase with height. Alternatively, if the minor ion is heavier, the electric field will have proportionately less opposing effect and the ion scale height will be closer to that of the neutral parent. This dependence may be investigated quantitatively by writing the differential equation for each ion species and summing. The resultant distribution for any one species is then found to be given by

$$d \ln n_i/dh = -(m_i - \overline{m}_i/2)g/kT, \tag{5.7}$$

where $\overline{m}_i$ is the average ion mass, and a common temperature T is assumed.

This equation shows, for example, that in a predominantly O^+ region, the effective mass for H^+ is -7, and for He^+ it is -4, in atomic units. A negative effective mass implies that the concentration of the corresponding ion increases with height, although as it does so $\overline{m}_i$ will decrease and will eventually reach $2m_i$. Farther up, the lighter constituent predominates and determines the electric field. The equation also shows that the effective mass for O^+ in a predominantly He^+ atmosphere is 14, which is more nearly the value 16 of the neutral oxygen atom than the value 8 for a purely O^+ atmosphere. This situation may be described by stating that the ions tend to separate into layers, with the lighter layers floating on the heavier ones. Ionized oxygen atoms predominate in the bulk of the *F* layer, but they give way to a zone in which He^+ is the major ion, at heights of 1000–1500 km [13].

Ionized hydrogen ultimately becomes the dominant ionic species of the atmosphere as a consequence of this process. And then, because its effective scale height is twice that of the neutral hydrogen (or even more, once the exospheric departure from a hydrostatic law for the latter becomes severe), it finally becomes the major constituent of the atmosphere. The region of its dominance is termed the 'protonosphere' or 'protosphere.'

The geomagnetic field has a strong influence on the distribution of the ionized constituents at great altitudes. Diffusion of charged particles can proceed without hindrance along the field lines but is impeded in the perpendicular directions (see Chapter 7). At high latitudes where the field lines are nearly vertical, diffusion may proceed in much the same way as for the neutrals, but at low latitudes the nearly horizontal field restricts vertical diffusion. Because of this, the analysis of the height distribution just presented is in fact valid only at high latitudes. For moderate and low latitudes, equations of the form (5.4) should be rewritten to yield a balance of forces along the geomagnetic field alone. The further requirement of co-rotation of the magnetospheric ionization with the earth, which will be discussed in the following chapter, leads to the centrifugal force becoming of greater importance in the outer regions. It can act to increase the concentration of ions at greater heights, and indeed a belt of enhanced particle density may surround the earth at a height of some 6–10 earth radii over the equator.

5.3.2. Whistler Studies of the Distant Ionosphere. The first evidence that an appreciable electron content extended to several earth radii was provided by Storey's interpretation of the 'whistler' phenomenon [14]. The whistler is so named because of the gliding tone, from high to low pitch, of audio-frequency electromagnetic signals that may be heard on occasion by simply connecting an antenna through an amplifier to a loud-speaker. The signals originate in lightning flashes and are propagated from one hemisphere of the earth to the other through the magnetosphere, approximately along a geomagnetic field line.

The propagation of whistlers is discussed in Appendix I, where it is shown that the travel time from one hemisphere to the other, t, is given approximately by

$$2cf^{1/2}t = \int f_0 f_H^{-1/2}\, ds, \tag{5.8}$$

where f is the radio frequency of interest, f_0 the local electron plasma frequency, f_H the local electron gyrofrequency ($> f$), c the velocity of light, and ds an element of path length; the integration extends along the geomagnetic field line. This integral receives its major contribution from regions where f_H is small, and so from the region of weakest geomagnetic field. The whistler method is therefore particularly advantageous for the study of the distant magnetosphere. If a single-parameter model of the electron distribution is assumed—for example, an exponential variation in which the scale height is assigned but the absolute value at any selected height is left as an unknown—then the single parameter may be determined by a very simple analysis of the observed frequency-time variation. Electron densities of order 10^2 or 10^3 cm^{-3} at three to four earth radii were revealed by this method.

In a more accurate approximation, the factor $f_H^{-1/2}$ in Eq. (5.8) is replaced by $f_H(f_H - f)^{-3/2}$. Examination will show then that there is a frequency, nearly equal to the minimum value of $f_H/4$ along the field line, for which t is a minimum. Frequencies higher and lower than this arrive with greater retardations, yielding a characteristic 'nose' shape to a frequency-time plot. Whistlers that exhibit this shape are called 'nose whistlers,' and the frequency for minimum t is the 'nose frequency.' Such whistlers are particularly useful, for the nose frequency provides a very accurate means of determining the minimum f_H along the path, and so the maximum height, which may then be coupled with the electron density that is revealed by the delay time. Depressions typically 15–20% in electron density have been found to be associated with severe magnetic storms by means of this technique, while annual and secular variations have been revealed as well [15]. We have seen earlier that both the $F2$ region and the neutral exosphere exhibit large diurnal changes in density. The diurnal changes in the protonosphere are smaller, a fact made possible by the loose coupling between the F region and the protonosphere [16].

At the lowest frequencies received in whistler studies heavy ions affect the propagation, as discussed in Appendix I. Careful analysis of whistler dispersion at these low frequencies has revealed the presence of protons [17].

Fine structure within individual whistlers has revealed that certain preferred paths of propagation exist, and these are identified as field-aligned columns of enhanced (or reduced) electron concentration [18]. It is now known that a ducting of the radio waves within such columns is more important than the natural propagation characteristics of those waves, in effecting a guidance of the whistler energy along the field lines.

5.3.3. Radio Probe Measurements. In addition to the whistler studies which require only the passive reception of naturally occurring radio signals, many active ground-based radio techniques of probing the higher ionization are now employed. The radio frequency used must be capable of complete penetration of the $F2$ peak; that is, it must either be a sufficiently low frequency (below the electron gyro frequency) propagating in the whistler mode, or a high frequency above the penetration frequency f_0F2.

The use of ground-based low-frequency probes provides data essentially similar to those described in the preceding section. There is, of course, a potential advantage in being able to control the point of origin, timing, and modulation of the transmissions.

Ground-based high-frequency probes make use of two distinct phenomena: Faraday rotation of the plane of polarization, and incoherent backscatter from individual electrons. The Faraday rotation is caused by the different speeds of propagation of the two nearly circularly polarized modes into which a linearly polarized signal is resolved in its passage through the ionosphere (see Appendix I). By utilizing high-power techniques, echoes from the moon have been obtained and the total Faraday rotation determined [19]. The Faraday rotation of satellite transmissions has also been studied. The total rotation is a measure of the total electron content along the transmission path, weighted in favor of the lower regions where the geomagnetic field strength and electron density are greatest. The result is generally expressed as a ratio of the electron content above the F-layer maximum to that below. Values range from 3 to 8, with the lower values more characteristic of daytime conditions. Errors arise from inaccuracies in the evaluation of the lower ionospheric profile from ionosonde data in the vicinity of the F maximum, and the technique provides little information about the distribution of the ionization.

The total power scattered from individual electrons provides a measure of the electron number density (see Appendix II). A high-power radar can provide a measurable return from the integrated scatter [20], and observations up to heights in excess of 5000 km have been achieved. The technique is of special importance because it permits continuous observations both in time and in height. It is also significant in that the spectral distribution of the scattered energy depends on the ion mass and temperature, and on the ion/electron temperature ratio, all of which may now be studied directly. Early results indicate, for example, that the electron temperature in and above the F layer may be as much as 1.6 times the ion temperature.

5.3.4. Rocket and Satellite Observations. Upper ionospheric studies by means of space vehicles have advanced rapidly in recent years, beginning with Berning's rocket-borne measurement of electron density to 1500 km [21]. He used a propagation method, measuring the wave velocity in the ionosphere. Another type of rocket measurement was made by Hanson and McKibbin [22] using an ion trap to measure the ion density near the rocket. Similar measurements have also been made with several satellites and 'deep space' probes.

Most recently, the technique of 'topside sounding' from a satellite has been accomplished [23]. Since ionosondes provide much of the information for the lower ionosphere, it can be confidently expected that the technique will greatly extend our knowledge of the upper part. In fact, better geographical coverage can be obtained now for the topside than for the bottom.

Figure 5.6 shows the contours of constant plasma frequency observed on a single satellite pass from south to north approximately along the 75°W meridian. At least three distinctive latitude regions can be identified: equatorial, mid-latitude, and high-latitude. In the equatorial region, the equatorial anomaly (see Chapter 4) can be seen within $\pm$ 20° of the magnetic equator. It extends above the peak of the *F* layer, disappearing in this instance at about 600 km, but it can be observed to extend to greater heights on occasion. Detailed analysis of the daily development of this anomaly has revealed the existence of a ledge or apparent excess of ionization, indicated by the dots in the figure, aligned along magnetic field lines. This ledge develops gradually after sunrise and is located along successively higher field lines. The domelike contours of electron density in this region suggest that ionization is lifted over the equator early in the day and then is distributed along the magnetic field lines; the ledge is then simply the upper boundary of this redistributed ionization.

In the middle-latitude region the ionization contours are relatively well behaved. So far, however, theoretical attempts to relate these ionization data to simple ionospheric models have failed, indicating that some of the assumptions made, such as that the region above 600 km is isothermal, or that the ion, electron, and neutral gas temperatures are all equal, are oversimplifications of the actual situation.

At geomagnetic latitudes in the range 55°–60° an abrupt drop in the ionization contours is usually observed during the night. This feature is

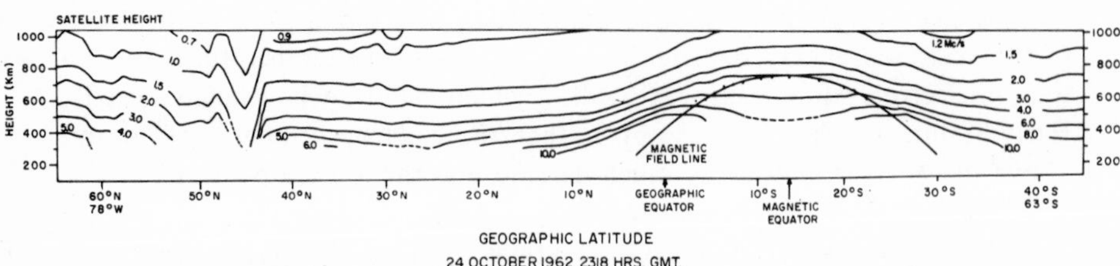

Fig. 5.6 Contours of constant plasma frequency above the *F*-layer maximum as observed by the top-side sounder in Alouette I during a single north-south pass in the early evening near the 75°W meridian. (From Nelms [59].)

clearly illustrated in Fig. 5.6 (at a geographic latitude of about 45°N), but its physical significance has not yet been fully assessed. (See also Sec. 4.2.3.) At higher latitudes, spread F becomes more prevalent, frequently extending from the F-layer maximum to heights of at least 1000 km, and this reduces the accuracy of the electron density contours derived from the ionograms. Nevertheless there is evidence that the high-latitude electron densities are rather variable, as indicated in the figure.

At the moment of writing, it is too early to summarize the topside-sounding results in a quantitative manner, since many features of the observations have only tentative explanations or none at all. The gross characteristics they reveal do confirm conclusions found by the other techniques; but a far more thorough study is now possible, and new areas of investigation have been exposed.

5.4. THE EARTH'S RADIATION BELTS: INTRODUCTION

For upper atmosphere physicists, the most important single result of the International Geophysical Year was probably the discovery of the geomagnetically trapped corpuscular radiation. This has introduced new and difficult problems concerning the origin and behavior of the trapped particles themselves, but it has also opened up lines of study which have led to a new perspective on geomagnetic storm phenomena and the aurora.

The existence of geomagnetically trapped energetic particles was established by observations from the earlier earth satellites, being reported first by the group led by Van Allen. Further investigations revealed the presence of two main zones of high radiation intensity (the 'inner' and 'outer' Van Allen belts) with apparently distinctive characteristics. The most recent observations show that this division is rather less clear-cut than was previously believed to be the case, but the notion of distinct inner and outer belts still retains much of its usefulness, and we use it in the following description of the trapped particle phenomenon. This description is necessarily brief, and it should be noted that details are likely to be changed as further observations are made.

A short review of some relevant elements of plasma physics has been included as a necessary adjunct to any understanding of the trapped particle phenomenon. The results are mostly stated without proof since more extensive accounts are available elsewhere. Within the present volume, the reader may find it necessary to refer to the chapters concerning geomagnetic variations, the geomagnetic storm effect, and the aurora.

5.5. THE MOTION OF CHARGED PARTICLES IN MAGNETIC FIELDS

The force exerted by a magnetic field on a moving charged particle, being normal to the particle's velocity vector, often complicates severely the trajectory that the particle will follow. In most cases that arise geophysically, the complication is sufficient to preclude exact analytic treatment. Nevertheless, examination of certain idealized cases and the application of appropriate approximations permit major advances in our general understanding of the motions, and indeed this procedure provides simplifications that are adequate for many pertinent quantitative calculations. Some of the simplified approaches that have been found of value are outlined in the present section.

5.5.1. The Case of Uniform Electric and Magnetic Fields. The vector equation of motion for a particle with charge q and mass m, moving with velocity $\mathbf{v}$ in a magnetic field of induction $\mathbf{B}$, is

$$m\, d\mathbf{v}/dt = \mathbf{F} + q\mathbf{v} \times \mathbf{B} \tag{5.9}$$

where $\mathbf{F}$ is the nonmagnetic force acting on the particle.*

When $\mathbf{F}$ vanishes and $\mathbf{B}$ is constant in space and time, the kinetic energy, T, of the particle does not change during the motion, since

$$dT/dt = m\mathbf{v} \cdot d\mathbf{v}/dt = 0.$$

Thus, if the velocity vector is written in the form $\mathbf{v} = (v_i, v_j, v_\parallel)$ where v_i and v_j are the components perpendicular to the magnetic field lines and $v_\parallel$ is the component parallel to the field, then

$$2T/m = v_i^2 + v_j^2 + v_\parallel^2 = \text{constant.} \tag{5.10}$$

Similarly, by taking the scalar product of (5.9) with $\mathbf{B}$, we find that $v_\parallel$ is constant. The equation of motion therefore reduces to

$$dv_i/dt = v_j qB/m, \qquad dv_j/dt = -v_i qB/m, \tag{5.11}$$

where $v_i^2 + v_j^2 \equiv v_\perp^2 =$ constant. These component equations have solutions

$$v_i = v_\perp \sin(\omega_c t + A), \qquad v_j = v_\perp \cos(\omega_c t + A), \tag{5.12}$$

where A is an arbitrary constant, and ω_c is the angular 'cyclotron frequency' or 'gyrofrequency' (including the sign of the charge), given by

$$\omega_c \equiv qB/m. \tag{5.13}$$

The trajectory of the particle is therefore a helix of pitch angle $\alpha = \tan^{-1}(v_\perp/v_\parallel)$ lying on a circular cylinder with its axis parallel to the magnetic field and radius

$$\rho \equiv |v_\perp/\omega_c| \equiv |mv_\perp/qB|; \tag{5.14}$$

ρ is called the 'radius of gyration' or 'Larmor radius.' If T is measured in electron-volts and B in gauss, then for electrons $\rho = 3.37\, T_\perp^{1/2}/B$ cm and for

*Unless expressly stated, mks units are used throughout. The treatment is nonrelativistic, although several results hold for relativistic particles, notably those with $\mathbf{F} = 0$, where v and $m \equiv m_0(1 - v^2/c^2)^{-1/2}$ are constants, m_0 being the rest mass.

protons $\rho = 145\, T_\perp^{1/2}/B$ cm, where $T_\perp = mv_\perp^2/2$. The gyrofrequencies are $|\omega_c| = 1.76 \times 10^7 B$ (radian sec^{-1}) for electrons, and $0.96 \times 10^4 B$ (radian sec^{-1}) for protons, where B is again measured in gauss.

Consider next the drift of a particle in the presence of fields **B** and **F** which are constant in space and time. If a velocity **v**′ is defined such that

$$\mathbf{v}' = \mathbf{v} - \mathbf{F} \times \mathbf{B}/qB^2, \tag{5.15}$$

then on substituting into (5.9) we obtain an equation for **v**′:

$$m\, d\mathbf{v}'/dt = \mathbf{F}_\parallel + q\mathbf{v}' \times \mathbf{B}. \tag{5.16}$$

Thus in a frame of reference that moves with velocity $\mathbf{F} \times \mathbf{B}/qB^2$, the particle motion consists of a gyration around the lines of force at the cyclotron frequency and a uniform acceleration along the lines of force due to $\mathbf{F}_\parallel$. Clearly **F** causes a drift of the center of gyration (or 'guiding center') of the particles at a speed $|F_\perp/qB|$, perpendicular to **F** and to the lines of force.

If **F** represents the effect of an electric field **E**, so that $\mathbf{F} = q\mathbf{E}$, then the drift is given by

$$\mathbf{v}_D = \mathbf{E} \times \mathbf{B}/B^2, \qquad v_D = E_\perp/B, \tag{5.17}$$

which is independent of the charge on the particle. In the case of a gravitational field, the drift is oppositely directed for positively and negatively charged particles; here $\mathbf{F} = m\mathbf{g}$, and thus

$$\mathbf{v}_D = m\mathbf{g} \times \mathbf{B}/qB^2, \qquad v_D = g_\perp/|\omega_c|. \tag{5.18}$$

These results are summarized in diagramatic form in Fig. 5.7. One can understand how these trajectories occur by noticing that T is not constant over a gyration, but decreases and increases as the particle 'rises' and 'falls' in the **F** field. Thus $v_\perp$ also varies, and since the gyrofrequency remains constant, the radius of curvature of the trajectory is a maximum when T is a maximum and vice versa.

5.5.2. The Störmer Theory of Motion in the Field of a Magnetic Dipole. As an introduction to the case in which the magnetic field is not uniform, we shall consider the problem of finding the trajectory of a charged particle in the field of a magnetic dipole. This problem was examined in great detail by Störmer [24] following the experiments of Birkeland, which suggested that the aurora could be explained on this basis. Störmer's work is now mainly of historical interest insofar as auroral theory is concerned, for it is recognized that the solar plasma is of sufficient density for collective interactions to be significant, but the results have an important application with regard to geomagnetic effects on cosmic rays and on the trapped radiation that is our immediate concern. In this section, we consider only that aspect of the theory which indicates that energetic charged particles can be trapped by a dipole field.

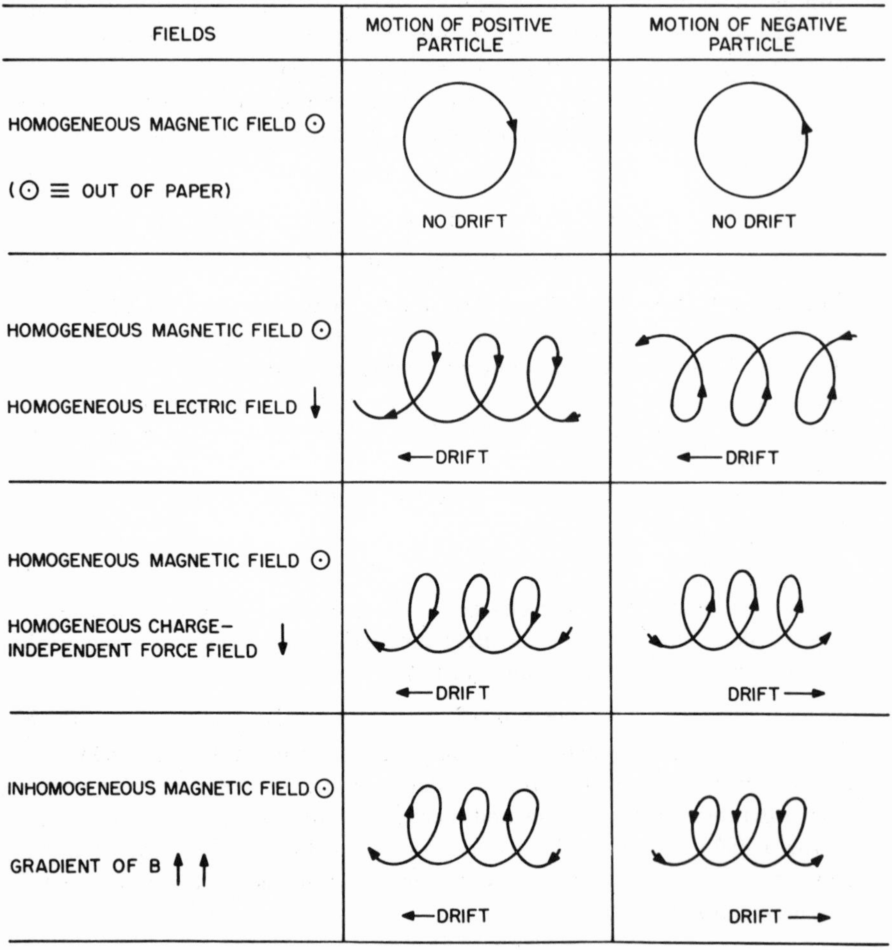

FIELDS	MOTION OF POSITIVE PARTICLE	MOTION OF NEGATIVE PARTICLE
HOMOGENEOUS MAGNETIC FIELD ⊙ (⊙ ≡ OUT OF PAPER)	NO DRIFT	NO DRIFT
HOMOGENEOUS MAGNETIC FIELD ⊙ HOMOGENEOUS ELECTRIC FIELD ↓	←DRIFT	←DRIFT
HOMOGENEOUS MAGNETIC FIELD ⊙ HOMOGENEOUS CHARGE-INDEPENDENT FORCE FIELD ↓	←DRIFT	DRIFT→
INHOMOGENEOUS MAGNETIC FIELD ⊙ GRADIENT OF B ↑ ↑	←DRIFT	DRIFT→

Fig. 5.7 Diagrammatic summary of charged-particle drifts.

In the absence of other fields, a particle moving in a nonuniform magnetic field experiences no force in the direction of its motion, and hence its kinetic energy and speed remain constant. The variation of angular momentum about the axis of symmetry of the dipole is described by an integral of the motion which is obtained as follows: In terms of cylindrical coordinates (r, φ, z) positioned appropriately with respect to the dipole axis, the φ component of the vector equation of motion is

$$\frac{d}{dt}\left(r^2 \frac{d\varphi}{dt}\right) = \frac{q}{m}\left(rB_r \frac{dz}{dt} - rB_z \frac{dr}{dt}\right). \tag{5.19}$$

With the magnetic field symmetrical about the z axis, $\mathbf{B}$ is derivable from a magnetic vector potential of the form $\mathbf{A} = (0, A_\varphi, 0)$ through the relations

$$B_r = -\frac{1}{r}\frac{\partial}{\partial z}(rA_\varphi), \qquad B_z = \frac{1}{r}\frac{\partial}{\partial r}(rA_\varphi). \tag{5.20}$$

These may be substituted into the right-hand side of (5.19) to show that the latter is a perfect differential, and the equation can then be integrated directly to give

$$r^2\, d\varphi/dt = -qrA_\varphi/m + \text{constant}. \tag{5.21}$$

For a magnetic dipole of moment $\mathbf{M}$ placed at the origin and aligned so that $q\mathbf{M}$ is in the direction of the positive z axis,

$$A_\varphi = \pm Mr/R^3, \tag{5.22}$$

where $R \equiv (r^2 + z^2)^{1/2}$ and the sign to be employed is that of q. We can write $ds = v\, dt$ and, since v is constant, introduce a unit of length C_{st} such that

$$C_{st} \equiv |qM/mv|^{1/2}. \tag{5.23}$$

When r, R, and ds are measured in terms of this 'Störmer unit,' (5.21) becomes

$$r^2\, d\varphi/ds = -2\gamma - r^2/R^3, \tag{5.24}$$

where 2γ is a constant of integration determined by the angular momentum of the particle at infinity.

It is not possible to solve completely the equations of motion for the general case in closed form, although analytic solutions can be obtained for the restricted problem in which the motion is confined to the plane $z = 0$. Störmer, however, has shown that, despite the necessity for numerical integration to solve the problem fully, some important characteristics of the orbits are determined by the value of γ alone. By putting $r\, d\varphi/ds = \sin\theta$ in (5.24) and using $|\sin\theta| \leq 1$, Störmer obtained the condition

$$S \equiv |2\gamma/r + r/R^3| \leq 1. \tag{5.25}$$

Observe that θ is the angle between the direction of motion and the meridian plane through a point in the particle trajectory. The condition $S = 1$ defines a surface of rotation which divides space into 'allowed' ($S < 1$) and 'forbidden' ($S > 1$) regions corresponding to particular values of γ; examples are shown in Fig. 5.8. If $-1 \leq \gamma \leq 0$, the allowed region is such that particles can reach the dipole from infinity, but if $\gamma > 0$ there are no trajectories which reach the dipole. If $\gamma < -1$, there are two allowed regions: one which stretches to infinity and another in the immediate vicinity of the dipole. The second, the 'inner allowed region,' is inaccessible to particles coming from infinity since they cannot cross the intervening forbidden region under the conditions assumed; if there is some means by which particles can be injected or scattered into the inner region by processes not treated here, however, then they can be trapped there and forced to move in quasi-periodic orbits.

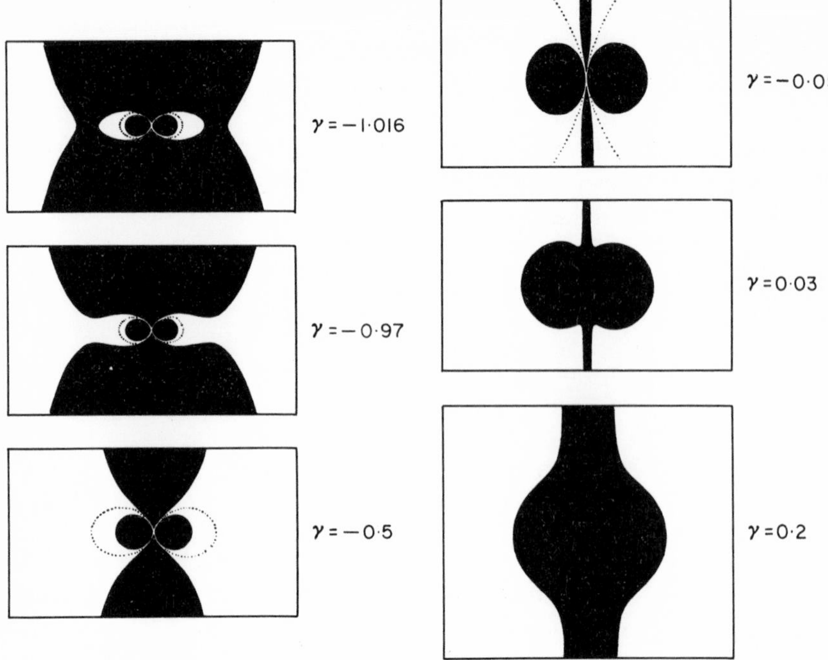

Fig. 5.8 Störmer's allowed and forbidden regions for various values of γ. The forbidden regions are shaded and the diagrams represent meridional sections of figures of revolution. Note that particles coming from infinity can reach the central dipole only if $-1 \leq \gamma \leq 0$. If $\gamma < -1$, a small allowed region exists within a main forbidden region, in which particles can be trapped if a means of injection is available. (After Störmer [24].)

Experiments on the interaction between a stream of charged particles and the field of a magnetized sphere have long shown the existence of trapped particles, presumably scattered into captive orbits by collisions with residual neutral molecules. The significance of such trapped particles to geophysical phenomena was not recognized, however, until comparatively recently when Singer [25] postulated their natural occurrence as a feature of geomagnetic storms (see Chapter 15). Particles more energetic than those invoked by Singer, but similarly trapped, have since been found to be continuously present in the exospheric region where they constitute the great radiation belts. Their origin and mode of trapping are still hotly debated, and it is clear that something more than the simple Störmer considerations must be involved. In particular, it is necessary to call upon distortions of the geomagnetic field, collective interactions of particles, large-scale electric fields, and the effects of hydromagnetic waves. The approximate techniques used in the analysis of these effects are described briefly in the following two subsections.

5.5.3. The 'Guiding Center' Approximation. To find the trajectories of particles of relatively low energy (having small gyro-radii) moving in inhomogeneous electric and magnetic fields, we use the perturbation theory developed originally by Alfvén [26]. In this theory, the particle motion is assumed to consist of a gyration at the local gyrofrequency and a drift of the guiding center due to the net effect of electric and gravitational fields, as already outlined, and to inhomogeneities in the magnetic field as discussed below. The approximation is accurate provided that the scale of inhomogeneities is large compared with the radius of gyration of the particle, and the variations with time are slow compared with the period of gyration. Clearly this method is of most value in considering low-energy particles which undergo many gyrations in the course of their motion and for which it would therefore be very difficult to compute trajectories by numerical integration of the basic equations.

Two effects combine to produce a drift of the guiding center of a particle in an inhomogeneous magnetic field. The first is due to variations of the field along the particle path, which change the radius of gyration so that a drift results, as can be seen from Fig. 5.7. The drift is in the direction $\pm \mathbf{B} \times \nabla B$, and is given in full by

$$\mathbf{v}'_D = \left(\frac{v_\perp^2}{2\omega_c B^2}\right)(\mathbf{B} \times \nabla B) \tag{5.26}$$

to the first order, where ∇B is the gradient of the scalar field B. Secondly, a particle moving along a curved field line experiences a centripetal force of magnitude $mv_\parallel^2/R$, where R is now the radius of curvature. This causes a further drift in the direction perpendicular to the plane of the curving field line, with speed

$$v''_D = \frac{v_\parallel^2}{\omega_c R}, \tag{5.27a}$$

found by substituting $F_\perp = mv_\parallel^2/R$ in (5.15). If $\nabla \times \mathbf{B} = 0$ locally, that is, if any local currents can be neglected, then it can be shown that

$$R^{-1} = \frac{|\mathbf{B} \times \nabla B|}{B^2}$$

and that $\mathbf{B} \times \nabla B$ lies in the direction normal to the plane of the curving field line. With this assumption (5.27a) may be replaced by

$$\mathbf{v}''_D = \left(\frac{v_\parallel^2}{\omega_c B^2}\right)(\mathbf{B} \times \nabla B), \tag{5.27b}$$

and hence the net drift in an inhomogeneous magnetic field becomes

$$\begin{aligned}\mathbf{v}_D = \mathbf{v}'_D + \mathbf{v}''_D &= \frac{v_\parallel^2 + (v_\perp^2/2)}{\omega_c B^2}(\mathbf{B} \times \nabla B)\\ &= \frac{T(1 + \cos^2 \alpha)}{m\omega_c B^2}(\mathbf{B} \times \nabla B).\end{aligned} \tag{5.28}$$

Since ω_c is proportional to q, positive and negative charges drift in opposite directions. In the case of the geomagnetic field, the drifts are westward for protons and eastward for electrons. At a geocentric distance of 2 earth radii, particles with flat pitches ($\alpha = \pi/2$) take approximately $3 \times 10^4/T_K$ minutes to drift around the earth, where T_K is the particle energy in Kev.

Further information about the motion of charged particles can be obtained by means of the so-called adiabatic invariants [27]. These are quantities that are approximately constant for a given particle if the time and space variations of the magnetic field are sufficiently slow. The most important is the magnetic moment, μ, defined as

$$\mu \equiv mv_\perp^2/2B \equiv \frac{T \sin^2 \alpha}{B}, \tag{5.29}$$

which is conserved, provided that the period of gyration is small compared with the transit time of the particle through any local nonuniformity in **B**. From this property, we can infer that a particle tends to be reflected from regions of increasing magnetic field. For example, in the absence of electric fields, a particle moving along a tube of force in the direction of increasing B will do so in such a way that $v_\perp$ is increased. But this increase must come about at the expense of $v_\parallel$, since both v and T must remain constant. A point of reflection or 'mirror' point is reached if $v_\parallel$ is reduced to zero. The magnetic induction required at the mirror point to achieve this is given by

$$B_M = T/\mu = B(v_\parallel^2 + v_\perp^2)/v_\perp^2 = B/\sin^2 \alpha. \tag{5.30}$$

This reflection process plays a part in retaining 'trapped' particles in their orbits, in the case of the dipole-like geomagnetic field, as is illustrated in Fig. 5.9.

The second ('longitudinal') adiabatic invariant is defined as

$$I \equiv \int v_\parallel \, ds, \tag{5.31}$$

where the line integral is taken along the particle's path between two successive mirror points. This quantity is conserved if the transit time of the particle through irregularities of the magnetic field is long compared with the time between reflections. As a consequence of the invariance of I, the guiding center of a particle drifts around the earth on a single 'longitudinal invariant surface,' and returns to the line of force from which it started (see Fig. 5.9).

These results remain true in the presence of a static electric field with potential φ, although the longitudinal invariant surface is altered, and the reflecting induction B_M varies with longitude, because of variations in T (such that the total energy $K = T + q\varphi$ remains constant). If the fields are not static, then the adiabatic treatment fails unless the variations are slow compared with the time taken by the particle to drift once around the invariant surface.

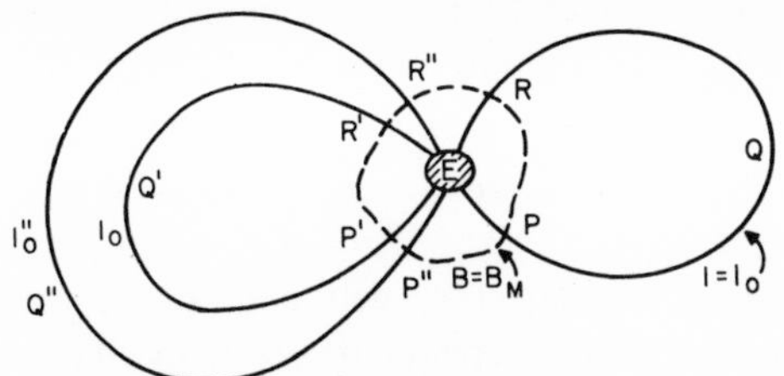

Fig. 5.9 A geomagnetic meridian plane showing the dipole-like field lines and the locus of constant magnetic field strength $B = B_M$. A particle moving on the field line PQR at the right is reflected at mirror points which are the intersections of the field lines with the line $B = B_M$. As the particle drifts in longitude, it moves to field lines for which the second invariant I is equal to the value (I_0) which it had on PQR. Thus on the left the particle finds itself on the segment of the field line P′Q′R′ for which $I = I_0$ and $B = B_M$ at P′ and Q′, rather than on any other segment of field line, such as P″Q″R″, for which $I = I_0'' \neq I_0$.

5.5.4. The Energization of Charged Particles [28]. The two basic processes that lead to changes in the kinetic energy of a charged particle moving in a magnetic field can be described as 'longitudinal' and 'transverse' compression of the space occupied by the trajectory of the particle. These processes, which are analogous to the ordinary adiabatic compression of a gas, require the presence of electric fields, since no work is done by a magnetic field acting alone. The magnetic field acts as a container in which changes of shape are associated with the electric fields, and the latter energize the particle.

The mechanism corresponding to longitudinal compression was proposed by Fermi and is often termed 'Fermi acceleration.' Consider a particle which is trapped between two mirror points on a tube of force: If these mirror points approach each other, then the longitudinal speed of the particle is increased at each reflection almost as it would be if the reflection were caused by an elastic impact on some approaching massive body. The longitudinal kinetic energy, $T_\parallel \equiv mv_\parallel^2/2$, increases in such a fashion that

$$T_\parallel \propto 1/L^2, \tag{5.32}$$

where L is the distance between the mirror points. If the cross section of the trapping region remains constant, then its volume V is proportional to L, and the law of compression is therefore $T_\parallel V^2 = \text{constant}$. This should be compared with the adiabatic compression of a monatomic gas when energy is transferred to only one translational degree of freedom, in which case the effective ratio of specific heats is 3 instead of the usual 5/3.

Acceleration by transverse compression (that is, strengthening) of the magnetic field is the mechanism used in the betatron, hence the process is often called 'betatron' acceleration. If the magnetic field is increased sufficiently slowly so that the magnetic moment is conserved, then

$$T_\perp \equiv mv_\perp^2/2 \propto B. \tag{5.33}$$

But $\rho \propto v_\perp/B$ from (5.14), and so the cross-sectional area enclosed by the trajectory, transverse to **B**, is proportional to $v_\perp^2/B^2$ and so to B^{-1}. The volume V occupied by the trajectory will similarly be proportional to B^{-1}; hence $T_\perp V =$ constant. This corresponds to a specific heat ratio of 2, as should be expected, since energy is transferred to only two of the translational degrees of freedom.

Both the foregoing processes are reversible and their effectiveness in accelerating particles to very high energies is limited. In the case of longitudinal compression, the acceleration continues only as long as the particles remain trapped between the mirror points—in fact trapping can eventually be lost since the pitch angle becomes steeper as the longitudinal energy increases—whereas with transverse compression the energy can increase only in proportion to the magnetic field strength. With the inclusion of irreversible processes, such as collisions, however, repeated compression cycles can lead to the general heating of a plasma as a whole. Consider, for example, a particle moving in a magnetic field which is more or less homogeneous apart from hydromagnetic waves. One effect of such a wave, with frequency ν small compared with the particle gyrofrequency, is alternately to energize and de-energize the particle by the betatron process, since the magnetic moment is conserved in the interaction. If, however, there are in addition interactions with waves of much smaller wavelength and higher frequency such that the magnetic moment is not conserved, these waves will act as scatterers tending to keep the velocity distribution isotropic and to exchange energy between the parallel and trasverse motions of particles. Thompson [29] has shown that, in such circumstances, if the velocity distribution is indeed kept isotropic by elastic scattering, there is a net gain of energy at an average rate given by

$$\frac{1}{T}\frac{dT}{dt} = \frac{2}{3}\nu\left(\frac{\delta B}{B}\right)^2, \tag{5.34}$$

where $(\delta B/B)$ is the fractional amplitude of the wave, and T the total kinetic energy of the particle.

The possibility of statistical acceleration of the type exemplified by Thompson's mechanism was first proposed by Fermi, who considered the effect of a series of collisions between energetic particles and moving lumps of magnetic field as a means of producing cosmic rays. In fact it appears that such processes are at work in all plasmas bearing magnetic fields, tending to produce 'suprathermal' ions as an enhancement of the high-velocity tail of the Maxwellian distribution [30, 31].

Electrons suffer from greater radiation losses than do ions of equal energy, because of their smaller mass, and so the ordinary Fermi mechanism is unlikely to be as effective in raising them to high energies. Moreover, the Thompson mechanism may fail for electrons owing to a lack of disturbances in the magnetic field with a scale sufficiently short, relative to the Larmor radius, to act as scatterers. Nevertheless, highly energetic electrons do occur naturally and this indicates that some heating processes must exist. Parker [32] has suggested that interpenetrating plasma streams could result in the production of high-energy electrons; other mechanisms have also been advanced, which involve acceleration of geomagnetically trapped particles by electromagnetic waves in the whistler range [33, 34], but the significance of these various processes has yet to be determined.

5.6. THE RADIATION BELTS [35, 36]

5.6.1. The Inner Radiation Belt. The most penetrating particles in the inner Van Allen belt are protons having energies in the range 1–700 Mev with an energy spectrum typically of the form shown in Fig. 5.10. The maximum particle flux, which occurs at a geocentric distance of about $1\frac{1}{2}$ earth radii in the equatorial plane, is of the order 4×10^4 cm^{-2} sec^{-1} for energies greater than about 40 Mev [38]. A striking feature of this belt of protons is that it does not change very much with time. Careful observations have recently indicated that changes do in fact occur [39], but these are not nearly as large nor as rapid as those occurring in the outer belt.

It is accepted by most scientific workers that these inner belt protons are the result of β-decay of neutrons 'back-splashed' when cosmic rays strike the upper atmosphere [40]. The decay process is

$$n \rightarrow p^{+} + e^{-} + \bar{\nu} + 780 \text{ Kev}, \tag{5.35}$$

with a neutron half-life of about 12 min. Most of the 780 Kev liberated is shared by the electron and the neutrino ($\bar{\nu}$), whereas the proton retains most of the kinetic energy of the original neutron. An advantage of this theory is that it explains very neatly how charged particles can be injected into stable trapped orbits without requiring them to cross Störmer's forbidden regions. Also the theory is such that a fairly detailed analysis can be made of the proton energy spectrum (at least for some types of removal mechanism), and the results compare favorably with observation except at the lower energies (see Fig. 5.10).

The objections to the neutron albedo theory are based largely on the fact that the average residence time for protons in the inner belt region must be of the order of 100 years if galactic cosmic rays produce the neutrons. This seems very long, especially in view of the observed changes in the intensity of the belt. It is likely, however, that in addition to the galactic cosmic radiation, high-energy solar particles, which produce polar cap

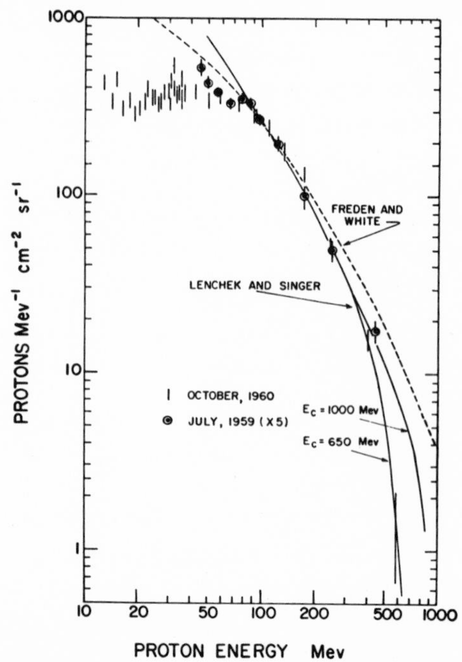

Fig. 5.10 Inner belt proton spectrum. (From Heckman and Armstrong [37].) Comparison of experimental data for July, 1959, and October, 1960, with theoretical curves of Freden and White and of Lenchek and Singer [40] (normalized to data at 100 Mev).

absorption (see Chapter 11), also contribute significantly to the neutron albedo. Other theories have been suggested which involve such processes as local acceleration [41] and temporary capture of cosmic rays in quasi-periodic orbits [42, 43]; however, the latter suggestion appears to violate Liouville's theorem. It has been pointed out [44] that if energetic α-particles were present in the inner belt then it would be difficult to defend the neutron albedo theory; in fact no α-particles have been detected to date.

The relative importance of various removal mechanisms for these particles is not very clear. Gradual energy losses and small-angle scattering due to collisions with atmospheric particles are significant, and catastrophic removal of the energetic protons may occur as a result of nuclear interactions and charge exchange. Presumably such processes are of prime importance in determining the structure of the belt at low altitudes. The protons may also be removed by scattering from hydromagnetic waves and due to a reduction in the probability of trapping occurring when the gyro-radius

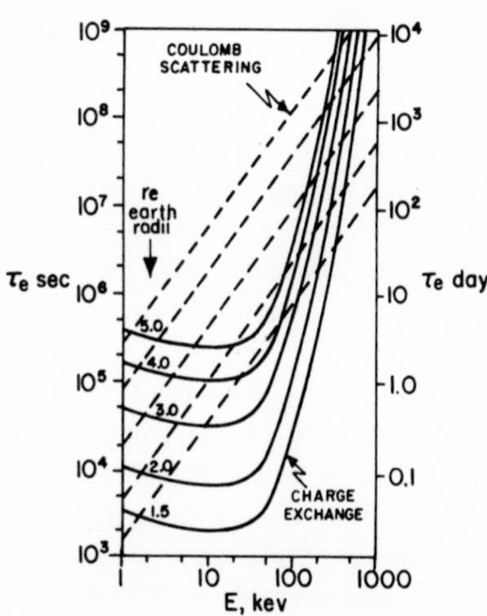

Fig. 5.11 Charge exchange and coulomb scattering lifetimes. The equatorial lifetime τ_e is plotted as a function of proton energy E for several altitudes r_e. (After Liemohn [46].)

becomes comparable to the length scale of the inhomogeneity of the geomagnetic field. These latter effects may explain the absence of very energetic protons beyond geocentric distances of about two earth radii.

An energy flux of the order of 50 erg cm^{-2} sec^{-1} steradian^{-1}, due to protons or other ions with energies in the range 0.5 Kev–1 Mev, was observed at altitudes of $\sim$ 1000 km in the region of the inner radiation belt by detectors flown in the polar orbiting satellite Injun I [45]. The lifetime of such protons under the influence of charge exchange and coulomb scattering is given as a function of energy in Fig. 5.11. It is clear that if the observed protons have a lifetime greater than a day or so, their energies must be of the order of hundreds of Kev, and the corresponding particle flux is therefore about 10^8 cm^{-2} sec^{-1} steradian^{-1}.

Measurements of the electron flux at low altitudes ($\sim$ 1000 km) on lines of force which extend to equatorial distances of 1.3–2.5 earth radii indicate an integral flux of 7×10^6 cm^{-2} sec^{-1} for energies greater than 50 Kev [47, 48]. The observed energy spectrum is in fair agreement with the spectrum deduced from the neutron-albedo theory, above 400 Kev, and there appears to be a cutoff at about 800 Kev which is consistent with the reaction given in Eq. (5.35). It seems clear, however, that the electrons with energies below 400 Kev and also the protons mentioned just previously cannot be satisfactorily explained on the basis of neutron albedo. Alternative theories are not well understood, but they may involve local acceleration by one of the mechanisms described in Sec. 5.5.4., or inward diffusion from the outer regions of the geomagnetic field where solar injection of the particles may occur more easily.

5.6.2. The Outer Radiation Belt. Early measurements of electron fluxes in the outer radiation belt tended to be misleading since usually only a single detector was flown, and this had a counting efficiency which varied by many orders of magnitude over the energy range of interest (10 Kev to 10 Mev). In order to interpret the measurements in terms of particle fluxes it was necessary to assume an energy spectrum; various assumptions for the spectrum, in combination with various measurements, gave estimates of the maximum electron flux in the range 10^{10} to 10^{11} cm^{-2} sec^{-1}.

Subsequent observations [49] showed that the maximum flux of electrons with energies above 200 ev in the outer belt could not exceed 3×10^7 cm^{-2} sec^{-1} at the time of the flights, so that the particles concerned must have been of much greater energies than the previously assumed value of some tens of Kev. This conclusion has been confirmed by observations using a number of different detectors from the earth satellite Explorer XII [50]. It now appears that in the heart of the outer belt the electron energy spectrum is more or less flat in the range 1–100 Kev and that most of the energy flux is carried by particles in the 100–1000 Kev range. The flux of electrons with energies greater than 1 Mev is of the order of 10^5 cm^{-2} sec^{-1}, and apparently it was these particles that contributed most to the counting rates previously observed in the outer zone. The spectrum varies considerably with position, however, and becomes 'softer' (that is, relatively more intense at lower energies) with increasing distance from the earth beyond the maximum of the outer belt ($\sim$ 3.5 earth radii). Near the boundary of the geomagnetic field at about 10 earth radii, most of the flux (10^8 cm^{-2} sec^{-1}) appears to be due to electrons with energies in the range 0.2–20 Kev.

Protons have been found in considerable abundance in the region of the outer belt by detectors carried in Explorer XII. Typical fluxes at 3–4 earth radii are of the order 10^8 cm^{-2} sec^{-1} for protons with energies of hundreds of Kev [51]; these constitute the largest energy density of any energetic trapped particles observed to date—perhaps as much as 10% of the local geomagnetic field energy density. The protons found in the inner belt region by Injun I (see Sec. 5.6.1) are presumably a continuation of this same population.

Temporal changes in the outer belt are not particularly well understood at present, as changes in both spectrum and flux are involved. It is clear that during geomagnetic storms large changes do take place (that is, changes of an order of magnitude or more in particle flux) and it seems that the flux of lower-energy electrons may be enhanced initially during the storm while the higher-energy electrons are lost. Later, as the storm decays, the higher-energy electrons reappear and the lower-energy component returns gradually to its original level [52].

Some form of solar control appears to be necessary to account for the trapped particles in the outer belt. It is also necessary to understand the connection between the outer radiation belt and the aurora, for the revised electron fluxes previously mentioned suggest that the radiation belts could not supply the energy requirements of the aurora for more than a few hours without replenishment. The trapped radiation may represent only a remnant of a larger population, which has survived precipitation into the auroral zone atmosphere, thus casting the outer radiation belt in the role of a 'splash catcher.'

Dessler, Hanson, and Parker [53] have suggested that hydromagnetic waves generated by the interaction between the solar wind and the geomagnetic field form shock waves in the magnetosphere and then dissipate their energy by heating the ambient exospheric protons to energies of the order of a few Kev. In this way energetic particles are generated on trapped orbits without the necessity for any rapid radial movement. The possibility of some energy being given to electrons as well is not ruled out and so the radiation belts (apart from the high-energy protons of the inner belt) could in principle be due to a mechanism of this type.

A theory of a different nature has been put forward by Axford and Hines [54], as one aspect of a unification of the combined phenomena of high latitudes and of the radiation belt. The existence of an electric field with a total potential drop of the order of 20 Kv is deduced from observations of ionospheric current systems (see Chapter 15). Because of the very high electric conductivity that exists above 100 km altitude, lines of force of the geomagnetic field are equipotentials and thus corresponding electric fields must occur throughout the magnetosphere. These fields lead to the inward convection and energization of low-energy ionization on the night side of the earth, by means of the processes already discussed in Sec. 5.5.4. The process is closely analogous to, although with a geometry different from, that discussed by Alfvén [26] in which an external (interplanetary) electric field was assumed. It can operate to produce ions and electrons of some 20 Kev at geocentric distances of four or five earth radii, from particles of only 1 Kev energy near the boundary of the magnetosphere. The particles will remain only transiently in their energized state, if static electric fields alone are operative, but they circulate continuously and so provide a constant distribution of partially energized particles near the heart of the outer zone. If small-scale, nonreversible scattering processes are operative, this distribution can provide a steady supply of particles suitable for further energization. There seems to be common agreement that such processes must be acting, at least in the course of auroral displays, at distances of five earth radii or so (see Sec. 15.2.3).

5.7. THE GEOMAGNETIC EFFECTS OF TRAPPED PARTICLES

A world-wide decrease of the horizontal component of the geomagnetic field is observed during the main phase of geomagnetic storms, and it has long been thought to be due to a westward ring current encircling the earth at a distance of several earth radii. This was considered by Singer [25] to be a manifestation of the temporary presence of moderately energetic particles, in sufficient quantity noticeably to distort the geomagnetic field, and it was in fact by this route that he was led to predict the presence of trapped particles at the time of storms. Their magnetic effects even in the absence of storms are now of major interest.

Some rocket magnetometer measurements have shown the existence of discrepancies between the observed and calculated geomagnetic field at five to seven earth radii, which may indicate the presence of a ring current [55]. Since these effects were not observed by Explorers X and XII [56], it is by no means clear yet that a ring current of significant magnitude ($\sim 10^6$ amp) does exist.

The net field perturbation caused by trapped particles can be regarded from the microscopic point of view as being due to a current resulting from the oppositely directed longitudinal drifts of protons and electrons in the inhomogeneous dipole field (which reduces the field inside the ring), together with the diamagnetic effect of the spiraling particles (which pushes the field away from the region occupied by the particles). Equivalently, from the continuum point of view, the field perturbations result from pressure gradients which must be balanced by a $\mathbf{J} \times \mathbf{B}$ force, where $\mathbf{J}$ is the electric current vector. By adopting model distributions of energy and density for the trapped particles, several writers have been able to calculate the distortion of the magnetic field so produced [57, 58]. Most of these calculations give only the first-order changes in the field, although terms of higher order can be taken into account in some circumstances by successive approximations.

The ring current of magnetic storms is not necessarily to be associated with the trapped particles which have been observed so far. Instead, it is commonly believed that the particles concerned are protons with energies of $\sim$ 10 Kev. These may be generated by the acceleration of thermal protons as proposed, for example, by Dessler, Hanson, and Parker [53], or they may be solar protons carried into the interior of the magnetosphere and consequently energized as suggested by Axford and Hines [54].

REFERENCES

1. Cook, G. E., D. J. King-Hele, and D. M. C. Walker, The contraction of satellite orbits under the influence of air drag. Part I. With spherically symmetrical atmosphere, *Proc. Roy. Soc. A*, **257** (1960), 224.

2. Nicolet, M., Structure of the thermosphere, *Planet. Space Sci.*, **5** (1961), 1.

3. Jacchia, L. G., Influence of solar activity on the earth's upper atmosphere, *Planet. Space. Sci.*, **12** (1964), 355.

4. Harris, I., and W. Priester, Heating of the upper atmosphere, in Space Research III, ed. W. Priester. Amsterdam: North-Holland Publishing Company, 1963, p. 53.

5. ———, and ———, Time-dependent structure of the upper atmosphere, *J. Atmos. Sci.*, **19** (1962), 286.

6. Jacchia, L. G., Electromagnetic and corpuscular heating of the upper atmosphere, in Space Research III, ed. W. Priester. Amsterdam: North-Holland Publishing Company, 1963, p. 3.

7. Paetzold, H. K., Solar activity effects in the upper atmosphere deduced from satellite observations, in Space Research III, ed. W. Priester. Amsterdam: North-Holland Publishing Company, 1963, p. 28.

8. CIRA 1961, COSPAR International Reference Atmosphere, 1961. Amsterdam: North-Holland Publishing Company, 1961.

9. Opik, E. J., and S. F. Singer, Distribution of density in a planetary exosphere, II, *Phys. Fluids*, **4** (1961), 221.

10. Herring, J., and L. Kyle, Density in a planetary exosphere, *J. Geophys. Res.*, **66** (1961), 1980.

11. Johnson, F. S., and R. A. Fish, Telluric hydrogen corona, *Astrophys. J.*, **131** (1960), 502.

12. Mange, P., The distribution of minor ions in electrostatic equilibrium in the high atmosphere, *J. Geophys. Res.*, **65** (1960), 3833.

13. Bourdeau, R. E., E. C. Whipple, Jr., J. L. Donley, and S. S. Bauer, Experimental evidence for the presence of helium ions based on Explorer VIII satellite data, *J. Geophys. Res.*, **67** (1962), 467.

14. Storey, L. R. O., An investigation of whistling atmospherics, *Phil. Trans. Roy. Soc. A (London)*, **246** (1953), 113.

15. Carpenter, D. L., Electron-density variations in the magnetosphere deduced from whistler data, *J. Geophys. Res.*, **67** (1962), 3345. (See also Carpenter, D. L., *J. Geophys. Res.*, **67** (1962), 135.)

16. Hanson, W. B., and I. B. Ortenburger, The coupling between the protonosphere and the normal F region, *J. Geophys. Res.* **66** (1961), 1425.

17. Barrington, R. E., and T. Nishizaki, The hydrogen ion effect in whistler dispersion, *Can. J. Phys.*, **38** (1960), 1642.

18. Helliwell, R. A., Whistler paths and electron densities in the outer ionosphere, Proc. Symp. Phys. Processes Sum-Earth Environment, DRTE Publ. No. 1025, Defence Research Board, Ottawa, 1960, p. 165.

19. Evans, J. V., The electron content of the ionosphere, *J. Atmos. Terr. Phys.*, **11** (1957), 259.

20. Bowles, K. L., G. R. Ochs, and J. L. Green, On the absolute intensity of incoherent scatter echoes from the ionosphere, *J. Res. NBS, Radio Propagation*, **66D** (1962), 395.

21. Berning, W. W., A sounding rocket measurement of electron densities to 1500 kilometers, *J. Geophys. Res.*, **65** (1960), 2589.

22. Hanson, W. B. and D. D. McKibbin, An ion-trap measurement of the ion concentration profile above the F2 peak, *J. Geophys. Res.*, **66** (1961), 1667.

23. Warren, E. S., Some preliminary results of sounding of the top side of the ionosphere by radio pulses from a satellite, *Nature*, **197** (1963), 636.

24. Störmer, C., The Polar Aurora. London: Oxford University Press, 1955.

25. Singer, S. F., A new model of magnetic storms and aurorae, *Trans. Am. Geophys. Un.*, **38** (1956), 175.

26. Alfvén, H., Cosmical Electrodynamics. London: Oxford University Press, 1950.

27. Northrop, T. G., and E. Teller, Stability of the adiabatic motion of charged particles in the earth's field, *Phys. Rev.*, **117** (1960), 215.

28. Spitzer, L., Physics of Fully Ionized Gases. New York: Interscience Publishers, Inc., 1956.

29. Thompson, W. B., On the acceleration of comsic-ray particles by magnetohydrodynamic waves, *Proc. Roy. Soc. A*, **233** (1955), 402.

30. Parker, E. N., and D. A. Tidman, Suprathermal particles, *Phys. Rev.*, **111** (1958), 1206.

31. ———, and ———, Suprathermal particles, II, *Phys. Rev.* **112** (1958), 1048.

32. ———, Suprathermal particles, III, *Phys. Rev.* **112** (1958), 1429.

33. ———, Trans-resonant electron acceleration, *J. Geophys. Res.*, **66** (1961), 2673.

34. Helliwell, R. A., and T. F. Bell, A new mechanism for accelerating electrons in the outer ionosphere, *J. Geophys. Res.*, **65** (1960), 1839.

35. Singer, S. F., and A. M. Lenchek, Geomagnetically trapped radiation, in Progress in Elementary Particle and Cosmic Ray Physics, Vol. VI. Amsterdam: North-Holland Publishing Company, (1960), Chap. III.

36. Farley, T. A., The growth of our knowledge of the earth's outer radiation belt, *Rev. Geophys*, **1** (1963), 3.

37. Heckman, H. H., and A. H. Armstrong, Energy spectrum of geomagnetically trapped protons, *J. Geophys. Res.*, **67** (1962), 1255.

38. Van Allen, J. A., and L. A. Frank, Radiation around the earth to a radial distance of 107,400 kilometers, *Nature*, **183** (1959), 430.

39. Pizella, G., C. E. McIlwain, and J. A. Van Allen, Time variations of intensity in the earth's inner radiation zone, October 1959 through December 1960, *J. Geophys. Res.*, **67** (1962), 1235.

40. Lenchek, A. M. and S. F. Singer, Geomagnetically trapped protons from cosmic ray albedo neutrons, *J. Geophys. Res.*, **67** (1962), 1263.

41. Alfvén, H., Momentum spectrum of the Van Allen radiation, *Phys. Rev. Letters*, **3** (1959), 459.

42. Gall, R., and J. Lifshitz, *Proc. I.U.P.A.P. Cosmic Ray Conference*, Moscow (ed. Syrovatsky), **3** (1960), 64.

43. Kelsall, T., Solar proton impact zones, *J. Geophys. Res.*, **66** (1961), 4047.

44. Morrison, P., Symposium on the exploration of space, *J. Geophys. Res.*, **64** (1959), 1693.

45. Freeman, J. W., Detection of an intense flux of low-energy protons or ions trapped in the inner radiation zone, *J. Geophys. Res.*, **67** (1962), 921.

46. Liemohn, H., The lifetime of radiation belt protons with energies between 1 Kev and 1 Mev, *J. Geophys. Res.*, **66** (1961), 3593.

47. Holly, F. E., and R. G. Johnson, Measurement of radiation in the lower Van Allen belt, *J. Geophys. Res.*, **65** (1960), 771.

48. Walt, M., L. R. Chase, J. B. Cladis, W. L. Imhof, and D. J. Knecht, Energy spectra and altitude dependence of electrons trapped in the earth's magnetic field, in Space

Research, ed. H. K. Kallmann-Bijl, Amsterdam: North-Holland Publishing Company, 1960, p. 910.

49. Gringauz, K. I., V. V. Bezrukikh, V. D. Ozerov, and R. E. Rybchinsky, Artificial earth satellites, *USSR Academy of Sciences*, **6** (1961), 101.

50. O'Brien, B. J., J. A. Van Allen, C. D. Laughlin, and L. A. Frank, Absolute electron intensities in the heart of the earth's outer radiation zone, *J. Geophys. Res.*, **67** (1962), 397.

51. Davis, L. R., and J. M. Williamson, Low-energy trapped protons, in Space Research III, ed. W. Priester. Amsterdam: North-Holland Publishing Company, 1963, p. 365.

52. Maehlum, B., and B. J. O'Brien, Study of energetic electrons and their relationship to auroral absorption of radio waves, *J. Geophys. Res.*, **68** (1963), 997.

53. Dessler, A. J., W. B. Hanson, and E. N. Parker, Formation of the geomagnetic storms main-phase ring current, *J. Geophys. Res.*, **66** (1961), 3631.

54. Axford, W. I., and C. O. Hines, A unifying theory of high-latitude geophysical phenomena and geomagnetic storms, *Can. J. Phys.*, **39** (1961), 1433.

55. Sonett, C. P., E. J. Smith, D. L. Judge, and P. J. Coleman, Current systems in the vestigial geomagnetic field, Explorer VI, *Phys. Rev. Letters*, **4** (1960), 161.

56. Smith, E. J. A comparison of Explorer VI and Explorer X magnetometer data, *J. Geophys. Res.*, **67** (1962), 2045.

57. Dessler, A. J., and E. N. Parker, The hydromagnetic picture of geomagnetic storms, *J. Geophys. Res.*, **64** (1959), 2239.

58. Akasofu, S.-I., and S. Chapman, The ring current, geomagnetic disturbance, and the Van Allen belts, *J. Geophys. Res.*, **66** (1961), 1321.

59. Nelms, G. L., Ionospheric results from the topside sounder satellite Alouette, in Space Research IV, ed. P. Muller. Amsterdam: North-Holland Publishing Company, 1964, p. 437.

6

C. O. *Hines*

Motions of the Neutral Atmosphere

6.1. INTRODUCTION

The preceding chapters have treated the upper atmosphere primarily as a stationary medium, whereas in fact it is in a continuous state of motion. It is appropriate now to consider in some detail the types of motion that occur and to examine certain of their consequences. This chapter deals with motions of the neutral atmosphere which are controlled largely by ordinary hydrodynamic forces, although in some cases they are modified by the presence of ionization. Motions of the ionization are subject to similar forces, but to a large extent they are controlled by collisional interaction with the neutral gas and by electrostatic and magnetic fields. Their general properties are discussed in the next chapter, together with specific examples that arise during normal conditions; modifications related to storm conditions will be described observationally in Chapter 14 and theoretically in Chapter 15.

6.2. ATMOSPHERIC ROTATION [1]

The dominant motion of the atmosphere is one of rotation. This fact is frequently ignored, and often with good reason, but its consequences should nevertheless be borne in mind, and some of them merit more study than has yet been given them.

The simple dynamical effects are, of course, well known and are normally taken into account by the adoption of a rotating coordinate system and the introduction (when significant) of Coriolis and centrifugal forces. The Coriolis force plays a prominent part in atmospheric circulation and tidal oscillations, for example, whereas the centrifugal force may be important in influencing the distribution of ionization in the outer magnetospheric regions as noted in Chapter 5.

The role of ionization in the rotation of the atmosphere should not be passed over lightly, since at present it gives rise to a degree of uncertainty. If ionization were absent, atmospheric rotation could be enforced with little difficulty by viscosity acting from below, for any drag that might be exerted from above by the interplanetary medium would be relatively unimportant. (The transition from a rotating atmosphere to a nonrotating interplanetary gas would occur in the exosphere, where individual atoms would maintain their angular momentum constant as they rose and fell, rather than their angular velocity.) With ionization present, ion-atom collisions must be taken into account, and they could lead to a substantial drag opposing rotation.

It appears in practice, however, that the ionization of low and middle latitudes is set into rotation by the neutral gas of the E region, the effect being carried up the geomagnetic field lines by a polarization charge which is itself established to offset the induction electromotive force that results from rotation within a magnetic field. The same may be true at high latitudes, if the configuration of polar field lines is such as to form a tail, as depicted in Fig. 1.5, although the rotation of the overlying ionization in that case would be about the curved axis of the tail rather than the earth's axis itself. On the other hand, if the polar field lines extend into the interplanetary medium (see Fig. 15.8), then the polarization charge may be drained away into that medium as rapidly as it is formed, and the ionization may not be able to maintain corotation. In that case, the neutral gas of the polar regions would be prevented from rotating freely at ionospheric heights. There is as yet no strong evidence to support either of these possibilities against the other.

6.3. PREVAILING WINDS [2]

The large-scale pattern of prevailing winds can be studied reliably, by present means, only to an altitude of 100 km or so. The pertinent data are derived primarily from balloon ascents in the lowest levels, and then by shell and rocket-borne smoke-puff experiments, rocket-released vapor trails, 'abnormal' sound propagation, and the drifting of meteor trails. These data have been augmented on occasion by apparent motions of noctilucent clouds at the mesopause and of ionization irregularities (including sporadic-E patches) at higher levels, but these motions are of doubtful relevance to a study of prevailing winds, as subsequent discussion will reveal. Successful determination of the wind system substantially above 100 km will probably hinge upon an extension of the rocket network to these greater altitudes.

The prevailing winds that have been detected in the upper atmosphere are predominantly zonal in that, on most occasions and at most sites, the direction of motion is essentially eastward or westward. (It should be remarked that the meteorologists' convention of naming such winds 'westerly' or 'easterly,' respectively, is avoided by most writers when discussing the upper atmosphere, in favor of a specification of the vector direction; but care must be exercised to avoid misinterpretation on some occasions.) The zonal flow varies appreciably through the course of a year, in a pattern that is found to repeat broadly in both hemispheres according to season. A composite of representative meridional sections [3–5] is displayed in Fig. 6.1, for solsticial conditions.

Prevailing zonal winds may be expected to be 'geostrophic'; that is, to be in quasi equilibrium under the combined effects of a pressure gradient, the Coriolis force introduced by the earth's rotation, and gravity. In a local cartesian coordinate system oriented with x axis eastward, y axis northward,

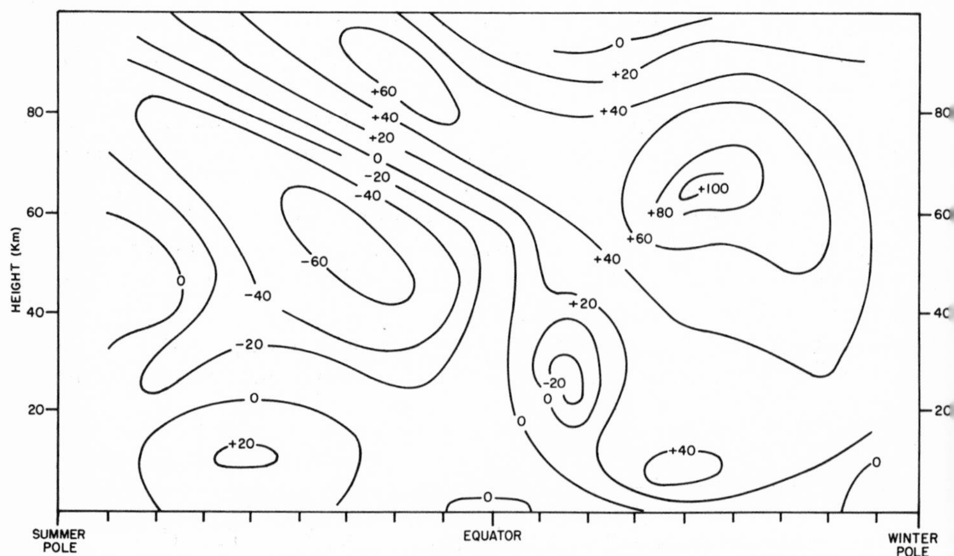

Fig. 6.1 A meridional section of the prevailing zonal winds (measured in m/s, positive toward the east) at the solstices—after Kochanski [3], Pant [4], and Murgatroyd [5]. The speed indicated at any selected point is determined only roughly, and little reliance should be placed on the form of the various contours in progressing from one point to another.

and z axis upward, the zonal wind speed u (measured as positive in the eastward direction) would then satisfy the equilibrium condition

$$2u\Omega\rho \cos \theta = -\partial p/\partial y, \tag{6.1}$$

where Ω is the earth's angular velocity, θ is the colatitude (measured from the north pole), ρ is the atmospheric density, and p the pressure. The equation of static equilibrium,

$$\rho g = -\partial p/\partial z, \tag{6.2}$$

would apply approximately, with g the acceleration due to gravity, an upward Coriolis force density equal to $2u\Omega\rho \sin \theta$ being negligible in relation to ρg. The density variable may be replaced by temperature T, by means of the gas law $\rho \propto p/T$, and the pressure may be eliminated as a variable by a suitable differentiation and combination of (6.1) and (6.2), whence

$$\partial T/\partial y = -[2\,\Omega(\cos \theta)T^2/g](\partial/\partial z)(u/T). \tag{6.3}$$

This 'thermal wind equation' indicates, for example, that the ratio u/T should increase with height in any region where the temperature is increasing toward the equator, and conversely.

By the application of the thermal wind equation to contours of the type depicted in Fig. 6.1, and with the adoption of a specific latitudinal distribution of temperature at a base height of 25 km, Murgatroyd [5] has derived the distribution of temperature at higher altitudes given in Fig. 6.2. This distribution is in substantial agreement with more direct data up to a height of 60 or 70 km, but there are few measurements available as a check at still greater heights. One rather startling feature is revealed: at 80–100 km, the winter pole is seen to be warmer than the equator, which in turn is warmer than the summer pole. These relative temperatures of the poles are contrary not only to first expectations, but also to the implications of a detailed

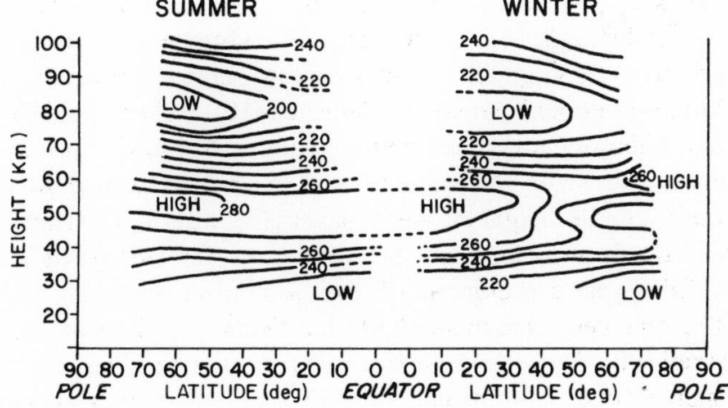

Fig. 6.2 Temperatures to the 100-km level, as deduced from zonal wind systems by Murgatroyd [5].

analysis of radiative energy sources and sinks in the upper atmosphere [6]. It has been suggested by Kellogg [7] that the winter polar regions might be maintained at their higher temperature by a subsidence of the atmosphere with an attendant release of energy from the recombination of oxygen atoms into molecules. The supply of atoms would have to be maintained by a flow from the sunlit regions of lower latitudes, and indeed some nonzonal flow directed toward the winter pole has been detected at meteor heights [8]. Airglow observations [9] tend also to confirm the proposed subsidence, so there is now a good prospect that this anomaly will be resolved shortly.

6.4 TIDAL OSCILLATIONS [1]

Superimposed on the prevailing winds of the upper atmosphere, and often exceeding them in magnitude, are the diurnally recurring motions caused by atmospheric tides. These motions are revealed most clearly by radar observations of drifting meteor trails at 85–105 km, for the interpretation of the meteor data is direct and the periodic components of motion stand out well [10, 11]. Supporting observations have been obtained for greater heights, and with a broader geographical distribution, from studies of moving irregularities in the background ionization of the *E* region. Such irregularities need not move with the same velocity as the neutral atmosphere, however, nor indeed with the same velocity as the ionized constituents, but they do reveal periodic components of motion which can be correlated with meteor-height tides and which are normally interpreted as tidal oscillations [12].

At low latitudes, the dominant high-altitude tidal oscillation appears to be provided by the solar 24-hr component, although the data that lead to this conclusion are derived mainly from the drifting of ionization irregularities, and it is possible that they are contaminated by the effects of other diurnal processes. At Adelaide, Australia, at a latitude of 35°S, meteor data indicate solar 24-hr and 12-hr components of about equal amplitude [11]. At higher latitudes, the solar 12-hr component appears to dominate, although a residual 24-hr component can still be detected [10]. Higher-order harmonics of the solar oscillation have been sought, but with limited and somewhat doubtful success. A lunar 12-hr component has been detected by a careful statistical study of the height of the *E* layer [13], although recent evidence indicates that this conclusion may be valid only for the sporadic-*E* component [14]. Of all the components of the oscillation, the solar 12-hr component is the one best documented observationally and most thoroughly studied theoretically. It will receive the greatest attention here.

The existence of a semidiurnal atmospheric oscillation at ground level has been known for more than two centuries now, having been revealed by early barometric measurements in the tropics. This oscillation was initially attributed to the gravitational attraction of the sun, and so was termed a 'tide' by obvious analogy, although there are now strong reasons for believing that thermal effects dominate the generation process. The question arises in either case as to why the solar 12-hr tide should be so strong: if the source is gravitational, why does the stronger tide-raising force of the moon not result in a stronger lunar 12-hr tide, and if thermal, how does the dominant diurnal component of heat flux fail to produce a stronger solar 24-hr tide?

Kelvin advanced the basis of an explanation toward the end of the last century, when he suggested that the atmosphere may have a natural mode of oscillation whose period approximates to 12 solar hours. A resonant response might then be expected in the presence of any semidiurnal excitation mechanism, which would amplify the resultant oscillation abnormally. The mathematical analysis of this suggestion has been pursued extensively but is still not complete. At best it can be said that the possibility of a resonance exists, sufficient to enhance the solar 12-hr oscillation over the solar 24-hr oscillation even if thermal sources are dominant, but that an adequate enhancement of a gravitationally excited solar 12-hr component relative to the lunar 12-hr component seems wholly unlikely. In view of separate evidence on the phase of the solar semidiurnal oscillation, which cannot be explained on the basis of a predominantly gravitational excitation [15], it seems safe to conclude that thermal sources are of greatest importance.

Since tidal theory is a complicated subject that cannot be done justice in the space available, it is not reviewed here, but an outline of the physical concepts it contains will be given. For further details, the reader may refer to Wilkes' monograph [16] and to the source material it draws upon.

The basic relations of tidal theory are the equations of motion,

$$\rho D\mathbf{V}/Dt = -\operatorname{grad} p + \rho\mathbf{g} + \mathbf{F}, \tag{6.4}$$

the equation of continuity,

$$\partial \rho/\partial t + \operatorname{div}(\rho\mathbf{V}) = 0, \tag{6.5}$$

and the adiabatic equation of state,

$$Dp/Dt = C^2 D\rho/Dt, \tag{6.6}$$

where ρ is the gas density, p the gas pressure, $\mathbf{g}$ the acceleration due to gravity, C the speed of sound, and $\mathbf{F}$ the assumed force that is taken to be driving the motion; D/Dt is the mobile operator, $\partial/\partial t + \mathbf{V}\cdot\operatorname{grad}$, of time differentiation following the motion. These equations are invariably analyzed in spherical coordinates rotating with the earth, and the inertial force density $\rho D\mathbf{V}/Dt$ then gives rise to an explicit Coriolis force term, which is of major importance to the development, and to a centrifugal term which is normally ignored. The equations are linearized, by an assumption that variations of $\mathbf{V}$, ρ, and p (from their steady-state values, in the absence of a tide) will be of only perturbation magnitude, so that their products with one another may be ignored. The vertical acceleration in the rotating system is assumed to be negligible; heat transfer and heat input are frequently ignored, and **F** is then taken to be derivable from a potential function. Finally, C^2 is taken to be dependent only on height.

With these assumptions, it is possible to achieve a separation of variables such that

$$\operatorname{div} \mathbf{V} = Z(z)\Theta(\theta) \exp i(\omega t + s\varphi), \tag{6.7}$$

where z again measures height (upward), θ is the colatitude, φ the longitude, and $2\pi/\omega$ the period; s determines the number of nodes that occur around a circle of latitude; it must be an integer in order that the solution should be single-valued as φ increases through 2π radians, and the ratio ω/s must conform to the apparent motion of the sun or moon as source. Individual components of the perturbation in $\mathbf{V}$, ρ, and p are related to $\operatorname{div} \mathbf{V}$ in a specific manner which incorporates the force term **F**. The Θ function satisfies a differential equation which need not be written here, but it obviously gives rise to a problem in eigenmodes in order to provide continuity at $\theta = 0$ and π. The solution of this problem is achieved by numerical computation, and it yields a family of eigenvalues h_r for any given ω and s; h_r has the dimensions of a length, and for the dominant mode observed at ground level its value is 7.9 km.

The eigenvalue $h_r(\omega, s)$ has a further significance which becomes clear when the vertical variation $Z(z)$ is considered. This function is found to be a solution of the differential equation,

$$C^2 \frac{d^2Z}{dz^2} + \left[\frac{dC^2}{dz} - \gamma g\right]\frac{dZ}{dz} + \left[\frac{dC^2}{dz} + (\gamma - 1)g\right]\frac{Z}{h_r} = 0, \tag{6.8}$$

which has the characteristics of a wave equation. Wavelike solutions can be found, of the form

$$Z \propto H^{-1/2} k^{-1/2} \exp \int \frac{dz}{2H} \exp \pm i \int k\, dz, \tag{6.9}$$

with

$$H \equiv C^2/\gamma g \text{ and } k^2 \equiv \left(\frac{dH}{dz} + \frac{\gamma - 1}{\gamma}\right)\Big/ Hh_r - 1/4H^2, \tag{6.10}$$

provided that Hk varies sufficiently slowly with height ($|dHk/dz| \ll Hk^2$).

The factor $\exp \int dz/2H$ in (6.9) represents a growth of the wave with increasing height, and it results physically from the corresponding decrease of gas density. It proceeds at just such a rate as to maintain the flux of energy in the wave essentially constant. The importance of tides in the upper atmosphere results primarily from this growth, which at 100 km represents an amplification by a factor of 1000 over ground-level values of the tidal velocity and of the fractional variations in density and pressure.

The second exponential factor in (6.9), in combination with the exponential in (6.7), represents a traveling wave if k is real and a spatial attenuation if k is imaginary. Examination of (6.10) will show that k may be real at one level and imaginary at another, and in such circumstances a 'reflection' of the wave at an intermediate height is to be expected. The value of k^2 clearly depends on h_r, and so on the particular eigenmode selected for study.

Pekeris [17], with an early temperature profile, and Weekes and Wilkes [18] with more recent data, have shown that the dominant mode observed at ground level should propagate as a wave in the lower atmosphere, but be reflected in the mesosphere and again propagate as a wave above the mesopause. They have, moreover, shown that multiple reflections at the mesosphere and ground may be so phased that the lower atmosphere can act as sort of resonance cavity for this mode and can thereby provide the enhanced response envisaged by Kelvin to account for the observed ratio of the 12-hr and 24-hr tides. The reflecting barrier provided by the mesosphere attenuates the energy flux by a factor of the order 100, and hence the amplitude by a factor of 10, as the tide penetrates through to ionospheric heights, but this is more than offset by the amplification factor previously mentioned.

Although this picture provides some satisfaction, it cannot be complete. Other modes than the resonant one are observed at ground level and are free from serious reflection in the mesosphere as determined from (6.10); they should then dominate over the resonant mode at ionospheric heights. The true problem is in fact not adequately specified by the model previously described for many reasons, but notably because the initial equations ignore the presence of the zonal wind systems. A full analysis should take those systems into account and would probably indicate a significant reflection of the secondary modes as well, but it could at the same time upset the resonance previously deduced. Again, the earlier calculations were based on a driving force derivable from a potential, whereas a heat source is now to be preferred. The appropriate calculations are complicated to an extreme, but at least have been initiated. They indicate that resonance is far less effective in determining the relative magnitudes than is the degree of matching that exists between the vertical profile of heat input and the vertical structure of the resultant tidal wave; this matching is poor for the 24-hr mode, but good for the 12-hr mode [19].

Apart from the question of resonance and despite the use of an inaccurate temperature profile, the calculations of Weekes and Wilkes provide a reasonable estimate of the variation of amplitude and phase in one mode of the solar 12-hr tide (see Fig. 6.3). The tendency toward a constant energy density will be noted, as will deviations from this tendency both at 20–40 km and at 50–100 km. The lower departure results from the occurrence of a node in the standing-wave pattern, and the recovery of the energy density

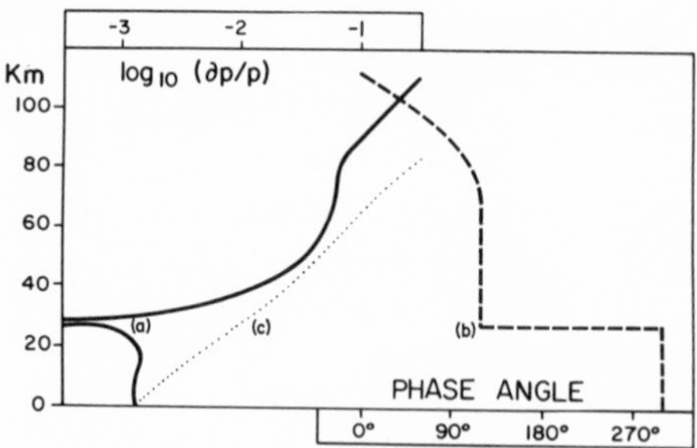

Fig. 6.3 The height variation of (a) amplitude and (b) phase angle ($= \phi$ in a variation of the form cos $[\omega t - \phi]$) deduced by Weekes and Wilkes [18] for the dominant mode of the 12-hr solar tide. The dotted line (c) represents the amplitude that would have obtained, had the tidal energy been distributed uniformly in height, given the temperature profile adopted by Weekes and Wilkes.

at 50 km to its ground-level value is indicative of this. The decrease of energy density above 50 km results from k^2 becoming negative, the relevant solution for Z being exponentially damped through a factor $\exp - \int |k| \, dz$. It is this region of negative k^2 that produces the reflection that in turn leads to a standing wave below 50 km and to the possibility of resonance. Above 80 km, k^2 increases and becomes positive again, whereupon the height-distribution of energy is again uniform but at a reduced level, corresponding to the small amplitude of the wave that leaks through the reflecting region. The abrupt change of phase at the node of the standing wave pattern may be noted, as may the gradual decrease of phase angle at greater heights where freely propagating conditions are resumed. This decrease corresponds to a downward propagation of phase, but to an upward propagation of energy.

The best available observational data on upper atmospheric tides are probably those provided by Greenhow and Neufeld [10], obtained at Jodrell Bank (53°N) by the radar detection of meteor-trail drifts. Their results for one 24-hr period are depicted in Fig. 6.4, together with the results of a Fourier analysis which reveals the prevailing, the 24-hr, and the 12-hr components of the atmospheric velocity. The growth of amplitude with height is clearly visible here, as is an advance of phase (or decrease of phase angle) at greater heights, particularly in the dominant semidiurnal component. The tidal wind vector rotates clockwise (as seen from above) as would be expected in the northern hemisphere; a counterclockwise rotation is expected and observed in the southern hemisphere.

Monthly averages of the phase and amplitude of the tidal winds are shown for a 1-yr interval in Fig. 6.5. For winter, Greenhow and Neufeld

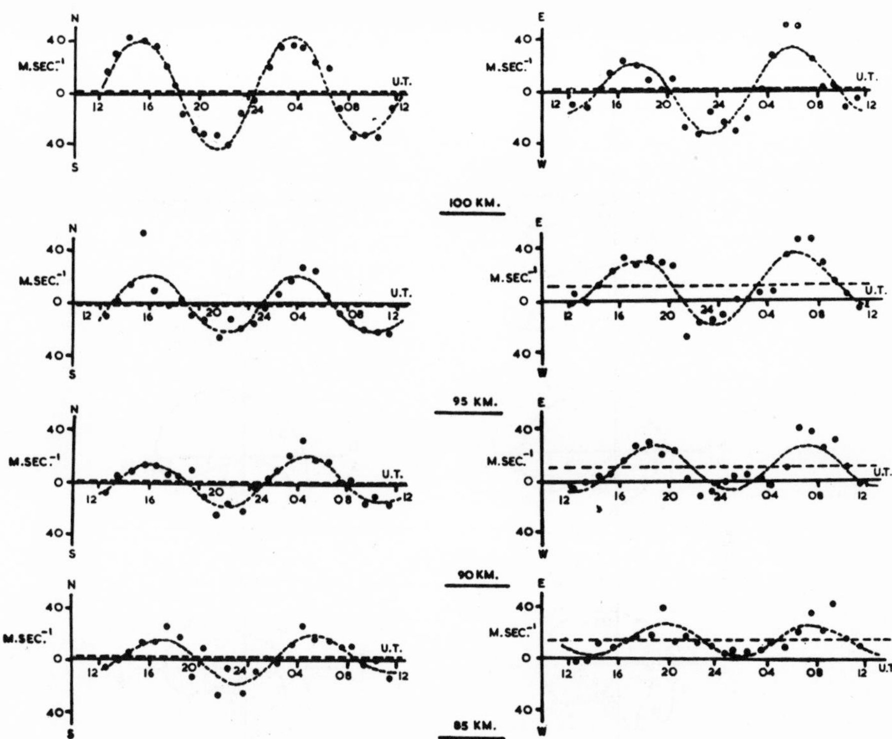

Fig. 6.4 Height variation of N-S and E-W wind components, as revealed by the meteor-drift observations of Greenhow and Neufeld [10]. The steady wind and sum of the diurnal and semidiurnal oscillations revealed by harmonic analysis are shown as broken lines.

quote a phase gradient of 7°/km and an amplitude gradient of 1.5 m/s/km as average values; for summer, the gradients reduce to 3°/km and 0.4 m/s/km, respectively. These gradients are roughly consistent with those derived by Weekes and Wilkes for the pressure variation at the same altitudes, and agreement is also found between the absolute magnitude of the observed and theoretical oscillations. In both cases, however, the agreement must be to some extent fortuitous, for additional modes must be expected in practice. Their presence can be inferred from a detailed comparison of the observed with the predicted phase changes or by a more cursory examination of the latitudinal variations [1].

The vertical variation of tidal phase has been observed by Jones [12] at greater heights, using the drifts of ionospheric irregularities as measured at two neighboring radio frequencies. This variation is quite comparable to that detected by Greenhow and Neufeld, and the absolute phase is compatible with an extrapolation of their data. The amplitudes detected by

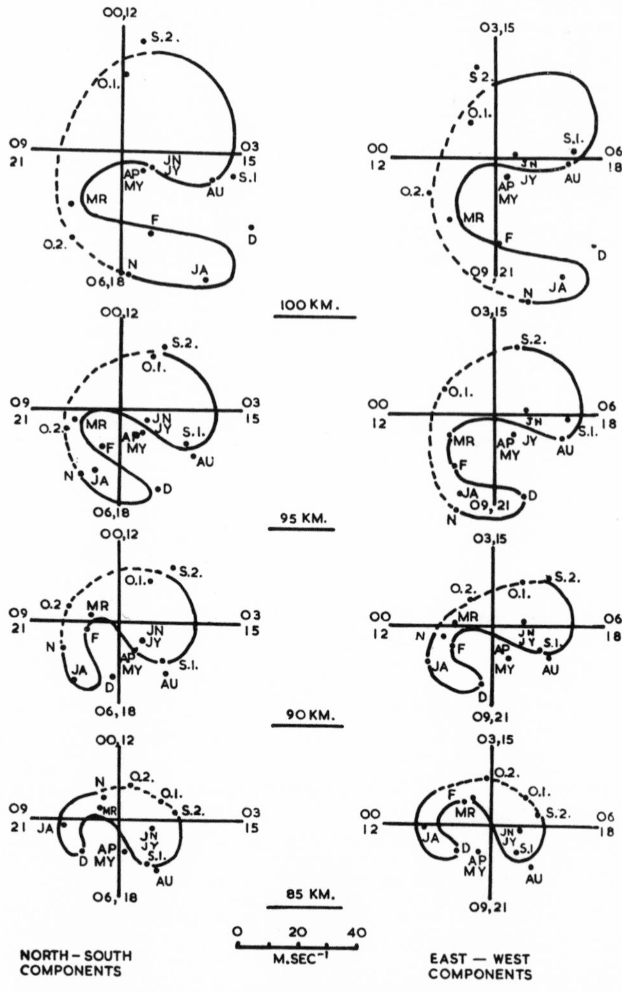

Fig. 6.5 Monthly averages of tidal amplitude (measured as a radial distance from origin) and time of maximum (measured as an hour angle), as revealed by the meteor-drift observations of Greenhow and Neufeld [10].

Jones at 110 km or so are not substantially greater than those found at meteor heights, however; hence the vertical gradient of amplitude revealed by the meteor measurements and predicted by theory cannot persist much above 100 km. The explanation may lie once again in the presence of a second mode of oscillation, it may result from an energy dissipation in the *Sq* current system that is to be discussed in the next chapter, or it could be a consequence of a breakdown in the basic theory. That theory, it will be recalled, assumes the oscillations to be of perturbation amplitude, whereas at heights of 100 km and more the amplitude predicted in this way has risen well above perturbation magnitude. Indeed, extrapolation of the meteor measurements upward to a height of 110–115 km would suggest 100% variations of atmospheric density there. Clearly, nonlinear terms must play a part to limit this amplification, but a mathematical treatment of the limitation has yet to be undertaken.

6.5 IRREGULAR WINDS AND INTERNAL GRAVITY WAVES [1, 20]

The motions depicted in Fig. 6.4 reveal a scattering of values about the smooth oscillation of the tidal winds. The scatter evidently results from a superimposed irregular motion of the atmosphere. This irregular motion has been studied in some detail by Greenhow and Neufeld by further analysis of the meteor data [21, 22]. For this purpose, they have grouped their observations in 20-min intervals to reveal more clearly the irregular fluctuation, with results typified by those displayed here in Fig. 6.6. The random or noiselike nature of the variation is clearly evident.

The temporal and spatial scales of these irregularities are of interest from both the practical and the theoretical point of view and are perhaps best described by autocorrelation functions. The temporal autocorrelation

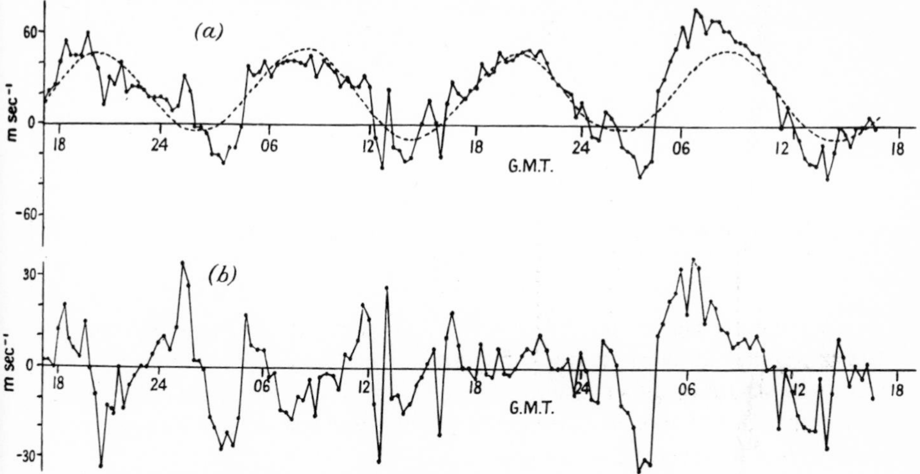

Fig. 6.6 Irregularly varying winds revealed by the meteor-drift observations of Greenhow and Neufeld [21]: (a) includes the steady wind and the diurnal and semidiurnal oscillations; (b) reveals the residual after those components are removed by harmonic analysis.

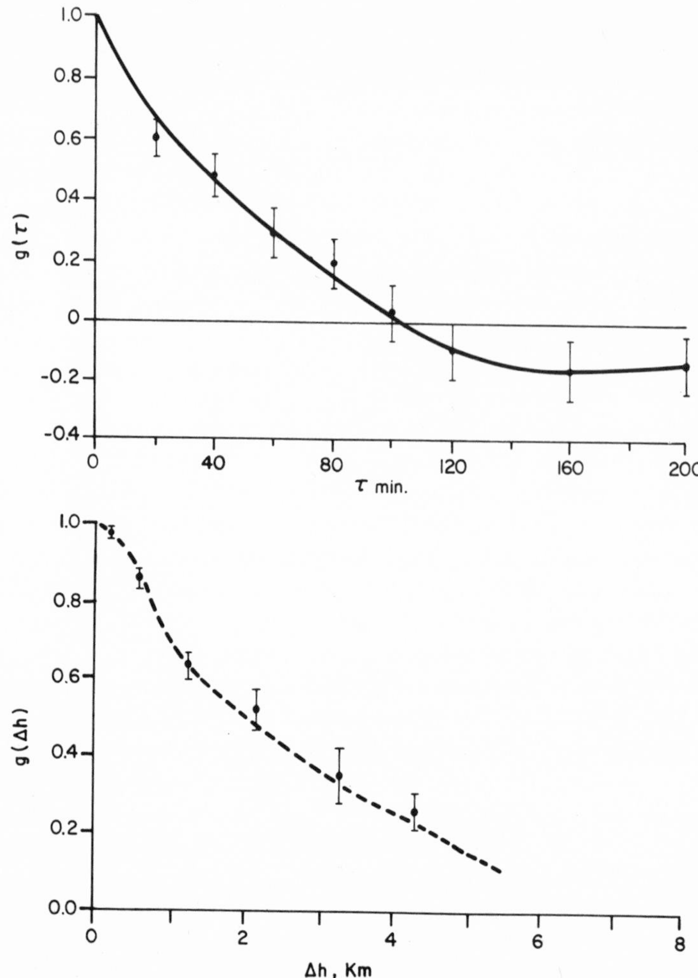

Fig. 6.7 Temporal and spatial autocorrelation coefficients, $g(\tau)$ and $g(\Delta h)$ of the irregular winds for time separations τ and vertical separations Δh, derived by Greenhow and Neufeld [22].

for the irregular variations of Fig. 6.6 is shown in Fig. 6.7, together with a vertical spatial autocorrelation for similar irregularities. The time scale is seen to be of the order of 100 min, and the vertical scale about 6 km. The horizontal scale cannot be determined directly, but it has been estimated to be substantially greater than 100 km.

A more direct measurement of the vertical scale of the irregular winds is provided by photographs of long-enduring meteor trails. These trails, which may persist for many seconds, are rapidly distorted from their initial straight-line shape into a rather sinuous form, such as that illustrated in

Fig. 6.8. The growth of wind amplitude with height which is seen here is quite characteristic, as is the growth of the dominant and minimum vertical scale sizes. The photographic observations indicate unambiguously that the winds are predominantly horizontal, and this conclusion is borne out by radar measurements. The meteor-trail observations have been extended upward in recent years by a number of studies of rocket-released vapor trails [23].

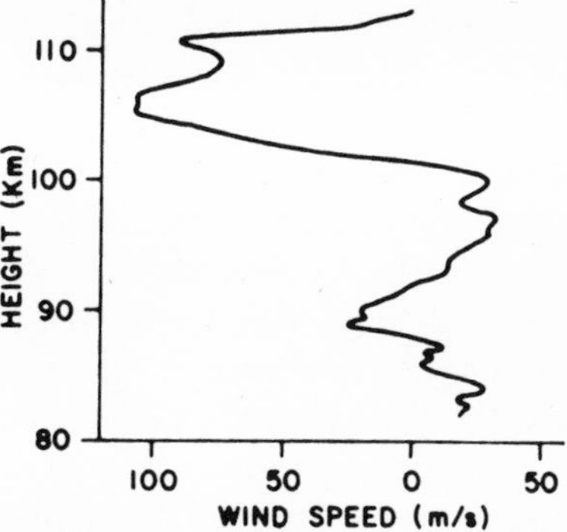

Fig. 6.8 The wind components at meteor levels in a vertical plane normal to the line of sight, on one representative occasion, derived by Liller and Whipple [26] from the distortion of a long-enduring meteor trail.

The large-scale pancake-shaped irregularities revealed by these observations were for some time attributed to turbulence, and much of the literature describing them employs the terminology and some of the mathematical formalism appropriate to such an interpretation. These accounts must be read with care, for the turbulence concept now appears to be inapplicable in this particular area and the earlier statements in many cases require rephrasing. The motion is now held to be of a more organized nature than true turbulence, although its exact character has still to be firmly established. The only attempt at a comprehensive theory yet available [20] assumes the motion to be produced by randomly superimposed atmospheric waves, closely akin to the tides but on a substantially smaller scale. This same theory seeks also to explain certain irregularities that occur in the distribution of the background ionization which are revealed both in the 'drift' measurements previously mentioned and in the large-scale traveling disturbances of the F layer that were described in Chapter 4.

The randomly variable ionization 'drift' irregularities are studied most extensively by means of fixed-frequency radio reflections, using a single transmitter and a system of at least three spaced receivers. The radio signal returned from the ionosphere is variable both in space and in time, as a consequence of the irregular ionization distribution and of its variations. Often the variations detected at the separate receivers do not show any substantial correlation with one another, but there are also periods when they do. On the latter occasions, the correlation is greatest if the records from the spaced receivers are shifted in time relative to one another, in the manner to be expected if an unchanging pattern of irregularities was drifting horizontally past the observing stations. The correlation is never perfect, of course, and departures from complete correlation can be attributed both to inherent changes in the pattern as it moves and to the fact that the spaced receivers would actually be observing slightly different parts of the pattern.

These various factors render the analysis and interpretation of the records somewhat uncertain and extremely complicated. Moreover, the data pertain directly only to the pattern of ionization irregularities—to its movement and distortion—and not necessarily to the movement of the ionization itself, let alone to the movement of the neutral constituents. As has been noted, the large-scale 12-hr and 24-hr variations revealed by this technique are normally interpreted as manifestations of the atmospheric tides, but a mental reservation must always be placed on this interpretation. The random fluctuations that are superimposed, and that are now under consideration, are even less likely to be simply related to the motion of the neutral gas.

To take an extreme example, a single mode of oscillation, propagating waves through the *E* region, would tend to distort surfaces of constant electron density into an oscillatory form about their normal horizontal positions as illustrated in Fig. 6.9. The pattern of distortion would appear to move horizontally as the wave train progressed obliquely, and radio waves reflected from any one of these surfaces would exhibit at ground level a pattern of intensity fluctuation that also moved horizontally. The motion in this case would be related to the phase progression of the atmospheric wave, and not to the actual perturbation velocity of the gas itself; the latter would affect only the amplitude of the intensity fluctuations.

Randomly superimposed atmospheric waves would lead to a random pattern of irregularities randomly changing in time. If the atmosphere itself were moving past an observer, as a consequence of a tidal motion, say, and if the 'randomness' were established with respect to the moving system, then

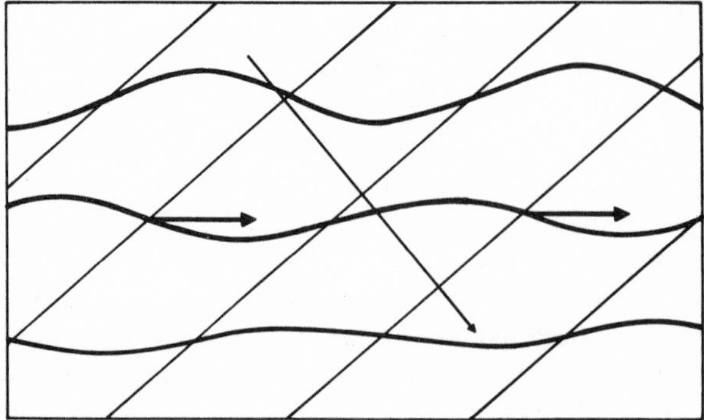

Fig. 6.9 Contours of constant electron density, represented by solid lines, will exhibit deformations that appear to move horizontally (heavy arrow) under the influence of an atmospheric wave system (illustrated by lines of constant phase, drawn lightly) propagating obliquely (light arrow).

the observer could detect the tide by averaging out the random part of the fluctuations he detects. On this basis, the extraction of tidal winds could be justified even if the irregularities and their irregular motions were produced by waves.

On the other hand, however, the waves need not be propagating randomly. Even with a stationary atmosphere in the *E* region, a preferred direction of wave propagation might arise, and this direction might be subject to diurnal and semidiurnal variations (as a consequence, say, of the effects of tidal wind shears at some lower level). In these circumstances, an apparent drift velocity would be obtained, and its direction and magnitude could change in a manner indistinguishable from that of a true *E*-region tidal wind.

The correlation between the phase of the 12-hr component of meteor drifts and *E*-region irregularity drifts, mentioned before, suggests that a tidal interpretation is in fact legitimate. No corresponding empirical justification exists, however, for assuming that the prevailing winds and the irregular component of motion inferred from *E*-region reflections are true winds. There are indeed theoretical reasons for believing them to be other than true winds, for true winds would operate in conjunction with the geomagnetic field to transport ionization with some velocity other than that of the wind itself, at heights above 100 km or so. Irregularities in the distribution of ionization might be transported with the velocity of the ionization itself or with some other velocity, but almost certainly not with the velocity of the neutral atmosphere at these heights.

As has been indicated, a single comprehensive wave theory can account for all the irregularities previously described and can in fact explain many of their characteristics. It seems to be relevant, too, to structure observed in noctilucent clouds, airglow emissions, and irregular height variations of temperature and density, but has not yet been applied in detail to these phenomena. It is still in its early stages of development, but many of its basic features are already quite clear. These will be summarized briefly.

The waves in question are internal waves of the atmosphere, propagating in a fashion closely analogous to that of the tidal oscillation. Their smaller scales and shorter periods render them less affected by the curvature of the earth and the Coriolis force, but somewhat more dependent on vertical acceleration. Their origin is not yet clear, but certainly the global boundary conditions applicable to tides are not crucial to their observed characteristics. Tropospheric and stratospheric wind systems, instabilities in the middle atmosphere, and nonlinear tidal interactions appear to provide the most likely sources in normal conditions, and free propagation away from such sources may be assumed.

The equations that govern the propagation are those of motion, of continuity, and of adiabatic state—Eqs. (6.4) to (6.6)—as with tides. The first of these may be recast in cartesian coordinates, however, to give

$$\rho_0 \partial u/\partial t = -\partial p'/\partial x \tag{6.11}$$

$$\rho_0 \partial v/\partial t = -\partial p'/\partial y \tag{6.12}$$

and

$$\rho_0 \partial w/\partial t = -\partial p'/\partial z - \rho' g \tag{6.13}$$

in linearized form; the x and y axes are horizontal and the z axis is vertically upward as before; u, v, and w are the corresponding velocity components; ρ' and p' represent the departures of density and pressure from their equilibrium values, ρ_0 and p_0 respectively.

A first understanding of the physical situation described by these equations can be gained by the adoption of plane-wave solutions and by an examination of their characteristics. Practical cases would, of course, involve more complex solutions, but these could be synthesized by the superposition of plane-wave modes. Normally, the only substantial qualitative change introduced by this process concerns the decrease of wave amplitude as distance from the source is increased; this can be taken into account, if ever a source is specified, by the insertion of an inverse distance dependence.

When C^2 is constant in height, plane-wave solutions of Eqs. (6.5), (6.6), and (6.11)–(6.13) can be found, in which ρ'/ρ_0, p'/p_0, u, v, and w all have the form $\exp(z/2H) \exp i(\omega t - k_x x - k_y y - k_z z)$, with

$$\omega^4 - \omega^2 C^2 (k_h^2 + k_z^2) + (\gamma - 1) g^2 k_h^2 - \gamma^2 g^2 \omega^2 / 4C^2 = 0 \tag{6.14}$$

where $k_h^2 \equiv k_x^2 + k_y^2$. The factor $\exp(z/2H)$ results in an upward increase in the amplitude of the oscillatory motion and plays the same role in maintaining energy flux constant as did the similar factor in tidal theory. The relative magnitudes of the wind, density and pressure may be found from the basic equations:

$$u \propto \omega k_x C^2 [k_z - i(1 - \gamma/2) g/C^2]; \tag{6.15}$$

$$v \propto \omega k_y C^2 [k_z - i(1 - \gamma/2) g/C^2]; \tag{6.16}$$

$$w \propto \omega [\omega^2 - k_h^2 C^2]; \tag{6.17}$$

$$p'/p_0 \propto \gamma \omega^2 [k_z - i(1 - \gamma/2) g/C^2]; \tag{6.18}$$

$$\rho'/\rho_0 \propto \omega^2 k_z + i(\gamma - 1) g k_h^2 - i \gamma g \omega^2 / 2C^2. \tag{6.19}$$

The factor of proportionality is the same in all of these relations, and comprises the exponential factors indicated immediately before (6.14) in addition to an arbitrary amplitude constant.

If attention is limited to the case of real k_h and k_z, then examination of (6.14) reveals that two distinct sequences of waves can propagate. The one, which arises when

$$\omega > \omega_a \equiv \gamma g/2C, \tag{6.20}$$

consists of acoustic waves, and when $\omega \gg \omega_a$, these waves simply propagate with the speed of sound. The other sequence arises when

$$\omega < \omega_g \equiv (\gamma-1)^{1/2} g/C, \tag{6.21}$$

and consists of internal gravity waves. When $\omega \ll \omega_g$ these waves attain a limiting 'horizontal phase speed' ($\equiv \omega/k_h$) approximating to $2(\gamma - 1)^{1/2}\, C/\gamma$ —or about $0.9C$—regardless of the inclination of the wave normal, except for waves that propagate nearly vertically. Only evanescent waves exist in the intermediate range, $\omega_g < \omega < \omega_a$, and such waves can also exist outside that range, provided that k_h is sufficiently large (if $\omega > \omega_a$) or small (if $\omega < \omega_g$).

The more general behavior of these wave sequences is represented by the contours of Fig. 6.10, which illustrate the phase speeds relative to C (refractive index $\equiv C$/phase speed) for various wave periods and directions of propagation. It may be noted that acoustic waves in general propagate with phase speeds exceeding C, and internal gravity waves propagate with phase speeds less than the limiting horizontal phase speed previously cited.

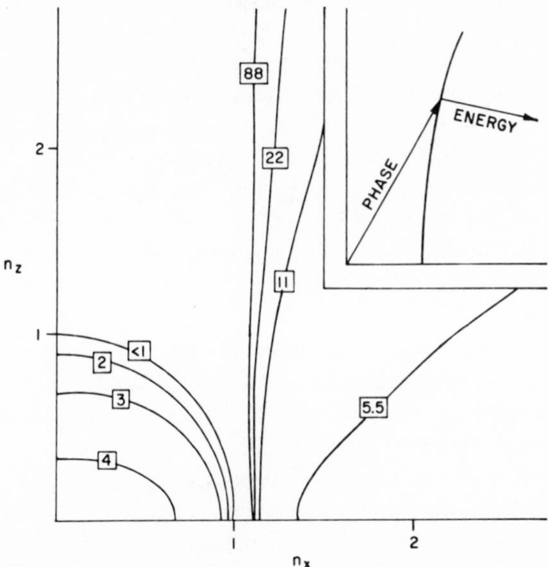

Fig. 6.10 The 'refractive index' ($\equiv$ speed of sound divided by phase speed), measured radially from the origin, as a function of angle of elevation of phase normal (measured from the horizontal) and wave period—measured in minutes, and shown in boxes on each contour in turn [20]. The inset illustrates the geometrical construction that yields the direction of energy flow, as discussed in Chapter 1.

The direction of energy flow in any of these waves can be determined as in the inset diagram, by drawing the outward normal at the appropriate point on a constant-period contour. Upward phase propagation is seen to correspond to upward energy flow in acoustic waves, whereas in internal gravity waves (as in tides) an upward component of phase propagation is accompanied by a downward flow of energy, and vice versa.

The insertion of appropriate values for E-region heights will reveal that $2\pi/\omega_g$ is of the order of 5 min there, whereas it is two or three times as great in the F region. The large-scale irregular winds that are revealed by meteor-trail deformation, with their time-scales of 100 min or so, and the large-scale traveling disturbances in the F region, with their quasi periodicities of 20 min, then lie in the part of the spectrum that provides internal gravity waves. It may be conjectured that the time scale of the 'drift' irregularities is similarly greater than $2\pi/\omega_g$, although no direct evidence exists on this point.

An explanation of the meteor-trail distortions on the basis of these waves can be supported on the following counts [20]: Given a periodicity of 100 min or more, and a vertical wavelength of the order 10 km as observed, a horizontal wavelength of some hundreds of kilometers can be deduced from (6.14) in conformity with observation. Similarly $(u^2 + v^2)^{1/2}$ will be found to exceed w by an order of magnitude, again in agreement with the observations. The observed increase of wind amplitude with height (Fig. 6.8) can be explained as a consequence of the factor $\exp(z/2H)$. Although not discussed here, the dissipative effects introduced by viscosity and heat conduction provide an explanation for the disappearance of the smaller-scale modes as height is increased and the corresponding lengthening of the dominant scale; these dissipative effects simply act more strongly on the smaller-scale modes and at greater heights (where the 'kinematic viscosity' is greater).

In application to the 'drift' measurements and to the large-scale traveling disturbances, the theory is again successful in accounting for many of the characteristics observed. Most points of comparison are numerical and need not be recited here. One point of qualitative interest warrants comment, however, concerning the traveling disturbances. It seems likely that the bulk of the energy responsible for these disturbances is trapped low in the upper atmosphere—probably beneath the thermal decline of 55–80 km, where tidal energy is so strongly reflected—and is propagated horizontally over great distances as a consequence. The actual deformation of the F layer is then produced by some small portion of the energy that leaks upward and out of the trapping region, with the amplitude of oscillation increasing, of course, because of the factor $\exp(z/2H)$. This upward flow of energy is accompanied by an obliquely downward progression of phase, and it is this progression that produces the downward movement that is apparent when

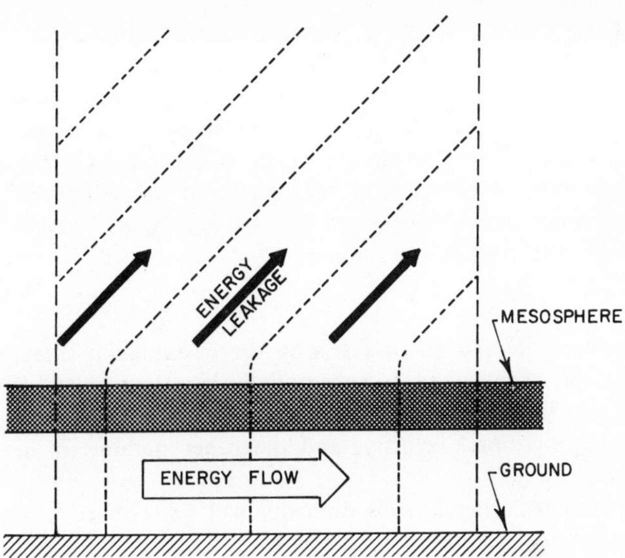

Fig. 6.11 Wave energy trapped below the mesopause may be propagated to great distances without substantial loss; that which does escape to higher levels does so in modes whose phase fronts are inclined forward at the top, and this leads to an apparent downward motion of the disturbance when viewed at a single site.

observations are confined to a single station (Sec. 4.5.1). The situation is illustrated in Fig. 6.11.

6.6. TURBULENCE

Although turbulence is not a strong contender for the explanation of the large-scale irregularities just discussed, its occurrence in the lower part of the upper atmosphere is reasonably well established. Turbulence appears to be necessary, for example, to explain the rapid diffusion of long-enduring meteor trails—a diffusion that proceeds at a much greater rate than can be accounted for on the basis of thermal molecular transport alone [24].

Some question exists as to whether the turbulence required for this might not be produced by the meteor itself, in its flight through the atmosphere. But sodium trails released from rockets also give evidence of turbulence, and numerical estimates of the turbulence energy deduced by this means agree with those obtained from meteor trails, about 10^{-2} watt/kg [25]. Such a coincidence could not be expected unless the energy were in fact intrinsic to the atmosphere itself, unsupplemented by any significant increase due to the passage of the meteor or the rocket.

There is some possibility that the turbulence is modified by the force of gravity and by the corresponding stratification of gas density, but its interpretation to date has been carried out on the basis of ordinary isotropic turbulence theory. A difficulty arises with this interpretation, for the atmosphere is stably stratified and would not be expected to generate turbulence spontaneously. The turbulence energy is then thought to originate in the shearing irregular winds previously discussed, but still a difficulty arises since the available shears appear to be inadequate as judged by a standard criterion: the 'Richardson number,'

$$\mathrm{Ri} \equiv g[dT/dz + (\gamma - 1)T/\gamma H]T^{-1}(dV/dz)^{-2}, \tag{6.22}$$

is commonly employed in assessing the destabilizing effect of shears, and is normally expected to be substantially less than unity before instabilities occur, but the observed values [25] are more of the order 10. (In Eq. 6.22, V is the horizontal velocity, and the other parameters are as previously defined.)

The means whereby this difficulty will be resolved are not yet certain. The relevance of a number such as Ri as a criterion for instability has been called into question [25], and indeed the precise 'critical' value (if one exists) is a matter of some debate; but it seems necessary that the energy should derive from the irregular wind systems and a comparison of the general type provided by Ri, between stabilizing and destabilizing influences, does seem to be required. It has been suggested [1] that a modification of form would be required, however, since the most important irregular winds are likely to be inclined at a substantial angle from the horizontal, whereas Ri itself is concerned only with horizontal winds. The necessary modification should lead to less stringent requirements on the shear and so should lead to a closer compatibility with the observations. A further source of modification arises from the perturbations of temperature that accompany the wind system, if the latter is indeed caused by internal gravity waves, for these perturbations should be included when (6.22) is being evaluated, and they can act to reduce it substantially.

The turbulence terminates abruptly at heights of 100–110 km, and this raises further questions of interpretation. According to one postulate [25], the Reynolds number of conventional hydrodynamic flow theory is relevant, and the termination results from a decrease of this number below some critical value. According to another [1], it results from the disappearance of the smaller-scale members of the wave system at the same heights, for it is these members that lead to the modifications of Ri just discussed.

The occurrence of turbulence, and its termination, bear on two other topics that warrant comment [1]. The rate of dissipation of turbulence energy cited above is adequate to heat the atmosphere at a rate of 1°/day, and enhancements over this value can be expected to occur on occasion or with a change of latitude. This rate is comparable to the heating rate effected directly by solar radiation, so the turbulence may be expected to play a part in establishing the thermal equilibrium of the region. Secondly, it seems probable that the transition from a chemically mixed state to a state of diffusive equilibrium occurs near the height of termination of the turbulence. As the latter varies in strength from time to time, or from one place to another, so the relative composition and the absolute gas density at all greater heights will be modulated.

REFERENCES

1. Hines, C. O., The upper atmosphere in motion, *Quart. J. Roy. Meteorol. Soc.*, **89** (1963), 1.
2. Kochanski, A., Circulation and temperatures at 70- to 100- kilometer height, *J. Geophys. Res.*, **68** (1963), 213.
3. Kochanski, A., Cross sections of the mean zonal flow and temperature along 80° W, *J. Meteorol.*, **12** (1955), 95.
4. Pant, P. S., Circulation in the upper atmosphere, *J. Geophys. Res.*, **61** (1956), 459. (Note: Plates 2 and 3 of this paper are interchanged.)
5. Murgatroyd, R. J., Winds and temperatures between 20 km and 100 km—a review, *Quart. J. Roy. Meteorol. Soc.*, **83** (1957), 417.
6. Murgatroyd, R. J., and R. M. Goody, Sources and sinks of radiative energy from 30 to 90 km, *Quart. J. Roy. Meteorol. Soc.*, **84** (1958), 225.
7. Kellogg, W. W., Chemical heating above the polar mesopause in winter, *J. Meteorol.*, **18** (1961), 373.
8. Elford, W. G., and E. L. Murray, Upper atmosphere wind measurements in the antarctic, in Space Research, ed. H. Kallman-Bijl. Amsterdam: North-Holland Publishing Company, 1960, p. 158.
9. Tohmatsu, T., and T. Nagata, Dynamical studies of the oxygen green line in the airglow, *Planet. Space Sci.*, **10** (1963), 103.
10. Greenhow, J. S., and E. L. Neufeld, The height variation of upper atmospheric winds, *Phil. Mag.*, **1** (1956), 1157.
11. Elford, W. G., A study of winds between 80 and 100 km in medium latitudes, *Planet. Space Sci.*, **1** (1959), 94.
12. Jones, I. L., The height variation of drift in the E region, *J. Atmos. Terr. Phys.*, **12** (1958), 68.
13. Appleton, E. V., and K. Weekes, On lunar tides in the upper atmosphere, *Proc. Roy. Soc., A*, **171** (1939), 171.
14. Matsushita, S., Interrelations of sporadic-E and ionospheric currents, in Ionospheric Sporadic-E, ed. E. K. Smith and S. Matsushita. New York: Pergamon Press, 1962, p. 344.
15. Chapman, S., The semidiurnal oscillation of the atmosphere, *Quart. J. Roy. Meteorol. Soc.*, **50** (1924), 165.

16. Wilkes, M. V., Oscillations of the Earth's Atmosphere. London: Cambridge University Press, 1949.

17. Pekeris, C. L., Atmospheric oscillations, *Proc. Roy. Soc. A*, **158** (1937), 650.

18. Weekes, K., and M. V. Wilkes, Atmospheric oscillations and the resonance theory, *Proc. Roy. Soc. A*, **192** (1947), 80.

19. Butler, S. T., and K. A. Small, The excitation of atmospheric oscillations, *Proc. Roy. Soc., A*, **274** (1963), 91.

20. Hines, C. O., Internal atmospheric gravity waves at ionospheric heights, *Can. J. Phys.*, **38** (1960), 1441.

21. Greenhow, J. S., and E. L. Neufeld, Large scale irregularities in high altitude winds, *Proc. Phys. Soc.*, **75** (1960), 228.

22. Greenhow, J. S., and E. L. Neufeld, Measurements of turbulence in the 80– to 100–km region from the radio echo observations of meteors, *J. Geophys. Res.*, **64** (1959), 2129.

23. Kampe, H. J. aufm, M. E. Smith, and R. M. Brown, Winds between 60 and 110 kilometers, *J. Geophys. Res.*, **67** (1962), 4243.

24. Greenhow, J. S., Eddy diffusion and its effect on meteor trails, *J. Geophys. Res.*, **64** (1959), 2208.

25. Blamont, J. E., and C. de Jager, Upper atmospheric turbulence near the 100 km level, *Ann. Geophys.*, **17** (1961), 134.

26. Liller, W., and F. L. Whipple, High-altitude winds by meteor-train photography, *J. Atmos. Terr. Phys., Spec. Supp.*, **1** (1954), 112.

7

J. A. Fejer

Motions of Ionization

7.1. INTRODUCTION

In the D region, the neutral gas is sufficiently dense to tend to carry with it in its motion any ionization that happens to be present. Such is not necessarily the case in the E region and above, however, for there the ions and electrons are subject to forces that can exceed by a large factor the collisional interaction with the neutral constituents. In this chapter, we turn to a study of the ionization movements at these higher levels.

The importance of charged-particle movements is twofold. Firstly, they lead to ionospheric currents if the mean drift velocities of positive ions and electrons are unequal. Such currents, concentrated mainly in the E region, are thought to be responsible for most of the short-term variations in the earth's magnetic field. Secondly, charged-particle movements redistribute the free electrons produced by solar ionizing radiation, before they are removed by recombination or attachment. The effect of such redistribution on the shape of the layers is particularly great in the F region where the lifetime of free electrons is measured in hours. The effect on the E region is smaller but is nevertheless thought to be appreciable.

The present chapter is divided into four parts. In Sec. 7.2, general expressions for the mean drift velocities of the charged particles are derived theoretically. The results are then used to determine the conductivity and to derive the equations governing ambipolar diffusion in the ionosphere.

In Sec. 7.3, the results of Sec. 7.2 are applied to the discussion of the different atmospheric current systems whose existence is inferred from magnetic observations. Stress is laid on the so-called dynamo current system which is thought to be the main cause of the daily variations (both solar and lunar) of the earth's magnetic field during magnetically quiet days. Other current systems arise, or at least are enhanced, during magnetically disturbed conditions, and they are discussed in later chapters.

It will be shown that, although the dynamo current system is generally restricted to heights below about 150 km, electric fields and electron drifts associated with it extend upward throughout the magnetosphere. The redistribution of electrons that then results, as modified by diffusion, is studied in Sec. 7.4. Stress is laid there on $F2$-layer effects. Finally, in Sec. 7.5 there is a discussion of the motions of ionization due to horizontal winds in the neutral gas.

7.2. THE MEAN VELOCITY OF CHARGED PARTICLES IN THE IONOSPHERE; CONDUCTIVITY AND DIFFUSION

The kinetic theory of gas mixtures leads, after some simplifying assumptions, to certain equations each of which may be interpreted as an equation of motion for one of the constituent gases. These equations of motion have the form [8],

$$N_r m_r \, d\mathbf{c}_r/dt = N_r m_r \mathbf{A}_r + \sum_s \theta_{rs} N_r N_s (\mathbf{c}_s - \mathbf{c}_r) - \nabla p_r \tag{7.1}$$

for the rth constituent gas. Here $d\mathbf{c}_r/dt$ is the total derivative of the local mean velocity $\mathbf{c}_r$ with respect to time; N_r is the number density; m_r, the particle mass; p_r, the partial pressure; and $\mathbf{A}_r$, the body force per unit mass acting on the rth-type particle. Encounters between the rth and sth-type particles are taken into account by a force density

$$\theta_{rs} N_r N_s (\mathbf{c}_s - \mathbf{c}_r)$$

exerted by the sth gas on unit volume of the rth gas. The parameter θ_{rs} characterizes friction between the rth and sth constituent gases and is (at least roughly) independent of the proportions of the mixture. The term ∇p_r represents the gradient of partial pressure which in static equilibrium would be equal to the force term $N_r m_r \mathbf{A}_r$.

In the present chapter, Eq. (7.1) is applied to those large-scale motions of the terrestrial ionosphere in which changes take place very slowly. In this 'quasi-equilibrium' case the inertial term on the left in (7.1) may be neglected.

The gas is arbitrarily divided into three constituents: singly charged positive ions, electrons, and neutrals. The ions and the neutrals are each assumed to consist of a single type of particle, and ion-electron collisions are neglected. This latter assumption is certainly permissible in a sufficiently weakly ionized gas, where collisions of charged with neutral particles predominate over collisions between charged particles. Below a height of 150 km or so, the ionosphere meets this criterion. Subsequent arguments will show that, for purposes of the present chapter, the neglect of ion-electron collisions remains a good approximation even at greater heights.

With the foregoing assumption, Eq. (7.1) for electrons may be written in the form

$$N_e m_e \mathbf{A}_e + N_e m_e \nu_e (\mathbf{c}_n - \mathbf{c}_e) - \nabla p_e = 0, \tag{7.2}$$

where the subscript e indicates electrons and the subscript n neutral particles. The notation $N_n \theta_{en} = m_e \nu_e$ is used. A similar equation for ions may be obtained by changing the subscripts e to i. The quantity ν_e (or ν_i) is closely related to (although in the case of ions it may differ by a factor of two from) the mean frequency of collisions of an electron (or an ion) with molecules of the neutral gas, and is often termed the 'collision frequency.'

In the ionosphere the force term $m_e \mathbf{A}_e$ is given by

$$m_e \mathbf{A}_e = q_e(\mathbf{E} + \mathbf{c}_e \times \mathbf{B}) + m_e \mathbf{g} \tag{7.3}$$

where q_e is the charge of an electron, $\mathbf{E}$ and $\mathbf{B}$ are the usual electric and magnetic field vectors, and $\mathbf{g}$ is the gravitational acceleration. Combination of (7.2) and (7.3) leads to the equation of motion of the electron gas

$$q_e(\mathbf{E} + \mathbf{c}_e \times \mathbf{B}) + m_e \mathbf{g} + m_e \nu_e (\mathbf{c}_n - \mathbf{c}_e) - N^{-1} \nabla p_e = 0 \tag{7.4}$$

where $N = N_e \simeq N_i$ since neutrality must be very nearly preserved. A similar equation may be written for the ions. It is sometimes convenient to introduce the relative velocity $\mathbf{v}_e = \mathbf{c}_e - \mathbf{c}_n$ of electrons with respect to the neutral gas and simplify notation by writing $\mathbf{u}$ instead of $\mathbf{c}_n$ for the velocity of the neutral gas. Then Eq. (7.4) assumes the form

$$q_e(\mathbf{E} + \mathbf{u} \times \mathbf{B} + \mathbf{v}_e \times \mathbf{B}) + m_e \mathbf{g} - m_e \nu_e \mathbf{v}_e - N^{-1} \nabla p_e = 0. \tag{7.5}$$

With the notation

$$\mathbf{F}_e \equiv q_e(\mathbf{E} + \mathbf{u} \times \mathbf{B}) + m_e \mathbf{g} - N^{-1} \nabla p_e, \tag{7.6}$$

Eq. (7.5) may be written as

$$m_e \nu_e \mathbf{v}_e - q_e(\mathbf{v}_e \times \mathbf{B}) = \mathbf{F}_e, \tag{7.7}$$

where the quantity $\mathbf{F}_e$ defined by (7.6) has the dimension of force. The first term $q_e (\mathbf{E} + \mathbf{u} \times \mathbf{B})$ on the right of (7.6) is the force exerted on an electron by the electric field $\mathbf{E} + \mathbf{u} \times \mathbf{B}$ that would be seen by an observer moving with the neutral gas. The field $\mathbf{u} \times \mathbf{B}$ is often called the 'dynamo field,' since it corresponds to the field seen by the armature of a dynamo moving at velocity **u** in a magnetic field of induction **B**, and it leads to currents in the same fashion. The second term on the right of (7.6) is the gravitational force acting on the electrons. The third term, which represents the effect of partial pressure, is important in the calculation of ambipolar diffusion.

If the force term $\mathbf{F}_e$ is known, then Eq. (7.7) determines the mean relative drift velocity $\mathbf{v}_e$ of the electrons. This velocity can be obtained for example by solving the three component equations of the vector Eq. (7.7) for the unknown cartesian components $v_{e\xi}, v_{e\eta}, v_{e\zeta}$. It is often convenient to employ for this purpose a coordinate system ξ, η, ζ, whose positive ζ axis is directed along **B** and whose η axis is perpendicular to $\mathbf{F}_e$. Then

$$v_{e\xi} = \frac{F_{e\xi}}{m_e} \frac{\nu_e}{\nu_e^2 + \omega_e^2}, \qquad v_{e\eta} = -\frac{F_{e\xi}}{m_e} \frac{\omega_e}{\nu_e^2 + \omega_e^2}, \qquad v_{e\zeta} = \frac{F_{e\zeta}}{m_e \nu_e}, \tag{7.8}$$

where $\omega_e = q_e B/m_e$ is the 'gyrofrequency' of electrons, including the sign (that is, ω_e is negative). A similar set of equations, with only the subscripts altered, applies to the mean drift velocity of the positive ions (but ω_i will be positive).

At ionospheric heights $-\omega_e \simeq 7 \times 10^6 \text{ sec}^{-1}$, whence $|\omega_e| \simeq \nu_e$ at a height of about 70 km (see Fig. 3.13). At heights sufficiently below 70 km, $\nu_e \gg |\omega_e|$ and Eqs. (7.8) are well approximated by

$$v_{e\xi} = F_{e\xi}/m_e \nu_e, \qquad v_{e\eta} = 0, \qquad v_{e\zeta} = F_{e\zeta}/m_e \nu_e. \tag{7.9}$$

The electrons then drift relative to the neutral gas in the direction of the force $\mathbf{F}_e$, with a relative velocity which is inversely proportional to the collision frequence ν_e. For a constant $\mathbf{F}_e$ this velocity will of course increase with increasing height since the density of neutral particles and hence ν_e decreases. In this approximation ($\nu_e \gg |\omega_e|$) the magnetic field has no effect on the mobility of the electron.

At heights sufficiently above 70 km, $\nu_e \ll |\omega_e|$ and Eqs. (7.8) are well approximated by

$$v_{e\xi} = 0, \qquad v_{e\eta} = -F_{e\xi}/m_e \omega_e, \qquad v_{e\zeta} = F_{e\zeta}/m_e \nu_e. \tag{7.10}$$

Equations (7.10) show that the drift velocity that is parallel to the magnetic field and caused by the parallel component of a constant driving force $\mathbf{F}_e$ continues to increase with height above 70 km, since again the collision frequency continues to decrease. The transverse component of the driving force, however, generates a drift which is perpendicular both to the driving force and to the magnetic field. The drift velocity is now independent of the collision frequency and thus, for constant $F_{e\xi}$ and for a uniform magnetic field, is independent of the height.

The continuous upward increase of $v_{e\zeta}/F_{e\zeta}$ would lead ultimately to an infinitely high electrical conductivity along the magnetic field lines, as will be seen shortly. In practice, however, the collisions between charged particles that were previously neglected will act to limit this conductivity at heights above about 200 km. Nevertheless, even if ion-electron collisions are taken into account, the conductivity parallel to the field remains many orders of magnitude higher than the conductivity perpendicular to the field, and for purposes of the present chapter the assumption of an infinitely high conductivity parallel to the field remains a sufficiently good approximation.

With the aid of Eq. (7.8) for the drift velocity of electrons and the corresponding equation for ions, the steady-state conductivity of the ionosphere may be calculated. In this calculation, the second and third terms on the right of Eq. (7.6), which are usually very much smaller than the first term, are neglected and the notation $\mathbf{E}_t = \mathbf{E} + \mathbf{u} \times \mathbf{B}$ is introduced. The 'total electric field' $\mathbf{E}_t$ is thus defined as the sum of the electrostatic field $\mathbf{E}$ (due to polarization charges) and of the dynamo field $\mathbf{u} \times \mathbf{B}$. It is the electric field seen by an observer who moves with the neutral gas. Equation (7.8) then assumes the form

$$v_{e\xi} = \frac{E_{t\xi}}{B} \frac{\nu_e \omega_e}{\nu_e^2 + \omega_e^2}, \qquad v_{e\eta} = \frac{-E_{t\xi}}{B} \frac{\omega_e^2}{\nu_e^2 + \omega_e^2}, \qquad v_{e\zeta} = \frac{E_{t\zeta}}{B} \frac{\omega_e}{\nu_e}, \tag{7.11}$$

and similar equations apply to ions. Figure 7.1(a), based on representative values of the collision and gyrofrequencies for middle latitudes, shows $v_{e\xi}B/E_{t\xi}$, $v_{e\eta}B/E_{t\xi}$, $v_{e\zeta}B/E_{t\zeta}$, $v_{i\xi}B/E_{t\xi}$, $v_{i\eta}B/E_{t\xi}$, and $v_{i\zeta}B/E_{t\zeta}$ as functions of the height [6].

Also marked on Fig. 7.1(a) is the height z_e for which $\nu_e = |\omega_e|$ and the height z_i for which $\nu_i = \omega_i$ in the model assumed. It may be seen that the heights z_e and z_i represent transitions for the motion of electrons and ions respectively. Below the critical height z_e, the ions move relative to the neutral gas at the velocity $\mathbf{E}_t q_i/m_i\nu_i$ in the direction of the electric field, whereas the electrons move at the much greater velocity $\mathbf{E}_t q_e/m_e\nu_e$ in the opposite direction; the magnetic field has no influence beyond that already included in $\mathbf{E}_t$. Above the critical height z_i, particles of both signs move with a common drift speed $E_{t\xi}/B$, or a common drift velocity $\mathbf{E}_t \times \mathbf{B}/B^2$, in a direction perpendicular to both the electric and the magnetic fields. (This expression gives the transverse drift velocity with respect to the neutral gas; $\mathbf{E} \times \mathbf{B}/B^2$ is the corresponding drift velocity with respect to the coordinate system in which $\mathbf{E}$ is measured.) In addition, the particles move parallel to the magnetic field at velocities which are independent of that field and which, for a given parallel component of the electric field, continue to increase with height.

In the intermediate height range between z_e and z_i, only the electrons move with the drift velocity $\mathbf{E}_t \times \mathbf{B}/B^2$, whereas the ions remain almost stationary in comparison. The resulting current, which flows in a direction perpendicular to both the electric and the magnetic fields, is called the 'Hall current.'

The current density $\mathbf{J}$ in the medium is given by $\mathbf{J} = N(q_e\mathbf{v}_e + q_i\mathbf{v}_i)$.

After substitution of $\mathbf{v}_e$ from Eq. (7.11) and $\mathbf{v}_i$ from the corresponding equation for ions, the current density is given by

$$J_\xi = E_{t\xi}\frac{Ne}{B}\left[\frac{\nu_i\omega_i}{\nu_i^2+\omega_i^2} - \frac{\nu_e\omega_e}{\nu_e^2+\omega_e^2}\right] = \sigma_1 E_{t\xi}, \tag{7.12 a}$$

$$J_\eta = E_{t\xi}\frac{Ne}{B}\left[\frac{\omega_e^2}{\nu_e^2+\omega_e^2} - \frac{\omega_i^2}{\nu_i^2+\omega_i^2}\right] = \sigma_2 E_{t\xi}, \tag{7.12 b}$$

$$J_\zeta = E_{t\zeta}\frac{Ne}{B}\left[\frac{\omega_i}{\nu_i} - \frac{\omega_e}{\nu_e}\right] = \sigma_0 E_{t\zeta}, \tag{7.12 c}$$

where $e = q_i = -q_e$ is assumed and where, as before, the gyrofrequencies ω_e and ω_i differ in sign.

These equations may be written in a somewhat more general form which permits the inclusion of an η component of the electric field

$$\mathbf{J} = \boldsymbol{\sigma} \cdot \mathbf{E}_t \tag{7.13}$$

where $\boldsymbol{\sigma}$ is a tensor given by

$$\boldsymbol{\sigma} \equiv \begin{bmatrix} \sigma_1 & -\sigma_2 & 0 \\ \sigma_2 & \sigma_1 & 0 \\ 0 & 0 & \sigma_0 \end{bmatrix} \tag{7.14}$$

in a coordinate system whose third axis is aligned in the direction of **B**. Equations (7.12a), (7.12b), and (7.12c) or Eqs. (7.13) and (7.14) determine the current that flows in the presence of a known total electric field. Three different conductivities are defined by Eqs. (7.12a), (7.12b), and (7.12c). The conductivity σ_0, which determines the current parallel to the magnetic lines of force, is that which would exist for all directions in the absence of the magnetic field. The conductivity σ_1, often called the 'Pedersen conductivity,' must be used to calculate the current parallel to that component of the electric field which is normal to the magnetic field. The Hall conductivity σ_2 determines the current which flows in a direction perpendicular to both the electric and the magnetic fields. Figure 7.1(b) shows $\sigma_0 B/Ne$, $\sigma_1 B/Ne$, and $\sigma_2 B/Ne$ as functions of the height for the same values of the collision and gyrofrequencies as were used in Fig. 7.1(a). In the F region and above, σ_0 is extremely large in comparison with σ_1 and σ_2, which become vanishingly small. It may then be inferred that $\mathbf{E}_t$ cannot be maintained with any substantial component along the magnetic field lines, and hence that the latter are very nearly lines of constant potential.

The steady-state current carried along a tube of force must be virtually independent of position on the tube, in the F region and above, since the current is strongly inhibited from flowing across the field lines and out of the tube. Whatever current is poured into the tube of force at one end, say in the northern hemisphere, must consequently pour out of it at the opposite end in the southern hemisphere. We may then simplify our further discussions by picturing a horizontal current system which flows in a relatively

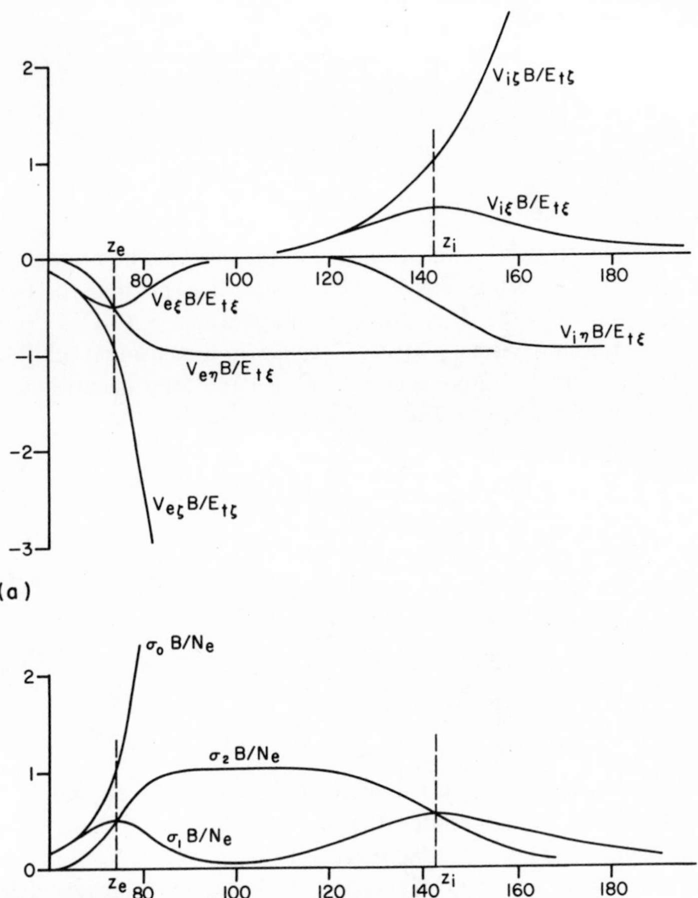

Fig. 7.1 (a) Components of the ionospheric drift velocities of positive ions and electrons in uniform electric and magnetic fields, as functions of the height. The curves represent certain dimensionless quantities, indicated by the labels and defined in the text, which are proportional to the drift velocity components of ions and electrons. (b) The dimensionless quantities, $\sigma_0 B/Ne$, $\sigma_1 B/Ne$, and $\sigma_2 B/Ne$, which are proportional to the ionospheric conductivities, σ_0, σ_1, and σ_2, as functions of the height.

thin spherical shell in the *E* and *D* regions and has conjugate sources and sinks in the northern and southern hemispheres.

If symmetry about the geomagnetic equator is assumed, both of the wind system and of the conductivity, then no currents flow along the tubes of force in the *F* region and above; the current system is constrained to flow entirely in the thin spherical shell provided by the *D* and *E* regions.

In this special case, the vertical current density can be ignored at all heights. It is then more convenient to use a coordinate system whose x, y, and z axes point to the south, the east, and the zenith respectively. In this new coordinate system, the components of the tensor $\boldsymbol{\sigma}$ are given by

$$\boldsymbol{\sigma} \equiv \begin{bmatrix} \sigma_1 \sin^2 I + \sigma_0 \cos^2 I, & \sigma_2 \sin I, & (\sigma_0 - \sigma_1) \sin I \cos I \\ -\sigma_2 \sin I, & \sigma_1, & \sigma_2 \cos I \\ (\sigma_0 - \sigma_1) \sin I \cos I, & -\sigma_2 \cos I, & \sigma_1 \cos^2 I + \sigma_0 \sin^2 I \end{bmatrix}, \tag{7.15}$$

where I is the magnetic dip angle (positive in the *northern* hemisphere).

Since the vertical current density J_z vanishes, it is possible to eliminate E_{tz} (for example) from the three component equations of (7.13), written in the x, y, z coordinate system. This leads to a two-dimensional relationship between the horizontal components E_{tx}, E_{ty} of the total electric field and J_x, J_y of the current density. This relationship may be written in the form,

$$J_x = \sigma_{xx} E_{tx} + \sigma_{xy} E_{ty}, \tag{7.16 a}$$

$$J_y = -\sigma_{xy} E_{tx} + \sigma_{yy} E_{ty}, \tag{7.16 b}$$

where

$$\sigma_{xx} = K^{-1} \sigma_1 \sigma_0, \tag{7.17 a}$$

$$\sigma_{xy} = K^{-1} \sigma_2 \sigma_0 \sin I, \tag{7.17 b}$$

$$\sigma_{yy} = K^{-1} (\sigma_1 \sigma_0 \sin^2 I + \sigma_1 \sigma_3 \cos^2 I), \tag{7.17 c}$$

$$K = \sigma_1 \cos^2 I + \sigma_0 \sin^2 I, \tag{7.17 d}$$

$$\sigma_3 = \sigma_1 + \sigma_2^2/\sigma_1. \tag{7.17 e}$$

Here σ_{xx}, σ_{xy}, σ_{yy} may be regarded as the components of a two-dimensional conductivity tensor which relates the horizontal current density to the horizontal components of the total electric field.

In the special case where $\mathbf{E}_t$ is independent of height, the height-integrated conductivity tensor with components $\int \sigma_{xx}\, dz$, $\int \sigma_{xy}\, dz$, $\int \sigma_{yy}\, dz$ relates the height-integrated horizontal current density $\int \mathbf{J}\, dz$ to the horizontal component of the total electric field. These components, which play an important part in theories of the dynamo current system [3, 12] are shown by Fig. 7.2 for typical midday conditions. Over most parts of the earth, the height-integrated conductivity $\int \sigma_{xy}\, dz$ is seen to predominate. At the magnetic dip equator, however, $\int \sigma_{xy}\, dz$ vanishes, and the height-integrated conductivities $\int \sigma_{xx}\, dz$, $\int \sigma_{yy}\, dz$ assume very large values. These large values are believed to be the cause of the observed very high values of the magnetic solar variation *Sq* and lunar variation *L* near the magnetic dip equator.

In the foregoing treatment of ionospheric conductivity, the gravitational and the pressure terms in Eq. (7.6) were arbitrarily neglected. These two terms are much smaller than the first term on the right of Eq. (7.6) and their

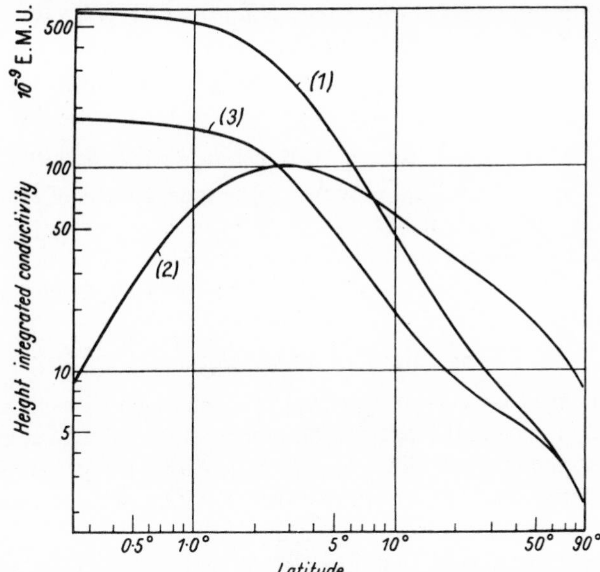

Fig. 7.2 The height-integrated conductivities (1) $\int \sigma_{xx} dz$, (2) $\int \sigma_{xy} dz$, and (3) $\int \sigma_{yy} dz$ as functions of the latitude. (After Fejer [12].)

neglect may seem always justified. More careful consideration shows, however, that the effect of these two neglected terms can be important for some purposes in the F region and above. This may be seen by the application of (7.10) and the corresponding equation for ions. Symmetry about the equator will again be assumed, so that the component of the current density parallel to the magnetic field in the F region and above may be set equal to zero.

The pressure and gravitational terms in the η component of Eq. (7.10) cause very weak currents, which are normally negligible and which will be ignored here. The η component of (7.10) then reduces once again to

$$v_{e\eta} \simeq v_{i\eta} \simeq -E_{t\xi}/B. \tag{7.18}$$

In vector notation this common transverse drift velocity, measured with respect to the neutral gas, is given by $\mathbf{E}_t \times \mathbf{B}/B^2$; the corresponding drift velocity with respect to the coordinate system in which $\mathbf{E}$ is measured, is $\mathbf{E} \times \mathbf{B}/B^2$.

In the ζ component of Eq. (7.10) and the corresponding equation for ions, the pressure and gravitational terms cannot be neglected. The condition $v_{e\zeta} = v_{i\zeta} = v_\zeta$ (which follows from $\mathbf{J} = 0$), combined with Eqs. (7.6) and (7.10) and the corresponding equations for ions, leads to

$$m_e \nu_e v_\zeta = F_{e\zeta} = -eE_\zeta + m_e g \sin I - N^{-1} \, \partial p_e/\partial \zeta, \tag{7.19}$$

$$m_i \nu_i v_\zeta = F_{i\zeta} = eE_\zeta + m_i g \sin I - N^{-1} \, \partial p_i/\partial \zeta, \tag{7.20}$$

where I is again the magnetic dip angle. Addition of Eqs. (7.19) and (7.20) and substitution of $p_e = p_i = kTN$ (where k is Boltzmann's constant and T is the temperature, assumed equal for ions and electrons) results in the velocity of 'ambipolar diffusion' along the lines of force

$$v_\xi = (m_e \nu_e + m_i \nu_i)^{-1}[(m_e + m_i)g + 2N^{-1}k\,\partial(TN)/\partial z] \sin I, \qquad (7.21)$$

where z is the height and TN is assumed to be independent of latitude. The vertical (upward) component of v_ξ, v_z, is given by $v_z = -v_\xi \sin I$. After the assumption of isothermal conditions and the introduction of the dimensionless height $h = z/H$, where $H = kT/m_i g$ is the ion scale height, Eq. (7.21) may be rewritten as

$$v_z = -(g/\nu_i)[1 + (2/N)(\partial N/\partial h)] \sin^2 I, \qquad (7.22)$$

where m_e and $m_e \nu_e$ have been neglected in comparison with m_i and $m_i \nu_i$. Equation (7.22) indicates the vertical component of the velocity of ambipolar diffusion along the magnetic lines of force, caused by the gravitational and the pressure terms in (7.6). Its practical application will be discussed in Sec. 7.4.

It must be remembered that Eqs. (7.18) and (7.21) indicate the drift velocity with respect to the neutral medium, which itself may move with a velocity $\mathbf{u}$ with respect to the earth. The assumption $\mathbf{u} = 0$ is usually made for the F region, and then Eqs. (7.18), (7.21), and (7.22) indicate velocities with respect to the earth.

7.3. THE DYNAMO THEORY

A wide variety of short-term fluctuations of the earth's magnetic field have been observed. Some of these are associated with solar corpuscular activity and are discussed in later parts of this book. Other more regular variations of a diurnal nature are related to the solar and the lunar day; they will be treated here.

Balfour Stewart [23] suggested that motions of the atmosphere induced by solar heating cause the small daily variations of the earth's magnetic field on magnetically quiet days. In his dynamo theory it is assumed that the air in the uppeı atmosphere is highly conducting and that currents are induced by dynamo action in this conducting air as it moves across the magnetic field of the earth. The solar component Sq and the much smaller lunar component L of the observed magnetic variations are supposed by the theory to be caused by the magnetic fields of these upper atmospheric currents. Figure 7.3 shows the current system which, if flowing at a height of 100 km, would produce the (average) observed Sq magnetic variations.

When the dynamo theory was first formulated mathematically [5, 22], little was known about the conductivity or the movements of the upper atmosphere. As more data on ionospheric electron densities became available from ionosonde records, the dynamo theory was successively revised [3, 12, 14, 15, 16]. These revisions take the anisotropic nature of ionospheric conductivity into account and show that the observed upper atmospheric wind velocities, electron densities, and magnetic variations are at least approximately consistent with each other in terms of the dynamo theory. Despite difficulties of detail which remain to be explored, that theory is at the moment the one most widely held.

Two theoretical approaches have been used to demonstrate its internal consistency. In the first approach the wind velocities and the conductivity are assumed; the resulting current system and magnetic variations are then calculated. In the second approach the observed magnetic variations provide the starting point and a conductivity distribution is assumed; the current system, the total electric field required to drive the current, and finally the wind velocities are calculated.

The first approach has the disadvantage that the dependence of upper atmospheric wind velocities on height and geographical position is not very well known. This disadvantage is avoided to some extent in the second approach which starts from the much better-known magnetic data. The second approach does retain certain arbitrary assumptions about the wind velocity and its height dependence, however, and the accuracy of its deductions is limited as a result. In both cases uncertainties as to the distribution of conductivities introduce further limitations.

In the first approach the problem is usually simplified by assuming the wind system to be symmetrical about the equator, and by supposing that

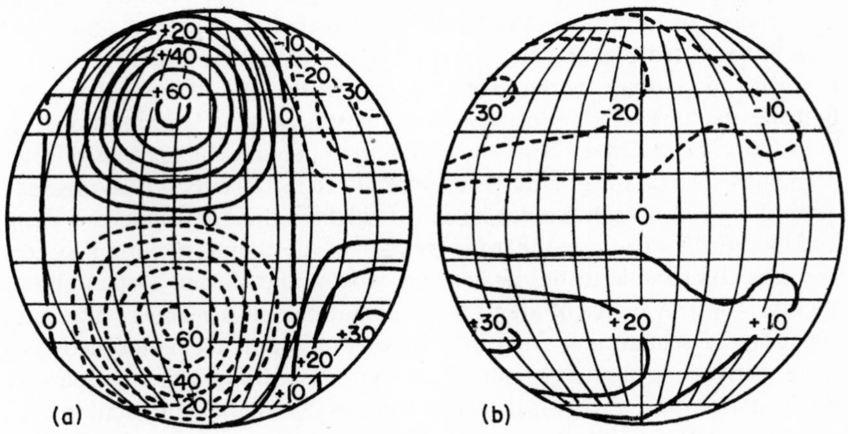

Fig. 7.3 Upper atmospheric current system over the sunlit hemisphere (a) and the night hemisphere (b) at a height of 100 km which may produce the observed *Sq* variation of magnetic elements during the equinoxes. A current of 10,000 amp flows between adjacent lines. (After Chapman and Bartels [7].)

the unperturbed geomagnetic field is that of a dipole at the center of the earth. The geomagnetic and geographical axes (and coordinates) are taken as identical. The current density at any point in the ionosphere is then given by

$$\mathbf{J} = \mathbf{J}_h = \boldsymbol{\sigma}_h \cdot \mathbf{E}_{th} = \boldsymbol{\sigma}_h \cdot [\mathbf{E}_h + (\mathbf{u} \times \mathbf{B})_h], \tag{7.23}$$

where the tensor $\boldsymbol{\sigma}_h$ is the two-dimensional tensor of Eqs. (7.16) and (7.17) and where the subscript h of the vector quantities signifies the horizontal components, treated as two-dimensional vectors. The horizontal component $\mathbf{E}_h$ of the unknown electrostatic field $\mathbf{E}$ may then be expressed as $\mathbf{E}_h = -\text{grad}\,\psi$ where ψ is the two-dimensional electrostatic potential on the thin current-carrying ionospheric shell.

In the quasi-stationary state, the (two-dimensional) divergence of the height-integrated current density in the ionospheric shell must vanish if the very small currents needed to build up the polarization charges, which are the sources of $\mathbf{E}$, are neglected. The equation div $(\int \mathbf{J}_h\,dz) = 0$ leads, after substitution of $\mathbf{J}_h$ from (7.23), to

$$\text{div}\left[\int \boldsymbol{\sigma}_h\,dz \cdot \text{grad}\,\psi\right] = \text{div}\left[\int \boldsymbol{\sigma}_h \cdot (\mathbf{u} \times \mathbf{B})_h\,dz\right]. \tag{7.24}$$

Equation (7.24) is a partial differential equation for the potential function ψ as a function of the latitude and local time. If the solution for ψ has been obtained, then the dynamo current density is given by (7.23).

The differential Eq. (7.24) has been further simplified by some authors [12, 15] by neglecting the diurnal variation of electron density; that is, by assuming that $\boldsymbol{\sigma}_h$ is a function only of the latitude and the height and is independent of local time. The longitudinal variation of grad ψ and $\mathbf{u}$ can then be separated out, and Eq. (7.24) becomes an ordinary differential equation with the latitude as the independent variable. The further assumption is made that the wind velocity in the ionospheric shell is proportional to the wind velocity derived from the semidiurnal pressure fluctuations of solar origin observed on the ground. The factor of proportionality is then regarded as an unknown constant, independent of height within the conducting shell, and its value is so adjusted that the strength of the computed current system becomes comparable to the semidiurnal part of the current system shown by Fig. 7.3(a). A factor of about 60 is obtained in this manner. The ratio between the semidiurnal wind velocities observed in the ionosphere and those derived from the pressure fluctuations on the ground is not very different from this theoretical factor. The results of the computation thus support the viewpoint that the magnetic variations are due to dynamo action.

The second approach has been used by other authors [14, 16] who took the diurnal variation of conductivity into account. This approach starts from a current system similar to that of Fig. 7.3. A height-integrated con-

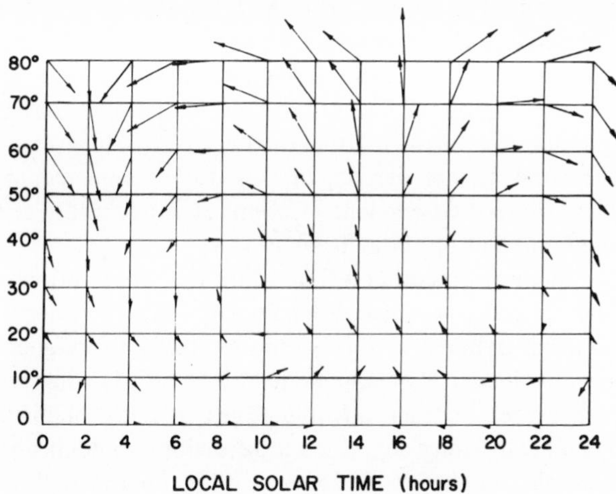

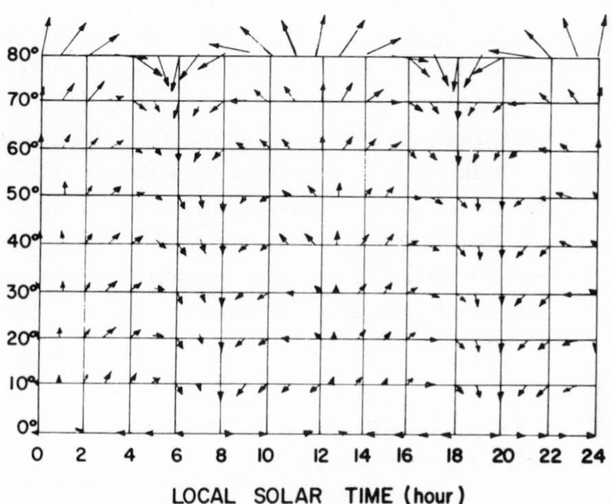

Fig. 7.4 Diurnal and semidiurnal wind systems in the dynamo region, as inferred from equinoctial magnetic variations. (After Kato [14].) Each chart depicts the northern hemisphere, but the winds of the southern hemisphere can be inferred by symmetry.

ductivity tensor, whose components $\int \sigma_{xx}\,dz$, $\int \sigma_{yy}\,dz$, and $\int \sigma_{xy}\,dz$ are functions of both latitude and local time, is assumed. The horizontal component $\mathbf{E}_{th} = \mathbf{E}_h + (\mathbf{u} \times \mathbf{B})_h$ of the total electric field $\mathbf{E}_t$ is determined with the aid of Eq. (7.16) from the current system, on the assumption that the wind velocity is independent of the height within the conducting shell. The additional assumption is made by one worker [16] that the wind velocity may be derived from a velocity potential. A partial differential equation for this velocity potential is derived from (7.24) and is solved numerically by expansion into spherical harmonics.

The assumption of a velocity potential in the foregoing analysis is equivalent to the neglect of Coriolis forces. In a somewhat modified but essentially similar treatment [14] the Coriolis forces have been taken into account. The wind system derived in this way is depicted in Fig. 7.4; it exhibits a large diurnal component of about 30 m/sec and a relatively weak semidiurnal component of about 10 m/sec.

Both the theoretical computations and the observations need to be carried further in order to test the dynamo hypothesis in detail. It is by no means certain that dynamo action is the only cause of magnetic variations. The distortion of the earth's magnetic field by a steady solar wind, depicted in Fig. 1.5, provides another possible cause of daily magnetic variations during a magnetically quiet day. Such a distortion would probably increase the magnetic field on the day side more than on the night side, and an observer on the ground would therefore see a diurnal variation. In these circumstances, the pertinent currents would be flowing at the outer boundary of the magnetosphere, well above the heights of present concern. The relevance of such currents, in competition with those of the dynamo system, has yet to be investigated in any detail for quiet conditions.

It should be pointed out here that, during magnetically disturbed periods, there are daily magnetic variations caused by currents (the so-called *DS* currents) which are believed to flow at much the same height as the dynamo currents but which are almost certainly not due to atmospheric dynamo action. (These magnetic variations, which are most intense in the auroral zone, are discussed observationally in Chapter 12 and theoretically in Chapter 15.)

7.4 THE EFFECT OF CHARGED-PARTICLE DRIFTS ON ELECTRON CONCENTRATION

It may be recalled from Chapter 4 that the shape of the *F*2 layer and certain of its anomalous features can be described only imperfectly on the basis of electron production and loss mechanisms alone, and that movements of the ionization are believed to be responsible for much of the remaining discrepancy. These movements arise from a variety of causes, and produce a correspondingly varied range of effects. The principal ones are reviewed here.

It was shown in Sec. 7.2 that if the neutral gas in the *F* region is assumed stationary, then the vertical velocity caused by diffusion is given by Eq. (7.22). The presence of the collision frequency ν_i in the denominator on the right of (7.22) leads to the important conclusion that the velocity caused by diffusion can become important at heights where there are relatively few neutral particles. This diffusive velocity, acting through the divergence term in the continuity equation,

$$\partial N/\partial t = \text{(production rate)} - \text{(loss rate)} - \text{div}\,(N\mathbf{v}), \qquad (7.25)$$

is thought to be essential in a description of the $F2$-layer shape.

The term in the square bracket on the right of Eq. (7.22) vanishes for a plasma which is in diffusive equilibrium in the gravitational field. Such equilibrium is thought to be nearly established at heights well above the F-layer peak, and the plasma density is then believed to decrease with increasing height at a rate determined by the appropriate scale height. At much lower heights diffusion is ineffective, and, as mentioned before, the decrease of the attachment coefficient causes the electron number density to increase with increasing height. Clearly a peak in the electron density must be established at some intermediate level. At moderate latitudes detailed analysis of Eqs. (7.22) and (7.25) shows [25] that the peak is formed at approximately 300 km. This height is not very different from the observed heights of the peak.

Near the magnetic dip equator diffusion is greatly reduced by the horizontal magnetic field [20] as the factor $\sin^2 I$ in (7.22) indicates. Theory then leads to the expectation that the peak of the $F2$ layer would be formed at a much greater height near the equator than at moderate latitudes. Observations confirm this prediction.

There are many other unusual aspects of $F2$-layer behavior which are not explained directly by the foregoing considerations. Martyn has suggested that many of these so-called anomalies may be caused by plasma drifts, with velocity $\mathbf{E} \times \mathbf{B}/B^2$ as from Eq. (7.18), engendered by the electric fields produced at dynamo levels, and he has successfully demonstrated lunar tidal variations in the virtual height and critical frequency of the $F2$ layer that can be attributed to this cause [18]. A corresponding analysis of drift effects induced by the solar tide is more difficult, because of complications introduced by the diurnally varying rate of electron production, but some attempts have been made.

Maeda [17], for example, has applied the results of dynamo analysis to the calculation of drifts in the F region and thence, with further assumptions about the production and loss processes, to a study of layer deformations. His results display some of the observed anomalies in the $F2$ layer—in particular, the so-called geomagnetic anomaly described in Chapter 4—but they are as yet of doubtful value because they depend critically on the assumptions made about the loss processes, and commonly accepted loss coefficients differ considerably from those employed by Maeda and cast doubt on the close agreement with observation he obtained.

An extension of the drift analysis has been proposed by Duncan [10], with specific application to the geomagnetic anomaly. He suggests that, near the geomagnetic equator, electrons are raised from the $F2$ layer to high levels by upward drift in the morning hours and then are driven by diffusion back down along the geomagnetic field lines to the $F2$ layer at higher latitudes, some ten or more degrees from the dip equator. Although this picture accounts qualitatively for the observations (see Sec. 5.3.4.), a more quantitative formulation will be necessary before it can be properly assessed.

The validity of the assumption implicit in all the foregoing theories, that the neutral air velocity remains vanishingly small in the *F* region despite the presence of drifting charged particles, has recently been questioned [9]. It has been pointed out that the drifting charged particles may, over a period of the order of hours, set the neutral air into motion and that this would in turn modify the motion of the charged particles. If the extreme assumption is made that the neutral particles move with the same horizontal velocity as the positive ions, then the predictions of the theory are very different. First of all, the factor $\sin^2 I$ disappears from Eq. (7.22) for ambipolar diffusion; secondly, the vertical drift velocity caused by the dynamo electric field vanishes. This extreme assumption is certainly not quite valid, but the opposite assumption of vanishingly small neutral air velocity in the *F* region is probably even less so.

It is safe to conclude that, although past investigations have established the importance of electromagnetic drifts in the *F*2 layer, the detailed nature of their effects is not yet known.

The foregoing discussion was restricted to those electromagnetic drifts which are generated indirectly by the tidal air motions. The arrival of solar particle streams in the vicinity of the earth generates similar drifts, associated with electric fields perpendicular to the lines of force, in the *F*2 layer and above. These drifts are associated with the *DS* current system mentioned at the end of Sec. 7.3, and this current system is discussed in Chapter 12.

Vertical drifts in the *E* layer are not as important as those in the *F* layer, because of the much shorter lifetime of the ionization and the greater drag of the neutral gas. Nevertheless, certain observed deviations from the simple Chapman-like layer characteristics are attributed to such drifts, generated again by the dynamo system [4]. The pertinent theory [1] shows that the drift motion itself leads always to a decrease in the peak electron density, although a vertical gradient in that drift can result in an increase or a decrease depending on the sense of the gradient. Since both increases and decreases are observed, varying with latitude, it appears necessary to assume that gradients are important.

7.5. VERTICAL DRIFTS DUE TO HORIZONTAL WINDS IN THE NEUTRAL GAS

As discussed in the preceding chapter, there is strong evidence of horizontal motions in the neutral gas at ionospheric levels. These can set the ionization into motion through collisional interaction, but the electrodynamic complications discussed in the present chapter then modify the motion. An important example is provided by the case of vertical shears in the horizontal motion, which can lead to the formation of dense ionized layers. The process was discussed initially, in its simplest form, by Dungey [11], in a manner illustrated by Fig. 7.5. At sufficiently great heights (above the E region), the charged particles are constrained to move along the lines of force of the magnetic field (dashed slanting lines). The horizontal neutral wind shown therefore forces the charged particles to move along the field lines in the direction of the small arrows. These motions cause an accumulation of charged particles in the vicinity of the dashed horizontal line where the wind reverses direction. Certain types of sporadic-E layers may be explained by this process although the theory for the E region [2, 24] is more complicated than the foregoing approximate considerations would indicate.

If the level at which the reversal in wind direction takes place changes with time, then the height of the dense ionized layer formed by the above process also changes. Such would be the case if the wind shears were produced by the internal atmospheric gravity waves discussed in the preceding chapter. It will be recalled that their phase velocity is approximately in the downward direction if the energy is propagating upward, and they could then generate downward-moving dense ionized strata by the foregoing process. Such downward-moving strata are often observed between the E and the F layers. It is interesting to note that in this case the ionization is actually trapped at the level of wind reversal and is carried downward with it, so that a true vertical convection of ions is produced by a purely oscillatory motion of the neutral gas [2].

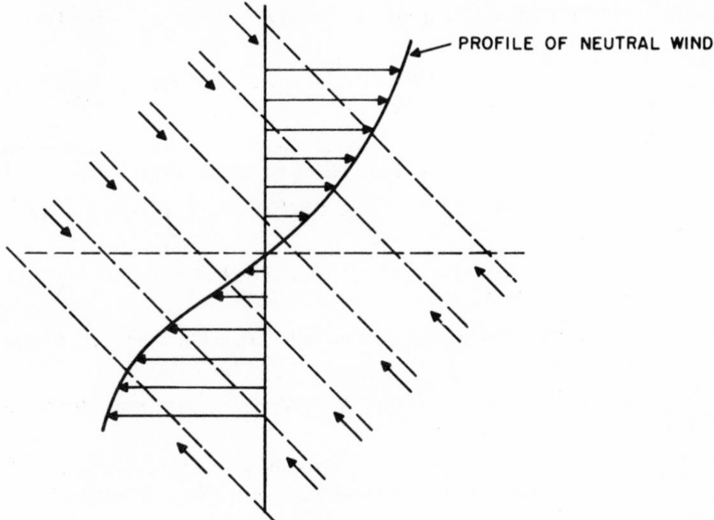

Fig. 7.5 Formation of a thin, densely-ionized layer by a reversal in the direction of horizontal wind velocity with height [2].

Although the effect of charged-particle drifts on the electron concentration in the E and F regions has been investigated in some detail, almost no studies of similar effects on the electron concentration high in the $F2$ layer exist at present. No theory of the ionosphere below the peak of the $F2$ layer will be complete until the electron distribution above the peak is known and explained. Motions high in the magnetosphere are likely to play a very important part in the explanation.

REFERENCES

1. Appleton, E. V., and A. J. Lyon, Ionospheric layer formation under quasi-stationary conditions, in The Physics of the Ionosphere, London: Physical Society, 1955, p. 20.
2. Axford, W. I., The formation and vertical movement of dense ionized layers in the ionosphere due to neutral wind shears. *J. Geophys. Res.*, **68** (1963), 769.
3. Baker, W. G., Electric currents in the ionosphere; Part II, The atmospheric dynamo, *Phil. Trans. Roy. Soc. A*, **246** (1953), 295.
4. Beynon, W. J. G., and G. M. Brown, Geomagnetic distortion of region E, *J. Atmos. Terr. Phys.*, **14** (1959), 138.
5. Chapman, S., The solar and lunar diurnal variation of the earth's magnetism, *Phil. Trans. Roy. Soc. A*, **218** (1919), 1.
6. ———, The electrical conductivity of the ionosphere: A review, *Nuovo Cimento*, **4** (1956), 1385.
7. Chapman, S., and J. Bartels, Geomagnetism. London: Oxford University Press, 1940, p. 696.
8. ———, and T. G. Cowling, The Mathematical Theory of Non-uniform Gases, 2nd ed. London: Cambridge University Press,1952.
9. Dougherty, J. P., On the influence of horizontal motion of neutral air on the diffusion equation of the *F* region, *J. Atmos. Terr. Phys.*, **20** (1961), 167.
10. Duncan, R. A., The equatorial F region of the ionosphere, *J. Atmos. Terr. Phys.*, **18** (1960), 89.
11. Dungey, J. W., The influence of the geomagnetic field on turbulence in the ionosphere. *J. Atmos. Terr. Phys.*, **8** (1956), 39.
12. Fejer, J. A., Semidiurnal currents and electron drifts in the ionosphere, *J. Atmos. Terr. Phys.*, **4** (1953), 184.
13. Ferraro, V. C. A., Diffusion of ions in the ionosphere, *Terr. Mag. Atmos. Electr.*, **50** (1945), 215.
14. Kato, S., Horizontal wind systems in the ionospheric E region deduced from the dynamo theory of the geomagnetic Sq variation. Part II. Rotating earth, *J. Geomag. Geoelectr.*, **8** (1956), 24.
15. Lucas, I., The dynamo theory of geomagnetic tides, *Archiv. Elek. Uebertr.*, **8** (1954), 123.

16. Maeda, H., Horizontal wind systems in the ionospheric E region deduced from the dynamo theory of the geomagnetic Sq variations. Part I. Non-rotating earth, *J. J. Geomag. Geoelectr.*, **7** (1955), 121.

17. Maeda, K., Theoretical study of the geomagnetic distortion in the F2 layer, *Rep. Ionos. Res. Japan*, **9** (1955), 71.

18. Martyn, D. F., Atmospheric tides in the ionosphere; III, Lunar tidal variations at Canberra, *Proc. Roy. Soc. A* (1948), 429.

19. ———, Processes controlling ionization distribution in the F2 region of the ionosphere, *Aust. J. Phys.*, **9** (1956), 161.

20. ———, The normal F region of the ionosphere, *Proc. I.R.E.*, **47** (1959), 147.

21. Rishbeth, H., and D. W. Barron, Equilibrium electron distributions in the ionospheric F2 layer *J. Atmos. Terr. Phys.*, **18** (1960), 234.

22. Schuster, A., The diurnal variation of terrestrial magnetism. *Phil. Trans. Roy. Soc. A*, **208** (1908), 163.

23. Stewart, B., Terrestrial magnetism. Encyclopaedia Britannica, 9th ed., **16** (1883), 159.

24. Whitehead, J. D., The formation of the sporadic-E layer in the temperate zones, *J. Atmos. Terr. Phys.*, **20** (1961), 49.

25. Yonezawa, T., On the influence of electron-ion diffusion exerted upon the formation of the F2 layer, *J. Radio Res. Lab.* (*Japan*), **5** (1958), 165.

8

R. E. Barrington

J. A. Fejer

Ionospheric Noise and Geomagnetic Micropulsations

8.1. INTRODUCTION

Terrestrial observations show the existence of a great variety of naturally occurring electromagnetic fluctuations over a wide range of frequencies. This chapter deals with two distinct classes of such fluctuations: ionospheric noise and micropulsations. Both classes of fluctuation may occur during undisturbed conditions. There is, however, considerable observational evidence that the occurrence of certain subclassifications is correlated with the stronger magnetic disturbances that contribute to 'storm' conditions. This suggests that at least some of the fluctuations are associated with the arrival of solar corpuscles in the vicinity of the earth. This, of course, does not preclude relationships to other geophysical events; for instance, an association between micropulsations and meteor activity has recently been claimed [1].

A wide variety of naturally occurring emissions is found in the frequency range 0.5–15 kc/s. Some of these, such as atmospheric noise ('sferics') and whistlers, are known to be of tropospheric origin and do not concern us here (see Sec. 5.3.2.). Other types are believed to originate in the ionosphere, since they are usually associated with magnetic disturbances. If reproduced by a loudspeaker, these emissions give a surprising variety of sounds. The name 'ionospheric noise' has become common for them and they form the subject of the first part of the present chapter.

The second part of the chapter deals with geomagnetic micropulsations, which are observed as relatively rapid fluctuations on a magnetometer. The pulsations occur in a much lower range of frequencies than ionospheric noise; their periods may extend from a fraction of a second to a few minutes. (See [38] for a recent comprehensive review of micropulsations.)

Both ionospheric noise and micropulsations are believed to be associated with waves in the magnetospheric plasma, but the mechanism by which the waves are generated is as yet uncertain. Waves propagating in the whistler mode are believed to play an important part in ground observations of ionospheric noise, whereas the micropulsations are thought to be a form of hydromagnetic oscillation. Theories of both phenomena must therefore first treat the waves that can exist at the appropriate frequencies and must then postulate a mechanism by which they are excited. The first step is well established in its essentials (see Appendix I), although its application to the complex situation presented in nature is still at an early stage of development; the second step is particularly difficult. It will become apparent from this chapter that much observational and theoretical work is still needed before firm conclusions can be drawn about the nature and origin of ionospheric noise and micropulsations.

8.2. IONOSPHERIC NOISE

Ionospheric noise in and around the VLF band has been studied more extensively than that at most other frequencies. This is partly owing to the high intensity of the noise generated in this band (field strengths of millivolts per meter are not uncommon) and partly to the coherence which it often exhibits. Generally, a spectrograph or some form of transducer which changes the electrical energy into sound is used in its study. With either of these techniques, it is possible to distinguish between ionospheric noise and noise of tropospheric origin, such as sferics and whistlers, both of which are also intense in the VLF band. The distinction is made by the different variations of frequency with time exhibited by the various phenomena. Sferics are of very short duration, milliseconds or less, and cover a wide frequency range. Whistlers decrease steadily in frequency with time, according to a quite precise law as described in Appendix I. In contrast, ionospheric noise shows great variety in the relationship between frequency and time or may cover a broad range of frequencies for periods varying from seconds to hours. The considerable effort which has been expended in recording and analyzing the ocurrence and form of ionospheric noise has established several of its gross features. These characteristics of the noise will be discussed first, to be followed by a consideration of the available studies of its correlation with other geophysical phenomena. The treatment concludes by discussing some of the theories which have been advanced to explain the origin of ionospheric noise.

8.2.1. Characteristics of Ionospheric Noise. Despite difficulties of rigorous classification, three distinct types of ionospheric noise are recognized by international agreement [2]. These are described as follows:

1. Hiss: a relatively steady noise which has many of the characteristics of thermal noise. Unlike thermal noise, however, the power spectrum of the hiss is usually frequency dependent, and it may change in shape and intensity (in periods of several seconds or more) with time.
2. Discrete emissions: well-defined (narrow-band) noise which may have a tonal quality and durations of the order of a few tenths to several seconds or more. A definite and repeating frequency-time relation is often observed.
3. Dawn chorus: a series of many discrete emissions, often overlapping, with time separations of less than 1 sec. Often abbreviated simply as 'chorus.'

A more comprehensive system of classifying discrete emissions, according to the specific form of the frequency-time variation [3], is illustrated by Fig. 8.1. Usually there is little difficulty in differentiating hiss or bands of random noise from the musical tones that ionospheric noise often exhibits. It is more difficult to allocate a given musical tone to one category or another, on the basis of its temporal variations alone. Thus there may be uncertainty in classifying some types of emissions according to the more comprehensive system. Nevertheless, the large number of classes used in it does serve to illustrate the wide variety found in the form of ionospheric noise. As yet these divisions are purely empirical, although it seems likely that some of them, at least, are related to different mechanisms of production or to different locations of the source.

In spite of the great variety in form just indicated, certain average or general characteristics of these emissions are found. Usually the hiss and the frequency variation of a discrete tone are confined to a frequency band 2 or 3 kc/s in width. This band may be centered anywhere from 2 to 10 kc/s, but is generally found at about 3.5 kc/s. The various types of emissions occur most frequently in groups with the discrete forms overlapping, although occasionally any of them will occur as isolated events. Hooks are the most

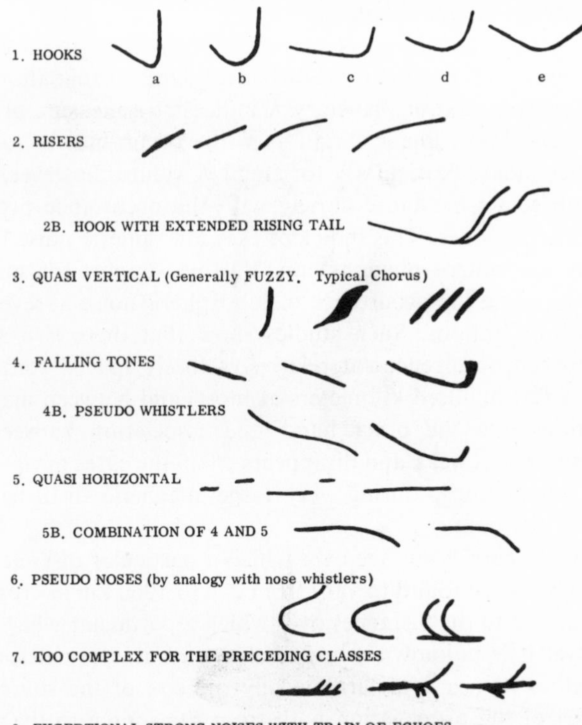

Fig. 8.1 Classification of discrete ionospheric noise emissions. Each trace is a spectral representation of frequency versus time. (After Gallet [3].)

common type of emission, but risers are almost as plentiful. Often a gradual transition from one type to another is found, the most usual being from hiss to some form of discrete tone or vice versa. Occasionally, whistlers seem to give rise to a chain of emissions or hiss, but as a rule these two phenomena are found independently of one another.

8.2.2. Relation to Other Geophysical Phenomena. Many investigations of the occurrence of ionospheric noise in relation to other geophysical phenomena have been undertaken. Usually a sampling technique is employed, in which magnetic-tape recordings are obtained for short periods at regular intervals. The tapes are then analyzed aurally; the presence or absence of the different types of noise is recorded, and an estimate of their intensity is made. Thus the results contain significant subjective factors which make large-scale cooperative studies difficult. Nevertheless, before and particularly during the IGY, large amounts of such data were recorded and much information concerning the frequency of occurrence, geographic distribution, and daily or seasonal variations of the emissions was obtained. Although the data processing continues, enough has already been learned to permit reliable discussion of certain features.

There is a fairly high degree of correlation between the occurrence of ionospheric noise and magnetic disturbance. One examination of this relationship [4], using local or planetary K indices as a measure of magnetic activity, shows an almost linear variation in the occurrence of ionospheric noise with either index. Particularly for small K values, however, the local indices correlate somewhat more closely with the occurrence probabilities than do the planetary ones. This indicates that ionospheric noise is, at least to some extent, a localized phenomenon. Further support for such a view is found by comparing the occurrence of ionospheric noise at several neighboring and distant stations. Such studies show that there is a significant association between occurrences at relatively closely spaced stations (with separations of a few hundred kilometers at most) and between magnetically conjugate stations. On the other hand, the association between distant nonconjugate stations is weak and disappears when the cases of simultaneous occurrence at all stations, during very large magnetic disturbances, are eliminated from the data.

The area on the earth's surface over which a particular discrete emission can be detected has been found to vary from 200 to 1000 km in cross section, which is comparable to the distances over which a particular whistler can be identified. As yet it is unknown whether this area is symmetrical. Nor is it decided whether its size is determined by the size of the source, by the ionospheric part of the propagation path from the source to the observing stations, or by the coupling into, and subsequent attenuation of, waves propagating below the ionosphere. Any or all of these factors could be of importance in determining the region of observability of a particular discrete emission.

A study of the average diurnal variation in the occurrence of ionospheric noise at a fixed location shows a reasonably well-defined maximum in the activity for a particular time of day. This peak has a half width of about 5 hr and its time of occurrence depends on the geomagnetic latitude of the observing station. Low-latitude stations experience the maximum activity early in the day; higher-latitude stations find it at somewhat later times (see Fig. 8.2). Middle-latitude stations experience no other well-defined temporal variations in the occurrence of ionospheric noise, but a winter maximum has been reported at high latitudes [5].

The relationship between ionospheric noise and the optical aurora is not well understood. The emissions occur more frequently with increasing geomagnetic latitude up to at least 60° and are known to be infrequent in the neighborhood of the geomagnetic poles. Such a geographic distribution is similar to that of the aurora and some connection might therefore be inferred, but such a conclusion would be debatable at best. There is increas-

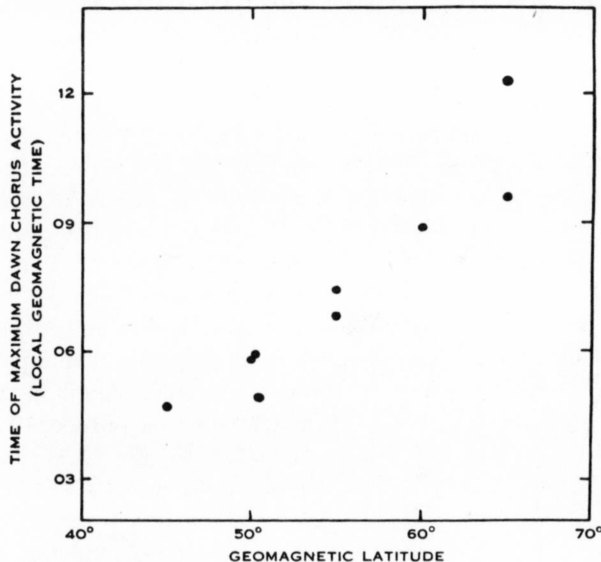

Fig. 8.2 The latitude variation of the time of maximum ionospheric noise emission. (After Allcock [4].)

ing evidence which indicates, for example, that the region of maximum occurrence of ionospheric noise lies at lower latitudes than that of maximum auroral activity. Also the change of VLF activity with latitude is much slower than that of the aurora; stations at 30° geomagnetic latitude frequently observe the radio emissions but only in exceptional circumstances see the aurora. There is, moreover, a widely different diurnal variation in the occurrence of the two phenomena. Nevertheless, it has been claimed [5] that in regions where aurora occurs frequently, the ionospheric noise activity correlates more closely with auroral activity than with the magnetic K index. Both phenomena are manifestations of a disturbance created in the ionosphere by solar matter, but the mechanisms by which, and the regions in which, each is generated probably differ considerably.

8.2.3. Theories of the Generation of Ionospheric Noise. An understanding of the mechanisms that produce ionospheric noise is essential before observations of this noise can provide any but the most approximate information about the upper atmosphere. Fortunately the generation is believed to occur in the ionosphere where many of the difficulties confronting investigations of laboratory plasmas can be avoided. This also opens the possibility that an understanding of ionospheric noise production may be an important contribution to the whole field of plasma physics. Before discussing some of the possible generation mechanisms, however,

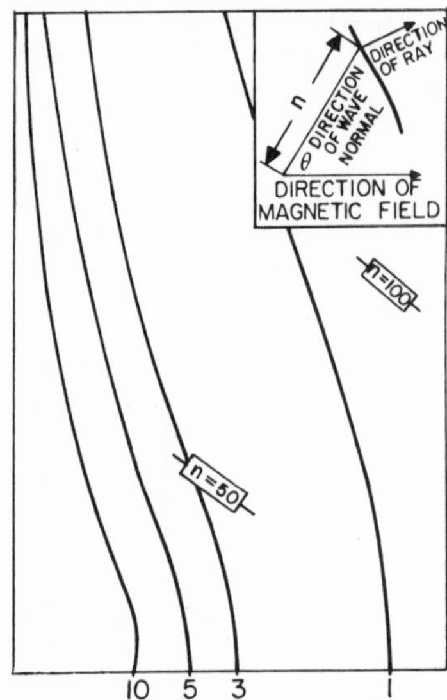

Fig. 8.3 The refractive index (n) and ray direction (given by the geometrical construction illustrated), as functions of the direction of phase propagation (at angle θ relative to the magnetic field), for waves of 1–10 kc/s in representative ionospheric conditions (electrons only). (Based on Hines [7].)

attention will be given to the factors that determine the regions in which they must operate.

The possible regions of origin of ionospheric noise can be determined by considering the flow of energy from an isotropic source of low-frequency radio waves situated somewhere in the magnetosphere. For the waves emitted by such a source, the ionosphere acts as a highly anisotropic medium. The propagation conditions are discussed in some detail in Appendix I, but for present purposes it is sufficient to refer to Fig. 8.3, in which the refractive index of a VLF wave is plotted as a function of the angle θ between its wave normal and the direction of the magnetic field; in this diagram, the effects of positive ions have been neglected. From this curve, the ray direction (the direction of flow of the energy) can be derived as described in Chapter 1 and as illustrated here. When this is done, it is found that all the energy leaving the source is confined to two relatively narrow cones, oppositely directed, which have as axis the magnetic line of force on which the source is situated. This confinement may be further enhanced, and even controlled, by ducting within the field-aligned columns of irregular ionization that were mentioned in Sec. 5.3.2 [6]. Thus in the ionosphere, the energy radiated from the VLF source can never travel far from the field line on which it originates.

At the lower boundary of the ionosphere the energy can couple into a 'waveguide mode,' when it is trapped between the ionosphere and the earth's surface. There it is free to radiate horizontally in any direction, although in fact the direction it follows is determined by its original wave-normal spectrum and the coupling process. The amplitude of waves propagating away from the coupling region via this mode, however, decreases rapidly with distance. Thus, unless the VLF source is unusually strong, radiation from it can be detected on the earth's surface only at or near the magnetic field line containing the source. This fact combines with a consideration of the shape of the geomagnetic lines of force, and with the rare occurrence of ionospheric noise at geomagnetic latitudes greater than 75°, to imply that ionospheric noise sources usually lie within 5 or 6 earth radii of the earth's surface.

It has been pointed out [7] that, if the motions of positive ions are considered in the treatment of VLF propagation, the preceding considerations must be modified slightly. The θ variation of refractive index is then changed from the form shown in Fig. 8.3 to that illustrated in Fig. 8.4. For small values of θ, the wave energy still tends to be guided along the magnetic field lines, but for large values of θ, energy flow transverse to the field direction is possible. For a typical region of the exosphere, the group velocity of this transverse mode decreases with increasing frequency as shown in Fig. 8.5. Hence a pulse propagating by this mode is dispersed into a rising tone comparable to that often observed in ionospheric noise.

There is, however, no natural confinement or guiding of electromagnetic energy in this mode, and it would not propagate from one point to another on the earth's surface in the manner of whistlers. The existence of transverse propagation does not, therefore, imply that sources of ionospheric noise

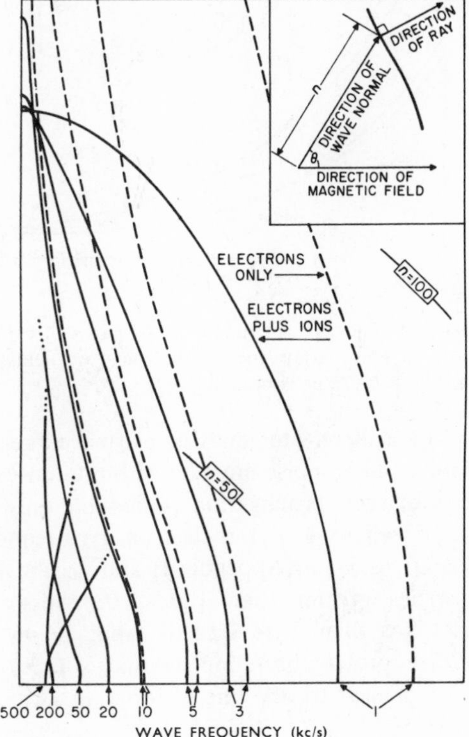

Fig. 8.4 As in Fig. 8.3, but with the effects of positive ions (here protons) included. (After Hines [7].)

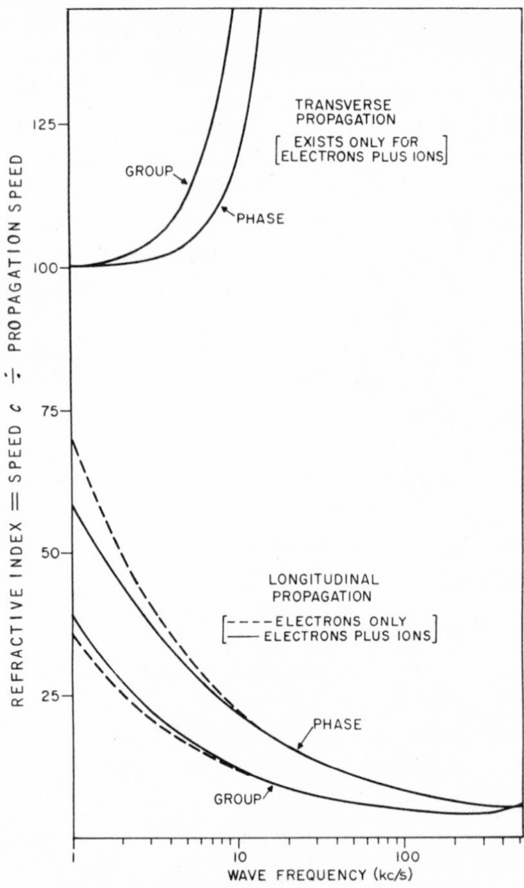

Fig. 8.5 Refractive indexes as functions of wave frequency, for propagation along and transverse to the magnetic field, under the conditions of Fig. 8.4. (After Hines [7].)

might lie below the ionosphere. Nor does its existence alter the conclusion that the sources of ionospheric noise must lie within a few earth radii of the earth's surface, because such propagation is possible only for frequencies less than about $(\omega_e \omega_i)^{1/2}$ where ω_e is the electron gyrofrequency (a positive quantity, in this chapter, $\equiv \omega_{II}$ in Appendix I) and ω_i the proton gyrofrequency; for frequencies greater than 1 kc/s, transverse propagation is limited to heights of less than 2 or 3 earth radii. Below this level, the existence of transverse propagation implies that sources of ionospheric noise need not lie on, or near to, the line of force on which the noise itself is observed.

The limits which have been set to the possible locations of sources of ionospheric noise preclude the possibility that such noise is generated by an oscillation of some region of the magnetosphere at its local gyro- or plasma frequency. These are naturally resonant frequencies of the ionosphere, and hence are likely to be excited by any disturbance of the medium, such as might be produced by the influx of streams of charged particles. (Some types of solar radio noise are often attributed to an excitation of the solar plasma at one of these frequencies, as will be discussed in Chapter 10.) The electron gyro- and plasma frequencies of the terrestrial ionosphere are fairly well established, at least up to heights of several earth radii, and are one or more orders of magnitude greater than the frequencies commonly observed in ionospheric noise. Thus, although oscillations of the terrestrial plasma at these frequencies may be excited, they do not contribute to the type of ionospheric noise now under consideration.

Amplification, similar to that which occurs in a traveling-wave tube [8], has been suggested as a possible source of ionospheric noise [9]. Such a process requires an electron or ion stream of high velocity traveling along some form of waveguide in which the velocity of phase propagation is comparable to the speed of the stream. In the exosphere, VLF radio waves have a velocity of phase propagation at least an order of magnitude below that of light, and as has already been pointed out, they tend to be guided along the direction of the earth's magnetic field. There is also accumulating evidence which shows that, at times of magnetic disturbance, streams of charged particles move with high velocities in this same direction. Present techniques do not detect directly the presence of electron streams with velocities as low as those of VLF waves, but much indirect evidence indicates that such streams exist in the exosphere under certain conditions. Thus the basic requirements of traveling-wave amplification probably exist in the earth's ionosphere.

In this case, it is important to consider what waves can be amplified by such a mechanism. The thermal radiation and natural radio noise of other sources which pervade the magnetosphere provide a continuous spectrum of possible waves, all of which are of low intensity. If the traveling-wave mechanism is operative, to amplify some part of this spectrum to detectable levels, then the waves of interest would be those whose phase velocity is in some region equal to the stream velocity; large amplification occurs only under this condition. The following relationship then obtains between the stream velocity V_0, the frequency of the amplified wave ω, the electron gyrofrequency ω_e, and the plasma frequency ω_0 of the medium:

$$c/V_0 = \left[1 - \frac{\omega_0^2}{\omega(\omega - \omega_e)}\right]^{1/2} \tag{8.1}$$

(cf. Eq. (I.28), with $\theta = 0$). Since ω_0 and ω_e vary throughout the ionosphere, different frequencies will be amplified at different levels. Following amplification, each frequency would be assumed to propagate, via the whistler mode, along a line of force to the ground.

On this basis it is possible to interpret the observed forms of discrete emissions in terms of the gyro- and plasma frequencies of the magnetosphere, and the velocity and extent of some of the electron streams that traverse it [3, 9]. A steady stream of ions would amplify a range of frequencies over an extended period of time, and these would be observed as a broad band of noise or hiss. The width and position of this band in the frequency spectrum then place limits on the stream velocity and the ionospheric levels at which amplification occurs. If, however, a cloud or blob of ions is moving along a line of force, it will amplify different frequencies at different times and heights. An observer on the ground would receive these frequencies in some sequence, depending on their instant of generation and the propagation time from their level of amplification to the observer. Thus a discrete type of emission of the form illustrated in Fig. 8.1 could be produced by such a high-speed ion cloud. The theory has been used, along with the assumption that the stream velocity remains constant during the amplification process, to derive plausible models of the ionization distribution from some observed discrete emissions [3].

In spite of this success, the traveling-wave theory has some difficulties. An examination of the conditions for amplification of VLF waves by ion streams shows that there is no increase in amplitude of waves whose normals lie precisely in the direction of the stream velocity and the magnetic field. Waves with normals in other directions may be amplified. Large amplification of such waves occurs only when their phase velocity is equal to the component of the stream velocity in the wave normal direction. But ionospheric propagation is anisotropic; hence, at any given level, a wide range of frequencies satisfies this condition. Thus a broad band of frequencies should be amplified at any height, making emissions of the discrete form difficult to explain by this mechanism alone. To overcome this difficulty it has been suggested that inhomogeneities of the medium might either limit the range of frequencies which are amplified at a given height, or prevent most of the frequencies amplified at a given level from reaching an observer on the ground.

Another difficulty facing the traveling-wave mechanism has been pointed out [10]. This difficulty arises because a very small velocity distribution in the ion stream is sufficient to eliminate the instability which gives rise to traveling-wave amplification. The tolerance is so small that it is doubtful whether any of the processes which occur in the sun-earth region is capable of producing an ion stream with a sufficiently small velocity spread. Thus, although traveling-wave amplification explains some of the general characteristics of ionospheric noise, the details of the process require closer investigation before its relevance can be accepted.

Another mechanism which may play a part in the generation of some forms of ionospheric noise is gyroradiation from energetic charged particles traveling, in spiral orbits, along the geomagnetic field lines [11, 12]. Already it has been indicated that such radiation at the local gyrofrequency of ionospheric electrons will not explain ionospheric noise, and similar arguments apply to radiation at the proton gyrofrequency. If protons or electrons move with high velocity along a magnetic field line, however, the frequency of their gyroradiation suffers a Doppler shift and this may be sufficient to bring it into the frequency range of ionospheric noise.

This process can be understood most easily by considering the motion of and radiation from a single charged particle (electron, or singly charged ion) in an ionized medium. If the particle has a velocity V_0 relative to the medium, in a direction which forms an angle θ with the magnetic field, its motion will be as shown in Fig. 8.6; $V_\parallel$ is the velocity parallel to the magnetic field and $V_\perp$ that transverse to the field. To an observer moving through the medium with velocity $V_\parallel$, the particle would appear to execute a circular orbit with frequency

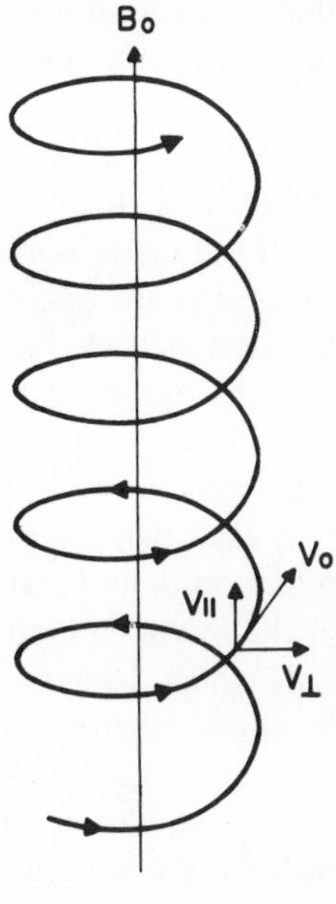

$$\omega_H = eB_0/m, \qquad (8.2)$$

where B_0 is the magnetic induction, e the charge of a proton, and m the mass of the particle. Such an observer would find the particle to be radiating at this frequency and its harmonics. An observer fixed with respect to the medium has a velocity $V_\parallel$ relative to the first observer, and hence would find the radiation to be Doppler-shifted to some new frequency. For propagation along the field lines, this observed frequency would be ω'_H, given by

$$\omega_H/\omega'_H = 1 \pm V_\parallel/V_W, \qquad (8.3)$$

where V_W is the phase velocity for waves of frequency ω'_H. (The plus and minus signs provide for particle motions either away from or toward the observer.)

Fig. 8.6 Geometry of particle paths in the emission of ionospheric noise, as discussed in text.

If waves emitted by a high-speed gyrating particle in the ionosphere are to be observed as ionospheric noise by a ground-based observer, their frequency must lie in the VLF band and their electric vector must rotate in the same sense as electrons gyrate in the magnetic field. (This sense of rotation is required by the polarization relations appropriate to the whistler mode of propagation, and only that mode can propagate freely in the ionosphere at the relevant frequencies; cf. Appendix I.) Examination shows that this condition can be met, if electron gyroradiation is to be a source of ionospheric noise, only if the electron is moving away from the observer with a velocity $V_{\parallel}$ much greater than V_W. For a proton to be the noise source, however, it must be moving toward the observer with a velocity $V_{\parallel}$ slightly greater than V_W.

Ionospheric noise is due not to a single radiating particle but to many. This raises the question of the phase relationship between the waves emitted by each particle, which in turn depends upon the manner in which the particles are set in motion and the forces which act on them as they move. Very little is known about the processes that give rise to high-speed ions in the magnetosphere. In the absence of such knowledge it might be assumed that each particle radiates independently. In this case the amplitude of the radiation is $n^{1/2}E$, where n is the number of radiators and E is the magnitude of the waves emitted by each. This may be considered as a minimum amplitude which the gyro process can produce and may be increased considerably by some coherence in the motions of the radiators. There is evidence that coherence is effected, on occasion, by other emissions, such as whistlers [13].

Gyroradiation and traveling-wave amplification may be complementary rather than mutually exclusive processes. Both can lead to roughly the same predictions as to the levels in the ionosphere at which different frequencies are produced by a given stream. Traveling-wave amplification is essentially a coherent process and requires a stream with an extremely small velocity spread, whereas gyroradiation may be incoherent and does not impose such a restriction on the stream's velocity distribution. Present observations of ionospheric noise do not provide a basis for rejecting either of these two possible mechanisms.

In concluding the discussion of ionospheric noise, it should be emphasized that attention here has been limited to such noise in and near the VLF band. The ionosphere in fact produces noise over a broad range of the radio spectrum; ionospheric noise even at frequencies of tens of megacycles has been reported and is under current study. The characteristics and generating mechanisms of this ever-expanding spectrum of natural noise is only beginning to attract serious scientific study. There has been, on the other hand, considerable research on natural noise in the frequency range that lies below the VLF band. Terminology changes, however, for this noise first came under study by those concerned with the geomagnetic field rather than radio propagation, and the noise itself is described as 'geomagnetic micropulsations.' The characteristics of these micropulsations are now to be discussed.

8.3. GEOMAGNETIC MICROPULSATIONS

Records of the earth's magnetic field show variations of many different types. The slowest of these, the so-called secular variations, are believed to originate in the earth's interior and are therefore outside the scope of this book. Other, somewhat faster variations of the order of minutes to hours, with durations ranging from a few minutes to a few days, appear to be closely related to solar activity and are discussed in Chapters 12 and 15. There are also variations of tidal nature with periods that are submultiples of the solar and lunar day; an account of these is found in Chapter 7.

In addition to all these slower variations, magnetic records often show a finer structure in the form of quasi-sinusoidal oscillations or trains of pulses, with periodicities ranging from a fraction of a second to a few minutes. These are the micropulsations with which this chapter is now concerned. They have been recorded by observatories in many parts of the world for several decades, but only in recent years has much attention been devoted to them. Kato and Watanabe [14] give a short history of the observational development. Balfour Stewart [15] appears to have been the first to recognize the existence of pulsations on normal geomagnetic records; Ebert [16] introduced the technique by which they are most commonly detected today. This consists of the measurement of the electromotive force that is induced in a large coil of wire by the changing magnetic field. An alternative technique is provided by so-called earth-current measurements, which, in fact, record the electromotive force that is established between two spaced electrodes sunk into the ground. Most workers believe that earth-current records and records obtained with the aid of induction coils both display the same micropulsations, although possibly with a different frequency response. It has also been asserted, however, that earth-current records show some variations which are not present on records taken with induction coils and are therefore influenced by different causes. This controversy has not yet been resolved because of the different frequency response and spatial integration of the two techniques.

A precise classification of micropulsations is difficult, in view of their great variety of form, but attempts have been made by some individuals and scientific bodies to distinguish different types. The distinctions are empirical ones based on the observed nature of the fluctuations rather than their origins (which are as yet not established). One of the earliest attempts at a rough classification distinguished three types and assigned the symbols P_c, P_t, and P_g to them. Unfortunately, precise definitions of these types were not given, with the result that, although they are used quite generally, they are not always employed with the same meaning. More recently the terms 'short irregular pulsations,' 'pearl type pulsations,' and 'sweepers' have been applied to forms of micropulsations not recognized in the earlier classification. As a rule, these last three terms are applied to fluctuations of shorter period than the preceding group.

There is still no general agreement as to the use of the foregoing terms, and many workers consider that some of them at least are superfluous; hence, the following remarks must be considered as only a rough outline of the various types and characteristics of micropulsations. They represent an attempt to indicate the most general usage of these terms, rather than the views of a particular observer or scientific body.

8.4. OBSERVATIONAL CHARACTERISTICS OF MICROPULSATIONS

8.4.1. P_c Pulsations. P_c or continuous pulsations are those which have a considerable element of continuity, periods of the order 10–100 sec, and durations of many hours. Figure 8.7 shows an example of a P_c pulsation.

There have been numerous recent observations and statistical studies of these pulsations [14; 17–27]. Their frequency of occurrence is greater in the summer than in the winter. It is also greatest in daytime, although the actual time of daily maximum appears to vary from one station to another [20, 21]. The diurnal variation depends in fact on both local and universal time, with the dependence on local time apparently predominating [21].

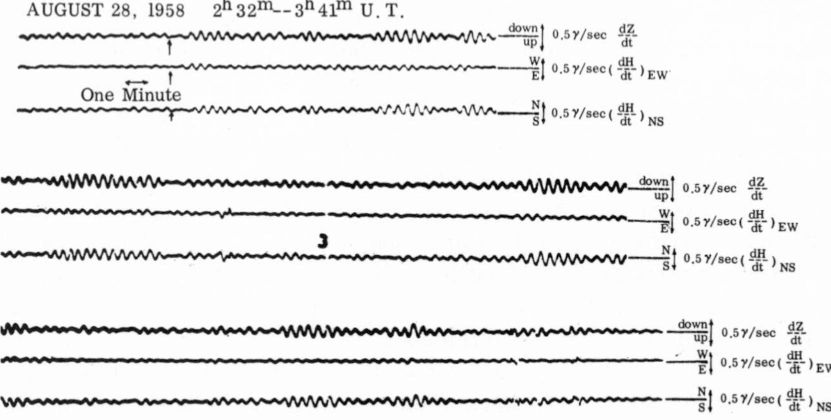

Fig. 8.7 Magnetograms of P_c pulsations. (After Kato [22].)

A positive correlation exists between the frequency of occurrence of P_c pulsations and the magnetic K_p index, with the maximum in P_c activity occurring about a day after the maximum in K_p [22]. A significant 27-day periodicity in the rate of occurrence of P_c pulsations has also been found [23, 24], and the amplitude of the P_c's appears to be greatest in the zone of maximum auroral occurrence [25]. This type of evidence strongly indicates an association of P_c's with some types of solar disturbance, and indeed a clear correspondence has been reported [26] between the occurrence frequency of these pulsations and the appearance of solar magnetic 'unipolar regions' (see Secs. 9.2 and 12.2.1).

The properties of P_c pulsations appear to vary with the relative amplitudes of their frequency components, although observers are not unanimous on this point. There seem to be two prominent frequency groups in the spectrum. One group, whose periods lie in the range 40–90 sec, occurs simultaneously over wide areas and can be represented by a large-scale overhead current system [25]. The second group, with periods of 10–30 sec, does not show widespread occurrence. According to some workers, the former group is restricted to the daylight hours whereas the latter occurs both by night and by day, but still preferentially during the day [25]. Others have found that the few persistent oscillations observed by them at night were of the longer-period variety [18]. The same set of data [18] shows a steady decrease in the period of micropulsations during the day, starting at dawn. Another study, confined to days of high magnetic activity, found that the period had a maximum at about local noon [22]. Perhaps some of these conflicting results are due to a different diurnal variation of the period, in different geographical locations.

The dependence of the period of micropulsations on the latitude has also been studied, and here too the results are conflicting. Some observers [18, 27] have found that the period increases with increasing latitude; others [19] find that the period does not depend significantly on the latitude. As will be seen shortly, certain hydromagnetic theories predict that the period should increase with increasing latitude.

This very brief account indicates that further observations of P_c pulsations, preferably on a world-wide scale, will be needed if their properties are to be established and their origins understood.

8.4.2. P_t Pulsations. The waveform of P_t pulsations may be described as a train of damped oscillations, of broad frequency spectrum, with a fundamental period of 60–100 sec and a duration that is usually less than an hour. An example of P_t pulsations is shown in Fig. 8.8.

These pulsations have amplitudes of the order 0.5γ at middle latitudes, rising to 100γ in the auroral zones [25]. They occur predominantly by night, their onset usually precedes a geomagnetic 'bay' (see Sec. 12.2) by a few minutes, and they last until the bay reaches its maximum intensity. There is evidence of correlation of P_t pulsations with pulsating aurora [28, 29].

P_t pulsations, like the long-period component of P_c, seem to occur simultaneously over the whole earth and may also be represented by a large-scale overhead current system. This current system closely resembles the equivalent current systems of magnetic bays and is particularly intense in the auroral zone [25].

8.4.3. Giant (P_g) Pulsations. P_g, or giant, pulsations are observationally distinguishable from P_c only by their greater amplitudes (rising to some tens of γ) and possibly by a closer confinement to high latitudes. Given the

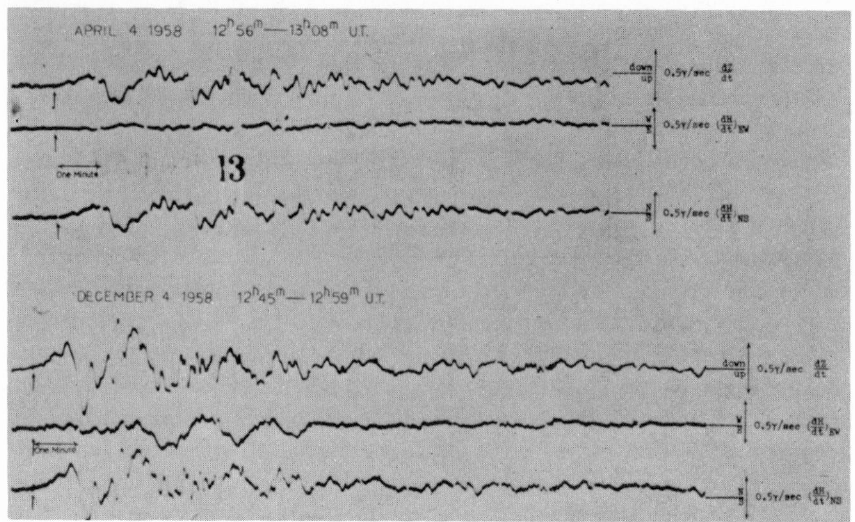

Fig. 8.8 Magnetograms of a P_t pulsations. (After Kato [22].)

recent evidence that the amplitude of P_c pulsations is enhanced in the auroral zone, it is possible that pulsations previously classisfied as P_g may have been simply strong examples of P_c. There is relatively little information on P_g occurrences, so the question is as yet difficult to decide with certainty.

8.4.4. Other Types of Micropulsations. Rapid pulsations are especially prominent on earth-current records [20, 30], although they also can be observed with induction-coil magnetographs [20, 31].

Short irregular pulsations (*SIP*'s) have a limited duration, usually of less than an hour. They precede magnetic bays and may be said to represent the microstructure of P_t pulsations with which they are closely associated. Their most prominent period is about 6 sec. Occasionally *SIP*'s occur in the absence of a magnetic bay, and they are then usually associated with the long-period component of P_c's [20].

There is often striking correlation between *SIP*'s and visible aurora; even the prominent period of the pulsating aurora (which may vary from event to event) coincides approximately with the prominent *SIP* period [20].

Pearl type pulsations (*PP*'s) are sinusoidal oscillations with regular amplitude variations and periods of about 0.2–5 sec. The name is derived from the resemblance of the envelope of the oscillation to a string of pearls, as illustrated in Fig. 8.9. These pulsations sometimes continue without interruption for a few hours; at other times, they occur in bursts which last only a few minutes. It has been reported [29] that they are often excited during periods of sharp increase in cosmic-ray intensity.

Analysis reveals that *PP*'s comprise two spectral components which

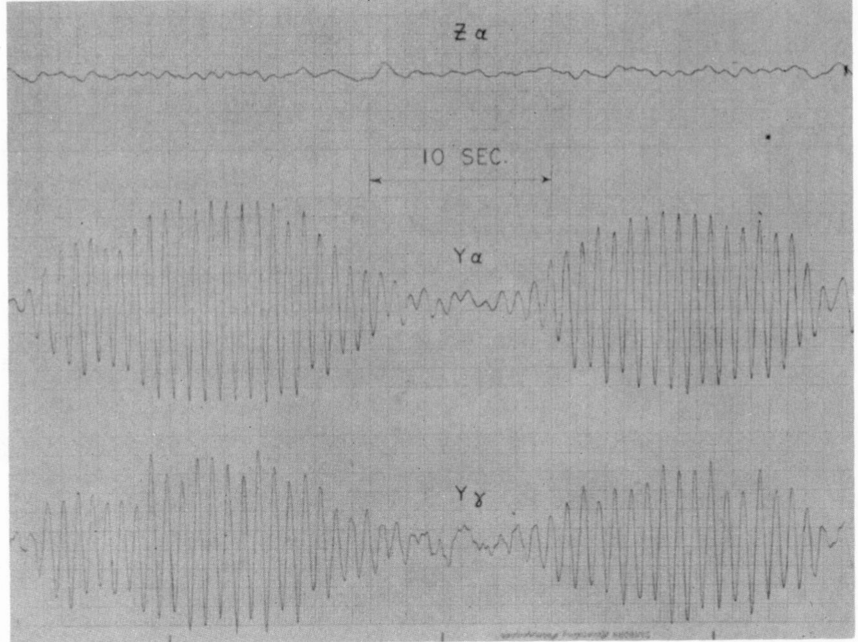

Fig. 8.9 An example of pearl pulsations (*PP's*) of the earth's magnetic field. (After Duffus, Shand, and Wright [17].)

'beat' together to produce the characteristic envelope. The two components may have fixed frequencies [33] suggestive of resonant oscillations, or they may sweep in frequency simultaneously, keeping a fixed frequency separation [32].

Sometimes rapid pulsations with several frequency components in the

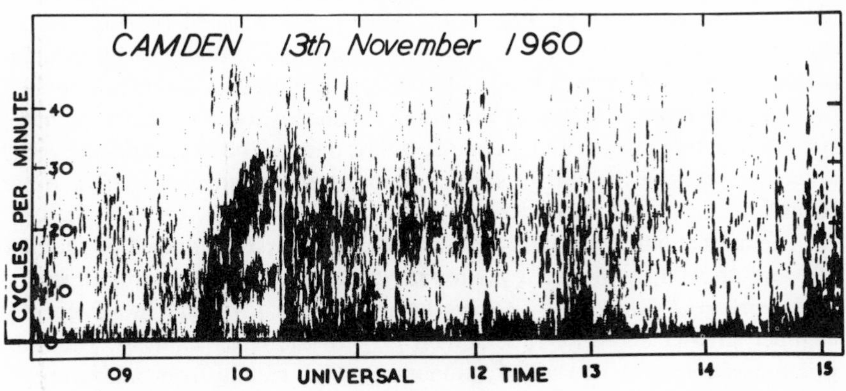

Fig. 8.10 Sonogram of a 'sweeper' recorded in the course of a magnetic storm on 13 November 1960. (After Duncan [18].)

range from 1 to 5 cycles per second are observed. The frequency of the individual components usually decreases slowly [34], and the components are not harmonically related.

During magnetic storms rapid pulsations with a progressive change of frequency during several minutes are observed [18, 20, 34]. A sonogram of such a 'sweeper' is shown in Fig. 8.10. Rapid pulsations are also observed at the time of a sudden commencement; see, for example, [18].

Pulsations excited by high-altitude atomic explosions have been detected [35]. Their starting times can be determined rather accurately, and if plotted as a function of distance from the explosion, they reveal an effective velocity of propagation of the first arrival (deduced for the shortest possible path) of about 3000 km/sec. A second group of pulses is also observed; from their starting times an effective velocity of the order of 500 km/sec is obtained.

8.5. THEORIES OF MICROPULSATIONS

Early investigators believed that micropulsations are caused by fluctuations in an existing current system such as the *Sq* system (Chapter 7), but this would not explain the observed periodicity of the pulsations. More recent theories attempt to explain the observed periodicity by the existence of resonant modes of hydromagnetic oscillation in the earth's outer atmosphere [27, 36].

The characteristics of hydromagnetic waves are discussed in Appendix I, where it is noted that two modes of propagation can be found in a homogeneous medium. In the actual magnetosphere, with its curved field lines and limited extent, these give rise to two classes of natural oscillation. In the one, the energy of a single characteristic wave oscillates backward and forward along the geomagnetic field lines, and for suitable frequencies a resonant standing wave can be established. The material motion is east-west, and is independent of longitude on any given magnetic 'shell' (that is, surface obtained by rotating a field line about the dipole axis): this class of resonant oscillation is often termed 'toroidal.' In the second class, termed 'poloidal,' the material motion occurs in meridional planes, with the whole magnetosphere pulsating inward and outward; the resonance then depends on energy reflection between the earth's surface (and lower ionosphere) and the outer boundary of the magnetosphere.

The mathematical analysis of these modes was first conducted by Dungey [36] and applied by him to a preliminary interpretation of micropulsations. This work was extended by Obayashi and Jacobs [27], and more recently in much greater detail by MacDonald [37]. In the latter analysis, attention was focused on a third type of resonance, which results from a ducting of wave energy between the earth's surface and a height low in the magnetosphere—at heights of 1000–2000 km—where the speed of hydromagnetic propagation reaches a maximum.

Little progress has been made in correlating these different types of resonant modes with the different kinds of micropulsations. The periods of resonant toroidal oscillations increase with latitude, and the reported observational increase in the periods of the P_c pulsations (if confirmed) may be explained on this basis. The strong enhancement of pulsations in the auroral zones tends to favor the toroidal oscillations as the basic form of disturbance in most cases, although coupling into poloidal and ducted modes may well contribute to the final observational pattern. The initial wave train arriving from nuclear explosions almost certainly propagates in ducted modes. More experimental and theoretical work is, however, clearly needed before any definite conclusions can be drawn about the hydromagnetic waves that are actually present in the various circumstances. Their manner of excitation remains as a further problem for study.

REFERENCES

1. Campbell, W. H., Magnetic micropulsations accompanying meteor activity, *J. Geophys. Res.*, **65** (1960), 2241.
2. *URSI Information Bulletin* No. 122, July–September (1960).
3. Gallett, R. M., The very low frequency emissions generated in the earth's exosphere, *Proc. IRE*, **47** (1959), 211.
4. Allcock, G. McK., A study of the audio-frequency radio phenomenon known as "Dawn Chorus," *Aust. J. Phys.*, **10** (1957), 286.
5. Pope, J. H., An investigation of whistlers and chorus at high latitudes, AFCRC—TN 355 ASTIA Doc. No. AD 216522 (1959).
6. Smith, R. L., Propagation characteristics of whistlers trapped in field-aligned columns of enhanced ionization, *J. Geophys. Res.*, **66** (1961), 3699.
7. Hines, C. O., Heavy-ion effects in audio-frequency radio propagation, *J. Atmos. Terr. Phys.*, **11** (1957), 36.
8. Pierce, J. R., Traveling-Wave Tubes, New York: D. Van Nostrand Co. Inc., 1950.
9. Gallet, R. M., and R. A. Helliwell, Origin of "very-low-frequency emissions," *J. Res. Nat. Bureau of Standards*, **63-D** (1959), 21.
10. Kahn, F. D., Velocity changes of charged particles in a plasma, *Astrophys. J.*, **129** (1959), 468.
11. McArthur, J. W., Theory of the origin of the very low-frequency radio emissions from the earth's exosphere, *Phys. Rev. Letters*, **2** (1959), 491.
12. Dowden, R. L., Doppler-shifted cyclotron radiation from electrons: A theory of very low frequency emissions from the exosphere, *J. Geophys. Res.*, **67** (1962), 1745.
13. Brice, N. M., Traveling-wave amplification of whistlers, *J. Geophys. Res.*, **65** (1960), 3840.
14. Kato, Y., and T. Watanabe, Studies on geomagnetic pulsation, Pc, *Sci. Rep. Tohoku Univ.*, **8** (1957), No. 3.

15. Stewart, B., On the great magnetic disturbance which extended from August 28 to September 7, 1859, as recorded by photography at the Kew Observatory, *Phil. Trans. Roy. Soc.*, **151** (1861), 425.

16. Ebert, H., Short-period pulsations in terrestrial magnetic field, *Terr. Mag.*, **12** (1907), 1.

17. Duffus, H. J., J. A. Shand, and C. S. Wright, Influence of geological features on very low frequency geomagnetic fluctuations, *Nature*, **186** (1960), 141.

18. Duncan, R. A., Some studies of geomagnetic micropulsations, *J. Geophys. Res.*, **66** (1961), 2087.

19. Ellis, G. R. A., Geomagnetic micropulsations, *Aust. J. Phys.*, **13** (1960), 625.

20. Troitskaya, V. A., Pulsation of the earth's electromagnetic field with periods of 1 to 15 seconds and their connection with phenomena in the high atmosphere, *J. Geophys. Res.*, **66** (1961), 5.

21. Jacobs, J. A., and K. Sinno, Occurrence frequency of geomagnetic micropulsations, Pc, *J. Geophys. Res.*, **65** (1960), 107.

22. Kato, Y., Investigation on the geomagnetic rapid pulsation, *Sci. Rep. Tohoku Univ.*, **11**, Supplement, (1959).

23. Kato, Y., J. Ossaka, M. Okuda, T. Watanabe, and T. Tamao, Investigation on the magnetic disturbance by the induction magnetograph, Part VI, On the daily variation and the 27-day recurrence tendency in the geomagnetic pulsation, *Sci. Rep. Tohoku Univ.*, **8** (1956), 19.

24. Burkhart, K., Mikropulsationen des erdstorms und der erdmagnetischen horizontal komponenten, *Ztschr. f. Geoph.*, **21** (1955), 57.

25. Jacobs, J. A., and K. Sinno, World-wide characteristics of geomagnetic micropulsations, *Geophys. J. Roy. Astr. Soc.*, **3** (1960), 333.

26. Kato, Y., and S. Akasofu, Relationships between the geomagnetic micropulsation and the solar UM region, *J. Atmos. Terr. Phys.*, **9** (1956), 352.

27. Obayashi, T., and J. A. Jacobs, Geomagnetic pulsations and the earth's outer atmosphere, *Geophys. J. Roy. Astr. Soc.*, **1** (1958), 53.

28. Campbell, W. H., Micropulsations in the earth's magnetic field simultaneous with pulsating aurora, *Nature*, **185** (1960), 677.

29. Terada, T., On rapid periodic variations of terrestrial magnetism, *J. College of Sci., Imperial Univ. of Tokyo*, **37** (1917), 9.

30. Hessler, V. P., and E. M. Wescott, Rapid fluctuations in earth currents at College, *Geophys. Inst., Univ. of Alaska, Sc. Rep. No. 1*, (1959).

31. Maple, E., Geomagnetic oscillations at middle latitudes, *J. Geophys. Res.*, **64** (1959), 1395.

32. Mainstone, J. S., and R. W. E. McNicol, Micropulsation studies at Brisbane, Queensland, I. Pearl pulsations and 'screamers,' *Proc. International Conference on the Ionosphere*, London: Inst. of Physics and Physical Society, 1963, p. 163.

33. Tepley, L. R., Observations of hydromagnetic emissions, *J. Geophys. Res.*, **66** (1961), 1651.

34. Duffus, H. J., P. W. Nasmyth, J. A. Shand, and C. Wright, Sub-audible geomagnetic fluctuations, *Nature*, **181** (1959), 1258.

35. Berthold, W. K., A. K. Harris, and H. J. Hope, World-wide effects of hydromagnetic waves due to Argus, *J. Geophys. Res.*, **65** (1960), 2233.

36. Dungey, J. W., Electrodynamics of the outer atmosphere, *Report of Conference on the Physics of the Ionosphere*, The Physical Society, London 1955, p. 229.

37. MacDonald, G. J. F., Spectrum of hydromagnetic waves in the exosphere, *J. Geophys. Res.*, **66** (1961), 3639.

38. Troitskaya, V. A., Rapid variations of the electromagnetic field of the earth, in Research in Geophysics, Vol. I: Sun, Atmosphere and Space, ed. H. Odishaw, Cambridge: The M. I. T. Press, 1964, Chap. 19.

9

W. C. Collins
L. Herzberg

Solar Activity and Short-lived Terrestrial Effects (SID)

9.1. INTRODUCTION

The foregoing chapters have dealt primarily with the upper atmosphere in its 'undisturbed' state. Much of the interest in upper atmospheric studies centers, however, on the varied conditions that are connected with disturbances. The remaining chapters will deal almost exclusively with these.

Disturbances in the upper atmosphere follow upon major disturbances on the sun and can be separated with little ambiguity into those produced by ultraviolet light and *X*-rays, and those produced by corpuscular radiation emitted by a disturbed region of the sun. The latter type of disturbance is, in general, very complicated, since the particles involved carry electric charges and their paths are severely affected by the solar and/or terrestrial magnetic fields. They comprise at least two major classes which require extensive discussion and which will be treated in subsequent chapters.

Ionospheric disturbances due to ultraviolet light and *X*-rays are more readily dealt with, if only because the radiation concerned follows a rectilinear path. They comprise only one major type of phenomenon, known as 'sudden ionospheric disturbance' (SID), and it is relatively short-lived. This class of disturbance is dealt with in this chapter. As a preliminary to the discussion of all classes, however, we begin with a broad survey of various facets of abnormal solar activity revealed by optical phenomena. (For a more extensive review, see [22].)

9.2. SUNSPOTS; SPOT GROUPS; THE SUNSPOT CYCLE

The most obvious indication of solar disturbance is the presence on the disk of dark spots, known as 'sunspots.' Since sunspots can be observed in white light, occasionally even with the naked eye, sunspot observations became possible long before most of the studies discussed in this book were undertaken. These observations now provide us with a record of solar activity that goes back for more than two centuries.

The general appearance of sunspots may be seen in the photograph reproduced here as Fig. 9.1. It shows a large group of spots of different size, some merging into one another, each surrounded by a filamentary structure which is called the 'penumbra.' Single spots, as well as whole spot groups, are always imbedded in regions slightly brighter than the rest of the disk. Bright regions of this type, which may or may not contain spots, are referred to as 'plage' areas. In white light, they are visible only near the limb.

The dark appearance of the spots indicates that the temperature in the area is lower than that in the spot-free region of the disk. This is confirmed

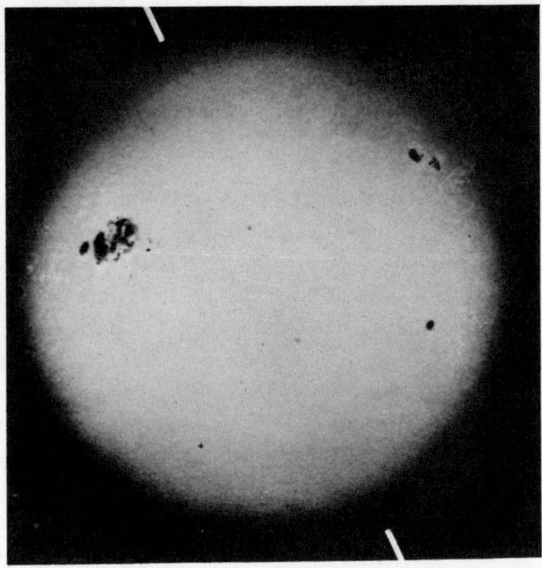

Fig. 9.1 The solar disk in white light. (Courtesy Dominion Observatory, Ottawa, Canada.)

by spectroscopic observation of enhanced molecular absorption in these areas. The temperature determined from sunspot spectra is of the order of 4000°K, some 2000°K lower than that derived from the undisturbed photosphere.

Sunspots are, above all, regions of exceptionally high magnetic field strength. Zeeman-effect measurements on absorption lines in sunspots show magnetic field strengths of several thousand gauss, more or less perpendicular to the solar surface. In contrast, the magnetic fields measured in other regions are of the order of 1 gauss. This holds both for the random photospheric fields and for the component of the general solar dipole field which can be measured at high heliographic latitudes [4].

The magnetic polarity of a single spot may be north or south. Complex spots may show a mixture of both polarities, which can be understood as the result of fusion of a number of smaller uncomplicated spots, though spots tend to occur in pairs of opposite polarity. There is, in fact, fairly good evidence to show that the bipolar spot pair is the basic phenomenon. When pairs occur, the two members form at much the same latitude but are separated in longitude (by about 10°, typically). Single spots, apparently unipolar, are as a rule accompanied by small plages, indicating the presence of a submerged or not fully developed spot, very likely the other component of a bipolar pair. (These apparently unipolar sunspots must not be confused with magnetic unipolar regions of much smaller intensity, which are observed in regions removed from the centers of activity, and which are at present thought by some to be identical with the hypothetical 'M regions' responsible for certain periodic geomagnetic disturbances as discussed in Chapter 12.)

It is now generally accepted that the strong magnetic fields in the spots, by their influence on the convective transport of energy, are the cause of the relatively low temperature within the spot area itself and of the relatively high temperature of the plage region surrounding it. Energy from the solar interior is conveyed upward, partly by radiation, and in the upper region (convective zone) by convection. The latter process is revealed by the granular appearance of the undisturbed solar surface, the brighter grains corresponding to columns of rising hot gases, the darker ones to columns of descending cooler matter. Since a strong magnetic field impedes convection, the equilibrium temperature on the surface of the photosphere will be less in the area of a spot than in the undisturbed region of the disk. The surplus energy will reach the surface in the region surrounding the spot and will there cause the appearance of a bright hot plage area.

The penumbra region around a sunspot is neither uniformly dark like the sunspot center, the umbra, nor does it show the regular granulation of the undisturbed disk. It shows a characteristic fibrous structure which can be understood as produced by the complicated turbulent motion of the

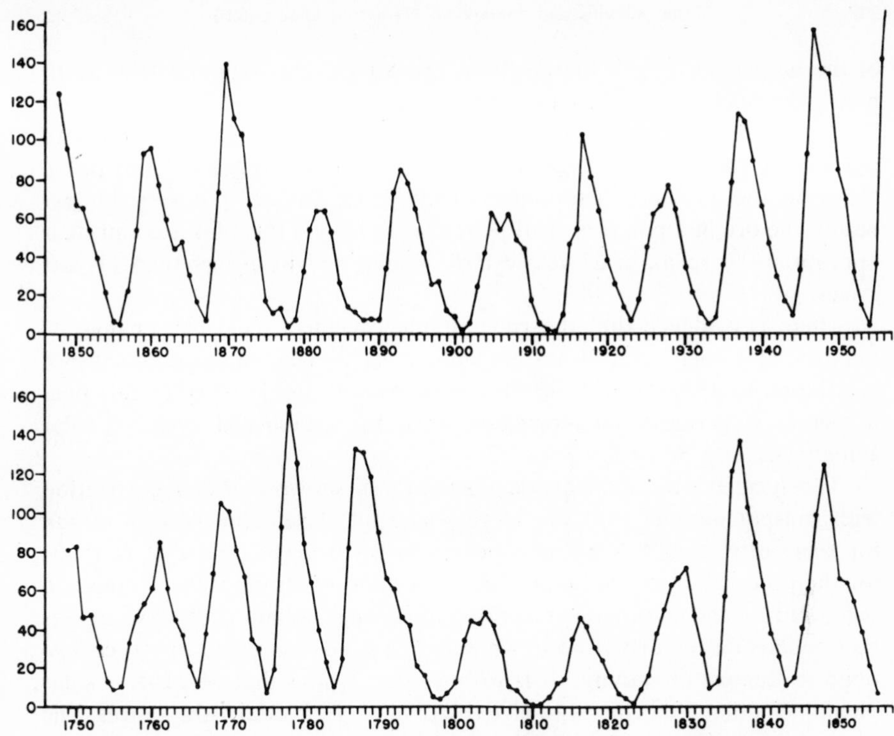

Fig. 9.2 Variation in sunspot numbers with time. (From Menzel [22].)

solar gases in the transition region between the relatively quiescent area of the umbra and the normally convective photosphere.

As has been recognized for a long time, the number of spots, their position on the disk, and their polarity are subject to a periodic variation, known as the 'sunspot cycle.' The total number of spots varies with a somewhat irregular period of approximately 11 years (see Fig. 9.2). At the time of 'solar minimum' (minimum number of spots), sunspots begin to form at a latitude of about 40° on the two solar hemispheres. As the cycle progresses, the number of spots first increases and then decreases, in a broad region which gradually moves toward the equator. The beginning of a new cycle is characterized by the reappearance of spots at higher latitudes. Individual spots may be recognizable for days or weeks in the course of this general development. Although the length of the cycles is roughly constant, there is a considerable difference in the total number of spots from cycle to cycle, indicating a long-term variation of solar activity superimposed on the classical sunspot cycle.

The cyclic variation of the number of sunspots and of their average position on the disk is paralleled by a periodic reversal of the magnetic polarity of sunspot pairs. If, during a given 11-year period, the leading spots of the bipolar groups in the northern hemisphere are, say, magnetic north poles, the leading spots on the southern hemisphere will be south poles. During the succeeding 11-year period this situation will be reversed, with the leading spots on the northern hemisphere being magnetic south poles, those on the southern hemisphere north poles. In the following 11-year period the original polarities will be restored. Taking this into account, it is appropriate to speak of 22-year cycles of solar activity rather than 11-year cycles.

There is evidence that the general solar magnetic field can change its polarity. One such reversal has been observed [3], near the time of sunspot maximum, in 1957–58. Further observations will decide whether this phenomenon is periodic and correlated with the established cycle of solar activity (see also Sec. 10.3).

The incidence of ionospheric disturbances shows a broad correlation with sunspot number over the 11-year sunspot cycle. The physical reason for this correlation has become clearer with the development of methods for the observation of the solar disk in the light of chromospheric emission lines, and for the continuous recording of coronal radiation. It now appears that regions on the disk, that in white light are marked by sunspots, correspond to 'centers of activity.' It is within these regions that we observe solar phenomena that are believed to give rise to many terrestrial disturbances. The most striking solar phenomena are the optical flares, with their accompanying enhancements in *X*-ray emission and outbreaks of corpuscular clouds.

A typical active center has a total lifetime of several solar rotations, the synodic period of solar rotation—i. e., the period of rotation as observed from the orbiting earth—being about 27 days at the pertinent heliographic latitudes. The first phase of its existence, lasting about a month, is characterized by the formation of spots in an expanding plage area and by sporadic outbreaks of flares. This period is followed by a second phase in which the sunspots disappear and the flare activity dies down. The plage area reaches its full expansion during this period, and during the following months gradually fades away.

As discussed before (Chapter 2), coronal radiation is enhanced over plage areas. This is true both of the discrete coronal lines and of the continuous *X*-radiation. Because of the close relation between the development of sunspot groups and plages, the total intensity of solar *X*-ray emission varies with the 11-year sunspot cycle [20]. This is paralleled by a slow variation in ionospheric conditions as a whole, which is apparently independent of the violent episodic disturbances following solar flares.

9.3. SOLAR FLARES AND RELATED PHENOMENA; THE SOLAR DISK OBSERVED IN MONOCHROMATIC LIGHT

Observation of spots in white light serves to give information on the general state of solar activity. With the exception of the occasional extraordinarily intense flare ('white light flare'), however, details of localized solar disturbances can be discerned only in the light of certain spectral lines whose intensities are especially sensitive to variations in temperature. Suitable for this purpose are mainly the intense red hydrogen emission line Hα, the ultraviolet and infrared lines of singly ionized calcium (Ca II), and an infrared line of helium.

Useful results from observation in the light of solar emission lines are obtained only if the narrow wavelength region in which intensity changes occur can be resolved from the surrounding continuum. This means that the bandpass of the monochromator employed in the case of Hα, for example, must be as narrow as 0.6 Å.

Until recently these stringent requirements could be satisfied only by the spectroheliograph, an arrangement of instruments in which a spectroscope of high resolving power serves as monochromator and where the solar image is scanned and recorded point by point. The spectroheliograph produces excellent results as far as detail is concerned, but the method is too time-consuming to obtain a continuous record of the rapidly changing aspect of the solar surface. This latter purpose is served very well by recently developed interference filters (Lyot filters) which make it possible to obtain a monochromatic image of the whole disk in a single exposure [14].

Photographs of the surface of the sun obtained at different wavelengths show differences in detail, because the temperature dependence of the intensity varies from line to line in the solar spectrum. At present, continuous systematic observation of the sun from a series of stations around the earth is made in the light of Hα. This patrol is very valuable mainly for the data it provides on the incidence of solar flares, their intensity, position on the disk, and duration.

Figure 9.3 represents an example of a solar-disk photograph made at wavelength 6562 Å, at the center of the Hα line of hydrogen. This picture shows much detail and a number of features which could not have been discerned in white light, whereas sunspots are recognized only with difficulty. The granular structure of the solar surface due to convective motions in the photosphere is revealed very clearly in the mottled appearance of the undisturbed regions of the disk. All this is characteristic of photographs obtained in monochromatic light.

Apart from the short-lived flares, to be discussed below, the most striking features seen in monochromatic disk photographs are irregular 'floccular' bright spots and long narrow dark filaments. The former are the plage areas, previously mentioned, which occur in connection with spot groups. These are the 'faculae' of the older literature. Although in white light these areas can be seen only near the limb, in monochromatic light they are visible anywhere on the disk, thus roughly marking out the extent and the distribution of centers of solar activity.

The features which appear dark against the bright background of the disk are due mostly to absorption of light by sheaths and streamers of solar

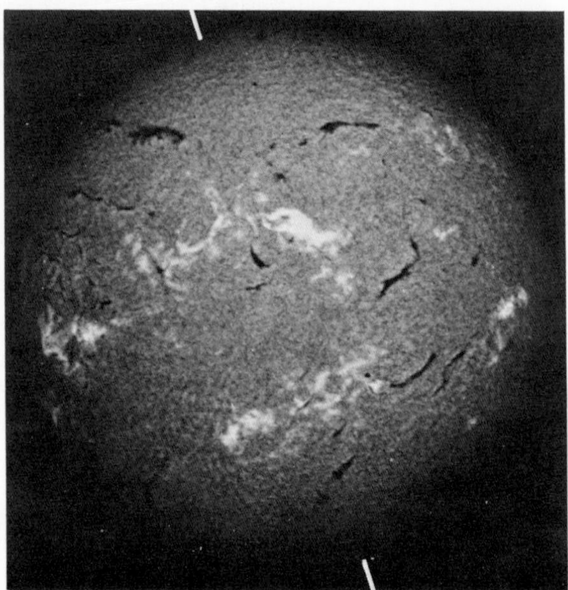

Fig. 9.3 The solar disk in light of Hα (λ = 6562.8 Å). The bright feature near the center of the disk is a class 3 flare at maximum brightness. (Courtesy Dominion Observatory, Ottawa, Canada.)

gases, known as 'filaments,' extending upward into the chromosphere and occasionally perhaps into the lower corona. Similar gas masses, when seen beyond the solar limb, appear as bright emission features and are then referred to as 'prominences.'

Detailed studies of prominences have shown the existence of a great variety of forms, ranging from quiescent clouds to short-lived loops and erupting jets. Correspondingly, one observes filaments of varying forms and stability, including 'dark surges' which can sometimes be seen to reach the limb and then to propagate outward in the form of bright eruptive prominences.

Experience has shown that bright flares are likely to be followed by distinctive ionospheric disturbances. For this reason, the observation of flares is of great geophysical interest. In the light of Hα, a flare appears as a sudden brightening near a sunspot. During its first 'explosive' phase it expands rapidly parallel to the solar surface and more slowly upward. Visual analysis of flares in Hα has shown that a fully developed flare, in general, appears as a quiescent layer of bright gas, extending from the upper photosphere through the chromosphere into the lower corona [28, 30]. The short 'explosive' phase of a flare is followed by a period of slow decline. The lifetime of a flare increases, in general, with area and with the width of the line in which it is observed. Any one of these parameters, used judiciously, can be taken as an indication of the 'importance' of a flare. Table 9.1 illustrates the classification of flares according to statistical average values of these characteristics.

Table 9.1.* FLARE CHARACTERISTICS

Class or 'importance'	Duration (min.) Average	Range	Area Limits (10^{-6} visible disk)	Average Line Width of Hα at Maximum (Angstrom)
1−	. . .	. . .	< 100	1.5
1	20	4–43	100–250	3.0
2	30	10–90	250–600	4.5
3	60	20–155	600–1200	8.0
3+	180	50–430	> 1200	15.0

*After Ellison [11] and Friedman [16].

Observations of flares from above the bulk of the atmosphere have revealed significant enhancements of the radiation in the *X*-ray region. This enhancement sets in at the start of the visible flare, and it consists of both an over-all intensity increase and an extension of the spectrum to shorter wavelengths (for details see [17]). This is illustrated by the set of data given in Table 9.2.

Table 9.2.* SOLAR X-RAY FLUX (erg cm^{-2} sec^{-1} at earth's orbit)

Wavelength Interval (Angstrom)	Background (14 Aug. 1959) 1600 UT	2 + Flare (31 Aug. 1959) 2253 UT
20–100	0.6	4.0
8–20	0.002	0.09
2–8	0.00055	0.03

*After Friedman [17].

All but a very small fraction of the *X*-ray energy emitted during a flare is contained in the wavelength region $\lambda \geq 1$ Å. It is possible to ascribe this main part of the *X*-ray spectrum to atomic emission (recombination spectrum) of the gas in a region of coronal condensation at a temperature of about 10^7 °K. Such a spectrum would have a short-wavelength limit of ~ 1 Å corresponding to the recombination energy of completely ionized iron.

Radiation at wavelength $\lambda \leq 1$ Å is observed only in the very first phase of flare development. Its contribution to the total energy is insignificant, but it is of interest nevertheless because of the high photon energies involved (up to, at least, 125 Kev). It has been suggested [17] that this high-energy tail of the *X*-ray spectrum might be bremsstrahlung from electrons thermalized at about 10^8 °K.

The energy expended in flares is very great. It has been estimated [12] that the energy released during the first few minutes of an intense flare event may be as high as 10^{33} ergs, a quantity which exceeds the entire heat energy stored in the solar chromosphere and corona. The source for this tremendous energy must be sought in the strong and complicated magnetic fields of solar active regions. Some observations [25] suggest that flares tend to appear at a neutral point in the magnetic field of a sunspot group and that, with the onset of the flare, the magnetic field in the immediate neighborhood breaks down. The effect occurs when the condition of the chromospheric plasma in the vicinity becomes unstable in the course of an increase in the gradient of the magnetic field strength. Such a situation may arise during the approach toward each other of two bipolar sunspot groups [13].

Order-of-magnitude estimates show that converted magnetic energy can account for the energy dissipated in various forms during a flare. Pressure variations accompanying the rapid changes of magnetic field strength during the initial phase of the event will increase temperature and turbulent velocities at photospheric and chromospheric levels and should also give rise to shock waves which propagate upward. These shock waves can carry sufficient energy to produce the hot coronal condensations in which the observed X-ray flux is believed to originate. Temperature increases at photospheric and chromospheric heights can account for the enhancement of visible radiation observed during flares.

As mentioned in Sec. 9.1, certain ionospheric events following major solar disturbances are not caused by ultraviolet light or X-rays, but by corpuscular radiation. On some occasions (see Sec. 10.4.3 for a more complete discussion) the corpuscular radiation is closely related in origin with the optical flare emission. About 1% of the energy released during an intense event could account for the necessary acceleration of the particles emitted [12]. Ejection of matter by the sun during a disturbance may be thought of as the result of the violent turbulence associated with a flare, though more coherent processes may also be involved.

Recently it has become possible to study the development of the dynamic chromospheric disturbance accompanying an optical flare in monochromatic (Hα) photographs of the disk [23]. It has been found that many of the flares, including those of small size, are accompanied by disturbances that travel over considerable distances on the solar disk. They are seen to interact with filaments which are far removed from the flare, occasionally causing their sudden disappearance. (Sudden disappearance of apparently unrelated filaments at the time of a flare has been noted for a long time.) Certain major flares have been found to be accompanied by disturbances traveling over distances of the order of 500,000 km, which is half the diameter of the solar disk, at velocities of about 1000 km/sec.

9.4. SUDDEN IONOSPHERIC DISTURBANCES: INTRODUCTION

One type of atmospheric disturbance which has long been related to enhanced solar emissions is called 'sudden ionospheric disturbance' (SID). This is the generic name given to a variety of short-lived abnormalities which occur during the daylight hours and which result from a marked increase in the electron density of the lower ionosphere. Named for their distinctive temporal variation, the effects usually reach their peak within a few minutes after starting although the return to normal conditions may take from 15 min to 2 hr. Optical observations of the solar flares on the sun and radio observations of the ionosphere frequently show similar temporal variations during SID's, as has been well established from statistical evidence for a number of years. But there are many flares which are not accompanied by an SID, and some effort has been made to determine the peculiar characteristics of the SID-producing flares [7, 10, 29]. There appears to be some relationship between the 'importance' of a flare and the occurrence of a terrestrial disturbance, in that SID's are found to accompany class 3 and 3+ flares more often than those of lesser importance, but this is hardly surprising. It has also been found that flares with SID's occur most frequently near the centre of the solar disk and that a flare does not seem to produce an SID unless the solar disturbance extends upward beyond a critical height in the chromosphere.

It is noteworthy that many ionospheric disturbances have been classified and treated as SID's although they could not be associated with any distinctive solar feature. For some events this was undoubtedly due to the observational difficulties involved in making optical measurements. From data obtained during the International Geophysical Year, it has been found that almost all SID's occurred at the time of a flare and that all but one of the others occurred when there were active Hα regions on the sun [8].

9.5. TYPE OF SOLAR RADIATION PRODUCING SID'S

The occurrence of an SID is always confined to the sunlit hemisphere. It must therefore be caused by an increase above normal of the solar ionizing electromagnetic radiation, that is, by an intensity enhancement in the short ultraviolet or X-ray region of the spectrum. It may be recalled from Chapter 2 that the main constituents of the upper atmosphere, N_2, O_2, and O, are ionized only by radiation of wavelength $\lambda < 1026$ Å. The molecule NO, however, which can be assumed to be present as a trace constituent in the upper atmosphere, can be ionized by radiation of longer wavelength ($\lambda < 1300$ Å) including the hydrogen Lyman α line at 1215 Å, and NO ionization by Lyman α is now widely accepted as the mechanism underlying ordinary D-layer ionization.

Because the Hα radiation is greatly enhanced at the time of a flare and the SID effects indicate an electron number density enhancement over an extended height range, it had been assumed until quite recently that SID's were caused by a parallel increase in the sun's Lyman α emission. This could be expected to produce an enhancement of the electron concentration down to about 70 km. Increases of ionization by a factor of three have been estimated from a study of some VLF and LF effects, and enhancements of this magnitude might possibly be accounted for on the basis of increased Lyman α radiation.

This mechanism, however, has never been entirely satisfactory for various reasons. Perhaps the most serious of these is provided by the change in reflection height that is observed with 16 kc/s transmissions—a change from normal daytime levels of 75 km or so to heights as low as 60 km on occasion. The intensity of Lyman α is diminished by a factor exceeding 10^4 in this height range, and the intensity of the incident radiation must increase by at least this factor if it were to explain the observations. Such an increase is considered most unlikely.

It is therefore reasonable to assume that solar radiation at still shorter wavelengths is the cause of the ionization observed during an SID. In fact, the high-altitude measurements of solar intensity which have been made to date at times of disturbance seem to indicate that ionization by X-rays is actually the dominant process.

One of the most interesting results to come from the American rocket program has been the detection of X-ray fluxes during SID's [26]. Data were obtained for a number of flares, most of which were accompanied by SID's. Substantially greater X-ray fluxes were recorded throughout the spectrum during solar flares than for quiet-sun conditions. Appreciable hardening of the X-ray spectrum was also observed, and it is suggested that the hardness is a more important factor than the total flux intensity in accounting for the occurrence of the SID's. No evidence was found for large increases in Lyman α emission although the firings were made to coincide with the maximum phase of the flares. Extensive observations made with the satellite 1960 Eta 2 have confirmed these earlier results and have added further detailed information [21]. The Lyman α radiation accompanying distinct solar events was found to be only a small fraction of the average Lyman α emission from the whole disk, and such small changes were not geophysically significant. On the other hand, a very good correlation was found between the $0-8$ Å X-ray flux associated with flares and other distinct events on the sun, and the occurrence of short-wave fadeouts and other related ionospheric effects on the earth.

Friedman [16] has put forward an explanation of these emissions in terms of intense heating of the coronal atmosphere above the visible flare. An equivalent temperature of 5×10^6 °K is suggested to account for the 8 Å radiation, and even higher temperatures for the solar processes which produce the emissions at 2 Å. He has also noted that there will be a limiting value of 1.4 Å for temperatures above 10^7 °K, which may account for the fact that the apparent maximum change in reflection height for VLF transmissions is 15 km (see Sec. 9.6.1), independent of the size of the flare. There is a difference of about 15 km between the depth of atmospheric penetration for Lyman α and 1 Å X-rays.

Although the rocket and satellite measurements are still relatively few, they leave little doubt that *X*-rays are the ionizing radiations responsible for SID's. Large variations in characteristics of SID's, which have hitherto been attributed to the relative intensities of Lyman α and *X*-rays, now seem more likely to be caused by variations in the *X*-ray emission alone.

9.6. DESCRIPTION OF SID'S

The increase in the electron number density in the ionosphere at the time of an SID has a marked effect on the propagation of radio waves. Because of the vertical extent of the enhanced ionization, the radio effects can often be observed on frequencies from a few kc/s up to almost 100 Mc/s. The SID is usually described in terms of these radio-wave effects, and the term is often used in reference to any one or to a combination of the radio-wave variations.

9.6.1. VLF and LF Effects. Low and very low frequency signals reflected from the ionosphere at both oblique and near-vertical incidence show anomalous change of phase at the time of the SID. This is called a 'sudden phase anomaly' (SPA) and it is interpreted as indicating a real decrease in the height of the reflection level. Many of the observations have been made at 16 kc/s [7]. Waves of this frequency are normally reflected from a height of about 75 km by day, where the electron density has a value of about 300 electrons cm^{-3}. Decreases of apparent reflection heights as great as 15 km have been recorded. From 16 kc/s to 113 kc/s the magnitude of the SPA seems to be independent of frequency, and the decrease of 15 km appears to be a limiting value which is independent of the size of the flare as already noted. At 150 kc/s the SPA's are very small. At this frequency the reflection takes place in the lower part of the *E* region and the phase change is probably due to the passage of the radio wave through the enhanced ionization below the reflection level as well as to the change in the reflection height.

The increase in the *D*-region ionization also causes pronounced changes in the signal strength of VLF atmospherics in the frequency range of 2 kc/s to 500 kc/s, which are propagated by the lower ionosphere from distant thunderstorms [10, 18]. At a lower limit of about 10 kc/s the intensity of the noise signals is increased, and this effect has been named 'sudden enhancement of atmospherics' (SEA). The maximum of the signal enhancement seems to occur most frequently at 22–30 kc/s, although SEA's vary greatly in this respect and maxima have been observed at much higher frequencies. Below 10 kc/s, the field strength of the atmospherics is usually decreased, and at 5 kc/s it may be reduced by as much as a factor of ten.

9.6.2. HF Effects. Waves in the HF band, which are propagated through the *D* region, usually suffer severe and rapid attenuation at the time of an

SID. This is termed 'short wave fade' (SWF) or 'fadeout.' Since the absorption of the HF signals is usually so great as to exceed the dynamic range of the recording equipment, it is difficult to obtain quantitative measures of the effect. A few measurements made with a vertical-incidence ionosonde operating in the frequency range of 1 to 5 Mc/s have shown [2] that during large fadeouts in the middle of the day at medium latitudes, the total absorption increased by a factor of between five and ten.

Similar decreases are observed in the intensity of extraterrestrial noise signals received in the frequency range 15 to 60 Mc/s. Such decreases are called 'sudden cosmic noise absorption' (SCNA). Measurements of the variations in the intensity of cosmic noise are extremely useful in the study of SID's because of the improved sensitivity, SCNA's of as little as 0.2 db being detectable. They have the further advantage, in the absence of solar noise, of giving the complete time variation of the absorption event. They do not, however, give any information about the height of the absorbing region since the SCNA represents the integrated absorption of the total enhanced ionization.

9.6.3. VHF Effects. It has been found in recent years that radio waves in the frequency range of 30–100 Mc/s, which are propagated by scattering from irregularities in the lower ionosphere, are also affected during an SID. Both increases and decreases in the intensity of the forward-scatter signal have been observed at different times. These apparently inconsistent results are usually attributed to variations in the intensity and the depth of penetration into the ionosphere of the ionizing radiations. During a weak SID, the electron number-density enhancement extends down only to the height at which the VHF waves are scattered, and a signal enhancement results. In a major SID, the electron number density is increased also below the scattering region, where the collisional frequency is high, and attenuation of the VHF signal is then observed.

9.6.4. Geomagnetic Effects. Many SID's are accompanied by anomalous variations in the earth's magnetic field, referred to as magnetic 'crochets' or geomagnetic 'solar flare effects' (SFE). The variations are not large, usually 20–30 gammas, and are mainly in the horizontal direction though observable on all three components of the field.

Crochets have been observed to occur mainly with large flares although not all large flares are accompanied by these magnetic variations; the correlation is in fact based largely on statistical studies. There is some evidence to show that flares which can be associated with crochets indicate special solar conditions. Such flares have been found to occur most frequently 35°–50° on either side of the sun's central meridian. It has also been found that, for these crochet-associated flares, the average width of the Hα line at maximum is large, typically 6–10 Å [9].

Crochets, like SID's, are observed over most of the sunlit hemisphere. But, unlike the SID intensities, the crochet amplitudes are sometimes quite different from station to station, and for these events there does not appear to be any simple dependence on the solar zenith angle. The amplitude-time variation of the crochet is somewhat similar to the SID, and the start is almost coincident with the start of the flare. The duration of the crochet, however, is usually much shorter than either the SID or the flare, and the peak in the magnetic deviation occurs about 2.5 min after the peak in the hydrogen emission.

The transverse conductivities of the ionosphere are largest in the *E* region (see Sec. 7.2 and Fig. 7.1). Little is known, however, about the exact height of the ionospheric currents believed to be responsible for the crochets. Current systems derived from crochet amplitudes at a number of widely separated observatories were found to be very similar to the current system derived from the normal quiet-day variations of the magnetic field, and until quite recently it was generally thought that the crochets indicated a simple increase in the intensity of normal quiet-day currents in the *E* region. Analysis of the development of SPA's and SEA's, involving the concept of a relaxation time in the ionosphere, has led to the derivation of heights of 120–130 km for the crochet currents, though heights as low as 70 km have also been suggested. In a comprehensive study of absorption in the *D* and lower *E* regions, Appleton and Piggott [2] presented several arguments for believing that the crochet and quiet-day currents could not flow at the same level. Recent synoptic studies have shown that there are probably two current systems contributing to the production of the crochets. One of these is the normal *Sq* system in the *E* region, which is enhanced during an SID, and the other is a flare-produced system at a slightly lower level in the *D* region. The contributions of these two systems to the magnetic effects are estimated to be about equal [27].

9.7. IONIZATION DURING SID'S

One of the problems in the study of SID's is the determination of the spatial distribution of the electron number-density increase at the time of the disturbance. One of the parameters useful for this study is f_{min}, the minimum frequency of total reflections observed by a vertical-incidence ionosonde. During an ionization enhancement in the lower ionosphere, radio-wave absorption is increased, especially at the low end of the HF band, and f_{min} rises. Measurements of f_{min} from a large number of medium and low-latitude stations have been used by Japanese scientists to determine the geographic extent of the SID. It was found that the intensity of the SID was a function of solar zenith angle but was not controlled by the geomagnetic latitude [31].

Very little is known with certainty about the electron density–height profile. It may be inferred from the variety of effects observed that the changes in the electron density cannot be very localized. Medium-frequency vertical-incidence soundings have shown partial reflections at heights as low as 56 km. Phase anomalies in the VLF transmissions indicate ionization changes at 70–75 km, and there must also be appreciable changes at 90 km to produce SPA's at 150 kc/s. Measurements of absorption of HF waves probably indicate changes between 80 and 100 km, and the magnetic SFE's suggest an even broader range of heights, as has been noted.

Vertical-incidence soundings on 2.28 Mc/s have revealed a rather complex structure of the lower ionosphere during SID's [18]. Both increases and decreases in the amplitudes of partial reflections are observed from levels below the E region. These have shown that very large increases in the electron density occur in the lower ionosphere and that the relative increases are greatest at the bottom. It has been estimated from this work that in a typical large SID, associated with a class 2 or 3 flare, the mean enhancement might vary from 20/1 at 65–70 km, through 3/1 at 90 km, to unity at 110 km. Measurements at 2.66 Mc/s and 6.275 Mc/s during a class 2+ flare showed that the electron number densities in the 60–75 km region had increased by about a factor of ten, and that the electron density gradient in this height region had increased by about a factor of two [5].

Most SID's show a rapid onset coincident with or soon after the start of the flare. The intensity of the radio-wave fadeout often follows the Hα variations of line width quite closely, whereas the SPA and the SEA do so only during the initial stages and then decay much more slowly. The maximum of all these radio-wave manifestations of an SID usually lags 5–10 min behind the maximum of the flare itself, presumably because of relaxation effects. The relaxation time is given approximately by $(2\alpha N_0)^{-1}$, where α is the recombination coefficient and N_0 the electron density at the time of maximum [1].

The determination of recombination coefficients from the time-lag of ionospheric layer variations has already been discussed with reference to normal diurnal variations, at the end of Sec. 3.4.1, and it provides a basis of comparison for SID studies. From the ratio of the relaxation time during the SID to the relaxation time during undisturbed periods, either the height of the disturbed region (as represented by α) or the magnitude of the ionization enhancement can be calculated if the other one is known. In view of the complex structure just discussed, though, the usefulness of this approach seems very limited. It has not in fact been extensively employed.

Values of the electron collisional frequency, ν, have been calculated by Findlay [15] from the measured changes in group and phase paths of radio waves near 2 Mc/s, reflected from the E region during fadeouts. The most probable value of ν was then used to compute a height of 101 ± 2 km.

This height was considered to be about the same as the level of the ionization enhancement. The analysis involved a number of somewhat doubtful assumptions, and Findlay stated that the height obtained should be regarded as an upper limit.

There are relatively few observations of SID effects in the *E* region. The changes of electron density at about 100 km are difficult to detect, in part because of the small magntitude of the effects and in part because of the *D*-region absorption. Bibl [6] has reported that, during the summer months of 1950, all enhancements of the *E*-layer penetration frequency that exceeded the median by at least 0.2 Mc/s coincided with SID's.

Part of the difficulty in obtaining a general picture of the SID is due to the lack of simultaneous multifrequency measurements. Comparisons between different frequencies must at present be confined almost entirely to observations made at different times and in different places. This leads to the assumption of a kind of 'average' SID which, because of the variability of the phenomena, often has very little meaning. The only investigation so far which has been based on a number of simultaneous measurements at different frequencies has been conducted by Morriss [24]. In this study, sudden phase anomalies were recorded on 16 kc/s and 19.6 kc/s, whereas changes of phase path were measured by vertical pulse transmissions on four frequencies. Two of the latter, near 2 Mc/s and 2.8 Mc/s, were chosen to give reflections from the *E* region, and the other two, approximately at 4 Mc/s and 6 Mc/s, were selected because they would be reflected from the *F* region. Variations in cosmic noise were also recorded on 16.5 Mc/s and 24.3 Mc/s. For details of the analysis of this comprehensive set of measurements see the original account of the work; only a few of the important results can be repeated here. Morriss concluded that most of the extra ionization at the time of the SID is produced in the *E* region, extending at least to the *E*-layer peak and probably up to 150 km. On the other hand, because of the variation of the collision frequency with height, the absorption of the radio waves takes place predominantly very low in the ionosphere, often at heights of about 65 km and on occasion even as low as about 50 km.

A few accounts of early investigations described changes in the *F* region at times of SID's, and two notable cases have been reported when increases of about 1 Mc/s were observed in the *F*2 critical frequencies. More recently, new techniques have been employed that permit the effects of solar flares to be studied in the height region between about 100 km and 200 km [19]. The observed effects are relatively small and comparatively short-lived but can be identified as due to an increase in the electron number density of the upper *E* and *F* regions. These manifestations tend to appear somewhat (from 2–8 min) earlier than the accompanying short-wave fadeout in those cases that show both effects. Not all flares are found to be accompanied by

F-region effects, just as not all flares are accompanied by fadeouts, but the probability of observing increased ionization effects in the higher ionosphere appears to increase with increasing flare importance.

REFERENCES

1. Appleton, E. V., A note on the "sluggishness" of the ionosphere, *J. Atmos. Terr. Phys.*, **3** (1953), 282.
2. Appleton, E. V., and W. R. Piggott, Ionospheric absorption measurements during a sunspot cycle, *J. Atmos. Terr. Phys.*, **5** (1954), 141.
3. Babcock, H. D., The sun's polar magnetic field, *Astrophys. J.*, **130** (1959), 364.
4. Babcock, H. W., and H. D. Babcock, The sun's magnetic field, 1952–1954, *Astrophys. J.*, **121** (1955), 349.
5. Belrose, J. S., and E. Cetiner, Measurement of electron densities in the ionospheric D-region at the time of a 2+ solar flare, *Nature*, **195** (1962), 688.
6. Bibl, K., The ionization of the E layer, its evaluation and its relation to solar eruptions, *Ann. Geophys.*, **7** (1951), 208.
7. Bracewell, R. N., and T. W. Straker, The study of solar flares by means of very long radio waves, *Mon. Not. Roy. Astron. Soc.*, **109** (1949), 28.
8. DeMastus, H., and M. Wood, Short-wave fadeouts without reported flares, *J. Geophys. Res.*, **65** (1960), 609.
9. Dodson, H. W., and E. R. Hedeman, Crochet-associated flares, *Astrophys. J.*, **128** (1958), 636.
10. Ellison, M. A., The Hα radiation from solar flares in relation to sudden enhancements of atmospherics on frequencies near 27 Kc/s, *J. Atmos. Terr. Phys.*, **4** (1953), 226.
11. Ellison, M. A., Report of the Working Group on flare classification, *Trans. I.A.U.*, **9** (1955), 146.
12. Ellison, M. A., Solar flares, *Nature*, **193** (1962), 532.
13. Ellison, M. A., S. M. P. McKenna, and J. H. Reid, The solar flares of 1960 April 1, *The Observatory*, **80** (1960), 149.
14. Evans, J. W., Birefringent filters, in The Sun, ed. G. P. Kuiper, Chicago University Press, 1953, p. 626.
15. Findlay, J. W., An investigation of sudden radio fadeouts on a frequency near 2 Mc/sec, *J. Atmos. Terr. Phys.*, **1** (1951), 367.
16. Friedman, H., The sun's ionizing radiations, in Physics of the Upper Atmosphere, ed. J. A. Ratcliffe, New York: Academic Press, 1960, p. 133.
17. Friedman, H., X-ray and ultraviolet radiation measurements from rockets, in Space Astrophysics, ed. W. Liller, McGraw-Hill, 1961, p. 107.
18. Gardner, F. F., The use of atmospherics to study the propagation of very-long radio waves, *Phil. Mag.*, **14** (1950), 1259.

19. Kanellakos, D. P., Origin and location of ionospheric perturbations affecting the instantaneous frequency and azimuthal angle of arrival of the waves, in Radio Astronomical and Satellite Studies of the Atmosphere, ed. J. Aarons, North-Holland Publishing Company, 1963, p. 525.

20. Kreplin, R. W., Solar *X*-rays, *Ann. Geophys.*, **17** (1961), 151.

21. Kreplin, R. W., T. A. Chubb, and H. Friedman, X-ray and Lyman-Alpha emission from the sun as measured from the NRL SR-1 satellite, *J. Geophys. Res.*, **67** (1962), 2231.

22. Menzel, D. H., Our Sun, Cambridge: Harvard University Press, 1959, p. 106.

23. Moreton, G. E., and H. E. Ramsay, Recent observations of dynamical phenomena associated with solar flares, *Publ. Astn. Soc. Pac.*, **72** (1960), 357.

24. Morriss, R. W., Observations of sudden ionospheric disturbances, *Proc. Phys. Soc.*, **76** (1960), 79.

25. Sverny, A. B., Nonstationary processes, in solar flares as a manifestation of the pinch effect, *Soviet Astronomy A. J.*, **2** (1958), 310.

26. U. S. Naval Research Laboratory Report, Rocket astronomy and astrophysics research at the U. S. Naval Research Laboratory, March 1959 to October, 1960, *Nat. Acad. Sc. IGY Bulletin*, no. 45, (1961).

27. Volland, H., and J. Taubenheim, On the ionospheric current system of the geomagnetic solar flare effect (SFE), *J. Atmos. Terr. Phys.*, **12** (1958), 258.

28. Warwick, C. S., Flare height and association with SID's, *Astrophys. J.*, **121** (1955), 385.

29. Warwick, C. S., and M. Wood, A study of limb flares and associated events, *Astrophys. J.*, **129** (1959), 801.

30. Warwick, J., Heights of solar flares, *Astrophys. J.*, **121** (1955), 376.

31. Kasuya, I., Y. Hakura, and H. Hajo, on the SWF phenomenon (Dellinger effect) and f_{min} in the world-wide distribution, *J. Radio Res. Lab.* (*Tokyo*), **6** (1959), 1.

10

T. R. Hartz

Particle Emissions from the Disturbed Sun, and the Sun-Earth Environment.

10.1. INTRODUCTION

In addition to the abnormal photon emissions discussed in Chapter 9, the solar disturbances can energize particles of matter and accelerate them away from the sun. In succeeding chapters, we shall consider the disturbances of the upper atmosphere that are associated with such solar particles when they arrive at the earth. These disturbances are prevalent at high geomagnetic latitudes, and there they may persist for many days on end. Even at middle latitudes, and occasionally at low, they can lead to effects that are, on the whole, of greater moment than those of the very short-lived SID's. What are these particles, in what solar phenomena do they originate, how do they travel to the earth, and how do they enter the earth's atmosphere and generate the observed disturbances? We shall attempt to shed some light on these questions in this chapter.

The latitude dependence of the disturbed conditions led to an early appreciation that incoming charged particles, controlled in some way by the magnetic field of the earth, were involved. This conclusion was supported to some extent by laboratory model measurements and by Störmer's extensive theoretical calculations previously outlined (see

Chapter 5). Because his theoretical model neglected particle interactions, Störmer's analysis can be of interest only in those cases where the flux of solar particles is sufficiently low that mutual interactions are not important, and such cases are now known to occur only infrequently. They arise, not as a part of the auroral process that Störmer had in mind, but rather during the incidence of the so-called solar cosmic rays. When such energetic charged particles enter the earth's upper atmosphere, they are able to produce significant additional ionization in the D region, and a characteristic condition known as polar cap absorption (PCA) then results; this subject is discussed in some detail in Chapter 11.

More frequent are the occasions on which the solar particle flux is great enough that particle interactions are important. Under such conditions the traveling cloud or stream behaves as a plasma, which on arrival at the earth generates magnetic, ionospheric, and auroral disturbances or storms (Chapters 12–14). It is convenient to apply the term 'storm plasma' to the ejected solar material in these cases. The chain of events that follows upon the arrival of the storm plasma in the neighborhood of the earth is undoubtedly complex; consequently, a great variety of suggestions and theories have been advanced to account for the abnormal conditions. Included among these, in earlier days, were some that avoided the assumption of a solar plasma, but all such have failed so far to gain more than transitory recognition. There now seems little doubt that the high-latitude disturbances have their origin in particle emissions from the sun; and the current theories of geomagnetic and auroral storms (Chapter 15) are based almost exclusively on this premise.

There is, likewise, little argument against a solar origin for the PCA particles. In their flight from the sun both classes of particles are influenced by the interplanetary gas and the magnetic field in the region between the sun and the earth. The PCA particles or solar cosmic rays are able to pass through the interplanetary gas and their motion in that region seems to be controlled by the magnetic field existing there. On the other hand, the storm plasma sweeps the interplanetary gas ahead of it, producing a blast wave of some description that travels from the sun in advance of the solar plasma cloud.

It is interesting to note that, historically, the storm particles were thought to take the form of a stream of like particles. Later, when it was recognized that such a stream should be dispersed by coulomb forces in the absence of a background gas, a neutral stream, consisting of equal numbers of positive and negative particles, was postulated. This neutral-stream concept has received most attention and currently is still the basis of most theoretical models. In recent years a number of variations of this concept have been proposed, and the current literature contains such descriptive terms as 'wind,' 'tongue,' 'bottle,' 'beam,' 'bubble,' 'cloud,' 'shock wave,' and 'blast wave.' The particular model chosen is dependent largely on the assumed conditions in interplanetary space, particularly in connection with the background gas density and the magnetic field in the region between the sun and the earth.

The following sections discuss the common environment of the sun and the earth and the influence this has on the solar particles in their flight. The near atmosphere of the sun is considered, as are some of the phenomena that occur in this atmosphere at times when solar particles are thought to be traveling through it. The meager observations that denote the passage of solar material through the interplanetary regions are reviewed and the causal relationship between unusual events on the sun and terrestrial disturbances is discussed. Note that many of the deductions drawn from the observations are necessarily argumentative and possibly may be subject to more than one interpretation. It is to be hoped that these uncertainties will soon be resolved with the acquisition of more data.

10.2. THE SOLAR CORONA AND THE INTERPLANETARY GAS

Any discussion of the transport of material particles from the sun to the vicinity of the earth must include a consideration of the intervening medium. The early workers in this field believed that the gas concentration was of negligible significance during usual conditions except in the immediate neighborhoods of the sun and the earth. Consequently, they did not think the interplanetary gas to be very important for the processes associated with a solar particle stream. Recently, this view has changed; this gas, with its associated magnetic field, now plays an important part in current theoretical models.

There is fairly extensive information on the gaseous atmosphere near the sun. Immediately above the visible photosphere (of radius R_0, the 'solar radius') and extending out to a heliocentric distance of about $1.02R_0$, lies the 'chromosphere,' described in Chapter 2, in which the gas is only partly ionized and across which there is a steep temperature gradient. Beyond this limit lies the approximately isothermal corona with a temperature of the order of 10^6 °K. The gas here is completely ionized, consisting predominantly of protons and electrons, and its concentration is usually given by the number density of electrons. The electron number densities in various parts of the corona have been measured, principally at times of eclipses, and fairly reliable data have been obtained out to distances of about $20R_0$ [1]. Average values for these densities as a function of radial distance are shown in Fig. 10.1. It is not intended to imply that these values are constant; on the contrary, there is evidence that near the sun the mean densities change by a factor of two or more between sunspot minimum and maximum. Moreover, the inner corona is not spherically symmetrical, being somewhat less dense over the polar regions and significantly (by upward of

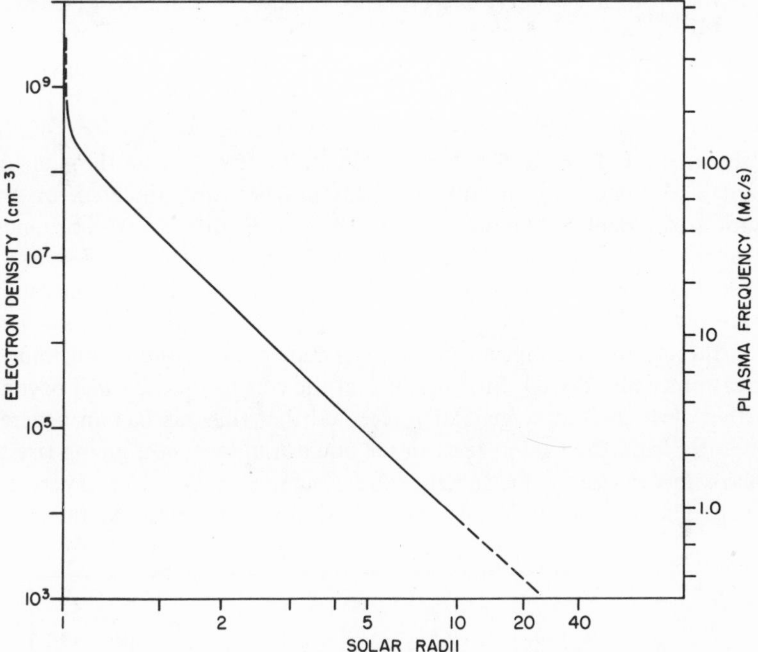

Fig. 10.1 Mean electron density, and corresponding plasma frequency, as a function of radial distance from the sun.

an order of magnitude) more dense over localized active regions on the sun. Nevertheless, the values shown in Fig. 10.1 are probably sufficiently representative of undisturbed solar conditions for present purposes. Also shown in Fig. 10.1 are the plasma frequencies that correspond to the respective electron densities: the significance of these frequencies is discussed in Sec. 10.4.2.

At heliocentric distances greater than about 20 R_0, the coronal densities are less certain. Not only does this represent a practical limit for measurements of the polarization of coronally scattered light, but the electron component cannot be reliably distinguished from the dust component of the scattered light. A number of workers have attempted to overcome the first of these difficulties by taking observations of the zodiacal light near the earth's orbit, but here, too, there is the problem of resolving only the electron component of the scattered radiation. The most recent observations in this connection are those of Beggs *et al.*, who conclude that almost all of the measured polarization is attributable to the dust; accordingly, they place an upper limit of 36 cm^{-3} on the electron number density in interplanetary space at one astronomical unit from the sun [2].

Other types of observations have led to similar conclusions regarding the charged-particle densities in the neighborhood of the earth. Kupperian *et al.*, on the basis of Lyman α observations, found a proton density between 15 and 45 cm^{-3} in the interplanetary regions [3]. Several space probes have measured fluxes of charged particles during undisturbed conditions from which proton densities of the order of 10 cm^{-3} have been obtained. These order-of-magnitude values are represented by the dashed portions of the curve shown in Fig. 10.2. The values due to Blackwell near the sun are indicated in the figure by the full line; this has been extrapolated, on the assumption of a density that varies with the inverse square of the distance, to conform with the meager data near the earth's orbit previously discussed. The dashed curve should be considered rather tentative until better measurements are obtained.

Even though the gas density in the extended solar corona is not known with great precision, there is little doubt that the corona extends well beyond the earth's orbit. It is now generally accepted that this gas has an ordered motion away from the sun, at least in the equatorial latitudes, giving rise to the 'solar wind' concept: this subject will be pursued in Sec. 10.5. There are also indications that a significant concentration of dust exists in the inter-

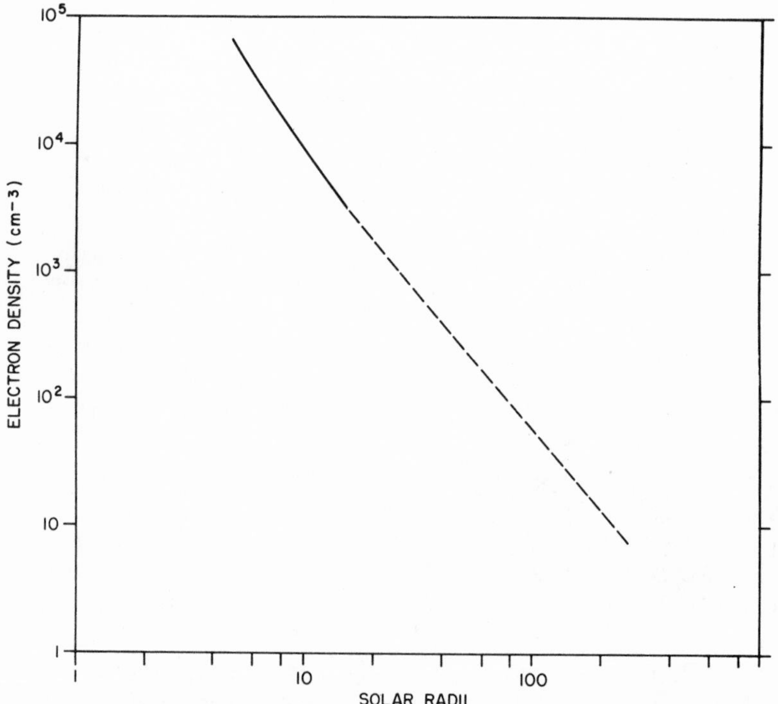

Fig. 10.2 Estimated electron densities in the inner solar system, plotted as a function of radial distance from the sun. The earth is at a distance of about 215 R_0 (=1 A. U.).

planetary regions, mainly in the invariant plane of the solar system of planets, but this is not considered to have much influence on the ejected solar particles.

So far we have been dealing with the corona during quiet or undisturbed conditions. During disturbed periods when excess solar material is traversing the interplanetary regions, some increase in electron density is expected; but the amount of the increase is still a controversial subject. A number of estimates have been made of the densities in a particle cloud or stream, and the values range from as low as 1 cm^{-3} to as much as 10^5 cm^{-3} for a large magnetic storm, but these are admittedly very uncertain. Unsöld and Chapman [4], who obtained the highest value, based their estimates on some measurements of an absorption spectrum believed to be due to ions between the sun and the earth. Not only were these measurements marginal, but they have since been repeated with negative results [5]. Consequently, there now seems little reason to postulate an increase in electron number density of more than one or two orders of magnitude in the solar particle cloud during a moderately intense geomagnetic storm.

In this connection, it was thought that the zodiacal light should brighten substantially if the electron density at the earth increased significantly. An increase in brightness by a factor of at least 100 has been suggested as a necessary consequence of a thousandfold increase in electron density. Blackwell and Ingham have indeed found an increase in brightness during an intense geomagnetic storm, but only by some 40%, which they tend to associate with the interplanetary dust [6]. Even under storm conditions, it seems that the electron component of the zodiacal light is not comparable to the dust component, in agreement with the preceding estimates for the electron density enhancement at about one astronomical unit (A.U.) from the sun.

The foregoing remarks apply, of course, only in connection with the storm particles. The particles that cause PCA events, the so-called solar cosmic rays, are not sufficiently numerous to affect significantly the interplanetary densities. In such circumstances, the electron number densities in the vicinity of the earth essentially remain at the undisturbed value until the arrival of the storm plasma and/or the associated shock wave.

Our incomplete knowledge of the particle densities, under both disturbed and normal conditions, is now being augmented by direct information from space vehicles. As we shall mention later, there are already a few such data, but not sufficient for a representative estimate at all phases of the solar cycle. Nevertheless, the exact value for the particle densities is less important than the fact that the background gas is a significant factor in the physical processes associated with the passage of the storm plasma and solar cosmic rays from the sun to the earth. Many of these processes are only now being considered and explored. Of particular significance in this connection are the solar wind concept and the frozen-in magnetic field concept, which will be discussed later.

10.3. MAGNETIC FIELDS IN THE EXTENDED SOLAR CORONA

The solar particles in the interplanetary regions, although in the form of an electrically neutral stream or cloud, are nevertheless ionized, and therefore cannot be considered independently of the magnetic field that exists there. The magnetic field will control the motion of the solar matter if the energy density of the field greatly exceeds that of the charged particles; that is, if $B^2/\mu_0 \gg \rho v^2$, where ρ is the density of solar matter moving with velocity v in a magnetic field of induction B. The PCA, or solar cosmic-ray particles fall into this category; despite their high energies, their concentration is usually sufficiently low that their motion is thought to be controlled by the interplanetary field. The low-energy storm-inducing particles, on the other hand, usually have a much greater flux, sufficiently so that their energy density exceeds that of the interplanetary field; hence they are thought to control the field. In particular, a cloud or stream of ionized storm-inducing material, propelled away from an active region on the sun, may carry away with it a 'frozen-in' portion of the magnetic field of the region: if the size of the cloud is large and the conductivity of the gas is high, this magnetic field will decay only very slowly with time. The interplanetary magnetic field, however, should be 'frozen-out' of the cloud, only slowly diffusing into it, so that the advancing plasma cloud should be preceded by a region containing swept-up interplanetary magnetic field and interplanetary plasma. So long as the energy density of the storm plasma cloud exceeds that of the interplanetary field, the latter cannot be expected to play a significant role in controlling the motion of the solar matter.

From the foregoing it is obvious that the interplanetary magnetic field is expected to vary with time and position. The direct measurements are not yet adequate to describe this field, and probably our best information is obtained from indirect observations. Their relevance may be appreciated in the light of the following theoretical model.

On the hypothesis that, during undisturbed conditions, the extended solar corona is in an ordered motion away from the sun—in a so-called 'solar wind'—Parker [7] has proposed a model for the magnetic field in these regions. According to his argument, the outward-moving ionized material from the sun would carry with it 'frozen-in' magnetic field lines, the ends of which necessarily would remain anchored to the emissive region on the sun. The rotation of that body will introduce a curvature to the field lines which can be represented, near the sun's equatorial plane, by the relation $\tan \phi = \omega r/v$. This applies in the case of a particular stream with frozen-in field lines that is moving radially from the sun with velocity v, where ω is

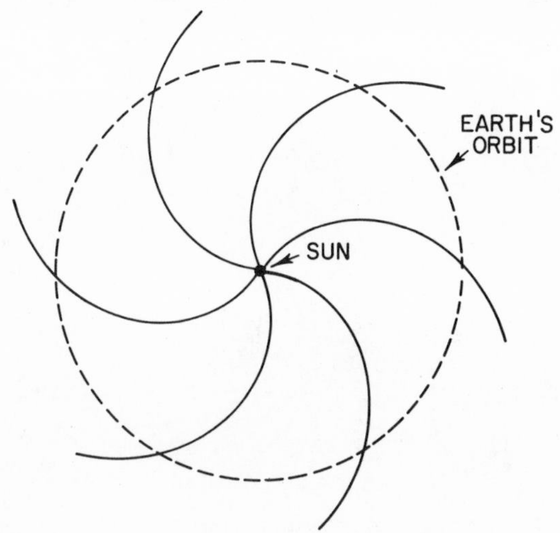

Fig. 10.3 Solar magnetic field lines as viewed from above the sun's north pole.

the sun's angular velocity and ϕ is the 'stream angle' between a radius vector **r**, drawn from the sun to the point in question, and the solar magnetic field line that passes through that point. If, now, there is a general particle emission from the surface of the sun, the resulting pattern for the magnetic field, projected into the sun's equatorial plane, is expected to have the configuration illustrated in Fig. 10.3.

Observations of the coronal structures at times of eclipses tend to show a radial pattern extending out to 2 or 3 solar radii, which is consistent with the foregoing model. At greater distances the coronal structures become invisible and can be studied only by means of their effect on radio waves that pass through the solar atmosphere. Emissions from certain discrete radio sources, such as Taurus A, are well suited for this study during the intervals when the sources are occulted by the solar corona. The irregular ionization structures in the corona diffract and scatter the radiations so that a measurement of the apparent shape of the discrete source can be interpreted in terms of the shape and orientation of the ionization irregularities. By this means the corona has been investigated out to heliocentric distances of $120R_0$ or more [8]. The results show that the scattering corona is ellipsoidal, extending to about $40R_0$ in the polar regions and to about $55R_0$ in the equatorial regions, although occasionally these latter regions show scattering out to $120R_0$: the greater equatorial extension probably is related to the active belt on the visible sun. Moreover, the shape of the irregularities out to distances of $60R_0$ has been found to be elongated approximately radially with respect to the solar axis of rotation. Some of the striking results obtained

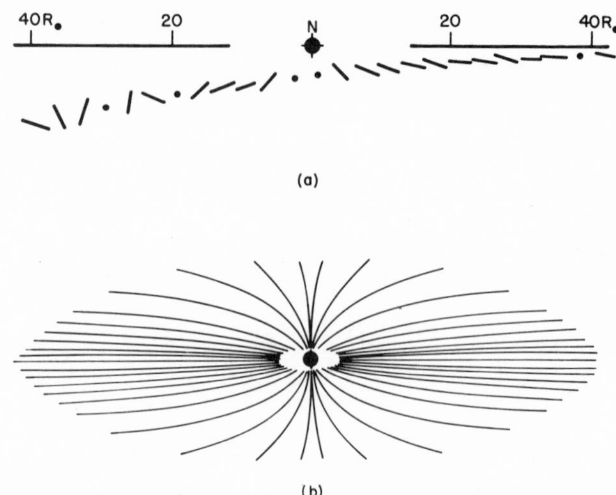

Fig. 10.4 (a) The direction of alignment of the scattering filaments plotted, as seen from the earth, relative to the equatorial plane of the sun. A point signifies no significant scattering anisotropy or solar interference. (From Gorgolewski and Hewish [9].)

(b) Idealized representation of solar magnetic field lines as viewed from the earth.

in June, 1959, by Gorgolewski and Hewish within $40R_0$ of the sun, have been reproduced here in Fig. 10.4(a) [9]. With the exception of those shown in the extreme left-hand side of the diagram, the observations indicate elongated ionization irregularities that are oriented more or less radially with respect to the solar axis, in agreement with the Parker model if the ionization is distributed along magnetic field lines. An idealized representation of such a field, as viewed from the earth, is shown in Fig. 10.4(b). It is significant that, with the exception of two very minor magnetic disturbances, the period during which the foregoing observations were made was one of geomagnetic inactivity: the inferred field pattern illustrated in Fig. 10.4(b) probably applies only at such times. The disordered field depicted in the left of Fig. 10.4(a) can be attributed to the presence of an active region on the southeast quadrant of the sun at the time: the corpuscular stream or tongue associated with that region caused a weak geomagnetic disturbance when it swept over the earth midway during the observing interval.

Much stronger evidence for the existence of the spiral field pattern is provided by the measurements of the directions in space from which solar cosmic-ray particles approach the earth. A study of the impact zones on the earth's surface in several cases of solar-flare-associated influxes has shown that the particles first arrive from a direction some 50 degrees west of the sun [10]. This observation is readily explained if the low flux of solar particles can be guided to the earth by a curved pattern of solar magnetic field lines as illustrated in Fig. 10.3.

During geomagnetically undisturbed conditions, then, the indirect observations of the magnetic field in the extended solar corona seem to be consistent with the theoretical model proposed by Parker. This pattern is represented in Figs. 10.3 and 10.4(b) which depict the expected field in, and at right angles to, the plane of the solar equator. As far as direct observations of the magnetic field are concerned, there have not yet been enough of these to confirm the expected model. The Pioneer V space probe obtained magnetometer data in interplanetary space, from which Coleman *et al.* deduced that the field during quiet conditions was oriented at right angles to the plane of the ecliptic [11]. It has since been pointed out, however, that a reinterpretation of the same data would yield an orientation similar to that shown in Fig. 10.3 but with a slightly greater curvature—say curved through an angle of about 50 degrees in 1 A.U. [12]. The space probes Explorer X and XII both carried magnetometers, but it is not certain that their orbits took them sufficiently far from the earth to get magnetic field measurements representative of interplanetary space [13]. Nevertheless, stream angles (ϕ) of about 50 degrees were observed during undisturbed conditions. The more recent and more extensive observations [50] by Mariner II during undisturbed conditions have confirmed the spiral field structure at times, but not always. That is, the instantaneous values show this general pattern at times and, at times, fluctuate considerably in direction, but a general average of these data indicates that the field has the spiral form shown in Fig. 10.3. The basic structure of the field appears to be a spiral pattern with a stream angle of about 45°, but there are many small-scale variations in this general pattern.

The magnitude of the interplanetary field during undisturbed conditions was found by Pioneer V to fluctuate between approximately 2 and 6 gamma, whereas the Explorer X values were about three times as great. The Mariner II data fluctuated in the range 2 to 10 gamma.

So far nothing has been said about the extremities of the swept-out field lines. Presumably, they form closed loops at some distance beyond the earth's orbit, although at what distance this happens is not clear. Arguments have been advanced which would place the limit where the solar-wind material becomes neutralized through charge exchange with the intergalactic matter. Other arguments suggest that the field lines cannot continue to build up indefinitely and therefore there must be a pinching-off of the magnetic field at some point and the escape of 'blobs' of solar matter with their frozen-in field. In this connection, we shall see in a later section that a correlation has been found between solar activity and some observations on the planet Jupiter, which would seem to indicate that ejected solar material and perhaps the magnetic field lines can reach at least that far.

The foregoing model seems to be consistent with the few available data and, lacking a better alternative, will be taken here to represent the field pervading the whole sun-earth space. As some space probes have shown, however, the field is not as regular as depicted and smaller-scale variations and a certain degree of distortion are to be expected as the distance from the sun increases, although major departures from this idealized model are not anticipated within an astronomical unit of the sun during quiescent solar conditions. Accordingly, this field pattern serves as a background for the disturbance emissions, both the storm plasma and the solar cosmic rays. The latter are guided to a large extent along the curved field lines, with the result that the particles that reach the earth do so, in most cases, from the sun's western hemisphere rather than the eastern. In the case of the storm plasma, additional magnetic field will be carried out from the active region on the sun in the form of a tongue, as suggested by Gold [51], if the energy density and conductivity of the plasma are great enough. Consequently, the resulting configuration in interplanetary space depends on the relative flux and energy of the normal and the abnormal particle emission. For a storm plasma with sufficiently great energy density and having a velocity greater than that of the normal solar wind, a situation similar to that illustrated in Fig. 10.5 is expected. The diagram shows the magnetic 'tongue' at three different times in the advance of the storm plasma. Although this must be considered as a rather idealized representation of the actual situation, it portrays the important physical processes involved. The ejected matter travels radially outward from the sun, but the magnetic tongue assumes a curvature due to the solar rotation. This is analogous to the curved stream in the case

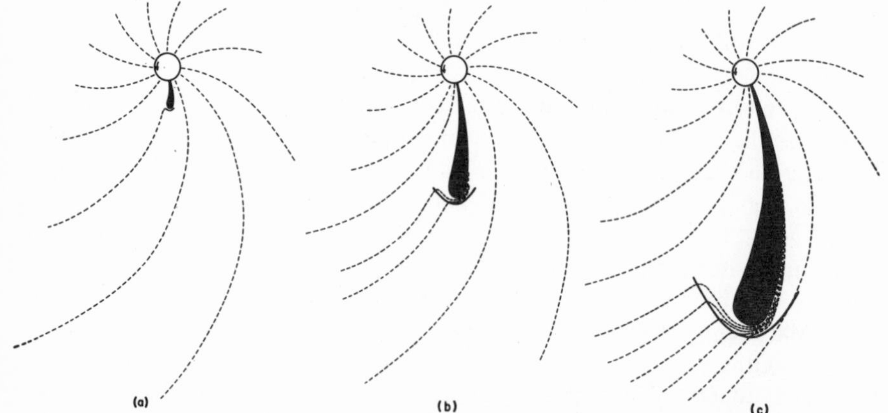

Fig. 10.5 An idealized representation of a magnetic tongue containing solar storm plasma at three different stages in its travel through the interplantary plasma, which itself is moving radially away from the sun but with a lower velocity. The thin spiralling lines represent the magnetic field lines, which are shown dashed outside of the tongue and continuous inside.

of a moving garden hose. (Note that we wish to portray a tongue, not a narrow stream, and since the tongue expands as it advances, the lateral dimension shown in the diagram may have been underestimated.) Because of the greater velocity of the storm particles, the interplanetary matter and existing magnetic field are swept up ahead of the plasma cloud to form a shock front, as indicated. This has a greater lateral extent than the particle cloud itself. Furthermore, the swept-up interplanetary matter exerts a pressure on one side of the plasma cloud or tongue, which may cause the storm particles to be deflected slightly from their otherwise radial trajectories.

This tongue configuration is the logical consequence of the ejection of ionized matter from a region on the sun that possesses a localized magnetic field. The question naturally arises as to whether the more or less radial (or spiral) magnetic field in the interplanetary region during quiet conditions is an extension of the field of the localized regions, that is, the remnants of decaying magnetic tongues, or does the sun have a general magnetic field that is extended because of continual emission from the whole surface? In the latter case the tongues from the localized emissive regions would introduce a transitory perturbation. This subject has not been satisfactorily resolved: the most reliable evidence for a general field seems to be the observation of a weak dipolar component near the poles, but the more recent observation of a period when both solar poles had the same sign followed by a reversal of the original magnetic polarity has not been satisfactorily explained, except perhaps in terms of a multiplicity of localized fields [14, 15].

10.4. OBSERVATIONS OF THE SOLAR PARTICLES NEAR THE SUN

The preceding sections have dealt briefly with the nature of the interplanetary regions during both undisturbed and disturbed conditions. In this and the following sections, we summarize some of the observations which have provided information on the ejected solar material at various distances from the sun. As already indicated, our main interest is in those emissions that can be linked to terrestrial disturbances or storms.

10.4.1. Optical Measurements. It will be recalled from Chapter 9 that optical instruments have revealed a number of unusual phenomena on the sun, some of which are thought to be associated with the emission of particles. Of special interest in this context are those features which collectively denote a 'center of activity,' since they have been found to correlate best with geomagnetic activity. Accordingly the flares, prominences, and other features that represent an evolutionary phase of a center of activity should show evidence of particles moving away from the sun, and in many cases such motions can be observed.

In the prominences, matter can be seen to rise and apparently fall back to the sun's surface. Occasionally the ascending motion becomes very pronounced and matter is ejected to great heights in what are known as 'eruptive' or 'surge' prominences. During such events the measured radial velocities are of the order of several hundred kilometers per second. Particles with velocities as great as this should be able to escape the sun's gravitational field and travel to the earth and beyond if no other forces operate to restrain them.

In some cases, surge prominences have been associated with flares that have appeared near the limb of the solar disk. This would indicate that flare material is ejected to great heights. Further substantiation for this conclusion has been found for flares appearing in other locations on the disk, mainly from measurements of the Doppler broadening and the Doppler shifts of hydrogen spectral lines, and from motion pictures of flare regions. Giovanelli and McCabe [16, 17] indentified two distinct ranges of velocity for the outward-moving solar matter: early in the life of the flare the high-speed 'puffs' move with velocities of the order of 50,000 km/sec; this is followed by a later surge phase in which a second cloud is seen to travel with velocities of the order of 1000 km/sec. Athay and Moreton also have indentified an 'explosive phase' for certain flares in which outward velocities of the order of 1500 km/sec have been noted for the clouds of matter [18].

It should not be taken that the particle motions just described represent the only observed motions in the solar atmosphere: only those have been mentioned that seem to be important for the terrestrial disturbances. There are numerous smaller-scale motions observable on the sun which are thought to have little likelihood of being associated with a particle efflux sufficient to disturb the terrestrial atmosphere. These may, however, have some significance in connection with the general emission that has been postulated to support the quasi-steady solar wind: this topic is beyond the scope of this book and will not be pursued further.

10.4.2. Radio Measurements. Some of the earliest observations of intense solar radio noise emissions were made at a time when a very large sunspot group was visible on the disk. The obvious conclusion that the noise was generated in the sunspots had to be rejected because it was realized that the intense ionization in the corona would not permit the observed radio frequencies to propagate outward from the photosphere. In order to be observable at the earth, the radiation must originate within the corona and above some minimum height, usually called the 'escape level,' which is determined by refractive effects. In a regular and spherically symmetrical corona, the height of the escape level above the photosphere is a function of the radio frequency, and also of the angle subtended at the sun's center by the observer and the radiation source. When this latter angle is small, that is, when the noise source is near the center of the apparent solar disk, the escape level coincides with the plasma level plotted in Fig. 10.1, whereas for larger angles the escape level will be somewhat higher: it also will be higher in the case of enhancements of electron number density, such as occur in the 'coronal condensations' over centers of activity. Accordingly, the values in Fig. 10.1 represent the minimum height from which a particular radio frequency can propagate to the earth, and because they are limital values, they probably are not severely dependent on the assumption of a regular corona.

From the foregoing, it is apparent that the observer can obtain information at various heights in the corona by a suitable choice of observing frequency, even though the electron densities may not be known with great precision. Moreover, by observing at a number of frequencies, he can trace the outward progress of sources of radio emission that are associated with disturbances on the sun. Such measurements can provide indirect information on ejected solar material at coronal heights where other, more direct measurements cannot be made.

The present discussion ignores the noise emissions from the quiet sun and deals only with the disturbance emissions which, at meter and decameter wavelengths, are usually considerably more intense. These long-wavelength emissions are thought to signal the passage of shock waves and clouds of charged particles through the corona, whereas the centimeter and millimeter wave emissions provide information on the very energetic processes close to the photosphere that accompany particle ejections. Within each of these wavelength ranges there are a number of characteristic types of radio noise, which may occur separately or in a sequential pattern. These types are described below, and their significance is discussed in regard to particle emissions.

Early measurements of the noise radiations at the time of a large flare disclosed that the noise bursts at the different frequencies were not always coincident in time: the lower-frequency bursts were sometimes delayed with respect to those at higher frequencies. Such observations are consistent with the outward movement through the corona of an agency that generates noise on successively decreasing frequencies as it advances, namely, the flare-ejected cloud of particles. Subsequent observations with sweep-frequency receivers, a technique pioneered by Wild and McReady [19], have identified a number of characteristic noise events, all of which seem to be associated with abnormal phenomena on the sun and probably with the ejection of ionized matter. They have also revealed that the noise emissions frequently exhibit a high degree of complexity, particularly at the longer wavelengths, as illustrated in Fig. 10.6, which is an idealized sketch of the noise spectrum associated with a major flare. Some of the features depicted here have been isolated and studied in detail as burst types II, III, etc. The main characteristics of these burst types and their relation to each other and to the flare are illustrated in the diagram. For an outstanding event, all these noise types may appear in a sequential pattern, as shown: for smaller

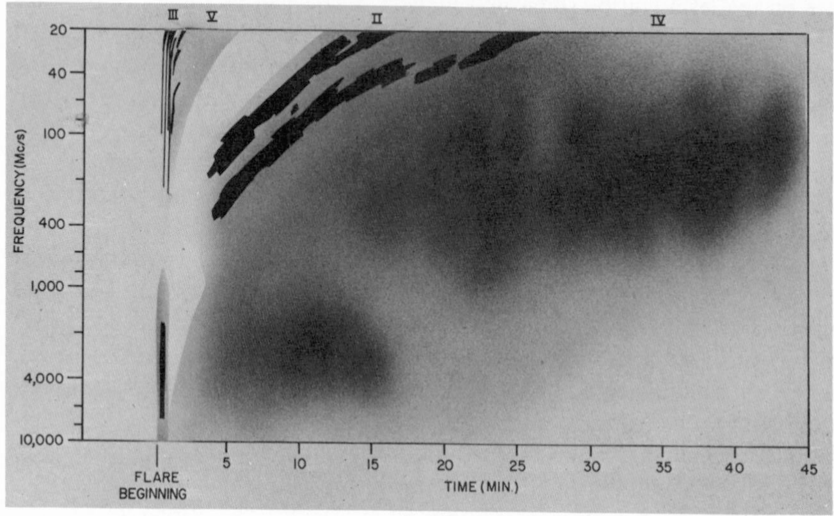

Fig. 10.6 Sketch of the dynamic spectrum of a radio noise outburst accompanying a major flare. The features at meter and decameter wavelengths are identified by the burst types II, III, IV, and V. At centimeter and decimeter wavelengths the distinctive features are the initial burst, sometimes called the M-type burst, followed by the enhanced continuum radiation.

events, not all of these features are expected, and in fact, many of the burst types usually appear separately in such cases.

The type II, or 'slow drift' burst has long been associated with the storm particles. The double-banded structure exhibited by many of these bursts has helped to identify the noise generation mechanism as a plasma oscillation of the coronal gas, thought to be excited by the ejected solar matter. Consequently, the data on electron densities in the corona permit the calculation of the velocities of the particles from the observed frequency drift of the bursts. The early computations yielded velocities of several hundred kilometers per second, which, though of the right order of magnitude, were too low to account for the delay of 1 to 2 days that is usually observed between large flares and geomagnetic storms. More recently, evidence has been found by Wood and Warwick for acceleration of the corpuscular clouds in the corona [20]. Furthermore, there is reason to believe that the coronal electron densities used in the earlier work were too low by almost an order of magnitude for the regions over centers of activity, and higher values can provide the correct range of velocities.

Nevertheless, there seems to be a basic difficulty in associating the type II bursts with the storm plasma. Although some of these bursts are followed within a day or two by a geomagnetic storm, there are others for which it is not possible to make such an identification. Moreover, this type of burst occurs much less frequently than do flares and geomagnetic storms. It would seem that the type II burst, by itself, cannot be considered necessary and sufficient evidence that a corpuscular cloud has been ejected from the sun. One recent hypothesis attributes this spectral feature to a shock wave that precedes the actual plasma cloud, rather than to the ejected particles, and this explanation, if correct, may account for some of the discrepancies.

The type III, or 'fast drift' noise burst likewise is thought to result from plasma oscillations of the coronal gas. From the observed frequency drifts have come estimates of velocity, originally of the order of 30,000 km/sec, but more recently these have been revised upward to an average of 150,000 km/sec, with a maximum in the neighborhood of 250,000 km/sec. Detailed studies have led Wild, Sheridan, and Neylan [21] to conclude that this type of noise originates from the interaction of relativistic electrons with the gas in the coronal streamers. They were able to trace the outward progress of the ejected electrons with a high-resolution radio telescope and showed that the source of the radiation moved away from the sun in a systematic manner. These high-energy electrons spiraling in the local magnetic field are themselves expected to radiate a characteristic type of noise known as 'synchrotron radiation.' This has been observed as a continuum emission, sometimes called a type V event, following the type III bursts, as indicated in Fig. 10.6.

The fast-drift bursts are associated with a large percentage of flares, and seem to be the only noise phenomenon accompanying the very small flares. From observations near the earth there seems little reason to believe that relativistic electrons in large numbers leave the sun as frequently as the type III bursts might lead us to conclude. No correlation between such bursts and geomagnetic storms has been found, and the PCA events have been shown to result from another type of particle. Consequently, the energetic electrons have either escaped direct detection so far, or else an alternative explanation exists for the fast-drift bursts.

The most promising type of noise for correlation with terrestrial disturbances is the so-called type IV event. As indicated in Fig. 10.6, this is a continuum radiation which has a long duration, occasionally persisting for more than a day. It is attributed to synchroton emission from electrons spiraling in a magnetic field. Radio studies of the source have shown the emissive regions to be quite extensive relative to the size of the generating flare, and to move away from the sun with velocities of the order of 1000 km/sec in the first few minutes of their lifetime. All type IV bursts are associated with flares, and are usually preceded by type II bursts. But, more important, when a type IV burst of great intensity occurs, it is usually followed within a period of 1 to 3 days by a geomagnetic storm [22, 23]. To be sure, the influence of the preceding type II cannot be overlooked in such cases, but the intense continuum emission seems to be the dominant parameter, since the type II–type IV combination correlates much better with subsequent terrestrial disturbances than does the occurrence of only the type II burst.

Observations of the type depicted in Fig. 10.6 made with sweep-frequency equipment are superior to those made with fixed-frequency receivers, but data from the latter have been available for a much longer period than from the former. There now seems little doubt that the classifications 'major' and 'major plus' bursts, first applied by Dodson, Hedeman, and Owren [24] to noise recordings made at a fixed frequency, signify, respectively, the presence of a type II burst and a type II–type IV burst combination. A number of studies have been made on the relationship between single-frequency noise bursts and geomagnetic activity, and their results have become much more meaningful because of the more recent burst classifications. Some of this work is summarized briefly here.

The general belief that the large solar flares are followed within several days by geomagnetic activity has been found to be conditional on the occurrence, at the time of the flare, of a 'major' or 'major plus' noise burst at frequencies below about 200 Mc/s. This is illustrated in Fig. 10.7, in which are plotted average geomagnetic indices following 76 major flares with, and 82 major flares without, such noise bursts [25]. It has been suggested that an

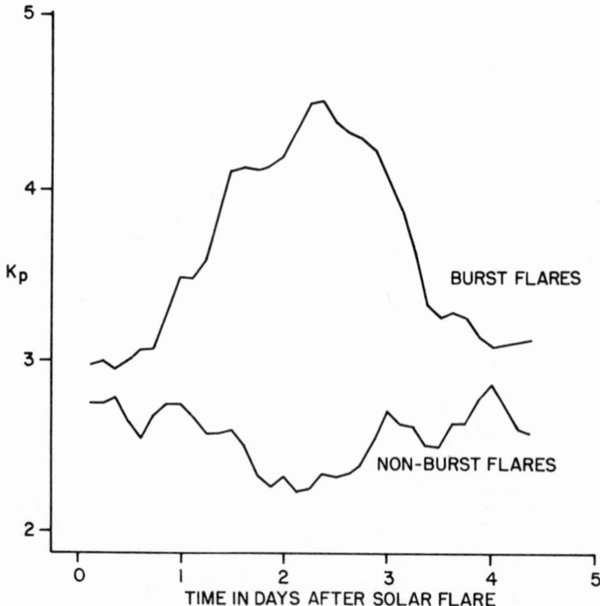

Fig. 10.7 Superposed epoch diagrams of the planetary magnetic indices following major flares that were, and were not, accompanied by major radio noise bursts at frequencies less than 200 Mc/s. (From Hartz and McAlpine [25].)

important requirement for positive correlation with terrestrial disturbances is that the burst occur in the premaximum phase of the optical flare, but subsequent work has not substantiated this. The location of the flare on the sun has been found to be an important factor, since the maximum correlation between burst flares and geomagnetic storms results from flares that cluster on the disk at about 20 degrees to the west of the sun's central meridian: similar flares near the solar limbs are generally followed by minor or no terrestrial disturbances [25].

The occurrence, at times of major flares, of the intense noise outbursts on fixed-frequency receivers—or of the intense type IV bursts on sweep-frequency equipment since their identification is more certain—at meter wavelengths is considered symptomatic of the ejection of plasma clouds from the sun. Such intense continuum radiation over a broad band of frequencies indicates a very high total energy content in the emissive region. The type II is a narrow-band emission which may relate only to the shock wave which advances through the corona ahead of the storm plasma. Occasionally the intense continuum radiation extends into the centimeter and millimeter wavelength regions of the spectrum, as illustrated in Fig. 10.6. In such cases a high degree of correlation has been found with the PCA events and with cosmic ray increases at the earth's surface [26]. It seems that the very intense, broad-band continuum radiation in the microwave region is symptomatic of the ejection of solar cosmic rays. On the other hand, the short wavelength bursts of lesser intensity seem to correlate well only with sudden ionospheric disturbances.

Besides the burst components of solar noise which occur in conjunction with flares, another type of noise fits into the present context. This is the long-enduring noise storm, type I noise. At meter wavelengths such a storm may be very intense and usually lasts for a number of days. It is found to accompany a large sunspot or large sunspot group. Statistical studies have revealed that the passage across the sun's central meridian of such noisy sunspots is correlated with subsequent increased geomagnetic activity, whereas the central meridian passage of quiet sunspots tends to be followed by a decrease in geomagnetic activity [27]. The significance of this decrease —and the role of the particular sunspot in inhibiting particle emission from the sun or, alternatively, in redirecting such emissions—has not yet been adequately assessed. It would seem, however, that noisy sunspots are associated with an increase in storm plasma emission from the sun.

The long-enduring noise enhancements extend to decimeter and centimeter wavelengths, but there they appear much less spiky in character and are much reduced in intensity relative to the meter-wavelength storm. These enhancements are usually referred to as the 'slowly varying component.' A high degree of correlation has been found between this type of noise and the centers of activity on the sun, and the noise is thought to originate in regions of exceptionally high electron number density in the chromosphere over such active centers. Such noise observations seem capable of defining the active solar regions; they also apparently provide a better index of the ultraviolet or *X*-radiation that is influential in the formation of the earth's ionosphere than is possible from sunspot data [28].

10.4.3. Particle Emission Mechanisms. Our knowledge of the solar processes that give rise to earth-reaching corpuscles is still very fragmentary and fraught with conjecture. There seems to be good reason for choosing meter-wavelength radio noise emissions as the most reliable criterion to denote particle ejection, since these radiations arise at high levels in the solar atmosphere: if the upper corona is not disturbed by ejected solar matter there seems little likelihood that the earth should be. The causal factors, however, probably are more closely associated with photospheric and chromospheric phenomena where optical observations can be more definitive. With the notable exception of the M-region particles (which are considered in Secs. 10.6 and 12.2.1), for which the solar source is still not certain, there now seems little doubt that the origin of the particles can be found in the centers of activity on the sun. But since each center undergoes an evolutionary cycle that may include such visual features as sunspots, plages or faculae, flares, filaments, prominences, etc. — many of which are present at the same time — it is difficult to determine what are the essential parameters for the emission of matter. In general, the most energetic phenomena appear very early in the life of the active center, and it is this early phase which includes the growth of most sunspots and the appearance of most of the flares. Since the terrestrial disturbances are linked more often than not with one or both of these two features, the circumstances surrounding the appearance and growth of an active center warrant investigation.

There is little difficulty in identifying a center of activity through one or other of its visual features, but it is not at all clear what underlying conditions produce such activity. Some theoretical models picture the active region as a magnetic disturbance that has reached the surface from within the sun. On this basis, the sunspots, flares, and other observed features are thought of as a consequence of the magnetic field disturbance and not as its cause. Accordingly, the study of magnetic fields in the region should prove quite fruitful in defining the various physical processes, and a number of investigations of this kind are going on. Zeeman splitting of certain spectral lines is observed, and for many years now the measurement and classification of sunspots according to their magnetic characteristics has been carried on. More recently it has been possible to explore, in detail, the field in the regions lying over active centers. The mappings that have been made show very irregular and highly variable field distributions in these regions at various phases, particularly in connection with sunspots and flares. For this reason many of the mechanisms suggested as responsible for the ejection of solar particles depend in some way on the complexities of the magnetic field associated with these features. We shall see later in Chapter 12 that observations made by Bell and Glazer [29, 30] show a greater probability of terrestrial disturbance when the sunspot group involved exhibits a complex magnetic field. Their results indicate that the complex (γ) sunspots are geomagnetically the most consistently disturbing of the various magnetic classes, and that the greatest percentage of the geomagnetically disturbing flares originate in the complex (γ) and semicomplex ($\beta\gamma$) regions.

Near the sun, at the lower heliographic latitudes the field is predominantly that of the localized areas. Here unipolar, bipolar, and multipolar spot groups are well known, and magnetic fields of several hundred to several thousand gauss have been found in such regions. Intense fields of this order led to an early suggestion that charged particles, while spiraling in the field, would give rise to electric fields sufficient to accelerate some of the particles to high energies and permit their escape from the sun. A popular suggestion was that the charged particles would be accelerated by a changing field of the kind observed in the complex spot groups, in a manner analogous to that employed in the betatron accelerator.

Dungey [31] has proposed a somewhat different mechanism. He pointed out that if the magnetic variability of the active center is such that 'neutral points' can develop where the field vanishes locally, then extremely high current densities can be expected; these would result in the transfer of energy from the electric field to the charged particles. In support of this mechanism, Severny [32] has reported observations of flares that have appeared at such neutral points and has noted that the field in these regions is markedly altered after the flares. (Other observations have been made which contradict Severny's findings, and the validity of this mechanism is not yet satisfactorily established.)

Gold and Hoyle [33] have proposed a rather attractive mechanism which requires that energy be stored in the form of twisted filaments, or twisted loops of magnetic field lines that protrude above the sun's surface. Such filaments normally are quite stable; the sudden release of energy observed in a flare is thought to occur when twisted magnetic loops of opposite sense and opposite twist meet. The loops attract each other, and these authors have shown that in the region of interpenetration the annihilation of the longitudinal component of the field should result in the release of energy and in the consequent acceleration of solar matter.

Yet another mechanism for the acceleration of charged particles is one first suggested by Fermi [34]. He pointed out that in a region of distorted and changing magnetic fields, some particles may gain energy through random collisions with irregularities of the field (as discussed in Sec. 5.5.4). Since other particles would lose energy, this process is a selective one in which only a few particles are accelerated at the expense of the remainder.

The processes summarized here should not be taken to constitute a complete list of those suggested, but in the light of existing observational data, they represent some of the more plausible ones that have come forth. Note that all these processes depend in some way on the magnetic field of the solar region concerned. So far no other means has been proposed to explain the concentration of energy in the flare region — estimated to be in the order of 50 joules/m^3 as compared to approximately 1 joule/m^3 for the normal thermal energy density in the chromosphere — or for its sudden transport there during the flare phenomenon itself. To be sure, flares are probably not the only solar features associated with particle emission, but they appear to contain the greatest amounts of energy — on the basis of optical data, the total integrated emission from a major flare has been estimated to exceed 10^{25} joules — and other possible phenomena have not received as much attention.

So far we have dealt only with the sporadic disturbance emissions: there is also the problem of the continous and long-enduring emissions that are postulated to account for the solar wind and for the recurrent geomagnetic storms (see Sec. 12.2.1.). Parker [35] has proposed that hydromagnetic waves from the sun's surface are able to transfer energy to a small fraction of the coronal matter, producing suprathermal particles that can escape from the sun. Another mechanism suggested by Milne [36] also may be of some importance in this connection. This consists of a form of radiation pressure involving the selective absorption of radiation to convert an atom to an excited energy state: the momentum of the absorbed photon is thought to be transferred to the atom and serves to accelerate it away from the sun, whereas the recoil the atom experiences on reradiation should be in a random direction and produce no net effect on the average. This mechanism might be expected to accelerate particles all the time, and therefore should be more applicable to the quasi-steady solar wind than to the discrete occasions preceding geomagnetic storms.

10.5. OBSERVATIONS OF THE CORPUSCULAR CLOUD IN THE SUN-EARTH SPACE

In the past few years it has become possible to obtain direct observations in the interplanetary regions through the use of space vehicles. Although the importance of such measurements should not be underestimated, they are still few in number; the bulk of our knowledge of these regions still rests on indirect evidence that is subject to inherent uncertainties of interpretation. The present section summarizes some of the observations and deductions pertaining to the solar matter in the sun-earth space.

10.5.1. Motions in Comet Tails. Biermann [37, 38] has argued that the observed motions of gaseous matter in the tails of comets cannot be explained on the basis of solar radiation pressure. Instead, he postulated a neutral stream of protons and electrons emanating from the sun which transfers momentum to the particles in the cometary tail. From a study of comet photographs he was able to estimate the rate of momentum transfer, and from this, managed to arrive at a density and velocity for the solar particles. His work has been criticized, however, mainly because the ion densities he deduced for the interplanetary regions did not agree well with other estimates. Perhaps the most uncertain part of his model had to do with the details of the momentum transfer from the solar stream to the comet material and it is on this point that his interpretation has been attacked by Alfvén [39] and others. In spite of this, it is difficult to negate the conclusion that in order for the comet tail always to exhibit the observed orientation and motions, there must be a continual outstreaming of solar material. This conclusion has given rise to the concept of a solar wind in the interplanetary regions. During undisturbed conditions, this wind appears to 'blow' fairly steadily. Following increases in the solar corpuscular emission, this wind is thought to be enhanced both in density and velocity, as we have mentioned earlier. Biermann found definite evidence for such enhancements in the comet data: he showed that the greatest accelerations in the tail of Halley's Comet could be linked with individual geomagnetic storms. The Mariner II data have shown increased particle densities and velocities associated with both sporadic and recurrent storms, lending support to the thesis that observations on the tails of comets in the inner solar system can provide valuable information on the storm plasma.

10.5.2. Forbush Decreases in the Cosmic Ray Flux. The energetic cosmic-ray particles that reach the earth's surface appear to arrive almost exclusively from outside the solar system, and only on rare occasions that are linked to specific solar flares can any of this flux be identified as solar in origin. Accordingly, there would seem little reason to expect a modulation of the cosmic rays by local conditions near the sun or the earth. In fact, however, characteristic decreases in the cosmic-ray flux have been observed to occur in time coincidence with some geomagnetic storms. It was long held that such Forbush decreases [40], as they are now generally known, occurred because of the distortion suffered by the earth's magnetic field on the arrival of charged particles from the sun. An instrumented space probe, however, measured a decrease in the particle counting rate outside of the magnetosphere at the same time that a similar decrease was observed on the ground, thereby establishing a more distant screening process as the cause [41]. The events are now attributed to the presence in interplanetary space of a screening mechanism that is capable of influencing such energetic particles.

Although the screening mechanism is not entirely understood, it is generally held that the enhancements of the solar wind, with their increased magnetic field 'frozen in,' are responsible: they serve to prevent cosmic-ray particles that would otherwise reach the earth from doing so. Under these circumstances, a study of variations in the cosmic-ray flux may provide data on interplanetary conditions and on the storm plasma, even though these data may be difficult to interpret. For instance, it is already known that there is an 11-year cyclic variation in the cosmic-ray data, such that maximum flux occurs at sunspot minimum and minimum flux at the maximum of the sunspot activity cycle. This seems to be excellent evidence that there exists a sunspot-cyclic variation in the magnetic field in interplanetary space that makes up the screening mechanism.

10.5.3. Direct Observations in Space. By far the most satisfactory measurements of the solar particles are those few that have been made from space vehicles outside of the magnetosphere. Ion-trap and plasma-probe measurements are of particular significance since they substantiate the solar wind hypothesis. Several U.S.S.R. space vehicles, particularly Lunik II, Lunik III, and the Venus probe [42, 43], have taken such measurements at great distances from the earth — in the case of the Venus probe the distance was almost 300 earth radii. These observations have revealed a flux of positive particles that varied between 2×10^8 and 10^9 cm^{-2} sec^{-1}, directed away from the sun. The Explorer X instrumentation also recorded proton fluxes, as great as 10^9 cm^{-2} sec^{-1}, at geocentric distances greater than about 22 earth radii, arriving from the general direction of the sun [44]. Large fluctuations in flux and in the energies of the particles were noted during the observing period, and number densities ranging from 6 to 20 protons per cm^3 were deduced from the data. The Mariner II plasma probe [49] has provided more than 100 days' data in interplanetary space at distances greater than 450,000 miles from the earth. The observations pertained to plasma moving within $\pm 10°$ of the radial direction from the sun, and some 40,000 measurements were made of the energy spectrum of the solar wind. The velocity was generally between 380 km/sec and 850 km/sec directed away from the sun, with no marked preference for any particular value in that range. The particle number densities fluctuated between about 0.3 and 30/cm^3, but were usually in the range 2–10/cm^3. Using these and other data obtained from space probes, we have the following reasonable values for the pertinent parameters: $B = 10$ gamma; $n = 10$ ions/cm^3; $v = 500$ km/sec. The energy density of the particles, ρv^2, can then be shown to exceed the energy density of the field B^2/μ_0, by a factor of about 40. This implies that the magnetic lines of force are carried along by the solar plasma. Also, the plasma velocity is significantly greater than the Alfvén velocity (see Sec. 15.2.1) so that shock-wave effects are to be expected.

Another interesting feature was noted by Explorer X within a few minutes of a magnetic storm sudden commencement that was observed on the earth. The particle flux increased markedly and the energy of the particles was found to be enhanced. An estimate of the particle concentration at this time showed an increase by a factor of about four or five over that noted immediately before the sudden commencement.

Mariner II also measured a magnetic storm sudden commencement almost 5 hr before the corresponding event was observed on terrestrial magnetometers. At the time, the space probe was some 8,600,000 km nearer to the sun than was the earth. On that occasion (7 October 1962) the normal solar plasma appeared to be overtaken and displaced by a plasma having particle energies some 25% greater and a number density about six times as great. Furthermore, the Mariner II data showed a general correlation of plasma velocity with K_p, and several 27-day recurrence patterns were evident in the velocity observations [49]. The magnetic field in the interplanetary regions has also been measured by several space probes, and values of the order of 5 to 10 gamma have been found. During geomagnetic storms, field increases of about an order of magnitude have been observed [11], and changes in the 'stream angle' — the angle ϕ defined in Sec. 10.3 — also have been noted [13].

In addition to the observations on the solar particles and the magnetic field, some other measurements of interest have been made, the most noteworthy of which have been the observations of cosmic-ray decreases, such as Pioneer V noted on entering a solar plasma cloud [41].

The preceding measurements represent a modest beginning only; they will be followed by many more in the future. Our present knowledge of the solar particles in the interplanetary regions, however, depends heavily on indirect measurements and will only slowly be supplanted by better data made possible by the space-probe technique.

10.5.4. Miscellaneous Measurements. Some marginal results have been obtained from the many exploratory attempts that have been made to detect the storm plasma outside of the earth's magnetosphere, and a few such are noted here.

A search of solar spectrograms obtained prior to, and during, geomagnetic disturbances was made for absorption bands that might be attributed to the solar particles. Some weak, Doppler-shifted lines were reported that indicated the presence of calcium ions in the interplanetary regions, moving toward the earth with mean velocities of about 600 km/sec [45]. More recently, similar measurements have not confirmed these results, and the original reports should be viewed with caution [5].

The reduced intensity of solar radio noise for sources on the sun's western hemisphere has been interpreted in terms of absorption by the intervening storm plasma [46].

A correlation has been found between geomagnetic activity and the intensity of the 10 Mc/s and 18 Mc/s radiation coming from Jupiter approximately nine days later [47]. It may then be concluded that solar particles, in addition to producing disturbances in the terrestrial atmosphere, are able to influence the Jovian transmissions when they have traveled as far as that planet.

10.6. SUMMARY

The dependence of two distinct types of upper atmospheric disturbances on abnormal activity on the sun can be explained on the basis of the transport of two classes of charged particles from the sun on sporadic occasions. For the polar cap absorption (PCA) events, the flux of particles is low, even though their individual energies are high; for the upper atmospheric storms, the particle energies are low but the flux is sufficiently great that plasma processes must be considered in the incoming stream. These two types of solar emission are in addition to the general outflowing of plasma that normally takes place and that is known as the solar wind. This solar wind consists of a tenuous gas which flows radially outward from the sun with a velocity of about 500 km/sec and which carries with it a frozen-in magnetic field having a curved quasi-radial direction with respect to the sun (at least for the low heliographic latitudes). There is evidence that this wind produces some of the minor disturbances, such as nightly aurora, geomagnetic fluctuations, sporadic-*E*, etc., at high geomagnetic latitudes. The large disturbances or storms are, however, associated with definite enhancements of the solar wind, and undoubtedly a gradation of storms and corresponding wind intensities occurs ranging from 'breeze' to 'gale.'

The disturbances originate in localized regions on the sun and, as we shall see in Chapter 12, can be designated as sporadic or recurrent according as the particle emission is short-lived or long-lived in comparison with the solar rotation period. In the former category are those disturbances, PCA events as well as upper atmospheric storms, that result from chromospheric flares; it also includes those nonrecurrent storms that are attributed to the passage across the sun's central meridian of centers of activity. The recurrent category includes those storms that repeat at intervals of about 27 days, for which long-enduring emissive regions exist on the sun. Some of these cases can be associated with the central meridian passage of recognized centers of activity, whereas many others cannot be linked with any distinctive solar features. To explain these recurrent storms, Bartels [48] inferred the existence of 'magnetically active' regions on the sun, unidentified in any other way, as the source of the particles. These M-regions, as he termed them, have remained almost as mysterious as when they were first postulated, although there is now some reason to consider the unipolar magnetic (UM) regions on the photosphere the likely source.

Since they can be linked to specific localized regions on the sun, the enhancements occur only in a limited volume and hence are usually thought of in the form of a stream or tongue. The solar cosmic-ray particles, likewise, are restricted to a limited volume, since the magnetic field channels them. Consequently, the question of the relative geometry enters significantly into solar-terrestrial relations, particularly in regard to the intensity of the disturbance.

The positive identification of the solar particles has been accomplished only for the PCA particles: these are known to be protons with a small percentage of heavier ions. The storm plasma particles are generally assumed to be protons and electrons, since hydrogen is the most abundant constituent of the sun and because protons and electrons have been detected entering the upper atmosphere during auroral disturbances.

There is considerable evidence that the character of the terrestrial disturbances varies somewhat with the sunspot activity cycle, and more will be said on this subject in Chapter 12. Only a part of this variation should be associated with a changing emission of the PCA and storm plasma particles: a significant influence may be produced by variations in the density of the interplanetary medium — due to a changing general emission from the sun — and in the strength of its magnetic field. There are good reasons to believe that these parameters have 11-year periodicities in step with the solar activity cycle, and the observed 11-year variation in the cosmic-ray flux, mentioned previously, would support this contention.

Finally, it should be pointed out that the role of hydromagnetic waves in solar-terrestrial relationships is not fully understood. Such waves are thought capable of propagating through the tenuous interplanetary gas from the sun to the earth and may contribute to a number of upper atmospheric processes. At the very least, the sudden impulses and sudden commencements recorded on magnetometers on the earth probably result from some form of hydromagnetic shock wave associated with solar plasma clouds traveling in interplanetary space.

REFERENCES

1. Blackwell, D. E., A study of the outer solar corona from a high altitude aircraft at the eclipse of 1954 June 30. II. Electron densities in the outer corona and zodiacal light regions, *Mon. Not. Roy. Astron. Soc.*, **116** (1956), 56.

2. Beggs, D. W., D. E. Blackwell, D. W. Dewhirst, and R. D. Wolstencroft, Further observations of the zodiacal light from a high altitude station and investigation of the interplanetary plasma, *Mon. Not. Roy. Astron. Soc.*, **127** (1964), 329.

3. Kupperian, J. E., Jr., E. T. Bryam, T. A. Chubb, and H. Friedman, Far ultraviolet radiation in the night sky, *Planet. Space Sci.*, **1** (1959), 3.

4. Unsöld, A., and S. Chapman, Optical and radiofrequency absorption by solar corpuscular bursts, *Observatory*, **69** (1949), 219.

5. Smyth, M. J., Photoelectric investigations of solar corpuscular radiation, *Mon. Not. Roy. Astron. Soc.*, **114** (1954), 137, 503.

6. Blackwell, D. E., and M. F. Ingham, Observations of the zodiacal light from a very high altitude station. III. The disturbed zodiacal light and corpuscular radiation, *Mon. Not. Roy. Astron. Soc.*, **122** (1961), 143.

7. Parker, E. N., Dynamics of the interplanetary gas and magnetic fields, *Astrophys. J.*, **128** (1958), 664.

8. Slee, O. B., Observations of the solar corona out to 100 solar radii, *Mon. Not. Roy. Astron. Soc.*, **123** (1961), 223.

9. Gorgolewski, S., and A. Hewish, The irregular structure of the solar corona during 1959 June, *Observatory*, **80** (1960), 99.

10. McCracken, K. G., The propagation of cosmic rays through interplanetary space on May 4, 1960, and during November 1960, *J. Phys. Soc. Japan*, **17**, Supp. A-II (1962), 310.

11. Coleman P. J., C. P. Sonett, D. L. Judge, and E. J. Smith, Some preliminary results of the Pioneer V magnetometer experiment, *J. Geophys. Res.*, **65** (1960), 1856.

12. Kellogg, P. J., *J. Phys. Soc. Japan*, **17**, Supp. A-II (1962), 18.

13. Heppner, J. P., N. F. Ness, T. L. Skillman, and C. S. Scearce, Magnetic field measurements with the Explorer X satellite, *J. Phys. Soc. Japan*, **17** Supp. A-II (1962), 546.

14. Babcock, H. D., The sun's polar magnetic field, *Astrophys. J.*, **130** (1959), 364.

15. Hoyle, F., and N. G. Wickramasinghe, A note on the origin of the sun's polar field, *Mon. Not. Roy. Astron. Soc.*, **123** (1961), 51.

16. Giovanelli, R. G., Flare-puffs as a cause of type III radio bursts, *Aust. J. Phys.*, **11** (1958), 350.

17. ———, and M. K. McCabe, The flare-surge event, *Aust. J. Phys.*, **11** (1958) 191.

18. Athay, R. G., and G. E. Moreton, Impulsive phenomena of the solar atmosphere. I. Some optical events associated with flares showing explosive phase, *Astrophys. J.*, **133** (1961), 935.

19. Wild, J. P., and L. L. McCready, Observations of the spectrum of high-intensity solar radiation at metre wavelengths, *Aust. J. Sci. Res.*, A, **3** (1950), 387.

20. Wood, M. B., and C. S. Warwick, Geomagnetic disturbance and velocity of slow-drift solar radio bursts, *Nature*, **184** (1959), 1471.

21. Wild, J. P., K. V. Sheridan, and A. A. Neylan, An investigation of the speed of the solar disturbances responsible for type III radio bursts, *Aust. J. Phys.*, **12** (1959), 369.

22. McLean, D. J., Solar radio emission of spectral type IV and its association with geomagnetic storms, *Aust. J. Phys.*, 12 (1959), 404.

23. Hakura, Y., and T. Goh, Pre-SC polar cap ionospheric blackout and type IV solar radio outbursts, *J. Radio Res. Lab.* (*Japan*), **6** (1959), 635.

24. Dodson, H. W., E. R. Hedeman, and L. Owren, Solar flares and associated 200 Mc/sec radiation, *Astrophys. J.*, **118** (1953), 169.

25. Hartz, T. R., and J. L. McAlpine, The dependence of ionospheric disturbances on large solar flares, *J. Atmos. Terr. Phys.*, **23** (1961), 13.

26. Kundu, M. R., and F. T. Haddock, A relation between solar radio emission and polar cap absorption of cosmic noise, *Nature*, **186** (1960), 610.

27. Simon, P., Centres solaires radioémissifs et non radioémissifs, *Ann. d'Astrophys.*, **19** (1956), 122.

28. Kundu, M. R., Solar radio emission on centimeter waves and ionization of the E layer of the ionosphere, *J. Geophys. Res.*, **65** (1960), 3903.

29. Bell, B., Major flares and geomagnetic activity, *Smithsonian Contrib. Astrophys.*, **5** (1961), 69.

30. ———, and H. Glazer, Sunspots and geomagnetism, *Smithsonian Contrib. Astrophys.*, **2** (1958), 161.

31. Dungey, J. W., Cosmic Electrodynamics. London: Cambridge University Press, 1958, p. 98.

32. Severny, A. B., Nonstationary processes in solar flares as a manifestation of the pinch effect, *Soviet Astronomy*, *A. J.*, **2** (1958), 310.

33. Gold, T., and F. Hoyle, On the origin of solar flares, *Mon. Not. Roy. Astron. Soc.*, **120** (1960), 89.

34. Fermi, E., Galactic magnetic fields and the origin of cosmic radiation, *Astrophys. J.*, **119** (1954), 1.

35. Parker, E. N., Suprathermal particle generation in the solar corona, *Astrophys. J.*, **128** (1958), 677.

36. Milne, E. A., Emission of atoms from stars, *Mon. Not. Roy. Astron. Soc.*, **86** (1926), 459.

37. Biermann, L., Kometenschweife und solare Korpuskularstrahlung, *Z. Astrophysik*, **29** (1951), 274.

38. ———, Über den Schweif des Kometen Halley im Jahre 1910, *Z. Naturforschung*, **7(a)** (1952), 127.

39. Alfvén, H., On the theory of comet tails, *Tellus*, **9** (1957), 92.

40. Forbush, S. E., On cosmic-ray effects associated with magnetic storms, *Terr. Mag. Atmos. Elec.* **43** (1938), 203.

41. Fan, C. Y., P. Meyer, and J. A. Simpson, Rapid reduction of cosmic-radiation intensity measured in interplanetary space, *Phys. Rev. Letters*, **5** (1960), 269.

42. Shklovskii, I. S., V. I. Moroz, and V. G. Kurt, The nature of the earth's third radiation belt, *Soviet Astronomy*, *A. J.*, **4** (1961), 871.

43. Gringauz, K. I., V. V. Bezrukikl, V. D. Ozerov, and R. E. Rybehinskii, A study of the interplanetary gas, high-energy electrons, and corpuscular radiation from the sun by means of the three-electrode trap for charged particles on the second Soviet cosmic rocket, *Soviet Phys. Doklady*, **5** (1960), 361.

44. Bridge, H. S., C. Dilworth, A. J. Lazarus, E. F. Lyon, B. Rossi, and F. Scherb, Direct observations of the interplanetary plasma, *J. Phys. Soc. Japan.* **17**, Supp. A-II (1962), 553.

45. Brück, H. A., and F. Ruttland, Some observations of the H and K lines in the solar spectrum during a magnetic storm, *Mon. Not. Roy. Astron. Soc.*, **106** (1946), 130.

46. Hey, J. S., S. J. Parsons, and J. W. Phillips, Some characteristics of solar radio emissions, *Mon. Not. Roy. Astron. Soc.*, **108** (1948), 354.

47. Carr, T. D., A. G. Smith, and H. Bollhagen, Evidence for the solar corpuscular origin of the decameter-wavelength radiation from Jupiter, *Phys. Rev. Letters*, **5** (1960), 418.

48. Bartels, J., Terrestrial-magnetic activity and its relations to solar phenomena, *Terr. Mag. Atmos. Electr.* **37** (1932), 1.

49. Snyder, C. W., M. Neugebauer, and U. R. Rao, The solar wind velocity and its correlation with cosmic-ray variations and with solar geomagnetic activity, *J. Geophys. Res.*, **68** (1963), 6361.

50. Coleman, P. J., L. Davis, E. J. Smith, and C. P. Sonett, The mission of Mariner II: preliminary observations; interplanetary magnetic fields, *Science*, **138** (1962), 1099.

51. Gold, T., Plasma and magnetic fields in the solar system, *J. Geophys. Res.*, **64** (1959), 1665.

11

G. C. Reid

Solar Cosmic Rays and the Ionosphere

11.1. INTRODUCTION

Since 1942 it has been known that particles can be accelerated to cosmic-ray energies in the neighborhood of the sun and can then travel to the earth and be detected at ground-level stations. These events are apparently always associated with the occurrence of intense solar flares, and until recently were considered to be extremely rare, only four events having been detected in the 14-yr period, 1942–55. It has also been known for many years that high-frequency radio communications circuits operating in high latitudes are subject to frequent interruptions which may be of long duration. During these periods, a standard vertical-incidence ionospheric sounder cannot receive any detectable echo from the ionosphere, and the condition known in radio terminology as 'blackout' exists. Not until the International Geophysical Year was it realized that there is a very intimate link between these two phenomena, and hence also between the previously distinct disciplines of cosmic-ray physics and ionospheric physics. The purpose of this chapter is to discuss the nature of this link and its implications for both disciplines.

The existence of the link came to be known largely through improvements in the available techniques for measuring ionospheric absorption of radio waves and through the use of these improved techniques at high latitudes. Since an understanding of the observational techniques is important to the discussion that follows, they will be described briefly at this point.

11.2. THE MEASUREMENT OF IONOSPHERIC ABSORPTION

For many years the only measurements of ionospheric absorption came from vertical-incidence ionospheric sounders operating in the high-frequency band, and before the IGY, only a few of these were operated on a routine basis at high latitudes.

Quite apart from the paucity of data, the conventional ionospheric sounder is inherently an unsuitable instrument for the investigation of intense ionospheric absorption. The very word 'blackout' implies that no information is obtainable. The amount of nondeviative absorption suffered by a radio wave in traversing an ionized region is inversely proportional to the square of the frequency provided that the frequency is large compared to the electron-molecule collisional frequency [see Eq. (I.27)]. This suggests that it should be possible to reduce the absorption to a measurable amount merely by increasing the radio-wave frequency sufficiently. The ionospheric sounder technique, however, requires that energy be reflected back to the ground from the upper levels of the ionosphere; obviously, once the frequency of the exploring wave exceeds the penetration frequency, no further information can be obtained, and if at this critical frequency the absorption is still too intense to allow a measurement of the returned signal, only the existence of blackout conditions can be recorded.

Despite the limitations of the technique, a considerable amount of information on high-latitude blackouts was obtained from sounding data prior to the IGY. Most of this material was treated statistically, however, rather than on the basis of individual events; as a result the picture that emerged was somewhat confusing and indicated the need for a new approach to the problem. More recently, as we shall see later, sounding measurements have regained their position as an extremely useful tool, the key to their interpretation having been provided primarily by the VHF techniques discussed in Sec. 11.2.1.

11.2.1. The Riometer.

As has been mentioned, the measurement of ionospheric absorption by means of ground-based sounding techniques is limited in its usefulness by the requirement that the exploring frequency be kept below the penetration frequency of the ionosphere. Obviously this difficulty would be removed if a transmitter were located outside the ionosphere; one could then measure relative ionospheric absorption on a continuous basis merely by recording the signal received at the earth's surface. The frequency limitation on such a technique would be complementary to that on the sounding method, that is, measurements would be possible only on frequencies *higher* than the penetration frequency of the ionosphere; lower frequencies would be reflected away from the earth before reaching the ground.

The radio noise emitted by the galaxy (so-called cosmic noise) provides a suitable source for this technique, and was first employed for the purpose by Shain [1] in Australia. The technique was adapted and refined for use at high latitudes by Little and his associates at the Geophysical Institute of the University of Alaska. The equipment has been given the name of 'riometer' (*r*elative *i*onospheric *o*pacity *meter*) and a complete description of the Alaskan model has been published [2]. The central feature of the riometer is a simple servomechanism which continuously compares the incoming cosmic noise signal with the output from a local noise diode. The resultant error signal is used to adjust the noise diode output to equality with that of the antenna, and the plate current of the diode is recorded. Variations of system gain are thus reflected merely in the amplitude of the error signal and not in the final output.

Ionospheric absorption reduces the output signal below its normal quiet-day level, and the intensity of the absorption can be measured in decibels by calibrating the equipment with an external noise source. Using this simple technique, the effective dynamic range is usually in the neighborhood of 15–20 db, with a maximum sensitivity of about 0.1 db. If we assume an inverse square frequency dependence of absorption, then 20 db at 30 Mc/s would correspond to about 180 db at 10 Mc/s in the center of the sounder frequency range. Since most conventional sounders show no detectable echo for absorption greater than 40–60 db, it can be seen that a 30 Mc/s riometer considerably extends the range of useful absorption measurements. The range can, of course, be extended at will by increasing the riometer operating frequency still further.

11.2.2. VHF Forward Scatter. In the last decade, the useful frequency range for beyond-the-horizon communications has been greatly extended by the use of scatter propagation. In the case of ionospheric scatter circuits, the frequencies used are generally in the VHF band, and the propagation mechanism depends on the existence of small-scale irregularities of ionization in the lower ionosphere, such as meteor trails. Ionospheric absorption is detected by these circuits if the absorbing region is located below the level of the scattering irregularities. As in the case of the riometer, the dynamic range is greater than that of the sounder because of the higher frequency. These circuits serve as good indicators of the occurrence of absorption events, but they do not give a useful absolute measurement of absorption because of their dependence on a reflection mechanism. Under some circumstances, an increase in ionization in the lower ionosphere can actually produce an enhancement in the scatter signal, owing to an increase in the reflection coefficient of the scattering region. The difficulty in obtaining quantitative measurements by this technique is further increased because the signal propagates at large zenith angles, so that the path-length through the ionosphere is not accurately known.

This technique has, however, proved extremely useful in identifying events of the type we shall discuss, and ionospheric scatter data provided the first evidence of the link between solar cosmic rays and ionospheric absorption.

11.3. IONOSPHERIC EFFECTS OF SOLAR COSMIC RAYS

The intensity of cosmic radiation has been continuously monitored for many years at several locations on the earth. Three main types of intensity variation have been identified: first, a slow variation with the period of the sunspot cycle, the intensity being lower at sunspot maximum than at sunspot minimum; secondly, decreases lasting for several days and coinciding with geomagnetic storms (called 'Forbush decreases'); and thirdly, comparatively rare increases, sometimes of several orders of magnitude, which appear to follow some intense solar flares. The additional particles in this last case are believed to originate at the sun and are termed 'solar cosmic rays' to distinguish them from the general background.

The fifth, and until then the largest, of the observed increases took place following an intense flare near the west limb of the sun on 23 February 1956. A second effect which followed the flare was the occurrence of very intense radio-wave absorption at high latitudes, starting within an hour of the flare time. This absorption was noticed by a number of workers, and its effects on VHF ionospheric scatter circuits in the Arctic were described in detail by Bailey [3, 4], who noted several unusual features concerning it. Among these were (1) its great geographical extent and uniformity; (2) its restriction to high geomagnetic latitudes (greater than 60°); (3) a very pronounced diurnal variation, the absorption being much more intense by day than by night; (4) the long total duration of the absorption (at least four days, the absorption diminishing with time); (5) the absence of any significant geomagnetic disturbance during the early stages.

These observations are consistent with the hypothesis that the radio-wave absorption was caused by an influx of charged particles which increased the electron density in the lower ionosphere. Charged particles in the appropriate energy range would be directed toward the polar regions of the earth by the action of the geomagnetic field and would penetrate into the lower ionosphere. Since the ground-based cosmic-ray observations showed that high-energy particles were indeed bombarding the earth, it was natural to link the increased absorption with the cosmic-ray enhancement.

In 1957, Reid and Collins [5] analyzed some of the recordings from a riometer located at Churchill (geomagnetic latitude 69°) and concluded that abnormal absorption events at this location could be classified into three fairly distinct types: Type I coincided in time with major solar flares and could be identified with the well-known sudden ionospheric disturbance (SID) discussed in Chapter 9. Type II was characteristically irregular in appearance, and the duration of individual events varied from a few minutes to several hours; it showed fairly good correspondence in time with the appearance of visible aurora and geomagnetic disturbance. Type III, on the other hand, was normally smooth and steady in appearance, and showed characteristics very similar to those Bailey had described for the event of February, 1956, with the important exception that no ground-level cosmic-ray increases had been observed to accompany the initiating solar flares. It was suggested that type III absorption events could be explained by a flux of low-energy solar protons emitted following certain flares, and the relative frequency of these events at Churchill suggested that such solar proton emissions were much less rare than would appear from the ground cosmic-ray data.

By general agreement, type II absorption is now usually referred to as 'auroral absorption' and type III as 'polar cap absorption' (PCA). This terminology will be used throughout the remainder of this chapter, which discusses PCA in particular.

Since 1957, many of these events have been described by various authors, and Hultqvist [6] independently proposed a flux of solar protons as an explanation of events which occurred in July and August, 1958. Reid and Leinbach [7] listed 24 PCA events which were identified in Alaskan riometer records in the 27-month period from May, 1957, through July, 1959; in this same period only one ground cosmic-ray increase was observed.

11.3.1. Ionization Produced by Solar Cosmic Rays. Before discussing the observational features of a typical PCA event and the current state of our knowledge concerning the nature of the bombarding particles, we shall describe briefly the expected atmospheric effects of an incoming flux of energetic charged particles.

While they are still at some distance from the earth (the distance depending on the momentum of the particle), the particles begin to deviate from their original paths because of the influence of the geomagnetic field. The problem of the motion of a charged particle in the geomagnetic field is a difficult and complex one. It can be simplified somewhat by approximating the geomagnetic field by that of a dipole, and in this form it was first attacked by Störmer in an extensive and famous series of papers, the main results and conclusions of which have more recently been compiled and summarized [8]. Here we are not concerned with the details of Störmer's theory (see Sec. 5.5.2) but merely with its predictions regarding the energy selection imposed by the field on a continuous spectrum of charged particles.

In dealing with the effects of a magnetic field on the motion of a charged particle, the *momentum* of the particle is a more useful concept to consider than the kinetic energy, since particles having the same momentum and charge behave in the same way in a magnetic field. Using Eq. (5.14), the 'radius of gyration' or 'Larmor radius' of a particle of mass m, charge Ze, and velocity v perpendicular to the direction of a uniform magnetic field of induction B is given by

$$\rho = \frac{mv}{ZeB} = \frac{p}{ZeB}, \tag{11.1}$$

where we have written the momentum as p. In dealing with cosmic rays, the particle speeds are often sufficiently great that relativistic effects must be taken into account. The relativistic kinetic energy of the particle, W, is related to p by the equation

$$W = (m_0^2 c^4 + p^2 c^2)^{1/2} - m_0 c^2, \tag{11.2}$$

where m_0 is the rest-mass of the particle and c the velocity of light. In the case of background primary cosmic rays, we are usually dealing with so-called relativistic particles (that is, particles whose kinetic energy is much larger than their rest energy, $m_0 c^2$), and in this case

$$W \approx pc. \tag{11.3}$$

It is customary to measure kinetic energy in electron volts (ev), and hence for simplicity to measure p in units of ev/c. From Eq. (11.3) it will be seen that for a truly relativistic particle, the energy in ev is numerically equal to the momentum in ev/c. For less energetic particles, the rest energy becomes appreciable, and (11.2) must be used. In this case the kinetic energy in ev is smaller than the momentum in ev/c. For nonrelativistic particles—that is, particles for which $pc \ll m_0 c^2$ — (11.2) reduces to the ordinary classical relation between kinetic energy and momentum.

As mentioned earlier, particles having the same charge and momentum behave in the same way in a magnetic field. The dependence on charge can be eliminated by using *rigidity* instead of momentum. The rigidity, R, is defined as pc/Ze, where Ze is the charge of the particle. It is usually measured in electron volts, in which case the definition becomes

$$R = pc/Z, \tag{11.4}$$

where Z is now the numerical charge of the particle in units of the electronic charge e.

Störmer's theory showed that there is a certain rigidity R_c corresponding to each geomagnetic latitude λ, such that particles of rigidity less than R_c cannot reach the earth at vertical incidence. It can be shown that

$$R_c = 14.9 \cos^4 \lambda, \tag{11.5}$$

where R_c is now measured in Bev (1 Bev $= 10^9$ ev). R_c then represents the minimum rigidity which a particle must have to arrive from a vertical direction at a point on the earth with geomagnetic latitude λ. R_c is usually known as the *cut-off rigidity* for vertically incident particles at geomagnetic latitude λ. The relationship between R_c and λ is shown in Fig. 11.1.

Particles with rigidity somewhat less than R_c can reach the earth at latitude λ at large zenith angles and at certain azimuths. For positively charged particles in the northern hemisphere, the minimum rigidity is reached for particles arriving from the western horizon. At the latitudes with which we are concerned, however, this true minimum rigidity does not differ much from R_c: the difference amounts to less than 10% at latitudes greater than 40° and to less than 1% at latitudes greater than 70°. For most practical purposes, then, we can regard R_c as a fairly sharp cut-off rigidity. The incoming particle flux is thus distributed in geomagnetic latitude according to its rigidity spectrum, all particles with rigidity less than R_c being confined approximately to latitudes greater than λ.

In order to penetrate the entire atmosphere and reach ground level, a vertically incident proton must have an initial energy of about 2 Bev, corresponding to a rigidity of about 3 Bev. Figure 11.1 shows that these protons are excluded from latitudes less than about 50°; thus all the atmospheric effects of protons that are stopped in the atmosphere are confined to latitudes higher than this. In fact, as we shall see, the most intense absorption effects are produced by particles which stop somewhat below the ionospheric *D* layer. For vertically incident protons, the required energy is less than 200 Mev, and the effects are confined to geomagnetic latitudes higher than 62°.

Protons that are incident on the atmosphere obliquely will stop at greater heights than vertically incident protons, but this departure becomes appreciable only at large zenith angles because of the steep increase in atmospheric density with depth of penetration. As we shall see later, protons with all zenith angles of incidence are usually present in PCA events, so that the latitude restriction previously deduced is only an illustrative approximation.

We must now consider the ionization produced by these particles in the atmosphere. A charged particle traversing a material medium loses energy by ionization and leaves a trail of ions and electrons behind it. In the case of protons, the rate of energy loss in standard air as a function of energy is well known, and from these data the variation of rate of energy loss with distance along the track of the ionizing particle can be readily calculated. This leads to the well-known 'Bragg curve,' illustrated in Fig. 11.2 for the

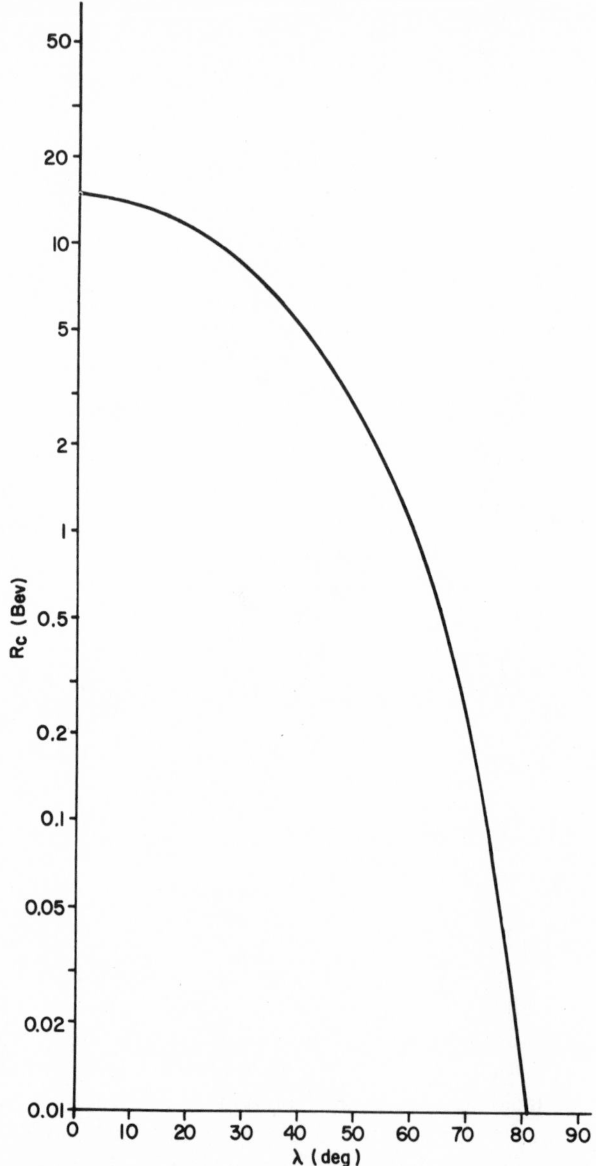

Fig. 11.1 Vertical cut-off rigidity as a function of geomagnetic latitude (centered dipole approximation).

case of a proton of initial energy 1.6 Mev (1 Mev = 10^6 ev), corresponding to a range in standard air of 5 cm. The interesting feature of this curve is that the greatest rate of energy loss, and hence the greatest rate of ion production, occurs near the end of its track. In the case of a heavy particle

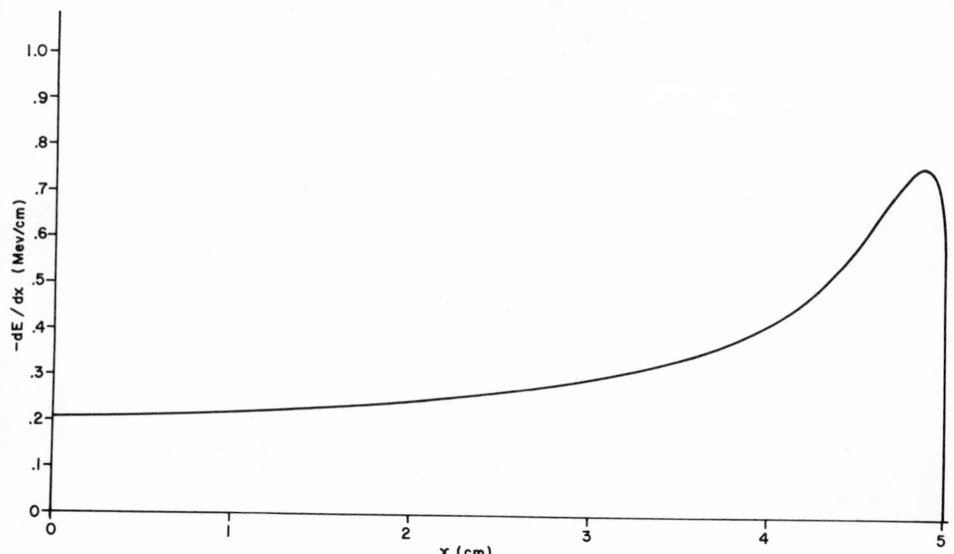

Fig. 11.2 Rate of loss of energy of a proton of initial energy 1.6 Mev in air at standard temperature and pressure.

entering the earth's atmosphere, where the density increases steeply with depth, this maximum would become even more pronouced, as is illustrated in Fig. 11.3. This shows the total energy lost by a vertically incident 50 Mev proton at various levels in the atmosphere. The first 10% of the initial energy is lost between the top of the atmosphere and a height of 56 km; the last 10% is lost between approximately 42.1 km and 42.0 km, a height interval of only 100 meters. Half the total energy of the proton is lost in the last 2.5 km of its path, so that the ionization it produces will be greatly concentrated near the end of its track. As we shall see later, the incoming flux during a PCA event contains protons with a wide range of initial energies and angles of incidence, so that ionization is produced at all heights in the atmosphere down to the lowest level that can be reached.

The equilibrium electron number density is determined not only by the rate of production of ionization by the incoming protons, but also by the relative rates of all the various reactions involving ions and electrons which take place in the atmosphere (see Sec. 3.5). Calculations of equilibrium electron density profiles were first carried out for an incident proton flux by Bailey [4] and have since been repeated by other authors, using different incident proton spectra and different values for the various rate coefficients. Besides dissociative recombination between electrons and molecular positive ions, the most important processes which affect the electron density are the attachment of free electrons to neutral atoms and molecules to form negative ions, and the removal of these ions by photodetachment, collisional detach-

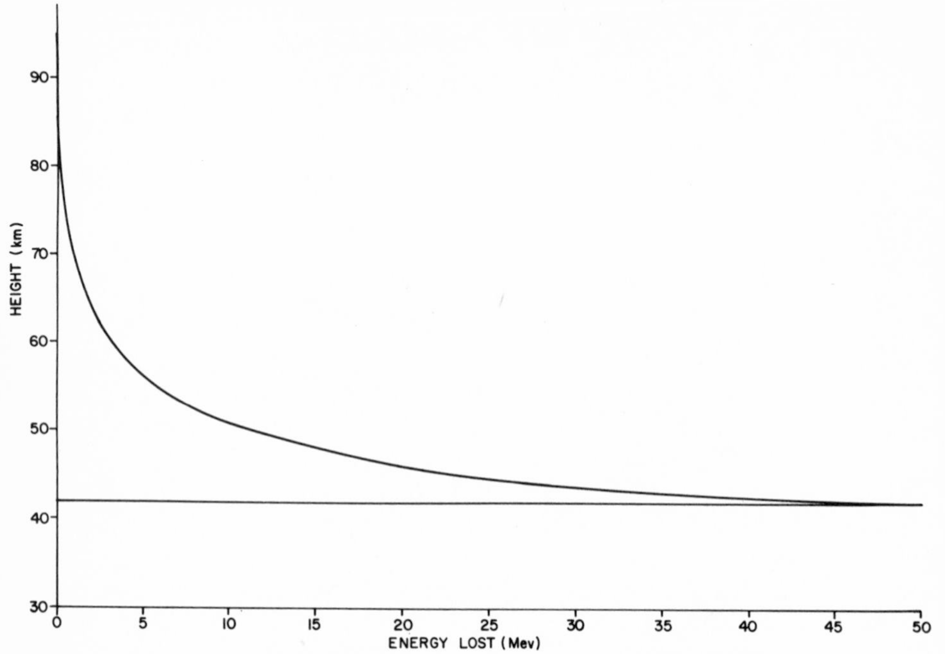

Fig. 11.3 Total energy lost by a vertically incident proton of initial energy 50 Mev in reaching a given height above the ground.

ment, and ionic recombination with positive ions. Unfortunately, none of the required rate coefficients is known to a high degree of accuracy, and there is even appreciable doubt concerning the nature of the dominant negative ion. Under these circumstances, calculations of theoretical equilibrium electron density profiles are necessarily approximate.

One of the most characteristic features of PCA is the existence of a large-amplitude diurnal variation. This variation can readily be explained qualitatively by the photodetachment reaction caused by sunlight. After sunset, photodetachment ceases, and the free-electron number density drops sharply throughout the lower ionosphere, causing a corresponding drop in absorption. On the assumption that O_2^- is the only negative ion present, Reid [9] has calculated equilibrium electron density profiles for both day and night conditions for a particular proton spectrum. The results show that the peak electron density is reached during the day at a height of about 75 km, and during the night at about 85 km. The electron density falls off above the peak because of the decreasing atmospheric density with height, and consequently decreasing electron production rate. The fall-off below the peak is caused by the rapid increase in the negative-ion attachment rate with depth. These factors are sufficiently strong that the heights of the peaks become roughly independent of the form of the proton spectrum over a wide range of possible spectra. With the same assumptions, it has also been shown that protons with energy in the neighborhood of 100 Mev have the maximum efficiency for producing 30 Mc/s radio-wave absorption. This efficiency drops very rapidly for proton energies less than 30 Mev and drops rather slowly for proton energies greater than 200 Mev. Vertically incident protons within this energy range penetrate the atmosphere to heights in the 25–45 km range.

From the preceding discussion, it is clear that three of the features of PCA previously described are consistent with the assumption of a flux of protons as the causative agency. First, the existence of strong radio-wave absorption is readily explained by the formation of an ionized layer in the *D* region, since the electron collision frequency is high in this region. Secondly, the pronounced diurnal variation can be explained by the formation of negative ions and the presence of daytime photodetachment. Thirdly, the confinement of the effects to high latitudes is quite consistent with our knowledge of the influence of the geomagnetic field on protons in the requisite energy range. Before discussing the remaining characteristic features of PCA, we shall briefly review our present knowledge concerning the solar particles themselves.

11.4. THE NATURE OF SOLAR COSMIC RAYS

It will be evident from what has already been said that the phenomenon of polar cap absorption provides a link between two hitherto unconnected branches of geophysics, since it demonstrates the effects of cosmic rays on the earth's ionosphere. The significance of this link was not immediately realized, and the first direct evidence for the bombardment of the polar ionosphere by solar particles was obtained independently by Anderson [10] from balloon measurements of cosmic rays at Churchill in August, 1958. Since then, many such events have been detected by balloons, rockets, satellites, and space probes, and much direct information has been obtained concerning the nature and properties of the solar particles responsible for polar cap absorption. A brief account of this work is given in this section.

11.4.1. Balloon Observations. Most of our information on solar cosmic rays has come from balloon measurements, and especially from those made by the groups at the State University of Iowa and the University of Minnesota. Instrumentation used in these balloon flights has included ionization chambers, Geiger counters, and nuclear emulsions. Following Anderson's identification of solar protons at Churchill in August, 1958, the Minnesota group [11] reinterpreted an anomalous increase in the cosmic ray flux over Minneapolis in March, 1958, as a solar cosmic ray event, an identification which was verified by the simultaneous presence of PCA at high latitudes.

This latter event was unusual, however, in two respects: first, no large solar flare had been observed for two days before the increase; secondly, the energy of the protons required to explain the observations was far below the normal cutoff at Minneapolis. The key to this latter point lay in the fact that a geomagnetic storm was in progress at the time of the observations, and it became evident that geomagnetic storms could deform the field sufficiently to change cut-off rigidities by large amounts at middle latitudes.

Since 1958, many balloon observations of solar cosmic rays have been made, both in the polar cap and at lower latitudes during geomagnetic storms. The principal results of these measurements can be summarized as follows:

1. The particles are mainly protons, though in many cases heavier nuclei and especially alpha particles are present. There is no direct evidence for the presence of high-energy electrons.
2. The proton energy spectrum for energies greater than about 80–100 Mev is usually steeply inclined toward the low-energy end and can be adequately represented by a power law of the form:
$$N(> E) = KE^{-\gamma}, \qquad (11.6)$$
where $N(> E)$ is the flux of protons with energy greater than E and the exponent γ is usually in the neighborhood of 4.
3. Except possibly during the early stages of an event the proton flux is nearly isotropic in direction for zenith angles less than 90°.

Balloon measurements carried out during the IGY have been summarized in a review article by Winckler [12].

11.4.2. Rocket and Satellite Observations. The balloon technique suffers from one major disadvantage: it is not at present possible to attain heights greater than 30–35 km. Thus the observations are confined to particles with sufficient initial energy to penetrate the residual atmosphere above this level. This sets the low-energy cutoff for balloon measurements of protons at 80–100 Mev. As we have seen, the protons which give rise to the most intense absorption effects have energies in the 30–200 Mev range. Because of the steep inclination of the energy spectra toward low energies, there are usually many more protons present at the low-energy end of this range than at the high-energy end, so that the most important part of the spectrum from the ionospheric point of view lies below the atmospheric cutoff for balloon measurements. These particles can be detected directly only by using rocket or satellite techniques and a few such experiments have now been conducted successfully.

Rocket firings carried out at Churchill [13] during PCA events in September and November, 1960, showed that the proton energy spectrum extended to energies at least as low as 1 Mev. The steepness of the spectrum decreased at lower energies, as had been expected from earlier reasoning based on the latitude distribution of PCA, and the approximate isotropy of the flux was verified. These measurements also showed the presence of heavier nuclei [14], and it was possible to show that the ratio of their flux to that of the protons was much closer to the ratio found spectroscopically in the sun than to that found in ordinary cosmic rays.

Rocket observations overcome the low-energy cutoff inherent in the balloon technique, but they suffer from the disadvantage that observations last for only a very short period of time. This disadvantage can be overcome to some extent by the use of satellites and space probes, and a few such observations have been carried out. Solar protons were detected in August, 1958, by counting equipment carried on Explorer IV [15], and subsequently a few observations have been made by other satellites. Equipment on board the space probe Pioneer V [16] in April, 1960, detected solar protons at a distance of 5,000,000 km from the earth. To date, however, observations of this type have not added much to our knowledge of these particles. Striking evidence of the intensity of some of these events and of their potential as a hazard for manned space flight came from the satellite Discoverer XVII, which was launched into polar orbit at the time of a very intense solar cosmic ray event in November, 1960. The satellite was recovered after two days in orbit, and was found to be highly radioactive, the activity presumably having been induced by solar particle bombardment.

11.5. THE CHARACTERISTIC FEATURES OF POLAR CAP ABSORPTION

In this section we shall discuss some typical features of PCA as observed on riometer recordings and attempt to give an account of current ideas concerning the interpretation of these features. To illustrate some of the characteristics, a fairly typical PCA is shown in the lower part of Fig. 11.4. Cosmic noise absorption as measured by a 30 Mc/s vertical incidence riometer at Fort Churchill is plotted at 30-min intervals for the period 22–25 August 1958.

The event was apparently initiated by a flare which appeared in the northwest quadrant of the sun at 0828 Local Standard Time (1428 Universal Time) on August 22. The start of the flare is indicated by the arrow at the left-hand side of the diagram. The flare was accompanied by a solar radio noise outburst which drove the riometer off scale and prevented any absorption measurements being made until about 1230. From this time on the absorption increased and reached a maximum of 8 db at 1630. This was followed by a rapid decrease, which accelerated as night conditions spread through the lower ionosphere. Next morning, as the sun rose, the absorption again increased, this time reaching a daytime maximum of only 5 db, followed

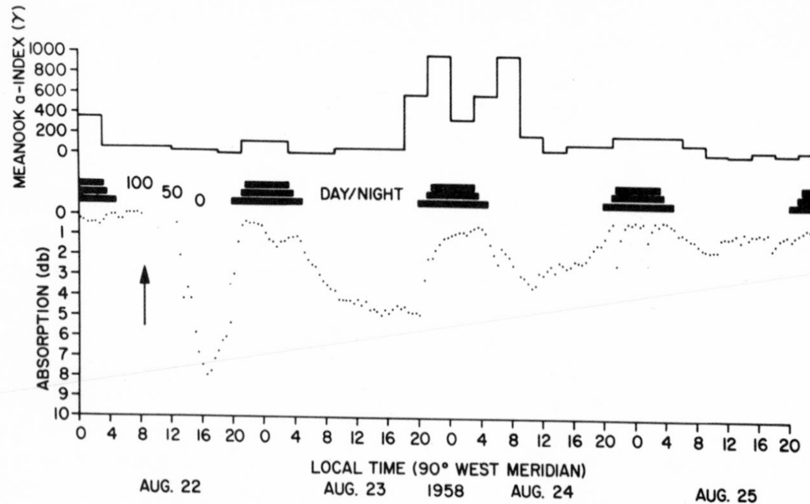

Fig. 11.4 The PCA event of 22–25 August 1958. The dots represent 30 Mc/s cosmic-noise absorption measured at Churchill; the shaded bars indicate periods of darkness at ground level and at altitudes of 50 km and 100 km; and the histogram represents the level of magnetic disturbance recorded at Meanook, Alberta. The arrow indicates the occurrence of the visible solar flare that probably initiated the event.

by a sharp evening decrease to a fairly constant nighttime value. With the exception of the late afternoon decrease visible on the first day, this pattern was repeated on the succeeding days, the amount of absorption decreasing from day to day. Some residual absorption still remained on August 26, when a second event took place, obscuring the termination of this event.

The event of August 22–25 shows many features which appear to be typical of PCA, and these will be discussed separately in the succeeding subsections.

11.5.1. The Correlation with Visible Solar Flares. When a large number of these events is considered, the correlation with the occurrence of intense solar flares becomes quite striking. In a study of 24 events, Reid and Leinbach [7] were able to identify the initiating flare beyond reasonable doubt in 18 cases (the occurrence of solar radio noise with the characteristics to be described was used as a criterion in the identification). In most of these cases the visual importance of the flare was rated as 3 or 3+. As we have seen, the primary cause of the absorption is thought to be ionization produced in the lower ionosphere by incident protons, and the flare correlation strongly suggests that these protons are accelerated in some way during the flare. At present, only speculation is possible concerning the acceleration mechanism and even concerning the location of the accelerating region relative to the flare. It seems likely, however, that the accelerating region is within the visible flare itself and that the energy required to accelerate the protons is supplied by the magnetic fields in this region. In particular, a mechanism involving successive reflections of the protons from randomly moving magnetic field inhomogeneities has been invoked by several authors; this type of acceleration was originally proposed by Fermi as an explanation of the very high particle energies found in background cosmic rays. A discussion of this and other acceleration mechanisms is beyond the scope of this book; for a detailed study of the application of the Fermi mechanism to solar protons see Parker [17].

In the event illustrated in Fig. 11.4, the delay time between the flare and the apparent onset of the absorption is some 3–4 hr. This is longer than would be expected if the protons traveled along direct paths between the sun and the earth. The rectilinear travel times for protons of energies 10 Mev and 100 Mev are, respectively, about 1 hr and about 20 min (the travel time for light from the visible flare is about 8 min). This discrepancy might be explained by postulating that the particle acceleration takes place only during the dying stages of the flare, but this seems unlikely. Much longer delays are occasionally observed in cases where there can be little doubt of the flare identification, and the delay seems to bear little relation to the velocity of the particles themselves. There is some evidence [18] that the delay is strongly influenced by the position of the flare with respect to the solar central meridian, being considerably longer for flares located east of the central meridian than for those to the west. It seems likely that the delay represents some kind of diffusion time for the particles. If, as some current theories suggest, the earth is usually connected magnetically to some point in the western hemisphere of the sun by a curved quasi-radial field line, then particles originating on the eastern hemisphere must diffuse on to this field line before they can reach the earth. This diffusion could be caused by the presence of magnetic irregularities in the solar corona.

11.5.2. The Correlation with Solar Radio Noise Outbursts. A large percentage of the flares which initiate PCA are accompanied by very intense solar radio noise over a wide range of frequencies extending from meter wavelengths down to centimeter wavelengths. It has been shown [19] that for the period May, 1958–July, 1959, 83% of all observed intense broadband centimeter wavelength outbursts were followed by PCA, and every PCA event was preceded by an intense centimeter wave outburst.

Broadband emission of this type has been tentatively explained as being due to synchrotron radiation by relativistic electrons spiraling in a solar magnetic field. If this explanation is accepted, it implies the existence of some acceleration mechanism associated with the flare which can raise electron energies to these levels. It seems reasonable that the same mechanism might accelerate protons to similar energies and that the protons would be able to escape the magnetic field because of their greater rigidity, whereas the electrons would remain trapped. The correlation between the broadband solar noise and PCA would appear to follow quite naturally from a mechanism of this kind.

11.5.3. The Correlation with Geomagnetic Disturbance. The histogram in the upper part of Fig. 11.4 shows the 3-hr *a*-indices of magnetic activity from Meanook, Alberta, for the period of the PCA. Meanook is sufficiently close to Churchill to show the same general magnetic disturbance features, and the *a*-index gives the range of variation of the horizontal component in any 3-hr period measured in gammas (1 gamma $= 10^{-5}$ gauss).

It will be observed that, during the early stages of the PCA, magnetic activity was at a very low level, and not until late on August 23 did conditions become disturbed (in fact a magnetic storm sudden commencement occurred at about 1945 Local Standard Time on August 23).

This behavior of the magnetic field is typical. Occasionally the field is disturbed during the early stages of a PCA, but this activity usually represents the later stages of a disturbance which began well before the flare and does not appear to be a consequence of the proton bombardment which gives rise to the PCA.

Since magnetic disturbance is usually attributed to the influx of particles from the sun, it may seem surprising at first sight that the large ionospheric effects of the PCA should be unaccompanied by any magnetic disturbance. The explanation lies in the comparatively small electron number density necessary in the lower ionosphere to produce large absorption effects. For instance, magnetoionic theory shows that a layer of electrons 10 km thick centered at a height of 65 km will produce 5 db absorption of 30 Mc/s radio waves if the electron density throughout the layer is about 4×10^4 cm^{-3}. It can be shown that this equilibrium electron density could be produced by a vertically incident flux of 15 Mev protons of about 1000 cm^{-2} sec^{-1}. (In actual fact, the protons are neither monoenergetic nor all vertically incident, but this does not materially change this order-of-magnitude estimate.)

The velocity of 15 Mev protons is about 5×10^9 cm sec^{-1}, and so their density in interplanetary space would be of the order of 2×10^{-7} cm^{-3} in this case. The kinetic energy density of the proton flux would then be about 4×10^{-12} erg cm^{-3}. Chapman and Ferraro [20] have estimated that a density of about 100 protons per cm^3 traveling at a velocity of 10^8 cm sec^{-1} will produce a moderate magnetic storm; the corresponding kinetic energy density is about 8×10^{-7} erg cm^{-3}, which is several orders of magnitude larger than the kinetic energy density of the proton flux we have been considering. Thus the lack of any apparent magnetic disturbance associated with PCA is hardly surprising. Chapman and Ferraro [21] have also given a criterion for the maximum stream density to which Störmer's theory can be strictly applied. This critical density is about 10^{-8} cm^{-3}. At higher densities, interactions between the particles must be considered, and the theory based on individual particles breaks down. The foregoing estimate of density shows that this critical value is probably exceeded during some PCA events, but the observations of the latitude dependence of the effects indicate that, at least qualitatively, the cutoff predicted by Störmer's theory is not seriously violated.

The magnetic storm shown in Fig. 11.4 as starting late on August 23 is not directly related to the PCA protons, but is probably due to the arrival at the earth of a relatively dense plasma cloud emitted at the time of the flare. The particles in this cloud have much lower velocities than those that cause the PCA, but their much higher density is responsible for the intense magnetic effects.

As mentioned earlier, the magnetic storm frequently has the effect of extending the region of proton bombardment to lower latitudes than before, allowing, for instance, balloon detection of the protons in middle latitudes. The effect of the magnetic storm on protons precipitating within the polar cap, however, has not yet been studied in detail. In the particular case illustrated, the storm appears to have had little effect.

11.5.4. The Diurnal Variation. It is evident from Fig. 11.4 that PCA exhibits a very pronounced diurnal variation. Immediately above the absorption plot, the presence of nighttime conditions at heights of 0, 50, and 100 km is indicated by shaded strips. The onset of night is here taken as the instant at which the shadow of the solid earth reaches the level in question, taking account of refraction of sunlight in the lower atmosphere. It can be seen that the nighttime absorption is very much less than the daytime absorption. This pronouced diurnal variation has been mentioned in Sec. 11.3, in connection with Bailey's observations of the event of 23 February 1956, and its probable explanation in terms of photodetachment of negative ions was discussed in Sec. 11.3.1.

The variation of the absorption during the sunrise and sunset transition periods is of considerable interest, and its interpretation is still open to controversy. Since the molecules N_2 and O_2 are by far the most numerous neutral constituents of the lower ionosphere and since N_2 cannot form a stable negative ion, it has generally been assumed that the dominant negative ion must be O_2^-. Although the precise values of the electron affinity of this ion and of its photodetachment cross section are still somewhat uncertain, it is known that photodetachment occurs at all visible wavelengths. The daytime electron number density, then, ought to prevail at any level in the atmosphere until the visible sun sets, or at least until it is sufficiently obscured by the lower atmosphere to reduce the photodetachment rate significantly. Riometer recordings made at sunset show that the daytime absorption starts to decrease when the solar zenith angle, χ, is about 90° (that is, ground sunset) and that most of the recovery is completed by the time the solid-earth shadow reaches the 50-km level ($\chi = 98°$). At sunrise the reverse situation occurs, with daytime conditions not becoming fully established until after ground sunrise. These observations strongly suggest that most of the absorption takes place at heights well below 50 km. On the other hand, as discussed earlier, calculations of the electron density profiles produced by a flux of solar protons show that most of the ionization is well above 50 km, with a peak density in the 75–85 km region. An attempt has been made to resolve this inconsistency by taking into account the obscuration of sunlight by the lower atmosphere when the sun is near the horizon [9]. This still leaves a large discrepancy between theory and observation, however, and it appears to be impossible to explain the early start of the sunset effect by this approach. At $\chi = 90°$, obscuration of visible sunlight is negligible throughout the absorbing region.

These difficulties would be resolved if the effective screen for sunlight were the ozone layer instead of the solid earth; that is, if the negative ion required ultraviolet light of wavelength less than 3000 Å for efficient photodetachment. At $\chi = 90°$ the shadow of the 'top' of the ozone layer lies at about 40 km; at $\chi = 98°$, it reaches about 90 km, so that the entire absorbing region is in the ultraviolet shadow. This explanation, however, implies that the dominant negative ion is not O_2^-, for which photodetachment occurs at much longer wavelengths, and it is by no means clear how a negative ion of a minor constituent can become dominant in the presence of O_2.

An alternative suggestion [22] is that the rate of formation of nitric oxide (NO) in the lower ionosphere might be greatly increased during a PCA event. Ionization of NO, which is thought to be largely responsible for the normal ionization of the *D* region, occurs under the influence of the ultraviolet Lyman α line of hydrogen, and this component of the ionization would show the ozone layer screening effect. At the time of writing, controversy still surrounds the interpretation of these twilight effects, and the final answer will probably come from rocket-borne mass spectrometer measurements.

11.5.5. The Duration of the Absorption. As can be seen from Fig. 11.4, the duration of a PCA event can be several days. In one or two events, durations of at least 8 days have been observed by riometers located at far northern latitudes, and solar protons were detected [23] at balloon heights over Resolute Bay for 11 days following the flare of 16 July 1959. These long durations are somewhat puzzling, since the initiating flare usually disappears after an hour or two. The possibility that the long duration is an atmospheric effect has been ruled out by the direct balloon observations. Another possibility would be the storage of solar protons in the geomagnetic field, in a manner analogous to the trapping of high-energy particles in the Van Allen belts. This is not likely, however, in view of the observations which have been carried out in the vicinity of the geomagnetic and dip poles. The lines of force from these points must certainly traverse regions of very weak field intensity and the storage of highly energetic particles along such lines would be difficult to visualize. There is also the difficulty of introducing these particles into the trapping domain; as we have seen, the early stages of a PCA event are often characterised by quiet magnetic conditions, and unless the field is distorted in some way, trapping would not be likely to occur.

We are forced, then, to one of two possible explanations for the long duration. Either the sun continues to emit protons for several days following the flares, or the protons are all emitted at the time of the flare and are then stored for a long period somewhere in the solar system, but outside the earth's geomagnetic domain. The former explanation does not seem very plausible. Although it is quite possible that a solar flare is merely a symptom of a more general disturbance and that this disturbance rather than the flare itself is directly responsible for accelerating the protons, this is unlikely. Indeed, convincing arguments have been presented [17] on the basis of the total energy involved which show that the most likely source of the protons is the flare itself. Furthermore, there have been instances (notably on 23 February 1956) of the flare region rotating around the west limb of the sun while the protons were still bombarding the earth. On the theory of continuous emission by the flare region, this would require that there exist some path by which protons emitted from the hidden hemisphere of the sun can reach the earth. Although one can certainly imagine magnetic fields which will provide such a path, it would be preferable if such an *ad hoc* hypothesis could be avoided.

It appears, then, that the most likely explanation of the long duration of the proton flux is that the protons cannot simply travel outward from the sun in straight lines and escape from the solar system, but are stored in some region from which they gradually leak out over a period of days. Various storage mechanisms have been proposed within the last few years, and two of these will be described briefly.

From observations of the long duration of the relativistic particle flux following the flare of 23 February 1956, Meyer, Parker, and Simpson [24] inferred the existence of a magnetic barrier in the outer solar system capable of reflecting charged particles. This barrier would take the form of a rather thick shell located well beyond the orbit of the earth and having the sun as its center. Following a cosmic ray flare, the hollow inside this shell would rapidly fill up with particles and then gradually be emptied as particles succeeded in diffusing through the barrier. During this entire period, the earth, located within the hollow, would be subjected to bombardment by the particles.

It was later [25] suggested that such a barrier could be set up by the solar wind which would drag out some magnetic field from the sun (see Sec. 10.3) and would set up an interplanetary magnetic field whose lines of force in the inner solar system would be radially outward with a curvature imposed by the solar rotation. The magnetic barrier is visualized as arising from instabilities which are inherently present in this outward stream of gas, and which grow to appreciable proportions somewhat beyond the earth's orbit, producing a region of tangled incoherent magnetic field. This situation is illustrated in Fig. 11.5.

If there were no magnetic field within the hollow, flares on the hidden solar hemisphere would be able to produce particles at the earth almost as efficiently as visible flares. The guiding effect of the curved field lines within the hollow, however, would prevent this, or at least inhibit it for a considerable length of time.

A model proposed by Gold [26] also involves a magnetic field of solar

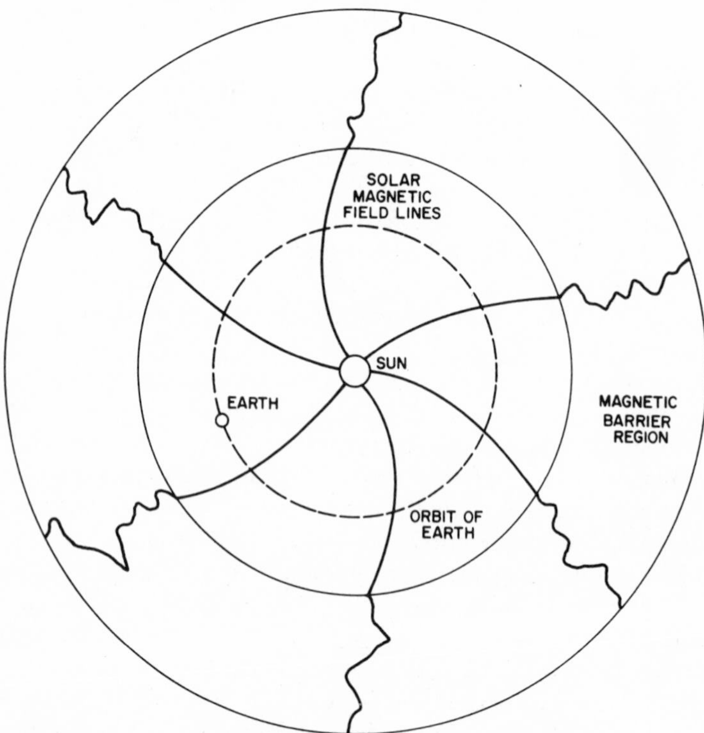

Fig. 11.5 The magnetic-barrier model of the interplanetary magnetic field.

origin, but is somewhat different from Parker's mechanism previously discussed. In this model, the clouds of relatively dense material which are sporadically ejected from the sun, and which give rise to magnetic storms on the earth, can drag out magnetic field from the sun. The field lines will remain connected at their base to the region of origin of the outburst, so that as the material travels outward it will drag out a long 'magnetic tongue.' A pictorial representation of such a tongue is shown in Fig. 11.6.

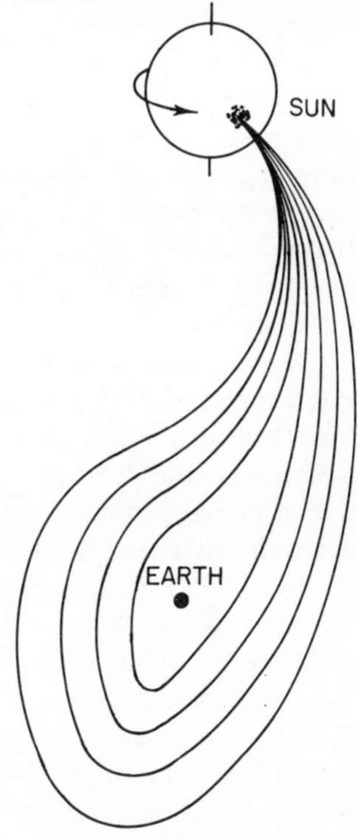

Fig. 11.6 The magnetic-tongue model of the interplanetary magnetic field.

Fast protons injected into this tongue by a flare at its base can be trapped in an analogous fashion to the Van Allen belt particles, and will spiral back and forth along the magnetic field lines. If the earth is located within the tongue, being thus magnetically connected to the sun, these fast particles will be observable, and their flux will last as long as the trapping continues or as long as the earth remains within the tongue. The solar plasma cloud emitted by the same flare would be expected to drag out a fresh magnetic tongue whose arrival at the earth would be signaled by the occurrence of a geomagnetic storm. The enhanced magnetic fields associated with this new tongue would serve to exclude some of the background cosmic rays, thereby explaining the Forbush decrease in cosmic-ray intensity often associated with geomagnetic storms.

It is beyond our present scope to criticize these and other models which have been proposed to explain the long duration of solar proton fluxes and PCA. More experimental data are needed, and in the near future it is likely that space-probe experiments will provide many of the answers on this and other problems connected with the existence of interplanetary magnetic fields and their terrestrial effects.

11.6. THE USE OF IONOSPHERIC SOUNDING TO INVESTIGATE PCA

As we saw in Sec. 11.1, the standard vertical-incidence ionosonde has severe limitations in its application to the measurement of high-latitude ionospheric absorption. Nevertheless, once the separation of absorption events into the distinct classifications of auroral and polar cap became clear from the VHF techniques, interpretation of ionosonde absorption data began to yield valuable results. In 1958, Japanese workers [27] discovered the existence of blackouts in the polar caps preceding the sudden commencement of geomagnetic storms. After the start of the storm, the blackout region appeared to move equatorward and form a band around the auroral zone. It is now clear from the riometer work that the prestorm blackout consists mainly of PCA, whereas the storm blackout in the auroral zone is mainly the quite distinct auroral absorption.

Several workers have now investigated ionosonde data with a view to extending available information on both types of absorption. These data do have two major advantages over the VHF data: first, the geographical coverage is considerably greater; second, ionosonde data are available over a long period of time. These features have been employed to advantage in a recent survey of blackouts during the entire sunspot cycle from 1949 through 1959 [28]. This survey showed marked differences in the variation of occurrence of the two types during the sunspot cycle, PCA being strongly concentrated about the time of sunspot maximum—as might be expected from its strict dependence on solar flare activity—and auroral absorption showing a maximum during the decaying years of the sunspot cycle.

An examination of the seasonal dependence of the occurrence of polar cap blackouts suggested the existence of an equinoctial maximum, with a low probability of occurrence in the northern winter. An important question which remains to be answered at the time of writing is whether this is truly a seasonal variation, or really an annual variation. A true seasonal variation would imply that occurrence in the southern hemisphere should be out of phase with that in the northern hemisphere; that is, there should be a very low probability of occurrence of PCA over the southern hemisphere during the northern summer. A definite answer on this question is hardly possible on the basis of the small amount of Antarctic ionosonde data currently available.

As has been mentioned previously, the standard ionosonde is not a suitable indicator of strong absorption since it merely records a total blackout under these conditions. This same limitation, however, makes it a more sensitive recorder of very weak absorption than the riometer. In particular, by using the minimum frequency on which an echo is obtainable (usually tabulated in ionospheric sounding data as f_{min}), absorption which is undetectable by the riometer can be measured. This only gives a relative measure of absorption, since the parameter f_{min} depends on such factors as the transmitted power, which varies from one ionosonde to another, and the reflection coefficient of the layers that return the echoes. The technique is especially valuable, however, in determining the starting time of PCA events by looking for the earliest time when f_{min} has increased significantly above its monthly median value for that hour.

11.7. EFFECTS ON LOW-FREQUENCY RADIO PROPAGATION

The ionization produced in the lower ionosphere by solar proton bombardment gives rise to very marked effects on the propagation characteristics of low-frequency radio waves in the affected areas. This is not unexpected, since these waves normally propagate by reflection in the *D* region, where the extra ionization is probably most intense. Little has been published at the time of writing on these effects, and only a very brief description will be given here.

The most noticeable effect is on the diurnal variation of the phase of the sky wave received from a low-frequency transmitter. Under normal conditions the nighttime phase lags behind the daytime phase, indicating that reflection is taking place at a greater height during the night. During an intense PCA, the diurnal variation disappears, and reflection apparently takes place day and night at a somewhat lower level than during an undisturbed day. According to Belrose and Ross [29], normal daytime reflection of 70 kc/s waves propagated over distances of about 2000 km occurs at a height of about 65–70 km. During the intense polar cap events of November, 1960, the reflection height became 50–55 km. Ortner *et al.* [30] have suggested the possibility of reflections from the 15–20 km height range to explain the effects seen at Kiruna, Sweden, on the 16 kc/s transmissions from Rugby, England, during intense polar cap events. Such an explanation would appear to be discounted by the phase measurements, though admittedly these refer to a considerably higher frequency.

The amplitude of the received signal is also affected, and can be either greater or less than normal during a polar cap event Unlike waves which have been transmitted through the absorbing region, low-frequency waves, which are reflected in the absorbing region, are affected predominantly at night. Under normal conditions, the daytime signal is considerably weaker than the nighttime signal, and the nighttime signal shows slow fading of large amplitude. The day-night transition occurs during twilight near the midpoint of the path. During a weak polar cap event, the nighttime signal is less than normal with an almost complete disappearance of fading, but the daytime signal is not much affected. During a strong polar cap event, or at the low-latitude edge of a very intense event, this diurnal variation is reversed, the daytime signal being enhanced above its normal level, and the nighttime signal being greatly attenuated. During a very intense event, the diurnal variation completely disappears, and the signal amplitude remains at about its normal daytime value throughout both day and night. Propagation characteristics for very low frequencies under these conditions may actually be better than the average for an undisturbed day.

The explanation of these low-frequency effects is by no means clear. Reflection of low-frequency waves depends critically on the vertical gradients in electron number density in the lower ionosphere, and the height range over which they are maintained, as well as on the absolute value of the density. The evidence previously quoted seems to show that, during an intense polar cap event, gradients of electron density sufficiently pronounced to reflect 70 kc/s waves exist in the neighborhood of 50–55 km both day and night. The lack of any diurnal variation suggests that the location of this critical gradient is independent of ionospheric processes, such as the attachment and photodetachment of electrons, and is probably determined mainly by the characteristics of the bombarding particles.

The measurements suggest that low-frequency waves are a very sensitive detector of solar protons and may show the existence of events which would not be detected by the standard riometer.

11.8. CONCLUSION

At the time of writing, our knowledge of polar cap absorption and of the solar particles that produce it has been expanding at a rapid pace. Although this pace may be slowed down by the approaching period of low solar activity and the consequent drop-off in the frequency of occurrence of these events, many of the questions that have been left unanswered in this chapter may have definite answers by the time of publication. Polar cap absorption as a distinct study may be said to have been born on 23 February 1956, so that the lapse of time between writing and publication of this chapter covers an appreciable fraction of its young life. An attempt has been made, however, to give an accurate picture of the subject as it stood three years after the end of the International Geophysical Year. Many of the minor details may be changed, but the broad outline and interpretation of these phenomena are not likely to be substantially altered.*

*This picture of a causal relationship between intense solar flares and polar cap absorption events appears to be firmly established, at least for the sunspot maximum epoch. More recently, with the advance of the solar activity cycle toward a minimum, new and more sensitive measuring techniques have revealed a number of smaller solar cosmic ray events, many of which are too small to be readily identified in ionospheric absorption data [31, 32]. The relationship of all of these weaker events to solar flares is not yet certain. In one such case an association with a solar M-region seems to have been established; satellite data showed four events (in a 27-day recurrent pattern) for which the proton flux in the 1 Mev to 7 Mev energy range increased significantly [33].

REFERENCES

1. Shain, C. A., Galactic radiation at 18.3 Mc/s, *Aust. J. Sci. Res., A*, **4** (1951), 258.
2. Little, C. G., and H. Leinbach, The riometer—a device for the continuous measurement of ionospheric absorption, *Proc. I.R.E.*, **47** (1959), 315.
3. Bailey, D. K., Disturbances in the lower ionosphere observed at VHF following the solar flare of 23 February 1956 with particular reference to auroral-zone absorption, *J. Geophys. Res.*, **62** (1957), 431.
4. ———, Abnormal ionization in the lower ionosphere associated with cosmic-ray flux enhancements, *Proc. I.R.E.*, **47** (1959), 255.
5. Reid, G. C., and C. Collins, Observations of abnormal VHF radio absorption at medium and high latitudes, *J. Atmos. Terr. Phys.*, **14** (1959), 63.
6. Hultqvist, B., On the interpretation of ionization in the lower ionosphere occurring on both day and night side of the earth within a few hours after some solar flares, *Tellus*, **11** (1959), 332.
7. Reid, G. C., and H. Leinbach, Low-energy cosmic-ray events associated with solar flares, *J. Geophys. Res.*, **64** (1959), 1801.
8. Störmer, C., The Polar Aurora. Oxford: Clarendon Press, 1955.
9. Reid, G. C., A study of the enhanced ionization produced by solar protons during a polar cap absorption event, *J. Geophys. Res.*, **66** (1961), 4071.
10. Anderson, K. A., Ionizing radiation associated with solar radio noise storm, *Phys. Rev. Letters*, **1** (1958), 335.
11. Freier, P. S., E. P. Ney, and J. R. Winckler, Balloon observations of solar cosmic rays on March 26, 1958, *J. Geophys. Res.*, **64** (1959), 685.
12. Winckler, J. R., Balloon study of high-altitude radiations during the International Geophysical Year, *J. Geophys. Res.*, **65** (1960), 1331.
13. Davis, L. R., C. E. Fichtel, D. E. Guss, and K. W. Ogilvie, Rocket observations of solar protons on September 3, 1960, *Phys. Rev. Letters*, **6** (1961), 492.
14. Fichtel, C. E., and D. E. Guss, Heavy nuclei in solar cosmic rays, *Phys. Rev. Letters*, **6** (1961), 495.
15. Rothwell, P., and C. McIlwain, Satellite observations of solar cosmic rays, *Nature*, **184** (1959), 138.
16. Arnoldy, R. L., R. A. Hoffman, and J. R. Winckler, Solar cosmic rays and soft radiation observed at 5,000,000 kilometers from earth, *J. Geophys. Res.*, **65** (1960), 3004.
17. Parker, E. N., Acceleration of cosmic rays in solar flares, *Phys. Rev.*, **107** (1957), 830.
18. Obayashi, T., and Y. Hakura, Propagation of solar cosmic rays through interplanetary magnetic field, *J. Geophys. Res.*, **65** (1960), 3143.
19. Kundu, M. R., and F. T. Haddock, A relation between solar radio emission and polar cap absorption of cosmic radio noise, *Nature*, **186** (1960), 610.

20. Chapman, S., and V. C. A. Ferraro, A new theory of magnetic storms. Part I—The initial phase, *Terr. Mag. Atmos. Electr.*, **36** (1931), 171.

21. ———, and ———, The theory of the first phase of a geomagnetic storm, *Terr. Mag. Atmos. Electr.*, **45** (1940), 245.

22. L. Herzberg, The possible importance of nitric oxide formation during polar cap ionospheric absorption events, *J. Geophys. Res.*, **65** (1960), 3505.

23. Anderson, K. A., and D. C. Enemark, Observations of solar cosmic rays near the north magnetic pole, *J. Geophys. Res.*, **65** (1960), 2657.

24. Meyer P., E. N. Parker, and J. A. Simpson, Solar cosmic rays of February, 1956, and their propagation through interplanetary space, *Phys. Rev.*, **104** (1956), 768.

25. Parker, E. N., Dynamics of the interplanetary gas and magnetic fields, *Astrophys. J.*, **128** (1958), 664.

26. Gold, T., Plasma and magnetic fields in the solar system, *J. Geophys. Res.*, **64** (1959), 1665.

27. Hakura, Y., Y. Takenoshita, and T. Otsuki, Polar blackouts associated with severe geomagnetic storms on Sept. 13th, 1957, and Feb. 11th, 1958, *Rep. Ionos. Res. Japan*, **12** (1958), 459.

28. Collins, C., D. H. Jelly, and A. G. Matthews, High-frequency radio-wave blackouts at medium and high latitudes during a solar cycle, *Canad. J. Phys.*, **39** (1961), 35.

29. Belrose, J. S., and D. B. Ross, Observations of unusual low-frequency propagation made on 12 November 1960, *Canad. J. Phys.*, **39** (1961), 609.

30. Ortner, J., A. Egeland, and B. Hultqvist, A new sporadic layer providing VLF propagation, *I.R.E. Trans. Antennas Prop.*, **AP-8**, (1960), 621.

31. Gregory, J. B., Particle influx at high latitudes. 2. Solar protons, *J. Geophys. Res.*, **68** (1963), 3097.

32. Bryant, D. A., T. L. Cline, U. D. Desai, and F. B. McDonald, New evidence for long lived solar streams in interplanetary space, *Phys. Rev. Letters*, **11** (1963), 144.

33. Burrows, J. R., Private communication.

12

I. Paghis

Magnetic and Ionospheric Storms

12.1. INTRODUCTION

Continuous measurements of the earth's magnetic field have been made for many decades, by a world-wide network of observatories. (See Chapman and Bartels [8] for a thorough summary of these measurements, and for many other discussions pertinent to the subject matter of this chapter.) In the 1930's, following the development of radio pulse-sounding techniques, a similar network was established to monitor electron number-density variations in the ionosphere. On some days, both the magnetic and ionospheric variations appear to be smooth and regular; such days are called 'quiet.' By contrast, the variations on other days are markedly irregular, or 'disturbed.' Disturbances may be divided into several distinctive types, such as magnetic micropulsations (Chapter 8), sudden ionospheric disturbances (SID, Chapter 9), polar cap radio absorption (PCA, Chapter 11), and the subject of this chapter, the magnetic and ionospheric storms. The last two types are specific manifestations of a more general disturbance, the 'upper atmospheric storm,' that includes a wide variety of related physical phenomena.

The terminology used here requires some explanation, because there are no generally accepted definitions of the various categories of storm. Historically, the name 'storm' arose from the occasional great severity and extent of abnormal variations in magnetic field strength and electron number density. We shall see that storms generally have a characteristic morphology and that the name has been extended to include much weaker disturbances of similar morphology. The category 'magnetic storm' is reasonably straight forward, since there are several international planetary magnetic indices that may be used to provide a quantitative definition of a magnetic storm. The category 'ionospheric storm,' however, presents some difficulty. Nearly all of the earlier ionospheric storm studies were restricted to electron number-density variations. As a result, in the literature the term 'ionospheric storm' is used instead of the more precise (but longer) term 'electron number-density variation storm'; this usage is followed throughout this book. There are no international planetary indices of electron density variation, and consequently no standardization in the definitions of 'ionospheric storm.'

The present chapter is primarily concerned with the observational aspects of magnetic and ionospheric storms, but much of the discussion has wider applicability. Visual and radio auroral phenomena, including radio-wave absorption, are considered in Chapters 13 and 14, and various theories of magnetic and auroral storms are outlined in Chapter 15. (The theory of ionospheric storms [25] is still in a very fragmentary state and is not discussed in this book. It is often assumed that once the magnetic and auroral observations are understood, the ionospheric behavior will fall into an appropriately neat pattern.)

What, precisely, is an upper atmospheric storm, and how can it be distinguished from other disturbances? Terrestrial observations alone do not provide an entirely satisfactory answer. The first storm phenomena to be extensively studied were the world-wide magnetic variations, along with associated visual auroral displays. Other ionospheric disturbances were identified at a later date, and these disturbances were considered to be part of the storm process only if they showed a close correlation with either the magnetic storm or the associated visual aurora. Specific disturbances which fail to correlate in this way include the sudden ionospheric disturbances (SID) of Chapter 9, some types of magnetic micropulsation (Chapter 8), and the polar cap radio absorption (PCA) events described in the preceding chapter.

A somewhat more satisfactory classification of terrestrial disturbances arises from a consideration of the cause of the disturbance. Evidence that active regions on the sun are the primary source of the photons and energetic charged particles which cause upper atmospheric disturbances has been discussed in Chapters 9 and 10. The SID's are produced on the earth's sunlit hemisphere by photon emissions at the time of solar flares. Certain flares also emit the energetic particles, mostly protons, which are now known as 'solar cosmic rays.' The concentration of these protons is relatively low, and their collective interactions can normally be neglected. They travel at velocities of the order of 10^5 km/sec and are responsible for the PCA events. The bulk of the solar particle emissions consists of protons and electrons which are less energetic than the solar cosmic rays. The density of the main emission is such that collective interactions are important and the charged particles form a neutral plasma. Plasma is emitted more or less continuously from the sun, and this 'solar wind' may play a significant role in the daily variations of the quiet upper atmosphere. Occasionally, relatively dense or energetic plasma clouds are emitted, with velocities of the order of 10^3 km/sec. The term 'storm plasma' is applied to these emissions (see Sec. 10.1) because they may interact with the earth's atmosphere to produce the type of disturbance we call a 'storm.'

Accordingly, whereas the more traditional definition of a storm is based solely on terrestrial observation, a more meaningful definition would appear to be possible by considering the causes of the storm. Unfortunately, in practice a one-to-one relationship between cause and effect is not found, and much arbitrariness has crept into the classification of storms. We shall see that 27-day recurrent storms are not flare associated; nevertheless, it is assumed that the recurrent events are caused by storm plasma emissions. Moreover, the cause of certain disturbances, such as magnetic micropulsations, is still not firmly established, and their relationship to storms is not yet clear. Another point that should not be overlooked is that the sun-earth medium is a further variable and we are unable as yet to assess its significance to the classification of upper atmospheric disturbances.

A major storm is readily identified by magnetic and/or ionospheric observations. The SID and PCA events which may occur during the storm also have readily identifiable characteristics and do not confuse the issue. The storm observations are very dependent on geomagnetic latitude and local time. The same storm appears to have very different characteristics at the equator, say, than in the auroral zones; or at noon, compared with midnight. Accordingly, a number of indices have been devised to indicate the average strength of a disturbance over a large geographic area. The most widely used index is the planetary 3-hr range of magnetic variation, K_p (see Sec. 1.4.2). Other measures of upper atmospheric activity are frequently compared with K_p in order to determine their relationship with storm phenomena.

As an example, the performance of a long-distance high-frequency radio communication circuit depends in a complicated way on conditions in the *D*, *E*, and *F* ionospheric regions. The performance of such a circuit, between Montreal and London, is continuously monitored and assigned a quality index, known as the 'transatlantic quality figure,' *TAQ*. This index ranges from 0 to 5, as the performance varies from excellent to complete blackout.

Figure 12.1 shows the daily mean values of K_p and TAQ, during May, 1959. The correlation is particularly strong during the stormier periods. Although SID's and PCA's occurred during this month, the smoothed K_p and TAQ indices were not significantly modified by these events.

Almost all storm analysis before the 1930's was based on magnetic field measurements and observations of visual aurora. Since then a wide variety of radio techniques has been developed for obtaining storm data, including, of course, the pulse soundings already mentioned. In addition, during the past decade there has been a rapidly increasing use of balloons, rockets, and satellites as remote laboratories within the upper atmosphere. Data obtained by these new experiments have provided considerable information about the nature of storms, but there are still serious gaps in our knowledge. What are the physical processes whereby a solar cause produces a terrestrial storm? How many kinds of storm are there, and how are the different storm phenomena related? How do storms vary with the latitude and longitude of the observer? We have as yet only the sketchiest of answers to these questions. When the solar sunspot (and flare) activity is high, storms are most frequent. But storms also occur when the solar disk is entirely free of visible spots. Some storms start suddenly, others have a very gradual commencement. Some end abruptly, others very slowly. Sometimes storms recur regularly with a period of about 27 days, corresponding to the rotation period of the sun's surface at low latitudes. Other storms appear to be isolated events. A few storms have clearly delineated phases, known as the initial, main, and recovery phases. Other storms are very irregular. Some storms last less than one day; others, as long as a week.

In the following sections, we first consider the relationship between solar

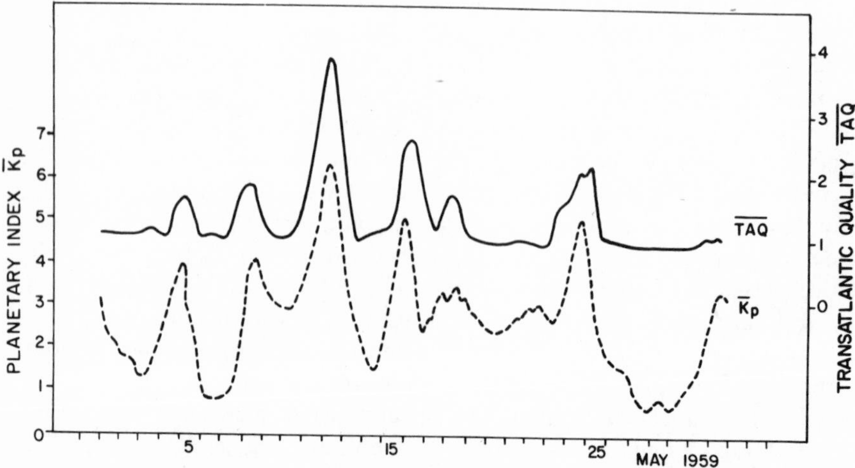

Fig. 12.1 Mean values of the magnetic indices $\overline{K}_p$ and the transatlantic quality figure $\overline{TAQ}$, during May 1959. (From Hartz and McAlpine [13].)

activity and storms, and the information this provides about the classification of storms. Then the magnetic and ionospheric storms are described, both as individual events and as averaged world-wide disturbances.

12.2. UPPER ATMOSPHERIC STORMS AND SOLAR ACTIVITY

The general nature of the evidence connecting solar corpuscular emissions with upper atmospheric storms was outlined in Chapter 10. That discussion emphasized solar observations, particularly those concerned with solar radio noise. The present section considers sun-earth relations from a different point of view, with the emphasis now being placed on terrestrial observations.

Storms may occur sporadically in time, or they may recur at fairly regular intervals. It will be recalled that both the sporadic and the recurrent storms are considered to be caused by the emission of solar storm plasma. Such emissions originate in localized regions of the solar surface, they are sometimes preceded by shock or blast waves, and they travel outward from the sun, generally in a radial direction. The solar storm plasma will either hit or miss the earth's magnetosphere, depending on the angular location of the earth with respect to the solar source, and the velocity of the plasma. Since storms are identified as 'sporadic' or 'recurrent' on the basis of terrestrial data alone, it follows that this arbitrary classification can provide only limited information on the occurrence and duration of solar corpuscular emissions. Precisely what happens at the boundary of the magnetosphere when the storm plasma arrives is uncertain. The experimental evidence is weak, and theoretical models are still in disagreement. Regardless of the mechanism, a disturbance travels through the magnetosphere toward the earth's surface, and upper atmospheric storms are observed.

These storms are exceedingly complex, and all regions of the ionosphere are involved. Changes occur in the temperature, atmospheric density, ion and electron density, ionospheric currents, flux of nonthermal particles, optical and X-ray emissions, and other related quantities. In spite of this complexity, certain systematic features are recognizable in most storms. These features are now summarized; a more detailed description of magnetic and ionospheric storms is given in later sections.

A storm appears to consist of separable high- and low-latitude components. At high latitudes, the most spectacular storm effects are the visual auroral displays, which spread out toward the poles and toward the equator from the zones of maximum auroral occurrence. The main extension is toward lower latitudes; the stronger the storm, the lower the latitude at which aurora occurs. The auroral occurrences, however, are far from uniform along a parallel of geomagnetic latitude, at any one time. Apparently localized patches of increased ionospheric conductivity are formed, and current vortices and auroral displays are observed [5]. The magnetic fields of the current vortices are observed on standard magnetograms as positive and negative deviations from normal, termed 'bays.' (The bays derive their name from their characteristic shape, which resembles the shore line of an ordinary bay, on standard magnetogram records.) Electron number density distributions are also altered in the general neighborhood of the auroral displays, and the normal D, E, and F layers are modified by irregularly and sporadically ionized regions. In general, these storm phenomena are dependent on the earth's magnetic field (more specifically, on the magnetic L coordinate described in Sec. 1.4.1), and there is correlation between observations made at magnetically conjugate points.

The horizontal component of the magnetic field is decreased during the main phase of the storm. This decrease is strongest at the geomagnetic equator and becomes smaller at high latitudes. At the same time, the vertical component of the field is increased in both the north and south polar regions. The vertical increase is considerably smaller than the corresponding horizontal decrease. It has been suggested that a current circling the earth in the equatorial plane would produce the observed magnetic field variations. Such a source would have to be far above the ionospheric current systems in the E region, and this source is the 'ring current' of various storm theories. The main phase of the storm is also characterized by variations in ionospheric electron density, but the ionospheric variations show little correspondence with the magnetic variations. The largest ionospheric disturbance occurs near the auroral zones, and there is relatively little disturbance at the equator or in the polar regions.

The storm plasma takes one or more days to reach the earth. This time interval is highly significant in studies of sun-earth relationships. Many solar events, each having the capability of producing a storm, so far as we know, may occur during this transit time. Present experimental techniques do not permit the tracking in any detail of a disturbance propagating from the sun to the earth. How, then, can we be certain that a particular solar event is responsible for a specific storm? There is substantial evidence that, during certain major disturbances, a particular flare ejected solar plasma, and that this solar plasma could (some days later) have caused the terrestrial storm. For the most part, however, the evidence connecting solar events with storms is still statistical and circumstantial.

12.2.1. Recurrent Storms. The solar rotational period is an important parameter in the analysis of recurrent storms; it is obtained by studying the surface features and is found to increase with latitude. The synodic period, that is, the rotation period as viewed from the earth, is about $26\frac{1}{2}$ days at the equator, 27 days at 20°, and 30 days at 40° latitude. Now, it has been observed that occasionally storms occur in a sequence, with a time interval of 25–30 days between adjacent members of the sequence. (Statistical analysis yields a mean recurrence interval of 27.3 days, and the phenomenon is normally referred to as 27-day recurrence.) It is therefore logical to look for storm-associated solar features, at heliographic latitudes of less than 40°, that could account for the 27-day recurrent storms.

Early attempts to establish a relationship between solar activity and storms did not, however, separate sporadic from 27-day recurrent events. Solar activity was measured by the 'sunspot number' (see Sec. 1.7) and this index was compared with the occurrence of world-wide magnetic storms. It did not matter particularly which magnetic storm parameters were used; the general results were similar. In Fig. 12.2(a), the *annual* mean values of magnetic activity are shown, for an idealized sunspot cycle. The linear cross-correlation coefficient is high, but in spite of this strong correlation, the curves differ in two major respects. During the quiet years, with negligible sunspot activity, storm activity remains appreciable; and the maximum of storm activity occurs about two years after the sunspot number maximum. If *monthly*, instead of annual mean values of magnetic activity are used, the linear cross correlation decreases. Detailed analysis shows that this decrease arises from a vanishingly small correlation during the years of low sunspot number. This result suggests that, at least during sunspot minimum years, storm occurrence cannot be directly linked with solar activity as measured by the sunspot index. This point was confirmed by Shapley [26] who found that the 27-day recurrence tendency of the daily International Magnetic Character Figure, C_i, is strongest during sunspot minimum years (see Fig. 12.2b).

An excellent survey of early work on the 27-day recurrence tendency is given by Chapman and Bartels [8]. Some of the storm sequences persist for more than one year, but more commonly a sequence lasts only about five or six months. Such sequences are most readily identifiable during years of low sunspot activity, because of the scarcity of sporadic storms.

One sequence of seven storms is illustrated in Fig. 12.3. The amplitude of the 3-hr linear planetary magnetic range index, a_p, is plotted for each storm. Storm duration varied from about 3 to 6 days, which is typical of the 27-day recurrent storms during years of low sunspot number. The time intervals between storms, shown on the right, were determined by cross correlation of 10-day segments of the a_p index. The linear correlation index was in the range 0.6–0.7 for the entire sequence.

The existence of recurrent storms, with recurrence intervals substantially different from 27 days, has been investigated for many years with inconclusive results. The shorter intervals could arise, for example, if storm-associated features, such as M regions (see below) and radio-noisy sunspots tend to maintain a constant angular separation on the sun's surface. Longer intervals could arise if storm-associated features occur at solar latitudes greater than

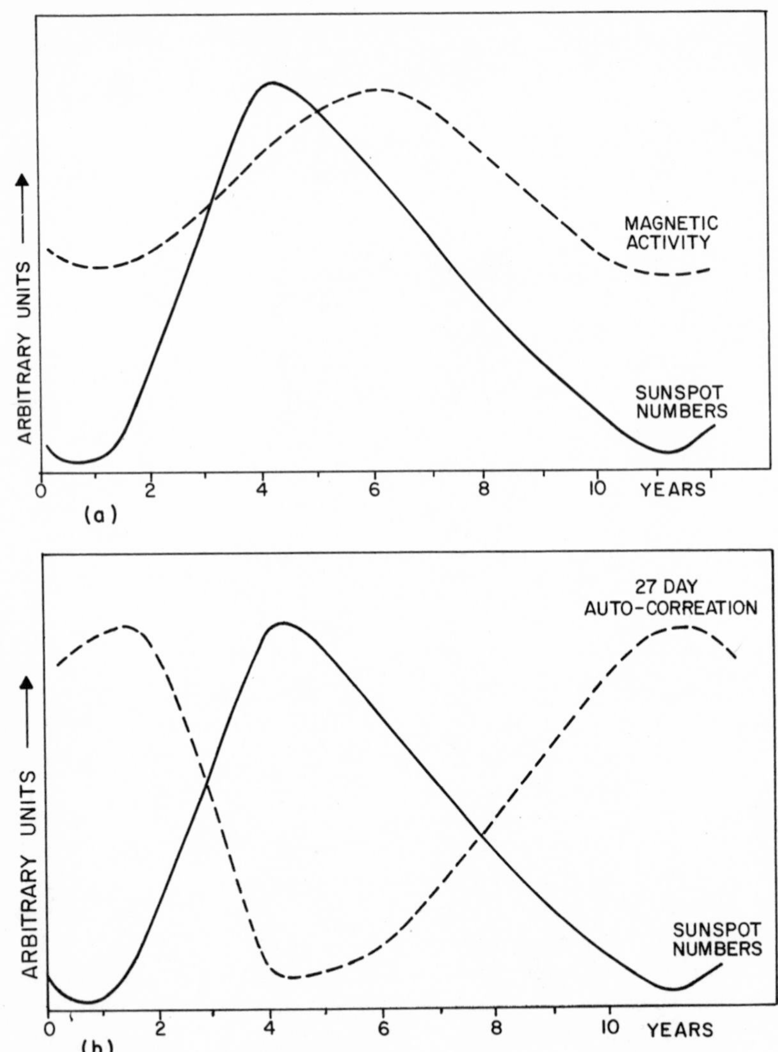

Fig. 12.2(a) Annual mean values of sunspot number and magnetic activity, for an idealized sunspot cycle. **(b)** Annual mean values of sunspot number and the 27-day autocorrelation of magnetic activity for an idealized sunspot cycle. (Based on Shapley [26].)

45°, since at these latitudes the rotation period of the photosphere is longer than 30 days. Recent analysis [23, 24] of recurrence intervals ranging from 3 days to more than 40 days shows that recurrent storm sequences with intervals in the range 30–40 days consist of storms whose duration is typically less than 3 days; that is, they are substantially shorter than the 27-day recurrent storms.

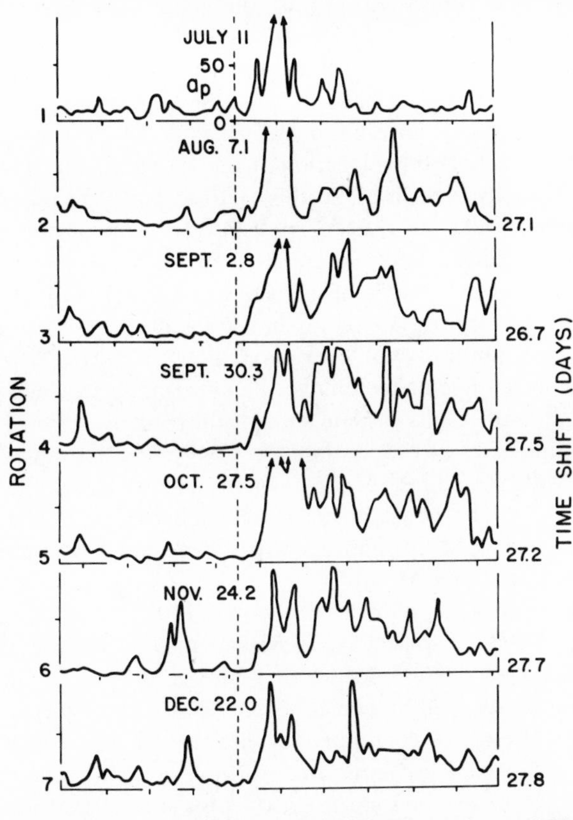

Fig. 12.3 The planetary magnetic range index a_p, for a sequence of seven 27-day recurrent storms in 1950.

Solar sources of recurrent storms have not yet been fully identified. As early as 1932, Bartels [2] gave the name 'M region' to the sources of the 27-day recurrent storms, but until recently little progress was made in determining the nature of these regions. Babcock and Babcock [1] have found that, in addition to the strong magnetic fields that appear in the vicinity of sunspots, weaker fields not linked to the centers of activity occur frequently on the solar surface. These weak fields may be classified as unipolar, bipolar, complex, etc. In 1953, a unipolar magnetic (UM) region was observed at about 15°N heliographic latitude for at least six solar rotations. The mean field intensity was only 0.5 gauss, and there were no sunspots nearby. On each rotation, the central meridian passage (CMP) of the UM region preceded the onset of a storm by about three days. There is, therefore, a distinct possibility that UM and M regions are identical, but more data are needed to verify this point.

12.2.2. Sporadic Storms. Sunspots and associated centers of activity, although not usually directly correlated with recurrent storms, may still be associated with sporadic storms. Two main possibilities have been investigated extensively. The occurrence of sporadic storms may depend on the previous occurrence of solar eruptions, such as flares, or it may be critically dependent on the heliographic location of the active region. These possibilities are not mutually exclusive, and this fact has made the analysis difficult.

Let us first consider the relationship between geomagnetic disturbances and the CMP of solar centers of activity. To reduce the effects of flares, Mustel [20] examined the years of low sunspot activity during five sunspot cycles. During each cycle, he found that a significant rise in geomagnetic activity occurred about six to seven days after the CMP of calcium-plage regions. It is more difficult to remove the effect of flares when the sunspot number is high, and results to date should not be considered as conclusive. The analyses indicate, however, that the CMP of solar centers of activity is correlated with variations in geomagnetic activity during all phases of the sunspot cycle. The geomagnetic activity appears to be reduced on the first day or so after CMP, following which it reaches a maximum at about five to seven days after CMP.

The solar centers of activity are the sources of the more spectacular solar flare events and their associated corpuscular and radio-noise emissions, as described in Chapter 9. The evidence that flare occurrence is connected with the production of sporadic upper atmospheric storms is very strong, particularly in isolated cases of great intensity, but it is difficult to establish a one-to-one relationship between flares and storms in general. The time interval between flare occurrence and storm production is measured in days, rather than hours, and there are very many more flares than storms. Thus during the sun-earth transit time many flares may be observed. And, equally important, not all storms can be attributed to observed flares. Many investigators have tried to establish criteria for identifying storm-producing flares, and this remains a very active field of research.

During years of high sunspot activity, an increase in geomagnetic activity occurs within about three days of the onset of an intense flare. This increase is particularly evident when additional solar parameters are considered in the analysis. As a result of many separate investigations, it has been shown that parameters significant in the production of sporadic storms include flare intensity and heliographic location, associated radio emissions at frequencies below about 200 Mc/s, and magnetic fields in the vicinity of the associated sunspot groups. This listing is not necessarily complete, but other parameters have been studied less extensively and will not be considered here.

Solar radio noise emissions were discussed in some detail in Sec. 10.4.2. An optical flare is evidence of a disturbance at the sun's surface; radio noise bursts at meter wavelengths confirm that the disturbance has penetrated outward into the solar atmosphere. It follows that solar radio noise can potentially provide detailed information about solar shock waves and corpuscular emissions. Figure 10.7 shows the geomagnetic activity following intense flares in 1956–59. Typically, a well-defined maximum in magnetic activity occurs for only those major flares which were accompanied by 'major' or 'major plus' radio noise bursts at frequencies below 200 Mc/s, and this maximum occurs about two days after flare onset. The association is increased markedly for those flares that are followed by PCA events [14]. Radio noise receivers with sufficient angular resolution to identify the noise-producing region have now been in operation for several years, and some progress has been made in interpreting the data [33]. In future work on sun-earth relations, the information provided by solar radio noise will certainly be of major significance.

Flare-storm analyses covering one or more sunspot cycles must, at present, be made without the benefit of appropriate solar noise data. Following earlier work by Hale [10], Newton [21], and others, Bell [3] made a detailed study of the two sunspot cycles 1939–59. About 95% of the 580 major flares, of importance 2+ or greater, occurred in the vicinity of sizable sunspots. The location, intensity, and magnetic type [11] of these sunspot groups were separately considered in the analysis.

Regardless of distance from the solar central meridian, about 50% of the major flares were followed within three days by a magnetic storm. (A 'storm' was listed if both the daily A_p and the daily K_p indices exceeded 25.) Maximum storm activity occurred on the second and third day after the flare. Although the overall probability of storm occurrence did not appear to depend on flare longitude, on the average the central flares were followed by stronger storms. More detailed investigation [14] of the probability of storm occurrence shows a small but consistent western bias of the storm-flares in both the northern and southern hemispheres. About three-quarters of the great storms followed flares that occurred within 45° of the central meridian.

Bell [3] considered separately the intensity of Hα emission and the area of the flare in heliographic square degrees. Neither the number nor the intensity of the storms occurring within three days of the flare appeared to increase systematically with either flare intensity or area. An active region, however, often produces several major flares in less than three days, and this would tend to make interpretation difficult. When the flare area exceeded 50 square degrees, or the Hα flare intensity was more than twice that of the neighboring continuum, both the relative number and intensity of the associated storms increased significantly.

The sunspot groups associated with major flares were divided into four magnetic categories: unipolar (α), bipolar (β), semicomplex ($\beta\gamma$), and complex (γ). The probability that a flare would be followed by a storm within three days was only 0.4 for α groups, but increased to 0.45 for β, 0.6 for $\beta\gamma$, and 0.7 for γ groups. This result might be due to the magnetic properties of the spot groups, or to some asymmetry in the location of the different groups on the sun. In examining this point, Bell found a marked asymmetry between the northern and southern hemispheres, such that the asymmetry increased with increasing storm intensity. From 1937 to 1959 about 62% of the 580 major flares occurred in the northern solar hemisphere, and these northern flares were followed by 86% of the great storms. Systematic flare observations are not available for earlier sunspot cycles, but analysis of sunspot data [4] indicates that the southern solar hemisphere, rather than the northern hemisphere, may have been dominant during the last half of the previous century.

To conclude, during the years of low sunspot activity, long-lived solar features (as yet unidentified) are predominant in their effects and cause recurrent storms. During the high-activity years, major flares are strongly associated with the occurrence of sporadic storms. As noted in Chapter 10, it is probable that the CMP of solar centers of activity is also associated with the occurrence of sporadic storms. Since 1937, and possibly for a much longer period, the solar northern hemisphere has been more effective than the southern hemisphere in producing intense, isolated storms. Although details of the physical processes are still uncertain, the occurrence of certain types of anomalous radio noise at meter wavelengths (see Sec. 10.4.2) appears to be symptomatic of the storm-producing solar activity.

12.3. THE AVERAGE CHARACTERISTICS OF MAGNETIC AND IONOSPHERIC STORMS

There does not appear to be a sharp dividing line between normal or quiet conditions and abnormal or storm conditions. Magnetic and ionospheric storms produce effects on a world-wide basis, but in the auroral zones smaller-scale disturbances occur almost every day. These disturbances are sometimes called 'elementary polar storms' because they may underlie the larger-scale effects. They are characterized by the occurrence of visual aurora and of isolated geomagnetic bays. Between the magnetic bays, whose duration is an hour or so, the magnetic field returns to its normal, undisturbed level. During a world-wide storm, the polar magnetic bays increase in number and magnitude until, as the storm increases in strength, the bays overlap and the polar magnetic field is continuously disturbed. Although isolated bays cannot be associated with solar events in quite the same way as the world-wide storms, they nevertheless have certain features in common with storms. The characteristics of bays will therefore be considered in parallel with the characteristics of storms.

The various geophysical phenomena which constitute an upper atmospheric storm must, by definition, be related to each other. The stronger magnetic storms are invariably accompanied by ionospheric disturbances. Storm phenomena, however, such as magnetic field variations and radio wave absorption, do not necessarily occur in the same volume of space, or in precise time coincidence, even if they do arise from the same external cause. Broadly speaking, magnetic storms are strongest in the auroral zones and near the geomagnetic equator. Ionospheric storms are also strongest in the auroral zones, but they become progressively weaker at lower latitudes. The study of space and time relationships between various storm features is a subject of intensive continuing research. These relationships are significant in the development and verification of storm theories, and are also of practical importance to the users of radio communications and to space travelers.

The main observational data are magnetic field variations, visual and radio aurora, radio wave absorption, and electron number density profiles up to the *F*-layer maximum. These measurements are usually made at fixed ground stations. Satellite-borne equipments now coming into use can observe the upper side of the ionosphere, and measure the incoming flux of energetic charged particles, along with the electron and ion densities. The continuous and rapid geographic coverage provided by a satellite makes it relatively easy to identify and map various types of irregularity, and this will permit a more direct approach to be made to the study of world-wide storm characteristics. To date, the satellite data on storms are scanty, and require careful interpretation.

Statistical analysis of storms often requires the separation of variations which are essentially independent of longitude, and which can therefore be identified as functions of universal time, from variations which are more directly associated with local time. Frequently, the time origin is taken at the start of a storm, and time measured from this origin is called 'storm time.' The optimum choice of spatial coordinates depends on the particular analysis, but because of the strong dependence of storm phenomena on the earth's magnetic field, geomagnetic latitude is generally used in preference to geographic latitude. To be consistent, geomagnetic local time should also be used. It is only at high latitudes, however, that the difference between geomagnetic and geographic local time becomes significant, so geomagnetic latitude and geographic local time coordinates are frequently employed for convenience.

In the following sections, magnetic storm classifications are discussed; then the regional and world-wide characteristics of magnetic and ionospheric storms are described. No generally accepted method of classifying storms exists. There is a strong tendency to classify in terms of the standard magnetogram observations, primarily because these data have been collected for many decades. In recent years, particularly since the IGY, world-wide data on other storm phenomena have become available and new classifications have been proposed. In time, some of these newer classifications may be widely adopted, but this chapter employs the conventional magnetic storm classifications.

12.4. MAGNETIC STORM CLASSIFICATION

Magnetic storms may be classified according to the characteristics of individual storms or according to their relationship to other storms. In the first case, the usual division is into sudden commencement (SC) and gradual commencement (GC); in the second, into isolated and 27-day recurrent storms. Despite many statements to the contrary, the relation between these two methods of division is not clear.

Intense flares nearly always occur one or two days before the strongest storms, and most of these storms are SC. Moreover, storm theorists have recently made substantial progress on physical models in which flares produce SC storms. There has therefore been an increasing tendency in the literature to assume that SC storms are isolated events, caused by flares, whereas GC storms are 27-day recurrent events not caused by flares. There is no direct evidence to support either this assumption or its converse; but in 1949–61 both GC and SC storms show a similar statistical association with flares of importance $\geqslant 2^+$, accompanied by major radio noise bursts [14]. Interpretation of the statistical evidence depends on the methods used to identify SC, GC, isolated, and recurrent storms.

The designation of a storm as SC depends only on the identification of a storm sudden commencement (SSC) inpulse (Fig. 12.5) occurring near the beginning of a storm. There is no precise definition of an SSC impulse. When a sudden change in the amplitude of a standard magnetogram record, with rise time of less than about ten minutes, is recorded simultaneously (within one minute or so) by several observatories, this event is called a 'magnetic impulse.' Similar impulses have more recently been recorded in space vehicles. Prevailing practice on storm classification seems to be to list a storm as SC if at least two widely separated stations record such an impulse at, or less than 24 hr before, the onset of other storm characteristics.

There are several complicating factors pertinent to this method of classification. Magnetic sudden impulses (SI), similar in all other respects to SSC's, often occur in the absence of storms. Many storms are preceded by several, rather than one impulse, and additional impulses frequently occur during the storm. Impulses preceding strong storms are generally larger than impulses preceding weak storms, although there are many exceptions. It follows that impulses preceding strong storms are less likely to be obscured by random fluctuations than are the impulses that precede weak storms. As noted earlier, the strongest storms are usually SC, and it is not known whether this effect arises primarily from the method of storm classification, or from an intrinsic difference between SC and GC storms.

A somewhat similar problem arises in attempting to separate isolated from recurrent storms. A storm is considered to be isolated unless it clearly forms part of a recurrent sequence. The selection of recurrent sequences depends entirely on terrestrial observations, and standard selection criteria have not been established. There is, moreover, a marked annual variation of terrestrial storm activity which makes it more difficult to identify storms during the solstitial months. These problems are not too serious during years or relatively low storm activity, when recurrent storm sequences are obviously the dominant phenomena. During the more active years, however, the selection of recurrent sequences becomes a very subjective process.

The 27-day recurrence tendency of storms is conveniently presented by arranging the data in successive rows of 27 days each, such that the twenty-eighth day is immediately underneath the first day, the twenty-ninth day under the second day, etc., as in Fig. 12.4. Recurrent storm sequences with three or more members, from 1948 to 1959, have been plotted. Only the starting times of the storms are shown. SC storms are indicated by a solid circle; GC storms by an open circle. Six of the sequences are entirely SC, ten are all GC, and twelve are mixed.

Although various authors have reported a number of statistical differences between SC and GC storms, these differences are not readily apparent for individual storms. One of the recurrent sequences of Fig. 12.4, extending from July to December, 1950, has already been shown in more detail in Fig. 12.3. Of its seven members, the second and fourth are listed internationally as SC's and the remainder as GC's, although the distinction is in no way apparent in the body of the storms.

Evidence of this type strongly suggests that the differences between SC

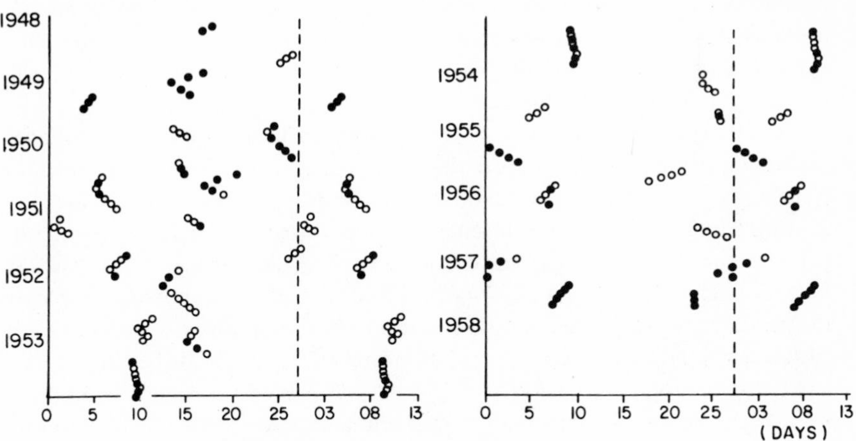

Fig. 12.4 The starting times of 27-day recurrent magnetic storms, 1948–1959.

●—●—● Starting times of SC storms

○—○—○ Starting times of GC storms

and GC storms are superificial, rather than basic. Such a conclusion, if fully accepted, would be helpful in morphological and synoptic studies of storms, for results derived from one class could then be ascribed equally to the other with little danger of error. In practice, SC storms have been analyzed much more extensively than GC storms, since it is a great convenience to have a well-defined starting time, but it seems from the foregoing that no serious limitation has resulted thereby.

During some storms a PCA event is also in progress. The occurrence of a mixed auroral–polar cap disturbance is of considerable interest, and one final storm classification would appear to be necessary. Since the solar cosmic-ray events are strongly correlated with the occurrence of visible solar flares (Sec. 11.5.1), these events are almost always either precursor to a magnetic storm or start during the storm. A flux of solar protons bombards the atmosphere, causing maximum ionization changes in the *D* region. The solar cosmic rays appear to do little that affects the characteristics of magnetic storms (Sec. 11.5.3), presumably because the magnetic variation currents flow at *E*-region heights and above, but they may have a drastic effect on storm phenomena in the *D* region. We shall call such a storm a 'mixed auroral–polar cap event,' or more concisely a 'mixed storm.' The existence of PCA events and mixed storms became apparent only after 1957 when the ionospheric effects due to solar cosmic rays were first appreciated. As a result, much of the earlier work on *D*-region storm phenomena requires reinterpretation.

12.5. LIFE HISTORY OF A STORM

Storms vary markedly from one another in their growth and decay and in the multitude of disturbance features they produce; yet they tend to show a life history that is broadly shared by all. The general features of that history, arbitrarily including the SSC impulse, are summarized here.

For the purpose, however, it is necessary to keep in mind the different latitude zones described toward the end of Sec. 1.4.1. This requirement is clearly revealed by the representative magnetogram traces exhibited in Fig. 12.5(a), which shows the development of an SC storm (1) in the polar regions, (2) near the zone of maximum occurrence of visual aurora, and (3) at low latitudes. The phases of the SC storm are indicated, and they are employed in the description of the overall development. For comparison, Fig. 12.5(b) shows a representative GC storm, as observed at low latitudes.

12.5.1. Before the Storm. At subauroral and polar latitudes, the magnetic field is relatively quiet, with only slow amplitude variations. Ionospheric parameters have their normal quiet-day values. Visual and radio aurora, auroral *X*-ray emissions, and abnormal HF radio-wave absorption do not occur.

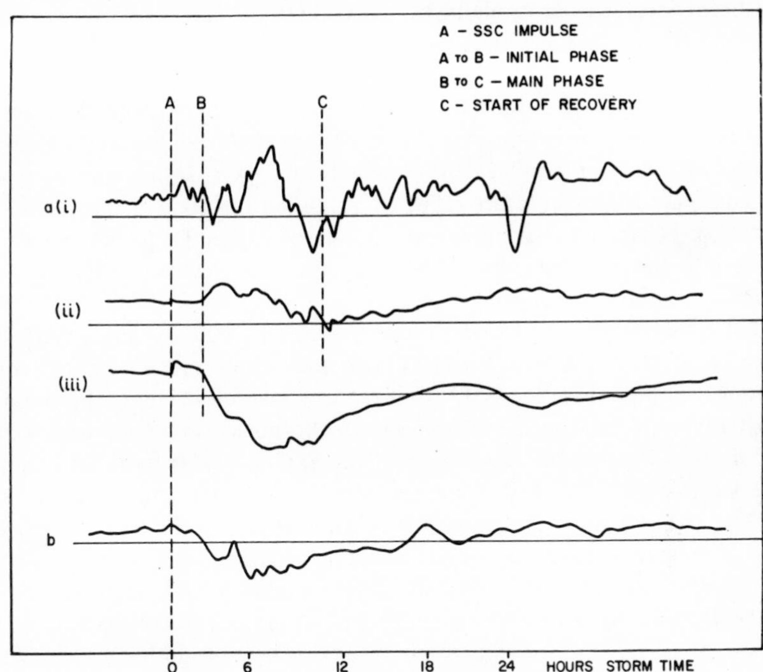

Fig. 12.5 Variations in the horizontal *H* component of standard magnetograms during storms:

(a) SC Storm

(i) in the polar cap.

(ii) near the auroral zone. (Vertical scale is reduced by a factor of ten.)

(iii) at low latitude.

(b) GC storm at low latitude.

Even though the upper atmosphere is 'quiet,' in terms of the mean worldwide activity, there are daily disturbances in the zone of maximum occurrence of visual aurora. Regular diurnal patterns of visual and radio aurora are observed, and auroral *X*-ray emissions are recorded at balloon heights. The first phase of the auroral disturbance starts in the late afternoon or early evening. Positive magnetic bays in *H*, of about $\frac{1}{2}$ hr duration, are accompanied by increased irregularity in the *F* layer (as revealed by spread-*F* on ionograms) and by the formation of auroral sporadic-*E* clouds. At about midnight, there is a transition from typically positive to typically negative magnetic bays. At the same time, active forms of visual aurora appear, and the density of sporadic *E* is increased, tending to obscure the *F* layer from study by ground-based radio ionosondes. The physical relationship between auroral emissions, magnetic bays, and abnormal HF absorption is still largely undetermined, even though clear-cut time and space correlations have been observed occasionally between different pairs of features; there are many more instances in which this local correlation does not appear to exist.

The main effect of the presence of solar cosmic rays before the start of a mixed storm is to increase the *D*-region electron density and electron-density gradients in the polar cap regions. Radio waves of low and very-low frequency, say 10–200 kc/s, are reflected at the bottom edge of this region by the steeper electron-density gradient. Waves of higher frequency penetrate further into the *D* region, but there the enhanced electron density causes abnormally large absorption.

12.5.2. Storm Onset. During the storm onset—that is, during the first 5–10 min after the start of the SSC impulse—there are no major storm phenomena other than the SSC itself, at low latitudes. Here, the impulse almost invariably produces an increase in the horizontal field, with a rise time of from 1 to 10 min. The shape of the SSC at higher latitudes is much more variable and is a current subject of much research [for example, 34]. The SSC is not always clearly visible in auroral and polar regions because of the increased background level of magnetic agitation.

Near the auroral-zone maximum, *X*-ray bursts have been observed at balloon heights [6] in time coincidence with some of the strong SSC's. An increase of *D*-region electron number density occurs in the auroral zone at this time [12, 22], and the resulting increase in radio-wave absorption is known as 'sudden commencement absorption' (SCA). The occurrence of visual and radio aurora does not seem to alter appreciably at the time of SC. There have been sporadic reports of large changes in the critical frequency and height of the *F*2 layer at the time of SC, but a consistent effect has not yet been confirmed. This may be due to the scarcity of suitable data; unlike magnetograms, which run continuously, the standard vertical ionosonde sweeps through its frequency range in about 15 sec, and usually does so only once every 15 min.

12.5.3. Initial Phase. At low latitudes, the mean value of *H* often remains above normal for several hours immediately before the main phase of the storm. This interval is called the 'initial phase.' In many (but not all) SC storms, the SSC impulse coincides with the start of the initial phase. The amplitude of the initial phase tends to decrease with increasing latitude, and a well-defined initial phase is not normally visible at auroral and polar latitudes. Small variations in amplitude, with a periodicity of minutes rather than hours, occur immediately following the SSC. These variations, or micro-pulsations, are usually strongest at auroral latitudes.

F-region disturbances begin at about the same time as the SC magnetic storm, but as already noted, it has not yet been shown that they consistently have a sharp onset. Anomalies in the normal *F* region make it difficult to obtain satisfactory quiet-day reference levels from which to compute the stormtime variations. This problem is less serious during the strongest magnetic storms, because of the large difference between quiet and disturbed conditions. The strongest storms, however, are usually those in which the initial phase has its shortest duration, and it often lasts for less than 1 hr. Moreover, analysis of the available data indicates that the direction of change of the critical frequency f_0F2 depends on local time, season, and latitude. For these reasons, the magnitude and direction of the ionospheric variations during the initial phase have not yet been determined. In particular, it is not known whether the reversal of direction of the magnetic H variation at the end of the initial phase is associated with a corresponding change in the ionospheric disturbances. Accordingly, further discussion of the F-region disturbances will be deferred until we consider the main phase of the magnetic storm.

During a mixed storm, the earth's magnetic cutoff for energetic charged particles apparently decreases, and solar cosmic rays arrive at latitudes appreciably below the normal polar cap region (see Chapter 11). This causes increased D-region ionization at these latitudes. There is still some question as to precisely when the change of magnetic cutoff occurs. The few well-documented cases have occurred after, rather than at, the time of SC, and have either preceded or occurred near the beginning of the main phase.

12.5.4. Main Phase. At low latitudes, the start of a large depression in H marks the beginning of the 'main phase' of the storm. At high latitudes, large-amplitude magnetic bay disturbances occur. The case illustrated in Fig. 12.5 is complex, with overlapping positive and negative bays. Irregularities in the shape of the low-latitude depression in H can often be correlated with details of the high-latitude bays.

The auroral disturbances which were largely confined to the auroral zone during the prestorm period and the initial phase now spread to much lower latitudes. Figure 12.6 shows the magnetic H component and the critical frequencies of the E and F regions at night during the main phase of a moderate storm at a station just below the auroral zone maximum. There is a typical positive bay before midnight and negative bay after midnight. The existence of spread-F echoes accounts for the range of values of f_0F2. During the positive bay, the increased critical frequency of sporadic-E prevents the reflection of radio waves from the F region. The positive bay is accompanied by relatively weak radio-wave absorption in the D region (not shown in Fig. 12.6). During the negative bay, the D-region absorption is sufficient to cause total ionospheric blackout at HF.

During the main phase of a storm there are marked changes in the distribution and density of ionization. Electron content can be measured by radio probes along a line of sight from the earth to the moon, or from the

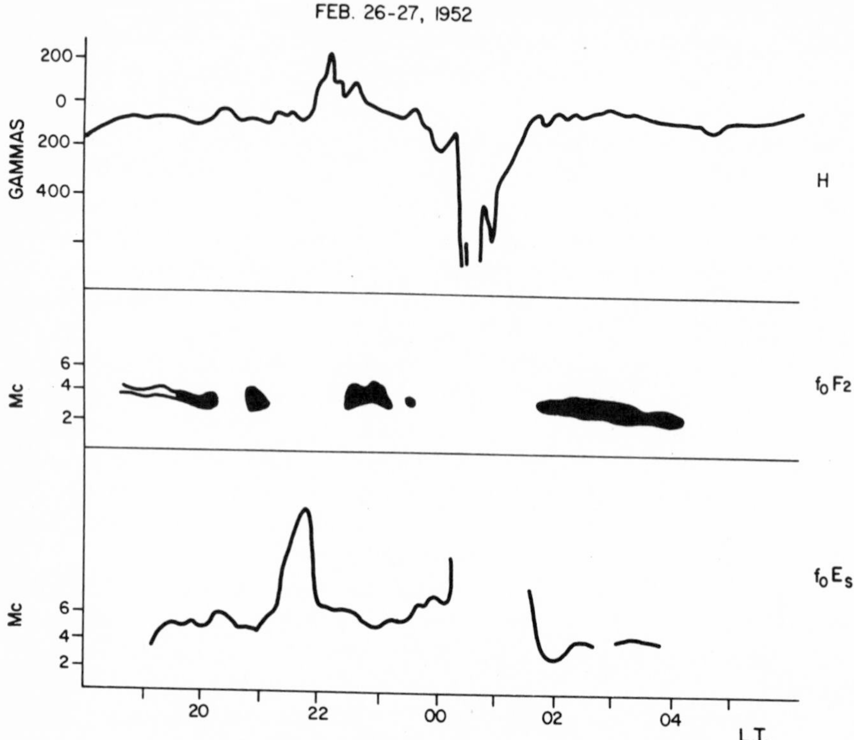

Fig. 12.6 Magnetic and ionospheric variations during a moderate storm, at Saskatoon 26–27 Feb. 1952; the shaded region on the central frame represents the range of the values recorded. (Based on Meek [17].)

earth to high-altitude artificial satellites, but these are recently developed techniques, they give only height-integrated results, and the storm data they provide are still scanty [18]. More extensive information on the ionospheric critical frequencies, electron number density variation with height, and the occurrence of various types of irregularities in electron density can be obtained from ground-based swept-frequency HF ionosonde records, though only up to the height of the *F*-layer maximum. Similar information above this height can also be obtained by the analysis of satellite-borne sweep-frequency ionosonde records. Again the observations are only recent, however, dating from the launching of the Canadian satellite Alouette I in September, 1962, and storms have been relatively weak and infrequent since that date because of the approaching minimum of the sunspot cycle in 1964–65.

The total electron content of the ionosphere, n_t, decreases during a storm at latitudes within the approximate range 30°–60° geomagnetic. At lower latitudes, there is evidence for a stormtime increase in n_t, but precise data are not yet available. At higher latitudes, n_t appears to decrease; the presence of irregularities makes quantitative analysis difficult, and very few results have been published to date. As an example of the marked effect at middle latitudes, n_t at Jodrell Bank (56°N geomagnetic) decreased to as little as one-tenth of the quiet-day value during the strong storm of 12–13 November 1960 [31]. Since most of the ionospheric electrons are produced below the F-layer peak, the reduced electron density observed at high latitudes could be due either to a decreased rate of production at the lower levels or to an increased rate of recombination there or at greater heights. In Sec. 4.2.1 it was remarked that the $F1$ ledge becomes more pronounced at all times when low values of f_0F2 occur, including periods of ionospheric storms, and in Sec. 5.2.3 that atmospheric drag on satellites increases during storms. All these results could be explained consistently if the basic storm effect were an increase in atmospheric temperature and density, in the upper F region if not at lower levels as well. Such an increase could cause a significant increase in the very low recombination rate above the $F2$ maximum, without a correspondingly large change in the rate of production of ionization in the lower F region.

Ionosonde data on stormtime electron densities at or below the F-layer maximum have been accumulating since about 1935. The parameters of particular interest here are the maximum electron density N_m, and the height at which it occurs, hN_m. Local time, seasonal, and latitude effects are all significant and these, taken together with the local irregularities present in most storms, have made data interpretation difficult.

In the polar cap and auroral zones, the F region is usually too disturbed during strong storms to permit the computation of valid electron density profiles, but N_m can be derived from measurements of the penetration frequency f_0F2. The main storm effect is a decrease of N_m, starting within a few hours of storm onset, and continuing throughout the storm. This decrease is strongest near noon, and as a result, the amplitude of the diurnal variation of N_m is greatly reduced from its normal value.

At the equator, N_m is increased when averaged over the entire storm, but there are also intervals during which N_m decreases below the quiet-day level. The average increase is about one order of magnitude smaller than the corresponding decrease at high latitudes. In the middle latitudes, either increases or decreases may occur, depending on a number of factors, including season. On the average, decreases occur in summer and increases in winter.

The stormtime variation of hN_m appears to be more irregular than variations in N_m. This irregularity may possibly be magnified by the scarcity of true-height data during storms. Height variations as large as 100 km may occur at all latitudes. Frequently the height changes correlate with changes in N_m; that is, a decrease in hN_m accompanies a decrease in N_m. There are also many exceptions.

Ionosonde data on storm effects above the F-layer maximum are just beginning to become available, and only preliminary analyses have been published to date [9, 19]. These results appear to confirm that there is a general reduction in electron number density during a storm at middle and high latitudes, but the existence of stormtime irregularities again makes it difficult to obtain complete vertical profiles of electron density.

12.5.5. Recovery phase. At low latitudes, the H component gradually returns toward the prestorm value during the storm 'recovery phase.' At high latitudes, the amplitude of the bay irregularities decreases and the bays are again isolated, as in the prestorm phase. The H component there is well below its prestorm value at the beginning of the recovery phase, and may remain below normal for several days. The 3-hr magnetic range index K is a much better indicator of ionospheric storm effects; it decreases at the beginning of the recovery phase and at about this time all the main ionospheric storm phenomena terminate.

12.6. WORLD-WIDE STORM CHARACTERISTICS

The world-wide characteristics of upper atmospheric storms are derived from simultaneous observations of the local characteristics at representative locations. Parameters whose planetary distributions have been extensively studied include magnetic field and electron density variations, the occurrence of high-latitude spread F, visual aurora, and anomalous radio-wave absorption. The present section considers only the magnetic field and electron number density variations. The occurrence of high-latitude spread F is discussed in Chapter 4, visual aurora in Chapter 13, and anomalous radio-wave absorption in Chapter 14.

Magnetic field variations observed at ground level, with time scales of a few days or less, are produced primarily by electric currents that flow above the earth's surface. This fact permits the representation of these field variations by an equivalent overhead current system [7]. Regardless of the actual location and configuration of the variation currents, it is convenient to place the equivalent current system in a thin shell, concentric with the earth's surface. This form of representation has already been met and justified for the quiet-day currents (Sec. 7.3); it is widely employed also for the currents of isolated polar magnetic bays $C(B)$, and for those of storms $C(D)$. The quiet and bay currents probably do flow in a restricted height range, in or near the E region, whereas the location of the stormtime currents is less certain, as will be discussed shortly.

Silsbee and Vestine [27] derived the average equivalent electric current system for a number of magnetic bays that occurred during the Polar Year 1932–33; it is shown in Fig. 12.7(a) for 00 hours U.T. The view is from

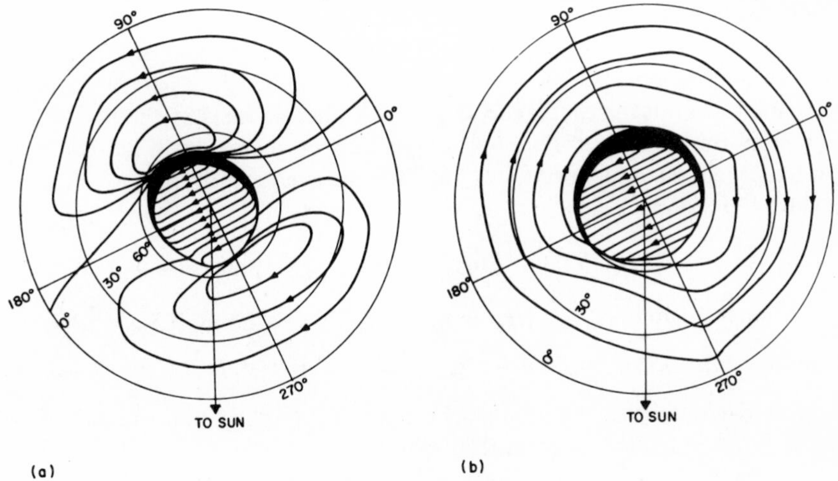

Fig. 12.7 Equivalent overhead current representation of magnetic field variations viewed from above the geomagnetic north pole.

(a) The mean current of magnetic bays, $C(B)$ at 00 hr U.T. during the Polar Year 1932–33. (After Silsbee and Vestine [27].)

(b) The current system $C(D)$ during the main phase of a storm, at 00 hr U.T., 1 May 1933. (After Vestine *et al.* [32].)

above the geomagnetic north pole, and equal currents flow between adjacent lines in the diagram. The mean $C(B)$ system is strongest at 60°–70° latitude, with a broad maximum from about 00–06 hours geomagnetic local time. It corresponds there to decreases in H, that is, to the occurrence of negative bays in H.

A very similar pattern is found at high latitudes during the main phase of a typical magnetic storm, as is illustrated by the $C(D)$ system shown in Fig. 12.7(b). Marked differences appear at the lower latitudes, and these are linked to the uncertainty in the location of the storm-time currents. The general uniformity of the low-latitude $C(D)$ system suggests that the related magnetic deviations are in fact due to some distant source, possibly a ring of current circling the earth high in the exosphere. This is the 'ring current' mentioned much earlier in the chapter, and it will appear again in the discussion of storm theories. For the present, we may note that some indication of such a stormtime current has been found by satellite measurements at heights of a few earth radii [28], although its common occurrence as a part of the storm process has not yet been firmly established.

If the magnetic deviations attributable to a ring current are removed before the equivalent $C(D)$ system is inferred, then a pattern much more closely resembling $C(B)$ is obtained. This suggests that isolated bays may be looked upon as evidence of low-intensity storm processes.

Many storm parameters, including $C(D)$, are often analyzed into two convenient components. The one comprises that part of the parameter that is symmetric about the geomagnetic axis; the other consists of the residuals. Thus a storm parameter D that is a function of geomagnetic latitude (λ) and longitude (φ), and stormtime (Tst), may be averaged over all longitudes to yield a component,

$$Dst(\lambda, Tst) \equiv (2\pi)^{-1} \int_0^{2\pi} D(\lambda, \varphi, Tst)\, d\varphi$$

that is independent of φ; it is termed the 'stormtime variation.' The residual is

$$DS(\lambda, \varphi, Tst) \equiv D(\lambda, \varphi, Tst) - Dst(\lambda, Tst),$$

and this is termed the 'longitudinal inequality.' In application to $C(D)$, for example, any ring-current equivalent would reside entirely in the stormtime component $C(Dst)$, whereas the baylike component would be found primarily in $C(DS)$. In application to other parameters, the parameter in question may be indicated parenthetically after the appropriate component symbol. Thus, the longitudinal inequality in H would be indicated by $DS(H)$.

Average storm characteristics, and so average Dst and DS components, are usually obtained by combining data from many stations for many storms. In practice, this process reduces the time resolution of the original data. Phenomena, such as SSC impulses, SC radio-wave absorption, magnetic bays, and auroral absorption bays, are some of the important storm features which may vanish as a result of the averaging process.

On the gross time scale, however, amplitude variations, such as those displayed in Fig. 12.8, are to be found, and they clearly reveal the main growth and decay stages of the world-wide deviations. Both curves represent averages over a range of low and middle latitudes (from 18°S to 50°N); curve 1 depicts the $DS(H)$ variation; curve 2 represents $Dst(H)$. The inherent longitudinal variation of $DS(H)$ is not shown here, but in the relevant latitude range it is closely approximated by a sin φ variation with φ measured from geomagnetic midnight [7].

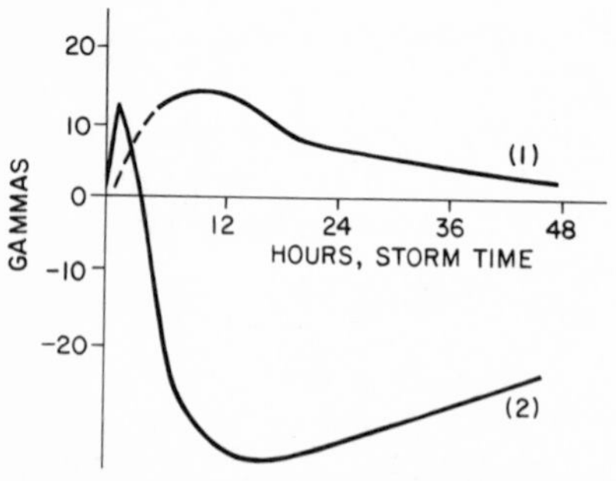

Fig. 12.8 The average variation of the horizontal magnetic field H for forty moderate magnetic storms; mean of eight observatories for mean geomagnetic latitude 37°. (After Chapman [7].)
(1) The amplitude of the longitudinal inequality $DS(H)$.
(2) The storm time variation $Dst(H)$.

In Fig. 12.9, the mean stormtime variation of the horizontal

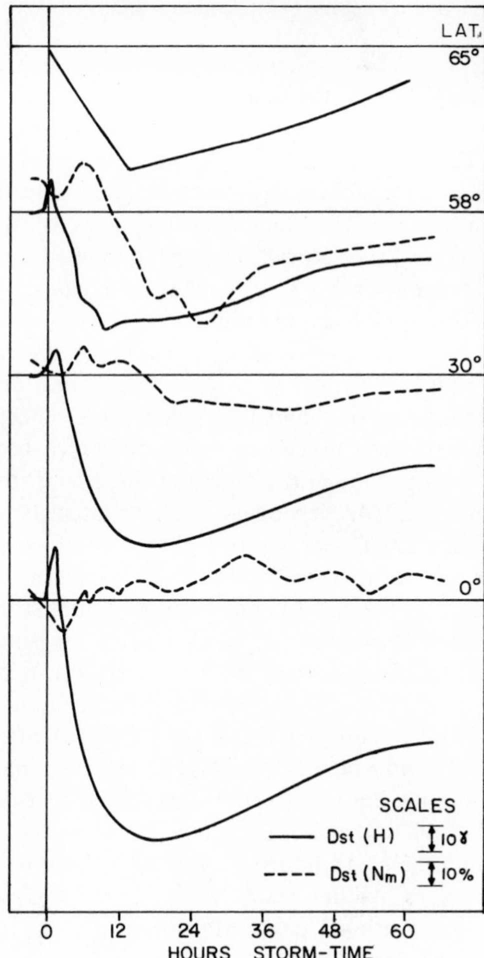

Fig. 12.9 The average world-wide characteristics of strong magnetic and ionospheric storms.

(a) *Dst(H)* for 74 magnetic SC storms 1902–45. (After Sugiura and Chapman [30].)

(b) The percentage variation of *Dst*(N_m) for 51 ionospheric storms, occurring during strong magnetic SC storms, 1946–55. (After Matsushita [16].)

magnetic field *Dst*(*H*) is compared with the mean stormtime percentage change of maximum electron number density *Dst*(N_m). The magnetic data are for the 74 strongest storms in 1902–45 [30]; the ionospheric data are for the 51 strongest storms in 1946–55 [16]. In general, hourly data were used, but at 65° the magnetic data were so irregular that only daily mean values of *Dst*(*H*) were plotted. The *Dst*(N_m) data are even more irregular at this latitude and have not yet been computed for stations above 60°.

Initial, main, and recovery phases are apparent in $Dst(H)$ at all latitudes below 65°. The amplitude of the main phase is greatest at the geomagnetic equator, and the maximum deviation occurs at about 18 hours stormtime at all latitudes. The $Dst(N_m)$ curve at 58° appears to follow the phases of the magnetic storm with some delay, the maximum deviation occurring at about 30 hours stormtime. The ionospheric storm, as measured by $Dst(N_m)$, weakens rapidly at the lower latitudes and at the same time the direction of the stormtime deviation changes. In equatorial regions, the deviations of $Dst(N_m)$ are positive during the main phase of the magnetic storm.

The $Dst(N_m)$ curves appear to have 'initial phases' several hours after the magnetic initial phase. This feature does not occur with any consistency in individual ionospheric storms, and its significance is uncertain.

There does not appear to be any basic difference between weak and strong magnetic storms, though the timing of the $Dst(H)$ maximum and the rate of recovery are markedly dependent on storm intensity [29]. The stronger the storm, the more rapidly the various phases occur, and the shorter the total duration of the storm. Thus the maximum of the magnetic main phase at middle latitudes was found to shift from 18 hours stormtime for great storms to 33 hours stormtime for weak storms. A similar relationship between strength and duration may hold for $Dst(N_m)$, but this has not yet been confirmed.

It is more difficult to compare $DS(H)$ and $DS(N_m)$, primarily because of a large scatter in the ionospheric data. $DS(H)$ reaches a maximum at about 09 hours stormtime and, unlike $Dst(H)$, this timing appears to be independent of the strength of the storm. $DS(N_m)$ for strong storms at high latitudes reaches a maximum at 12–18 hours stormtime. Variations with latitude, or with strength of storm, are uncertain. Much, therefore, remains to be done to complete the observational description of storms, quite apart from the subsequent theoretical interpretation.

REFERENCES

1. Babcock, H. W., and H. D. Babcock, The Sun's magnetic field, 1952–54, *Astrophys. J.*, **121** (1955), 349.

2. Bartels, J., Terrestrial magnetic activity and its relations to solar phenomena, *Terr. Mag. Atmos. Electr.*, **37** (1932), 1.

3. Bell, Barbara, Major flares and geomagnetic activity, *Smithsonian Contrib. Astrophys.* **5**, No. 7 (1961).

4. Bell, Barbara, North-south asymmetry in solar spottedness and in great-storm sources, *Smithsonian Contrib. Astrophys.*, **5**, No. 12 (1962).

5. Bless, R. C., C. W. Gartlein, D. S. Kimball, and G. Sprague, Auroras, magnetic bays, and protons, *J. Geophys. Res.*, **64** (1959), 949.

6. Brown, R. R., T. R. Hartz, B. Landmark, H. Leinbach, and J. Ortner, Large-scale bombardment of the atmosphere at the sudden commencement of a geomagnetic storm, *J. Geophys. Res.*, **66** (1961), 1035.

7. Chapman, S., The morphology of geomagnetic storms and bays, in Vistas in Astronomy, ed. A. Beer, **2** (1956), p. 912.

8. ———, and J. Bartels, Geomagnetism. Oxford: Clarendon Press, 1940, Chap. XII.

9. Hagg, E. L., A preliminary study of the electron density at 1000 kilometers, *Can. J. Phys.*, **41** (1963), 195.

10. Hale, G. E., Solar eruptions and their apparent terrestrial effects, *Astrophys. J.*, **73** (1931), 379.

11. ———, and S. B. Nicholson, Magnetic observations of sunspots, 1917–1924, *Carnegie Inst. Publ.* No. 498, 1938.

12. Hartz, T. R., Multi-station riometer observations, in Radio Astronomical and Satellite Studies of the Atmosphere, ed. J. Aarons. Amsterdam: North-Holland Publishing Company, 1963, p. 220.

13. ———, and J. L. McAlpine, The dependence of ionospheric disturbances on large solar flares, *J. Atmos. Terr. Phys.*, **23** (1961), 13.

14. Jenkins, R. W., and I. Paghis, Criteria for the association of solar flares with geomagnetic disturbances, *Can. J. Phys.*, **41** (1963), 1056.

15. Lawrence, R. S., and D. J. Posakony, The total electron content of the ionosphere at middle latitudes near the peak of the solar cycle, *J. Geophys. Res.*, **68** (1963), 1889.

16. Matsushita, S., A study of the morphology of ionospheric storms, *J. Geophys. Res.*, **64** (1959), 305.

17. Meek, J. H., AGARD-NATO: AGARDograph 29, Polar disturbances, in Polar Atmosphere Symposium, part II, Ionosphere, ed. K. Weekes, London: Pergamon Press, 1957, p. 120.

18. Mendonca, F. de, Ionospheric studies with the differential doppler technique, in Radio Astronomical and Satellite Studies of the Atmosphere, ed. J. Aarons. Amsterdam: North Holland Publishing Company, 1963, p. 289.

19. Muldrew, D. B., The relationship of F-layer critical frequencies to the intensity of the outer Van Allen belt, *Can. J. Phys.*, **41** (1963), 199.

20. Mustel, E. R., *Soviet Astronomy, A. J.*, **5** (1961), 19.

21. Newton, H. W., Solar flares and magnetic storms, *Monthly Notices Roy. Astron. Soc.*, **103** (1943), 244.

22. Ortner, J., B. Hultqvist, R. R. Brown, T. R. Hartz, O. Holt, B. Landmark, J. L. Hook, and H. Leinbach, Cosmic noise absorption accompanying geomagnetic storm sudden commencements, *J. Geophys. Res.*, **67** (1962), 4169.

23. Paghis, I., Magnetic impulses and sun-earth relations, *J. Phys. Soc. Japan*, **17**, Suppl. A-1 (1962), 21.

24. ——————, Solar rotation and geomagnetic disturbances, (in preparation).

25. Sato, T., Disturbances in the ionospheric *F*2 region associated with geomagnetic storms, *J. Geomag. Geoelectr.*, **8** (1955) 129; **9** (1957), 1, 94.

26. Shapley, A. H., The recurrence tendency and forecasts of magnetic activity, *Trans. Am. Geophys. Un.*, **28** (1947), 715.

27. Silsbee, H. C., and E. H. Vestine, Geomagnetic bays, their frequency and current systems, *Terr. Mag. Atmos. Electr.*, **47** (1942), 195.

28. Smith, E. J., and C. P. Sonett, Satellite observations of the distant field during magnetic storms: Explorer VI, *J. Phys. Soc. Japan*, **17**, Suppl. A-1 (1962), 17.

29. Sugiura, M., and S. Chapman, A study of the morphology of magnetic storms, in Great Magnetic Storms. *Geophys. Inst. Alaska*, AF 19(604)-2163, 1958.

30. ———, and ———, The average morphology of geomagnetic storms with sudden commencement, *Abh. Akad. Wiss. Gottingen, Math-Phys. Klasse*, Sonderheft Nr. 4, 1960.

31. Taylor, G. N., The total electron content of the ionosphere during the magnetic disturbance of 1960 Nov. 12–13. *Nature*, **189** (1961), 740.

32. Vestine, E. H., I. Lange, I. Laporte, and W. E. Scott, The Geomagnetic Field, its Description and Analysis. Carnegie Institution of Washington, No. 580, 1947, p. 371.

33. Wild, J. T., K. V. Sheridan, and G. H. Trent, The transverse motions of the sources of solar radio bursts, in Paris Symposium on Radio Astronomy, ed. R. N. Bracewell. Stanford: Stanford University Press, 1959, p. 176.

34. Wilson, R. W., and M. Sugiura, Hydromagnetic interpretation of sudden commencements of magnetic storms, *J. Geophys. Res.*, **66** (1961), 4097.

13

R. Montalbetti

Optical Aurora

13.1. INTRODUCTION

The aurora may be described as visible glows emanating from the upper atmosphere, of varying shape, size, and color, which last for times of a few minutes or more, and on occasion even from sunset to sunrise. Although no two displays are ever exactly alike, a few appear to follow a general pattern. At Churchill, Manitoba, for instance, one of the major centers of auroral observations, a strong display would typically be seen first as a faint white transparent arc situated some 30 degrees above the southeastern horizon in the early evening and would remain stationary for a half hour or so. Then, for no apparent reason, it begins to move up toward the zenith, becoming brighter and taking on a pale yellow-green color. Behind it, one or more similar arcs develop and appear to separate from the initial one. Figure 13.1 shows a representative display at this stage. As these arcs rise, they develop folds, loops, become rayed, change to irregular forms, and at the same time in other parts of the sky, new bright forms appear, such as those shown in the frontispiece and in Fig 13.2. Many of the forms move rapidly and show enhanced color effects, with yellow-green and red being most prominent but including blue, yellow, and violet. At the height of a spectacular display, the forms change and move so quickly that it is not possible to view the scene in its entirety. After many minutes or even hours, the forms gradually fade and give way to diffuse, cloudlike forms filling most of the sky. These too may

Fig. 13.1 Early evening auroral display.

eventually disappear before the sun rises, but on occasion they gradually blend with the light of dawn.

No theory exists which explains all that is seen in the many varied auroral displays, but it is fully agreed that the aurora is fundamentally an electrical phenomenon associated with disturbed conditions in the upper atmosphere. The visible glows result from the excitation of the atmospheric atoms and molecules, either by direct particle bombardment from above or by bombardment coupled with local discharge mechanisms. It is also clear that charged particles ejected from the sun are in some way responsible, but only after complicated interactions with the earth's magnetic field. Some of the theories of these interactions are discussed in Chapter 15.

Most of our knowledge of the aurora comes from studies made with optical instruments and from compilations of visual reports from many observers throughout the world. The work is often hampered by adverse sky conditions, and data are necessarily incomplete, as the instruments cannot be used during daylight hours or even when the sky is overcast. In the past decade, increasing use has been made of radio techniques which overcome the difficulties of the optical systems but which are subject to limitations of their own. For instance, auroral radar echoes have been observed only at elevation angles less than 20 degrees above the horizon, and

Fig. 13.2 Bright active auroral forms.

at these low elevations it is difficult to locate precisely and simultaneously the reflecting regions and any related region of luminosity that might be present. Accordingly, as a matter of caution, the term 'radio aurora' has been introduced to indicate that the echoes may not arise in precisely the same locations as the visible manifestation of the '(optical) aurora' itself, although a close physical connection between the generating processes of the two is generally accepted. The present chapter is confined to a discussion of the optical aurora; the next treats the related radio measurements. Much more comprehensive discussions of the aurora may be found in the monographs of Störmer [17] and Chamberlain [6], in review articles by Bates [2], and in a popularized book by Petrie [16].

13.2. GEOGRAPHICAL DISTRIBUTION

The geographical distribution of auroras in both the northern and southern hemispheres is such that contours of equal frequency of occurrence of aurora, called 'isochasms,' are essentially concentric ovals about the geomagnetic poles. The peak isochasm, that is, the region of greatest frequency of occurrence, has an average distance of some 23 degrees from the pole in the northern hemisphere and perhaps 18 degrees from the pole in the southern hemisphere. To the north and south of these peak isochasms, the frequency of occurrence decreases sharply. The differences in location and shape of the isochasms in the two hemispheres is believed to reflect only the regional irregularities of the earth's magnetic field.

The near-symmetry of the distribution immediately raises the question of whether auroras occur simultaneously in both hemispheres. Recent studies suggest that displays often do occur at the same time but that individual forms do not. The observations are far from conclusive, however, as several borderline cases and a few exceptions have been noted, and exact points of conjugacy are not yet known.

The particular distribution of auroral occurrence strongly suggests that the aurora is controlled by the geomagnetic field and that the primary cause of the aurora is a flux of charged particles. Indeed because of this apparent connection, almost all the auroral theories are concerned with the interaction of electrons and protons with the earth's magnetic field, and with the origin of the particles (see Chapter 15).

The frequency of occurrence of aurora as described is the average of observations taken over a few hundred years. Over a shorter interval, measured in days or weeks, say, the distribution may depart markedly from this, so much so that the 'auroral zone' appears to expand or contract depending on the level of solar activity. The 'auroral zone' is taken here as the region where the auroral frequency of occurrence, based on the long-term statistics, is greater than 50%. In the northern hemisphere it lies roughly between geomagnetic latitudes 60°N and 70°N with most of the land area underneath it lying in northern Canada. The peak isochasm, mentioned previously, is also called the 'auroral zone maximum.' Some observations of recent years indicate that this maximum is displaced toward the equator during disturbed periods, whereas other observations show no such displacement but rather a broadening of the auroral zone.

13.3. FORM AND BRIGHTNESS

There are several typical forms of the aurora and a number of ways in which they may be classified, depending on what characteristics are considered the most important. The classification generally accepted today distinguishes forms on the basis of the general shape and structure of the luminosity and on certain characteristic time and spatial variations. An attempt has been made to relate the classification of shapes to familiar objects, the terms arc (A), band (B), ray (R), drapery (D), glow (G), and surface (S) being used. A drapery, for example, looks like a pleated curtain hanging down, with the lower edge undulating. The forms that exhibit a rayed structure are so labeled (R); the nonrayed ones are termed 'homogeneous (H)' if they have a sharply defined lower edge, or 'diffuse (D)' if the edges are indistinct. The main auroral forms are described by the pertinent shape characteristic, modified when appropriate by an indication of the structure: HA (homogeneous arc); HB (homogeneous band); RA (rayed arc); RB (rayed band); R (ray); DS (diffuse surface); D (drapery); G (glow).

At times nonrayed arcs and surfaces remain essentially stationary in the sky but fade and brighten in rhythmic manner. These are called 'pulsating arcs (PA)' and 'pulsating surfaces (PS).' Certain other forms exhibit characteristic motions that are best described as waves of luminosity moving rapidly upward one after the other toward the magnetic zenith. These are termed 'flaming (F) aurora.' Unlike the other forms, the occurrence of flaming aurora seems to have a marked dependence on location. During one 5-yr observing period which included sunspot maximum, for example, no displays of flaming aurora were ever observed at Churchill although several were noted at stations of lower latitude.

The remaining form recognized in the classification system is the corona (C). It looks like a mass of parallel rays apparently converging to a point very near the magnetic zenith, and frequently resembles a fan. The point where the rays appear to converge is known as the 'radiant point' or the 'auroral zenith.' The corona is not a unique form but rather a rayed form viewed almost along the direction of the rays, and so is more indicative of the observer's position than of the form itself.

The classification system in use is not entirely satisfactory as it is mainly subjective and not necessarily related to auroral mechanisms. It does, however, permit uniform reporting so that observations from different places throughout the world can be combined and analyzed. (A new system of terminology and notation is described in the International Auroral Atlas [10].)

Two types of auroral displays are recognized as being unusual, primarily because of the color associated with part or all of the forms. They have been designated as type A and type B aurora. Type A consists of diffuse red glows having no sharply defined edges; type B refers to displays where the lower edges of arcs and bands are distinct and red. The importance of the two types is that they occur infrequently and suggest that some special event is in progress. Type A aurora tends to occur during large geomagnetic storms, and there is some evidence that links it to polar cap absorption (PCA) events, whereas type B aurora is indicative of a rare low-altitude display.

As mentioned in the introduction, some auroral displays may follow a general pattern. In the early evening, the forms tend to be quiet and homogeneous. Around the midnight hours, the forms become rayed, move rapidly in all directions, and in general create the impression of chaos. Observers refer to this particular phase as the 'break-up' phase of an auroral storm. Toward morning, diffuse forms tend to predominate. This sequence of events is not common to all displays, for the experience of auroral observers shows that the unexpected occurs more often than the expected.

The brightness of auroral displays varies over wide limits and is usually expressed in terms of the international brightness coefficients, I to IV. A faint aurora, about as bright as the Milky Way, is designated as having intensity I. One having a brightness of a thin moonlit cirrus cloud is of intensity II, and auroras as bright as moonlit cumulus cloud are of intensity III. An aurora would be of intensity IV only if its illumination were equal to that of the full moon. It is generally accepted that this is reached, if ever, only on very rare occasions.

In preparation for the International Geophysical Year of 1957–58, a comprehensive scheme of visual observations was devised. Many simple instruments were used to record the elevation and azimuth of the auroral forms and to discriminate between aurora and illuminated clouds [4].

Measurements of the height of auroral forms, their particular orientation in space, the distribution of luminosity, and motion of displays as a whole or of the individual forms give considerable information about the disturbed atmosphere and are necessary in formulating auroral theories. These characteristics, as measured by photographic and photometric techniques, are described briefly in the following sections.

13.4. HEIGHT

The height distribution of the lower edges of forms has been measured by a number of researchers using parallactic photography [9]. This method consists of photographing the aurora simultaneously from two stations separated by some 20 km or more, and then measuring the difference in the apparent position of the form relative to the background of stars. With the exception of sunlit type A and type B auroras which occur infrequently, most of the lower borders are at about 105 km above the earth regardless of geographic location. An example of measurements made at Churchill, on homogeneous and rayed arcs and bands, is shown in Fig. 13.3(a). The frequency distribution of the measured heights shows a characteristic double peak. This is probably due to an intensity effect, since a division of the data into weak and strong aurora (Fig. 13.3(b)) yields singly peaked distributions, with the stronger forms being 7 km lower than the weaker ones. Several factors have been suggested that could possibly influence the height of aurora, such as tidal motions and temperature variations, but the evidence for this is rather inconclusive.

Measurements of the height of type A and B auroras are few but they do show a marked difference from the usual forms. Diffuse type A glows are several hundred kilometers above the earth, whereas the lower edges of type B arcs and bands are as low as 70 km.

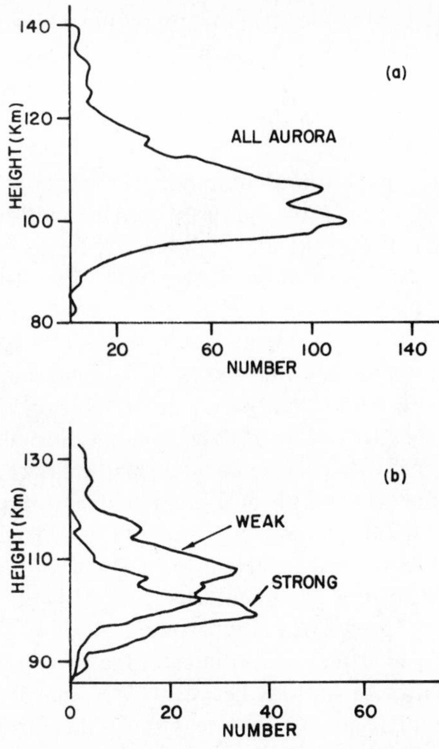

Fig. 13.3 Height distribution of lower edges of homogeneous and rayed arcs and bands: (a) showing all measured points and (b) showing weak and strong auroras only.

At high latitudes, and particularly during the summer months, aurora is visible in the sunlit portion of the upper atmosphere after ground sunset or before ground sunrise. It is usually white-violet or blue-violet in color and has been found to be at great heights. Sunlit rays have been measured extending up to about 1000 km, with the lower border at approximately 250 km, in contrast to rays in shadow which have their lower edge at about 110 km. Note, however, that not all sunlit auroras have these characteristics; many forms in the sunlit regions appear no different than those in shadow.

13.5. ORIENTATION

Auroral forms tend to be oriented along the magnetic field lines. This is most clearly seen in rays and draperies, but measurements using parallactic photography show that arcs and bands are also aligned approximately to include the field lines. The orientation of rays is most easily measured by comparing the radiant point of coronas with the magnetic zenith of the observing site. In most cases these points are within 1 degree of each other but on some occasions may be separated by as much as 7 or 8 degrees and may vary during a strong auroral display. This behavior is not understood; indeed, the whole problem of vertical field alignment has not been examined to any great extent.

A greater effort has gone into determining the horizontal orientation of arcs and bands with respect to the geomagnetic meridian. The earlier measurements showed that in the auroral zone the forms lie approximately perpendicular to this meridian, or in other words, along the circles of geomagnetic latitude. Attempts were made to find diurnal and seasonal variations in the orientation but the results were inconclusive. With the more extensive material gathered during the International Geophysical Year, Davis [7], working with data from the northern hemisphere, and Denholm and Bond [8], working with Antarctic data, found a diurnal variation which is more pronounced the higher the geomagnetic latitude. At stations near the geomagnetic poles, the average auroral alignment is approximately in the direction of the sun at all times, and arcs there will often appear to rotate through about 300° in the course of a 20 hour night. At stations between 68°N and 80°N the alignment changes gradually up to the time that auroral break-up occurs, usually around local midnight, and then changes rapidly in the next few hours; later in the morning the orientation remains about constant. At stations between 55°N and 68°N there is only a very small and gradual change in orientation; the forms being aligned geomagnetically east-west. Davis also noted that, during break-up, forms with alignment nearly north-south appear in the auroral zone. These and other observations may be interpreted in terms of a pattern of auroral forms fixed in space, under which the earth revolves. The pattern as deduced by Davis is shown in Fig. 13.4. The dashed line indicates the discontinuous nature of the forms after the break-up phase of auroral displays. There is a very close similarity between this pattern and the idealized current system that corresponds to the mean geomagnetic disturbance in the polar regions

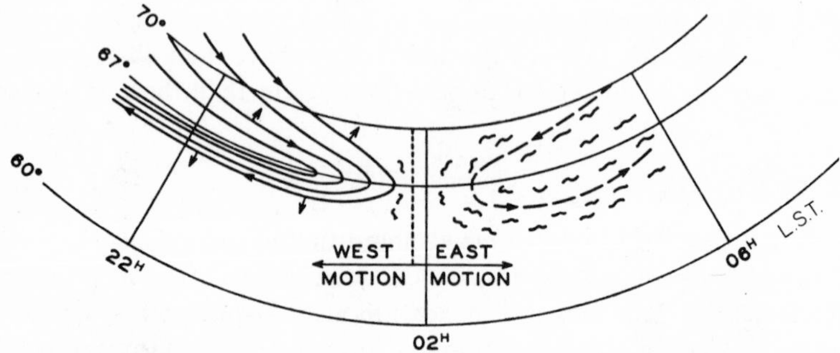

Fig. 13.4 The pattern of auroral forms deduced by Davis [7].

[5]. Both are considered in more detail from the theoretical point of view in Chapter 15.

13.6. LUMINOSITY

The intensity of the emitted light varies with height in an auroral form. For arcs and draperies, a maximum is reached about 10 km above the lower edge and the emissions fade into the night sky background some 50 km above this edge. For the case of rays, the luminosity rises gradually and is more or less constant over a height range of 100 km or more.

The horizontal thickness of relatively quiet auroral arcs as measured at Churchill is usually about 8 km but may vary over the range 1–20 km. On the other hand, some very active rayed arcs have been measured in Alaska to be only of the order of 300 meters in thickness. The horizontal length of arcs may exceed 2000 km on occasion, whereas rays have a cross-section diameter of only about 500 meters and extend vertically to great heights. These figures clearly indicate the great differences that exist between forms, and they present one of the main problems in attempting to formulate a suitable theory of the aurora.

13.7. MOTION

A relatively detailed study of the motion of aurora has recently been made possible by the use of 'all-sky cameras,' for which the most common design is a 16-mm or 35-mm motion-picture camera mounted above a convex mirror. The image of the entire sky seen from one station, formed by the mirror, is photographed, usually at the rate of one frame per minute. From a sequence of these frames, the speed and direction of motion of auroral forms are deduced.

Because magnetic field fluctuations and the aurora are known to be closely related, all the studies consider motions along, and perpendicular to, the geomagnetic parallels of latitude. Usually a height must be assumed in order to deduce a velocity; this is taken as 100 km and is considered to be constant throughout the period of observation. Although such an assumption is not valid in all cases, the height variations that have been measured would not greatly influence the deduced velocities.

Two types of movement of auroral luminosity are observed with all-sky cameras: one is the motion of irregularities within the auroral forms; the other is the motion of the forms themselves. The broad average characteristics of both types of motion have been partially determined by Davis [7] in the study referred to in Sec. 13.5. In agreement with earlier work, he found that in early evening the forms generally move westward, as would be expected if the pattern of Fig. 13.4 were stationary with the earth rotating beneath.

The motion of the irregularities, however, is eastward along the northern limb and westward along the southern limb of the pattern. The arrows in Fig. 13.4 indicate the directions of motion of the irregularities. During the break-up phase, the motions are not systematic as both east-moving and west-moving forms occur together. In the morning hours the auroral forms are generally discontinuous and diffuse, with the motion of the irregularities being reversed to that of early evening. The speed at which irregularities move relative to the earth has been found to average around 500 m/sec [11] and to be esssentially the same in both the eastward and westward direction. On occasion, both forms and irregularities have been measured to be traveling at speeds of up to 2000 m/sec.

Although some of the statistical properties of *E*-layer winds are similar to the motion of auroral forms, they are in general of substantially lower velocity. Moreover, the lack of distortion in rays and draperies makes it unlikely that motions of aurora are due to atmospheric motion. It seems rather that they result from greatly enhanced electric fields in *E*-region heights during disturbed conditions or that the source causing the aurora moves relative to the earth. As in the case of orientation, it seems that auroral motions are closely linked to the current systems that flow in the auroral regions. These points will be discussed again, in relation to the general theory of storms.

13.8. SOLAR INFLUENCE

It is evident from a wide variety of observations that solar disturbances cause major geomagnetic and auroral storms. The occurrence of auroras at low geomagnetic latitudes, on rare occasions down to 18°, is visible evidence that unusual solar disturbances have occurred. A marked correlation exists between sunspot number and the occurrence of aurora at moderate geomagnetic latitudes, to such an extent that the 11-yr cycle of sunspot numbers is clearly manifest in the auroral statistics. The peak of auroral activity lags the peak of the sunspot maximum by about two years but the minima coincide. Also type A auroras are more numerous during the times of large sunspot numbers.

The influence of solar activity is reversed in stations poleward of the auroral zone. For example, at Godthaab, Greenland, a minimum in auroral occurrence is observed during a maximum in sunspot number. Such a reversal very likely results from the auroral zone moving to lower latitudes as the solar activity increases.

There is some tendency for auroras to recur after a lapse of about 27 days, corresponding to the (apparent) period of rotation of the solar photosphere at low heliographic latitudes (see Sec. 12.2.1). In the auroral zone auroras occur almost every night, so the 27-day period is not as apparent as at the lower-latitude stations.

In addition to the 11-yr and 27-day periods associated with solar behavior there are diurnal and seasonal variations in the frequency of occurrence of aurora. For stations within the auroral zone the peak in occurrence is around local midnight. As the geomagnetic pole is approached, the time of the maximum becomes earlier (see Fig. 13.8).

At moderate and low-latitude stations, the auroral frequency is a maximum in the equinoctial months and a minimum in both summer and winter months. This particular seasonal variation has been well established by observations made in the Scandinavian countries and in northern United States. Poleward of these regions, the summer minimum apparently becomes progressively deeper whereas the winter minimum gives way to a maximum. The decrease in frequency of occurrence observed in summer as a function of latitude may be due entirely to the longer observing time of the winter nights. Again the seasonal variation could result from a motion of the auroral zone toward the equator at the equinoctial periods.

13.9. ASSOCIATED PHENOMENA

A number of geophysical phenomena are known to be closely allied to auroral activity, and many others may be, but their connections have not yet been firmly established. Sporadic-E clouds, ionospheric irregularities, and particular types of ionospheric absorption of radio waves are specific examples of the latter.

The close connection with the magnetic field has already been mentioned with regard to orientation and distribution of aurora. Further observations show that, as the auroral intensity increases from a negligible magnitude to very bright, the magnetic field changes from quiet to highly disturbed conditions, and at subauroral latitudes the elevation of aurora in the observer's sky, above the poleward horizon, correlates with the degree of variation of the local field. Detailed correlations are not completely satisfactory, however, since arcs have been observed when no magnetic field disturbances occur and disturbances occur when aurora is absent. Similar difficulties arise in the interpretation of ionospheric effects, but they will be discussed more fully in the next chapter.

13.10. AURORAL SPECTRUM

The auroral spectrum consists of a large number of lines and bands due to the excitation of both neutral and ionized atoms and molecules. It was by the identification of these features that constituents of the atmosphere at auroral heights were first deduced. Today the studies relate mainly to the role of protons and electrons in the production of auroral emissions and to the various collisional deactivation processes.

The identification problem was not simple. Some of the emissions from the aurora were unknown in spectra produced in the laboratory, and in some cases key auroral lines were obscured by bands. However, by further work on laboratory discharges, by comparisons with synthetically constructed spectra, and by resolution of the auroral features with better instruments, the constituents responsible for the lines and bands have been largely determined. It should not be assumed, however, that this reveals all the constituents present at auroral heights at all times. The existence of a particular spectral feature only implies that a particular type of atom is present, on occasions, during times of aurora. For example, a collision of a fast proton or electron with a nitrogen molecule may break it up into two nitrogen atoms which in turn may radiate characteristic lines of atomic nitrogen. On the other hand, the absence of a particular spectral feature does not necessarily imply that the atom or molecule is absent from the atmosphere. The spectral feature can occur only if both the constituent and a suitable exciting mechanism are present.

One of the modern tools used to study auroral emissions is the scanning spectrometer. This is similar to a spectrograph except that a photoelectric detector replaces the spectrograph's camera, and instead of all the spectral features being recorded simultaneously on film, the detector scans the spectral interval and reproduces the features on a paper chart recorder. In Fig. 13.5 a spectrum* taken with a scanning spectrometer located at Churchill is shown. The interval 3100 Å to 6700 Å is scanned in 20 sec so only the strongest features are observed. All these emissions arise from neutral atomic oxygen [OI], neutral molecular nitrogen N_2, and ionized molecular nitrogen N_2^+, with the so-called auroral green line of oxygen at 5577 Å and the 3914 Å band of N_2^+ being the two most intense features. Long exposures with spectrographs reveal many weaker features in the same wavelength interval arising from excited atomic nitrogen and neutral and ionized molecular oxygen. The characteristic yellow-green color of the aurora arises from excitation of atomic oxygen which emits 5577 Å radiation in returning to its ground state. The red color that sometimes is very prominent is due also to excitation of atomic oxygen, but in this case to a less energetic level which gives rise to the 6300 Å and 6364 Å lines, or to the excitation of molecular nitrogen which produces a band system in the 6400 Å–7000 Å region known as the first positive group (1PG). At times the red color is due to both. The violet and blue colors arise primarily from the excitation of ionized molecular nitrogen. The emitted band system is known as the first negative group (1NG) of which the strongest bands are at 3914 Å, 4278 Å, and 4709 Å.

*For a description of the spectral notation see Herzberg, G. H., Molecular Spectra and Molecular Structure. I. Spectra of Diatomic Molecules. New York: D. Van Nostrand Co., Inc., 1950, Chapter II.

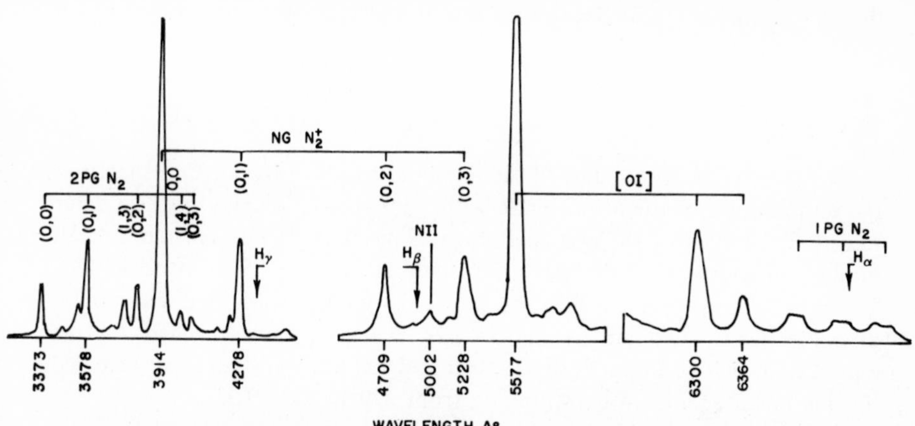

Fig. 13.5 Example of auroral spectrum taken with scanning spectrometers at Churchill, Manitoba.

The relative intensity of the various features of the auroral spectrum varies considerably with type of aurora, latitude, and height of the auroral display. For example, the intensity ratio I (6300): I (5577) is largest in type A auroras; the ratio I (5577): I (4278) measured from Oslo is larger than at the higher-latitude station, Tromso, and the ratio I (5577): I (3914) is greater near the lower border than in the upper portions of an auroral form. Such information is valuable in differentiating between various possible excitation and deactivation mechanisms and in determining some of the atmospheric properties.

Auroral spectra can be classified into three types [12]. The first type is common to the night sky and shows mainly intense red lines of OI and the 5200 Å line of NI. The emissions arise in the high rarefied layers of the atmosphere which are mostly atomic in composition. A second type is characterized by intense 5577 Å and numerous N_2 and N_2^+ emissions. Its origin is in the regions where molecular nitrogen is predominant and where aurora is easily seen visually. The third type arises in regions where molecular oxygen becomes important and shows, besides the emissions of the other types, bands of ionized oxygen molecules. Unfortunately, actual height measurements of individual spectral features are not available. If, however, there is such a height difference as suggested by the classification, it could result from the influx of streams of charged particles whose maximum energy varies. The more energetic the particles, the greater the penetration into the atmosphere.

On occasions the Balmer lines of atomic hydrogen, Hα, Hβ, and Hγ, are observed in auroral spectra. Their position in the spectrum is shown by ys in Fig. 13.5. Because of their importance they are considered in ail in Sec. 13.12.

13.11. TEMPERATURES

By detailed measurements of the lines and bands of the auroral spectrum, the temperature of the atmosphere within an auroral display may be determined. Theoretically, the best method is to measure by interferometric techniques the widths of forbidden lines, such as those at 5577 Å and 6300 Å. The long lifetime of the excited state in such cases insures that the number of collisions is adequate for the excited atoms to have reached thermal equilibrium before emission. The green and red auroral lines have revealed, by this means, temperatures ranging from 220°K to 700°K.

In practice, interferometers are rather difficult to construct and especially to operate on a continuous basis, so a much greater effort has gone into determining rotational temperatures. The (0, 0) band of N_2^+ is particularly suited for this although the (0, 1) band is also used. The method consists simply of measuring the intensity distribution of the rotational fine structure of the *R* branch. This method has led to estimates of temperatures as low as 150°K and as high as 700°K.

There is some question as to whether rotational temperatures correspond to the kinetic temperatures of the gases in thermal equilibrium. The situation is different from that of the forbidden lines, as the transitions giving rise to the (0, 0) and (0, 1) bands are allowed. The lifetimes of the excited states are so short that radiation occurs before thermal equilibrium can be established by collisions. Only when the excitation mechanism does not disturb the original conditions are the rotational temperatures equal to the kinetic temperatures. This is very likely the case for electron impact but it may not be if the excitation is by heavy-particle impact. The two methods described above give similar results, evidence that rotational temperatures are in fact equal to the kinetic temperatures.

Most of the temperature measurements by spectroscopic means are limited in application by uncertainties as to the height of the region where the various emissions arise. In a few cases, however, the temperature and the height have been measured simultaneously for different forms and during times when a particular form varied in height during its lifetime. If height measurements are not made, they are assigned on the basis of the statistical relation between intensity and the height of auroral displays. Without going into detail it may be stated that in the 100–160 km region the temperature increases with height at a rate of some 6°K/km. At 115 km the temperature is about 250°K. Sunlit auroras that extend to great height exhibit temperatures of 1000°K at about 250 km and 2000°K in the 400–500 km region.

13.12. HYDROGEN EMISSIONS

As mentioned previously, hydrogen emissions, in particular the Hα, Hβ, and Hγ lines, have been detected in some auroral spectra. The lines appear broadened in comparison to the other atomic lines and, when viewed in the direction of magnetic zenith, are asymmetrical and displaced several Angstroms toward the ultraviolet. This can be seen in Fig. 13.6 where the Hβ line observed during a particular night at Churchill is compared with the emission arising from a hydrogen-filled discharge tube. When viewed in

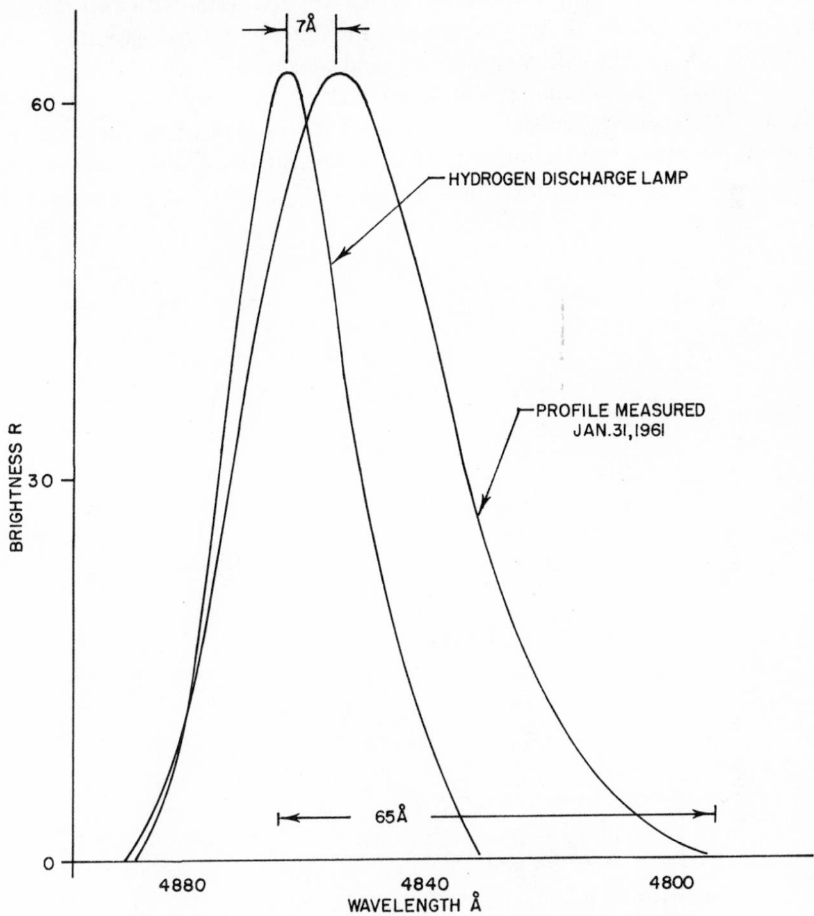

Fig. 13.6 The displacement and broadening of the Hβ line observed over Churchill, Manitoba in the direction of the magnetic zenith, compared to that observed in a hydrogen-filled discharge tube.

the direction of the magnetic horizon, the emission lines appear symmetrical and unshifted but still broadened. This shows quite definitely that protons are spiraling downward along the field lines and is direct experimental evidence that the upper atmosphere is being bombarded by charged particles.

When these results were first discovered, it was thought that protons could be responsible for certain forms of the aurora, such as arcs. Now, however, it is considered quite unlikely that any of the more common auroral forms are produced by such bombardment. Within the auroral zone, no systematic relationship exists between the various forms and the hydrogen emissions. On some occasions, strong hydrogen emissions have been observed during times of no visible aurora. The lack of correlation with aurora is also evident in a statistical study made at Churchill. A diurnal variation in the intensity of the Hβ emissions is observed as shown in Fig. 13.7, and with it is depicted the diurnal variation of auroral intensity measured for the same winter period. A local minimum in Hβ intensity occurs at the time of the auroral intensity maximum. Further evidence against correlation is found in spectroscopic data concerning the intensity of the hydrogen emissions

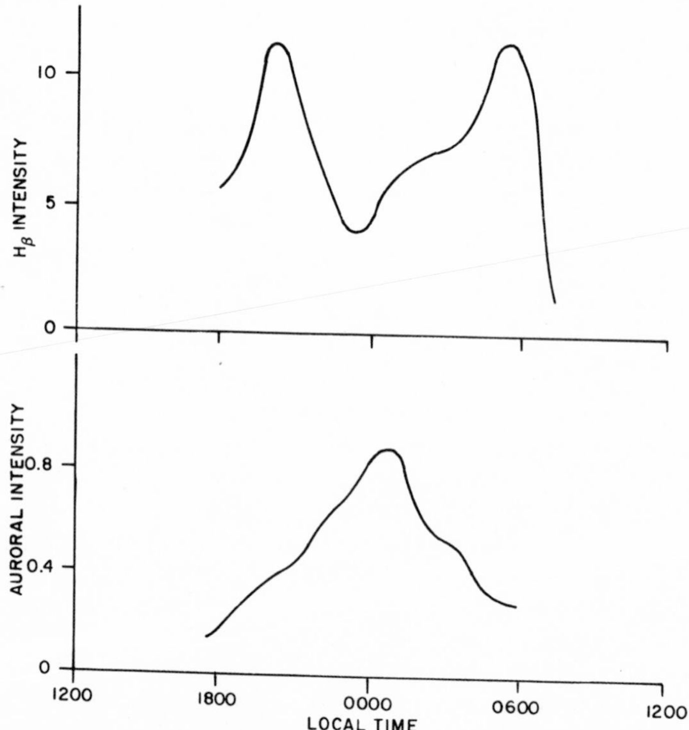

Fig. 13.7 The diurnal variation in the zenithal intensity of Hβ emissions and in the intensity of zenithal aurora measured at Churchill, Manitoba.

relative to the bands of the N_2^+ first negative group. The latter system results from simultaneous ionization and excitation of the nitrogen molecules in fast collisions. If the collisions were with protons, the intensity ratio of the 4709 Å band to the Hβ line should be about unity, but the measured value in an ordinary aurora is invariably greater than ten.

It seems, then, that proton bombardment is a phenomenon which sometimes accompanies normal auroral displays but is not directly associated with the luminous glows. 'Normal aurora' must be emphasized in this context as the situation may be different for type A red aurora occurring at times of PCA's and of large geomagnetic disturbances. On the few occasions when such auroras were seen at Churchill, marked radio-wave absorption and strong hydrogen emissions were measured. Protons with energies greater than some 10 Mev were probably responsible for the absorbing layer in the *D* region of the ionosphere, and perhaps protons of lower energy caused the type A aurora at higher altitudes but this is far from certain.

Attempts have been made to explain the line profiles observed both in the zenith and near the horizon, by considering the interaction of the incoming protons with atmospheric constituents. Initially the particle is slowed down by collisions to a speed near that of the outer orbital electrons of the atoms and molecules (about 2000 km/sec). At this point it has the highest probability of capturing an orbital electron so the proton may then become an excited hydrogen atom, which would in turn quickly cascade to the ground state with the emission of characteristic hydrogen lines. It would then undergo further collisions, become ionized, and recapture an electron. The sequence would be repeated many times. A proton with an initial energy greater than 90 Kev would undergo about 700 captures and reionizations on the average and would emit a total of some 10 quanta of Hβ photons in its travel through the atmosphere.

The first attempts to reproduce the zenithal line profile considered fast monoenergetic protons traveling rectilinear paths. Since most of the emissions would occur when the protons were reduced to a speed of 2000 km/sec the maximum of the Hβ profile should be displaced some 30 Å toward the ultraviolet. Observations such as that given in Fig. 13.6 show a displacement of about 10 Å or less. The discrepancy could be resolved by assuming that the incident protons had either a specific energy spectrum or that the particles had a particular dispersal in direction. When, however, the magnetic horizon profile was considered together with the zenithal one, it was found that both velocity and angular dispersion were required to get agreement with the observed profiles.

A velocity dispersion is of some importance in connection with the origin of the particles. The protons could not come directly from the sun, as there would be a long time difference between the arrival of the fast and slow particles. The implication is that the protons either have a range of velocities on reaching the earth and then get stored in the earth's magnetic field, to be dumped at some later time into the auroral zones, or they reach the vicinity of the earth with low velocities and are accelerated various amounts by some local mechanism.

Studies of hydrogen emissions at a number of stations should make it possible to determine the time and spatial characteristics of the impinging proton stream. A start has been made by comparing the diurnal variation of emissions observed at Churchill with that at College, Alaska [15]. The variation at Churchill, already given in Fig. 13.7, shows a maximum in the evening and morning with a well-defined minimum at local midnight, whereas at College the diurnal variation shows a single maximum at local midnight. These two-station results have been augmented by observations on the behavior of different types of sporadic-E clouds. There appears to be a close association between hydrogen emissions and one type of E_s layer, the so-called r type, on the one hand, and on the other between a second type of E_s layer (type f) and the incidence of aurora. The times of maximum occurrence or intensity of the four phenomena vary with geomagnetic latitudes in a pattern presented in Fig. 13.8. This pattern is to be considered fixed in space with the earth revolving underneath. The proton precipitation zone (P) is displaced from the zone where auroral activity is a maxi-

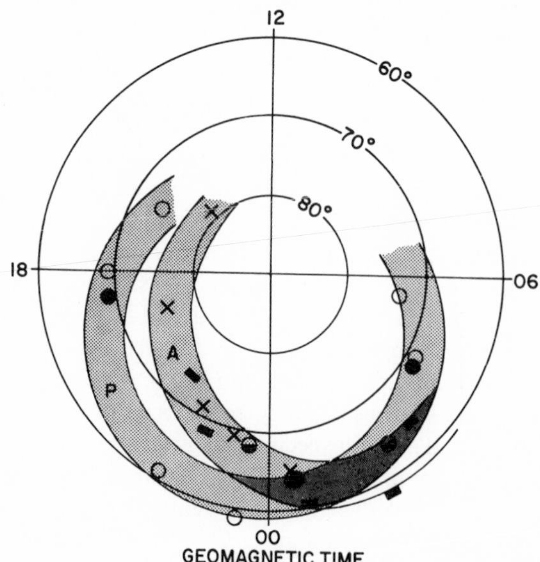

Fig. 13.8 The position of diurnal maxima of various phenomena in geomagnetic coordinates. Two distinct curves are shown: the curve marked P includes hydrogen line emissions (●) and type r sporadic E (○); the curve marked A includes visual aurora (◒, X) [13], and type f sporadic E (■).

mum (A), the latter being, perhaps, the zone of electron precipitation. The location and extent of the zones probably depend on the level of the solar activity and may even fluctuate over short time intervals. To explore fully the existence of these precipitation zones and their behavior requires many more observations from a large number of stations.

13.13. AURORAL PARTICLES

In recent years rocket, balloon, and satellite techniques have been developed which have greatly extended the type of measurements made on the aurora. Rockets flown directly into visible forms have given results of considerable importance on the nature of auroral particles. McIlwain [14], using two well-instrumented Nike-Cajun rockets, found that the luminosity is due to the incidence of energetic electrons upon the atmosphere. In one flight into a faint auroral glow, the energy of the electrons ranged from 3 Kev to 30 Kev, whereas in a second flight, into a bright rayed arc, the electrons appeared to be nearly monoenergetic with an energy of about 6 Kev. Additional equipment within the rockets showed that the proton flux incident on the atmosphere was very much less than the electron flux, although in the weak glow it was at least 10 times greater than in the bright arc. The total energy flux in the bright arc was as much as 50 times greater than in the glow. Thus luminosity is decidedly dependent on the electrons.

The bombardment of the atmosphere by electrons of the observed energies and fluxes can readily account for the absolute intensity and altitude distribution of the auroral emissions within the arc and glow. It may then be inferred that atmospheric discharge is unimportant in the production of auroral light in these two forms. Note, however, that this conclusion cannot be extended automatically to the quite different auroral rays.

Balloon techniques have also been used to study the energetic electrons incident in the high atmosphere, but somewhat indirectly as balloons only reach altitudes of around 30 km. The balloon-borne instruments measure the X-ray radiation produced by electrons that are stopped in the 80–100 km region. Thus they detect only X-rays with energies greater than 25 Kev, radiation of lower energy being absorbed by the atmosphere between the balloon and the source.

A sufficient number of balloon flights have been made both north and south of the northern auroral zone to determine the variation of the X-rays and their association with other phenomena [1, 3, 18]. At Minneapolis, geomagnetic latitude 55°, X-ray bursts correlate well with auroral rayed arcs and bands observed in the zenith. They are primarily a nighttime phenomenon and occur during strong magnetic bays or during the main phase of a strong geomagnetic storm. Within the auroral zone, X-rays are present at least 40% of the time and are spread throughout the 24-hr period.

Moreover they do not correlate with visible aurora, and when bursts occur they are less intense than at the lower-latitude station. The interpretation of these observations is that lower-latitude auroras may be due to the precipitation of energetic electrons having a mean energy of around 55 Kev, whereas the normal polar aurora is largely due to the electrons of substantially less energy. Extensive satellite observations of auroral particles are still not available, but rapid progress is being made (see Ch. 16).

REFERENCES

1. Anderson, K. A., Balloon observations of X-rays in the auroral zone, *J. Geophys. Res.*, **65** (1960), 551.
2. Bates, D. R., General character of auroras, in Physics of the Upper Atmosphere, ed, J. A. Ratcliffe. New York: Academic Press, 1960, p. 269.
3. Brown, R. R., Balloon observations of auroral zone X-rays, *J. Geophys. Res.*, **66** (1960), 1379.
4. Chapman, S., Annals of the International Geophysical Year, **IV**. London: Pergamon Press, 1957.
5. ———, and J. Bartels, Geomagnetism. London: Oxford University Press, 1940.
6. Chamberlain, J. W., Physics of Aurora and Airglow. New York: Academic Press, 1961, p. 441.
7. Davis, T. N., The morphology of polar aurora, *J. Geophys. Res.*, **65** (1960), 3497.
8. Denholm, J. V., and F. R. Bond, Orientation of polar aurora, *Aust. J. Phys.*, **14** (1961), 193.
9. Harang, L., The Aurora. Oxford: Clarendon Press, 1951.
10. International Auroral Atlas, published for the International Union of Geodesy and Geophysics. Edinburgh: University Press, 1963.
11. Kim, J. S., and B. W. Currie, Horizontal movements of aurora, *Can. J. Phys.*, **36** (1958), 160.
12. Krasovskii, V. I., Some results of investigations of aurorae and night airglow during the IGY and IGC, *Planet. Space Sci.*, **8** (1961), 125.
13. Malville, J. M., Antarctic auroral observations, Ellsworth Station, *J. Geophys. Res.*, **64** (1959), 1389.
14. McIlwain, C. E., Direct measurements of particles producing visible aurora, *J. Geophys. Res.*, **65** (1960), 2727.
15. Montalbetti, R., and D. J. McEwen, Hydrogen emissions and sporadic-E layer behaviour, *J. Phys. Soc. Japan*, **17** Supp. A-I (1962), 212.
16. Petrie, W., KEOEEIT—The Story of the Aurora Borealis. Oxford: Pergamon Press, 1963.
17. Störmer, C., The Polar Aurora. Oxford: Clarendon Press, 1955.
18. Winckler, J. R., Balloon study of high altitude radiations during the International Geophysical Year, *J. Geophys. Res.*, **65** (1960), 1331.

14

B. C. Blevis
W. C. Collins

Radio Aurora

14.1. INTRODUCTION

The occurrence of abnormal ionization in association with aurora was first reported by Appleton and his colleagues [1] following their studies during the second International Polar Year. The next few years witnessed only minor interest in this subject, although radio amateurs did continue to report occasions of anomalous propagation in the VHF band during periods of visible aurora. During the early 1940's, military radars from time to time obtained echoes from aurorally excited regions, but there was little active research work in the field until about 1947. Since that time, an increasing number of investigations, employing a great variety of radio techniques, have probed this aspect of the auroral phenomenon. It has been found convenient to apply the term 'radio aurora' to the ionization concerned, and this term will be employed generally here without regard to the specific nature of the radio observations.

Many of the pertinent measurements have been made with vertical incidence ionosondes operating between 1 Mc/s and 20 Mc/s. Such data have been extremely useful, since they exist also for normal ionospheric conditions and so permit comparisons to be made between disturbed and undisturbed periods. In these data, radio aurora may be revealed by an increase in the maximum frequency returned to the earth from the *E* region, and then it is often thought of as 'auroral sporadic-E' ionization. It also results at times in an increased attenuation of the radio signals, due to an enhancement of absorption in the D region. During intense disturbances, all HF radio waves may be so severely attenuated as to be undetectable at the ionosonde receiver; then a 'blackout' is said to be in progress. Such conditions are readily discerned in standard tabulations of ionosonde data (where they are denoted simply by a B symbol) and have provided the basis of many studies of radio aurora. Such studies are now complemented by VHF riometer techniques (see Sec. 11.2.1) which permit the intensity of absorption to be measured at all times. The distinction between auroral absorption and PCA was discussed in Sec. 11.3; the present interest lies only in the auroral effects, insofar as they can be distinguished from PCA.

Transmissions at VHF and UHF, although relatively free of critical reflection and severe absorption, often experience strong scattering from irregularities of the enhanced E-region ionization, and much of our present knowledge of the structure of radio aurora has come from investigations at these higher frequencies. Monostatic radars, in which the transmitter and receiver are located at the same site, have been most widely employed for the purpose, but significant contributions have also been derived from bistatic systems in which the transmitter and receiver are widely separated. In both cases, the geometry of the radio path is of considerable importance to the interpretation of the data. At these higher frequencies, Faraday rotation of the plane of polarization of a radio signal provides a further means of study, and has to some extent been exploited for this purpose [22]. (See also Sec. 5.3.3.)

The present chapter outlines results obtained by these techniques. It will describe briefly the general characteristics and structure of radio aurora, their relationship to other geophysical phenomena, and their likely generation mechanisms. An intimately related topic, that of radio emissions from aurora, is also touched upon.

14.2. REFLECTION AND SCATTERING IN RADIO AURORA

This section is concerned with the information that can be obtained from a study of the reflection and scattering of radio waves—the processes that lead to an echo return—both for HF ionosondes and for VHF and UHF radar systems. At the outset, note that it is often most difficult to compare in any quantitative sense the results of independent investigations, because of large differences in the parameters of the radio systems used. This is a major problem in the consolidation of our knowledge of radio aurora, and one which is likely to remain for some years to come. Even results obtained at different times on the same equipment can be compared only with reservations, for the mechanism of reflection or scattering may change with the physical conditions. In the light of these difficulties, attention here is directed toward a limited set of general characteristics of the radio aurora which are not strongly dependent on the observational equipment; emphasis is placed on their interpretation in terms of the actual ionization involved. An overly simplified picture will emerge, but any reader in pursuit of a more detailed description will find it (along with apparent inconsistencies) in the extensive literature on the subject, only a small portion of which is cited here.

14.2.1. General Characteristics. Perhaps the most obvious instance of radio aurora is found in HF ionosonde recordings of auroral sporadic-*E* echoes. These are observed mainly at high latitudes, usually during the night hours, and are associated with auroral and magnetic activity. They give evidence of thin layers of ionization at heights corresponding roughly to the lower boundary of the visual aurora. The ionization appears to exist in the form of irregular patches or blobs, for it permits partial transmission of the radio waves, and the vertical incidence ionosonde records often indicate stratification and diffuse (or spread) echoes above the lower boundary of the reflecting layer.

The ionization densities for auroral sporadic *E* are frequently great enough for critical reflection to occur at frequencies in excess of 5 Mc/s. Studies of such high-density cases have revealed [16] a spiral-like occurrence pattern at high latitudes that is very similar to the precipitation pattern found for visual aurora, thereby pointing to a close association between the two (see Fig. 13.9).

Only rarely do normal ionosondes detect auroral sporadic *E* in the zenith at frequencies exceeding 10 Mc/s, although on long-distance propagation paths it may be observed even up to 20 Mc/s because of an obliquity effect on the radio propagation (see Sec. II.3). At frequencies higher than those for which critical reflections are expected—in the VHF range and above—echoes are still observed even on monostatic equipment, but their character is somewhat altered. These echoes tend to arrive from directions for which the aspect angle, that is, the angle between the radar beam and the geomagnetic lines of force at the echoing region, approaches perpendicularity. When the probability of occurrence of an echo depends on the aspect angle in this way, the reflection (or scattering) process and the echoes themselves are said to exhibit 'aspect sensitivity.' The sensitivity may be weak or strong, depending on specific conditions, but it is invariably thought to arise when the ionization producing the radar echoes is in the form of irregularities aligned preferentially along the earth's magnetic field. (Note, however, that some characteristics attributed to aspect sensitivity have also been interpreted on other lines in which the magnetic field plays no part [11].)

The degree of aspect sensitivity has been found to increase markedly with increasing frequency, but even in the lower part of the VHF band it limits the echoing region to elevation angles of 30° or less. As the operating frequency is increased, aspect sensitivity becomes more important and echoes are obtained from only a small range of angles near the orthogonal situation. Figure 14.1 shows a comparison of the probability of occurrence of 55 Mc/s radar echoes, obtained at Invercargill, with the contours of constant aspect angle as determined for an echoing height of 110 km [30].

Aspect-sensitive echoes typically appear as rapidly fading signals, having fading rates in the range from ten to several hundred cycles per second. The amplitude distribution has been found to be approximately Rayleigh [10] from which it may be deduced that the echo consists of many scatter contributions combining in random phase.

Two main types of echoes have been distinguished in many of the investigations (see, for example, [5]). These are referred to as 'diffuse' and 'discrete' echoes, but the precise significance of the terms has varied considerably between authors. In spite of this, the following general distinction may be made: Discrete echoes appear to have a well-defined leading edge and are somewhat restricted both in their range-depth and in time duration of occurrence. Diffuse echoes, on the other hand, are extended in range and in time; they are observable over range intervals of several hundred kilometers and may persist for several hours. The diffuse echoes are usually weaker than the discrete echoes and also fluctuate more rapidly. It has been suggested that the diffuse echoing regions extend over great distances at

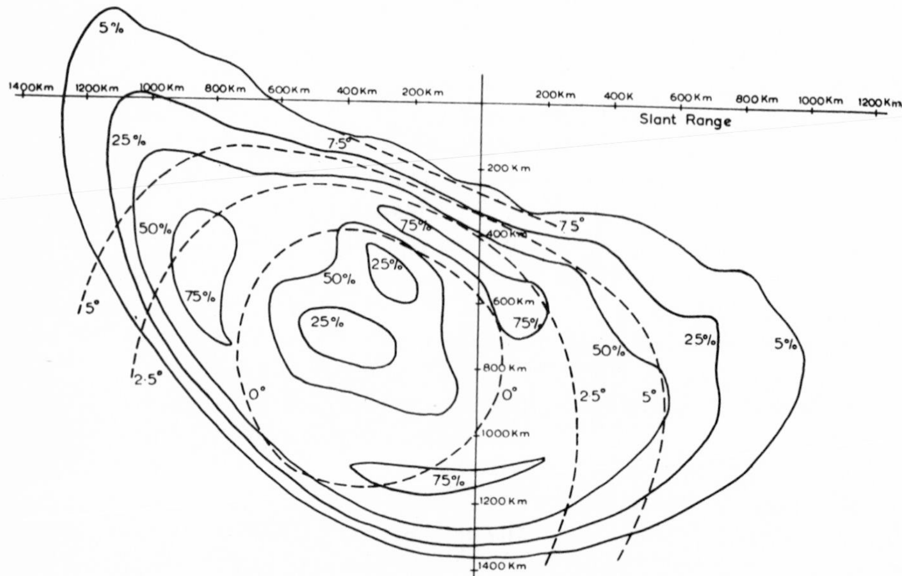

Fig. 14.1 Probability of occurrence of echoes on range-azimuth display as observed from Invercargill (46.6°S, 168.3°E). Dashed lines are contours of of constant aspect angle at 110 km. (From Unwin [30].)

almost constant height, whereas the discrete ionization regions lie along lines of magnetic latitude [28].

On VHF forward-scatter circuits in the vicinity of the auroral zone, a somewhat different classification of radio aurora has been made. Collins and Forsyth [7] identified three types, called by them A_1, A_2, and A_3 events, which they distinguished mainly on the basis of the fading characteristics. The A_1 events have a high rate of fading, of the order of 100 cps; the A_2 signals show deep irregular fades that are much slower than in the case of A_1, whereas the A_3 events display slow regular fading and generally persist for several hours. It is tempting to associate the A_1 and A_2 forward-scatter signal enhancements with the discrete echoes observed on UHF backscatter equipment, and the A_3 events with the diffuse echoes. There is an apparent height discrepancy between the A_3 and the UHF echoes, however, as will be discussed shortly, and therefore this association between the forward-scatter and backscatter signals is questionable.

Studies of the spatial distribution of radio aurora have been complicated by a number of factors. Not the least of these is the effect of aspect sensitivity, which serves to emphasize echoes from some regions of occurrence, as observed by any one radar system, and suppress echoes from others. The height and height range of the auroral ionization are important in this context, for they influence the location and extent of the regions, if any, in which an aspect angle close to 90° can be achieved for the radar in question. This situation is further complicated, in that data obtained at different frequencies are not immediately comparable because of the frequency dependence of the aspect sensitivity. In the case of bistatic systems, moreover, the former requirement for orthogonality gives way to a more general specification for a 'specular' (that is, mirror-like) relation between the directions of the incident and scattered waves, whereas more complex relations become applicable for the strength and frequency dependence of the scattered signal. And, finally, the forward-scatter observations indicate that the three types of auroral events exhibit varying degrees of aspect sensitivity, with one type, the A_3, showing none. In spite of these difficulties, the results presently available from both monostatic and bistatic equipments would indicate that the latitude distribution of auroral ionization does not differ substantially from that of the visual aurora.

Measurements of the heights of the auroral ionization, carried out by means of narrow-beam antennas or by correlation with features of the visual aurora, have shown that most echoes originate in the height range 100–120 km, although instances for which these limits are exceeded are not uncommon [28]. Some echoing regions are very restricted in height with average thicknesses less than 5 km, whereas others are reported to extend some tens of kilometers. In general, these observed heights correspond to those of the lower borders of the visual aurora.

A noteworthy exception to the preceding generalization seems to be the case of the A_3 forward-scatter signal enhancement, for which the responsible ionization regions may be below 85 km [7], and for which therefore the association with visual aurora is somewhat problematic.

Studies of the temporal variation of radio aurora have produced a rather confused picture because of the many dependent parameters involved in each investigation. It would seem, at first glance, that general agreement has been reached on only one distinguishing feature—the existence of a minimum in echo occurrence just before local noon—but even here the depth and breadth of the minimum is found to vary with time, location, and parameters of the radars used.

If we consider in turn the different latitude ranges, it is possible to make additional generalizations on the diurnal variation. At medium latitudes, a maximum in echo occurrence appears somewhat before midnight, with a second maximum in the early morning [3], as in Fig. 14.2. The relative importance of the two maxima seems to vary from one investigation to another; in this particular instance the morning peak is slightly greater than the evening maximum. At higher latitudes near the maximum of the auroral zone, the doubly peaked nighttime distribution curve is replaced by a singly peaked distribution, having a maximum at about local midnight [30]. This behavior is more in accord with the observations of visual aurora. At certain locations near the auroral zone maximum, the situation seems somewhat more complicated and three or more diurnal peaks in echo occurrence have been observed [10, 28].

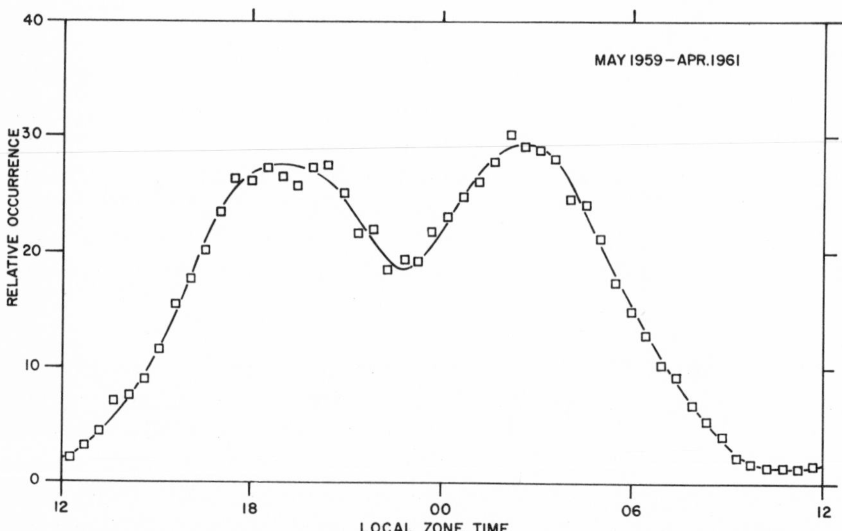

Fig. 14.2 Diurnal variation in the occurrence of auroral radar echoes as observed from Ottawa at a frequency of 500 Mc/s.

The auroral events observed on forward-scatter circuits show a strong nighttime maximum near the auroral zone, with a tendency for a subsidiary maximum to appear at lower latitudes. The time of occurrence of the main maximum (and also of the A_2 events) is in the vicinity of local midnight but depends on the geomagnetic latitude of the midpoint of the propagation path, appearing earlier with increasing latitude [13]. The subsidiary maximum, which seems to appear on mid-latitude paths at about 1800 hr local time, is due almost entirely to A_1 events. The A_3 events tend to peak later in the night—in the range 3–6 hr after midnight—although this time also may vary with latitude.

The long-term variation in radio aurora seems to follow closely that of the visual aurora. Equinoctial maxima in occurrence, as well as the 11-yr periodicity of the solar activity cycle, are found in both the back and forward-scatter observations at medium latitudes.

Motions of auroral ionization have been deduced from measurements of Doppler shift, of changes in range, and of fading rates. All these methods yield results that are quite similar, although it is sometimes found that the velocities obtained by the first two methods are oppositely directed. This situation could come about if the observed range changes were due to movements of the source of ionization, say, and if the Doppler measurements referred to electron motions within the disturbance current system.

The motions generally are observed to be directed more or less eastward and westward, nearly along parallels of geomagnetic latitude [5], although north-south components are also found [30]. The general pattern shows a predominantly westward motion in the evening, which changes to a predominantly eastward motion about an hour or so before geomagnetic midnight, at low auroral latitudes. This changeover appears to coincide with the nighttime minimum in the occurrence of echoes at medium latitudes. The velocities involved in the motions are usually in the range 100–600 m/s, although occasionally they have been observed to exceed 2 km/s. Such maximum velocities are one or two orders of magnitude greater than those of the normal E-region drift motions. (An extensive review of observations on radio auroral motions and their relationship to ionospheric current systems is given by Cole [9].)

Because of difficulties of comparison between different investigations, many estimates of the frequency dependence of the occurrence and strength of auroral echoes are questionable. The situation is further complicated by the probable existence of more than one reflection mechanism, whose relative importances vary with location, time, and operating frequency. By assuming that the echoing region does not fill the antenna beam, signal strengths can be expressed in terms of equivalent cross sections for purpose of comparison. Alternately, the echo strength can be expressed in terms of a reflection coefficient for a reflecting surface larger than the area illuminated by the antenna beam. Each of these methods permits the comparison of echoes at different frequencies, with conclusions that are largely independent of equipment parameters. The results obtained on multiple frequencies, with scaled systems where the dependence on equipment parameters has been removed, however, appear to be most reliable. One such study at UHF disclosed that the received power varied as about the seventh power of wavelength, but this value is probably dependent on aspect angle [3].

At VHF the situation is complicated by two competing reflecting mechanisms. On many occasions the signal amplitude at one frequency is found to be many times greater than at an adjacent higher frequency, whereas at other times the signals are comparable in amplitude. After due allowance had been made for aspect sensitivity, these results were interpreted to show that critical reflections are important, at times, at the lower frequencies, in addition to the more normal weak scattering from the ionization irregularities [15, 24].

14.2.2. Physical Processes. As implied in the foregoing discussion, several processes have been postulated to explain the observed characteristics of auroral radio reflections. This topic has evoked much debate, and to a large extent still remains unresolved, as no theory has yet been proposed that can explain adequately all aspects of the observed phenomena. This situation will likely persist until more consistent and definitive observations on radio aurora are available.

The argument that critical reflections from intensely ionized regions are involved at the lower end of the VHF spectrum is rather convincing. This would imply the existence of ionization irregularities of substantial size in which the electron density exceeded the critical density given by the usual formula—cf. Eq. (1.18):

$$N_c = 4\pi^2 \epsilon_0 m f^2 / e^2,$$

where e and m are the electronic charge and mass and f is the wave frequency. The existence of critical reflections at, say, 50 Mc/s implies electron densities as high as 3×10^7 cm^{-3}.

Since it is almost inconceivable that electron densities substantially in excess of this figure can be maintained in the E region, some process other than critical reflection must be sought for the higher frequencies. A process of partial reflection at the boundary of the ionized region was proposed by Herlofson [20]. This process was presumed to occur where the radar beam was perpendicular to the interface of an auroral drapery. To avoid the restriction of a plane surface, Aspinall and Hawkins [2] considered partial reflections from a cylindrical surface analogous to the situation obtaining in the case of auroral rays. This treatment also was too restrictive since it limited severely the positions from which echoes were possible.

Booker [4] proposed that the observed auroral radar echoes could be attributed to scattering from nonisotropic irregularities that are elongated along the earth's magnetic field. According to this theory, the nature of the irregularities can be described statistically in terms of the mean square deviation of the electron density from the average value. The postulation of short columns permits deviations from orthogonality to exist, and the permitted deviation varies with wavelength. This scattering process does not include the assumption of overdense ionization, even at the low end of the VHF band, and requires only that a small part of the incident energy be actually scattered by the irregularities.

This scatter theory was shown by Booker to be compatible with early radar data on the basis of an average electron density of 10^6 cm^{-3}, a fractional mean square deviation of 3×10^{-7}, and column sizes of about 40 meters in length and about 1 meter in diameter. Although radar data over a wide frequency range seem to substantiate column sizes of this order, it is doubtful that such ionization features can be associated directly with any features of the visual aurora (cf. Sec. 13.6). It is also questionable whether turbulence, which Booker proposed to explain the origin of such irregularities, can give rise to the particular configurations assumed. In addition, more recent measurements indicate that values some three orders of magnitude greater might be more appropriate for the mean square fractional deviation of electron number density [27]. Nevertheless, some theory of weak scattering by nonisotropic field-aligned irregularities appears to be the most satisfactory explanation for the behavior of auroral radar echoes.

A more generalized theoretical treatment of the scattering process has now been presented by Moorcroft [26] with results which include those of Booker as a special case. Moorcroft concludes that an assembly of scatterers of different sizes, having dimensions of the order of a few meters transverse to the field lines, axial ratios between 5 and 10, and peak electron densities of about 3×10^7 cm^{-3}, can explain many of the observations of radio aurora.

A general treatment for oblique scattering from anisotropic ionization irregularities (not circularly symmetric about the field lines) has also been given recently by Egeland [10].

14.3. AURORAL ABSORPTION OF RADIO WAVES

Although most of the radio auroral observations pertain to *E*-region heights, the ionization associated with aurora frequently extends well down into the lower ionosphere, to heights of 70 km or less. In these regions, radio waves suffer attenuation because of the high collisional frequency of the electrons, and the increased ionization at times of radio aurora results in abnormal radio wave absorption, usually referred to as 'auroral absorption.'

The presence of such absorption at high latitudes has long been known. Early statistical studies based on obliquely propagated HF signals and vertical incidence ionosonde data showed that the absorbing regions were very large and that they corresponded roughly to the visual aurora. Moreover, periods of intense absorption were found to correlate well with large magnetic bays and with the more active of the visual auroral forms. As outlined in Chapter 11, however, it was not until the introduction of the riometer at high latitudes that significant progress was made in this field. Data from such equipments indicated that the previously known 'polar blackouts' included at least two distinct types of absorption, and also permitted a quantitative assessment of each type.

The absorption events referred to here as auroral usually occur during those periods that show visual aurora and magnetic disturbances, but close correlation throughout the course of an event is not usually found. A part of this lack of agreement can be attributed to differences in the geometry involved in the different measurements, but other factors undoubtedly enter as well.

The main distinguishing characteristic of auroral absorption is its variability; the time scale involved may range from a few minutes to several hours, but on the average has been shown to be shorter at high latitudes, such as Resolute Bay, than at medium latitudes, such as Ottawa. This absorption occurs most frequently in a belt which is approximately parallel to the auroral zone maximum, but which is displaced a few degrees toward low latitudes [18]. Moreover, the location of this auroral absorption zone is dependent on geomagnetic activity, shifting to lower latitudes at times of disturbances, in a manner similar to the shift of the auroral zone. The seasonal variation shows maxima at the equinoxes analogous to those found in the case of the visual and other radio aurora. The secular variation over one sunspot cycle shows a maximum which lags the sunspot maximum by about four years, followed by a broad minimum centered approximately three years after the sunspot minimum [8]. The diurnal occurrence pattern shows a maximum in the morning and a minimum in the evening, with indications of a secondary maximum in the vicinity of midnight. This is illustrated in Fig. 14.3 which shows contours of percentage time occurrence of auroral absorption as a function of time of day.

Some attempts have been made to determine the size of the absorbing regions through the use of data from several stations or from complex antenna systems. Such studies show that the absorbing region is usually more widespread than the region of luminosity, and no evidence has been found for structures having a horizontal dimension much smaller than about 100 km [21]. Further, the results indicate that the ionization regions are somewhat more extensive in an east-west than in a north-south direction [23].

Although the effective height of the absorbing regions is not yet firmly established, there is evidence to show that it is less than 100 km. VHF signals, scattered by ionized meteor trails, show the effects of auroral absorption,

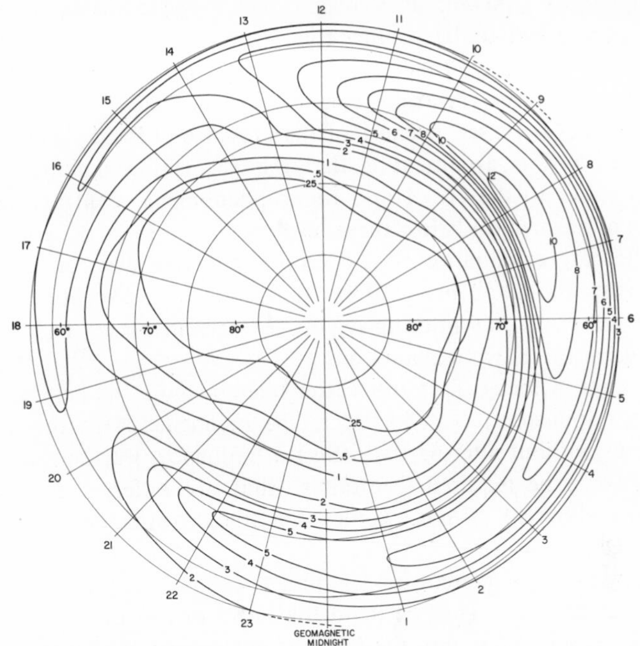

Fig. 14.3 Contour diagram showing the time percentage of occurrence of 30 Mc/s auroral absorption of 1.0 db or more as a function of geomagnetic latitude and mean geomagnetic time. (After Hartz, *et al.* [18].)

thus indicating that the absorbing ionization occurs below approximately 90 km, at least on occasion [15]. Rocket measurements made at Churchill during one auroral absorption event showed that most of the absorption was in the height interval of 70–75 km [19]. Values of the absorption ratios at several frequencies have been interpreted as showing that the responsible ionization at times extends below 50 km [31], but such results should be viewed with caution, since ionization at greater heights that has horizontal structure can lead to similar values for the absorption ratios.

It would seem, therefore, that the height and vertical extent of the absorbing region have not yet been determined with any accuracy, or that they vary greatly from event to event. Since the absorption is proportional to the product of the electron number density and the electron collision frequency, integrated over the height region involved, a variation in the height and vertical extent of the associated ionization is also implied. However, attempts to relate the enhancements of ionization that are deduced from the radio-wave scattering observations to the absorption measurements have met with little success, and that only for the special case of the A_3 data. Generally, the scattering data indicate that the irregularities are located principally above 100 km, at a height where the collision frequency is normally considered to be so low that little absorption would result. To overcome this difficulty, Reid and Collins [29] have suggested that during such disturbances the electron temperature and hence the collision frequency become increased because of the presence of local electric fields. A consequence of this argument is that the absorption region is expected at heights closer to the visual and radar phenomena, contrary to the observations of absorption below these heights.

An alternate explanation would require that the electron densities decrease slowly enough below 100 km that sufficient absorption can occur *below* the reflecting or scattering region. At present no clear choice can be made between these two explanations.

In the case of the A_3 forward-scatter phenomenon, the height region for the relevant ionization (< 85 km) can be reconciled with the absorption observations without altering the collision frequency. Further investigation, however, would be required to establish that two different processes, with significantly different height profiles for the disturbance ionization, are indeed involved.

A mechanism suggested by Chapman and Little [6] in this regard should be mentioned. They contend that electrons in the energy range of 10–100 Kev, precipitating into the E region at the time of an aurora, produce X-radiation in addition to the extra ionization produced in this height region by collisions. The X-rays are able to penetrate much deeper into the atmosphere, producing ionization of neutral molecules along their path. This theory not only introduces ionization at lower heights than the aurora, but also is capable of locating such ionization over a much more extensive region than that covered by the visual phenomenon. This explanation has not yet been found adequate on a quantitative basis, however, even though rocket and balloon-borne instrumentation has shown the presence of X-rays in association with aurora and auroral absorption. The results of McDiarmid *et al.* [25] seem much more significant in this connection. They obtained data on the flux of electrons with energies greater than 30 Kev during a rocket flight at Churchill which also measured the height profile of auroral absorption [19]. On comparing the two sets of data for that flight, they concluded that the measured electron flux was by itself sufficient to produce the observed absorption-height profile.

14.4. RADIO NOISE EMISSIONS FROM THE AURORA

Beginning in the late 1940's, there have been a number of scattered reports of emissions from the aurora. The emissions have ranged in frequency from about 30 Mc/s to 3000 Mc/s and have generally been characterized as consisting of short bursts of broadband noise. These reports have been viewed with some skepticism because they occurred so sporadically and because of the possibility that they involved auroral echoes from ground-based transmitters. A detailed examination of the characteristics of the observed signals can reduce or obviate this possibility, and occasionally some convincing identifications of auroral noise have been made. Such instances, however, are quite few, and the occasions when the emissions were sought but not observed are numerous. It has been suggested that the emissions may occur only when the solar activity is high, and some of the more reliable identifications have indeed been made near sunspot maximum and were associated, specifically, with very active auroral forms [14] and with type A red aurora [17].

Of the possible mechanisms suggested to explain such observations, a few appear somewhat more probable than the rest. The first is the occurrence of transient plasma oscillations arising from local perturbations in the charge distribution. The second is Čerenkov radiation generated from the influx of energetic particles into a region where the velocity of the wave propagation is comparable to the particle velocity. Both these processes appear to require local electron densities of at least 10^9 cm^{-3} in order to generate 3000 Mc/s radiation, and values as great as this are thought to be most unlikely in the auroral ionization. Yet a third explanation is synchrotron radiation from electrons spiraling in the geomagnetic field, but the adequacy of this process has still to be assessed.

14.5. CONCLUDING REMARKS

A number of authors have reported a close association between the probability of observing auroral echoes and the degree of local magnetic disturbance: for K indices greater than about five the probability of echo occurrence approaches unity at medium-latitude stations. It would seem that the enhanced ionization that gives rise to the radar echoes is associated with ionospheric currents responsible, at least in part, for the magnetic field variations observed on the ground. Some observations, [5] for instance, have shown diffuse evening echoes associated with positive magnetic disturbances and westward motion of the ionization; these give place to discrete morning echoes which are associated with negative magnetic disturbances and eastward motions, with the changeover occurring between 21 hrs and 22 hrs, local time.

It has been implicit in all the foregoing discussion that a close correspondence exists between radio aurora and the occurrence of visual aurora. Many attempts have been made to establish the degree of this correspondence, but the results are far from conclusive. As noted in the preceding sections, the gross occurrence patterns of the two phenomena exhibit many similarities, but the detailed correlation is rather disappointing. The spatial structures appear to differ substantially, the amplitude of the echoes and the intensity of the luminosity do not agree closely (however, see [12]), and some radio aurora apparently have no observable visual counterpart.

A part of the difficulty, at least, is due to the incompatibility of the radio and optical observing techniques at the same station. Because of aspect sensitivity, the radar observations are restricted to low angles of elevation, whereas atmospheric extinction limits the optical measurements to high angles of elevation. Accordingly, many of the results obtained to date may be revised when optical observations are available from stations located under the regions that give rise to the radio echoes.

REFERENCES

1. Appleton, E. V., R. Naismith, and L. J. Ingram, British radio observations during the second international polar year 1932–1933, *Phil. Trans. Roy. Soc. A*, **236** (1937), 191.
2. Aspinall, A., and G. S. Hawkins, Radio echo reflections from the aurora borealis, *J. Brit. Astr. Assoc.*, **60** (1950), 130.
3. Blevis, B. C., J. W. B. Day, and O. S. Roscoe, The occurrence and characteristics of radar auroral echoes at 488 and 944 Mc/s, *Can. J. Phys.*, **41** (1963), 1359.
4. Booker, H. G., A theory of scattering by nonisotropic irregularities with application to radar reflections from the aurora, *J. Atmos. Terr. Phys.*, **8** (1956), 204.
5. Bullough, K., and T. R. Kaiser, Radio reflections from aurorae—II, *J. Atmos. Terr. Phys.*, **6** (1955), 198.
6. Chapman, S., and C. G. Little, The nondeviative absorption of high-frequency radio waves in auroral latitudes, *J. Atmos. Terr. Phys.*, **10** (1957), 20.
7. Collins, C., and P. A. Forsyth, A bistatic radio investigation of auroral ionization, *J. Atmos. Terr. Phys.*, **13** (1959), 315.
8. Collins, C., D. H. Jelly, and A. G. Matthews, High-frequency radio-wave blackouts at medium and high latitudes during a solar cycle, *Can. J. Phys.*, **39** (1961), 35.
9. Cole, K. D., Motions of the aurora and radio-aurora and their relationships to ionospheric currents, *Planet. Space Sci.*, **10** (1963), 129.
10. Egeland, A., Studies of auroral reflections in the VHF band. 1. Experimental investigations, with special regard to time variations, fading rate, azimuthal distributions, and polarization characteristics, *Arkiv för Geophysik*, **4** (1962), 103.
11. Forsyth, P. A., On the geometry of radio reflections from aurora, *Can. J. Phys.*, **38** (1960), 593.
12. Forsyth, P. A., On the association of radio reflections with optical aurora, *Can. J. Phys.*, **39** (1961), 1721.
13. Forsyth, P. A., F. D. Green, and W. Mah, The distribution of radio-aurora in central Canada, *Can. J. Phys.*, **38** (1960), 770.
14. Forsyth, P. A., W. Petrie, and B. W. Currie, Auroral radiation in the 3000-megacycle region, *Nature*, **164** (1949), 453.

15. Forsyth, P. A., and E. L. Vogan, The frequency dependence of radio reflections from aurora, *J. Atmos. Terr. Phys.*, **10** (1957), 215.

16. Hagg, E. L., D. Muldrew, and E. S. Warren, Spiral occurrence of sporadic-E, *J. Atmos. Terr. Phys.*, **14** (1959), 345.

17. Hartz, T. R., Auroral radiation at 500 Mc/s, *Can. J. Phys.*, **36** (1958), 677.

18. Hartz, T. R., L. E. Montbriand, and E. L. Vogan, A study of auroral absorption at 30 Mc/s, *Can. J. Phys.*, **41** (1963), 581.

19. Heikkila, W. J., and S. R. Penstone, Rocket measurements of auroral radio absorption, *Can. J. Phys.*, **39** (1961), 1875.

20. Herlofson, N., Interpretation of radio echoes from polar auroras, *Nature*, **160** (1947), 867.

21. Holt, C., B. Landmark, and F. Lied, Analysis of riometer observations obtained during polar radio blackouts, *J. Atmos. Terr. Phys.*, **23** (1961), 229.

22. Ingalls, R. P., J. C. James, and M. L. Stone, A study of UHF communications through an aurora using the moon as a reflector, *Planet. Space Sci.*, **7** (1961), 272.

23. Leinbach, H., and R. P. Basler, Ionospheric absorption of cosmic noise at magnetically conjugate auroral zone stations, *J. Geophys. Res.*, **68** (1963), 3375.

24. Lyon, G. F., and P. A. Forsyth, Radio-auroral reflection mechanisms, *Can. J. Phys.*, **40** (1962), 749.

25. McDiarmid, I. B., D. C. Rose, and E. Budzinski, Direct measurement of charged particles associated with auroral zone radio absorption, *Can. J. Phys.*, **39** (1961), 1888.

26. Moorcroft, D. R., Models of auroral ionization. Part I. Auroral ionization models and their radio-reflection characteristics, *Can. J. Phys.*, **39** (1961), 677.

27. Nichols, B., Auroral ionization and magnetic disturbances, *Proc. I.R.E.*, **47** (1959), 245.

28. Presnell, R. I., R. L. Leadabrand, A. M. Peterson, R. B. Dyce, J. C. Schlobohm, and M. R. Berg, VHF and UHF radar observations of the aurora at College, Alaska, *J. Geophys. Res.*, **64** (1959), 1179.

29. Reid, G. C., and C. Collins, Observations of abnormal VHF radio wave absorption at medium and high latitudes, *J. Atmos. Terr. Phys.*, **14** (1959), 63.

30. Unwin, R. S., Studies of the upper atmosphere from Invercargill, New Zealand. Part I. Characteristics of auroral radar echoes at 55 Mc/sec, *Ann. de Géophys.*, **15** (1959), 377.

31. Ziauddin, S., and P. A. Forsyth, Three-frequency measurements of auroral absorption, *J. Geophys. Res.*, **66** (1961), 2315.

15

C. O. *Hines*
G. C. *Reid*

Theory of Geomagnetic and Auroral Storms

15.1. INTRODUCTION

The preceding chapters have given some indication of the tremendous variety of features that go to make up a typical geomagnetic or auroral storm, and have indicated as well the departures from 'typical' behavior that are commonplace when individual occurrences are considered. It would be rash to suppose that the theoretical explanation of the various phenomena could be embodied in a single chapter, even if that explanation were known. Actually, many theorists have advanced many theories for one aspect or another, and these have yet to be incorporated into a widely accepted comprehensive description. We can attempt to provide here only an outline of the theoretical approaches that we think to be most pertinent, as judged by general principles and by consistency with the observational data currently available.

The geomagnetic aspects have advanced rapidly in recent years, primarily as a consequence of a growing understanding of hydromagnetic processes and of charged-particle drifts in inhomogeneous magnetic fields. They are discussed in turn under the headings of sudden commencements, initial phase, main-phase *DS* behavior, main-phase *Dst* behavior, and elementary polar storms. Although a variety of approaches to some of these problems will become apparent, certain underlying threads of agreement should not go unnoticed and will in fact receive specific comment.

The theory of the aurora polaris is, if anything, beset by an even wider range of starting points. Certainly the most spectacular phenomenon of the earth's upper atmosphere, the aurora has posed some of the most elusive and fascinating problems in the study of those regions. A complete survey of the literature of auroral theory would cover the entire history of civilization and would convince the reader that the aurora is not an unexplained phenomenon but rather one with such a multiplicity of possible explanations as to produce a sense of complete bewilderment. Each of these theories is, however, more or less unsatisfactory in accounting for some of the major features of the observed aurora, and one is left with the impression that some completely new approach is required, or that fragments of existing theories must be unified in some manner not yet clear. Here we merely describe some of the major theories that have been put forward, and attempt to indicate their principal successes and shortcomings.

Those who wish to pursue these theoretical discussions further, other than through the original research papers, will find a current monograph edited by Matsushita and Campbell [1] to be of value for the magnetic aspects and an excellent survey article by Chamberlain [2] to provide a corresponding but more compact treatment of auroral theories.

15.2. GEOMAGNETIC STORMS

15.2.1. Sudden Commencements. It will be recalled that many geomagnetic storms are initiated by sudden deviations of the geomagnetic field from a previously quiescent state. These deviations are known collectively as 'sudden commencements,' or SC's, though individually they exhibit such a range of characteristics that a subsystem of classification has been established to facilitate their description. The theory of sudden commencements as a class is still rudimentary, and that of the subclasses almost nonexistent; only the former warrants discussion here.

The most striking feature of SC's is the rapidity of the changes they produce, even at the very onset. The first (and sometimes sole) stroke of the sudden commencement may be completed within a minute or so, even though it occurs a day or more after the initiating solar event. This disparity of time scales must play a critical role in any evaluation of possible mechanisms, and it has led to the belief that sudden commencements are caused by shock waves. We may conceive of an expanding cloud of ejected solar matter as in Fig. 15.1, pushing ahead of it the more quiescent coronal gas of the steady solar wind. After a period of time, this ejected matter might reach the position indicated by the solid line in the figure, which is called a 'contact surface,' whereas the somewhat compressed gas ahead of it would be confined

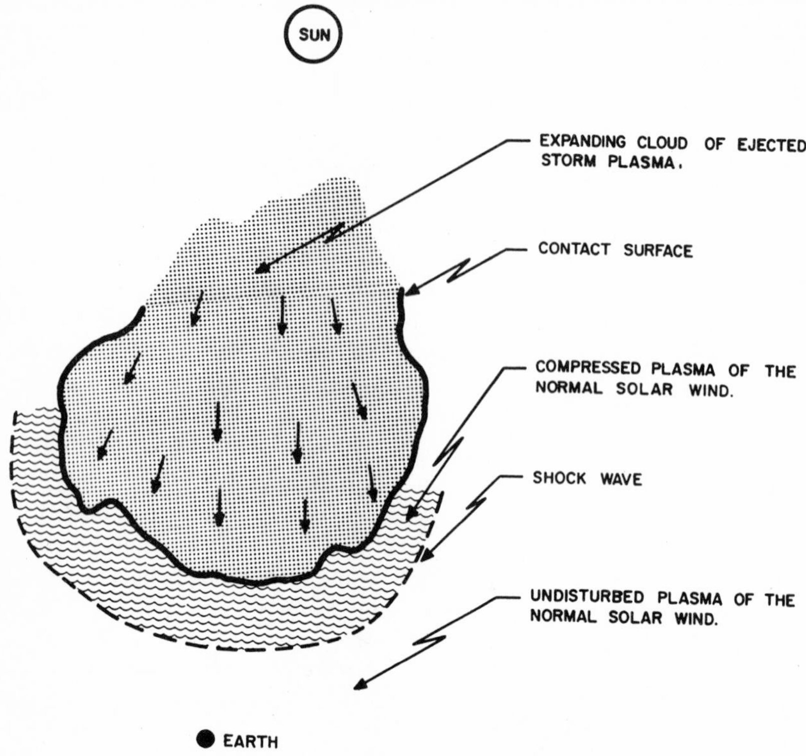

Fig. 15.1 Conceptual view of an expanding cloud of ejected solar matter, compressing ahead of it the gas of the normal solar wind.

between that line and some other advancing line—the broken line in the figure. The latter would be a shock front, if the speed of the newly ejected matter exceeded by a sufficient margin that of the quiescent solar wind. The arrival of the shock front at the earth would then correspond to the sudden commencement, whereas the subsequent arrival of the relatively diffuse contact surface would introduce a later stage in the development of the storm.

Although Fig. 15.1 provides adequate illustration for the case of an isolated storm, it can meet the demands of a sudden-commencement storm within a recurrent sequence only if repeated outbursts of matter from a single solar source are contemplated. It is more in keeping with present views to visualize a steady outstreaming in the case of a recurrent sequence; then a picture more of the form given in Fig. 15.2 becomes pertinent. A shock front can still be formed in these circumstances, although it seems likely that the necessary disparity of speeds between the quiescent and storm plasma would be greater in this case. (A shock is to be expected if the disparity of velocity components normal to the contact surface exceeds the maximum speed of wave propagation in the quiescent plasma, which is probably the Alfvén speed, of the order 100 km/s.) Conversely, when a sudden commencement is *not* observed—that is, in the case of gradual-commencement storms—it must be assumed that the disparity of speeds is not adequate to produce a shock front, whether the geometry is that of Fig. 15.1 or that of Fig. 15.2; the different geometries can account for the more frequent occurrence of SC's in the case of isolated storms.

Shock fronts in nonionized gases are of the order of one mean free path in thickness. A mean free path in the sun-earth region is typically of the order 10^7 km, and the shock front would sweep through this distance in 10^4 sec if it moved with the sun-to-earth speed of 10^3 km/s usually associated

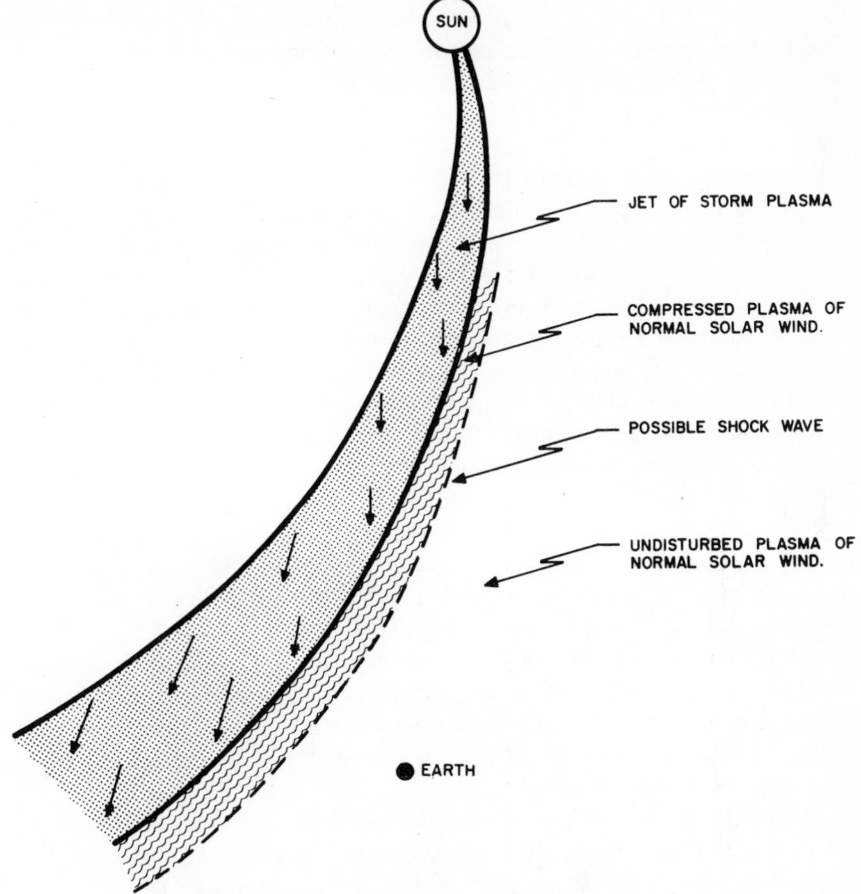

Fig. 15.2 Conceptual view of a continuing jet of solar matter, ejected at a speed exceeding that of the normal solar wind.

with magnetic storms. Even this time scale is too great to account for the rapid onset of sudden commencements.

This difficulty is generally evaded with the assumption that ionized gases can support shock fronts much thinner than the conventional mean free path. Laboratory experiments have already given some evidence in support of this contention, and its theoretical explanation is currently under intensive study [3]. In simple plasmas, it appears that collective interactions generate unstable irregularities and that these irregularities are able to transfer energy more rapidly than do simple interparticle collisions. Estimates of the thickness of the shock front derived on this basis range down to an interpenetration distance of the order of $(m_e V^2 \epsilon_0 / Ne^2)^{1/2}$ for two colliding plasmas, each of particle density N and relative velocity V. If $N = 10\ \text{cm}^{-3}$ and $V = 10^6$ m/s, for example, this yields a scale of 10 meters which is clearly much smaller than that needed to account for the observations. More conservative estimates, based on differently detailed reasoning, replace V^2 by c^2 in the foregoing formula, where c is the speed of light, but even they are consistent with the observed rise times.

A second mechanism is available for decreasing the thickness of a contact surface in a jet, or of a shock front in a shock wave. It depends on the existence of interplanetary magnetic fields, which could act to transfer momentum in distances of the order of an ion gyro radius. In a magnetic field of 1γ, for example, a 1000 km/s proton would have a gyro radius of 100 km or less. This is of the same order of magnitude as that suggested by the observed onset of a sudden commencement. In this picture, the broken-line front (shock front) in the earlier figures must be envisaged as a surface in which the magnetic field varies rapidly from its normal strength and direction to some new value imposed by the solar activity.

Note that almost all discussions of these collision-free shock waves contemplate only positive enhancements of particle and/or magnetic pressure, whereas negative impulses are also observed [4]. The negative magnetic impulses are analogous to SI's (see Sec. 12.4) rather than SC's, since they are not followed by appreciable magnetic disturbances, and these negative impulses may demand corresponding negative shocks.

Although the properties of shock waves in the interplanetary region require further elucidation, still other problems remain in the explanation of sudden commencements. These concern the nature of the interactions that occur in the immediate environment of the earth and their relation to the observed disturbances in detail.

According to one school of thought, the interplanetary shock wave—whatever its nature—generates hydromagnetic waves in the outer reaches of the magnetosphere. These then propagate down through the magnetosphere and penetrate the lower ionosphere, to emerge into the regions below, where we observe them as sudden commencements. The disturbance would be modified severely by the propagational processes of refraction, reflection, diffraction and absorption; and induced earth currents would add to the complication.

The propagation itself would also be anisotropic in part, for one of the modes of the hydromagnetic wave system can transmit energy only along the geomagnetic field lines (see Appendix I). The energy of this mode would then travel from the outer magnetosphere to high latitudes, and indeed these latitudes do exhibit SC effects most strongly. A detailed account of the wave progression has been given by Piddington [5]; Sugiura and Wilson [6, 7] present observational confirmation of the hydromagnetic nature of the disturbance at high latitudes.

The second hydromagnetic mode propagates isotropically and, when combined with certain unique conditions which arise in the case of vertical incidence, can account for a localized equatorial enhancement that is observed [8]. Calculations of the travel time of the waves from the outer magnetosphere to various points on the equator are consistent with observed differences of onset time at different locations and with the observed rise times [9], though additional factors undoubtedly contribute to the same observations and may even dominate them.

Although the hydromagnetic-wave theory is now widely accepted as the one most pertinent to SC's, it is incomplete in that the method of generation and certain aspects of the wave form remain open to debate. Moreover, the effects of other possible processes cannot be ignored entirely and may have some part to play. Chief among these is the precipitation of charged particles into the lower ionosphere from the outer magnetospheric regions, with attendant modification of the ionospheric electric fields and conductivities.

15.2.2. Initial Phase. It is heartening to note, in a subject replete with controversy, one feature on whose explanation there is almost complete agreement. This is the increase of (horizontal) magnetic field strength that constitutes the 'initial phase.'

The modern theory of the initial phase has grown out of the early work of Chapman and Ferraro [10] and indeed is very little different from that work. The model they adopted for the solar particles is similar to that depicted in Fig. 15.2, except that the jet emitted from the sun was taken to sweep through an otherwise empty region of space. They examined in considerable detail certain aspects of the interaction between the jet and the geomagnetic field and found that the more direct consequences of this interaction could reasonably be associated with the initial phase. They found, in particular, that currents would be induced in the leading face of the jet as it approached the geomagnetic field, of such a nature as to 'shield' the interior of the stream from that field. The magnetic effects established by these currents in the region outside the jet were, in the simplest case, equivalent to those that

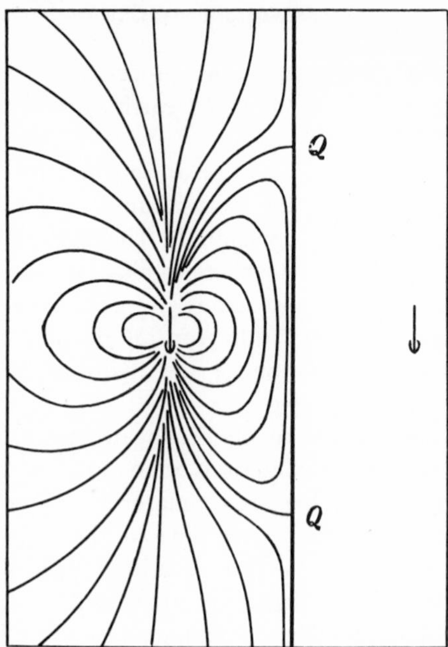

Fig. 15.3 A cloud of highly conducting plasma, with planar front QQ, proceeding from right to left into a plasma-free region that contains a magnetic dipole parallel to the front, introduces a modification of the magnetic field lines into the configuration illustrated here, as if carrying within it an image dipole which is also shown. (After Chapman and Ferraro [10].)

would be produced by a magnetic dipole acting in free space, the dipole having the same magnetic moment as the earth's and being located at a point as far within the jet as the earth was outside. The net pattern of field lines is illustrated in meridional section in Fig. 15.3, for an infinite plane front that has penetrated to the vicinity of the earth.

Associated with the induction of current systems on the face of the jet, there was a retarding force exerted on the solar gas. This force was expected to carve a hole out of the jet, as shown in Fig. 15.4. The solar gas would be deflected around the earth on all sides and might leave behind a sort of 'shadow' region initially devoid of ejected matter. The gas was expected to penetrate on the sunward side to a depth where the density of the geomagnetic field energy would be comparable to the kinetic energy density of the jet. Its penetration would in general not be so deep over other parts of the earth, except for a possible localized penetration which will be discussed later in connection with the production of aurora.

The modern approach to the problem of the initial phase differs only slightly from the foregoing. It recognizes the newly known fact that the region occupied by the geomagnetic field is filled with ionized material. This implies

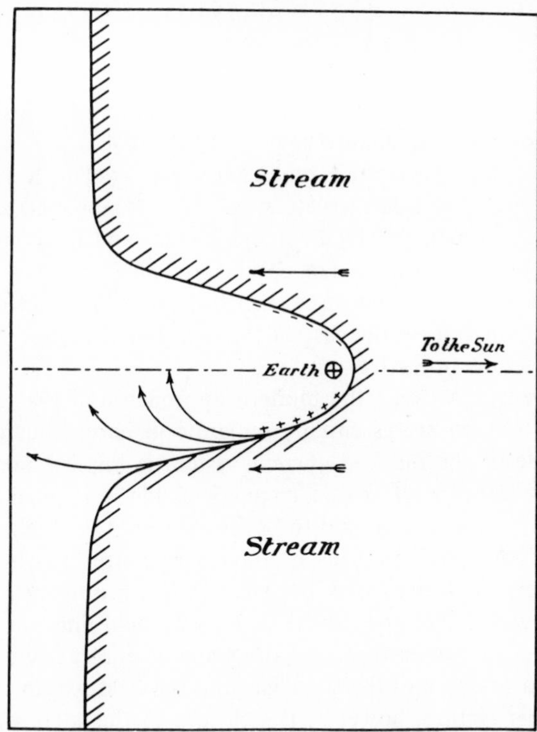

Fig. 15.4 A cloud such as that depicted in Fig. 15.3 would suffer retardation in the regions nearest the dipole and would then distort round it and tend to envelope it as illustrated here. (After Chapman and Ferraro [10].)

that, before the magnetic effects established by the current system can be detected at ground level, they must propagate hydromagnetically down to, and penetrate through, the lower ionosphere. Propagation through the magnetosphere may tend to enhance the disturbance at high latitudes, for the reason noted in the case of sudden commencements, though the bulk of the energy incident on the sunward face should be carried by the isotropically propagating mode; the penetration of the lower ionosphere was of course an implicit part of the earlier picture. Since the effects of these modifications have not been examined in detail, they have not yet altered in any practical way the theory originally presented.

A second modification, also of little importance, results from the current view that the background interplanetary gas has a sensible effect on the outer magnetosphere and that the geomagnetic field is distorted from a dipole pattern even before the incidence of the jet (as discussed in Chapter 1). The effect of the enhanced stream of solar particles would then be to carry more field lines from the low-latitude torus of Fig. 1.5 into the high-latitude family of lines, and perhaps to reorient this family, rather than to create a high-latitude family where none existed before. If Fig. 1.5 is indeed applicable, then the enhanced stream must also be expected to close behind the earth and so terminate the shadow region of Fig. 15.4.

Finally, the transition from a quiescent solar wind to a storm plasma takes place through the intermediate stage of a compressed solar plasma, lying between the shock front (when one exists) and the contact surface. The Chapman-Ferraro process can come into effect whenever the energy density of the solar plasma increases; hence it need not await the arrival of the newly ejected matter (in the case of Fig. 15.1) or the jet of storm plasma (Fig. 15.2) to become operative.

Other differences between the modern approach and that employed by Chapman and Ferraro are essentially semantic in nature but useful nevertheless. The role of the induced current system is implied rather than expressed, for the concept of frozen magnetic fields is applied in its place. Thus, the geomagnetic field is said to be frozen out of the highly conducting solar gas and compressed by it as its impact pressure increases. Although more geomagnetic field lines may be swept into a geomagnetic tail and so may appear to give some relief to the underlying field lines on the sunward side, nevertheless the forward face of the geomagnetic cavity is compressed by the enhanced pressure of the solar gas and the field within is everywhere increased. In this picture, however, the closure of the solar stream behind the earth must play a part, for it will affect the pressure that is exerted on the night side of the magnetosphere and so will help to determine the strength of the disturbance field there. Unfortunately, in common with other aspects of the updated picture, the observable implications of this concept have not been determined in detail, though some model calculations have shown the closure to be important even at ground level [11].

15.2.3. Main-phase *DS* System. The main phase of a geomagnetic storm exhibits two separable components, as described in Sec. 12.5: a *Dst* part, from which longitudinal variations have been excluded, and a *DS* part. It is convenient to discuss the longitude-dependent *DS* system first, and indeed there is reason to believe that this system is the more basic. The main magnetic deviations it reveals appear to be caused by 'auroral electrojet' currents in the ionosphere, flowing eastward in the afternoon or early evening hours, and more strongly westward near midnight or shortly after, in a narrow band of latitudes near the zones of maximum auroral occurrence. Less obvious, but nevertheless evident from the observations, is a return current flow of relatively weak intensity over the polar caps and through the lower-latitude ionosphere—see Fig. 12.7(b).

Much of the early effort at an explanation of these currents was directed to dynamo mechanisms, analogous to those that are believed to produce the *Sq* system of quiet days (Chapter 7). Such theories were forced to adopt objectionably high enhancements of conductivity or of ionospheric winds, however, if they were to meet the quantitative demands of the storm observations [12], and they have failed to find widespread acceptance on this account. A novel approach to the dynamo analysis has recently been introduced by Fejer [13], who notes that the electric fields of the *Sq* system will be modified by the presence of energetic trapped particles higher in the magnetosphere, and who deduces modifications to the corresponding currents that are similar in form to those of the *DS* system. These currents would be enhanced if the distribution and numbers of trapped particles were suitably modified during a storm, but quantitative difficulties may yet remain.

The tendency of recent years has been to seek an energy source for the *DS* system in interactions that involve solar corpuscular emissions directly, rather than in ionospheric winds. One of the first attempts was due to Alfvén [14], who undertook to trace the trajectories of individual noninteracting particles that swept from the sun (with velocity $\mathbf{V}_s$) as they passed by the earth. He postulated a magnetic induction ($\mathbf{B}_s$) external to the geomagnetic field and superimposed on it, directed northward through the plane of the geomagnetic equator, and then inferred an external electric field ($\mathbf{E}_s = \mathbf{B}_s \times \mathbf{V}_s$) which would be established by space-charge accumulations at the boundaries of the solar stream. The calculation of particle trajectories was confined to the equatorial plane and took into account the drift motions that would result from the inhomogeneity of the net magnetic field (Chapter 5).

A representative pattern of electron trajectories is illustrated in Fig. 15.5. The curvature of the paths in the vicinity of the earth results from the '∇B' drifts; it is modified in the course of the passage both by virtue of changes in ∇B and by the consequences of energy changes produced by the motion in the $\mathbf{E}_s$ field.

Proton trajectories would be similar in form to those depicted here, except that their departures from uniform flow would be oppositely directed with respect to the direction of $\mathbf{E}_s$; they may be visualized by a mental mirroring of the electron-flow pattern about the sun-earth line. A temperature-dependent scaling factor would also be applicable, and Alfvén took this to be such that the protons would tend to penetrate the geomagnetic field more deeply than the electrons before suffering strong deflection. As they do so, however, they would establish an excess of positive charge on the sunward side, and he concluded they would then be precipitated into the atmosphere along geomagnetic field lines. A part of the ion population thus having been removed, an excess of negative charge was inferred on the night side and a corresponding precipitation of electrons there was implied. The flow of

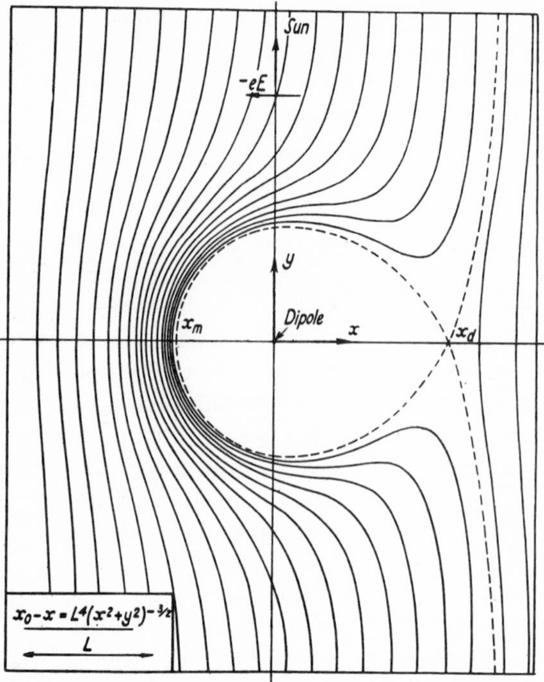

Fig. 15.5 Representative pattern of solar electron trajectories after Alfvén [14]. The total magnetic field consists of that from a dipole directed into the page and a superimposed constant field directed out from the page; the electrons are incident from the sun at the top, and are subject to a force of magnitude eE in the $-x$ direction, caused by an electric field **E** directed toward the right; the electrons are found to be excluded from a central 'forbidden region,' $x_m\, x_d$. Protons from the sun would follow similar paths, mirror-symmetric about the y axis. The spatial scales for both electrons and protons are dependent on their respective energies.

current that was thereby established was taken to be completed at ionospheric levels, by an eastward current on the evening side of the earth and a westward current on the morning side, in conformity with the electrojets.

Alfvén's theory, which included other aspects still to be discussed, has met with objection on several grounds. Quite apart from the loose arguments that characterize it at several points, it suffers from a degree of internal inconsistency—$\mathbf{E}_s$ alone is used in computing trajectories, whereas resultant polarization fields alone are used in discussing precipitation and ionospheric currents, for example—and of course it fails to take account of information subsequently gained, such as the high conductivity of the magnetosphere (which would rapidly discharge the $\mathbf{E}_s$ field) and the major importance of Hall currents in the ionosphere (which, if the polarization fields were operative, would lead to a current system almost opposite to the one inferred observationally). Interest in Alfvén's theory, though not yet abandoned, is now largely historic, save for one essential aspect yet to be discussed.

The prevalent present view is that the observed *DS* system represents primarily a flow of Hall current, though, of course, associated Pedersen currents (of weaker intensity) must also flow and must be completed by currents along the geomagnetic field lines to the distant magnetosphere. Several mechanisms have been proposed whereby such a system of currents might be set up, but none is as yet widely accepted. They all imply, however, the existence of ionospheric electric fields, and these fields have further implications. A preliminary assessment of the effects has been made by Axford and Hines [15], and several areas of interest have thereby been established. A brief outline of their analysis follows here; further aspects will be discussed in context in subsequent sections.

Axford and Hines begin with the picture of a solar plasma sweeping past a magnetosphere shaped as in Fig. 1.5 and, for conceptual purposes, postulate a continuous viscous-like interaction at the boundary, though they note that almost all the other mechanisms currently postulated would operate as effectively for their purposes. They then infer a sweeping of the outer magnetospheric ionization toward the geomagnetic tail, and a return flow through the interior. The topology of the convective pattern is necessarily of the form depicted in Fig. 15.6, whereas the precise pattern is inferred somewhat empirically. The motion is of the hydromagnetic type, and so is associated with an electric field $\mathbf{E}_{DS}$ given by $\mathbf{B}_E \times \mathbf{V}_{DS}$, where $\mathbf{B}_E$ is the geomagnetic induction and $\mathbf{V}_{DS}$ the imposed velocity of the magnetospheric plasma; the flow lines of $\mathbf{V}_{DS}$ are then contours of constant potential, as are the magnetic field lines (within the relevant order of approximation). The electric potential implied by the flow lines is carried down the field lines to ionospheric heights, where it drives the Hall currents that constitute the bulk of the observed *DS* system. The leakage of space charge that results from the associ-

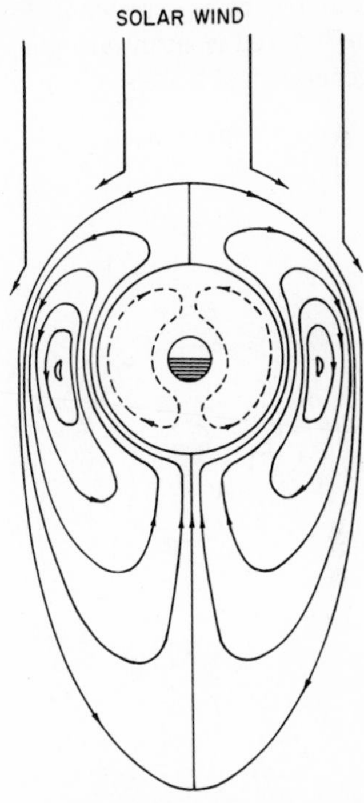

Fig. 15.6 Representative convective pattern in the earth's magnetosphere, in equatorial section, inferred by Axford and Hines [15]. The flow lines also represent equipotentials, each differing from its neighbor by about 2 Kv in the case of a moderate storm, but variable from quiet to storm conditions.

ated Pedersen currents must be replenished continuously by the initial driving mechanism, if the Hall currents are to be maintained, and some balance must be struck which determines the general intensity of the *DS* system as a whole. Within the limits of the postulated driving mechanism, departures of the observed Hall currents from symmetry about the sun-earth axis are attributed to longitudinal variations in ionospheric conductivity and to the action of ionospheric winds which are themselves established as a result of the current flow, but some other possible mechanisms are freer from a constraint to symmetry.

Axford and Hines have also stressed the role that must be played by rotation, through the action of an electric field of the type mentioned in Sec. 6.2. When its potential is added to that of $\mathbf{E}_{DS}$, and co-rotation of the polar regions is assumed, the net pattern of magnetospheric circulation is found to be as depicted in Fig. 15.7. Among the consequences that may now be inferred is an inward convection of any irregularities that may have been generated at the magnetospheric boundary, or of solar plasma that may have been captured there, along a sinuous band that follows the flow lines of Fig. 15.7 inward through the geomagnetic tail to the interior of the magnetosphere. This band maps down to ionospheric levels (along magnetic field lines) into another which curves down from polar to auroral latitudes in the hours immediately preceding and following local midnight, and which may be associated with an observed 'spiral' zone (marked *A* in Fig. 13.8) of enhanced magnetic irregularity, auroral production, and type *f* sporadic *E*. The occurrence of the zone may then be a natural consequence of the same processes that give rise to the *DS* current system, whatever their nature may ultimately prove to be.

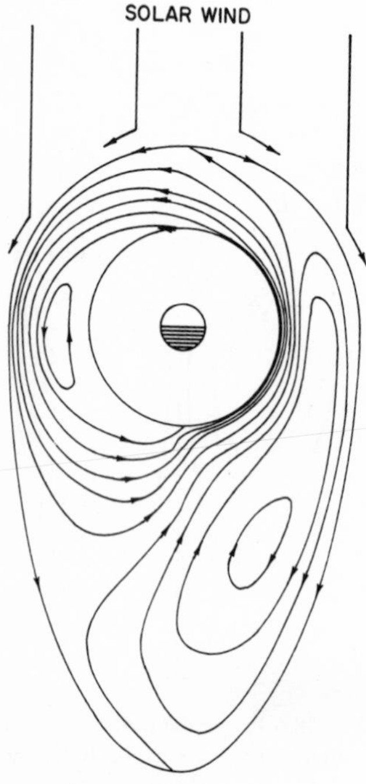

Fig. 15.7 Composite convective pattern, in equatorial section, that results from the superpositioning of the pattern in Fig. 15.6 and the normal rotation of the magnetospheric material. (After Axford and Hines [15].)

15.2.4. Main-phase *Dst* System. The longitude-independent *Dst* component of the main phase varies sufficiently slowly with latitude to suggest that its principal origin lies at some very great distance, well above the lower ionosphere. Its most characteristic feature—a decrease in the horizontal magnetic component at ground level, at low to middle latitudes—could be produced by a ring of electric current in the equatorial plane, flowing westward around the earth at a height of several earth radii, provided that the intervening medium did not shield the earth from the direct magnetic effects. This proviso can be met if the current is established appropriately, within the region where the geomagnetic field is dominant. The concept of a ring current was introduced by Störmer in connection with auroral theory, but it was first incorporated in geomagnetic storm theory by Chapman and Ferraro [16]. Their approach was admittedly provisional, as was a subsequent extension by Martyn [17] to account for related *DS* effects, and both have been abandoned. The concept of a ring current nevertheless remains, though in greatly altered form, as a central feature of most theories of the main phase.

The starting point of modern ring-current theory was provided by Alfvén, in his analysis of drifts due to inhomogeneities of the magnetic field. His particular application of that analysis to storm theory has already been given in a partial outline, but the point that is now of specific interest was suppressed there: the electron trajectories depicted in Fig. 15.5 depart from straight lines by virtue of velocity components which are directed more or less eastward round the earth, while the corresponding proton velocity components are directed more or less westward. The shared motion $\mathbf{V}_s$ of course leads to no effective current flow, but these oppositely directed azimuthal components imply a net westward current at great height, in harmony with the requirements of the main-phase *Dst* variation.

The next major step in the development of ring-current theory was made by Singer [18], who avoided the less attractive aspects of Alfvén's development and so focused attention more sharply on the importance of drifts. He postulated the actual trapping of solar plasma within the geomagnetic field, and hence its continuous circulation there, in contrast to the partial circulation of transitory particles as envisaged by Alfvén. This trapping was to occur within the normally inaccessible but nevertheless 'allowed' inner region of Störmer's theory (Chapter 5).

Singer's description made use of Alfvén's 'guiding center' approximation, and was exemplified most clearly by the drift component,

$$\mathbf{v}'_D = \left(\frac{v_\perp^2}{2\omega_c B^2}\right)(\mathbf{B} \times \nabla B), \tag{15.1}$$

of Eq. (5.26), applied for particle velocities confined to the equatorial plane. In this, $v_\perp$ was taken to be 2000 km/sec, whereas $\mathbf{B}$ was taken to be the unperturbed dipole induction $\mathbf{B}_E$. It may be deduced from (15.1) that positive ions will drift westward around the earth and electrons, with much smaller velocity, eastward. A westward current will then flow, in conformity with the characteristic magnetic variation of the main phase.

Singer also took some account of the drift component,

$$\mathbf{v}''_D = \left(\frac{v_\parallel^2}{\omega_c B^2}\right)(\mathbf{B} \times \nabla B) \tag{15.2}$$

of Eq. (5.27), which derives from the component of a particle's motion along the magnetic field and which is directed in the same sense as $\mathbf{v}'_D$. Subsequent investigations, [19] for example, have tended to lay more stress on this component than on $\mathbf{v}'_D$ since

$$\frac{v''_D}{v'_D} = \frac{2v_{\parallel}^2}{v_{\perp}^2} \tag{15.3}$$

—that is, a given particle speed parallel to $\mathbf{B}_E$ is of greater consequence than the same speed perpendicular to $\mathbf{B}_E$ in producing a drift motion. The effectiveness of this imbalance depends, of course, on the distribution of motions between the parallel and perpendicular components, and this distribution has yet to be established for the full spectrum of relevant particles.

A further complication is introduced by the diamagnetic influence of the spiraling charges. This influence has been evaluated for certain models by Dessler and Parker [19]. They find, for example, that if the trapped particles are confined to the equatorial plane, the diamagnetic effect cancels a third of the magnetic field produced by the drift $\mathbf{v}'_D$, for a measurement made at the center of the current system (or at ground level, in practice). In another model it opposes the measurable field of $\mathbf{v}'_D$ even more strongly. Since the diamagnetic effect and the drift $\mathbf{v}'_D$ both derive from the transverse velocity component $v_{\perp}$, these conclusions further attenuate the role attributed to the $v_{\perp}$ component and enhance that of $v_{\parallel}$.

Dessler and Parker go on to consider the consequences of the diamagnetic behavior at the mirror points of the trapped particles. These are such as to reduce the vertical component of field strength at ground level directly below. A decrease is indeed observed at latitudes of 55°–65°, as a part of the main-phase *Dst* behavior. For this decrease to be caused in the manner suggested, the belt of relevant trapped particles would have to extend between geocentric distances of about four and six earth radii in the equatorial plane.

Although this new model of the ring current appears capable of explaining the gross structure of the main-phase *Dst* system empirically, there remains the problem of the initial introduction of particles into the trapped orbits. Singer's original suggestion was that the geomagnetic field becomes sufficiently distorted during the early stages of a storm to permit the entry of solar particles into otherwise inaccessible regions. On recovery to its more normal distribution, the field would then enclose and trap the particles.

A variant of this was incorporated into the work of Dessler and Parker, who expected that instabilities at the interface between the magnetosphere and the solar gas would result in the formation of small blobs of solar plasma and that these could distort the geomagnetic field locally and push their way into the trapping region. There they would diffuse onto the field lines and become trapped as a consequence of collisional interactions. This description is now more or less abandoned, though it has been replaced by an alternative [20]: hydromagnetic shock waves, generated by the impact of the storm plasma on the magnetosphere, act to energize the ambient terrestial ionization in the geomagnetic tail region. When energized, this ionization will tend to drift faster, according to (15.1) and (15.2), and so will produce an enhanced current flow. This proposal, taken by itself, faces the difficulty that energetic ionization in the tail region is not suitably located to produce a ring current girding the earth.

Axford and Hines [15] have stressed that the electric fields of the *DS* system are likely to play a part in the production of a ring current. For, as should now be noted, the magnetospheric ionization becomes energized in the course of its inward convection on the night side of the earth, and so becomes more susceptible to '∇B' drift motions. The energization process may be thought of hydromagnetically as a consequence of compression, the ionization being 'frozen' within tubes of magnetic flux whose dimensions are diminishing as they move inward (to bring them into conformity with the geomagnetic field as it exists in the interior); alternatively, it may be described more classically as a consequence of the $\mathbf{E}_{DS}$ field, and may be calculated in a manner analogous to that of Alfvén (but with $\mathbf{E}_{DS}$ replacing Alfvén's $\mathbf{E}_s$, and the ionization now incident from the night side by virtue of convection rather than directly from the sunward side).

Simultaneously, of course, ionization of the interior regions is being carried outward and de-energized on the day side of the magnetosphere, so its contribution to a ring-like current is lost. Whether there results a net enhancement or diminution of the current is a question that cannot yet be answered, for it depends on the pre-storm distribution of ionization and this is not adequately known; but there is reason to believe that little change would result from this process acting alone.

On the other hand, if the ionization of the geomagnetic tail is first energized by shock waves and then convected to the interior, a net increase of ring current should result. The same is true if ionization from the external storm plasma should become entrapped in the outermost regions of the magnetosphere, by small-scale processes of the type envisaged by Singer or by Dessler and Parker, for it too would be carried inward and energized further. In both of these cases, the ring-like behavior of the current would be more of the nature described by Alfvén than that described by Singer, for the effective ionization would only be in transit through the interior of the geomagnetic field (but now *toward* the sun) as it makes its contribution.

The convection process can give rise also to a trapped component of ring current, however, if it can lead to an irreversible energization of ionization within the low-latitude torus of field lines. This seems to be possible by means of the turbulence that is carried to the interior of the magnetosphere, or as a consequence of temporal changes in the *DS* system, both of which can lead to variations of the otherwise 'invariant' parameters of the energized ionization (see Sec. 5.5).

Within the framework provided by these views, the 'main phase' proper would come to an end when the mechanism that drives the *DS* system ceases to operate. Any properly 'trapped' component of the ring current that was established during the main phase would remain, however, and could contribute to the 'recovery' phase of the *Dst* variation. This component would gradually be lost, probably predominantly through the action of charge-exchange with neutral atoms at thermal energies [19].

15.2.5. Elementary Polar Storms and Bays. The foregoing discussion of storm theories has been concerned primarily with the large-scale, statistically important features of storms, whereas much evidence points to the importance of bursts of activity, localized in space and time, as a fundamental feature [21]. These 'elementary polar storms' or 'polar substorms' exhibit strong effects for a period of an hour or so, largely concentrated in the zones of maximum auroral occurrence and most often in the early morning hours. Similar bursts of lesser intensity are observed, even in the absence of storms, as isolated magnetic bays.

There has been a tendency among theorists to ignore these events, in the hope that they might be explained as some minor fluctuation of the larger pattern once the latter itself is understood. They may however represent a fundamental change of conditions. This suggestion can be based on a theory advanced by Dungey [22, 23] to account for the *DS* system. He postulates a magnetic field exterior to the earth's and directed southward, and then infers a topology of field lines and a pattern of plasma flow as illustrated in Fig. 15.8. This leads to a distribution of electric fields, and to

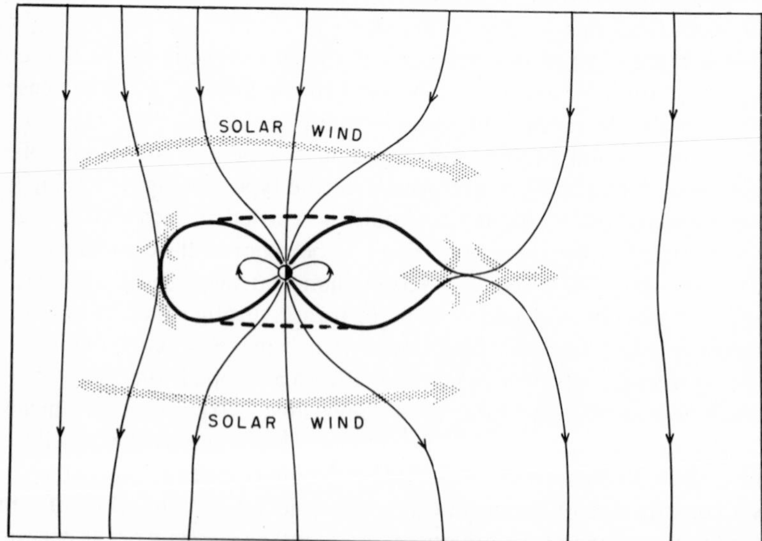

Fig. 15.8 Magnetic field-line configuration (thin lines) and solar plasma flow (shaded arrows) envisaged by Dungey [22].

secondary processes, of a type already discussed in connection with the work of Axford and Hines, save only for modifications imposed by the topological change in the configuration of field lines. This change is of major import, however, in that it provides a direct coupling between the storm plasma and the magnetospheric ionization and leads to a direct injection of solar material at a magnetic 'neutral point' (or neutral line) on the night side of the earth.

Dungey's mechanism has met objection primarily on the ground that the external magnetic field should not normally be as he describes, both theory and observation pointing more strongly to an external field that is confined primarily to a spiral direction outward from the sun (Chapter 10). Departures from this direction are to be expected in the body of a storm plasma, however, and irregular fluctuations of the external magnetic field are detected even during solar quiet. The topology of Fig. 15.8 may then suddenly be 'switched on' in the course of a storm, or even in its absence, and so may account for the intensifications observed as elementary polar storms or isolated bays.

15.3. AURORAL THEORY

The basic phenomenon which has to be explained by an auroral theory is the emission of light from the earth's upper atmosphere. The characteristics of these emissions have been described in Chapter 13; in Chapter 14 we saw that they are frequently accompanied by the appearance of abnormal amounts of ionization in the ionosphere. The production both of light and of ionization could be explained by the bombardment of the upper atmosphere by a suitable flux of either electromagnetic radiation or high-energy charged particles. It would be extremely difficult to explain the often sharply defined forms of the aurora and its tendency to occur most frequently in a certain range of geomagnetic latitudes on the basis of electromagnetic radiation as a cause, and nearly all serious theories to date have postulated particle bombardment of the upper atmosphere as the immediate cause of the aurora. This much, then, we may take as reasonably certain, and it is from this point that the theories start to diverge. Broadly speaking, the theories can be divided into two major groups: those that visualize the bombarding particles as being extraterrestrial in origin and those that propose the acceleration of particles already present in the ionosphere by the application of a suitable electric field, which can arise in a variety of ways. The current state of our observations of the aurora and of the development of the various theories is such that a decision in favor of one or other of these broad groups cannot yet be made.

Among the major features which any auroral theory must attempt to explain are:

1. The characteristic forms, heights, and spectra which have been described in Chapter 13;

2. The characteristic features of radio aurora described in Chapter 14;
3. The tendency for aurora to occur most frequently in zones centred at geomagnetic latitudes of about $\pm 67°$;
4. The close association between aurora and geomagnetic storms.

A few theories have taken this last feature as a starting point, and have developed an explanation of the aurora as an offshoot of a much more comprehensive theory of geomagnetic storms. These theories say very little about the detailed features of the aurora, which do not appear convincingly as a necessary consequence of the storm theory. Indeed there has been a distressing tendency to assume that the aurora is basically explained, except for details, if one can invent a mechanism for injecting particles into the atmosphere at approximately the correct location. In fact, most of these mechanisms would produce an enhancement of airglow, rather than aurora. Such an enhancement at high latitudes probably exists, but its connection with aurora has not been demonstrated.

Other theories have attempted to explain the visible auroral features, without discussing in any detail the magnetic storm effects that accompany them. Such an approach can be just as strongly criticized, but it is only by a thorough and painstaking examination of the successes and faults of all of these theories, and of new ones as they arise, that we can hope to arrive eventually at a successful explanation of these intriguing phenomena.

15.3.1. Störmer's Theory. Historically the first serious attempt at a detailed theory of the aurora was made by Störmer [24], who was led by the experiments of Birkeland and others to investigate mathematically the trajectories of charged particles in a dipole magnetic field. This theory has already been discussed in Chapter 5; here we merely consider its possible application to the aurora. For more complete details the reader is referred to Störmer's book.

The theory met with its greatest success in its explanation of many of the characteristic auroral forms, and especially the common rayed and homogeneous arcs. Störmer showed conclusively that if noninteracting charged particles were emitted in a group from a source of small angular dimensions, such as the sun, they would precipitate on the earth in the form of a long narrow arc inclined at a slight angle to the parallels of geomagnetic latitude, provided that certain conditions were fulfilled. The most important of these were that the particles had to have the same velocity, which is not inconceivable, since they arrive at the earth simultaneously, and that the source should have certain preferred declinations. This latter condition is not so easy to fulfill, since auroral arcs can be seen at all seasons of the year, during which the sun occupies a variety of declinations.

The theory encounters more fundamental difficulties in attempting to explain the location of the auroral zones. It can be shown from the theory that the lowest geomagnetic latitude l_0, at which a particle of mass m, charge q, and velocity v is capable of reaching the earth (radius r_e), is given by

$$\cos l_0 = (2r_e/C_{st})^{1/2} \tag{15.4}$$

where C_{st} is the Störmer unit of length, defined in Chapter 5, Eq. (5.23). When auroral particles are considered, l_0 may be taken as the lower latitude of the normal auroral zone, say 67°; it may then be inferred that the relevant particles would have to have energies of at least 60 Mev. Protons with this amount of energy would be capable of penetrating the atmosphere down to a height of about 40 km, and it becomes difficult to explain the normally observed confinement of auroral luminosity to heights of 100 km or more. The occasional appearance of aurora at latitudes much lower than 67° is even more difficult to explain on this basis.

To avoid these difficulties Störmer postulated the existence of a permanent ring current around the earth. Such a current would have the effect of reducing the total field in the neighborhood of the ring, and thus would allow particles to approach the earth at lower latitudes than would otherwise be possible. This ring current should not be confused with that just discussed; to have its maximum effect, the Störmer ring would have to be located at about 1 Störmer unit from the earth. In the case of a proton of speed 10^7 m/sec, which can just penetrate to auroral heights, we have for the radius of the ring $R = 2.8 \times 10^8$ m $= 44r_e$. The ring current postulated in magnetic storm theory is thought to have a radius of less than $10r_e$ and would not have a large enough effect on auroral particles.

Apart from this difficulty in accounting for the location of the auroral zones, the basic assumptions on which Störmer's theory is built are such that any application of the theory to the aurora must be regarded with great suspicion. In particular the interactions between the incoming particles have been neglected, each particle being treated as though there were no other particles present. In fact, consideration of magnetic storm effects points fairly conclusively to the density of the incoming stream being much too high to justify this point of view. The stream must rather be regarded as a plasma capable of supporting currents which will in turn give rise to additional magnetic fields. Despite these arguments, Störmer's theory is still cited from time to time to explain certain observed details of auroral phenomena, and indeed the state of our knowledge is not yet such that these explanations can be rejected out of hand. Auroral theory over the last three decades, however, has swung away from Störmer's theory to theories which, though much less exact, do take some account of the interactions between the particles and of their effect on the geomagnetic field.

15.3.2. The Chapman-Ferraro and Martyn Contributions. As mentioned above, Chapman and Ferraro [10] investigated the advance of a neutral ionized stream into the geomagnetic field and concluded that the stream would be brought to a halt in front of the earth, at the point where the magnetic energy density became equal to the kinetic energy density of the stream. The resultant magnetic field in the neighborhood of the earth would be the resultant of the geomagnetic field and the field due to the currents induced in the stream-front, and this could be inferred approximately from an image-dipole model. It can easily be seen that the original and image fields cancel in two regions, symmetrically situated on either side of the equatorial plane, where the dipole lines of force meet the stream front at right angles (see Fig. 15.3). Chapman and Ferraro visualized the development of 'horns' of ionized material protruding toward the earth from these field-free regions. These horns might seem to have some significance from the point of view of introducing material into the magnetosphere, but there is no apparent mechanism for accelerating the particles to the energies necessary to penetrate to auroral heights in the atmosphere. Furthermore, the horns should be present only on the sunward side of the earth and would not explain the nocturnal occurrence of aurora.

Martyn [17] investigated some of the consequences of the existence of a ring current in the earth's equatorial plane, of the type postulated by Chapman and Ferraro [16]. He presented arguments for the location and intensity of the ring current, and pointed out that the instability of the surface charges on the ring could explain the precipitation of energetic charged particles in the auroral zone. These surface charges were inferred to be under the influence of a repulsive electric field of the order of 10^{-1} volt/m, applied over a distance of about 10^7 m, so that they could be accelerated to energies of 1 Mev, which is ample to account for their penetration to auroral heights. Also they would be guided along the lines of force of the earth's magnetic field, which from Martyn's proposed location of the ring current would carry them into the auroral zone. No attempt has been made to expand this proposal to account for the details of auroral morphology, and indeed the basis of it has now been abandoned.

15.3.3. Alfvén's Theory. It will be recalled that Alfvén envisaged electrons and ions from a solar stream following paths of the form depicted in Fig. 15.5, except that precipitation of these particles was thought to occur at the boundary of the 'forbidden region' in the centre of the diagram. His views on auroral production followed from this picture, for he suggested that the aurora is a consequence of the precipitation process and then identified an auroral arc as the projection of the boundary of the forbidden region down the magnetic field lines into the earth's atmosphere. The direct precipitation process could be augmented by a discharge mechanism at auroral heights, established in connection with the closing currents he took to flow there.

This theory has the advantage of a local acceleration mechanism (in the field $\mathbf{E}_s$) which could raise the 1000 km/sec particles of the storm plasma to the energies required for precipitation to auroral heights, and it does permit the formation of an auroral zone at about the right latitudes. But from several points of view, it is also subject to severe criticism of a type already indicated, and the criticisms weigh most heavily against some of the details of the argument on which closest observational support is claimed. Even if Alfvén's general thesis were accepted, moreover, it would do little to advance the explanation of auroral morphology.

15.3.4. *DS*-associated Theories. As indicated in the preceding sections, theory for the main-phase *DS* system of a magnetic storm is now mainly based on the use of Hall current systems driven by an electric field $\mathbf{E}_{DS}$. Any such theory can be extended to include some aspects of auroral production, as Axford and Hines have argued. The energization provided by $\mathbf{E}_{DS}$, or by 'compression' in hydromagnetic terms, has already been discussed in connection with the ring current, but it is equally effective for the production of auroral primaries. The potential from which it derives is estimated to be a few tens of kilovolts, from the strength of the currents observed, and individual particles are then susceptible to energization by a few tens of kiloelectron volts. This is certainly adequate to permit electrons to reach auroral heights, or, if added to the energy of previously trapped protons, may be adequate for them as well.

Moreover, in contrast to Alfvén's theory, it can be directly inferred and not merely postulated that precipitation would be enhanced, for a further consequence of the compression process is a lowering of the mirror heights of trapped particles.

This lowering is of a relatively slow and large-scale nature, however, and it must be augmented by some smaller-scale process if it is to account for the relatively sharp auroral forms that are observed (though it may be adequate, of itself, to account for large-scale stable emissions, such as those of hydrogen discussed in Sec. 13.12). Turbulence convected to the interior, in a manner already indicated, may serve this latter function, and indeed enhanced auroral emissions and ionization are to be found along the expected path. That path reaches conventional auroral latitudes near midnight and persists there in the hours immediately following, just at the times of maximum auroral agitation.

A further feature that would be shared by all these *DS*-associated theories is an explanation of the pattern of motion revealed by small-scale auroral irregularities. This pattern is of much the same form as the inferred *DS* current system, though oppositely directed, and it then corresponds closely (after upward mapping along the geomagnetic field lines) to the pattern of convection high in the magnetosphere that is illustrated by Fig. 15.6, or by Fig. 15.7 with rotation included. This suggests that the observed irregularities move as a direct consequence of $\mathbf{E}_{DS}$, whether they are formed only locally at ionospheric heights or caused by precipitation from unobserved irregularities at greater heights. The relevant motion is that described in Chap. 7, as an $\mathbf{E} \times \mathbf{B}/B^2$ drift.

To these various attributes of *DS*-associated auroral production, Dungey's theory adds the further, perhaps useful, complication of a neutral point from which fresh solar particles may be supplied continuously.

15.3.5. The Self-focused Stream Theory. Bennett and Hulburt [25] proposed the existence of solar ion streams with completely different properties from those we have been discussing. They visualized the emission from the sun of a neutral cloud of ions and electrons, as before, but they argued that particles would be removed by scattering from the cloud, during the latter's passage through the corona, and that this process should be much more effective for the electrons than for the ions. After its passage through the corona, then, the cloud would consist predominantly of fast positive ions, which would draw in thermal electrons from the nearby interplanetary medium to preserve its electrical neutrality. Such a cloud of ions would constitute a current and must have a magnetic field associated with it. According to Bennett and Hulburt, this magnetic field may be strong enough to constrict the cloud into a narrow beam by the mechanism now generally known as the 'pinch effect.'

This mechanism appears to have two major advantages in its application to the aurora: (1) it provides a means of sending a beam of particles with one sign of charge from the sun to the earth, thereby perhaps preserving some of the features of Störmer's theory; (2) it provides for a very narrow beam of particles, a feature which appears to be required to explain some observational aspects of auroral occurrence and duration. The first of these advantages is dubious at best, however, and indeed it is not at all certain that Störmer's theory would apply to such a beam.

Again this theory says little about the details of auroral morphology, though perhaps Störmer's explanation of many auroral forms could be preserved. Bennett has carried out a series of experiments involving the bombardment of a magnetized sphere by a narrow beam of ions and has claimed that the results demonstrate many of the observed features of the aurora. All such experiments using models, however, are open to the criticism that one cannot interpret what is happening in the experiment any more than one can interpret the aurora; consequently their usefulness is strictly limited.

15.3.6. Discharge Theories. The auroral theories we have been discussing so far have one feature in common: they attribute the aurora to the direct impact of solar particles on the earth's atmosphere. They differ widely in the properties they attribute to the solar beam, and unfortunately the closer these properties seem to approach to physical reality, the less exact the theory becomes, and the more difficult it is to find a criterion on which to accept or reject a theory. Störmer's theory, which is as exact as one can possibly expect, deals with individual noninteracting particles and is physically applicable only to beams of exceedingly low density, such as cosmic rays. Chapman and Ferraro approached closer to reality by considering dense beams in which electrostatic and electrodynamic forces played a part. Alfvén was less concerned with the particle interactions, but introduced a magnetic field into the beam, which certainly does exist. Bennett and Hulburt returned to a Störmer-like approach and took account of the ambient interplanetary medium, but they ignored the electrodynamic effects that would arise in the vicinity of the earth. Axford and Hines treat the plasma properties of the magnetosphere extensively but leave for separate discussion the means by which these properties are called into play by the passage of the solar stream; although several mechanisms have been proposed, both by them and independently by others, the relevant ones have yet to be determined and Dungey's at best is complicated by the further uncertainties that arise with neutral points present. No theory has yet been proposed which combines all of the desirable features and discusses their interactions with each other and with the geomagnetic field; indeed the complexity of the problem is such that we can probably never hope to have an exact physical description of the effects of storm plasma on reaching the earth.

In recent years there has been a certain amount of speculation concerning the possible role of electrical discharges in the upper atmosphere as an alternative explanation of the aurora. As just mentioned, Alfvén's theory invokes a discharge, but the characteristic features it would be expected to show are not discussed.

Lebedinski [26] has attempted to explain the ray and arc forms of the aurora as a direct consequence of a discharge. He assumes that a solar ion stream flowing past the earth will leave a hollow around the earth, and that this hollow will contain an electric field of approximate strength $|\mathbf{V}_s \times \mathbf{B}_e|$ where $\mathbf{V}_s$ is the velocity of the stream as before (Sec. 15.2.3) and $\mathbf{B}_e$ is the value of $\mathbf{B}_s$ at the edge of the (spherical) hollow. He thereby obtains an estimate of the total potential drop across the hollow. This potential is applied to the ionosphere via the highly conducting lines of force, and there it causes electrical breakdown of the gas and hence the auroral luminosity. Rays are thought to arise where the current flows vertically down the lines of force, whereas arcs represent the horizontal flow which completes the discharge. Chamberlain [2] has pointed out justly that the concept of breakdown potential applies only to a gas which has no free ions present (or at least only a few, such as would be produced by cosmic rays or local radioactivity). It cannot be applied to the ionosphere, where free electrons already exist in sizable numbers and must merely be accelerated to produce luminosity. The theory could possibly be modified to meet this objection, but this has apparently not yet been done.

Wulf [27] has proposed that aurora (and also airglow) might be due to a glow discharge produced by dynamo action in the earth's upper atmosphere. The prime energy source in this theory is a zonal wind which blows ionization across the magnetic field, setting up a $\mathbf{B}_E \times \mathbf{V}$ electric field which causes a meridional polarizing current flow in the lower ionosphere. Wulf suggests that the luminosity is produced by a glow discharge representing the closing of the current loop through the upper ionosphere.

This suggestion has been supported and extended by Vestine [28], who further suggested that the variability of the zonal winds can, if the conductivity is high enough, cause a variable magnetic field capable of accelerating auroral particles by a betatron mechanism. This suggestion removes the question of solar ion beams from the picture entirely, except possibly as a means of creating the high auroral-zone wind velocities and high conductivity. The betatron mechanism would accelerate positive ions downward and electrons upward from about the 150-km level, thereby explaining the observed Doppler shift of the hydrogen lines in the auroral spectrum. A major disadvantage, pointed out by Vestine himself, is that positive ions other than hydrogen should also be accelerated downward, and their radiation should also be Dopper-shifted. This has not been observed.

Atmospheric dynamo theories of the aurora have been suggested by other authors, most recently by Cole [29], who attempted to explain auroral motions and magnetic bays by this mechanism.

Chamberlain [30] has made an attempt to develop a quantitative discharge theory of auroral rays. Using the observed luminosity of the 5577 Å line of oxygen and the constancy of the luminosity of a ray with height, he deduced the steady electric field necessary to produce the ray as a discharge. If the base of the ray is at 120 km, the required electric field is about 5×10^{-3} volt/m at this height, assuming the electron number density to be about 10^6 cm^{-3}. Electric fields of this magnitude could be set up readily by dynamo action. Unfortunately, however, no account was taken of the presence of the geomagnetic field in this theory, so the conclusion can be applied only to electric fields whose direction is along the magnetic field. For electric fields in other directions, the electron energy distribution would be radically altered by the presence of the magnetic field, and the computed electric field strength would no longer be applicable. Using Chamberlain's expression for the ionospheric current density created by an electric field, Reid [31] has attempted to give a qualitative description of the development of a typical auroral display, assuming the prime cause to be a potential difference somehow maintained between regions in the earth's magnetic field at great distances from the earth. This approach appears to give some hope of explaining the seasonal and diurnal characteristics of the aurora, as well as the temporal variations during a single display, but it has not yet been put on a firm theoretical and quantitative basis.

15.3.7. Trapped Radiation and Auroral Theory. The discovery by Van Allen and his co-workers of the great radiation belts surrounding the earth immediately raised the hopes of auroral theorists. Here was a new source which could presumably inject particles into the upper atmosphere and create the aurora. Indeed Van Allen suggested this link in his first reports on the discovery of the radiation belts. Unfortunately the hopes for an early and complete solution of the auroral problem on the basis of trapped particles entering the earth's atmosphere have not yet been realized. It is probable, however, that any future auroral theory must take account of the existence of energetic trapped particles in these regions. As we have seen earlier, magnetic storm theory has made considerable progress by introducing the concept of trapped particles, and presumably this progress must reflect on auroral theory in some way not yet evident.

One specific suggestion in this connection bears mention, though its relevance is highly controversial. Akasofu and Chapman [32] have argued that the trapped-particle intensity may rise to such strength during a storm, and produce such a strong ring current, that the geomagnetic field is reduced to the vanishing point and even reversed high in the magnetosphere. They visualize the formation of 'neutral lines' extending over a wide range of longitudes on the night side, at geocentric distances of five or six earth radii. At such lines, energetic trapped particles that normally mirror well above the dense atmosphere could be deflected and precipitated down to auroral levels: Akasofu and Chapman argue that this is the mechanism of auroral arc formation. The existence of the requisite neutral lines is not generally accepted, however, and many feel that they could not be established in the magnetosphere in any stable manner. This question has yet to be resolved.

As we have seen in Chapter 13, rocket flights into visible aurora have demonstrated the existence of large fluxes of electrons with energies in the 10–20 Kev region. If we accept for the moment that the excitation of the atmospheric gases by these electrons is sufficient to cause the auroral luminosity (a point which is not yet certain), we must then explain the presence of the electrons, and why they appear only in the characteristic forms of the aurora (rays, arcs, etc.) and not over wide areas of the sky, where they would merely produce a diffuse glow. We must also explain such features as the diurnal variation and the equinoctial maximum of auroral occurrence. Little progress has so far been made along these lines, although one or two hopeful clues have appeared. Present indications are that the outer portions of the trapped radiation belts normally contain a large flux of electrons whose energy is in the range required to explain the auroral electrons. At the onset of a magnetic storm, this flux apparently drops sharply, perhaps indicating that electrons have somehow been dumped into the earth's atmosphere, producing auroral luminosity. The drop in the flux is followed by a rapid rise during the next day or two, up to a value several times the pre-storm flux. The explanation of this rise, which would seem to be of fundamental importance, is by no means clear. It could arise either from the replenishment of the outer belt by fresh particles, presumably of solar origin, or from an acceleration of particles already existing in the region up to energies high enough to be recorded by the measuring equipment. In the former case, we must explain the continued arrival of these particles for a day or two after the main force of the storm is over; in the latter, we must provide an acceleration mechanism in the earth's magnetosphere. In any case, the connection between these observations and the aurora is only by inference and is not established.

The outer Van Allen belt can show a considerable amount of fine structure during a magnetic storm [33], and on at least one occasion this fine structure was apparently mapped down to the earth's atmosphere in the form of fine structure in the auroral luminosity [34]. If verified by other observations, this would seem to suggest that the characteristic auroral forms may merely be the result of mapping the characteristic fine structure of the trapped radiation down the field lines from the magnetosphere to the ionosphere. This would be a result of great importance to auroral theory.

15.4. CONCLUSION

Few natural phenomena have given birth to such a wide range of theoretical speculation and development as have magnetic storms and auroral emissions—and with so little conclusive to show for it, we might add. The developments of recent years have, however, narrowed the range of study and provided the tools whereby it may be pursued more effectively. As our understanding of hydromagnetic processes and trapped-particle behavior grows, the areas of possible theoretical maneuver become lessened; and as rockets, satellites, and space vehicles provide further data of incontrovertible nature, those areas will be narrowed to specific channels. For the present, however, a wide variety of processes must be kept in mind for the discussion of these storm events and tested against the new observations as they become available. The phenomena remain among the most fascinating available in the world around us.

REFERENCES

1. Matsushita, S., and W. H. Campbell, (eds.), Physics of Geomagnetic Phenomena. New York: Academic Press (on press).
2. Chamberlain, J. W., Theories of the aurora, in Advances in Geophysics, eds. H. E. Landsberg and J. Van Mieghem. New York: Academic Press, Vol. IV, 1958, p. 109.
3. Frenkiel, F. N., and W. R. Sears, (eds.), Symposium on magneto-fluid dynamics, *Rev. Mod. Phys.*, **32**, No. 4, (1960).

4. Nishida, A., and J. A. Jacobs, World-wide changes in the geomagnetic field, *J. Geophys. Res.*, **67** (1962), 525.

5. Piddington, J. H., A theory of polar geomagnetic storms, *Geophys. J.*, **3** (1960), 314.

6. Sugiura, M., Evidence of low-frequency hydromagnetic waves in the exosphere, *J. Geophys. Res.*, **66** (1961), 4087.

7. Wilson, C. R., and M. Sugiura, Hydromagnetic interpretation of sudden commencements of magnetic storms, *J. Geophys. Res.*, **66** (1961), 4097.

8. Jacobs, J. A., and T. Watanabe, The equatorial enhancement of sudden commencements of geomagnetic storms, *J. Atmos. Terr. Phys.* **25** (1963), 267.

9. Francis, W. E., M. I. Green, and A. J. Dessler, Hydromagnetic propagation of sudden commencements of magnetic storms, *J. Geophys. Res.*, **64** (1959), 1643.

10. Chapman, S., and V. C. A. Ferraro, A new theory of magnetic storms. Part I. The initial phase, *Terr. Mag. Atmos. Electr.*, **36** (1931), 171.

11. Mead, G. D., Deformation of the geomagnetic field by the solar wind, *J. Geophys. Res.*, **69** (1964), 1181.

12. Maeda, H., Wind systems for the geomagnetic S_d field, *J. Geomag. Geoelectr.*, **9** (1957), 119.

13. Fejer, J. A., Theory of auroral electrojets, *J. Geophys. Res.*, **68** (1963), 2147.

14. Alfvén, H., Cosmical Electrodynamics. Oxford: Clarendon Press, 1950.

15. Axford, W. I., and C. O. Hines, A unifying theory of high-latitude geophysical phenomena and geomagnetic storms, *Can. J. Phys.*, **39** (1961), 1433.

16. Chapman, S., and V. C. A. Ferraro, A new theory of magnetic storms. Part II. The main phase, *Terr. Mag. Atmos. Electr.*, **38** (1933), 79.

17. Martyn, D. F., The theory of magnetic storms and auroras, *Nature*, **167** (1951), 92.

18. Singer, S. F., A new model of magnetic storms and aurorae, *Trans. Am. Geophys. Un.* **38** (1957), 175.

19. Dessler, A. J., and E. N. Parker, Hydromagnetic theory of geomagnetic storms, *J. Geophys. Res.*, **64** (1959), 2239.

20. Dessler, A. J., W. B. Hanson, and E. N. Parker, A mechanism to establish the magnetic storm ring current, *J. Phys. Soc. Japan*, **17** Supp. A-I, (1962), 178.

21. Nagata, T., and N. Fukushima, Constitution of polar magnetic storms, *Rep. Ionos. Res. Japan*, **6** (1952), 85.

22. Dungey, J. W., The interplanetary field and auroral theory, *J. Phys. Soc. Japan*, **17**, Supp. A-II, (1962), 15.

23. Dungey, J. W., Interactions of solar plasma with the geomagnetic field, *Planet. Space Sci.*, **10** (1963), 233.

24. Störmer, C., The Polar Aurora. Oxford: Clarendon Press, 1955.

25. Bennett, W. H., and E. O. Hulburt, Magnetic self-focussed solar-ion streams as the cause of aurorae, *J. Atmos. Terr. Phys.*, **5** (1954), 211.

26. Lebedinsky, A. J., Electrical discharges and the interpretation of auroral types, in The Airglow and the Aurora, eds. E. B. Armstrong and A. Dalgarno. London: Pergamon Press, 1956, p. 222.

27. Wulf, O. R., On the production of glow discharges in the ionosphere by winds, *J. Geophys. Res.*, **58** (1953), 531.

28. Vestine, E. H., Winds in the upper atmosphere deduced from the dynamo theory of geomagnetic disturbance, *J. Geophys. Res.*, **59** (1954), 93.

29. Cole, K. D., A dynamo theory of the aurora and magnetic disturbance, *Aust. J. Phys.*, **13** (1960), 484.

30. Chamberlain, J. W., Discharge theory of auroral rays, in The Airglow and the Aurora, eds. E. B. Armstrong and A. Dalgarno. London: Pergamon Press, 1956, p. 206.

31. Reid, G. C., Electric field theory of aurorae, *Nature*, **182** (1958), 1791.

32. Akasofu, S. I., and S. Chapman, A neutral line discharge theory of the aurora polaris, *Phil. Trans. Roy. Soc. A*, **253** (1961), 359.

33. O'Brien, B. J., and G. H. Ludwig, Development of multiple radiation zones on October 18, 1959, *J. Geophys. Res.*, **65** (1960), 2695.

34. O'Brien, B. J., J. A. Van Allen, F. E. Roach, and C. W. Gartlein, Correlation of an auroral arc and a subvisible monochromatic 6300 A arc with outer-zone radiation on November 28, 1959, *J. Geophys. Res.*, **65** (1960), 2759.

16

Epilogue

The preceding chapters have tried to present a balanced and meaningful summary of existing knowledge of the physics of the earth's upper atmosphere. Attention has been concentrated largely on those physical phenomena that seemed particularly relevant to a unified picture. In the process relatively little attention was given to the many gaps, or 'areas of ignorance' in this picture. In this chapter we try to make up for this deficiency by listing some of the more important gaps and emphasizing those areas where the need for further research is strongly indicated.

Until recent years our knowledge of both the extent and the constitution of the upper atmosphere may be best described as sketchy. The lack of adequate data was a serious handicap in the construction of atmospheric models. Moreover, in retrospect, it appears that the earlier models neglected two vital features: the important role played by ionization—both thermal and energetic—at levels above the F-layer peak, and interaction effects between the atmosphere and its interplanetary environment. The use of sounding rockets, satellites, and deep-space probes to make measurements from above the bulk of the atmosphere has been a dominant factor in upper atmospheric research during the past decade. Equipment design for these purposes is still in its infancy, and it has not yet been possible to obtain adequate measurements of some of the important atmospheric parameters. Nevertheless, it has become quite apparent from the observations made to date that the two features previously mentioned are indeed vital and must be taken into account in any realistic model of the upper atmosphere. It should be emphasized that many of the pertinent geophysical and interplanetary measurements have been made over only relatively short intervals, or more specifically, for substantially less than one sunspot cycle. Extrapolation of the results to other epochs of the sunspot cycle, and to other sunspot cycles, must be considered as a speculative, rather than an analytic process. The theoretical difficulties are also still enormous, and it will be many years before a truly comprehensive picture of the upper atmosphere emerges.

Radiant energy from the sun has long been recognized as a controlling factor in many upper atmospheric processes, and continues to be intensively investigated for that reason. In addition to energy supplied by direct solar radiation, however, significant amounts of energy enter the upper atmosphere through dynamical coupling from the lower atmosphere, by interactions between the magnetosphere and the interplanetary medium, and possibly by the direct entry of energetic solar particles. None of these phenomena is particularly well understood.

Much of the gravity-wave spectrum that originates at lower levels is rapidly attenuated at heights above 100 km, but a preliminary assessment of the energy transferred by such waves, and of the importance of this energy to upper atmospheric phenomena, is only now becoming possible [7].

The mechanisms by which energy is transferred across the magnetospheric boundary are also uncertain. Two known complicating factors are the production of a 'standing shock front' by the normal solar wind, [4, 5], and the occasional occurrence of major disturbances in the flow of the solar wind. The standing shock front is at a distance of several earth radii 'upwind' of the magnetospheric boundary. The region between this shock front and the magnetosphere appears to differ substantially from both the interplanetary medium and the interior of the magnetosphere. During upper atmospheric storms, some solar material probably enters the magnetosphere, and both direct and indirect observations leave little doubt that large and rapid changes occur in the boundary of the magnetosphere and in the configuration of the magnetic field. In considering energy transfer problems, it would obviously be helpful to have more information on the nature, configuration, and extent of the standing shock front and the magnetospheric boundary and also on the fluxes of energetic particles in these regions. Plasma measurements made in deep-space probes from 1959 to 1962 provided only fragmentary data relating to these points. Attempts to obtain more detailed information are now in process, notably in the Interplanetary Monitoring Platform (IMP) series of satellites. The first of these was launched by the United States National Aeronautics and Space Administration in November, 1963, and quickly confirmed the existence of a standing shock front on the sunward side of, and somewhat 'upstream' from the magnetopause [6]. Furthermore, it revealed that the shock front randomizes the interplanetary magnetic field and the flow of solar plasma immediately outside the magnetopause proper, and that it apparently also leads to the production of electron energies of several Kev. These observations (along with others more extensive and more detailed that can be expected from future satellites) will undoubtedly be of major importance to an understanding of the total upper atmospheric storm process, but their full significance cannot yet be assessed.

Although particle energization processes in the magnetosphere are still not fully understood, efforts are being made to identify the energetic particles associated with the storm process and to correlate in detail the energetic particle fluxes with various upper atmospheric disturbance phenomena. The two following examples illustrate the rapid progress being made by direct measurements from earth satellites. Figure 16.1 shows the strong correlation between the intensity of auroral luminosity and the flux of energetic electrons observed by the Injun III satellite. Separate curves are given for electrons trapped in the radiation belts and for electrons that are being 'dumped' into the lower ionosphere where they are presumed to initiate the auroral pheno-

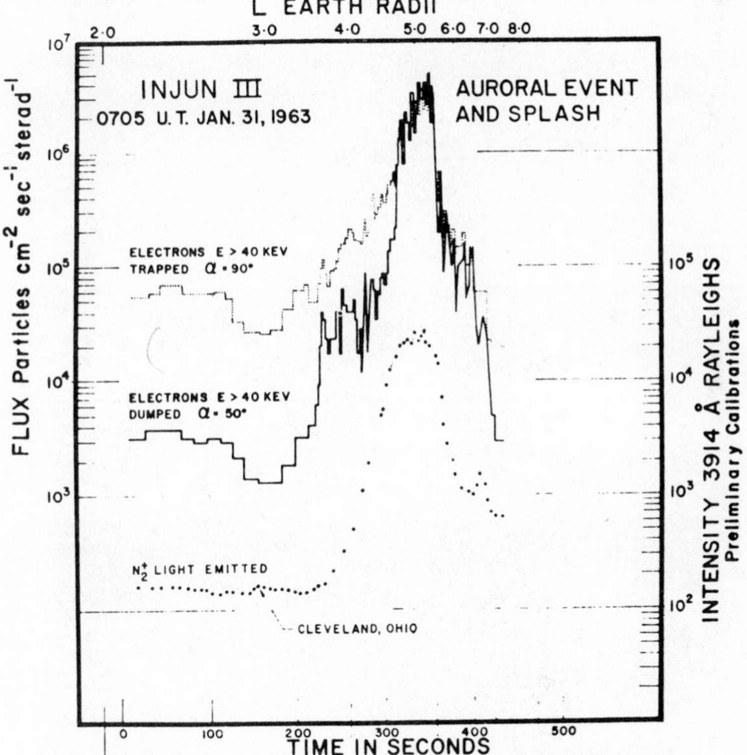

Fig. 16.1 The flux of energetic electrons on a field line and the intensity of auroral luminosity near the base of this field line, recorded by the Injun III satellite. (After O'Brien [2].)

mena. Another and quite different type of observation also shows great promise of providing information on processes in the magnetosphere. Satellite measurements of VLF emissions frequently show noise bands that are not observable on the ground, but which appear to depend on the properties of the plasma near the satellite: the noise bands are occasionally seen to depend on the geomagnetic field as illustrated in Fig. 16.2. Such data are being used to study the mechanism of generation of VLF noise and the structure and composition of the magnetosphere [8, 9].

The composition of the upper atmosphere is another area in which our present knowledge is inadequate for many purposes. The predominant neutral constituents are now believed to be known, and this neutral composition is directly related to problems of density variation with height and of airglow and auroral emissions. The lack of detailed information on the ionic constituents and on certain neutral trace constituents, however, seriously hampers analytic studies of the ionization production and loss processes. The more important ionization processes have probably been identified correctly, at least during quiescent conditions at low and middle

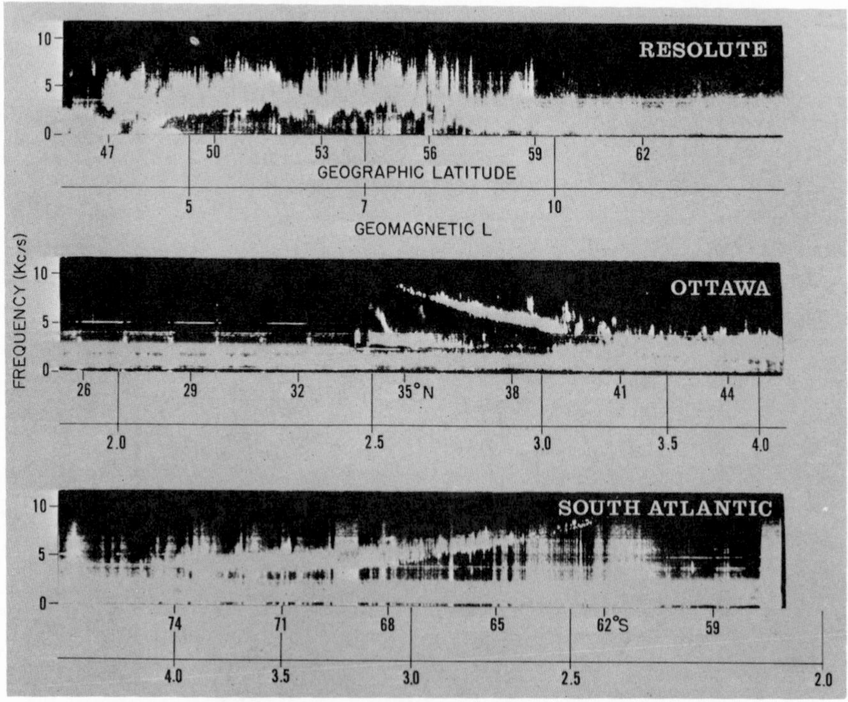

Fig. 16.2 Spectrogram of VLF ionospheric noise received by the Alouette I satellite on 31 January, 1963, at 1057–1148 U.T., at a height of 1000 km. Captions on the three segments refer to the telemetry stations where the data were recorded. (After Barrington *et al.* [3].)

latitudes, but no comprehensive quantitative treatment has yet been carried out.

During undisturbed conditions, most of the ionization in the lowest part of the *D* region is attributed to cosmic rays; in the intermediate part, to Lyman α radiation; in the upper *D* region and in the *E* region, to *X* radiation; and in the *F* region, to ultraviolet radiation. The production of ionization by cosmic rays, *X* rays, or ultraviolet radiation depends on the density of the dominant constituents, and it is not particularly sensitive to variations in atmospheric composition. The Lyman α radiation, however, specifically ionizes the trace constituent NO, and a detailed knowledge of the number density of NO is essential to any quantitative analysis of *D*-region ionization. During some types of disturbed conditions, major changes may occur in the spectrum and intensity of solar ultraviolet and *X* radiation, and the ionosphere may be bombarded by energetic charged particles of both solar and exospheric origin. Moreover, significant changes in temperature and density (and therefore changes of the composition in a given height region) are likely to occur during the disturbance. Thus, a quantitative study of ionization during a disturbance would appear to require considerable knowledge of the variations of atmospheric temperature and density, as well as detailed information on the solar radiation.

The equilibrium ionization density of a region, of course, depends not only on the rate of production of ionization, but also on the electron loss processes and on movements of ionization. Disregarding for the moment the question of movements, since they are not particularly dependent on atmospheric composition, it is probable that the electron loss processes, at all heights, depend on trace constituents as well as on the dominant components. The reaction rates of several of the loss processes are known to within only one order of magnitude. With increasing height, and therefore decreasing density and collision frequency, the most important electron loss process appears to change from negative-ion formation to dissociative recombination with positive molecular ions, and then to direct recombination with positive atomic ions. The ratio of negative ions to electrons has been estimated to exceed unity in the lower *D* region, but direct measurements of negative-ion composition are still not available. The situation is considerably better in regard to measurements of positive ions. Improvements in technique, in particular the reduction of gas contamination from the rocket vehicles, are now beginning to produce consistent data and progress is expected to be rapid. As an example, Fig. 16.3 shows the positive-ion composition recorded over White Sands, New Mexico, during two rocket soundings, one by day and one by night.

The polar ionosphere provides another example of our present state of ignorance with respect to upper atmospheric ionization. During the long polar night, analytic problems should be greatly simplified by the complete

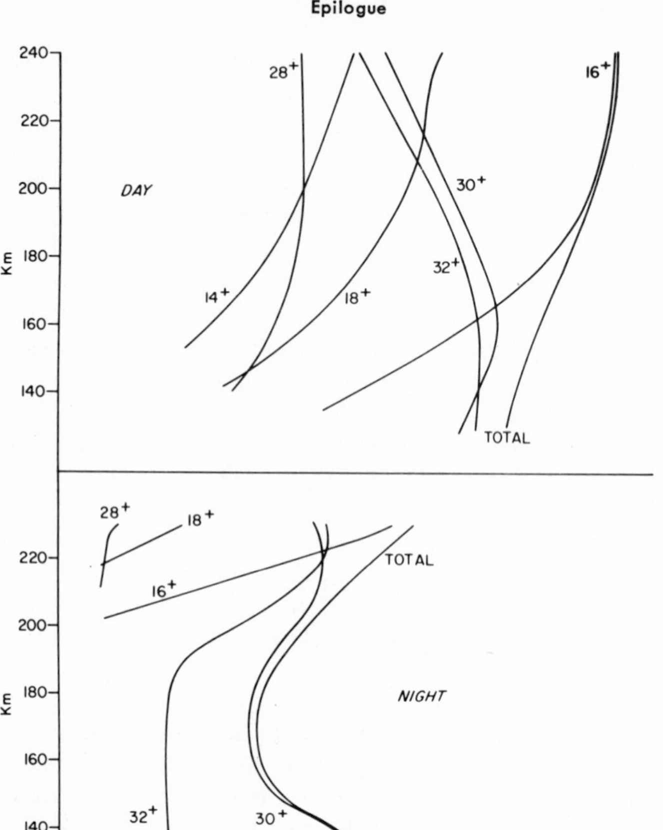

Fig. 16.3 Data recorded by a rocket-borne ion mass spectrometer over White Sands, New Mexico. (After Holmes and Young [1].)

absence of direct solar illumination. Polar ionization at night may be attributed to diffusion of ionization from other (sunlit) regions or to bombardment by energetic particles, but these processes still await proper evaluation. Diffusion of ionization depends on the magnetic field and proceeds particularly readily along the field lines, but the configuration of the magnetic field lines that rise from the polar regions is still undetermined. In addition, there are no direct measurements of either temperature or composition over the polar regions, and there are reasons to suspect that the temperature-height profile of the polar upper atmosphere differs substantially from that at lower latitudes. In any case, at the time of writing the relative importance of diffusion and of ionization by particle bombardment has not been established.

The difficulties of obtaining data on upper atmospheric processes are gradually being reduced, thanks to the ingenuity of the researcher, although, as is common in research, new problems are revealed by every success. Paradoxically, the area that is proving particularly difficult to explore is the height region below about 100 km. Between the balloon ceiling (at about 35 km) and the satellite 'floor' (at about 110 km) direct measurements are possible on only a short-term basis with rocket- (or gun-) launched instruments: the sporadic data so obtained are often difficult to interpret and do not permit a continuous study of any one phenomenon. Similarly, indirect observations by radio probes are difficult to interpret in this height range; the pertinent theoretical models are very complex, and a detailed knowledge of the atmospheric constituents is required in order to check observation against theory. This height region, spanning the lower and upper atmospheres, has become perhaps the least understood of all. In comparison both with the underlying and with the overlying regions, it has been investigated to only a slight extent, and then merely in connection with isolated phenomena, such as movements and radio-wave absorption.

The subject of movements is one of the most challenging that currently faces the upper atmospheric physicist. Unquestionably, winds of a conventional meteorological nature are present, at least to the base of the *F* region; these are under study by refined meteorological techniques employing rockets, and by meteor and noctilucent-cloud investigations. Moreover, the winds unquestionably interact with the ionization of the region and cause irregular deformations of the electron distribution. On the other hand, the ionization is subject to electrodynamic forces which impress upon it motions of a type unfamiliar to conventional meteorology, and by collisions the ionization may transfer to the neutral gas some of the influence of those forces. At the lower levels just discussed, the meteorological processes tend to hold sway, whereas at great heights the electrodynamic effects can dominate. The transition is a complicated one whose understanding will require intense efforts on the part of both meteorologists and ionospheric physicists.

C. O. Hines
I. Paghis
T. R. Hartz
J. A. Fejer

REFERENCES

1. Holmes, J. C., J. M. Young, and C. Y. Johnson, Ionospheric chemistry, in COSPAR, Space Research V. Amsterdam: North-Holland Publishing Company, (on press 1965).
2. O'Brien, B. J., High-latitude geophysical studies with satellite Injun 3. Part 3. Precipitation of electrons into the atmosphere, *J. Geophys. Res.*, **69** (1964), 13.

3. Barrington, R. E., J. S. Belrose, and D. A. Keeley, Very-low-frequency noise bands observed by the Alouette I satellite, *J. Geophys. Res.*, **68** (1963), 6539.

4. Axford, W. I., The interaction between the solar wind and the earth's magnetosphere, *J. Geophys. Res.*, **67** (1962), 3791.

5. Kellogg, P. J., Flow of plasma around the earth, *J. Geophys. Res.*, **67** (1962), 3805.

6. Ness, N. F., C. S. Scearce, and J. B. Seek, Initial results of the Imp 1 magnetic field experiment, *J. Geophys. Res.*, **69** (1964), 3531.

7. Hines, C. O., Dynamical heating of the upper atmosphere, *J. Geophys. Res.*, (on press).

8. Brice, N. M., and R. L. Smith, Recordings from satellite Alouette I: a very-low-frequency plasma resonance, *Nature*, **203** (1964), 926.

9. Barrington, R. E., J. S. Belrose, and G. L. Nelms, Ion composition and temperatures at 1000 km as deduced from simultaneous observations of a VLF plasma resonance and topside sounding data from the Alouette I satellite, *J. Geophys. Res.*, (on press).

Appendix I

R. E. Barrington

Wave Propagation in a Homogeneous Ionized Gas

I.1. INTRODUCTION

The theory of wave propagation in an ionized gas is an important and rapidly developing subject with applications in such diverse fields as radio astronomy, microwave electronics, fusion reactors, and radio propagation in the upper atmosphere. This appendix does not treat the theory in a general form applicable to all wave types and all ionized gases. Instead, it introduces several idealizations which are applicable in ionospheric problems. These assumptions reduce the discussion to a consideration of waves in an infinite, partially ionized low-temperature gas pervaded by a steady magnetic field. The mathematical description of plane waves in such a medium is relatively simple, but it must always be remembered that such idealized waves are only an approximation to the waves which actually exist in the ionosphere.

Several wave types can propagate in the ionosphere but only two, radio waves and hydromagnetic waves, are considered here. This limitation is imposed, not because other wave types, such as shock waves, plasma waves, acoustic, and quasi-acoustic waves, play no part in ionospheric behavior, but because, in a brief treatment, only the wave types which at present are thought to be most important in ionospheric studies can be considered. The same principle explains why most of this appendix is devoted to radio waves, whereas the treatment of hydromagnetic waves is at best sketchy.

I.2. THE HYDRODYNAMIC APPROXIMATION

Any analytical treatment of a gaseous medium requires some form of simplification, its nature being determined by the problem under consideration and the desired accuracy. Here, as in the early treatments of ionospheric radio waves, a hydrodynamic approximation is employed. Although this is far from the most rigorous approach, it does illustrate the important features of radio and hydromagnetic waves. Before using this approximation, however, its basic assumptions and limitations must be considered.

In a gaseous medium, each particle moves in a field of force which is the sum of the forces due to all other particles plus those arising from externally applied fields. Thus, as a particle moves among its neighbors it experiences an irregular and rapidly fluctuating force which is difficult to describe mathematically. To overcome this, the hydrodynamic approximation considers that each constituent of a gas may be replaced by a continuous fluid whose properties at any point are the same as the average properties of the gas particles contained in a volume centered on the point in question, which contains many particles but whose dimensions are much smaller than any wavelength of interest. Thus the discrete nature of a gas and the thermal motions of the particles that constitute it are ignored, in spite of the fact that the rms thermal velocities of the particles are usually very much larger than their average or organized velocity. Such a theory can be applied only to waves whose characteristic length is much greater than the mean interparticle distance. It also does not treat accurately effects that depend on the thermal motions of the particles. These will receive some consideration in Appendix II, with respect to the 'incoherent scattering' of radio waves.

Included in the mean force which determines the average or organized particle velocity are contributions from two different types of particle interactions. In one type, large momentum transfers are delivered in a time which is short compared with a wave period. Such encounters are thermal collisions and involve only two particles at any given instant. Interactions between neutral particles, or ions and neutral particles, are all of this type because the force fields surrounding neutral particles are of very short range. Ions, on the other hand, are surrounded by long-range coulomb fields so that ion-ion encounters involve a whole range of behavior extending from that of two-body 'collisional' interactions to that of long-range interactions in which only small momentum changes are involved and in which a given particle interacts simultaneously with many others. The long-range collective interactions play a role in the behavior of an ionized gas that is quite different from that of short-range collisions.

Collisions give rise to a friction-like force which tends to reduce any differences in the organized motions which two interacting groups of particles may have. This may be understood by considering a collision between an electron and a much heavier particle. The electron's vector velocity will be altered markedly in such an encounter, so that, statistically at least, its new direction bears no relation to its old. Such encounters, then, convert the ordered component of an electron's motion into random or thermal motion, but the loss by some electrons of their ordered velocity means that the average ordered velocity of all the electrons is reduced. Collisions between particles of approximately the same mass have a similar effect, although the process is complicated by the fact that only a part of the organized velocity is given up at each collision. The magnitude of the average frictional force due to an electron collision with stationary heavy molecules has been shown [2] to be approximately $m\nu\mathbf{V}$, where $\mathbf{V}$ is the ordered electron velocity, ν is the average number of collisions experienced by an electron per second, and m is the electron mass.

In determining the frictional force due to collisions, no account is taken of the fact that not all electrons possess the same thermal velocity and that ν may depend on this velocity. This is not usually of importance [8], except when the wave frequency is close to the collision frequency ν. Under such circumstances, the hydrodynamic theory is inaccurate and recourse must be had to more detailed considerations of electron collisions. This requires the solution of the difficult integro-differential 'Boltzmann's equation,' and accurate laboratory measurements of the collisional cross section and its energy dependence [11, 9]. Such considerations are beyond the scope of this appendix.

In contrast to collisions, the long-range interactions between the charged particles of a plasma contribute only to the average or organized properties of such a medium. In the absence of disturbances it is these long-range interactions which preserve the over-all electrical neutrality of an ionized gas, although the ions composing it do move almost freely and randomly. If, for example, the positive and negative charges of the medium are separated in a macroscopic sense, these long-range interactions produce a macroscopic electric field which tends to restore the medium to neutrality. In addition to such purely electrostatic forces, ions may interact by electromagnetic radiation fields. If the ions in some region of the medium are set oscillating, each ion acts as a source of elementary wavelets. These wavelets may then move throughout the medium and exert forces on ions in other regions. Thus the electric field which exists at any point in an ionized medium is composed of components due to sources outside the medium and a component due to the long-range electromagnetic and electrostatic interactions of the particles that constitute the medium.

Macroscopic forces may arise from pressure gradients in a constituent of a gas. Such a force produces organized motions of the gas particles and is basic to all acoustical phenomena and plasma waves. The magnitude of the pressure force per particle is given by $N_i^{-1}\,\nabla P_i$ where P_i is the pressure and

N_i the number per unit volume of the ith constituent of the gas. Pressure forces need normally be considered only for waves whose speed of propagation is comparable to, or less than, the rms thermal speed of the gas particles. With rare exceptions, this condition does not arise in ionospheric radio waves, and pressure gradients will be neglected in due course. The pressure may play a part in some types of hydromagnetic waves and must be considered in the treatment of such waves.

Once the manner of treatment of the interparticle forces has been decided, it is possible to determine the (arithmetic) average or organized motion of each constituent of a gas. It is sufficient for present purposes to confine attention to motions describable by the following equation:

$$\frac{d\mathbf{V}_i}{dt} = m_i^{-1}[q_i\mathbf{E} + q_i\mathbf{V}_i \times \mathbf{B} - N_i^{-1}\nabla P_i + \mathbf{F}_{\text{fric}}], \tag{I.1}$$

where $\mathbf{V}_i$ is the average velocity, m_i the mass per particle, q_i the charge per particle, N_i the number density and P_i the partial pressure of the constituent considered, $\mathbf{F}_{\text{fric}}$ the frictional force per particle due to collisions, and $\mathbf{E}$ is the electric field and $\mathbf{B}$ the magnetic induction in the medium. This equation is often referred to as the 'equation of motion,' the 'equation of momentum transfer,' or the 'force equation,' and it is one of the constitutive relations of the medium.

Equation (I.1) as it stands is nonlinear. This introduces considerable mathematical difficulty which can be avoided by a perturbation treatment in which the variations from static conditions are assumed small and their products negligible. In such a treatment the acceleration term of Eq. (I.1), which may be written $\partial\mathbf{V}_i/\partial t + (\mathbf{V}_i \cdot \nabla)\mathbf{V}_i$, reduces to $\partial\mathbf{V}_i/\partial t$, and N_i may be replaced by its value in the absence of any wave. Similarly, the term $q_i\mathbf{V}_i \times \mathbf{B}$ can be written $q_i\mathbf{V}_i \times \mathbf{B}_0$, where $\mathbf{B}_0$ is some dominant constant magnetic field (in practice, the earth's), since any contribution due to a magnetic field associated with the perturbation is negligible when multiplied with the perturbation velocity $\mathbf{V}_i$. Thus Eq. (I.1) assumes the linear form

$$\frac{\partial\mathbf{V}_i}{\partial t} = m_i^{-1}[q_i\mathbf{E} + q_i\mathbf{V}_i \times \mathbf{B}_0 - N_i^{-1}\nabla P_i + \mathbf{F}_{\text{fric}}], \tag{I.2}$$

where N_i is now to be interpreted as the unperturbed number density. A second constitutive relation must also be linearized, that for the macroscopic current density $\mathbf{J}$:

$$\mathbf{J} = \sum_i N_i q_i \mathbf{V}_i. \tag{I.3}$$

Perturbations of the medium may cause small variations in N_i. The contributions of such variations to the mean current density are ignored, since they are multiplied by the perturbation velocity, so again N_i is to be interpreted as an unperturbed quantity. Equations (I.2) and (I.3) give then, to the order of approximation of the linearized hydrodynamic theory, a relationship between the macroscopic electric field and the current of any perturbation existing in an ionized medium.

I.3. THE DISPERSION EQUATION OF RADIO WAVES

A dispersion equation, relating the frequency and wavelength of the plane waves which can exist in an infinite homogeneous medium, is a valuable tool for the study of wave propagation. The usefulness of such an equation is not limited because it relates only to plane waves, for since the equations governing the medium have been linearized, more complex disturbances can be synthesized from such waves by Fourier integration. Plane waves, on the other hand, have the great advantage that they reduce the relevant differential equations to algebraic ones. This simplifies the task of determining whether waves are possible in an ionized gas, and, if so, their properties. It is to this task, then, that attention will now be given.

When consideration is limited to the propagation of radio waves in an ionized gas, it is not necessary to take into account the motions of all the medium's constituents or the pressure gradients. Radio waves are usually of such high frequency that only electrons, with their relatively small inertia, attain appreciable velocities due to the wave fields. Thus in treating such waves the positive ions and neutral particles can be assumed stationary. These assumptions, coupled with the fact that consideration is limited to disturbances which have a variation with time of the form $A\ e^{i\omega t}$, allow Eqs. (I.2) and (I.3) to be written

$$i\omega\mathbf{V} = -\frac{e}{m}[\mathbf{E} + \mathbf{V} \times \mathbf{B}_0] - \nu\mathbf{V} \tag{I.4}$$

$$\mathbf{J} = -Ne\mathbf{V} \tag{I.5}$$

where e is the charge of a proton and N is the electron density, and where the previously discussed expression $-m\nu\mathbf{V}$ was substituted for the frictional force $\mathbf{F}_{\text{fric}}$. These may be combined to yield

$$\mathbf{J} = \boldsymbol{\sigma} \cdot \mathbf{E}, \tag{I.6}$$

where $\boldsymbol{\sigma}$ is known as the 'conductivity tensor.'

Before the components of this tensor can be determined, a set of axes must be chosen. It will be convenient to align the axes in such a way that $\mathbf{B}_0$ lies entirely in the yz plane, and the angle between $\mathbf{B}_0$ and the positive z axis will be designated θ (measured positively in the sense depicted in Fig. I.1). Such a choice in no way limits the generality of the treatment but substantially simplifies the determination of the tensor components. The latter become

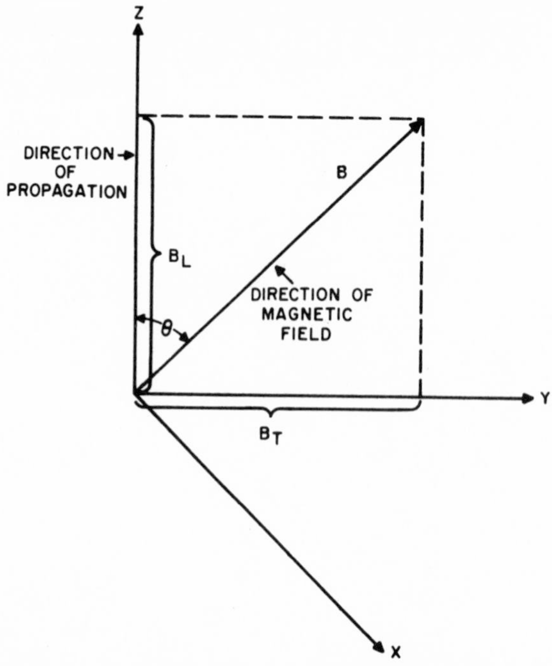

Fig. I.1 Relation of the magnetic field direction to the coordinate axis.

$$\left\| \begin{matrix} \dfrac{(\nu+i\omega)\,\omega_0^2\,\epsilon_0}{(\nu+i\omega)^2+\omega_H^2} & \dfrac{\omega_0^2\,\omega_H\,\epsilon_0\cos\theta}{(\nu+i\omega)^2+\omega_H^2} & \dfrac{-\omega_0^2\,\omega_H\,\epsilon_0\sin\theta}{(\nu+i\omega)^2+\omega_H^2} \\[2ex] \dfrac{-\omega_0^2\,\omega_H\,\epsilon_0\cos\theta}{(\nu+i\omega)^2+\omega_H^2} & \dfrac{\omega_0^2\,\epsilon_0}{(\nu+i\omega)}\left[1-\dfrac{\omega_H^2\cos^2\theta}{(\nu+i\omega)^2+\omega_H^2}\right] & \dfrac{\omega_0^2\omega_H^2\,\epsilon_0\sin\theta\cos\theta}{(\nu+i\omega)[(\nu+i\omega)^2+\omega_H^2]} \\[2ex] \dfrac{\omega_0^2\,\omega_H\,\epsilon_0\sin\theta}{(\nu+i\omega)^2+\omega_H^2} & \dfrac{\omega_0^2\,\omega_H^2\,\epsilon_0\sin\theta\cos\theta}{(\nu+i\omega)[(\nu+i\omega)^2+\omega_H^2]} & \dfrac{\omega_0^2\epsilon_0}{(\nu+i\omega)}\left[1-\dfrac{\omega_H^2\sin^2\theta}{(\nu+i\omega)^2+\omega_H^2}\right] \end{matrix} \right\| \tag{I.7}$$

where $\omega_0 = (Ne^2/\epsilon_0 m)^{1/2}$ and $\omega_H = |e|\,B_0/m$.

This tensor uses two parameters, ω_H and ω_0, both of which have the dimensions of frequency, to describe the properties of the medium. The first of these is the angular frequency with which an electron executes a circular motion in a magnetic field, and is called the 'gyrofrequency' or 'cyclotron frequency'; its magnitude depends on the magnetic field strength and the charge-to-mass ratio of the electron. The second, known as the 'plasma frequency,' is determined by the density, the charge, and the charge-to-mass ratio of the electrons. This frequency describes the collective interactions between the charged particles. If in some region the medium is disturbed in such a way that positive and negative charges are separated, a net space charge is produced, giving rise to an electric field which tries to restore the region to neutrality. This causes the particles to rearrange themselves so as to eliminate the space charge forces. In such a rearrangement, the particles acquire a net velocity which carries them through their positions of neutrality and a space charge is again built up. An oscillation is produced, whose frequency in the absence of a magnetic field is ω_0. Both ω_H and ω_0 represent natural resonance frequencies of an ionized gas, though in practice, interactions occur which render the resonances of an actual plasma dependent on some functions of these resonant frequencies determined by the manner of excitation.

Equation (I.6) depends only on the forces that exist locally and on their temporal variations. To examine the possibility of wave propagation, a relation between **E** and **J** depending on both their temporal and spatial variations is required. This is provided by Maxwell's equations, which may be written in general as

$$\begin{aligned} &\text{(a)} \quad \nabla \times \mathbf{E} + \frac{\partial \mathbf{B}}{\partial t} = 0, \qquad &\text{(c)} \quad \nabla \cdot \mathbf{B} = 0, \\ &\text{(b)} \quad \nabla \times \mathbf{H} - \frac{\partial \mathbf{D}}{\partial t} = \mathbf{J}, \qquad &\text{(d)} \quad \nabla \cdot \mathbf{D} = \rho, \end{aligned} \tag{I.8}$$

where **H** is the magnetic field, **D** the electric displacement, and ρ the space-charge. The free electrons are taken to be the only source of current, and their contribution is incorporated entirely in **J**, so the relationships

$$\mathbf{D} = \epsilon_0 \mathbf{E}, \qquad \mathbf{B} = \mu_0 \mathbf{H}, \tag{I.9}$$

apply where ϵ_0 and μ_0 are the free-space electric and magnetic permittivities. Equations (I.8a) and (I.8b) may be combined to yield

$$\nabla \times \nabla \times \mathbf{E} = -c^{-2} \frac{\partial^2 \mathbf{E}}{\partial t^2} - \mu_0 \frac{\partial \mathbf{J}}{\partial t}, \tag{I.10}$$

where $c \equiv \epsilon_0^{-1/2} \mu_0^{-1/2}$ is the speed of light in a vacuum.

Only the fields of plane waves are under consideration, as was indicated at the beginning of this section: hence the dependence of the variables in Eq. (I.10) on time and space may be represented in the form

$$A_0 \, e^{i(\omega t - \mathbf{k} \cdot \mathbf{r})}$$

(or as the real parts of such forms, the distinction being trivial since all present equations are linear in the variables). For such fields, Eq. (I.10) assumes the form

$$k^2 \mathbf{E} - \mathbf{k}(\mathbf{k} \cdot \mathbf{E}) - \frac{\omega^2}{c^2} \mathbf{E} = -i\omega \mu_0 \mathbf{J}. \tag{I.11}$$

Choosing the direction of propagation as the z direction of the coordinate system illustrated in Fig. I.1, Eqs. (I.6) and (I.11) may be combined to yield three simultaneous equations relating the components of the electric field. These are

$$\left[k^2 - \frac{\omega^2}{c^2} + \frac{i\omega(\nu + i\omega)\omega_0^2}{c^2[(\nu + i\omega)^2 + \omega_H^2]}\right] E_x + \left[\frac{i\omega\omega_0^2\omega_H \cos\theta}{c^2[(\nu + i\omega)^2 + \omega_H^2]}\right] E_y - \left[\frac{i\omega\omega_0^2\omega_H \sin\theta}{c^2[(\nu + i\omega)^2 + \omega_H^2]}\right] E_z = 0,$$

$$-\left[\frac{i\omega\omega_0^2\omega_H \cos\theta}{c^2[(\nu + i\omega)^2 + \omega_H^2]}\right] E_x + \left[k^2 - \frac{\omega^2}{c^2} + \frac{i\omega\omega_0^2}{c^2(\nu + i\omega)}\left\{1 - \frac{\omega_H^2 \cos^2\theta}{(\nu + i\omega)^2 + \omega_H^2}\right\}\right] E_y + \left[\frac{i\omega\,\omega_0^2\omega_H^2 \sin\theta\cos\theta}{c^2(\nu + i\omega)[(\nu + i\omega)^2 + \omega_H^2]}\right] E_z = 0,$$

$$\left[\frac{i\omega\omega_0^2\omega_H \sin\theta}{c^2[(\nu + i\omega)^2 + \omega_H^2]}\right] E_x + \left[\frac{i\omega\omega_0^2\omega_H^2 \sin\theta\cos\theta}{c^2(\nu + i\omega)[(\nu + i\omega)^2 + \omega_H^2]}\right] E_y + \left[k^2 - \frac{\omega^2}{c^2} + \frac{i\omega\omega_0^2}{(\nu + i\omega)c^2}\left\{1 - \frac{\omega_H^2 \sin^2\theta}{[(\nu + i\omega)^2 + \omega_H^2]}\right\}\right] E_z = 0. \quad \text{(I.12)}$$

The theory of simultaneous linear equations shows that if Eqs. (I.12) are to be satisfied for a nonvanishing value of the electric field, the determinant of the bracketed coefficients in these equations must equal zero. This determinant involves only ω, k, θ, and the parameters which describe the medium, ω_0, ω_H, and ν; its vanishing yields the dispersion equation of the characteristic waves, the waves which can exist in the medium:

$$\left(\frac{ck}{\omega}\right)^2 = 1 - \frac{X}{1 - iZ - \dfrac{Y^2 \sin^2\theta}{2(1 - X - iZ)} \pm \left[\dfrac{Y^4 \sin^4\theta}{4(1 - X - iZ)^2} + Y^2\cos^2\theta\right]^{1/2}} \quad \text{(I.13)}$$

where $X = (\omega_0/\omega)^2$, $Y = \omega_H/\omega$, $Z = \nu/\omega$.

The form of this equation has been chosen to yield explicitly the refractive index $n \equiv ck/\omega$, since it is in terms of this parameter that the propagation, reflection, and absorption of the waves will be discussed. Generally, Eq. (I.13.) yields four possible values for this index, once a specific set of parameters is introduced on the right. These occur in pairs which have the same magnitude but opposite sign. Each of these pairs represents different types of waves, whereas each component of a single pair describes the same wave type but with opposite directions of propagation. As a rule, Eq. (I.13) yields complex values of the refractive index, the real part describing the phase velocity of the characteristic waves and the imaginary part their attenuation. As might be expected from the discussion of the role played by collisions, energy dissipation is absent if collisions are ignored, although attenuation in nondissipative 'evanescent' waves is still possible, as will be discussed. The neglect of collisions is often permissible, but it must be kept in mind that collisions always occur in any actual gas.

The characteristic waves are subject not only to the dispersion equation but also to certain 'polarization relations' which specify the relative magnitudes of the components of the fields associated with them. These may be found with the aid of Eqs. (I.12) and (I.13). One of the most striking features of the characteristic waves, which can be seen from Eq. (I.12), is that they have an electric field component in the direction of propagation, except in the special case when this direction coincides with that of the magnetic field. Thus in contrast to radio waves in a vacuum, which possess only transverse fields, such waves in an ionized gas usually have longitudinal fields as well.

In spite of this longitudinal component, it is customary, in determining the polarization of the characteristic waves, to consider only the transverse electric field. Thus the polarization R of a wave traveling in the z direction is defined as E_x/E_y. Sometimes it is simpler to use the definition $R = -H_y/H_x$, since the magnetic vector of the characteristic waves is always transverse. When R vanishes, E_x vanishes and the wave is linearly polarized with its electric vector in the yz plane. When R is infinite, E_y vanishes and the wave is again linearly polarized but with its electric vector in the xz plane. In general, R is complex, signifying that the wave is elliptically polarized. Such polarization is termed 'right-handed' when the sense of rotation of the electric vector is clockwise if viewed in the direction of propagation, and 'left-handed' when it appears anti-clockwise. Circular polarization is a special case of elliptical polarization and occurs when $R = \pm i$. Unlike the amplitude, the polarization of the characteristic waves remains constant as the waves propagate through a homogeneous medium, even in the presence of

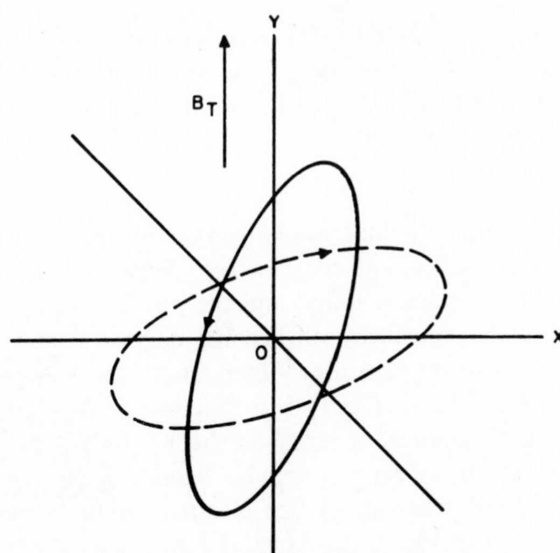

Fig. I.2 The relation between the electric-field polarization ellipses of the two characteristic curves. The xy plane is the plane of the wave front, and the wave normal is directed into the paper.

high absorption. Thus polarization is a convenient parameter with which to study the propagation of the characteristic waves.

The polarization of such a wave may be evaluated by substituting the wave number k, determined from Eq. (I.13), into (I.12) and then by solving these equations for E_x/E_y. This gives

$$R = \left\{\frac{-i}{Y\cos\theta}\right\}\left\{\frac{Y^2\sin^2\theta}{2(1-X-iZ)} \mp \left(\frac{Y^4\sin^4\theta}{4(1-X-iZ)^2} + Y^2\cos^2\theta\right)^{1/2}\right\}. \tag{I.14}$$

The product of the two polarizations given by this equation is unity, which indicates that they are reciprocally related. The polarization ellipse of one wave is obtained from that of the other by reflection in a line making an angle of 45° with the Ox and Oy axes as illustrated in Fig. I.2. It may also be found from Eq. (I.14.) that the electric field vectors of the two characteristic waves rotate in opposite directions.

I.4. GRAPHICAL REPRESENTATION OF THE DISPERSION EQUATION

The complexity of, and number of parameters in, the dispersion equation (I.13) make it impractical to illustrate graphically its general behavior. Two special cases, however, will be discussed with the aid of graphs and from them considerable insight into the full equations can be gained. More general summaries are provided by the monographs of Budden [3] and Ratcliffe [10].

The simplest of these special cases is an ionized gas which has no steady magnetic field and in which collisions are so infrequent that they can be neglected. For such a gas $Y = 0, Z = 0$, and the dispersion equation assumes the simple quadratic form,

$$n^2 - 1 + X = 0, \tag{I.15}$$

from which it may be seen that the two types of characteristic waves are identical in such a medium. If the electron density is also zero (that is, $X = 0$), the refractive index is unity, and the phase velocity c. Thus in free space the waves under consideration become normal electromagnetic ones. In a nonmagnetic ionized gas, they differ from electromagnetic waves in free space since their phase velocity is a function of frequency and greater than c. This is not a violation of relativity theory; for the velocity of energy propagation, the group velocity, given by $d\omega/dk = c[1 - X]^{1/2}$, is always less than c. Hence the presence of free electrons reduces the velocity of a radio-wave packet or pulse, particularly at frequencies only slightly above the plasma frequency.

Figure I.3. shows a plot of n^2 as a function of X (that is, of $[\omega_0/\omega]^2$) for these waves. From such a plot, it is seen that the refractive index is purely

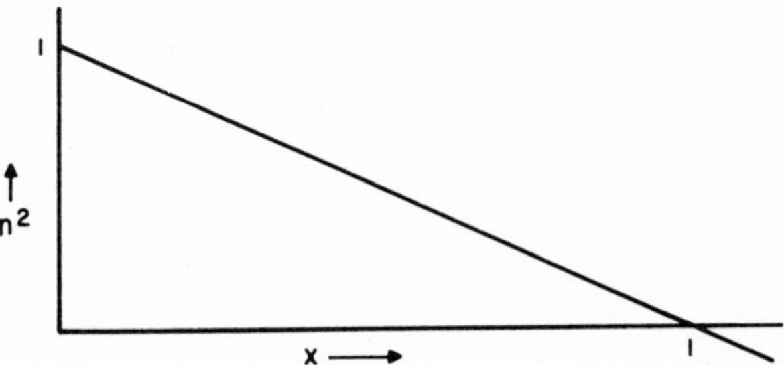

Fig. I.3 The variation of the square of the refractive index with X when the magnetic field is zero.

real for frequencies above the plasma frequency and purely imaginary for frequencies below. Waves for which the refractive index is imaginary are called 'evanescent.' If such waves are excited in a medium, the amplitude of their fields decays exponentially with distance from the source. This behavior is similar to that encountered in a waveguide working beyond cutoff. In neither case is energy propagated in the medium nor transferred from the source to the medium. Instead all the energy given to the medium during part of the wave cycle is reflected back into the source during the rest of the cycle. Again, if a wave is incident from free space on an ionized region in which the plasma frequency lies above the wave frequency, it is totally reflected at the interface between the two media.

From Eq. (I.12) it may be seen that, in a collisionless nonmagnetic plasma, radio waves are purely transverse. Moreover, the transverse field components are independent, hence such waves may have any polarization. This is quite different from the characteristic waves of a magnetic plasma, which have a unique polarization, and is a direct consequence of the fact that the two types of characteristic mode are indistinguishable in the circumstances now considered.

The presence of a magnetic field in a collisionless ionized medium leads to the phenomenon of double refraction, and therefore two possible values for the refractive index as given by the dispersion equation (I.13). These two indices refer to physically different wave types which become identical, in the collisionless case, only when the magnetic field approaches zero. In studying the nature of these waves it is convenient to consider separately the case of waves of frequency greater than and less than the gyrofrequency ω_H.

The variation of n^2 with $(\omega_0/\omega)^2$, as the angle θ between the magnetic field lines and the wave normal direction is changed from 0° to 90°, is shown in Fig. I.4 for $\omega_H/\omega < 1$. Typical curves are drawn for a fixed value of θ and, as might be expected, they always lie in the shaded areas between the limiting cases of longitudinal and transverse propagation. For one of the waves, n^2 is always less than 1, whereas for the other, n^2 assumes all values

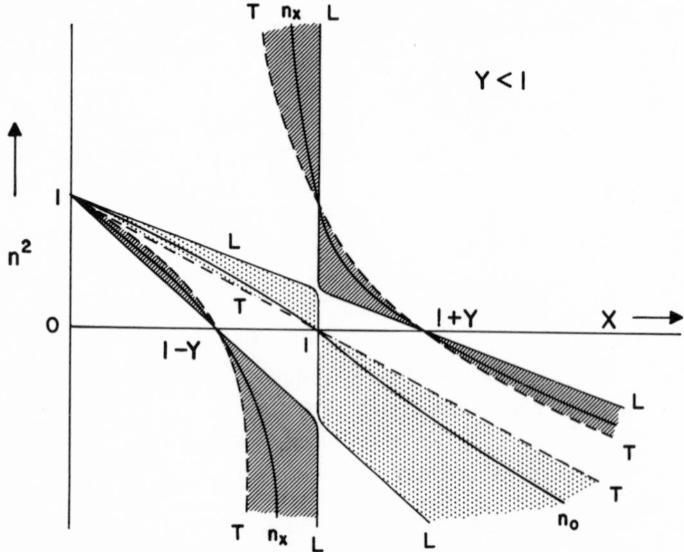

Fig. I.4 Behavior of the square of the refractive index for propagation in an arbitrary direction when $Y < 1$. The solid and dashed lines indicate the limiting cases of longitudinal (L) and transverse (T) propagation respectively. The shaded areas show the regions within which the curves for other directions of propagation must lie, and the solid curves in these areas indicate the behaviour of the refractive index for a particular value of θ.

between plus and minus infinity. There are only three values of X, $X = 1$, and $X = 1 \pm Y$, for which the refractive index is zero, and these values of X are all independent of the angle θ. When $X = 1$, the refractive index of one of the waves is zero and that of the other is unity. There is only one finite value of X for which n^2 is infinite, and this is $X = (1 - Y^2)/(1 - Y^2 \cos^2 \theta)$. Thus, this infinity always lies between $X = 1 - Y^2$ and 1.

Figure I.5 is drawn in the same manner as Fig. I.4 but applies when $\omega_H/\omega > 1$. Here again one of the waves assumes almost all values of n^2 between plus and minus infinity, whereas n^2 for the other wave may rise to values only moderately greater than 1. The zeros of the refractive index in this case occur at exactly the same values of X as when $\omega_H/\omega < 1$ except that, for $X = 1 - Y$, the zero occurs at a physically unrealizable negative value of X and is not shown. The refractive index of one of the waves is infinite when $X = (Y^2 - 1)/(Y^2 \cos^2 \theta - 1)$. This may occur for either negative or positive values of X, but only the case of a positive X value is shown. It can be seen from Figs. I.4 and I.5 that the presence of a magnetic field makes propagation possible at frequencies less than ω_0, that is, $X > 1$, whereas in

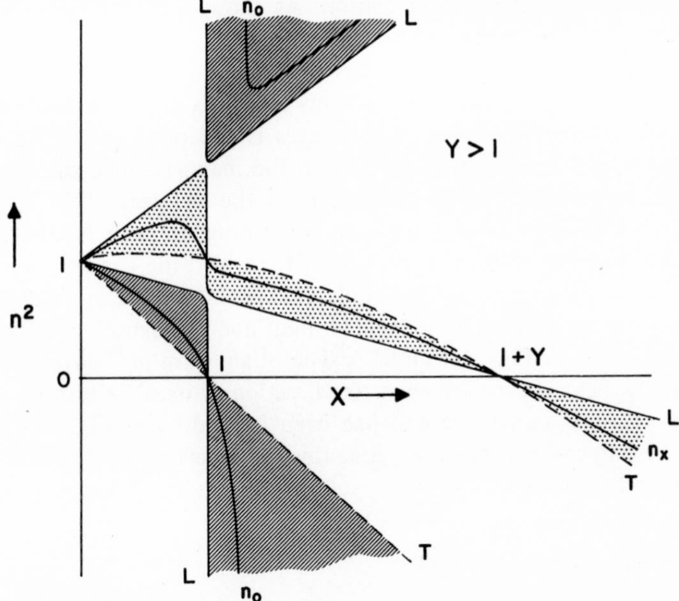

Fig. I.5 Behavior of the square of the refractive index for propagation in an arbitrary direction when $Y > 1$. The solid and dashed lines indicate the limiting cases of longitudinal (L) and transverse (T) propagation repectively. The shaded areas show the regions within which the curves for other directions of propagation (θ) must lie and the solid curves in these areas indicate the behaviour of n^2 for a particular value of θ.

a nonmagnetic plasma such propagation is impossible; in the case $\omega_H/\omega > 1$, propagation is in fact possible at all values of X.

The problem of naming or differentiating between the two types of radio waves of an ionized gas has created considerable confusion. Usually the names 'ordinary' and 'extraordinary' are adopted from the theory of optically birefringent crystals, but the basis on which these names are applied is far from uniform. In crystal optics no ambiguity arises: the ordinary wave has the same directions of phase and group velocity, whereas the extraordinary wave does not. The two types of ionospheric radio waves, as a rule, have different directions for their group and phase velocities; hence the distinction used in optics is not readily applicable. Generally the names are applied on the basis that the ordinary wave is the one less affected by the magnetic field, and hence resembles more closely the propagation of waves in a non-magnetic ionized medium.

To make such a criterion more precise, it is convenient to consider the limiting case of transverse propagation. As shown in Figs. I.4 and I.5, the variation of n^2 with X for one of the wave types, in this limit, becomes a straight line through $X = 1$. Thus this wave type resembles the waves which propagate in a nonmagnetic plasma. This similarity arises because, in transverse radio propagation, one of the waves is polarized so that its electric field sets the electrons in motion only in the magnetic field direction. The electrons then experience no force due to the magnetic field, and their behavior is the same as in a medium containing no such field. Here it is considered that the ordinary wave is that for which the variation of n^2 with X changes continuously, as the angle between the wave normal and the magnetic field approaches 90°, into a straight line through $X = 1$. This wave is denoted by n_O in Figs. I.4 and I.5. The other wave is always affected by the magnetic field, no matter what the direction of its wave normal may be. It is the extraordinary wave and has been labeled n_X in Figs. I.4 and I.5. It must be emphasized, however, that this nomenclature is not universal in ionospheric literature.

I.5. REFLECTION CONDITIONS

In principle the theory of radio wave propagation, developed so far, applies only to a homogeneous ionized gas. The ionosphere, however, is a varying medium and the preceding theory must be generalized if it is to take this into account. The variations are predominantly in the vertical direction and may be approximated by a number of plane homogeneous layers whose physical properties change very little between successive strata. A wave traveling through such a layered medium is often assumed to have the phase velocity and polarization in each layer that it would have if the layer were infinitely thick. This is equivalent to assuming that, as a wave propagates in a varying medium, its phase velocity and polarization change continuously, corresponding to the continuous changes in the properties of the medium. Such a simplified picture of the propagation is valid provided that the properties of the medium do not vary appreciably in a wavelength. It is termed the 'ray' or 'geometric optics' theory of radio-wave propagation, and it serves many purposes adequately, including those of the present appendix. Its foundations and region of validity are discussed more fully in Appendix II, together with an indication of the more sophisticated analyses that must in general be applied.

When a radio wave, propagating in the assumed stratified medium with its normal perpendicular to the layer boundaries, reaches a stratum in which the refractive index is zero, it is almost totally reflected. In the discussion of Figs. I.4 and I.5, it was pointed out that the zeros of the refractive index occur only when $X = 1$ or $X = 1 \pm Y$. These are frequently referred to as the 'reflection conditions for vertical incidence,' and are independent of the angle between the wave normal and the magnetic field. It must be remembered that these conditions apply strictly only in the collision-free approximation. As will be seen later, the presence of collisions prevents the refractive index from ever reaching zero, though even in this case a nearly total reflection occurs in the region where the real part of n is very small. For waves with normals which are not perpendicular to the layers of the medium, reflection is still possible but the conditions determining the level at which it occurs are somewhat more complicated.

It has sometimes been stated or implied that a radio wave is reflected at the level in the ionosphere where the refractive index is infinite. The expression for X at such a level is accordingly termed the 'fourth reflection condition.' It has been found [3], however, that there is no reflection here, but rather an absorption of the wave energy, even when there are insufficient collisions to account for such absorption. This anomaly occurs because the macroscopic approach used in deriving Eq. (I.13) neglects the thermal velocities of the electrons and hence is not valid when the velocity of a characteristic wave is comparable with the mean velocity of such particles. A more rigorous treatment, using Boltzmann's equation [6], shows that strong attenuation is present in these circumstances. This damping is associated with the conversion of the radio-wave energy into plasma waves, a subject which is beyond the scope of this appendix. Such considerations do, however, provide a basis for concluding that no fourth reflection condition exists.

I.6. QL AND QT APPROXIMATIONS

In the application of Eqs. (I.13) and (I.14) to ionospheric problems, their complexity makes them cumbersome. For this reason two approximations called quasi-transverse (QT) and quasi-longitudinal (QL) are, in practice, used more frequently than the full equations.

The QL approximation is valid when

$$\frac{Y^2 \sin^4 \theta}{4 \cos^2 \theta} \ll (1 - X)^2 + Z^2. \tag{I.16}$$

Under this condition, the refractive index and polarization may be written

$$n_{\mathrm{QL}}^2 = 1 - X/(1 - iZ \pm |Y \cos \theta|), \tag{I.17}$$

$$R_{\mathrm{QL}} = \mp i. \tag{I.18}$$

Thus in this approximation the waves have circular polarization no matter what angle their wave normals form with the magnetic field direction. (For more complete discussions of the QL and QT approximations see [10, 14].)

For QT propagation, it is necessary that

$$\frac{Y^2 \sin^4 \theta}{4 \cos^2 \theta} \gg (1 - X)^2 + Z^2. \tag{I.19}$$

The refractive index and polarization may now be written

$$n_{QT}^2 = 1 - \frac{X}{1 - iZ + (1 - X - iZ)\cot^2\theta}$$

or (I.20)

$$n_{QT}^2 = 1 - \frac{X}{1 - iZ - (1 - X - iZ)^{-1}\,Y^2\sin^2\theta}\,,$$

$$R_{QT} = 0 \quad \text{or} \quad \infty. \tag{I.21}$$

In this case the polarization is linear, and again independent of θ, whereas the refractive index in both cases depends on this angle.

The QL and QT approximations are so named because they apply to waves having polarizations which approximate closely to those of truly longitudinal or truly transverse waves. These names do not imply that the approximations are valid only for propagation which is almost transverse or almost longitudinal. This can be seen from the conditions (I.16) and (I.19) which depend not only on θ but also on X, Y and Z and hence on the electron density, gyro-frequency, and collision frequency. In fact, the QL approximation is often a very good one, even when the direction of the wave normal is considerably different from that of the magnetic field.

For a given value of Z and θ, it is in the neighborhood of the reflection level $X = 1$ that the QL approximation is first likely to fail. Accordingly, reflections at this level are termed QT or QL, depending on which of the approximations can be used to discuss the waves there. If at this level the QL approximation holds, it is valid for all other heights as well. In contrast, if at the $X = 1$ level the QT approximation is satisfied, it usually applies only over a limited height interval, whereas, at heights considerably removed from the reflection level, the QL approximation is again valid. To investigate fully the levels of the terrestrial ionosphere at which each approximation is valid, a model ionosphere must be chosen [10].

I.7. EFFECTS OF COLLISIONS ON THE REFRACTIVE INDICES

In the absence of collisions it has been found that the refractive index of a radio wave may assume a real or an imaginary value but never a complex one. When collisions occur, the refractive index is always complex, the real component describing the phase propagation and the imaginary part the attenuation of the waves. It is not practicable to develop a general set of curves illustrating the effect of collisions on the real part n_r and the imaginary part n_i of the refractive index. Instead n_i, and the magnitude of the absorption it gives in some special cases, will be discussed. Then the alterations in n_i and n_r which collisions cause, particularly in the neighborhood of the reflection level $X = 1$, are considered qualitatively, and the resulting difficulties of nomenclature are outlined.

In an absorbing medium, the fields of plane waves may be represented by

$$A = A_0 \exp\left(\frac{\omega n_i z}{c}\right) \exp i\left(\omega t - \frac{\omega}{c} n_r z\right), \tag{I.22}$$

where $-\omega n_i/c$ is the absorption coefficient, usually denoted by K. Thus if a wave propagates from A to B in an absorbing medium the ratio of its amplitude at B to that at A is

$$\exp\left(-\int_{\text{A}}^{\text{B}} K\,dz\right). \tag{I.23}$$

Rarely is K determined from the full dispersion equation. Instead it is usually obtained from the QL or QT approximation, and frequently the magnetic field is ignored completely.

If the QL approximation is considered, K is found by equating the imaginary components of Eq. (I.17): thus

$$2n_r n_i = \frac{-XZ}{[1 \pm Y\cos\theta]^2 + Z^2}, \tag{I.24}$$

whence

$$K = \frac{\omega_0^2 \nu}{2cn_r\{[\omega \pm \omega_H \cos\theta]^2 + \nu^2\}}. \tag{I.25}$$

A similar expression may be derived from the QT approximation and for the case $\omega_H = 0$.

In discussing absorption, it is customary to distinguish between the deviative and nondeviative types. In regions where $n_r \approx 1$, the absorption is considered nondeviative because at such levels appreciable refraction or deviation of the wave cannot occur. When n_r is considerably different from unity, the absorption is termed 'deviative,' though it should be remembered that even in this case only waves traveling obliquely to the stratifications of the medium suffer appreciable deviation. Much more important, in the deviative case, the group velocity is usually much smaller than c. Thus a wave packet may suffer appreciable absorption because of the long time it spends in the deviative region, rather than because the medium in this region can rapidly convert the wave energy into thermal energy. In the nondeviative case, high absorption occurs only in regions where the medium can quickly dissipate the wave energy.

It might be thought that, since collisions are necessary for absorption, the higher the collision frequency, the greater the absorption. This is not so in general, as can be seen from Eq. (I.25) for the case of nondeviative absorption. When ν is very much greater than $\omega \pm \omega_H \cos\theta$, K is given by

$$K \approx \omega_0^2/2c\nu, \tag{I.26}$$

indicating that a very high collision frequency results in very little absorption. The reason for this is that a very large number of collisions render an electron almost motionless in the field of a radio wave, and hence prevent it from acquiring appreciable wave energy which can subsequently be converted to thermal energy by collisions. Thus in the lowest levels of the ionosphere, where the collision frequency is very high in relation to other levels, very little absorption occurs. When ν is very much less than $\omega \pm \omega_H \cos\theta$, the absorption index reduces to

$$K \approx \frac{\omega_0^2 \nu}{2c(\omega \pm \omega_H \cos\theta)^2}, \tag{I.27}$$

and is again small, though now proportional to ν. For a fixed electron number density and wave frequency, nondeviative absorption is a maximum if the collision frequency is approximately equal to $\omega \pm \omega_H \cos\theta$, and decreases as the collision frequency is raised or lowered from this value. In practice there exists a corresponding height of maximum absorption efficiency, though its actual relevance depends on the distribution of electron density (as represented by the ω_0^2 factor).

Generally, deviative absorption is important near the reflection levels where the group retardation is high. A satisfactory treatment of absorption at such levels is complicated and will not be considered here [3, 10].

It has been noted that collisions complicate the reflection conditions for radio waves. They also introduce difficulties into the naming of such waves. This may be seen from Fig. I.6 which shows n_r and $-n_i$ as a function of X for several values of ν and constant values of Y and θ. In Fig. I.6(a) the collision frequency is small, and the curves for n_r resemble the positive part of the curves of n^2 shown in Fig. I.3, except that here n_r never quite reaches zero, the infinity has disappeared, and the curves are continuous. In Fig. I.6(b), ν is larger and has the value $Y \sin^2\theta/2\cos\theta \equiv \nu_c$, known as the 'critical collision frequency.' For such a collision frequency, n_r and n_i assume the same values for both waves at $X = 1$. Thus for this electron density, the two types of radio waves are physically indistinguishable. In Fig. I.6(c), ν is greater than the critical collision frequency and the waves are again distinct for all values of X. In all three of these cases, the n_r and n_i versus X curves are continuous, but in going from the first case to the third, an interchange has occurred in the connections between the two curves lying to the left of the $X = 1$ line and the two lying to the right. A similar effect is often observed if ν and Y are kept constant and θ is altered.

In Sec. I.4, the ordinary wave was defined as the one that changed continuously into the mode which, in purely transverse propagation, is unaffected by the magnetic field. A simple method of extending this definition to the case with collisions is to use the name 'ordinary' for the wave that changes continuously into the ordinary wave of the collisionless case, as ν is decreased. Since such a definition is consistent and easily applied, it is employed in this

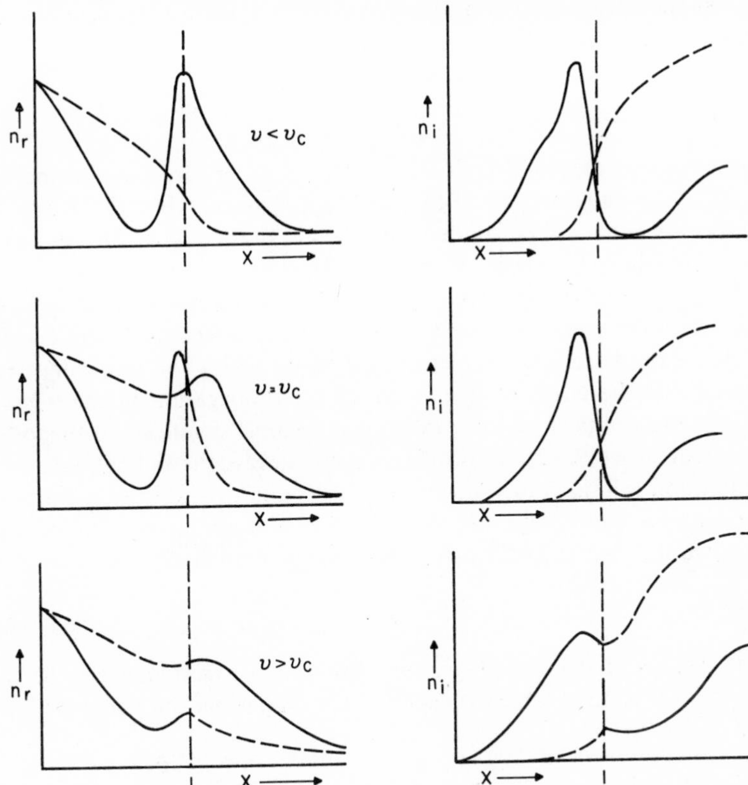

Fig. I.6 Variation of n_r and $|-n_i|$ with X for three values of the collision frequency, (a) $\nu < \nu_c$, (b) $\nu = \nu_c$, and (c) $\nu > \nu_c$, and for fixed values of Y and of the propagation direction.

appendix. It leads, however, to the peculiar result that, when $\nu > \nu_c$, the sections of the continuous curves for n_r and n_i which lie to the left of the line $X = 1$ have a different name from the sections of the same curves which lie to the right of this line. Some authors find this unattractive and prefer to use the same name for all sections of the curves of Fig. I.6. In such a system, the name of a wave depends not only on the criterion used to distinguish the ordinary and extraordinary waves, but also on whether this is applied to the right-hand or left-hand branches of the refractive-index curves.

An entirely different alternative is to name the waves in terms of their polarization instead of the behavior of their refractive indices. One such system defines the ordinary wave as that for which $|E_x/E_y| < 1$. Sometimes the sense of rotation of the electric vector is used, and then the terms 'ordinary' and 'extraordinary' are often replaced by 'electronic' and 'ionic' to distinguish the sense of rotation. Any consistent system of nomenclature can, of course, be used.

I.8. WHISTLER DISPERSION

It has been pointed out in Chapter 5 that whistlers are a useful tool for the study of the outer regions of the earth's ionosphere. Here the properties of this phenomenon will be studied with the aid of the theory of radio-wave propagation which has been developed. This will serve not only as an example of the application of the theory to a particular case but will also illustrate such concepts as group velocity and ray direction, both of which may be developed from the dispersion equation (I.13). The following treatment considers the effect of free electrons on propagation in the whistler mode. The effect of positive ions, which may become significant at the lowest whistler frequencies [7, 12], is considered briefly toward the end of this section.

If attention is limited to whistler propagation in the exosphere, collisions may be ignored, and the QL approximation is valid for nearly all directions of propagation. Thus the refractive index may be written

$$n^2 = 1 - \frac{X}{1 \pm Y\cos\theta}\cdot \tag{I.28}$$

In most regions of the exosphere, the plasma and gyrofrequencies lie well above the VLF band in which whistlers occur, and hence the refractive index may be derived from

$$n^2 = \pm\frac{X}{Y\cos\theta}\cdot \tag{I.29}$$

Only the plus sign gives a real value of n; hence only one mode propagates at low frequencies. This is the ordinary mode, illustrated in Fig. I.5, and is the mode responsible for whistlers. X greatly exceeds Y in practice, so $n \gg 1$ in the case of whistlers.

A whistler is believed to originate in a lightning discharge which radiates a broad band of low frequencies, known as a 'sferic,' in a wide range of directions. Some of these waves are reflected by the ionosphere and hence propagate away from the source via a waveguide mode below the ionosphere. Waves with normals directed close to the zenith direction, however, sometimes propagate through the lower ionosphere and emerge into the exosphere. Such waves are limited in both temporal and spatial extent; hence their propagation must be determined from their group velocities and ray directions. Analysis shows the ray direction of the whistler mode to lie close to the direction of the magnetic field. The wave packet is constrained to move along the magnetic field line, and it expands only very slowly in the direction transverse to this motion. Thus energy from a sferic may enter the ionosphere in one hemisphere, be confined, and guided to a region in the other hemisphere which is magnetically conjugate with the sferic; all the waves comprising a whistler wave packet travel approximately the same path through the ionosphere. As discussed in Chapter 5, this confinement is further enhanced and possibly even dominated by a ducting process.

The velocity with which the path is traversed is the group velocity, given by

$$V_g = d\omega/dk, \tag{I.30}$$

which can be found from Eq. (I.29). Using this velocity, the time taken by a whistler component of frequency $f(\equiv \omega/2\pi)$ to travel along a geomagnetic field line from one hemisphere to the other is found to be

$$t = \frac{1}{2cf^{1/2}} \int \frac{f_0}{f_H^{1/2}}\, ds, \tag{I.31}$$

where the integral is taken over the entire path; ds is an element of length along this path; $f_0 \equiv \omega_0/2\pi$; $f_H \equiv \omega_H/2\pi$; c is the velocity of light; and f is assumed to be very much less than either f_0 or f_H. This expression shows that the higher-frequency components traverse the path more quickly than the lower-frequency components; thus it explains the characteristic change of frequency with time exhibited by whistlers. More important is the fact that t and f are quantities which can be observed, and Eq. (I.31) shows that they are directly related to the plasma and gyrofrequencies and hence to the electron density and magnetic fields along the path. Thus by evaluating the quantity $tf^{1/2}$, which in the present approximation is a constant known as the 'dispersion' of a whistler, much can be learned of the electron densities and magnetic fields existing in the exosphere.

The equations which have been developed here to describe whistler propagation are approximate. These approximations fail for whistlers which travel to very great heights, since the wave frequencies lie close to the gyrofrequency at the top of the path. This leads to the phenomenon of 'nose whistlers' which include both rising and falling tones and do not have a constant dispersion. Such whistlers have a more involved dispersion equation than (I.31), which can be derived from Eq. (I.28), and are of great value in the determination of exospheric electron densities [13].

For very low frequencies, the present treatment of whistler dispersion also fails, since no account has been taken of the motions of positive ions. When such motions are considered, it is found that there is a continuous transition, as the frequency is lowered, from radio waves into hydromagnetic waves. As may be inferred from the discussion in Chapter 8, positive ions may affect the ray direction and hence the ray path (see Figs. 8.3 and 8.4). Positive ions also cause the whistler dispersion to vary as the frequency is decreased to very low values. More specifically, the dispersion increases as the wave frequency approaches the gyrofrequency of an abundant positive ion of the medium. Such an increase is barely detectable [12] because most whistlers do not have components of sufficiently low frequency. This effect is, however, an indication of the transition from radio to hydromagnetic propagation.

I.9. THE DISPERSION EQUATION OF HYDROMAGNETIC WAVES

Throughout this book it has been indicated several times that hydromagnetic waves are currently thought to play an important role in many ionospheric phenomena. Such waves are closely related to ionospheric radio waves; hence the method which has been used in this appendix can be extended to yield the dispersion equation of both wave types. Hydromagnetic waves differ from radio waves mainly in the frequency range in which they occur, and in the fact that the motions of the positive ions and occasionally neutral particles of the medium must be considered in determining their characteristics. The motions of the heavy ions considerably complicate the derivation of the dispersion equation, so only an indication of the manner in which this equation can be obtained will be given. Then some special cases and general characteristics of hydromagnetic propagation, which can be inferred from the dispersion equation, are discussed. It must be remembered, however, that the theory treats plane waves in a homogeneous gas, containing a uniform magnetic field. For hydromagnetic waves with their low frequency and long wavelength, the ionosphere is often a very poor approximation to such a medium.

If an equation similar to Eq. (I.2) is applied to determine the positive-ion motion, a conductivity tensor including the effects of such motions can be obtained. In this calculation [5], ion-electron collisions, pressure terms, and the organized motion of neutral particles are usually neglected. It can be shown that these three approximations are generally valid in the terrestrial ionosphere for periods much shorter than about an hour. For longer periods, in the F region and above, the ionization and neutral gas move together. By making the three foregoing approximations, waves of the acoustic type are ignored.

With the use of the modified conductivity tensor obtained in this manner, a dispersion equation can be found, of which Eq. (I.13) is a special case. This dispersion equation may be written

$$\alpha_4 n^4 + \alpha_2 n^2 + \alpha_0 = 0, \tag{I.32}$$

which is a quadratic equation in n^2, the square of the refractive index, for propagation in a direction forming an angle θ with the magnetic field. The coefficients are given by

$$\alpha_4 = K_0 \cos^2 \theta + K_1 \sin^2 \theta, \tag{I.33}$$

$$\alpha_2 = K_0 K_1 (1 + \cos^2 \theta) + (K_1^2 + K_2^2) \sin^2 \theta, \tag{I.34}$$

$$\alpha_0 = (K_1^2 + K_2^2) K_0, \tag{1.35}$$

where

$$K_0 = 1 - \frac{X_e}{1 - iZ_e} - \frac{X_i}{1 - iZ_i}, \tag{1.36}$$

$$K_1 = 1 + \frac{X_e(1 - iZ_e)}{Y_e^2 - (1 - iZ_e)^2} + \frac{X_i(1 - iZ_i)}{Y_i^2 - (1 - iZ_i)^2}, \tag{I.37}$$

$$K_2 = \frac{-iX_e Y_e}{Y_e^2 - (1 - iZ_e)^2} + \frac{iX_i Y_i}{Y_i^2 - (1 - iZ_i)^2}, \tag{I.38}$$

and where X_e, Y_e, Z_e, X_i, Y_i, Z_i have the same meaning as previously with the collision frequency and gyrofrequency of electrons or ions substituted into the expression for X, Y, and Z.

A relatively simple and important approximation to these equations exists in and above the F region, where the collision frequencies are much smaller than the corresponding gyrofrequencies ($Z_e \ll Y_e$, $Z_i \ll Y_i$), if the angular frequency is well below the ion gyrofrequency and therefore $Y_e \gg 1$, $Y_i \gg 1$. For propagation in directions not nearly perpendicular to the magnetic field one then obtains for the refractive indices n_1, n_2 of the two modes (hydromagnetic waves),

$$n_1^2 = K_1 \tag{I.39}$$

and

$$n_2^2 = K_1/\cos^2\theta, \tag{I.40}$$

where

$$K_1 = 1 + X_e Y_e^{-2}(1 - iZ_e) + X_i Y_i^{-2}(1 - iZ_i). \tag{I.41}$$

Before considering Eqs. (I.39), (I.40), and (I.41) in full, let the approximation be carried one step further by neglecting losses ($Z_e \ll 1, Z_i \ll 1$). Then $K_1 \approx 1 + N(m_e + m_i)/(B_0^2\,\epsilon_0)$, and the mode indicated by Eq. (I.39) has a velocity independent of frequency, given by

$$(\epsilon_0\mu_0 K_1)^{-1/2} = [\epsilon_0\mu_0 + \mu_0 N(m_i + m_e)/B_0^2]^{-1/2}. \tag{I.42}$$

The second term in the bracket on the right of Eq. (I.42) is much larger than the first even at exospheric heights (that is, the velocity of hydromagnetic waves is very much smaller than the velocity of electromagnetic waves in free space), so the velocity of the mode indicated by (I.39) in the absence of collisions is given by

$$B_0[\mu_0 N(m_i + m_e)]^{-1/2} = B_0(\mu_0\rho_c)^{-1/2}, \tag{I.43}$$

where ρ_c is the mass density of charged matter. The expression on the right of Eq. (I.43) is analogous to the formula originally derived by Alfvén [1] for the velocity of hydromagnetic waves in an incompressible perfectly conducting liquid, though ρ_c here replaces the total density of the conducting medium which appeared in Alfvén's case.

The velocity of the mode indicated by (I.40) is $B_0(\mu_0\rho_c)^{-1/2}\cos\theta$, and depends on the direction of propagation. This mode is guided along the magnetic lines of force in much the same way as whistlers.

In the absence of collisions, the two hydromagnetic modes represented by (I.39) and (I.40) can be shown to be identical to the waves that occur in a compressible fully ionized gas, if pressure terms are neglected.

If losses are taken into account [4], then the refractive indices of the two modes are given by Eqs. (I.39), (I.40), and (I.41). The refractive index is determined almost entirely by the ionic term in (I.41), which is much greater than the electronic term or unity with the present assumptions. If the angular frequency of the wave is much greater than the collision frequency of an ion with neutral particles (that is, $Z_i \ll 1$), then the refractive index is very nearly real as already discussed; the attenuation in a wavelength is correspondingly small. If the angular frequency is substantially smaller than the collision frequency of an ion with neutral particles, then the waves suffer very heavy attenuation in a wavelength and their velocity is reduced. The foregoing arguments about attenuation are valid only for periods under about an hour in the ionosphere. The more exact theory would show that at sufficiently low angular frequencies the attenuation again decreases. This happens when the angular frequency is lower than the collision frequency of a neutral particle with ions; the neutral particles then move with the ions and the total density of the gas must be substituted into Alfvén's formula.

At E and D-region heights the gyrofrequency of ions is not greater than the collision frequency of an ion with neutral particles, and therefore the approximations (I.39), (I.40), and (I.41) are invalid. These regions, in which the dynamo currents flow, probably play an important part in reducing the hydromagnetic wave energy that reaches terrestrial observers, particularly in daytime.

REFERENCES

1. Alfvén, H., On the existence of electromagnetic-hydrodynamic waves, *Nature*, **150** (1942), 405.
2. Appleton, E. V., and S. Chapman, The collisional friction experienced by vibrating electrons in ionized air, *Proc. Roy. Soc. A*, **44** (1932), 246.
3. Budden, K. G., Radio Waves in the Ionosphere. London: Cambridge University Press, 1961.
4. Dessler, A. J., Large amplitude hydromagnetic waves above the ionosphere, *J. Geophys. Res.*, **64** (1959), 397.
5. Fejer, J. A., Hydromagnetic wave propagation in the ionosphere, *J. Atmos. Terr. Phys.*, **18** (1960), 135.
6. Gersham, R. N., V. L. Ginsberg, and N. G. Denison, The propagation of electromagnetic waves in plasma (ionosphere), *Usp. Fiz. Nauk. Mask.*, **61** (1957), 561. (Translation by U.S. Atomic Energy Commission.)

7. Hines, C. O., Heavy-ion effects in audio-frequency radio propagation, *J. Atmos. Terr. Phys.*, **11** (1957), 36.

8. Pfister, W., Studies of the refractive index in the ionosphere; the effect of the collision frequency and of ions, in Internat. Conf. on the Physics of the Ionosphere. London: Physical Society, 1955, p. 394.

9. Phelps, A. V., and J. L. Pack, Electron collision frequencies in nitrogen and in the lower ionosphere, *Phys. Rev. Letters*, **3** (1960), 340.

10. Ratcliffe, J. A. The Magneto-ionic Theory. London: Cambridge University Press, 1959.

11. Sen, H. K., and A. A. Wyller, On the generalization of the Appleton-Hartree magnetoionic formulas, *J. Geophys. Res.*, **65** (1960), 3931.

12. Storey, L. R. O., A method to detect the presence of ionized hydrogen in the outer atmosphere, *Can. J. Phys.*, **34** (1956), 1153.

13. Helliwell, R. A., J. H. Crary, J. H. Pope, and R. L. Smith, The "nose" whistler—a new high-latitude phenomenon, *J. Geophys. Res.*, **61** (1956), 139.

14. Hibberd, F. H., Q. L. and Q. T. approximations to the magneto-ionic equations and their validity, *J. Atmos. Terr. Phys.*, **24** (1962), 843.

Appendix II

J. A. Fejer

Wave Propagation in an Inhomogeneous Medium

II.1. INTRODUCTION

Appendix I dealt with the propagation of radio waves in an infinite homogeneous ionized medium. In practice, the properties of the medium usually vary with position. In studies of ionospheric propagation of high-frequency radio waves, it is often reasonable to suppose that the properties are relatively slowly varying functions of height and that the path of a wave packet can be traced through the ionosphere very much like the path of a light ray through an optical system. It is shown in Secs. II.2 and II.3 how double refraction by the earth's magnetic field complicates this ray-tracing procedure by splitting up an incident wave packet into two separate packets, corresponding to the two characteristic waves defined in Appendix I.

For the most part these two wave packets propagate quite independently of each other after separation. There are, however, certain special levels in the ionosphere where the independent propagation of the characteristic waves breaks down even in a slowly varying medium. These levels, in which the simple ray solutions are no longer valid, are discussed in Sec. II.4. A medium, whose properties vary considerably in a wavelength and in which therefore ray solutions are invalid everywhere, is also considered in Sec. II.4.

Superimposed on the regular variation of ionospheric properties with height and the slower variation with geographical position, there are often irregular local variations. Fluctuations caused by turbulence exemplify this type of irregular variation, which is best described by statistical methods. Sections II.5–II.10 treat such irregular variations. A detailed introduction to the methods used for dealing with irregular variations will be deferred to Sec. II.5.

II.2. PROPAGATION IN A HORIZONTALLY STRATIFIED MEDIUM

The propagation of radio waves in a horizontally stratified medium is treated in considerable detail in a recent excellent book by Budden [13]. Sections II.2–II.4 of this Appendix are intended only as a rather elementary introduction to this subject; for further details consult Budden's book.

In propagation over not too long distances it is often sufficiently accurate to neglect the earth's curvature and to treat the ionosphere as stratified along horizontal planes. If the z axis of a cartesian coordinate system is taken in the vertical direction, then the properties of such a horizontally stratified medium depend only on the z coordinate, that is, on the height.

It was seen in Appendix I that the electrical properties of an ionized gas in a magnetic field can be expressed by a conductivity tensor $\boldsymbol{\sigma}$, whose components under the present assumptions depend only on the angular frequency ω and the height z. It was also seen in Appendix I that the differential equations of propagation may be written, after the elimination of $\mathbf{H}$ from Maxwell's two curl equations, in the form

$$\nabla \times \nabla \times \mathbf{E} - (\omega^2/c^2)\mathbf{E} + i\omega\mu_0\boldsymbol{\sigma} \cdot \mathbf{E} = 0. \tag{II.1}$$

In a homogeneous medium $\boldsymbol{\sigma}$ is independent of z. It is then possible to seek plane-wave solutions for E_x, E_y, and E_z, in which a factor $\exp[i(\omega t - k_x x - k_y y - k_z z)]$ is assumed. The spatial differentiations indicated in Eq. (II.1) can then be replaced by factors $-ik_x$, $-ik_y$, $-ik_z$. In this way the three component equations of the vector differential Eq. (II.1) are reduced to a system of three simultaneous linear algebraic equations, as was shown in Appendix I. These equations can have solutions for E_x, E_y, E_z only if the determinant of their coefficients vanishes and even then only if the ratios E_y/E_x and E_z/E_x, which express the polarization of the wave, are appropriate. The algebraic equation that expresses the vanishing of the determinant is called the 'dispersion relation.' This relation indicates the condition that must be satisfied by the angular frequency ω and propagation vector $\mathbf{k}$ of a plane wave in the homogeneous medium considered.

In a horizontally stratified medium the conductivity tensor $\boldsymbol{\sigma}$ is a function of z. Plane-wave solutions can then no longer satisfy Eq. (II.1) though it is still possible to seek solutions for E_x, E_y, and E_z, in which a factor

$\exp [i(\omega t - k_x x - k_y y)]$ is assumed. Then differentiation with respect to x and y can still be replaced by factors $-ik_x$, $-ik_y$, but that with respect to z cannot be treated in a similar manner. In this case, the vector differential equation is reduced to a system of three simultaneous linear differential equations for the dependent variables E_x, E_y, E_z in the single independent variable z. In general therefore, it is necessary to solve these differential equations; the solutions will be different functions of z, each multiplied with the factor $\exp [i(\omega t - k_x x - k_y y)]$.

In an ionospheric problem the values of k_x and k_y are frequently determined by the angle of incidence of a plane wave which enters the ionosphere from a non-ionized region, usually from below.* If the xz plane is chosen so that it contains the wave normal, which forms an angle θ with the z (vertical) axis, then clearly $k_x = (\omega/c) \sin \theta$, and $k_y = 0$.

The retention of the factor $\exp [i(\omega t - k_x x - k_y y)]$ in all oscillating parameters may be regarded as a rather general form of Snell's law which indicates that the horizontal component of the propagation vector $\mathbf{k}$ remains constant. Remember, however, that although the wave variation in the horizontal direction is purely sinusoidal, the same is not generally true in the vertical direction.

Note also that outside the ionosphere there are two possible plane waves whose propagation vectors have the horizontal components $k_x = (\omega/c) \sin \theta$, $k_y = 0$; one of these could correspond to a wave incident on the ionosphere, the other to a reflected wave.

In summing up the present section, it may be stated that in a homogeneous medium the solutions of the differential equations of propagation are plane waves whose angular frequency and propagation vector must satisfy the dispersion equation. In a horizontally stratified medium, the solutions are not plane waves although their variation in the horizontal direction is that of a plane wave; their variation in the vertical direction is obtained by solving a system of three simultaneous linear differential equations.

The solution of these differential equations can often be greatly simplified when the medium is slowly varying, that is, when there is little variation in the properties within a wavelength. These simple solutions, called 'ray solutions,' are discussed in the next section.

II.3. RAY SOLUTIONS

In a horizontally stratified medium whose properties vary sufficiently slowly with height, the solution of the differential equations, over any given relatively narrow range of heights, must resemble closely the plane-wave solution for a homogeneous medium. By the arguments of Sec. II.2, the solution contains a factor, $\exp [i(\omega t - k_x x - k_y y)]$, which is independent of

*In Secs. II.2–II.4, a wave propagating in the direction of increasing electron number density is called 'upgoing'; in the opposite direction, 'downcoming.'

the height. Therefore the vertical component k_z of the propagation vector **k** of a plane wave, that over a narrow range of heights closely approximates the solution of the differential equations, must be a root of the equation derived from the local dispersion equation by substitution of the values k_x, k_y, and ω of the incident wave. For an ionized medium in the presence of a magnetic field this equation may be shown [7] to be of the fourth degree and is usually called 'Booker's quartic.' It is usually written in terms of the dimensionless quantity $q = k_z c/\omega$, whose use corresponds to the use of the complex refractive index $n = kc/\omega$ in Appendix I. In general, the four roots are all different. In the special case of $k_x = k_y = 0$ (vertical incidence) Booker's quartic becomes a quadratic equation in k_z^2 or q^2, the roots of which are given by the Appleton-Hartree formula, Eq. (I.12).

The preceding discussion shows that in the vicinity of any given height the field of a radio wave of frequency ω is well approximated by the sum of the fields of four plane waves. The vertical components $k_{z1}, k_{z2}, k_{z3}, k_{z4}$ of the propagation vectors of these four waves are the four roots of the Booker quartic; the horizontal components are those appropriate to the incident wave.

The four roots of the Booker quartic are in general functions of the height; the question naturally arises whether the local solutions belonging to one of these four roots at different heights could not be joined together to form a single solution of the differential equation over a wide range of heights. Booker [7] noted that usually this is possible for a slowly varying medium. He showed that in such a solution the vertical component of the propagation vector gradually changes with height in such a way that the local dispersion equation is approximately satisfied everywhere; in addition, the polarization of the wave also changes gradually with height so that it is almost identical at all heights to the polarization of the appropriate characteristic wave. The field produced in a slowly varying ionosphere by a plane wave incident from below is therefore in general the sum of four such 'ray solutions' corresponding to the four roots of the Booker quartic.

If collisional losses are absent, the four roots of the Booker quartic are either real or occur in conjugate complex pairs. The real roots are shown in Fig. II.1 as a function of the dimensionless parameter $X = Ne^2/\epsilon_0 m\omega^2$ of Appendix I, for a relatively simple case of high-frequency ionospheric radio-wave propagation. Since the electron number density, which is proportional to X, increases with height at the bottom of the ionosphere, a plot which used height in place of X as the independent variable would be rather similar to Fig. II.1 for heights below the electron density maximum in the F layer. At the bottom of the ionosphere where $X = 0$, there are only two real roots, $k_z = \pm(\omega/c)\cos\theta$ or $q = \pm\cos\theta$, corresponding to the upgoing and downcoming waves in free space, with an angle θ between the wave normal and the zenith.

Still restricting our attention to heights below the F-layer maximum, in

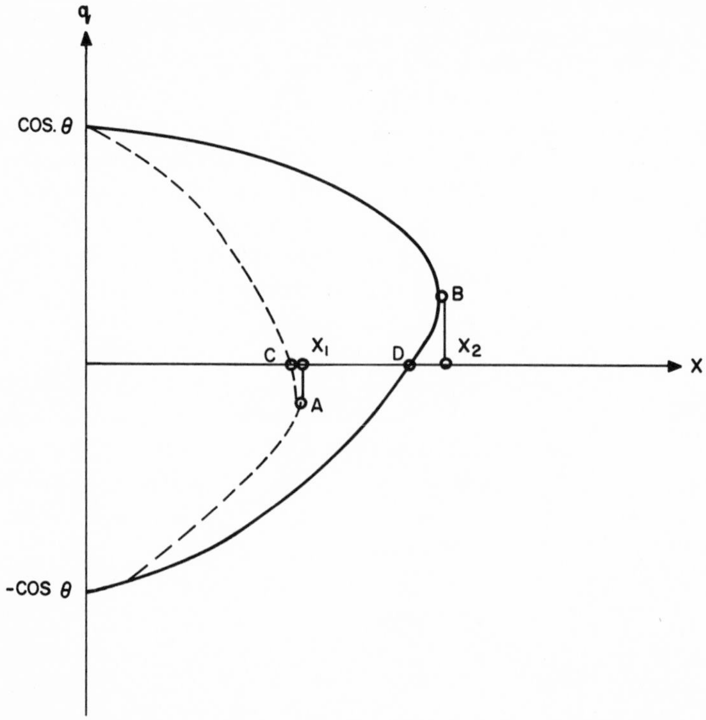

Fig. II.1 Real roots of the Booker quartic for the ordinary (solid line) and extraordinary (dashed line) rays as functions of the dimensionless parameter X. (After Budden [13].)

the height range where $0 < X < X_1$, there are four real roots for q, corresponding to upgoing and downcoming ordinary and extraordinary waves. In the range where $X_1 < X < X_2$, if it exists, there are only two real roots corresponding to upgoing and downcoming ordinary waves. For still greater heights (in the range where $X > X_2$, if it exists) there are no real roots.

It is clear from Fig. II.1 that the extraordinary wave is reflected (changes from an upgoing to a downcoming wave) at point A whereas the ordinary wave is reflected at point B, since the roots for the upgoing and downcoming waves coincide at these points. Note, however, that these are not the points at which the vertical component k_z of the propagation vector changes its sign: the change of sign occurs at the points C and D. Thus we have the rather peculiar situation that between the points A and C the extraordinary wave is still an upgoing wave, but the vertical component of the propagation vector already points downward. Similarly, between B and D, the ordinary wave is already downcoming but the vertical component of its propagation vector still points upward.

This apparent paradox is explained by the fact that the directions of phase and group propagation are in general not the same in a magnetoionic medium. It is easily ascertained that the vertical component of the group velocity (which indicates the direction of energy propagation) changes sign at points A and B and not at C and D. It is the direction of energy propagation which determines whether the wave is going up or coming down.

Group propagation is also of considerable practical interest because our knowledge of ionospheric layers is, to a large extent, obtained from ionosonde measurements of the travel time of a reflected radio wave packet. A graphical construction for the determination of the direction of the group velocity, for a given direction of phase propagation, was given in Chapter 1. If the group velocity vector has been determined for an incident wave packet as a function of the height, then the path of a ray can be determined through the ionosphere by a simple point-to-point tracing procedure.

The situation is particularly simple if we consider the case in which both the collisional losses and the magnetic field can be neglected. The dispersion equation (I.12) is then reduced to

$$k_x^2 + k_y^2 + k_z^2 = \frac{\omega^2}{c^2}\left(1 - \frac{Ne^2}{\epsilon_0 m\omega^2}\right),$$

and it is easily shown that the directions of group and phase propagation coincide. Substitution of $k_x = (\omega/c)\sin\theta$, $k_y = 0$ leads to the rather simple equation,

$$k_z^2 = \frac{\omega^2}{c^2}\left(\cos^2\theta - \frac{Ne^2}{\epsilon_0 m\omega^2}\right),$$

for k_z. As the wave penetrates further into the ionosphere, k_z decreases with increasing N and the ray direction becomes less steep until eventually k_z vanishes for $\cos^2\theta = Ne^2/\epsilon_0 m\omega^2$. At this height the direction of group (and phase) propagation becomes horizontal and reflection takes place.

In the presence of the magnetic field, an incident wave packet is in general separated into an ordinary and an extraordinary wave packet upon entering the ionosphere, corresponding to the two different roots of the Booker quartic shown by Fig. II.1.

In the special case of vertical incidence, the curves of Fig. II.1 are symmetric about the horizontal axis (since the Booker quartic becomes a quadratic in k_z^2) and therefore points A and C and similarly B and D coincide. In this case the phase velocity remains vertical because $k_x = k_y = 0$. The direction of group velocity may then be determined by the graphical construction described in Chapter 1, which shows that the path of a wave packet deviates from the vertical but remains in the magnetic meridian plane. At the top of the trajectory, the group velocity vanishes (hence the large group delay on ionospheric records) and from there the wave packet retraces its path backward. At the reflection point, the trajectory is generally oblique.

Since the path of the wave packet is not vertical and since the deviation from the vertical is different for the different magnetoionic components, the reflection points for these two components are generally displaced from each other horizontally as well as vertically. This is illustrated by Fig. II.2 which shows typical ray paths for the ordinary and extraordinary wave packets in the magnetic meridian plane for vertical incidence. Quite large horizontal separations (of the order of 10 km) of the reflection points are possible.

In the case of oblique incidence, the wave packet does not remain in the plane of incidence unless the latter coincides with the magnetic meridian plane; in the northern hemisphere the ordinary ray deviates to the north, the extraordinary ray to the south of the plane of incidence.

Usually the ray path becomes horizontal at the top of the trajectory, but not always. For example, if the wave packet is incident in the meridian plane, the path of the ordinary ray behaves in the rather peculiar manner indicated in Fig. II.3. As the direction of incidence becomes more oblique, up to a certain limiting angle, the level of reflection does not change with the angle of incidence and the wave does not become horizontal at the top of the trajectory but has a cusp there [13, 33]. The extraordinary ray has no similar cusp at oblique incidence.

Although the present discussion of ray tracing has been restricted to plane stratification, the methods can be extended to general slowly varying

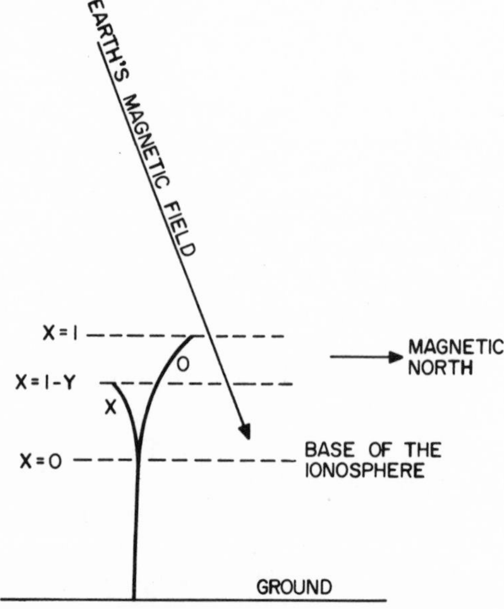

Fig. II.2 The paths of vertically incident wave packets in the northern hemisphere for a frequency greater than the gyrofrequency. The observer is looking towards the magnetic west. (After Budden [13].)

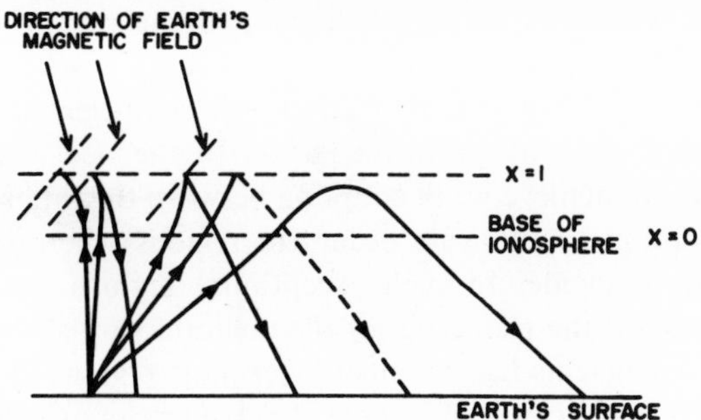

Fig. II.3 Typical ray paths for the ordinary ray in the magnetic meridian. (After Budden [13].)

media [27] since any such medium can be regarded as stratified along parallel planes over a limited region. The constancy of k_x and k_y, however, disappears in this more general case.

II.4. LIMITS OF THE RAY APPROXIMATION

In Sec. II.3 certain approximate solutions of the differential equations of propagation for a horizontally stratified medium, the ray solutions, were described. It was mentioned that a derivation of these solutions in a slowly varying medium was given by Booker [7] who also investigated the conditions of their validity. Later Forsterling [21] and, with greater generality, Clemmow and Heading [15] derived these ray solutions by different methods.

Clemmow and Heading's method of derivation is particularly instructive and elegant; some indication of its principles is given here. They showed that it is possible to define four different linear combinations f_1, f_2, f_3, and f_4 of the four components E_x, E_y, H_x, H_y of the electric and magnetic field vectors in such a manner that, in a slowly varying medium, the system of differential equations for the new variables f_n separates into four weakly coupled first-order linear differential equations for the four variables. The coefficients in the linear combinations definining the new variables f_n are suitably chosen functions of the frequency, the angle of incidence, and the properties of the medium. The resulting system of differential equations for the f_n are then of the form,

$$\frac{df_n}{dz} + ik_{zn}f_n = \sum_{m=1,2,3,4} L_{nm}f_m, \tag{II.2}$$

where the factor $\exp[i(\omega t - k_x x - k_y y)]$ is taken for granted in the variables f_n, the suffix n assumes the values 1, 2, 3, 4 in turn. The k_{zn} are the four roots of Booker's quartic and are functions of the frequency, the angle of incidence, and the properties of the medium. The coupling coefficients L_{nm} in the new differential Eqs. (II.2) are functions of the frequency, the angle of incidence, the properties of the medium, and the rate of change of these properties.

In a sufficiently slowly varying medium the coefficients L_{nm} are in general vanishingly small since the transformation to the new variables has been specially chosen to achieve weak coupling between the differential equations. The only exception to this rule occurs in regions where two roots of the Booker quartic coincide. In such exceptional regions the coefficients L_{nm} remain large even if the properties of the medium vary slowly with distance. Although the coefficients L_{nm} are small over most regions of a slowly varying medium, their neglect can lead to considerable errors over long propagation paths.

More accurate results are obtained if solutions are sought in which one of the variables f_n predominates over the others. The characteristic wave corresponding to that f_n will in fact generate the three other characteristic waves even in a slowly varying medium, but it is reasonable to assume that their amplitudes will be relatively weak since the coupling is weak. It is then reasonable to neglect all coefficients L_{nm} where $m \neq n$ but not the coefficient L_{nn} in Eqs. (II.2). The resulting solution for f_n is then

$$f_n = \exp\left(-i \int^z k_{zn}\, dz + \int^z L_{nn}\, dz\right)$$

or, including the omitted factor, the solution is proportional to

$$\exp\left[i\left(\omega t - k_x x - k_y y - \int^z k_{zn}\, dz\right) + \int^z L_{nn}\, dz\right]. \tag{II.3}$$

Four such solutions are obtained as n assumes the values 1, 2, 3, 4 in succession; they are the ray solutions which were described qualitatively in Sec. II.3.

It is to be remembered that the quantities f_n are obtained by a linear transformation from the quantities E_x, E_y, H_x, H_y. If one considers only the solution for one of the variables f_n, say f_2, this is equivalent to setting $f_1 = f_3 = f_4 = 0$. These three equations define the polarization of the wave associated with the root k_{z2} of the Booker quartic. Since the coefficients in the linear combinations defining f_1, f_3, and f_4 are all slowly varying functions of z, the polarization of the wave associated with k_{z2} changes slowly along the propagation path, as described in the previous section. The ray solutions defined by (II.3) are analogous to the well-known WKB-type solutions of quantum theory. Over a limited region where k_{zn} is approximately constant, these solutions have the properties of one of the characteristic waves appropriate to a homogeneous medium.

The existence of ray solutions of the type discussed in Sec. II.3 is mathematically verified with the aid of the four first-order coupled wave equations of Clemmow and Heading. The same equations show, as mentioned previously, that some of the coupling terms remain large even for a slowly varying medium in a region where two roots of the Booker quartic almost coincide. In such a region those ray solutions which correspond to the two neighboring roots break down; the other two ray solutions given by (II.3) remain valid. 'Coupling' is then said to occur between two of the characteristic waves.

It is convenient to differentiate between three different types of coupling. In the first type, which occurs at points A and B of Fig. II.1, the roots corresponding to the upgoing and downcoming waves of the same magnetoionic mode coincide (if losses are neglected). This form of coupling is merely another name for ionospheric reflection. Energy is transferred here from one characteristic (upgoing) wave to another characteristic (downcoming) wave. In a slowly varying medium the reflection coefficient may be obtained by a mathematical technique, called the 'phase-integral method,' which is also applicable to other coupling problems. The method may be illustrated by its application to the reflection of a wave vertically incident on the ionosphere.

The analytic extension of the function $n(z)$, where $n(z)$ is the complex refractive index, as a function of the real height z, must first be obtained. In the presence of losses, $n(z)$ does not vanish for any real height z which could be regarded for convenience as the reflection level. There is, however, always a complex solution z_0 to the equation $n(z) = 0$. The phase-integral formula [13] for the reflection coefficient R is then

$$R = i\exp\left(-2i\frac{\omega}{c}\int_0^{z_0} q\,dz\right),$$

and z_0 is sometimes said to be the 'complex height of reflection.'

In a second type of coupling, two roots of the quartic corresponding to an ordinary and extraordinary wave coincide for a value of X different from zero. At vertical incidence this type of coupling is possible only in the presence of losses. The roots corresponding to ordinary and extraordinary waves coincide at vertical incidence where $X = 1$ (that is, at the reflection level for the ordinary wave) if at the same time the collision frequency is equal to the so-called critical collision frequency defined in Appendix I. At such a level, if it exists, the independent propagation of characteristic waves breaks down and a wave packet, which before entering the coupling region had one of the characteristic polarizations, gives rise to two characteristic wave packets leaving the region; they have the different polarizations of the two coupled modes and follow different ray paths. This type of coupling appears to play an important part in the reflection of 150 kc/s radio waves at vertical incidence [16].

The second type of coupling can play an even greater part in propagation at oblique incidence, where two roots of the Booker quartic can coincide even in the absence of collisions. Conditions for such coincidences may be seen by examining the solutions of the Booker quartic in cases more complicated than those of Fig. II.1. A typical example is shown by Fig. II.4 where

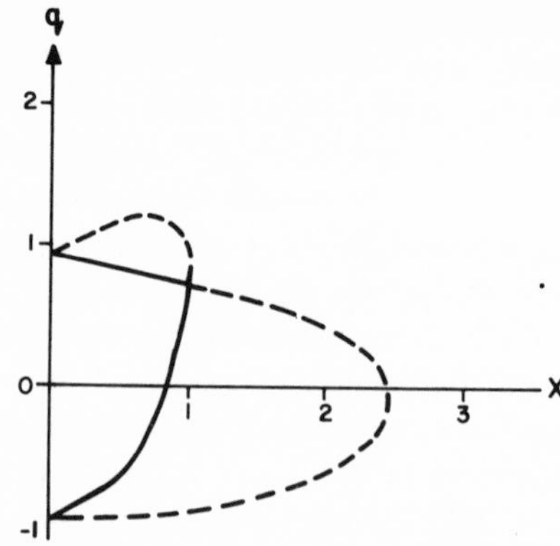

Fig. II.4 Real roots of the Booker quartic for north-south propagation when $Y = 2$ and the earth's field is inclined at 30° to the vertical. The angle of incidence has the critical value 24.2° so that the curves for the ordinary (solid line) and extraordinary (dashed line) rays meet on the line $X = 1$. (After Budden [13].)

the curves for the ordinary and extraordinary waves meet on the line $X = 1$. These curves represent the real roots of the Booker quartic and they do not show the effect of losses.

The third type of coupling occurs in regions where the frequency of the wave is well above the plasma frequency. The roots corresponding to ordinary and extraordinary components then almost coincide, since propagation occurs very nearly in free space. It is clear that the polarization of an actual wave cannot change in these regions. The polarizations of the characteristic waves of the magnetoionic theory—as given by Eq. (I.14)—continue, however, to change with height even if the number density of free electrons (and therefore X) becomes negligibly small, since the collision frequency (and therefore Z) changes with height. Coupling here has the purely formal function of insuring that the actual polarization of a traveling wave packet does not change, in spite of the change in the polarization of characteristic waves. The division into characteristic wave packets is itself highly artificial under these conditions, of course. The point at which coupling causes the splitting up of an originally pure downcoming characteristic wave into a combination of two characteristic waves, whose resultant does not change polarization, cannot be obtained from a ray approximation. The so-called limiting polarization, attained by such a wave after its emergence from an ionized medium, can only be determined from full-wave solutions [13].

If the properties of a stratified medium vary a great deal within a wavelength, then it is not possible to use either the ray approximation or the phase-integral method. For example, full-wave solutions are required to solve propagation problems for VLF radio waves whose wavelengths in free space are of the order of 20–30 km. At heights where such VLF waves are reflected, the ionospheric properties change substantially over distances of only a few kilometers, that is, in distances that are short compared with the wavelength. Full-wave solutions of the differential equations (II.1) for VLF wave propagation have been obtained by both analytical and numerical methods [2, 13]. The numerical solutions were based on models of the ionosphere derived from observations at higher frequencies, and the computations were used to test the different models by a comparison of the solutions with the results of VLF observations. The model that was in closest accord with the observations has been found and suggestions for its improvement have been made [2].

The propagation of VLF waves, other than those propagating in the whistler mode, must always be treated by full-wave theory in terrestrial applications; ray solutions and the phase-integral method are usually adequate for the treatment of higher-frequency propagation. Exceptions to this rule occur in regions where the rate of change in the properties of the medium with height is particularly rapid. For example, a very thin layer of intense ionization could be partially transparent even though ray theory would indicate total reflection. (The case is analogous to the well-known tunnel effect in quantum theory.) Such very thin layers of intense ionization are believed to be responsible for certain types of sporadic-E echoes observed on ionograms, as noted in Sec. 3.4, and a full-wave solution is required to determine their reflection and transmission properties [13].

The exospheric propagation of whistlers is believed to be guided by refraction in ducts aligned along the lines of force of the earth's magnetic field (see Sec. 5.3.2). Certain observations have been interpreted as evidence to indicate that occasionally even radio waves with frequencies of the order of 15 mc/s may be propagated in such exospheric ducts [24]. In all these cases, ray solutions indicate whether there is sufficient refraction for ducting, but full-wave theory is necessary to determine whether, with a given amount of refraction, the duct is sufficiently wide to support wave propagation at the frequency of interest. Similar problems have been thoroughly investigated in the theory of microwave propagation in tropospheric ducts [10]. Ducted propagation is discussed in considerable detail by Budden [13].

II.5. PROPAGATION IN AN IRREGULAR MEDIUM

In Secs. II.2–II.4, some of the methods available for solving problems of radio wave propagation in a variable medium were outlined. These methods are useful if the properties of the medium are relatively simple functions of position. The properties, however, often vary in a rather complicated and irregular manner with position. In other cases irregular variations are superimposed on larger variations of a more regular nature.

Many observations indicate the existence of irregularities superimposed on the more regular stratified distribution of electrons in the ionosphere. The best known of these is the irregular amplitude fluctuation or fading of ionospherically reflected radio waves. Signals received from satellite-borne transmitters also show irregular fluctuations. The so-called scintillation of radio stars falls into the same category. Spread echoes on ionosonde records are another manifestation of irregularities, and ionospheric echoes observed by VHF and UHF radar installations operating near the auroral zone are usually attributed to similar causes.

Communications engineers have exploited the existence of ionospheric irregularities. Scattering by such irregularities makes possible the propagation of VHF radio waves to distances well beyond the horizon, even when the operating frequency exceeds the maximum frequency that could be transmitted over the same path by simple reflection (the so-called maximum usable frequency, or MUF). Tropospheric irregularities in the dielectric constant of neutral air have been exploited in a similar manner for communication on even higher frequencies [14].

There are two related but rather different methods of studying the effects of an irregular ionosphere on radio wave propagation. In the one method [9], it is assumed that a statistical description of the field of the downcoming waves is available on a horizontal plane just below the ionosphere. It is then possible to determine the field in the free-space region which is assumed to exist below that plane. The field in that region may always be represented as a sum of an infinite number of plane waves, of different amplitudes and traveling in different directions, as specified by the so-called angular spectrum. A study of the relationship between this angular spectrum and the statistical properties of the field on the horizontal plane just below the ionosphere is a good introduction to a more general study of propagation in irregular media.

The other method [8] considers random three-dimensional irregularities in the properties of the medium. A description of the medium in terms of such irregularities may often be expected to be more useful than the description in terms of an irregular planar screen used in the first method.

The mathematical methods used in the treatment of propagation in irregular media are merely outlined in the following sections. The emphasis is on the physical ideas behind the mathematical methods and on the conclusions of the theory. Many of the subjects discussed in the following sections are treated in more detail in an excellent survey by Ratcliffe [36].

II.6. THE PHASE-CHANGING SCREEN

As mentioned in Sec. II.5, it is often convenient to assume that the field of a downcoming 'irregular' radio wave is known on a horizontal plane just below the ionosphere. One of the main effects of an irregular ionosphere on an incident wave, whether it is reflected or transmitted, is an irregular change of phase along the wave front. It therefore seems reasonable to represent the effect of such an ionospheric layer on a normally incident wave by a phase-changing screen, parallel to the wave front, situated at about the height where the wave emerges from the layer. In the absence of irregularities, the phase would be constant along such a screen. The effect of the irregularities may be represented, in the first approximation, by a phase change which is a function of position along the screen. Representation of ionospheric irregularities by such a phase-changing screen has been used in investigations of radio star scintillation [28].

Let such a screen be situated in the $z = 0$ plane of a cartesian coordinate system. A wave normally incident from the negative z direction is assumed and for simplicity the phase change impressed by the screen on the wave is taken to be independent of the y coordinate. (For the ionospheric application previously cited, it is the negative z axis that now represents the upward direction.) The electric field vector is taken to be parallel to the y axis; its magnitude $E(x, z)$ is a function of both x and z whose value, $E(x, 0) = E_0 \exp[i\phi(x)]$, is given on the $z = 0$ plane. Here $\phi(x)$ represents the phase change introduced by the screen, whereas the factor $\exp(i\omega t)$ is taken for granted in E_0.

It is convenient to consider first the relatively simple case where $\phi(x) = \phi_0 \cos(ax)$ and to assume further that $\phi_0 \ll 1$. The exponential in the expression for $E(x, 0)$ can then be expanded to give

$$\begin{aligned} E(x, 0) &= E_0 \exp[i\phi_0 \cos(ax)] \simeq E_0[1 + i\phi_0 \cos(ax)] \\ &\simeq E_0[1 + \tfrac{1}{2}i\phi_0 \exp(iax) + \tfrac{1}{2}i\phi_0 \exp(-iax)]. \end{aligned} \tag{II.4}$$

It is known that plane waves of the form $\exp[-i(k_x x + k_z z)]$ are solutions of the wave equation in free space (that is, for $z > 0$), where $k_z = (\omega^2/c^2 - k_x^2)^{1/2}$. It is clear from the form of Eq. (II.4) that $E(x, z)$ is the sum of three such plane waves with $k_x = 0$, $k_x = -a$, and $k_x = a$, respectively. Thus the field beyond the screen is

$$\begin{aligned} E(x, z) = {} & E_0 \exp[-i(\omega/c)z] + \tfrac{1}{2}iE_0\phi_0 \exp\{i[ax - (\omega^2/c^2 - a^2)^{1/2}z]\} \\ & + \tfrac{1}{2}iE_0\phi_0 \exp\{i[-ax - (\omega^2/c^2 - a^2)^{1/2}z]\}. \end{aligned} \tag{II.5}$$

The first of these three plane waves has the same direction as the incident wave, and in the case of an irregular screen it would be called the 'specular component.' The wave normals of the remaining two waves form the angle $\sin^{-1}(ac/\omega)$ with the wave normal of the incident wave as shown in Fig. II.5. These two diffracted waves, caused by the sinusoidal phase change, are of the propagating type if $ac/\omega < 1$. If this latter condition is not satisfied then the two diffracted waves are evanescent.

It follows from Eq. II.5 that, if the spatial extent a^{-1} of the corrugations

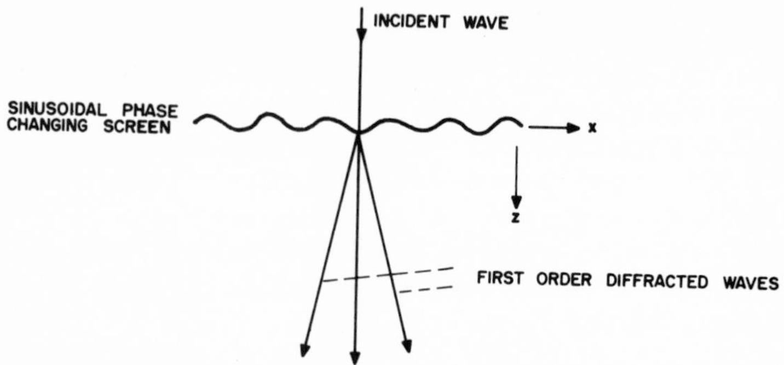

Fig. II.5 Wave normals of incident and first-order diffracted waves for a sinusoidal phase-changing screen.

of the phase screen is large, then the angle between the diffracted waves and the incident wave is small. As the spatial extent of the corrugations becomes smaller (that is, the screen structure becomes finer), so the angle between the diffracted waves and the incident wave increases until eventually the diffracted waves are evanescent.

If all three waves are nonevanescent, it is interesting to use Eq. (II.5) to examine the variation of the magnitude $E(x, z_0)$ along planes $z = z_0$ parallel to the screen. Inspection shows that the variation is one of only phase if $[\omega/c - (\omega^2/c^2 - a^2)^{1/2}]z_0 = n\pi$ and that it is a variation of only amplitude if $[\omega/c - (\omega^2/c^2 - a^2)^{1/2}]z_0 = (n + \frac{1}{2})\pi$, where n is an integer. The sum of these three plane waves thus leads, on different parallel planes, to different field distributions, which change periodically from pure phase variation to pure amplitude variation, as the distance from the phase-changing screen is varied.

If the second and third waves in Eq. (II.5) are evanescent, then the field $E(x, z)$ of these two waves decreases in amplitude very rapidly with the distance z from the screen, and at a distance of a few wavelengths, the first term alone in (II.5) has appreciable amplitude.

The three waves of Eq. (II.5) in this example form the angular spectrum of the phase-changing screen. This screen is of a rather special nature in that the variation of phase is much smaller than a radian and is purely sinusoidal. In reality the phase variation is unlikely to be sinusoidal and there will probably be an irregular variation of both amplitude and phase. It is, however, always possible to express the variation of the field on the screen in terms of a Fourier integral (which would be two-dimensional [18] if the present assumption of one-dimensional symmetry were dropped),

$$E(x, 0) = (2\pi)^{-1/2} \int_{-\infty}^{\infty} P(k_x) \exp(-ik_x x)\, dk_x, \tag{II.6}$$

where the individual terms still resemble the terms of (II.4) although there is in general an infinite number of terms. Each Fourier component of the field distribution (II.6) corresponds to a wave whose wave normal forms an angle $\sin^{-1}(k_x c/\omega)$ with the wave normal of the incident wave. For some of these waves the angle is complex; these waves are evanescent and their effect is negligible at great distances from the screen. The field beyond the screen (for $z > 0$) is given by an equation similar to (II.5), derived from (II.6).

Before leaving the subject of the sinusoidal phase-changing screen it is instructive to remove the previous restriction on the phase change ϕ_0 which was assumed to be much smaller than a radian. Instead of the approximate expression (II.4) one then has the Fourier expansion

$$E(x, 0) = E_0 \exp(i\phi_0 \cos ax) = E_0 \sum_{p=-\infty}^{p=\infty} i^p J_p(\phi_0) \exp(ipax),$$

where J_p is the Bessel function of the first kind of order p. For $\phi_0 \ll 1$ one has $J_1(\phi_0) \simeq \frac{1}{2}\phi_0 \gg J_2(\phi_0) \gg J_3(\phi_0) \ldots$, and the two first-order diffracted waves of Eq. (II.4) are regained. If, however, $\phi_0 \gg 1$, then the higher-order diffracted waves ($|p| \gg 1$), which form angles $\sin^{-1}(pac/\omega)$ with the wave normal of the incident wave, can no longer be neglected; most of the energy is contained in those waves for which $p \approx \phi_0$.

This is illustrated by Fig. II.6 which exhibits the components of the angular spectrum for $\phi_0 = 0.1$ and $\phi_0 = 10$. Figure II.6 shows that the propagation direction of the waves which are most prominent in the angular spectrum depends not only on the structure a^{-1} of the phase variations but also on the amount of the phase change ϕ_0. The greater ϕ_0 is in comparison to unity, the greater (for the same value of a) is the angle between the strongest diffracted waves and the incident wave. For $\phi_0 \ll 1$, however, the angle between the incident wave and the two diffracted waves depends only on the value of a, that is, on the spatial structure of the phase screen. Thus,

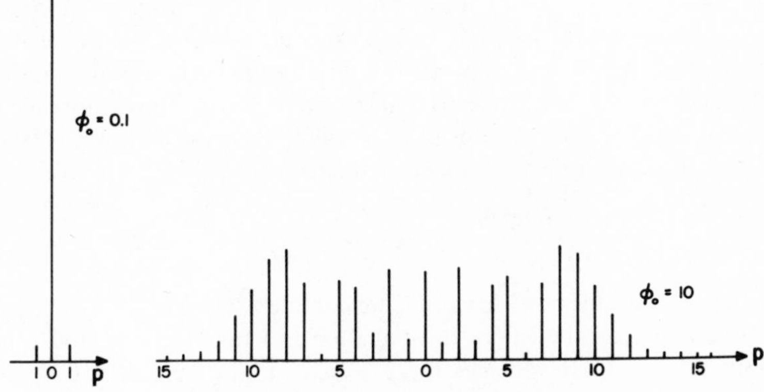

Fig. II.6 Magnitudes of the components of different order p in the angular spectrum of a sinusoidal phase-changing screen for sample cases in which $\phi_0 = 0.1$ and $\phi_0 = 10$.

although the distribution of power in the angular spectrum is closely related to the distribution of power among the spatial Fourier components of the field distribution on a plane, it would be quite wrong to infer that the distribution of power in the angular spectrum is determined only by the spatial extent of the irregularities in the ionosphere. This is clearly not true of a phase-changing screen with a phase deviation much larger than a radian. A more general discussion of the relations between the angular spectrum and the field distribution on a plane is given in the next section.

II.7. THE ANGULAR POWER SPECTRUM AND THE AUTOCORRELATION FUNCTION

Section II.6 discussed the example of a sinusoidal phase-changing screen in considerable detail. The methods used in the solution of that particular problem can be generalized, as was already indicated. Thus it is always possible to express the field $E(x, 0)$ on the $z = 0$ plane (still assuming one-dimensional symmetry for simplicity) as a Fourier integral of the form (II.6). The corresponding field on the free-space ($z > 0$) side of the screen may then be expressed as a sum of plane waves which form angles $\sin^{-1}(k_x c/\omega)$ with the z axis. Some of these waves may be evanescent. The quantity $|P(k_x)|^2$ indicates the distribution of power in this assembly of plane waves; it is usually called the 'angular power spectrum,' in which case it is thought of as a function of the angle $\sin^{-1}(k_x c/\omega)$. In the case of an antenna, a polar plot of the angular power spectrum is called the 'polar diagram.' In principle the angular power spectrum of waves coming from the ionosphere could be determined experimentally by means of a highly directional steerable antenna system situated on the ground.

The angular power spectrum is given by the inverse Fourier transformation of Eq. (II.6) which expresses $P(k_x)$ in terms of $E(x, 0)$. Unfortunately, $P(k_x)$ is usually a very rapidly varying function of k_x for a screen of large size (indeed, the integral for $P(k_x)$ diverges as the screen becomes infinitely large), and therefore $|P(k_x)|^2$ does not seem to be a particularly useful quantity for the characterization of a large irregular screen. Fortunately, however, it is possible to show [9, 39] that if (II.6) is valid, then the following 'Wiener-Kintchine theorem' follows from it mathematically:

$$\frac{\int_{-\infty}^{\infty} E^*(x, 0)E(x + \xi, 0)\, dx}{\int_{-\infty}^{\infty} |E(x, 0)|^2\, dx} = \frac{\int_{-\infty}^{\infty} |P(k_x)|^2 \exp(-i\xi k_x)\, dk_x}{\int_{-\infty}^{\infty} |P(k_x)|^2\, dk_x}. \tag{II.7}$$

The asterisk indicates here the conjugate complex value.

The quantity on the left of this equation is a function of ξ and is equal to unity for $\xi = 0$. It vanishes for $\xi = \pm\infty$ if the field $E(x, 0)$ vanishes outside a finite area of the screen. In future discussion such a screen will be called a 'finite screen.'

The function of ξ defined by the left-hand side of Eq. (II.7) is called the 'autocorrelation function' $\rho(\xi)$ of the field on the screen. The usefulness of the autocorrelation function becomes evident when it is used for very large irregular screens. For such a very large statistically uniform irregular screen, the value of the autocorrelation function for a particular value of ξ can be given a simple statistical interpretation, which incidentally shows how the autocorrelation function could be determined experimentally.

The real part of the expression on the left of Eq. (II.7) could be determined by averaging, for pairs of points separated by the same distance ξ in the x direction, the product of the amplitudes of the electric fields and of the cosine of the phase angle between them, over the whole screen. This average value, regarded as a function of ξ, is then normalized by dividing it by its value for $\xi = 0$. In the determination of the imaginary part of the same expression, the sine must be substituted for the cosine of the phase difference. This procedure is in accordance with the adopted definition:

$$\rho(\xi) \equiv \frac{\int_{-\infty}^{\infty} E^*(x, 0)\, E(x + \xi, 0)\, dx}{\int_{-\infty}^{\infty} |\, E(x, 0)\,|^2\, dx}. \tag{II.8}$$

The autocorrelation function therefore indicates the values of certain statistical averages taken over a large and statistically uniform irregular screen. In terms of this definition it is always necessary to use a screen very much larger than ξ in order to determine $\rho(\xi)$ for a given value of ξ. In practice the averaging process must be carried out only for values somewhat in excess of the largest irregularities present in the screen. For larger values of ξ, the autocorrelation function either vanishes or, as will be seen later, is a periodic function or a constant. Another property of the autocorrelation function follows from its definition: its absolute value never exceeds unity.

In addition to these mathematical approaches, the autocorrelation function may be described in a more intuitive manner: it indicates the size and shape of the irregularities in the field distribution on the screen. Qualitatively the approximate distance, beyond which $\rho(\xi)$ approaches its value (or behavior) at infinity, is related to the size of the irregularities. The irregular parts of the field at points closer to each other than the size of the irregularities are correlated, whereas the irregular fields at points further from each other are uncorrelated.

Intuitive descriptions of this nature are useful as long as their limits are realized. It will be clear from subsequent arguments that the autocorrelation function often does not fully describe the shape of the irregularities even in a statistical sense. Moreover, the intuitive description is not very useful if irregularities of many different sizes are present simultaneously.

Returning now to the mathematical formulation, we may combine Eqs. (II.7) and (II.8) into the form

$$\rho(\xi) = \frac{\int_{-\infty}^{\infty} |P(k_x)|^2 \exp(-i\xi k_x)\, dk_x}{\int_{-\infty}^{\infty} |P(k_x)|^2\, dk_x}. \tag{II.9}$$

This equation indicates that the autocorrelation function $\rho(\xi)$ is proportional to the Fourier transform of the angular power spectrum $|P(k_x)|^2$. Similarly $|P(k_x)|^2$ is proportional to the inverse Fourier transform of the autocorrelation function. It is interesting to note that, if the angular power spectrum is determined by taking the Fourier transform of the autocorrelation function of a large irregular screen, a smoothly varying function of k_x is obtained. In contrast to this, it has been pointed out earlier that if the angular power spectrum is determined for a large irregular screen from the field distribution itself, using the inverse form of Eq. (II.6), then a very rapidly varying function of k_x is obtained for $|P(k_x)|^2$.

This apparent contradiction is resolved when it is remembered that, although the definition using the inverse of (II.6) is meaningful only for a finite screen (since the defining integral diverges as the size of the screen approaches infinity), the definition using the inverse of (II.9) is statistically meaningful only for an infinitely large screen over which a statistical average $\rho(\xi)$ can be taken for any finite value of ξ. For a given finite screen, the two definitions are identical. The discussion here is restricted to screens over which Eq. (II.8) for $\rho(\xi)$ yields a statistical average value and the angular power spectrum will be taken as defined by the inverse of (II.9). The rapid fluctuations are thus averaged out in the angular power spectrum, and the use of divergent integrals is avoided.

The autocorrelation function does not necessarily vanish at infinity. It follows from Eq. (II.9) that if the angular power spectrum contains one or more δ-functions, that is, if there are plane waves containing a finite amount of power in the angular spectrum, then the autocorrelation function remains finite at infinity. This is clear from the nature of the Fourier transform of a δ-function. It is also clear from the example of the sinusoidal phase-changing screen treated in Sec. II.6 and from the theory of scattering by volume irregularities treated in Sec. II.8 that the angular spectrum may contain such plane waves. The so-called specular component would indeed be the only wave in the absence of irregularities, and a significant amount of power often remains in this specular component even in the presence of irregularities.

The relation expressed by Eq. (II.8) has another useful application. It was mentioned previously that one method for the measurement of the angular power spectrum of waves leaving the ionosphere would be the use of a large steerable highly directional antenna system. For long wavelengths this is obviously impractical. It is, however, sufficient to measure the autocorrelation function defined by (II.8) and then to calculate its Fourier transform. The measurement of the autocorrelation function is made convenient in practice with the aid of two receivers separated by an adjustable distance ξ. The averaging can be carried out in time rather than in space, since the ionospheric irregularities usually drift with respect to the observer and in any case change with time. By repeated measurements of the expression given by (II.8) for different distances ξ, it is possible to determine experimentally the autocorrelation function $\rho(\xi)$, at least in principle. Two separate measurements must be carried out to determine the real and the imaginary parts of $\rho(\xi)$, as was outlined in the discussion preceding Eq. (II.8).

It must be stressed that the autocorrelation function alone does not describe the field distribution fully, even in a statistical sense. This is clear from the example of the sinusoidal phase-changing screen where the field distribution on planes parallel to the screen changes periodically from a field of constant amplitude to a field of constant phase as the distance from the screen is varied. The angular power spectrum and therefore the autocorrelation function are the same for all these parallel planes. The same type of situation is possible with irregular field distributions; an irregular variation of the amplitude could lead to the same autocorrelation function as an irregular variation of phase.

There are, however, certain situations in which the autocorrelation function determines the statistical nature of the field distribution fully. For example, the field over a finite area of a plane parallel to an irregular diffracting screen (or scattering layer) of infinite lateral extent is fully determined statistically by the autocorrelation function, if the distance from the parallel plane to the screen is very large compared to the area of observation which itself is large compared to the size of the largest irregularities of the screen. This is true even if a specular component (that is, a δ-function) is present in the power spectrum although the phase of the specular component is not determined.

It is easy to understand why the statistical properties of the far field are determined by the power spectrum or the autocorrelation function; at a very distant point, waves propagating in different directions come from sections of the screen which are very far removed from each other and which are therefore uncorrelated. The statistical properties of the field produced by such a randomly phased angular spectrum are fully determined by the autocorrelation function or by the power spectrum. The theory of these statistical properties is rather similar to the theory of random noise in electrical circuits (in which it is assumed that the components of the frequency spectrum have random phases), although there are differences in detail owing to the two-dimensional nature of angular spectra [11].

II.8. WEAK SCATTERING BY THREE-DIMENSIONAL IRREGULARITIES

The previous sections attacked the problem of wave propagation in an irregular medium in a rather indirect manner, with the assumption that the field distribution is known after emergence from the medium containing the irregularities. In this section a more direct attack will be made by assuming that the irregular distribution of the dielectric constant in an isotropic medium is known in a statistical sense as a function of position within a certain scattering volume V. The field of the scattered waves may then be regarded as the sum of the radiation fields of elementary oscillating electric dipoles of moment $\mathbf{E}\,\Delta\epsilon\,dV$ where $\Delta\epsilon$ is the deviation of the dielectric constant from its mean value and $\mathbf{E}$ is the oscillating electric field inside the volume element dV. The problem will be simplified in the present section by assuming that the field of the scattered waves may be neglected in comparison with the field of the incident wave inside the volume V; the electric field $\mathbf{E}$ in the foregoing expression for the moments of elementary oscillating dipoles is thus taken to be the field of the incident wave alone. This approximation of 'weak scattering' is also known as the 'Born approximation.'

The field of the scattered waves at a point very far from the scattering volume V may then be expressed as a volume integral over V of the radiation fields originating from the dipoles of moment $\mathbf{E}\,\Delta\epsilon\,dV$. The analysis is not carried out here in detail and only the final result is given; more details are available in a paper by Booker and Gordon [8].

A quantity of particular interest is the angular distribution of the scattered power. It may be shown that this angular distribution can be expressed in terms of a three-dimensional autocorrelation function of the irregular deviations $\Delta\epsilon$. This autocorrelation function is defined as

$$\rho(\xi, \eta, \zeta) = [V\overline{(\Delta\epsilon)^2}]^{-1} \int_V \Delta\epsilon(x, y, z)\, \Delta\epsilon(x + \xi, y + \eta, z + \zeta)\, dx\, dy\, dz, \tag{II.10}$$

in much the same way as the one-dimensional autocorrelation function of the previous section. The deviation $\Delta\epsilon$ is assumed real so that there is no need now for the conjugate complex sign of the earlier expression. The averaging must be carried out over a volume very much larger than the size of the irregularities, keeping the vector (ξ, η, ζ) between the pair of points (x, y, z) and $(x + \xi, y + \eta, z + \zeta)$ constant.

It is usual to express the angular distribution of the scattered power in terms of the scattering cross section σ of the medium, defined as the power scattered per unit scattering volume, unit incident power density, and unit solid angle. The following relationship, similar to the inverse form of Eq. (II.9), may then be shown [8] to be valid:

$$\sigma\epsilon^2\lambda^4/\pi^2\overline{(\Delta\epsilon)^2} = \iiint \rho(\xi, \eta, \zeta) \exp i[(k_x - K_x)\xi + (k_y - K_y)\eta + (k_z - K_z)\zeta]\, d\xi\, d\eta\, d\zeta, \tag{II.11}$$

where λ is the wavelength, $\mathbf{K}$ is the propagation vector of the incident wave, and **k** is the propagation vector of the scattered waves. This is a three-dimensional Fourier transform relationship between the two quantities

$$\sigma(k_x - K_x, k_y - K_y, k_z - K_z)$$

and $\rho(\xi, \eta, \zeta)$. If the autocorrelation function $\rho(\xi, \eta, \zeta)$ and the mean square deviation $\overline{(\Delta\epsilon)^2}$ are known, then the scattering cross section σ may be calculated from Eq. (II.11) as a function of the difference between the propagation vectors of the scattered and the incident waves.

One interesting property of Eq. (II.11) is that it leads to a useful equivalence theorem relating the scattering cross section at one frequency and scattering geometry to the scattering cross section for any different frequency and geometry for which $\mathbf{k} - \mathbf{K}$ is unchanged. A typical example would be backscatter on a frequency f and forward scatter at an angle θ with the vertical on a frequency $f \sec \theta$. In such a case, the ratio of the scattering cross sections is equal to the ratio of the factors $\overline{(\Delta\epsilon)^2}/\lambda^4 \epsilon^2$ at the two frequencies. This ratio is unity for scattering by an ionized gas at frequencies well above the plasma frequency, where $\epsilon^2 \simeq \epsilon_0^2 =$ constant, and $\overline{(\Delta\epsilon)^2}$ is proportional to f^{-4} or to λ^4. This means that the scattering cross section of such an ionized gas is the same for backscatter at a frequency f as for forward scatter at an angle θ with the vertical at a frequency $f \sec \theta$. For example, the scattering cross section for beyond-the-horizon propagation to distances of the order of 1500 km by ionospheric forward scatter on a frequency of 50 Mc/s, say, must be the same as the scattering cross section for vertical incidence backscatter at the midpoint of the path on a frequency of about 10 Mc/s, if weak scattering alone is involved.

A similar equivalence exists for forward scatter by tropospheric irregularities, except that for them $\overline{(\Delta\epsilon)^2}$ is independent of the frequency, and therefore the scattering cross section for the frequency f for vertical incidence backscatter is smaller by a factor $\cos^4 \theta$ than the scattering cross section for the equivalent frequency $f \sec \theta$ for forward scatter.

Equation (II.11) cannot be used for quantitative predictions of the scattered power until some assumptions are made about the autocorrelation function. In particular, the frequency dependence of the scattering cross section (which is hidden in its dependence on $\mathbf{k} - \mathbf{K}$) is entirely determined by the dependence of ρ on ξ, η, and ζ. Only if the function $\rho(\xi, \eta, \zeta)$ can be determined either theoretically or experimentally, is it possible to predict the scattered power and its dependence on frequency using Eq. (II.11). Alternatively, if the dependence of the scattered power on frequency and on the scattering geometry can be determined experimentally, then the shape of the autocorrelation function may be calculated from the inverse relation corresponding to (II.11).

Equation (II.11) has been used to explain the aspect sensitivity of auroral radar echoes by assuming that the correlation of auroral irregularities decreases more slowly in a direction parallel to the magnetic field (say, in the ζ direction) than in a direction perpendicular to it (the ξ and η directions). This is equivalent to the assumption that the auroral irregularities are elongated in the direction of the magnetic field, as discussed in Chapter 14.

II.9. MULTIPLE SCATTERING

In Sec. II.8 it was assumed that the field of the scattered waves is much weaker than the field of the incident wave at all points in the scattering medium. If the thickness of a scattering layer of a given type is increased above a certain critical value, the assumption of weak scattering breaks down. The problem then becomes one of multiple scattering and is not easily solved, except in certain special cases. For example, the angular power spectrum for small-angle multiple scattering by a thick scattering layer has been determined [18] for an isotropic gaussian autocorrelation function. Also it has been shown [12] that the identical result is obtained if the thick scattering layer is simply replaced by a thin phase-changing screen, if the phase change at each point of this screen is defined as the total phase delay suffered by a ray during its passage through the thick scattering layer.

The conclusions of the theory of small-angle multiple scattering are best understood by using this concept of an equivalent phase-changing screen. Whenever the total phase delay is less than a radian, the angular power spectrum is entirely determined by the size of the irregularities. If, however, the total phase delay is much greater than a radian, then the angular power spectrum broadens, as suggested by the results obtained in Sec. II.6 for the example of the sinusoidal phase-changing screen.

II.10. INCOHERENT SCATTERING

Even in the absence of turbulent and similar irregularities, an ionized gas contains irregularities in electron number density. A qualitative understanding of these irregularities is obtained by considering a volume V, which is much smaller than the volume of the ionized gas but nevertheless contains a very large number of charged particles. There will be VN electrons on the average in such a volume, where N is the mean number density of electrons. If, however, samples of volume V were taken from different parts of the gas at the same instant, they would not all contain the same number of electrons even if the gas were in thermal equilibrium. On elementary statistical ground one would expect a spread in the result with a standard deviation $(VN)^{1/2}$. The more exact theory approximately confirms this estimate although the results are somewhat less simple.

The scattering of radio waves by such irregularities, which are present even in thermal equilibrium, is usually called 'incoherent scattering' [25].

Theories of incoherent scattering have recently been developed independently by a number of authors [5, 17, 19, 34, 37]; only the results are outlined here. Observations of incoherent backscatter of radar pulses from upper atmospheric ionization have been used to determine the electron density and ion temperature in the F layer, and even above its peak, as indicated in Sec. 5.3.3, and further experiments with more powerful radars are being planned.

For an understanding of the theoretical results it is necessary to appreciate the tendency of an ionized gas to maintain electrical neutrality. The arguments used in our estimate for the standard deviation of the number of electrons within the sample volume V may be applied to positive ions. If the ions and electrons carried out their thermal motion independently of each other, then the deviations from the mean of the number of ions and electrons within the volume V would be uncorrelated and therefore deviations from neutrality would occur. Such deviations would generate electrostatic fields which could perturb the motion of ions and electrons appreciably. Calculations show that, if the linear dimensions of the sample volume V are much smaller than the 'Debye length' $l_D \equiv (\epsilon_0 kT/Ne^2)^{1/2}$ introduced by Debye in the theory of electrolytes, then the effect of these perturbations is insignificant and the deviations are indeed uncorrelated. (Here k is Boltzmann's constant and T is temperature.) If, on the other hand, the linear dimensions of the sample volume are much larger than the length l_D, then the electrostatic fields become important and the deviations are strongly correlated. The ion and electron deviations are then nearly equal and are smaller than they would have been in the absence of the perturbations. If the ion and electron temperatures are equal, then the theory shows that the previously mentioned standard deviation is reduced by a factor of $2^{1/2}$, from $(VN)^{1/2}$ to $(VN/2)^{1/2}$.

In the absence of an external magnetic field and for wavelengths much smaller than the Debye length (which is a few millimeters in the $F2$ region), the scattered power may also be calculated by simple reasoning. The power backscattered by each electron is then simply determined by its classical (Thomson) cross section, and since the phases are incoherent, the powers scattered by the individual electrons are added algebraically.

Alternatively, the same result can be derived by considering the scattering as caused by the random irregularities in electron density already mentioned. This alternative approach becomes necessary when the wavelength of the radio wave is much larger than the Debye length, for then the electrostatic interactions cannot be neglected and the phases of the scattered waves are no longer completely incoherent. The first approach could be made to lead to the correct result only if it were assumed that the cross section of each electron has been reduced by a factor of two, or if some similar arbitrary assumption were made.

Because of the thermal motions of the electrons, the signal scattered from a wave of a particular frequency will contain new frequency components and the theory can predict the shape of the spectrum of scattered power. If the wavelength is much smaller than the Debye length, the spectrum of scattered power is obtained correctly by assuming that each electron scatters with a Doppler shift corresponding to the thermal velocity. The width of the spectrum of scattered waves is then determined entirely by the distribution of thermal velocities of electrons, and the shape of the spectrum is gaussian if the velocity distribution is Maxwellian. If, however, the wavelength is much larger than the Debye length, then the width of the spectrum is influenced more strongly by the thermal velocities of ions than of electrons. This is again a consequence of the electrostatic forces, which couple the electron density fluctuations to the much slower fluctuations of the ion density. There results a very great reduction in the width of the spectrum, and also a change in shape. The spectrum is no longer gaussian but has two very broad maxima symmetrically located about the frequency of the incident wave. These maxima are due to scattering by highly damped ion acoustic waves, and their position is dependent on the temperature. The theory thus shows that the number density of electrons may be determined from measurements of the total scattered power and that the temperature of the plasma may be deduced from measurements of the shape of the spectrum.

Under certain conditions the plasma may not be in full thermal equilibrium and the temperature of the electrons may exceed that of the ions. Under these conditions the theory shows that the two very broad maxima previously mentioned become very much sharper as a result of reduced damping of the ion acoustic waves. From the shape of the spectrum the temperature of both the electrons and the ions may then be inferred. It should be mentioned that the total scattered power is greatly reduced under these conditions.

The presence of a magnetic field will affect the irregularities and the scattering process, with consequences that have now been investigated theoretically [20, 23, 26, 30, 35, 38]. If the radar beam is nearly perpendicular to the field, sharp spikes in the spectrum are predicted, separated from the frequency of the incident waves by whole multiples of the electron or ion gyrofrequency. This opens the possibility of mass spectrometry by means of spectrum analysis. Close collisions between charged particles, especially ion-ion collisions, broaden these spectral spikes. Although no full theory of this broadening has yet been published, it is generally believed [6] that the spectral lines, separated by the gyrofrequencies of the heavier ions like atomic oxygen, will not be observable on account of the broadening in the lower and denser regions of the ionosphere. An accurate theory of the broadening of these spectral spikes would show whether it will be possible to detect the presence of helium ions and protons in the higher, more rarefied regions.

Observations have confirmed the theory of incoherent scattering within the accuracy of the measurements. The double-humped shape of the spectrum has been experimentally confirmed. Observations of the total scattered power, the shape of the spectrum, and the Faraday rotation of the scattered waves, have been combined in attempts to determine the number density, the electron and ion temperatures, and the composition [6]. Research in this field is still at a very early and active stage but electron number-density profiles up to heights of 5000 km and above, as well as useful information about the temperature of the ions and the electrons at heights below 1000 km, have already been obtained.

REFERENCES

1. Bailey, D. K., R. Bateman, and R. D. Kirby, Radio transmission by scattering and other processes in the lower ionosphere, *Proc. I.R.E.*, **43** (1955), 1181.
2. Barron, D. W., The numerical solution of differential equations governing the reflection of long radio waves from the ionosphere. IV, *Proc. Roy. Soc. A*, **260** (1961), 393.
3. Bowhill, S. A., The fading of radio waves of frequencies between 16 and 2400 kc/s, *J. Atmos. Terr. Phys.*, **8** (1956), 129.
4. Bowles, K. L., Observation of vertical incidence scatter from the ionosphere on 41 Mc/s, *Phys. Rev. Letters*, **1** (1958), 454.
5. ———, Incoherent scattering by free electrons as a technique for studying the ionosphere and the exosphere: some observations and theoretical considerations, *J. Res. Nat. Bureau of Standards*, **65D** (1961), 1.
6. ———, Incoherent backscatter from the ionosphere, *Rep. XIV Gen. Ass. URSI* (1963).
7. Booker, H. G., Oblique propagation of electromagnetic waves in a slowly varying non-isotropic medium, *Proc. Roy. Soc. A*, **155** (1936), 235.
8. ———, and W. E. Gordon, A theory of radio scattering in the troposphere. *Proc. I. R. E.*, **38** (1950), 401.
9. ———, J. A. Ratcliffe, and D. H. Shinn, Diffraction from an irregular screen with applications to ionospheric problems, *Phil. Trans. Roy. Soc. A*, **242** (1950), 579.
10. ———, and W. Walkinshaw, The mode theory of tropospheric reflection and its relation to wave guides and diffraction, in Report of Meteorological Factors in Radio Wave Propagation. London: Physical Society, 1946, p. 80.
11. Bramley, E. N., Diversity effects in spaced aerial reception of ionospheric waves, *Proc. Inst. Elec. Engrs.*, Pt. 1, **98** (1951), 91.
12. ———, The diffraction of waves by an irregular refracting medium, *Proc. Roy. Soc. A*, **225** (1954), 515.
13. Budden, K. G., Radio Waves in the Ionosphere. London: Cambridge University Press, 1961.

14. Chisholm, J. H., P. A. Portmann, J. T. de Bettencourt, and J. F. Roche, Investigations of angular scattering and multipath properties of tropospheric propagation of short radio waves beyond the horizon, *Proc. I.R.E.*, **43** (1955), 1317.

15. Clemmow, P. C., and J. Heading, Coupled forms of the differential equations governing radio propagation in the ionosphere, *Proc. Camb. Phil. Soc.*, **50** (1954), 319.

16. Davids, N., and R. W. Parkinson, Wave solutions for critical and near critical coupling conditions in the ionosphere, *J. Atmos. Terr. Phys.*, **7** (1955), 173.

17. Dougherty, J. P., and D. T. Farley, Theory of incoherent scattering of radio waves by a plasma, *Proc. Roy. Soc. A*, **259** (1960), 79.

18. Fejer, J. A., The diffraction of radio waves passing through an irregular refractive medium, *Proc. Roy. Soc. A*, **220** (1953), 455.

19. ———, Scattering of radio waves by an ionized gas in thermal equilibrium, *Can. J. Phys.*, **38** (1960), 1114.

20. ———, Scattering of radio waves by an ionized gas in thermal equilibrium in the presence of a uniform magnetic field, *Can. J. Phys.*, **39** (1961), 716.

21. Forsterling, K., Über die Ausbreitung elektromagnetischer Wellen in einem magnetisierten Medium bei senkrechter Inzidenz, *Hochfr. Elek.*, **59** (1942), p. 110.

22. Frihagen, J., and J. Troim, Scintillations of signals transmitted from earth satellites, *Tech. Note* No. 1, Norwegian Defence Research Establishment, Oslo, Norway, October, 1960.

23. Farley, D. T., J. P. Dougherty, and D. W. Barron, A theory of incoherent scattering of radio waves by a plasma. II. Scattering in a magnetic field, *Proc. Roy. Soc. A*, **263** (1961), 238.

24. Gallet, R. M., and W. F. Utlaut, Evidence on the laminar nature of the exosphere obtained by means of guided high-frequency wave propagation, *Phys. Rev. Letters*, **6** (1961), 591.

25. Gordon, W. E., Incoherent scattering of radio waves by free electrons with applications to space exploration by radar, *Proc. I.R.E.*, **46** (1958), 1824.

26. Hagfors, T., Density fluctuations in a plasma in a magnetic field, with applications to the ionosphere, *J. Geophys. Res.* **66** (1961), 1699.

27. Haslegrove, J., Ray theory and a new method for ray tracing, in Report of the Conference on the Physics of the Ionosphere. London: Physical Society, 1955, p. 355.

28. Hewish, A., The diffraction of radio waves in passing through a phase-changing ionosphere, *Proc. Roy. Soc. A*, **209** (1951), 81.

29. ———, The diffraction of galactic radio waves as a method of investigating the irregular structure of the ionosphere, *Proc. Roy. Soc. A*, **214** (1952), 494.

30. Laaspere, T., On the effect of a magnetic field on the spectrum of incoherent scattering, *J. Geophys. Res.*, **65** (1960), 3955.

31. Millman, G. H., A. J. Moceyunas, A. E. Sanders, and R. F. Wyrick, The effect of Faraday rotation on incoherent back-scatter observations, *J. Geophys. Res.*, **66** (1961), 1564.

32. Pineo, V. C., L. G. Kraft, and H. W. Briscoe, Some characteristics of ionospheric backscatter observed at 440 Mc/s, *J. Geophys. Res.*, **65** (1960), 2629.

33. Poeverlein, H., Strahlwege von Radio Wellen in der Ionosphäre, *Z. Angew. Phys.*, **2** (1950), 152.

34. Renau, J., Scattering of electromagnetic waves from a non-degenerate ionized gas, *J. Geophys. Res.*, **65** (1960), 3631.

35. ———, H. Camnitz, and W. Flood, The spectrum and the total intensity of electromagnetic waves scattered from an ionized gas in thermal equilibrium in the presence of a static quasi-uniform magnetic field, *J. Geophys. Res.*, **66** (1961), 2703.

36. Ratcliffe, J. A, Some aspects of diffraction theory and their application to the ionosphere, *Rep. Prog. Phys.*, **19** (1956), 188.

37. Salpeter, E. E., Electron density fluctuations in a plasma, *Phys. Rev.* **120** (1960), 1528.

38. ———, Plasma density fluctuations in a magnetic field. *Phys. Rev.*, **122** (1961), 1663.

39. Wiener, N., Generalized harmonic functions, *Acta Math.*, **55** (1930), 118.

Index

A

Absorption:
  auroral, 327–30 (*see also* Aurora, radio):
    height, 328–30
    latitude, 328
    and optical aurora, 328, 331–32
  deviative, 387
  in exosphere, 100, 102
  measurement, 246–48
  microwave, 38
  nondeviative, 387
  optical, 37–42
  polar cap, 221, 222, 241 (*see also* Cosmic rays, solar; Flares; Protons, solar):
    characteristics, 257–65
    geomagnetic control, 249–51
    and LF propagation, 267–68
    and solar cosmic rays, 248–49
    time variation, 254–55, 261–66
  of solar radiation, 100, 102
  sudden commencement, 288
  sudden cosmic noise, 210
Absorption coefficient, 37, 387
Acceleration of charged particles, 123, 124
Acoustic waves, 151, 420
Adiabatic invariant, 122
Air mass, 36
Airglow, 3, 42–45, 352
Albedo theory, neutron, 125–27
Allowed regions, 119
α-Chapman layer, 50–51 (*see also* Chapman layer)
Alpha particles, 126, 256
Ambipolar diffusion, 84, 160, 166
Amplification, traveling-wave, 185–86, 188
a_p, 20
A_p, 20, 102
Aspect sensitivity, 321–23, 417
Atmosphere:
  structure, 6–13
    chemical, 7–8
    from ionization dynamics, 9–13
    from static ionization, 8–9
    thermal, 6–7
  transmission, 35–37
  upper, 1–2, 4
Atmospherics, 209 (*see also* Noise; Whistlers)
Attachment, 50, 55
Attachment coefficient, 50, 85
Attenuation, 35, 36, 52 (*see also* Absorption)
Aurora:
  and radiation belt, 128–29
  and storms, 275
Aurora, optical, 299–318
  break-up, 303
  brightness, 304
  classification, 302–4

Aurora, optical (*Cont.*):
electrons in, 317–18, 365
geographical distribution, 301–2
height, 304–5, 312
hydrogen in, 313–17
luminosity, 307
magnetic conjugacy, 302
motion, 307–8
orientation, 305–7
proton bombardment in, 314–16
and solar disturbances, 308
spectra, 309–17
and sporadic *E*, 316
temperature, 312
time variation, 308–9
and winds, 308
and *X*-rays, 317–18
Aurora, radio, 301, 319–33 (*see also* Absorption):
absorption, 327–30
aspect sensitivity, 321–22, 323
classification, 322–23
frequency dependence, 325–26
and magnetic disturbances, 331
motions in, 325
physical processes, 326–27
radio noise from, 330–31
spatial distribution, 323
temporal variation, 324–25
Aurora, theory, 351–60
discharge, 356–58
DS-associated, 355–56
and geomagnetic storms, 352
and model experiments, 356
and trapped radiation, 358–60
Auroral zone, 4, 19, 302
Autocorrelation function, 413–16

B

Backscatter, 113, 417
Balance, chemical, 32
Ballistic trajectory, 97
Bands:
frequency, 24
molecular, 38, 43, 44
Barrier, magnetic, 263–64
Bay, magnetic, 276, 282, 289, 350
and storms, 287
Betatron mechanism, 124, 358
Blackout, 245, 246, 320 (*see also* Absorption):
polar, 328
Brooker's quartic, 399
Born approximation, 416
Breakdown, electrical, 357
Bursts, solar radio noise, 229–34 (*see also* Noise):
and magnetic activity, 231–33
and SID's, 233
and solar flares, 231–33

C

Center of activity, 202, 227–28, 234–35
Center of gyration, 117
Central meridian passage, 279, 280
Centrifugal force, 111, 135
Cerenkov radiation, 331
Chapman layer, 48–51
α-, 55, 59, 62, 74–75, 86
Character figure:
ionization, 65
magnetic, 20, 277
Characteristic waves, 378–79
Charge exchange, 127
Charge, polarization, 168
Chemiluminescence, 44
Chromosphere, 33, 218
CIRA, 103
C layer, 54–55
CMP, 279, 280
CO, 39
CO_2, 52
Coherence, 188
Collision frequency, 69, 90, 159, 160
and absorption, 387–88
critical, 388, 405
and hydromagnetic waves, 393
and SID's, 272
Collisions, 372–73
ion-electron, 159
and refractive indices, 385–90
Comet tails, 237
Conductivity:
electrical, 160–61
diurnal variation, 168
Hall, 162
Pedersen, 162
tensor, 162, 164, 375–76, 397
thermal, 100

Conjugacy, magnetic, 17, 302
Contact surface, 335–36
Continuity equation, 50, 84, 139, 150
Convection, 345, 349
Coordinates, 14, 17, 18
  geomagnetic, 14
  McIlwain, 17
  pseudo-polar, 18
Coriolis force, 135, 139, 170
Corona, solar, 33, 35, 218–22
  dust, 219
  electron density, 218–19, 221
  hydrogen, 108
  magnetic fields, 222–27
  proton density, 220
  structure, 222–24
  variability, 35
  X-rays, 208
Cosmic noise, 247 (*see also* Noise)
Cosmic rays, 55
  galactic, 125
  solar, 4, 255–56 (*see also* Absorption, polar cap; Flares; Protons, solar):
    ionospheric effects, 248–55
    and storms, 286, 288
COSPAR, 29, 103
Coupling, 405
Critical frequency, 51, 74 (*see also* Penetration frequency; Collision frequency)
Crochets, 210–11
Cross section, 37, 48
Current density, 161–62, 164, 168, 374
Current system, 292–93 (*see also* *DS*, *Dst*)
Currents (*see also* Conductivity):
  dynamo, 13 (*see also* Dynamo)
  ionospheric, 65, 211
  magnetospheric, 170
Cusp, 67, 402
Cutoff, magnetic, 289
Cyclotron frequency, 116 (*see also* Gyrofrequency)

D

Dawn chorus, 178
Dayglow, 42
Debye length, 419
December anomaly, 77
Density, 99–108
  extrapolation, 107–8
  height variation, 7, 8, 103–6
  measurement, 99–100
  temporal variation, 101–3
Diamagnetic effect, 348
Diffusion, 171
  ambipolar (plasma), 84, 87, 160, 166
  in magnetic field, 111, 166
  of meteor trails, 153
  polar, 368
  of solar protons, 259
Diffusive separation, 52, 59, 73, 96
Dip angle, magnetic, 78–80
Dip equator, 164, 171
Dip pole, 15
Dipole, approximation, 16
Dipole, magnetic, 14, 117
Discharge, 356–58
Dispersion equation, 24, 375, 378
Disturbance:
  magnetic, 260–61 (*see also* Storms)
  solar, 2, 4 (*see also* Flares; Sunspot)
  traveling, 152
Diurnal anomaly, 77, 88
D layer, 55, 56
Doppler shift, 187
Double refraction, 381
Downgoing wave, 398n., 399–400
Downward movement, 152
Drag, satellite, 99–100
D region, 3, 9, 51–58
  constitution, 51, 52
  electron distribution, 52–56
  high-latitude, 57
  meteorology, 57–58
  seasonal changes, 56–57
  and SID's, 209–10, 212
  in storms, 288–89
Drift:
  apparent, 149
  charged-particle, 117, 121, 130, 347–48
  in *F*2 layer, 171
  vertical, 63, 172–74
Drift velocity, 160, 161, 165–66, 172
DS, 170, 294–96, 342–46, 355–56
Dst, 294–96
Ducting, 112, 182, 391, 407
Dumped electrons, 359, 365
Dust, 219
Dynamo current, 166–67, 357–58

Dynamo field, 159, 172
Dynamo mechanism, 343
Dynamo region, 13
Dynamo theory, 166–70

E

Earth currents, 189
E layer, 9, 61, 66, 67
Electric field, 110, 122, 123
  in aurora, 355–57, 358
  components, 378–79
  in hydrodynamic theory, 374–75
  ionospheric, 345–46
  in magnetosphere, 129
  and neutrality, 373
  and ring current, 349
  total, 161
Electrojet, 342
Electron content, 290–91
Electron density (*see also* Electrons; Ionization; Ions):
  coronal, 218–19, 221
  gradients, 268
  maximum, 291
  in radio aurora, 326
  and reaction rates, 253–54
  in SID's, 207, 211–13
  storm, 295
  from whistlers, 112, 391
Electron streams, 185
Electron temperature, 89
Electrons:
  attachment, 50
  auroral, 359–60
    and luminosity, 365
  distribution, 50, 51
    D-region, 52–56
    E-region, 59–62
    F-region, 80–84
  loss, 50, 84–86, 88–89, 367
  production, 48–49, 84–86
  radiation-belt, 127, 128
  recombination, 50, 85 (*see also* Recombination)
Emissions, 178, 186 (*see also* Noise; Radiation; Radio waves)
Energy:
  balance, 52
  loss, 251–53
Equator:
  dip, 164, 171
  geomagnetic, 14
  magnetic, 16, 164
Equatorial anomaly, 77, 81, 87, 88, 114
Equilibrium:
  diffusive, 171
  hydrostatic, 7
  ion distribution, 110
  static, 137
  thermodynamic, 107
Equivalent height, 60 (*see also* Virtual height)
E region, 3, 9, 59–67
  electron distribution, 59–62
  in SID's, 212–13
E_s, 59 (*see also* Sporadic *E*)
Escape, 96–98, 228–29
Evanescent wave, 381
Exosphere, 8, 97, 107 (*see also* Outer ionosphere)
Extraordinary wave, 60, 383 (*see also* Ordinary wave)

F

f_oE, 62–65
f_oF1, 75–76
f_oF2, 76–80
*F*1 ledge, 74, 75, 86
*F*2 peak, 9, 73–74, 76, 86–87
Fadeout, 210
Fading, 408
Faraday rotation, 97, 113
Fermi acceleration, 259
Filaments, 204
Flare patrol, 203
Flares, solar, 202–6, 232–33 (*see also* Absorption; Cosmic rays, solar; Noise):
  classification, 28
  energy, 205–6
  importance, 204
  and noise bursts, 232–33
  and prominences, 228
  and protons, 258–59
  and solar cosmic rays, 248–49
  storm-producing, 280–82

Flares, solar (*Cont.*):
white-light, 203
F layer, 9, 74–84, 171, 291
Fluctuations, 408
Forbidden region, 119
F region, 3, 73–93 (*see also* Outer ionosphere):
anomalies, 77, 87, 88
collision frequency, 90
composition, 73, 85, 86, 89
electron distribution, 80–84
electron loss, 88–89
formation, 73, 74
irregularities, 90–93
layer formation, 84–88
nocturnal, 80–84
in SID's, 213–14
in storms, 288–91
temperature, 89–90
Forbush decrease, 237–38
Force density, 158
Force equation, 374
Forward scatter, 417
Frequency bands, 24
Friction, 158
Frozen-field approximation, 10
Full-wave solutions, 406–7

G

Gamma (γ), 20
Gas law, 7, 97
Geomagnetic anomaly, 15, 77, 81, 87–88, 171
Geomagnetic coordinates, 14
Geomagnetic field, 13–20 (*see also* Magnetic field; Storms):
main field, 14–19
variation field, 19–20
Geometric optics, 384
Geostrophic winds, 136
Gradual commencement, 284
Gravitational term, 159, 164–66
Gravity waves, 100, 149–53, 173, 364
Group, 24, 25
velocity, 380, 383, 401 (*see also* Packet velocity)
Guiding center, 117, 121
Gyrofrequency, 116, 160, 185, 376
Gyroradiation, 186–88
Gyro radius, 338

H

H, 9, 34, 43
auroral, 313, 317
in outer ionosphere, 105–6
H+, 110, 111 (*see also* Protons)
Hall current, 161, 345–46, 355
Hα, 203, 281
He, 9, 34, 105
He+, 110, 111
Heating, 124
Height, virtual, 21, 60
Heterosphere, 8
Hiss, 178
Homosphere, 8
Hooks, 178–79
Hydrodynamic approximation, 372
Hydromagnetic waves, 100
dispersion equation, 392–94
in outer ionosphere, 124, 126, 129
and storms, 338–39
velocity, 393
and whistlers, 391
Hydrostatic law, 7, 97, 110

I

IGY, 29
Importance, flare, 204
Impulse, magnetic, 284, 338
Indices, magnetic, 20
International Geophysical Year, 29
International organizations, 29
International Years of the Quiet Sun, 29
Invariant, 18, 122
Inversion, temperature, 58
Ionization (*see also* Ions; Electrons):
character figure, 65
field-aligned, 112
magnetospheric, 349, 351
processes, 367
by protons, 251–55
during SID's, 211–14
Ionosonde, 21, 60, 61
use in PCA, 265–67

Ionosphere, 3 (*see also D, E, F* regions; Outer ionosphere; Storms)
Ions (*see also* Electrons; Ionization):
distribution, 110, 111
escape, 98
negative, 68
suprathermal, 124
and VLF waves, 183
and whistlers, 390, 391
IQSY, 29
Irregular medium, 407–8
Irregularities, 112, 138, 408
Isochasms, 301

J

Jupiter, 240

K

K index, 20, 273

L

L (*see* Lunar variation; McIlwain coordinates)
Larmor radius, 116
Latitude:
geomagnetic, 14
invariant, 18
magnetic, 15
solar, 201
zones, 19
Layers, 46–51 (*see also D-, E-, F-* regions):
solar, 32–35
LF radio waves, 24, 54–55
in PCA, 267–68
in SID's, 209
Light, 32
Long-range interaction, 372–73
Longitude, geomagnetic, 14
Longitudinal inequality, 294–96
Low frequency, 24 (*see also* LF)
Lunar variation, 138, 164
Lyman α, 34, 40, 43, 44
D-region, 55
E-region, 67
and SID's, 207–8
Lyman continuum, 67

M

McIlwain coordinates, 17–18
Magnetic field (*see also DS*; *Dst*; Geomagnetic field; Storms):
and charged particles, 250–51
dipole, 14, 117
earth's:
components, 276
diurnal variation, 166–70
guiding radio waves, 112
secular variation, 188
from whistlers, 391
frozen, 9–13, 222
interplanetary, 222–27
particle motions in, 115–25
Magnetic field:
solar coronal, 222–27
curvature, 222, 224–25
energy density in, 222
magnitude, 225
neutral points, 235
Magnetic moment, 122
Magnetic tongue, 226–27, 265
Magnetogram, 19
Magnetosphere, 13, 364 (*see also* Outer ionosphere)
Main field, 14–19
Maxwell's equations, 377
Mean free path, 97
Mesopause, 7
Mesophere, 7
Meteor trails, 138, 146–47, 152, 153
Meteorology, *D*-region, 57–58
Micropulsations, 4, 188–95
characteristics, 190–94
pearl-type, 192–93
theories of, 194–95
Mirror point, 122
Mixing, 8, 9 (*see also* Diffusion)
Mobile operator, 139
Momentum transfer equation, 374
Motion, equations of, 116, 139, 150, 158, 374
M region, 200, 241, 279

N

N, 105
N_2, 38, 40, 41, 105, 310
$N_2{}^+$, 40–41, 67, 84–86, 310

Na, 43
Negative ions, 68
Neutral line, 351, 359
Neutral particles, 98–108 (*see also* Outer ionosphere)
Neutral point, 235, 351, 356, 357
Neutrality, electrical, 97, 373
Neutron albedo theory, 125–27
Night glow, 42
NO, 55, 367
NO+, 68, 84–86
Noise, radio (*see also* Radio waves):
  cosmic, 247
  ionospheric, 177–88
  and aurora, 180
    characteristics, 178–79
    frequency bands, 178
    generation, 181–88
    and magnetic disturbance, 180
    and particle streams, 185
    spectrum, 188
    temporal variation, 180
    VLF, 4
  solar, 259–60, 280–81
  tropospheric, 177
November effect, 57, 58

O

O, 42, 84–86, 103, 105, 310
O+, 84–86, 110, 111
O_2, 9, 38, 41, 42, 105
O_2+, 84–86
O_2−, 261–62
O_3, 39, 41, 52
OH, 43, 44
Orbit, satellite, 99
Orbital paths, 108
Ordinary wave, 60, 383, 387–88
Oscillations, tidal, 138–45 (*see also* Tidal oscillations)
Outer ionosphere, 96–130 (*see also* Exosphere):
  ionized, 109–15
    ion distribution, 110–11
    measurements, 113–15
    whistler studies, 111–12
  neutral, 98–108
    composition, 100, 105–6
    height variation, 103–7
Outer ionosphere (*Cont.*):
  neutral (*Cont.*):
    measurements, 99–100
    temporal variation, 101–3

P

Packet velocity, 26 (*see also* Group)
Particles, charged:
  in magnetic fields, 115–25
  thermal, 109–15
  neutral, 98–108 (*see also* Outer ionosphere)
  relativistic, 116n., 250
  solar, 4, 125, 343
    and drifts, 172
    emission, 234–36
  trapped (*see* Trapped radiation)
Patrol, flare, 203
PCA, 249 (*see also* Absorption, polar cap)
Pearls, 192–93
Pedersen current, 162, 345–46
Penetration depth, 39
Penetration frequency, 51, 62–65
Penumbra, 199, 200
Phase integral method, 405–7
Phase velocity, 380, 383, 401
Photosphere, 32
Plage, 199, 202, 280
Plane waves, 375, 397–98
Plasma, 4, 217, 351
Plasma frequency, 185, 376
Polar cap, 19
Polar cap absorption, 249 (*see also* Absorption, polar cap)
Polarization, 379–80, 389
  of coupled waves, 406
  QL and QT, 385–86
Polarization charges, 168
Pole:
  dip, 15
  geomagnetic, 14
Potential:
  electrostatic, 99, 167
  velocity, 169–70
Pressure gradient, 158, 373–74
Pressure, radiation, 99
Pressure term, 159, 164–66
Prominences, 204, 227–28
Protonosphere, 9, 111

Protons (*see also* H+; Cosmic rays):
auroral, 314–16
energy loss, 251–53
ionization by, 251–55
radiation-belt, 125, 127, 128
and ring current, 130
solar, 249, 251, 343
acceleration, 258–59
coronal, 220
D-region, 55
observations, 255–57
storage, 263–65
Protosphere, 9, 111
Pseudo-polar coordinates, 18

Q

Quasi-longitudinal (QL) approximation, 385–86
Quasi-transverse (QT) approximation, 385–86

R

Radar, 320
Radiation (*see also* Lyman α; Particles; Trapped radiation; *X*-rays):
solar, 32–35, 102
absorption, 37–42
corpuscular, 90, 102, 206
microwave, 101
ultraviolet, 39–42, 74
Radiation belts, 115, 120, 125–29 (*see also* Trapped radiation)
Radiation pressure, 103, 236, 237
Radio noise emissions (*see* Bursts; Noise; Radio waves)
Radio-star scintillation, 408
Radio waves (*see also* Noise):
ducting, 112, 182, 391, 407
escape from corona, 228
as probes, 113
VLF, 182–85
confinement, 182
full-wave solutions, 406–7
and particle streams, 185
and positive ions, 183
in SID's 209–10
Radius of gyration, 116
Ray direction, 26, 390
Ray path, 401–2
Ray solution, 398–406
Ray theory, 384
Reaction rates, 253–54
Recombination, 50, 67–68, 85, 291
coefficient, 62, 85–87, 212
Reflection, 399–402
complex height of, 405
critical, 326
Reflection conditions, 384–85
Refraction, 37, 381
Refractive index, 378, 380–86
Relativistic particles, 250, 116n.
Resonance, 139, 141, 377
Reynolds number, 154
Richardson number, 154
Rigidity, 250–51
Ring current, 98, 129–30, 276, 347–50, 353–54
Riometer, 246–47, 257–58
Risers, 179
Rotation, atmospheric, 134–35

S

SCA, 288
Scale height, 7, 62, 110
Scattering:
coefficient, 37
cross section, 416
forward, 247–48
geometry, 417
incoherent, 418–21
multiple, 418
in radio aurora, 326–27
three-dimensional, 415–18
Scintillation, radio-star, 408
SCNA, 210
Screen, phase-changing, 408–15, 418
angular power spectrum, 412–15
autocorrelation function, 413–15
finite, 412
Screening, interplanetary, 237–38
SEA, 209
Seasonal anomaly, 77, 88
Secant law, 35, 36
Self-focused stream, 356
Separation, diffusive, 52, 59, 73
SFE, 210
Sferics, 177, 390